3rd International Conference on Electrical Systems, Technology and Information (ICESTI 2017)

MATEC Web of Conferences Volume 164 (2018)

Bali, Indonesia
26 – 29 September 2017

Editors:

E. Alasaarela
F. Pasila
G. Chan
S.-G. Lee

ISBN: 978-1-5108-6197-8

Printed from e-media with permission by:

Curran Associates, Inc.
57 Morehouse Lane
Red Hook, NY 12571

Some format issues inherent in the e-media version may also appear in this print version.

Printed by Curran Associates, Inc. (2018)

For additional information, please contact EDP Sciences – Web of Conferences at the address below.

EDP Sciences – Web of Conferences
17, Avenue du Hoggar
Parc d'Activité de Courtabœuf
BP 112
F-91944 Les Ulis Cedex A
France

Phone: +33 (0) 1 69 18 75 75
Fax: +33 (0) 1 69 28 84 91

contact-edps@webofconferences.org

Additional copies of this publication are available from:

Curran Associates, Inc.
57 Morehouse Lane
Red Hook, NY 12571 USA
Phone: 845-758-0400
Fax: 845-758-2633
Email: curran@proceedings.com
Web: www.proceedings.com

TABLE OF CONTENTS

GEOGRAPHIC INFORMATION SYSTEM FOR HIGHER EDUCATION VIA DATA SCRAPPING 1
Alfiansyah Agung, Azhar Anas

IOT-BASED CAR'S PARKING MONITORING SYSTEM 8
Dwiputra Albertus Ega, Khoswanto Handry, Sutjiadi Raymond, Lim Resmana

MODIFIED WELCH BERLEKAMP ALGORITHM TO DECODE REED SOLOMON CODES 19
Mahmudi Ali, Achmadi Sentot, Michael

BIG DATA ANALYTICS: TOWARDS A MODEL TO UNDERSTAND DEVELOPMENT EQUITY FOR VILLAGES IN INDONESIA 30
Vijaya Annas, Angreani Linda Salma, Hariyadi Mokhamad Amin

DESIGN AND DEVELOPMENT OF RUNFORFUN MOBILE APPLICATION 36
Anci Anthony, Wiradinata Trianggoro

INFORMATION SYSTEM USER INTERFACE DESIGN IN SOFTWARE SERVICES ORGANIZATION: A SMALL-CLAN CASE STUDY 52
Jitnupong Boonchoo, Jirachiefpattana Waraporn

ENERGY SAVING POTENTIAL FROM SHADING DESIGN FOR RESIDENTIAL HOUSE IN RURAL AREA 64
Perwita Sari Dany, Chiou Yun-Shang

CONGESTION MITIGATION SCENARIO THROUGH PUBLIC TRANSPORTATION IMPROVEMENT 72
Suryani Erma, Agus Hendrawan Rully, Fasrter Eka Adipraja Phillip, Puspa Dewi Lily

PARTIAL-FACTOR ENERGY EFFICIENCY MODEL OF INDONESIA 84
Nugroho Fathul, Syaifudin Noor

GREEN INDUSTRIAL SYSTEM IN INDONESIA 93
Handoko Fourry, Nursanti Ellysa, Gatot, Edwin Tjahjadi Martinus, Hutabarat Julianus, Mulyadi Lalu, Kustamar

GEOMETRIC DEVELOPMENT OF POINT ABSORBER WAVE ENERGY CONVENTER 100
Saptono Warpindyasmoro Heri, Gunadi Kartika

TURBINE DESIGN FOR LOW HEAT ORGANIC RANKINE CYCLE POWER GENERATION USING RENEWABLE ENERGY SOURCES 106
Susanto Herry, Abdullah Kamaruddin, Saepul Uyun Aep, Muhammad Nur Syukri, Meurah Indra Mahlia Teuku

THE ROLE OF TANGIBLE INTERFACES IN ENHANCING CHILDREN\'S ENGAGEMENT IN LEARNING 123
Rante Hestiasari, Lund Michael, Caliz Doris

UNIFORM AND NON-UNIFORM IMAGE ENLARGEMENT BASED ON THE WINDOW KERNEL 132
Somawirata I Komang, Prio Hartono Bambang, Herbasuki Teguh, Soetedjo Aryuato

UNDERSTANDING A DEEP LEARNING TECHNIQUE THROUGH A NEUROMORPHIC SYSTEM A CASE STUDY WITH SPINNAKER NEUROMORPHIC PLATFORM 140
Sugiarto Indar, Pasila Felix

OPTIMIZATION TWIST ANGLE OF DARRIUS WIND TURBINE WITH COMPUTATIONAL FLUID DYNAMICS (CFD) SIMULATION FOR HIGHWAY AREA APPLICATION 159
Ismail, Augupta Pane Erlanda, Soleh

DESIGN OF MONITORING TOOL HEARTBEAT RATE AND HUMAN BODY TEMPERATURE BASED ON WEB 167
Jalinas, Kusuma Raharja Wahyu, Putra Emas Wijaya Bobby

INFORMATION SYSTEM STRATEGIC PLANNING FOR DEPARTMENT OF HOUSING AND SETTLEMENT REGION IN THE JAKARTA PROVINCIAL GOVERNMENT - INDONESIA 186
Sembodo Suroso Jarot, Harisno, Mauritsius Tuga, Setyawan Agung

DATA MINING APPLICATION USING ASSOCIATION RULE MINING ECLAT ALGORITHM BASED ON SPMF 194
Reynaldo Jason, Boy Tonara David

RFID AND IOT FOR ATTENDANCE MONITORING SYSTEM 204
Dedy Irawan Joseph, Adriantantri Emmalia, Farid Akh

INVESTIGATION ON VOLTAGE QUALITY PROBLEMS ON THE PROCESS OF CEMENT INDUSTRY PRODUCTION IN INDONESIA: A CASE STUDY OF CEMENT KUPANG FACTORY - INDONESIA 212
Sentosa Setiadji Julius, Rohi Daniel, Flantine Mozes Yoanne

EXPERIMENTAL INVESTIGATION OF AIR CONDITIONER USING THE DESICCANT COOLING SYSTEM IN EQUATORIAL CLIMATES 217
Abdullah Kamaruddin, Saepul Uyun Aep, Muhammad Nur Syukri, Bamahry Alie, Imanda Rino, Meurah Indra Mahlia Teuku

MODIFIED FLOATING SEARCH FEATURE SELECTION BASED ON GENETIC ALGORITHM 225
Homsapaya Kanyanut, Sornil Ohm

THE INTEGRATION OF GASIFICATION SYSTEMS WITH GAS ENGINE BY DEVELOPING WET TAR SCRUBBERS AND GAS FILTER TO PRODUCE ELECTRICAL ENERGY FROM BIOMASS 235
Siregar Kiman, Alamsyah Rizal, Ichwana, Sholihati, Tou Saminuddin, Cristian Siregar Nobel

THE ENCYCLOPEDIA OF VIRTUAL ART CARVING TORAJA - INDONESIA 245
Sudianto Lande, Simon Petrus

PRODUCTION CAPACITY OF SEVERAL HYBRID GENOTYPES OF JATROPHA CURCAS LINN. FOR FIVE YEARS IN PASURUAN, EAST JAVA – INDONESIA. 253
Maftuchah, Zainudin Agus, Ikhwan Ali, Purnama Adi, Kok Kuan Lim

SIMULATION STUDY OF BIO-METHANE CONVERSION INTO HYDROGEN FOR GENERATING 500 KW OF POWER 259
Mel Maizirwan, Riyad Hussein Abdeen Fouad, Mohd Salleh Hamzah, Izan Ihsan Sany, Adyani Ahmad Fuad Fazia, Hendroko Setyobudi Roy

DEVELOPMENT OF PRESENTATION MODEL WITH CLOUD BASED INFRASTRUCTURE 265
Magdalena Widiantari Maria, Budiman Arief

BROADCASTING THE STATUS OF PLANT GROWTH CHAMBER USING BLUETOOTH LOW ENERGY 275
Al-Azam Moh Noor, Achlaq Mochamad Mizanul, Nugroho Aryo, Gabriel Sooai Adri, Winaya Aris, Maftuchah

DESIGN AND DEVELOPMENT OF SMART AQUACULTURE SYSTEM BASED ON IFTTT MODEL AND CLOUD INTEGRATION 286
Dzulqornain Muhammad Iskandar, Harun Al Rasyid M. Udin, Sukaridhoto Sritrusta

INDONESIAN STOCK PREDICTION USING SUPPORT VECTOR MACHINE (SVM) 297
Santoso Murtiyanto, Sutjiadi Raymond, Lim Resmana

THE IMPORTANCE OF CREDIT PROGRAM SCHEME ON WASTE TO ENERGY PROGRAM IN INDONESIA: CASE STUDY ON TOFU INDUSTRY 302
Syaifudin Noor, Nurkholis, Handika Rangga, Hendroko Setyobudi Roy

FORMULATING INTEREST SUBSIDY PROGRAM TO SUPPORT THE DEVELOPMENT OF ELECTRICITY GENERATION FROM PALM OIL MILL EFFLUENT (POME) BIOMASS: AN INDONESIAN CASE STUDY 312
Syaifudin Noor, Nurkholis, Handika Rangga, Hendroko Setyobudi Roy

WEB-BASED ROBOTICS LABORATORY 321
Santoso Petrus, Khoswanto Handry, Njoto Sandjaja Iwan

BIOMASS AND SUGAR CONTENT OF SOME VARIETIES OF SORGHUM (SORGHUM BICOLOR L. MOENCH) ON DRY LAND FOREST AS FEEDSTOCK BIOETHANOL 327
Gamawati Adinurani Praptiningsih, Rahayu Sri, Sulistiyo Budi Luluk, Nindita Anggi, Soni Peeyush, Mel Maizirwan

A MATHEMATICAL PROOF CONCERNING THE GEOMETRICAL ASPECT OF VERY LOW INDEX OF DIFFICULTY IN MULTIDIRECTIONAL TAPPING TASK OF THE ISO 9241 - PART 411 332
Marsya Quita Reyna, Budhi Widodo Romy

AUTOMATIC ESSAY SCORING IN E-LEARNING SYSTEM USING LSA METHOD WITH N-GRAM FEATURE FOR BAHASA INDONESIA 340
Setiadi Citawan Rico, Christanti Mawardi Viny, Mulyawan Bagus

ENERGY DEMAND ANALYSIS AND DESIGN OF A HYBRID POWER SYSTEM IN BAWEAN ISLANDS, INDONESIA 357
Hantoro Ridho, Budiono Cahyun, Kipkoech Ketter Ronald, Ade Satwika Nyoman

CHARACTERISATION OF ARABICA COFFEE PULP - HAY FROM KINTAMANI - BALI AS PROSPECTIVE BIOGAS FEEDSTOCKS 367
Hendroko Setyobudi Roy, Krido Wahono Satriyo, Gamawati Adinurani Praptiningsih, Wahyudi Ahmad, Widodo Wahyu, Mel Maizirwan, Adhi Nugroho Yogo, Prabowo Bayu, Liwang Tony

REVISITING RENEWABLE ENERGY MAP IN INDONESIA: SEASONAL HYDRO AND SOLAR ENERGY POTENTIAL FOR RURAL OFF-GRID ELECTRIFICATION (PROVINCIAL LEVEL) 380
Agung Wahyuono Ruri, Magenika Julian Miga

DETERMINATION OF GENERATOR STEADY STATE STABILITY LIMIT FOR MULTIMACHINE SYSTEM BASED ON NETWORK LOSSES CONCEPT 391
Rusilawati, Budi Sulistiawati Irrine, Soeprijanto Adi, Seto Wibowo Rony

DESIGN AND BANDWIDTH OPTIMIZATION ON TRIANGLE PATCH MICROSTRIP ANTENNA FOR WLAN 2.4 GHZ 404
Sotyohadi, Afandi Riken, Rachmad Hadi Dony
THE BENEFIT OF DECISION SUPPORT SYSTEM AS SUSTAINABLE ENVIRONMENT TECHNOLOGY TO UTILIZE COASTAL ABUNDANT RESOURCES IN INDONESIA 418
Hermawan Surya
A STUDY OF MOBILE ROBOT CONTROL USING EEG EMOTIV EPOCH SENSOR 426
Victorio Yasin Timothius, Pasila Felix, Lim Resmana
FUEL SAVING ON DIESEL GENSET USING PV/BATTERY SPIKE CUTTING IN REMOTE AREA MICROGRID 437
Dwi Atmaja Tinton, Ardath Kristi Ant, Risdiyanto Agus, Susanto Bambang, Andriani Dian, Fujita Makoto, Hirono Atsushi
V2G DEVELOPMENT ON PUBLIC VERTICAL PARKING LOT TO SUPPORT COMMUNITY ENERGY MANAGEMENT SYSTEM 446
Dwi Atmaja Tinton, Susanti Vita, Mirdanies Midriem, Muharam Aam
SPELLING CORRECTION FOR TEXT DOCUMENTS IN BAHASA INDONESIA USING FINITE STATE AUTOMATA AND LEVINSHTEIN DISTANCE METHOD 457
Christanti Mawardi Viny, Susanto Niko, Santun Naga Dali
IMPLEMENTATION OF WINNOWING ALGORITHM BASED K-GRAM TO IDENTIFY PLAGIARISM ON FILE TEXT-BASED DOCUMENT 473
Nurdiansyah Yanuar, Nur Muharrom Fiqih, Firdaus
THE DESIGN OF E-COMMERCE SYSTEM IN THE SHRIMP PASTE INDUSTRY USING THE METHOD OF STRUCTURED ANALYSIS AND DESIGN TECHNIQUE (SADT) TO INCREASE MARKETING 484
Nurdiansyah Yanuar, Wijayanto Feri, Firdaus
Author Index

3RD ANNUAL 2017

ICESTI

INTERNATIONAL CONFERENCE ON ELECTRICAL SYSTEMS, TECHNOLOGY & INFORMATION

PREFACE

This proceeding includes the original, peer-reviewed research papers from the 3rd International Conference on Electrical Systems, Technology and Information (ICESTI 2017), held in 26 – 29 September 2017 in Bali, Indonesia.

The primary objective of this proceeding is to provide references for dissemination and discussion of the topics that has been presented in ICESTI 2017. The presented topics includes work related to Electrical Engineering, Technology and Information towards their sustainable development. Engineers, researchers as well as lecturers from universities and professionals in industry and government [(Australia, Germany, Indonesia, Japan, Malaysia, Nederland, People's Republic of China, Taiwan (Republic of China), Uni Arab Emirates, and United Kingdom], will gain valuable insights into interdisciplinary solutions in the field of Electrical Systems, Technology and Information, and Renewable Energy its applications.

The topics of ICESTI 2017 provide a forum for accessing the most up-to-date and authoritative knowledge and best practices in the field of Electrical Engineering, Technology and Information towards their sustainable development. The Scientific and Editorial Boards have selected the high quality papers from conference that passed through minimum three reviewers, with the acceptance rate of 40.7 %. The conference also classified the Technology Innovation topics in several parts, such as: "Technology Innovation in Robotics, Image Recognition and Computational Intelligence Applications", "Technology Innovation in Electrical Engineering, Electric Vehicle and Energy Management", "Technology Innovation in Electronic, Manufacturing, Instrumentation and Material Engineering", "Technology Innovation in Internet of Things and Its Applications", "Technology Innovation in Information, Modeling and Mobile Applications", "Bioengineering", "Renewable Energy", "Energy Planning and Policy", "Energy Science and Technology", and "Green Architecture - Energy in Building"

In addition, we thankful for the contribution and spending valuable time in the review process of our Advisory Boards, and Scientific - Editorial Boards. Also we really appreciate to our collaboration partners (Petra Christian University, Surabaya; University of Ciputra, Surabaya, Institute of National Technology, Malang and MATEC Web of Conferences), our Supported Institution (Oulu University, Finland, and Dongseo University, Korea) and our Sponsor (Continuing Education Centre, Petra Christian University, Surabaya).

Surabaya, April 1, 2018
Easter Sunday, 2018

Felix Pasila, Ph.D
General Chairman

SCIENTIFIC and EDITORIAL BOARDS

Statement of Peer review

In submitting conference proceedings to *Web of Conferences*, the editors of the proceedings certify to the Publisher that

1. They adhere to its **Policy on Publishing Integrity** in order to safeguard good scientific practice in publishing.
2. All articles have been subjected to peer review administered by the proceedings editors.
3. Reviews have been conducted by expert referees, who have been requested to provide unbiased and constructive comments aimed, whenever possible, at improving the work.
4. Proceedings editors have taken all reasonable steps to ensure the quality of the materials they publish and their decision to accept or reject a paper for publication has been based only on the merits of the work and the relevance to the journal.

Title, date and place of the conference

Title: The 3rd International Conference on Electrical Systems, Technology and Information (ICESTI 2017).
Date: 26- 29 September 2017
Place: Mercure Bali Harvestland, Kuta, Denpasar, Bali – Indonesia.
Web side: http://www.icesti.org/

Proceedings editor(s):

Editor in Chief : Roy Hendroko Setyobudi, Malang – IND
Board of Editor:
Esko Alasaarela, Oulu - FIN
Felix Pasila, Surabaya - IND
Gary Chan, Hongkong - HKG
Song-Gon Lee, Busan - KOR

Date and editor's signature

Malang, March 30, 2018
(Good Friday 2018)

ICESTI

(Roy Hendroko Setyobudi)

Geographic Information System for Higher Education via Data Scrapping

Agung Alfiansyah[1,*], and *Anas* Azhar[2]

[1]School of Applied STEM, Prasetiya Mulya University, BSD City Kavling Edutown I.1, Jl. BSD Raya Utama, BSD City, Kabupaten Tangerang 15339
[2]Dinas Pendidikan Kota Palembang, JL. Pramuka No. 929 Km. 5,5 Kel. Srijaya Kec. Alang-alang Lebar, Kota Palembang, Sumatera Selatan 30151

Abstract. This paper aims to build a database that can be used as the most important part of a geographic information system by using data from reliable sources. Data collection is done through process scrapping on some official website of Indonesia government. In addition to collecting quantitative data of higher education, this paper also mapping geographically from the high level of existing in Indonesia. It is expected that this data will be able to help the community and government in observing and analyzing the quantity and distribution of universities. The result of this research is one database that is ready to be integrated in more complex geographic information system. In addition, the scrapping method used allows us to perform the upgrade of data that has been obtained previously.

Key words: Data scrapping, geographic information system, higher education in Indonesia, spatial data.

1 Introduction

Indonesia is a large country with a population of almost 235×10^6, covering an area of 1 910 931 km^2. The country comprises more than 17 504 islands, makes it the largest archipelago in the world. The population is still dominated by young generation, whereby 44.72 % of its population is younger than 25 yr. This is particularly important due to the increasing needs to provide education and employment for the young.

As an emerging economy, Indonesia is considered as a low middle-income country entering the third stage of economic development, called the "efficiency driven economy" by the World Economic Forum (WEF 2012). Indonesia needs to address many complex issues to improve its competitiveness as it makes the transition to a new phase of economic development. In 2014 Indonesia is ranked at 34th by the World Competitiveness Index. Well-educated human resources, excellence in scientific research and better linkages to industry and government are regarded as key policy priorities in nearly all countries in this stage.

To achieve that, higher education programs are offered by five types of institution namely: academy, polytechnic, college, institute and university. The first two are specializing in vocational education stream, whilst the last three are more comprehensive and allowed to offer all education streams. A college (*Sekolah Tinggi*) is a specialized institution focusing on one particular academic discipline. Unlike universities, institutes are specialized in a particular group of disciplines such as sciences and technologies, arts or agriculture.

Universities in Indonesia are largely offered by the private sector. Out of around 3 500 institutions, only around 150 institutions are public (established and operated by the government). The public institutions in Indonesia are mostly under the Ministry of Education and Culture (98 institutions) and Ministry of Religion Affair (52 institutions). In the last 5 yr, the government has also established a number of new public institutions by converting the status of existing private institutions. The database of higher education directory are actually accessible online via https://forlap.ristekdikti.go.id/ [7].

*Corresponding author: agung.alfiansyah@prasetiyamulya.ac.id

2 Problem formulation

This paper aims to explain the ways used to obtain a database used to build a GIS that can be used to map the situation of higher education in Indonesia. The data is collected through the scrapping process of the official website of Ministry of Research, Technology and Higher Education (*Kementrian Riset dan Pendidikan Tinggi*) so that all important data can be obtained. In addition to quantitative data, the process offered will also be able to obtain spatial data from the geographical position of the university recorded on the website of the Ministry of Research, Technology and Higher Education.

Ultimately, this study aims to help people gain real insights, values, and benefits quickly, and precisely because much of the information can be explored and then processed and presented better in the form of GIS in its database pages. In addition, this study also aims to find out how to obtain record information/college data in Indonesia that has good and credible accuracy, design efficient data structures to create GIS, and know visualization of geographic data of Indonesian universities to be easily accessible and neatly presented to the general public.

3 Related works

This study explains how Wikipedia users choose places by identifying the correlation between conditions and locations based on social media objects Flickr and Twitter. This study focuses on the potential of geographic information on Wikipedia that should be able to customize its documents with the coordinates of photos on Flickr and corresponding Twitter messages, and also allows modeling of experimental languages on Flickr and Twitter that can fit in Wikipedia articles. The result is that the language can be used as a gazetteer-based data retrieval method (used by Yahoo!) and approaches on Wikipedia itself [1].

This study aims to improve the techniques for crawlers through the World Wide Web on search engines that focus on hierarchical crawling techniques, where crawlers are created dynamically at runtimes for different domains with resource sharing essences [2]. Swastika [3] developed a web based GIS for tourism in Gianyar Regency (Bali) that integrated google manually gathered data based to the google maps. For our case, this approach is not applicable as we have a big amount of highly dynamic data.

3.1 Geographic's information systems (GIS)

There several definition of GIS definitions and somehow the definition of GIS depends on who uses and processes it, from the user's background and point of view. In short, GIS is a computer system capable of storing data and using it to describe the places on the surface of the earth using the data from Geographic Positioning System [5]. In general, the definition of GIS includes three main components of hardware, software, and spatial data. In general, GIS should able to increase the performance of following tasks:

i). Speed and easiness to access a large amount and volumes of data;
ii). Ability to select data with specific areas or themes;
iii). Ability to analyze the characteristics of spatial data;
iv). Ability to look for certain characteristics in an area and then update data quickly.
v). Modeling alternative data and calculations;

As GIS is designed to store spatial data there are the following type of Information:

i). Latitude and Longitude as reference geography;
ii). Details of relationships as appropriate;
iii). Non-spatial attributes, such as data corresponding to usage.

The functions that exist in the GIS, one of which is there is enter data, storage, management, transformation, analysis and output. In general, outcomes of a GIS are: maps, graphs, addresses, lists and statistical summaries.

3.2 Google maps

Google visualization tools used by developers with HTML5 and JavaScript knowledge can already utilize up to 90 % of the overall functionality (Application Programming Interface). Some methods for visualization do not even require full code writing skills. A developer also needs the capability to change the source database in web server including SQL language communication and jQuery.

For data bound by geographic location, map visualization is often considered attractive to use. Unlike the graphite bar and the line drawing, it will be difficult to redraw the geographic area as desired. In visualization, Google Maps provides a basis for spatial data, and there are two types of graphics, namely geo-chart visualization and geo-map visualization. The two types of graphs are a delivery model according to the intensity and quantity of geographic access of each required area.

The difference between geo-map and geo-chart is the method used to render the actual image on the map. The rendering technique that geo-map uses Adobe Flash quickly but lacks the options for certain configurations. While geo-chart is rendered in VML (Vector Markup Language) or SVG (Scalable Vector Graphics), the configuration is detailed [5, 6].

4 Proposed method

To obtain credible data, we retrieve the necessary data through the official website pages issued by the technology research and higher education ministries by means of website scrapping. We gather the needed data from two official sites which are: FORLAP Website (Higher Education Databases): https://forlap.dikti.go.id/ [7] and BAN-PT (*Badan Akreditasi Nasional Peguruan Tinggi* — Board of Higher Education Accreditation): https://banpt.or.id/direktori/prodi/pencarian_prodi [8]. The workflow to build databases for higher education application using data scrapping can be illustrated using this scheme:

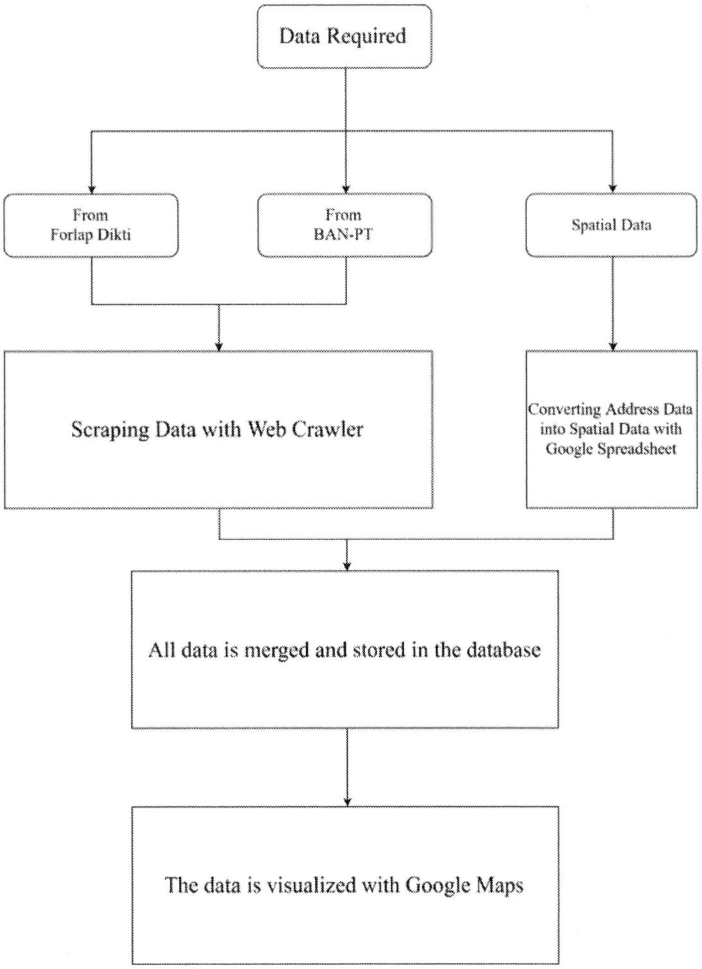

Fig. 1. Workflow in GIS database acquisition via website scrapping.

The workflow to build databases for higher education application using data scrapping can be illustrated using this scheme:

Table 1. Different data acquired from official governmental websites.

Data Source	Gathered Data
[7]	Institution, University Code, University, Study Program Code, forlap code University Status, Level, Permanent Lecturer, Lecturer with Doctoral Degree, Lecturer with Master Degree, Number of Students, Establishment year, Establishment Letter Number, Date of Establishment, Address, City, Postal Code, Telephone Number, Facsimile, email address, websites, study program url, University url.
[8]	Study Program name, accreditation level, Letter reference number, expired date, accreditation status.

To perform this data retrieval task, we use data retrieval using web crawling. This method is a stage that developed and used by a search engine to download web pages on the internet. Once downloaded, the next process is parsing on a web page and converted into a database on the server. Web crawlers also provide indexing to get valuable information about the web page.

4.1 FORLAP data acquisition

In retrieving data process in the FORLAP site, the website page it could not be scrapped only in one process as there are many site map sharing to get various data in the website. Therefore we did the workflow sub-division of the process described in Figure 2. This following chart describe the data collection diagram.

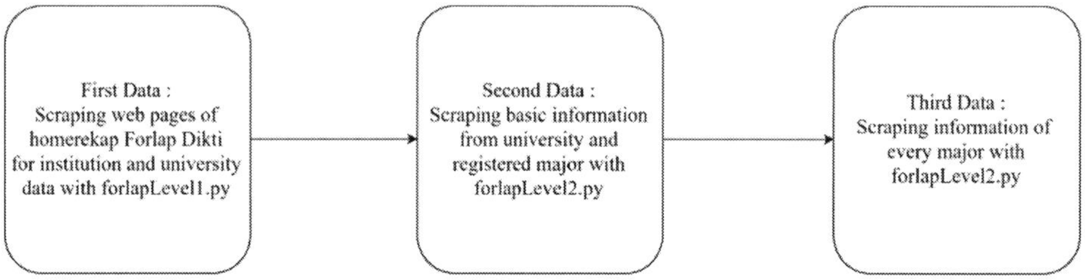

Fig. 2. Sub-process to perform data scrapping in FORLAP website.

4.2 FORLAP data acquisition

On the BAN-PT website, the accreditation data is displayed by the POST method in the PHP script which is then forwarded in html. This results in the absence of a query set in the site address section of the page. Therefore, we saved the pages of BAN-PT site into the local server in order to be processed and cleaned data. This method should be enhanced for the next application in order to increase the performance of the methods.

4.3 Spatial data conversion

The data that has been obtained by scraping and then stored in the database is processed as such, then there is some data that is used to obtain spatial data. This process is intended to convert the data from a university/institute physical address to its geospatial location. This data location is usually given in terms of the value of the position in latitude and latitude of the position on earth. To perform this process, we use the function available in google sheet, ie geocode. So that the address data that has been obtained from the forlap needs to first be tabulated in the spreadsheet to then be transformed automatically.

This spatial data helps us to visualize our gathered data on the online map. Most of conversion result give the right location, but some of them are not exactly in the correct location. This error is caused by the fact that the function cannot find the location with the defined name demanded by user, which is then done in wider location search. However, this type of error can be overcome by doing several experiments with different queries with the same meaning.

5 Implementation

To perform the appropriate tasks that have been described in the specifications, we use the following implementations of the following flows:

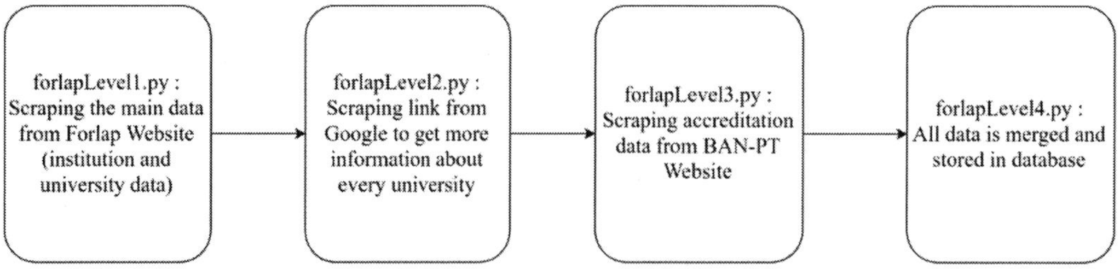

Fig. 2. Different level of scrapping in higher education data acquisition.

Overall step task performed by data scrapping in highest level (university), can be describe as follows:

```
Time initialization
Connect to MySQL databse
Access forlap web using urllib
Scrap data using beautifulSoup
Build University dataframe
for each link in datafram do
  for all data with <tr> tag do
    for all data with in tag <a> href=true do
        get university store to dict.
        get link and store to dict
Build data dict using Pandas
Build data dict in MySQLPandas
Print runtime execution
```

Fig. 3. Data scrapping in python-like *psudocode.*

Algorithm used in other parts is not too different from the first part, the difference is there because the structure of web pages are not the same, so it takes a different way of digging the data, although it is actually the same. Next step of the scrapping method is data address conversion from physical address to the latitude-longitude which performed using google sheet web application. Some of the results of this address conversion can be observed in the following figure:

R	S	T
Addr	Lat	Long
Universitas Gadjah Mada Kec. Depok - Kab. Sleman - Prop. D.I. Yogyakarta 55281	-7.7713847	110.3774998
Universitas Indonesia Kota Jakarta Pusat - Prop. D.K.I. Jakarta - Indonesia 10430	-6.1949311	106.848885
Universitas Sumatera Utara Kota Medan - Prop. Sumatera Utara - Indonesia 20155	3.5653554	98.6567748
Universitas Airlangga Kec. Mulyorejo - Kota Surabaya - Prop. Jawa Timur 60115	-7.2698208	112.784576
Universitas Hasanuddin Kota Makassar - Prop. Sulawesi Selatan - Indonesia 90245	-5.13241	119.488
Universitas Andalas Kota Padang - Prop. Sumatera Barat - Indonesia 25163	-0.914559	100.4595468
Universitas Padjadjaran Kota Bandung - Prop. Jawa Barat - Indonesia 40132	-6.893941	107.617288
Universitas Diponegoro Kec. Tembalang - Kota Semarang - Prop. Jawa Tengah 50275	-7.0520829	110.4399777
Universitas Sriwijaya Kota Palembang - Prop. Sumatera Selatan - Indonesia 30662	-2.9846917	104.7335316
Universitas Lambung Mangkurat Kota Banjarmasin - Prop. Kalimantan Selatan - Indonesia 70123	-3.2975189	114.5864305

Fig. 5. Address to geo-location conversion result.

It is rather difficult to check the thoroughness of this conversion result thoroughly. At this stage we only check a few (just a few) of the several universities that we know and examine as far as we know. This method may be very unreliable and inaccurate, but so far if the results obtained from the conversion process still exist in one sub-district area, it is in our opinion still quite good.

6 Results

We tested our proposed approach to acquire the data and we have following results (as 17 July 2017):

i). 4 027 universities and higher education institutions across Indonesia with a 2.5 MB SQL data load;

ii). 25 087 study programs from all universities and educational institutions in Indonesia with a load of 15.5 MB SQL data;

iii). 1 130 accredited information of the university and the institute of education of Indonesia with the contents of SQL data 192 KB;

iv). 19 102 Accreditation information from all Study Programs of all Universities and Institutions of Higher Education in Indonesia with a 3.5 MB SQL data load.

That result represents 88.3 % of the scrapped data from the total data in FORLAP website. The rest there is some of the data that cannot be scrapped as they were hidden from google crawler thus, cannot be found using google. It is possible that this happens because that the university has just submitted data into the FORLAP, so it is not indexed in the google search engine. In a short time, the data will be retrieved once google has done the indexing.

And finally, the visualization was performed on the Google Maps so that it can be publically accessed online. Intuitively, this technique makes easier for us to process data on the map. We do not need to build from scratch again or even do not need any API access code on google maps. Google maps themselves already provide layers, so users will be expected to query by checking on the slides tab to get the desired information, although obviously the functionality is limited and cannot be customized anymore. Google itself only gives 2 000 lines for each layer, this makes it difficult for us to add exploratory data on the map, because the data will be inserted more than 20 000 rows. Finally, we only add data that can be inserted in 2 000 line only.

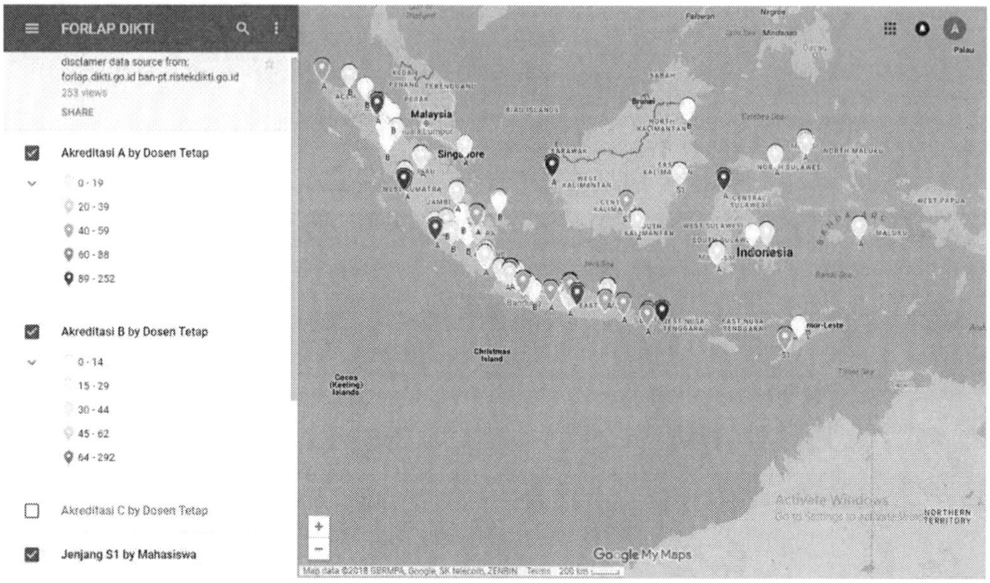

Fig. 5. Higher education visualization in google map with simple query.

We consider this limitation is a drawback for that should be solved for the next step of development, we proposed to build a dedicated server to accommodate the amount of data and also capability to perform complex data query and visualization.

7 Conclusion

The results of data retrieval using robot crawlers are data obtained from the forlap site pages and BAN-PT as well as data conversion in google docs. Acquisition of data achieved from the total data reached 4 027 of the 4 557 universities registered in the forlap dikti or in percentage reached 88.3 %. Approximately 11.7 % more data cannot be scrapped, this is because data cannot be found when searching using google. Search in google is done to pass through the security gap in the forlap site that is a captcha. Google does not or has not indexed a small portion of the Forlap site page that the crawler requested, so no data was found.

Annex

Partial visualized data in google maps with limited query can be found in: http://bit.ly/forlapdikti [9]. Source code and acquired data base can be forked in github from https://github.com/azharnian/forlapDikti [10].

Reference

[1] O.V. Laere, S. Schockaert, V. Tanasescu, B. Dhoedt, C.B. Jones. ACM Transaction on Information System. **33**,2(2014). https://dl.acm.org/citation.cfm?id=2629685
[2] A. Kundu, R. Dutta, R. Dattagupta, D. Mukhopadhyay. International Journal of Intelligent Information and Database Systems, **3**,1:90–106(2009). https://dl.acm.org/citation.cfm?id=1810808
[3] I.W. Swastika. *Sistem informasi geografis berbasis web untuk pemetaan pariwisata Kabupaten Gianyar: Studi kasus pada Dinas Pariwisata Kabupaten Gianyar*. [Web based geographic information system for tourism mapping of Gianyar Regency: A case study at Gianyar Regency Tourism Office]. [Undergraduate Thesis] Teknik Informatika, Universitas Pembangunan Nasional Veteran Yogyakarta (2011). [in Bahasa Indonesia]. 56 http://repository.upnyk.ac.id/905/1/SKRIPSI.pdf
[4] I. Heywood, S. Cornelius, S. Carver. *An introduction to geographical information system*. Third Edition. London: Pearson (2006). 18-27 https://www.amazon.com/Introduction-Geographical-Information-Systems-3rd/dp/B0041W4PSG
[5] T.L. Ruthkoski. *Google visualization API essentials*. Birmingham: Packt (2013). 7-18 https://www.safaribooksonline.com/library/view/google-visualization-api/9781849694360/
[6] B. Fry. *Visualizing data*. Sebastopol: O'Reily Media (2008). 6-14 https://www.amazon.com/Visualizing-Data-Explaining-Processing-Environment/dp/0596514557
[7] Kementrian Riset, Teknologi dan Pendidikan Tinggi, Pangkalan Data Pendidikan Tinggi [Online] from https://forlap.ristekdikti.go.id/ (2018). [Accessed on March 15th 2018]. [in Bahasa Indonesia]

[8] BAN-PT, Direktori Hasil Akreditasi Program Studi, [Online] from https://banpt.or.id/direktori/prodi/pencarian_prodi (2018). [Accessed on March 15th 2018]. [in Bahasa Indonesia]
[9] A. Alfiansyah, A. Azhar. *Visual Forlap Dikti*. [Online] http://bit.ly/forlapdikti [Accessed on March 15th 2018].
[10] A. Alfiansyah, A. Azhar. *Project of scraping web http://forlap.dikti.go.id/ with Python2.7* [Online] from https://github.com/azharnian/forlapDikti [Accessed on March 15th 2018].

IoT-Based Car's Parking Monitoring System

Albertus Ega Dwiputra[1], *Handry* Khoswanto[1], *Raymond* Sutjiadi[2], and *Resmana* Lim[1,*]

[1]Electrical Engineering Department, Faculty of Industrial Technology, Petra Christian University, Jl. Siwalankerto 121-131, Surabaya, 60234, Indonesia
[2]Informatics Department, Faculty of Information Technology, Institut Informatika Indonesia, Jl. Pattimura 3, Surabaya, 60189, Indonesia

Abstract. Internet-of-things-based technologies have advanced so much and helped public necessities. The use of IoT at a parking lot will help vehicle users to know the availability of a parking location through smartphones. This IoT-based parking system is created by using controllers, sensors, servers and cloud. Controllers and sensors will be placed on the ceiling of each parking slots to detect the presence of a car. Server collect the results of the sensors and store them in Cloud. System test is conducted by installing three sensor circuits and server in a parking lot. The tests consist of measuring time that required for data transmission and the rate of success of data transmission from the parking lot to the Cloud. Based on above tests, it is observed that the sensor circuit and Radio Frequency Identification are able to transmit the parking lot data without error. This system require maximum 1 min to update parking lot data. The process of obtaining data until the data being stored in Cloud takes 12 s and the process of acquiring parking condition data from Cloud to smartphone takes 30 s. The accuracy level of parking lot data transfer is 100 %.

Key words: Internet of things, IoT cloud, parking lots, smart parking system.

1 Introduction

Along side with the development of information technology, the Internet of Things (IoT) become more popular at this time. IoT is a concept to connect various devices (smart house, car, mobile phone and household device) and enable communication between them [1]. The IoT device is equipped with electronic components, sensors, actuators and network connectivity [2]. With these components, IoT device can send data or even be controlled remotely by utilizing the internet network infrastructure.

When the concept of IoT is applied in urban life, a new concept of Smart City is introduced. Although there is no clear definition of Smart City yet, the exact goal of Smart City is to create services to facilitate access to public facilities and improve their quality [3]. This aim can be realized by spreading the use of IoT technology on the infrastructure of public facilities in urban (Urban IoT) [4]. One example of an important public facility in urban areas is public parking for four-wheeled vehicles.

There are several technologies that have been created for parking systems in Indonesia, and some of them have been used in shopping areas. For example, the concept of a smart parking lot by adding sensors, actuators, and microcontrollers. Users only need to put the vehicle at a certain location, then the microcontroller will instruct the actuator to drive the vehicle to an empty parking location [5]. This concept is very interesting, but it needs a considerable cost because it takes a total physical renovation if anyone wants to apply it on an existing public parking lot. There is also a concept of another smart parking lot using sensors, microcontrollers, and Light-Emitting Diode (LED) displays [6]. The sensor will read the amount of vacant parking space and send the data to the microcontroller. Then the microcontroller will display the amount of vacant parking spot and display it to the LED display [7].

In this part of the IoT concept can be used to improve the accessibility of parking lot for the community [8]. People do not have to go to the location to find out how much parking space is available and where the parking lot is empty.

*Corresponding author: resmana@petra.ac.id

The use of mobile application connected with cloud can tell where the parking spaces are empty. The use of Radio Frequency Identification (RFID) can be added to the parking lot to increase the ease of data collection that can be used for the analysis process [9].

Therefore it is necessary to create a smart parking system that can connect with cloud. This parking system can help many vehicle users to find parking space more easily. Data obtained from this parking system can be sent to mobile phones or other applications. Communities can monitor vacant parking lots remotely and in real-time.

2 System design

The developed parking system is a system that is able to calculate and detect the presence of cars in the parking area. The data obtained in the parking area will be sent to the cloud database. The data will be used by Android application to inform the users where parking space they should go to. Figure 1 shows the mechanism of the parking system.

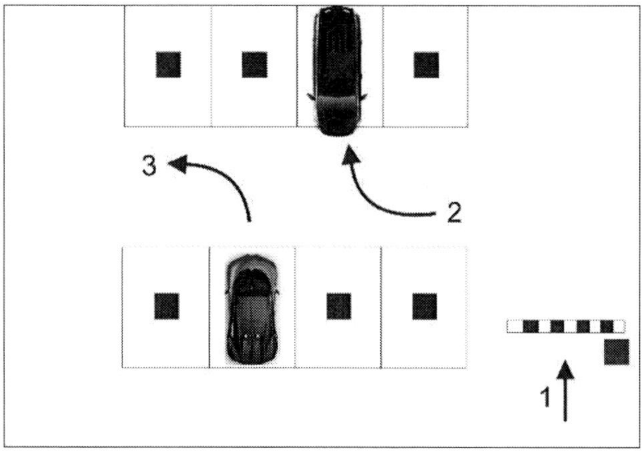

Fig. 1. Mechanism of parking system.

There are three main processes that become the core of this parking system design:
(i) Payment process at the entrance gate.
(ii) Signing in to the parking slot.
(iii) Processing out of the parking slot.

The first process is payment at the entrance, where at the entrance gate will be placed RFID reader and controller with Liquid Crystal Display (LCD). Car driver needs to have RFID card that has a function as e-money. The car driver only needs to tap the card on the scanner and data in the card will be sent to the local server and cloud then the gate will open. In this chapter, only a series of data readings and transmissions will be created and does not involve the development of a parking gate bar. However, if necessary, the microcontroller and RFID reader circuit can be connected to the parking gate bar because the relays are provided in the circuit.

The second process is the process of getting into the parking slot. In each of the parking slots will be installed car detection sensors and additional sensors on the parking marker to keep the car park tidiness. Each slot has a unique address for the parking lot mapping process. If a car is detected at a specific slot address, then the system will send the latest data to the cloud for updating. The third process is the process of getting out of the parking slot. This process is almost the same as the second process. If the sensor detects the car exits a certain parking slot, then the system will update the existing data in the cloud according to the slot address under changing conditions.

3 Circuit design

This system consists of two main circuits, i.e. sensor circuit and RFID sensor.

3.1 Sensor circuit

The controllers used in this system are Arduino Pro Mini and the modules are ESP8266, two HC-SR04, 16 × 2 LCD and a SHARP GP2Y0A710K0F proximity sensor. Other supporting components are 2N2904 transistor, 3.3 volt 1N4728A zener diode, LED, buzzer and resistor. Input for microcontroller comes from three sensors: two HC-SR04 ultrasonic and one GP2Y0A710K0F proximity sensor. Both sensors are used to detect the presence of the car. Proximity sensor is used to detect the distance of the existing parking limit on the side. If there is a car occupy more than its own parking area then the output value of the sensor will be processed by the controller, then the buzzer will be turned on to let the driver knows that the car's position is improper.

Two LEDs are used only to provide information visually about the presence of the car. If there is no car in parking slot, then one LED will light up, and if the parking slot occupied, another LED will light up. LCD is also used as a visual information that reads the three sensors. LCD does not need to be always installed, because the position of the circuit located in the ceiling of the parking area. ESP8266 WiFi Module serves as a data sender medium from the microcontroller to the local server.

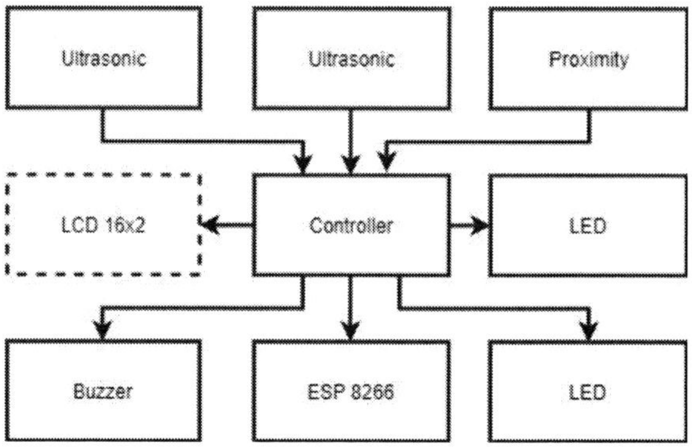

Fig. 2. Sensor circuit scheme.

3.2 RFID circuit

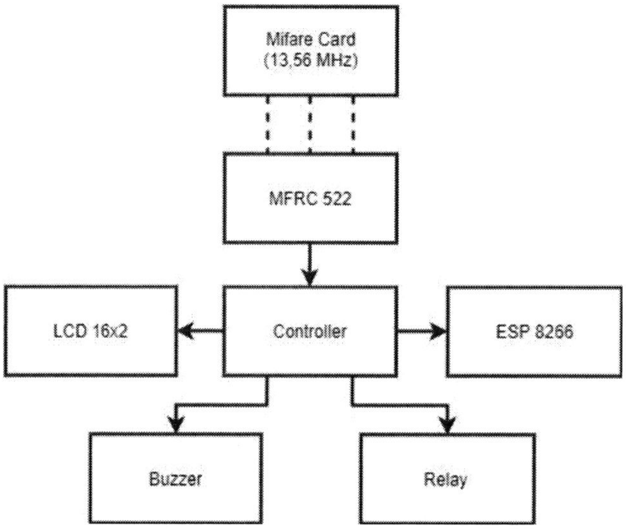

Fig. 3. RFID circuit scheme.

Figure 3 is a circuit diagram used for RFID card processing. In this system, the RFID reader is MFRC522 and the RFID card that can be used is the card which suits the 13.56 MHz protocol. ESP-8266 is used as a communication medium between local and Arduino servers.

4 Software design

Software design is divided into three parts: software for sensor circuit, software for RFID circuit and software for server.

4.1 Sensor circuit software

Figure 4 below illustrates how the system starts by initializing variables, I/O ports, and libraries used. By default, the sensor circuit will assume the parking slot is empty. Once all are initialized, the Arduino will calibrate the sensor by sampling the sensor readout data hundreds times. The average reading result will be a normal distance when no car is detected.

When calibration is complete, the Arduino will enter the network using ESP8266. Once connected with the network, the Arduino is ready to perform sensor readings. First, Arduino will read the existence of the car using both ultrasonic sensors. If both sensors detect a distance difference of approximately 1.3 m, then it means there is a car in that blocks and the presence status of the car will be changed to one. But if there is no car, the presence status of the car will be changed to zero.

If parking status has been obtained, the Arduino will check the status of the previous car with the current car status. If previously there was no car and now there is a car, or otherwise, then Arduino will make a connection to the local server and send the data of the parking slot. However if current and previous conditions are the same, Arduino will not establish a connection with the server. The next process is checking the parking tidiness. The circuit will do the distance reading on the proximity sensor to detect parking that is untidy. If the car is detected then the buzzer will be sounded, otherwise the buzzer will be turned off. After that, the program will perform a delay for one second then do the repetition checking the existence of the car.

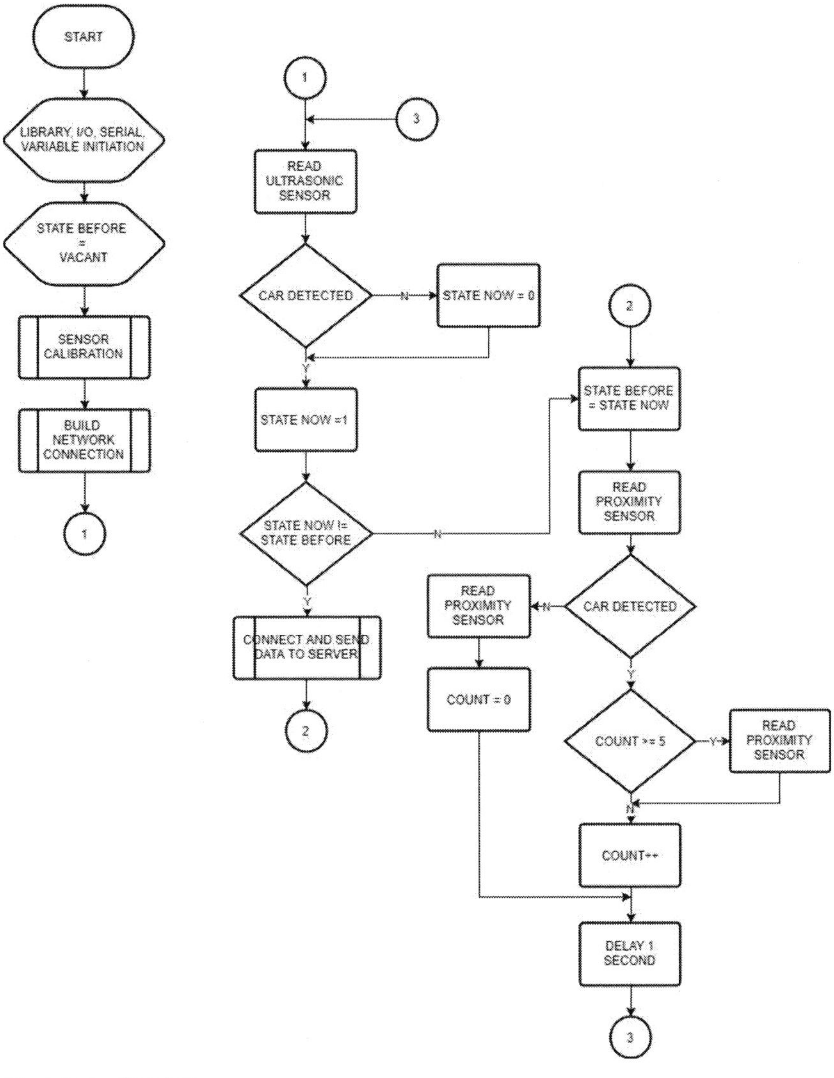

Fig. 4. Sensor flowchart.

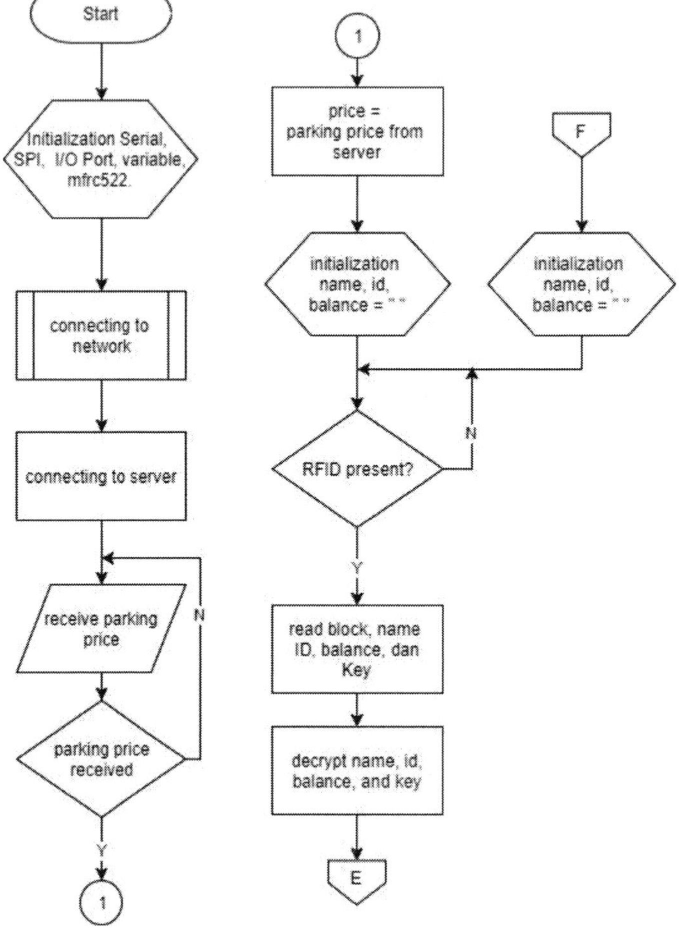

Fig. 5. RFID flowchart (part 1).

As shown in Figure 5, at the beginning, the program will initialize variables and libraries. After that, the circuit will be connected to WiFi network. In contrast to the sensor circuit design software, the circuit will be directly connected to the server to request parking fee from the server. If the fee is accepted, the process will resume. But if not yet, the request will be resent. If the parking fee has been successfully received, the data will be stored in a variable.

Once the connection is established and the fee is received, the program will initialize the variables to store the existing data on the RFID card. The variable will be emptied and the program will start the RFID card readings if any card is detected. If the card is detected then the data in the card will be read, decrypted and stored into the variables that have been provided. The received variables will be converted according to the needs because some data needs an integer or double and string type, while the reading data is a char array.

Continue to Figure 6 below, after the data is saved, card checking will be done to check whether the balance is sufficient or not. If not pass the existing requirements, then the card will be rejected and the circuit will be ready again to read the next card. But if the card complies with the existing requirements, then the connection to the server will be reconnected and data will be sent. After the data delivery is complete, the balance will be deducted, encrypted, and re-written to the card. Then the circuit will be prepared to read the next card.

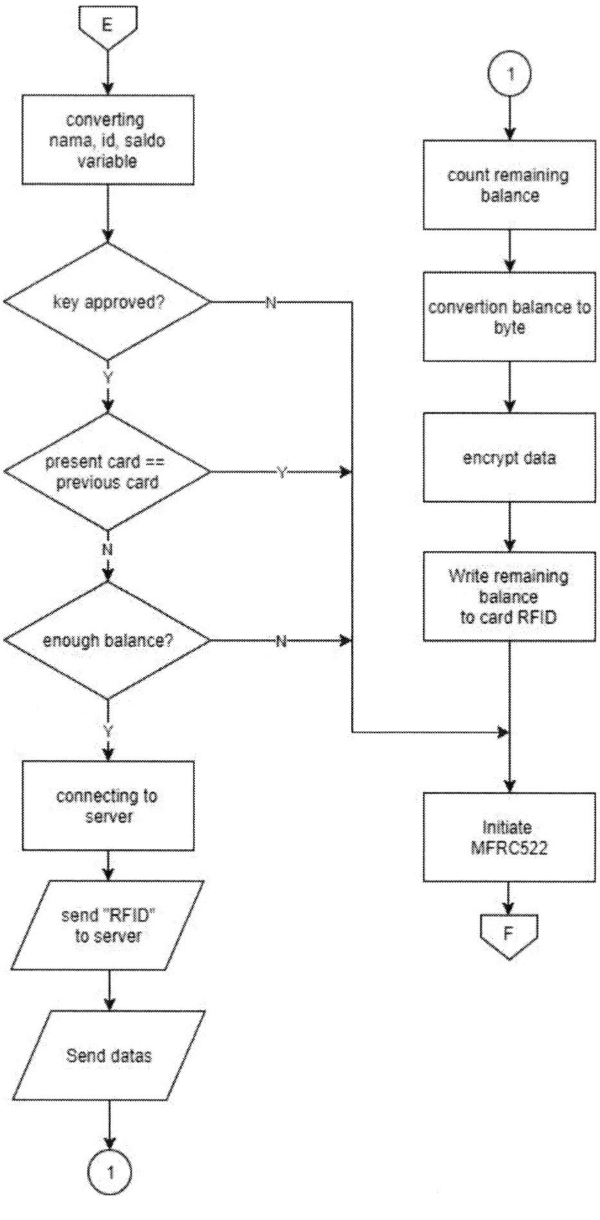

Fig. 6. RFID flowchart (part 2).

4.3 Local server software

The languages used on the server are Java and Python languages. The server works as a temporary receiver of data from sensors installed in the parking area. The data will be sent to cloud with the help of internet network. Figure 6 is the server program logic.

The server is designed using multithread Transmission Control Protocol (TCP) so it can handle more than one connection [10]. The first thing to do is to initialize the variables, sockets and classes needed for receiving and sending data streams. After that the server will take the fee of parking space stored in the cloud. Once the fee is stored in the server, a socket for a TCP connection will be established. If there is a connection request, then a new thread will be formed and run the server function.

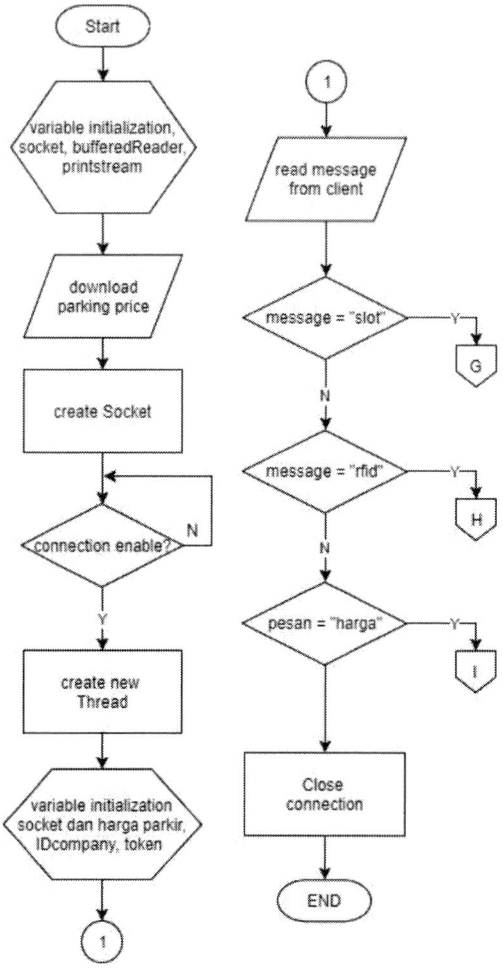

Fig. 7. Server flowchart part 1.

In the new thread, socket variables will be initialized, the parking fee, the company ID, and the token used. After that, the server will wait for data confirmation from the client connected to the server. There are three types of client requests to the server i.e. slot, RFID and parking fee. If the server can not identify the data sent, the connection will be disconnected by the server.

(i) Slot: If the request slot provided by the client, the server will again wait for data to be sent by the client. The data sent will be separated first and stored into several variables. The data received is the address and status of the parking slot. After that the server will take the data address of the variable ID in the database. Once the data is found, variable ID address of the database will be used to send the latest data to the server.

(ii) RFID: If the RFID request provided by the client, the server will wait for data to be sent by the client. The data sent will be separated first and stored into several variables. The data received are name, ID card and balance. After that, the server will retrieve the ID variable stored in the database. The existing variable ID will be used to send the RFID card ID to the cloud according to the address.

(iii) Parking fee: If the fee request provided by the client, the server will wait for one and a half seconds then the server will send the fee data back to the client. A one-and-a-half-second delay is done to allow the RFID circuit time to readily read the data serially.

After the process of one of the above three processes is completed then the server will disconnect and the program is completed.

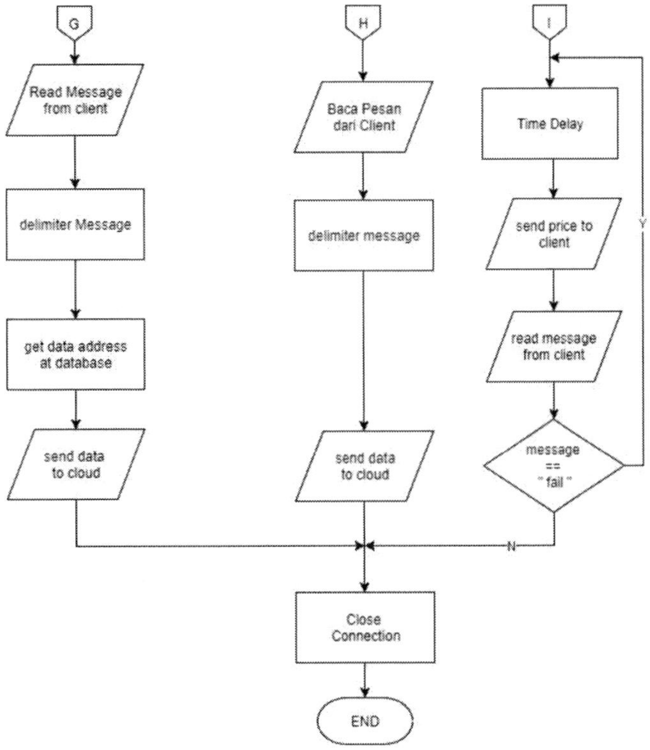

Fig. 8. Server flowchart part 2.

In the new thread, socket variables will be initialized, the parking fee, the company ID, and the token used. After that, the server will wait for data confirmation from the client connected to the server. There are three types of client requests to the server i.e. slot, RFID, and parking fee. If the server can not identify the data sent, the connection will be disconnected by the server.

(i) Slot: If the request slot provided by the client, the server will again wait for data to be sent by the client. The data sent will be separated first and stored into several variables. The data received is the address and status of the parking slot. After that the server will take the data address of the variable ID in the database. Once the data is found, variable ID address of the database will be used to send the latest data to the server.

(ii) RFID: If the RFID request provided by the client, the server will wait for data to be sent by the client. The data sent will be separated first and stored into several variables. The data received are name, ID card and balance. After that, the server will retrieve the ID variable stored in the database. The existing variable ID will be used to send the RFID card ID to the cloud according to the address.

(iii) Parking fee: If the fee request provided by the client, the server will wait for one and a half seconds then the server will send the fee data back to the client. A one-and-a-half-second delay is done to allow the RFID circuit time to readily read the data serially.

After the process of one of the above three processes is completed then the server will disconnect and the program is completed.

5 System testing

This system testing is conducted in two main circuits, i.e. sensor circuit and RFID sensor.

5.1 Sensor circuit testing

The test of the circuit data communication of the whole circuit to and from cloud is done by detecting the existence of the car 10 times with the assumption of 150 cm car height and floor to ceiling distance of 350 cm. The measuring point of this test is the success of the circuit in sending data, the length of time required, and the validity of the data. Calculation of respond time on the Arduino and server is done by the program by recording the difference between the start and end time of the program. The calculation of respond time on cloud is done by calculating the difference between server sent time and Ubidots received time. Based on the testing result as shown in Table 1 below, The sensor circuit has 100 % success rate for sending data to cloud with an average total required time of 6.4004 s for each data. Data errors were not found during the test.

Table 1. Sensor circuit testing result.

Test	1010001	Response Time			Total Time (s)	Data Error
		Arduino (ms)	Server (ms)	Ubi dots (s)		
1	Pass	237	228	4	4.465	0
2	Pass	249	315	6	6.564	0
3	Pass	312	226	6	6.538	0
4	Pass	369	235	6	6.604	0
5	Pass	253	234	6	6.487	0
6	Pass	245	209	6	6.454	0
7	Pass	232	210	6	6.442	0
8	Pass	274	229	6	6.503	0
9	Pass	233	225	6	6.458	0
10	Pass	268	221	7	7.489	0
Avg	100 %	267.2	233.2	5.9	6.400 4	0 %

5.2 RFID circuit testing

The method used to test RFID circuit communications to cloud is by tapping RFID cards ten times. In the program, there are already methods of calculating the respond time such as testing the sensor circuit. The measured points are the success of the circuit sending the data, the time it takes to send from the circuit to cloud, and the validity of the data sent with the received.

Table 2. RFID circuit testing result.

Test	RFID 1	Response Time			Total Time (s)	Data Error
		Arduino (ms)	Server (ms)	Ubi dots (s)		
1	Pass	1 396	751	7	9.147	0
2	Pass	925	362	8	9.287	0
3	Pass	1 406	776	7	9.182	0
4	Pass	1 303	550	7	8.853	0
5	Pass	2 156	500	2	4.656	0
6	Pass	1 488	603	7	9.091	0
7	Pass	1 714	622	8	10.333 6	0
8	Pass	1 214	161 4	6	8.828	0
9	Pass	1 062	121 1	3	5.273	0
10	Pass	1 302	546	6	7.848	0
Avg	100 %	1 396.6	753.5	6.1	8.250 1	0 %

RFID circuits have 100 % success rate in sending data to Ubidots cloud with the percentage of sent data error is 0 %. The average time it takes to send data from scratch when the card is detected until the data received by Ubidots is 8.2501 s. The process in Arduino takes an average of 1 396.6 ms and 753.5 ms is on the server. The longest time spent when sending data from the server to Ubidots is 6.1 s.

5.3 Car detection

Testing the accuracy of sensor readings conducted by car detection test with the assumption that the car has a height of 150 cm. Testing is done as much as ten times for each circuit of sensors by shifting obstacles. If there is a parking car, then the obstacles will be placed between the sensor and the floor. If the condition of the parking slot is empty, then the barrier will be removed so that the sensor will immediately detect the floor.

Table 4. Car detection testing with occupied parking slot condition

Car Present (Car Height 150 cm) - (Ceiling distance 350 cm)						
Test	1010001	1010002	1010003	1010004	1010005	1010006
1	Detected	Detected	Detected	Detected	Detected	Detected
2	Detected	Detected	Detected	Detected	Detected	Detected
3	Detected	Detected	Detected	Detected	Detected	Detected
4	Detected	Detected	Detected	Detected	Detected	Detected
5	Detected	Detected	Detected	Detected	Detected	Detected
6	Detected	Detected	Detected	Detected	Detected	Detected
7	Detected	Detected	Detected	Detected	Detected	Detected
8	Detected	Detected	Detected	Detected	Detected	Detected
9	Detected	Detected	Detected	Detected	Detected	Detected
10	Detected	Detected	Detected	Detected	Detected	Detected

Table 5. Car detection testing with unoccupied parking slot condition.

Car Not Present - (Ceiling distance 350 cm)						
Test	1010001	1010002	1010003	1010004	1010005	1010006
1	Empty	Empty	Empty	Empty	Empty	Empty
2	Empty	Empty	Empty	Empty	Empty	Empty
3	Empty	Empty	Empty	Empty	Empty	Empty
4	Empty	Empty	Empty	Empty	Empty	Empty
5	Empty	Empty	Empty	Empty	Empty	Empty
6	Empty	Empty	Empty	Empty	Empty	Empty
7	Empty	Empty	Empty	Empty	Empty	Empty
8	Empty	Empty	Empty	Empty	Empty	Empty
9	Empty	Empty	Empty	Empty	Empty	Empty
10	Empty	Empty	Empty	Empty	Empty	Empty

There are six circuits that are used for the testing process. From the two tables of sensor testing, it can be concluded that the whole circuits of managed sensors is able to detect the presence of the car accurately.

6 Conclusion

The development of a prototype of the internet-based smart parking system works well in detecting, processing parking data, and sending parking data to the cloud. Here are the key points that can be deduced from testing data are sensor and RFID circuits can send data to Ubidots IoT cloud without any data error under twelve seconds. The second is the RFID circuit is capable of reading and writing data back to the card with no data error under two seconds. The third is sensor, RFID, and server circuits can process data in less than two seconds. The last is data delivery to cloud takes longer than sending data from circuit to server, with maximum time is 20 s.

References

1. G. Lobaccaro, S. Carlucci, E. Löfström. Energies, **9**(5):1–33 (2016). http://www.mdpi.com/1996-1073/9/5/348.
2. P. Sethi, S.R. Sarangi. Journal of Electrical and Computer Engineering, **2017**(9324035):1–25 (2017). https://www.hindawi.com/journals/jece/2017/9324035/
3. Economic and Social Council, United Nations. *Smart cities and infrastructure: Report of the secretary-general*. Geneva: Commission on Science and Technology for Development (2016). http://unctad.org/meetings/en/SessionalDocuments/ecn162016d2_en.pdf
4. A. Zanella, N. Bui, A. Castellani, L. Vangelista, M. Zorzi. IEEE IoT Journal, **1**,1:22–32 (2014). http://doi.org/10.1109/JIOT.2014.2306328
5. I. Winarsih, R. Mahendra. JETri, **8**,2:21–36 (2009). [in Bahasa Indonesia]. http://download.portalgaruda.org/article.php?article=253389&val=6824&title=SISTEM%20PARKIR%20OTOMATIS%20MENGGUNAKAN%20RFID%20BERBASISKAN%20MIKROKONTROLER%20AT%2089S51

6. M. Priyatham M, S. Mandal S., M.S. Lakshmi, L. Ashwani, B.M. Sandhya. IJERCSE, **4**(6):360–363 (2017). http://technoarete.org/common_abstract/pdf/IJERCSE/v4/i6/Ext_03295.pdf
7. A. Anita. *Perancangan dan implementasi sistem alokasi tempat parkir berbasis mikrokontroler ATMega8535*. [Design and implementation of ATMega8535 microcontroller based parking allocation system] [Thesis]. Teknik Telekomunikasi, Fakultas Ilmu Terapan, Universitas Telkom (2011). [in Bahasa Indonesia]. http://repository.telkomuniversity.ac.id/pustaka/97105/perancangan-dan-implementasi-sistem-alokasi-tempat-parkir-berbasis-mikrokontroler-atmega8535.html
8. Z. Ji, I. Ganchev, M. O'Droma, L. Zhao, X. Zhang. Sensors **14**:2272–22393 (2014). http://www.mdpi.com/1424-8220/14/12/22372/pdf
9. P.C. Jain, K.P. Vijaygopalan. *RFID and wireless sensor networks*. Proceedings of ASCNT (Noida, India, 2010). https://pdfs.semanticscholar.org/47ae/cbb03c54d74911e11266d24289586ac72e2a.pdf
10. T.J. Andersson. *Single SCTP association with multiple streams vs. multiple TCP connections: A performance evaluation* [Thesis]. Department of Computer Science, Karlstad University (2005). https://www.cs.kau.se/cs/education/courses/davddiss/Uppsatser_2005/D2005-08.pdf

Modified Welch Berlekamp Algorithm to Decode Reed Solomon Codes

Ali Mahmudi[*], *Sentot* Achmadi, and *Michael*

Departement of Software Engineering, National Institute of Technology (ITN Malang). Jalan Sigura-gura 2, Malang 65145, Indonesia.

Abstract. In this paper, the Reed Solomon Code is decoded using the Welch-Berlekamp Algorithm. The RS Decoder is implemented using Hardware Description Language VHDL (VHSIC hardware Description Language) and simulated on Modelsim software. Some modifications have been carried out on the Welch Berlekamp algorithm in such a way that it is easier to implement. A pilot design double error correction RS(63, 59) decoder has been written in VHDL and simulated. The XILINX FPGA layout RS(63, 59) is then obtained.

Key words: FPGA, hard decision decoding, Reed Solomon Code, Welch Berlekamp algorithm

1 Introduction

The introduction of error control codes in data transmission and data communication is due to the addition of unwanted noise over the noisy channel. These error control codes are used to minimize the error. These codes are capable of detecting and correcting errors to achieve minimum error level.

Decoding Reed Solomon codes can be classified into two categories: soft decision decoding and hard decision decoding. The soft decision decoding is quite complex and very hardware intensive to implement. Generalized Minimum Distance Decoding is one example of the soft decision decoding. The hard decision decoder is very popular because it is very simple to implement [1, 2]. The Berlekamp-Massey Algorithm and the Euclidean Algorithm are the two well-known algorithms to solve the key equation in hard decision decoding [3–5]. However, the use of the Welch Berlekamp Algorithm to solve the key equation is not much presented [1, 6].

RS code is a cyclic linear block code that has been used in many modern applications. Advanced television [7], DVD applications [8], data hiding [9, 10] and data transmission with nano satellite [11] are some few applications in our modern life.

This paper presents the hard decision decoding for RS codes RS(63, 59), especially on the VHDL implementation of the Welch Berlekamp algorithm to solve the key equation for RS(63, 59) decoder.

This paper is primarily concerned with the VHDL implementation of the Welch

[*] Corresponding author: amahmudi@hotmail.com

Berlekamp algorithm to decode Reed Solomon Codes over GF(2^6), especially RS(63, 59). Some modifications have been carried out on the algorithm so that it is easier to implement. This paper is organized as follows. In section 2, a brief explanation of RS codes is given. Section 3 presents the RS encoder and section 4 deals with the RS decoder. Section 5 and section 6 deal with the implementation and results, respectively. Finally, section 7 is the conclusions.

2 RS code

The *RS* code is normally specified as *RS*(n, k) where $n = 2^m-1$ and $k = n-2t$ are the number of symbols in every codeword and the number of information symbols in every codeword [1, 2, 4], respectively. It works over $GF(2^m)$ with m bits per symbol.

RS(n, k) is able to correct up to t symbols. Then,

$d = 2t + 1$ is the designed distance

n-k is the number of redundancy or parity check symbols. The relation between t and n-k can be written as

$$2t = n-k$$

The RS code can be shown in Figure 1 below.

k symbols data	n-k parity check symbols

Fig. 1. The systematic *RS* code.

In the case of RS(63, 59), this code works over $GF(2^6)$ with 6 bits per symbol. It has 63 symbols in every codeword, where it has 59 information symbols and the rest is four parity check symbols. This code can correct up to two symbols.

3 RS encoder

The *RS*(n, k) code, is easily explained by using its special polynomial, called *generator polynomial*, $g(x)$. The general form of the *RS*(n, k) generator polynomial is shown in Equation 1, Equation 2, and Equation 3

$$g(x) = \prod_{i=0}^{n-k-1}(x-\alpha^{b+i}) \quad (1)$$

where b is a non-negative integer selected by the designer. In this paper, it is assumed that $b = 0$. In the case of *RS*(*63*, *59*), the generator polynomial $g(x)$ is

$$g(x) = (x-\alpha^0)(x-\alpha^1)(x-\alpha^2)(x-\alpha^3) \quad (2)$$
$$g(x) = x^4 + \alpha^{18}.x^3 + \alpha^{39}.x^2 + \alpha^{21}.x + \alpha^6$$

All valid *RS*(n, k) code words can be regarded as being polynomials of degree (n-1) over $GF(2^m)$ which are divisible by its generator polynomial $g(x)$.

$$I(x) = i_0 + i_1 x + ... + i_{k-1}x^{k-1} \quad (3)$$

Let be the information polynomial to be encoded. The systematic encoding works by multiplying the information polynomial $I(x)$ by x^{n-k}. The result is then divided with $g(x)$ to obtain the remainder polynomial of degree n-k-1. The encoded signal is then formed by subtracting $r(x)$ from $I(x)x^{n-k}$. It can be written as Equation 4

$$c(x) = I(x).x^{n-k} + (I(x).x^{n-k} \bmod g(x)) \quad (4)$$

It should be noted that the remainder polynomial is, in fact, the parity check polynomial. This generalized encoding scheme is shown in Figure 2.

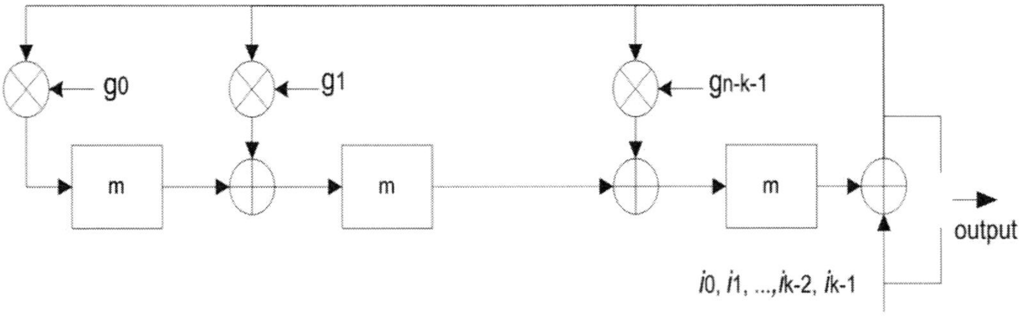

Fig. 2. The structure of *RS* encoder.

4 RS decoder

The RS decoder has three main stages: Re-Encoder, the Welch-Berlekamp algorithm and Chien Search and Error Evaluation

4.1 Re-Encoder

The Re-Encoding [2, 4, 12, 13] is similar to the encoding process. This Re-Encoding process is similar to the syndrome computation process. In the case of RS(63, 59) codes, this Re-Encoding process takes 59 received symbols. It internally generates four check symbols. The re-encoder output will be the mod two addition of four internally generated check symbols and four received check symbol. This is then called the 'parity check' symbol.

In the case of RS(63, 59), the parity check location is **H**= $\{\alpha^0, \alpha^1, \alpha^2, \alpha^3\}$ and the parity check is **R** = $\{R0, R1, R2, R3\}$.

4.2 Welch-Berlekamp algorithm

The check pair input to the Welch-Berlekamp algorithm will be (R_d, α_d): (R_0, α^0), (R_1, α^1), (R_2, α^2) and (R_3, α^3) consecutively. This algorithm is shown in Figure 3.

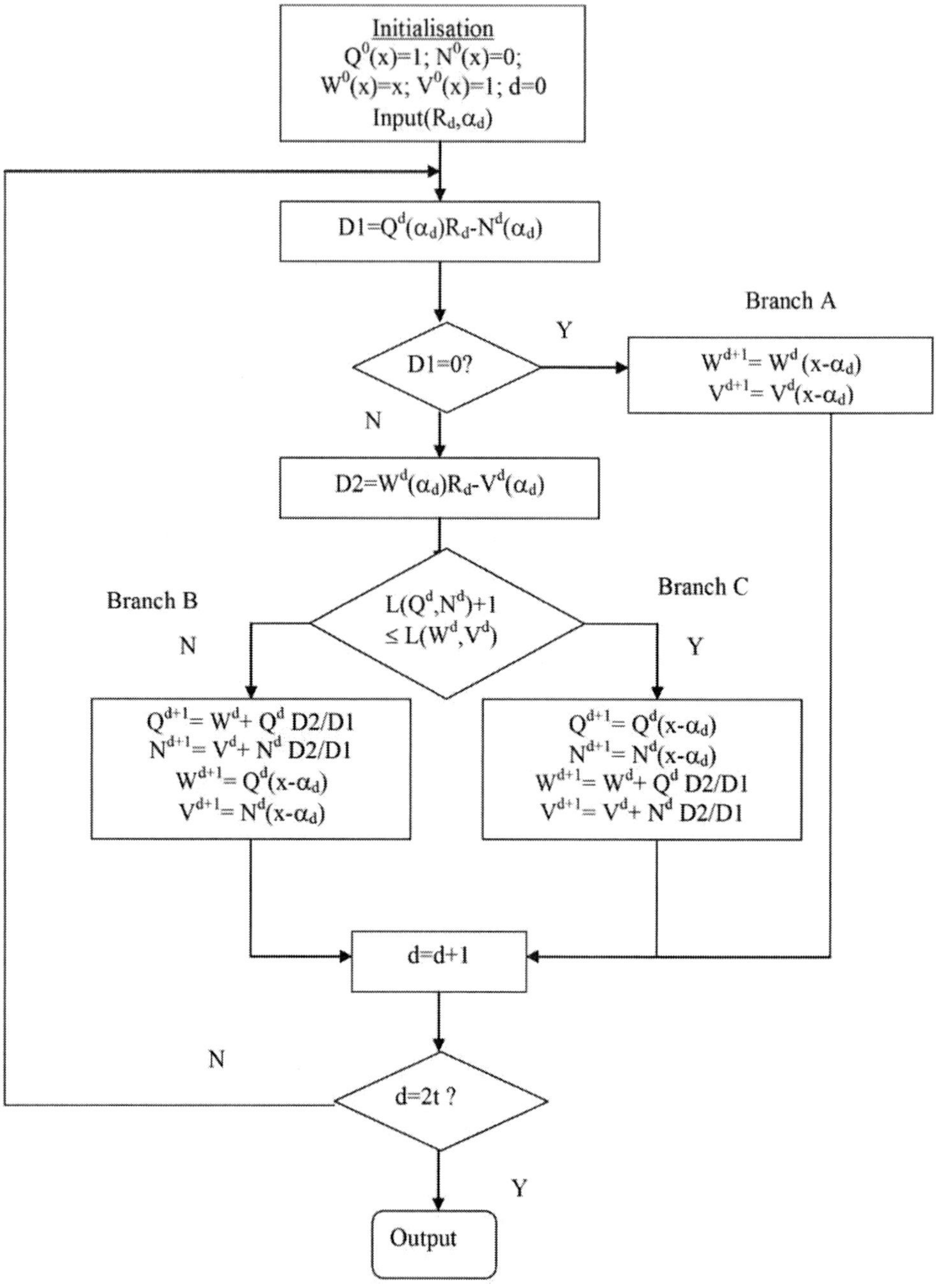

Fig. 3. The Welch Berlekamp algorithm.

The Figure 3 above can be written as shown on Listing 1.

```
1.    ---- Initialisation
2.    Q^0(x)=1; N^0(x)=0
3.    W^0(x)=x; V^0(x)=1
4.
5.    Input = (Rd, αd)
6.    for d=0 step 1 until less than 3
7.    begin loop
8.    D1= Q^d (αd)Rd- N^d (αd)

9.    if D1=0 then % Branch A
10.   W^(d+1)=W^d (x-αd).       & V^(d+1)=V^d (x-αd)
11.   Q^(d+1)=Q^d.              & N^(d+1)=N^d
12.

13.   Else
14.   D2=[W^d (αd)Rd- V^d (αd)]

15.   If L(Q,N)+1 ≤ L(W,V) then % Branch C
16.   W^(d+1)=W^d+Q^d. D2/D1 & V^(d+1)=V^d+N^d. D2 / D1
17.   Q^(d+1)=Q^d (x-αd)       & N^(d+1)=N^d (x-αd)
18.

19.   Else % Branch B
20.   W^(d+1)=Q^d(x-αd)        & V^(d+1)=N^d(x-αd)
21.   Q^(d+1)=W^d+Q^d .D2 / D1 & N^(d+1)=V^d+N^d. D2 / D1
22.

23.   End if
24.   End if
25.   End of loop
```

Fig. 4. Pseudocode Welch Berlekamp algorithm.

4.2 Modified Welch-Berlekamp algorithm

Then, if variable $\mathbf{J = L(W^d,V^d) - L(Q^d,N^d)}$ is defined. The modification process of Figure 4 above Listing 1 above can be explained as follows:

Line 4

As the polynomial $Q^0(x)=1$ and $N^0(x)=0$ then $L(Q^0,N^0) = 0$. The polynomial $W^0(x) = x$ and $V^0(x) = 1$ then $L(W^0,V^0) = 1$. Hence

$L(W^0,V^0) - L(Q^0,N^0) = 1$

$J = 1$.

```
4.  J = 1
```

Line 12

As in line 10, it means that

$$L(W^{d+1},V^{d+1}) = L(W^{d},V^{d}) + 1$$

As in line 11, it means that

$$L(Q^{d+1},N^{d+1}) = L(Q^{d},N^{d})$$

Hence J = J + 1

9.	if D1=0 then % Branch A	
10.	$W^{d+1}=W^{d}(x-\alpha_d)$	& $V^{d+1}=V^{d}(x-\alpha_d)$
11.	$Q^{d+1}=Q^{d}$	& $N^{d+1}=N^{d}$
12.	**J = J+1**	

Line 18

As in line 16, it means

$$L(W^{d+1},V^{d+1}) = L(W^{d},V^{d})$$

As in line 17, it means

$$L(Q^{d+1},N^{d+1}) = L(Q^{d},N^{d})+1$$

Hence J = J - 1

15.	If $L(Q,N)+1 \leq L(W,V)$ then % Branch C	
16.	$W^{d+1}=W^{d}+Q^{d}.D2/D1$	& $V^{d+1}=V^{d}+N^{d}.D2/D1$
17.	$Q^{d+1}=Q^{d}(x-\alpha_d)$	& $N^{d+1}=N^{d}(x-\alpha_d)$
18.	**J = J – 1**	

Line 22

As seen on line 15, the condition on Branch C is $L(Q,N)+1 \leq L(W,V)$, it can be shown that the condition on Branch B is $L(W,V) < L(Q,N)+1$ which means $L(W,V) = L(Q,N)$.

Then $L(Q^{d+1},N^{d+1}) = L(Q^{d},N^{d})$ because of line 21 and also $L(W^{d+1},V^{d+1}) = L(W^{d},V^{d}) +1$ because of line 20.

Hence J = 1.

19.	Else % Branch B	
20.	$W^{d+1}=Q^{d}(x-\alpha_d)$	& $V^{d+1}=N^{d}(x-\alpha_d)$
21.	$Q^{d+1}=W^{d}+Q^{d}.D2/D1$	& $N^{d+1}=V^{d}+N^{d}.D2/D1$
22.	**J = 1**	

Hence, the modified Welch Berlekamp algorithm can be shown as on Figure 5 and also on Figure 6.

The Welch Berlekamp algorithm output will be Q(x) and N(x) polynomials, the error locator polynomial and the error evaluation polynomial consecutively. These polynomials are able to correct up to t errors at the received signal. It will correct up to two errors, in the case of Q(x) and N(x) polynomials. Then, the Q(x) polynomial will be solved using a Chien-Search to find the root of Q(x).

---- Initialisation
$Q^0(x)=1;\ N^0(x)=0$
$W^0(x)=x;\ V^0(x)=1$
$J=1$
Input = (R_d, α_d)
for $d=0$ step 1 until less than $2t-1$
begin loop
$D1= Q^d(\alpha_d)R_d - N^d(\alpha_d)$

if $D1=0$ then % Branch A
$W^{d+1}=W^d(x-\alpha_d)$ & $V^{d+1}=V^d(x-\alpha_d)$
$Q^{d+1}=Q^d$ & $N^{d+1}=N^d$
$J=J+1$

Else
$D2=[W^d(\alpha_d)R_d - V^d(\alpha_d)]$

If $L(Q,N)+1 \leq L(W,V)$ then % Branch C
$W^{d+1}=W^d+Q^d.D2/D1$ & $V^{d+1}=V^d+N^d.D2/D1$
$Q^{d+1}=Q^d(x-\alpha_d)$ & $N^{d+1}=N^d(x-\alpha_d)$
$J=J-1$

Else % Branch B
$W^{d+1}=Q^d(x-\alpha_d)$ & $V^{d+1}=N^d(x-\alpha_d)$
$Q^{d+1}=W^d+Q^d.D2/D1$ & $N^{d+1}=V^d+N^d.D2/D1$
$J=1$

End if
End if
End of loop

Fig. 5. Pseudocode modified Welch Berlekamp algorithm

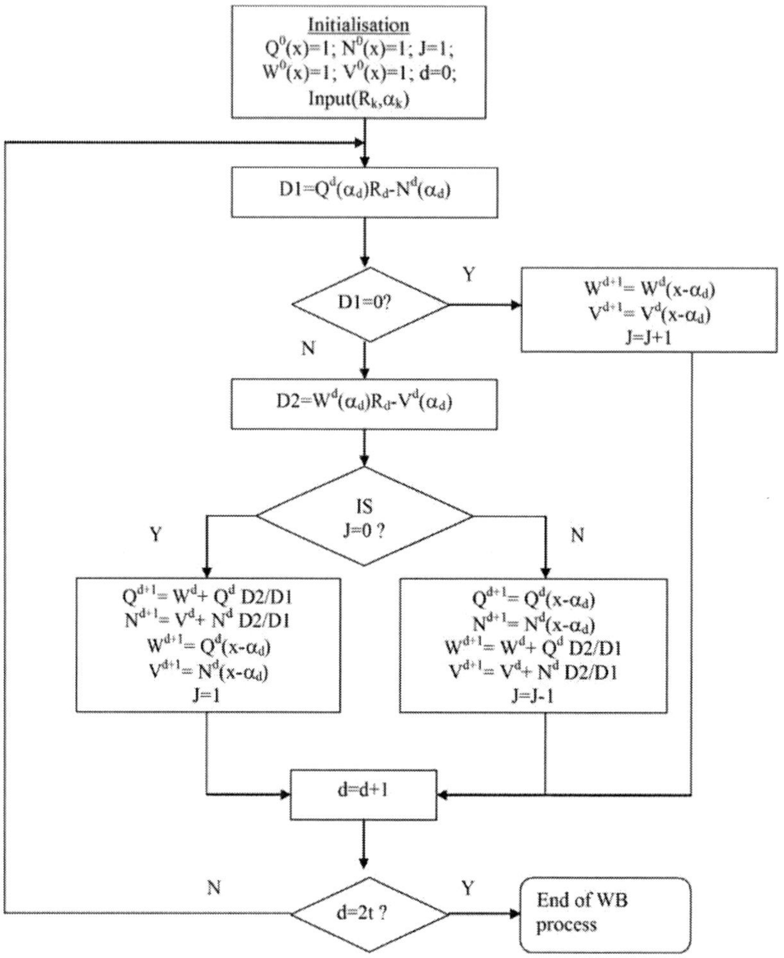

Fig.6. Modified Welch Berlekamp algorithm.

4.3 Chien search and error evaluation

Chien search [1, 3] is then used to find the root of $Q(x)$ polynomial. A Horner's rule is normally used to perform Chien Search (where $Q(x)$ is a polynomial of degree d, $d \le t$)

$$Q(x) = \sum_{i=0}^{d} q_i x^i = (\ldots(q_d x + q_{d-1})x + \ldots)x + q_0 \qquad (5)$$

This process requires at most t multipliers and it takes at most tm clock cycles. In the case of RS(63, 59), this Chien search process requires two multipliers (since, $t = 2$) and it takes 12 clock cycles to complete the process. However, the Chien search can be modified as follows

$$Q(x) = q_d x^d + q_{d-1} x^{d-1} + \ldots + q_0 \qquad (6)$$

Define $Q_l(x) = q_l x^l$ for $0 < l \le d$. Then

$$Q(x) = Q_d(x) + Q_{d-1}(x) + \ldots + q_0 \qquad (7)$$

and it can be shown that

$$Q(\alpha^p) - Q_d(\alpha^{p+1})\alpha^{-d} + Q_{d-1}(\alpha^{p+1})\alpha^{1-d} + \ldots + q_0 \qquad (8)$$

This modified Chien search requires *d* multipliers; however, whatever degree of the polynomial, it only takes *m* clock cycles. In the case of RS(63, 59), this modified Chien search needs two multipliers, but it only takes six clock cycles, whatever degree of the polynomial. Similar process is applied to the $N(x)$ polynomial.

If $Q(\alpha^g) = 0$ then α^g is the root of the error locator polynomial $Q(x)$. Then the error value E_g to the symbol s_g is given by [1, 3].

$$E_g = \begin{cases} \dfrac{N(\alpha^g)}{P(\alpha^g)Q'(\alpha^g)} : \text{if } \alpha^g \notin H_2 \\ n_g + \dfrac{N'(\alpha^g)}{P'(\alpha^g)Q'(\alpha^g)} : \text{if } \alpha^g \in H_2 \end{cases} \tag{9}$$

$$P(x) = \alpha^{10}x^4 + \alpha^{28}x^3 + \alpha^{49}x^2 + \alpha^{31}x + \alpha^{16}$$

Once the error value E_g is found using the Equation (9) at location α^g, the corrected symbol in that particular position can be found by

$$c_g = E_g + s_g \tag{10}$$

5 Implementation

A VHDL design of RS(63, 59) decoder has been designed and it is then synthesized onto a Xilinx XCV600 device.

How the RS decoder works is explained in the following steps.

Step 1: First of all, the received word is first re-encoded to obtain the remainder (parity check). This step needs *nm* clock cycles. It takes 63x6 clock cycles for RS(63, 59).

Step 2: The Welch-Berlekamp algorithm to solve the key equation. The output of the Welch-Berlekamp algorithm is *Q*(x) and *N*(x) polynomials, the error locator polynomial and the error evaluation polynomial consecutively.

Step 3: Find the roots of *Q*(x) polynomial using Chien search is the next step. If *Q*(x) = 0 at a certain location, the *N*(x) polynomial is then evaluated to find the error value. It is then added to the received symbol using modulo twoaddition to doing the correction.

6 Results

The resulting RS(63, 59) decoder circuit can do up to two errors corrections. The corresponding FPGA layout is shown below in Figure 5. This design requires 16 % (1 161 out of 6 912) of the total slices inside a Xilinx XCV600 package fg680 running at clock speed up to 27.343 MHz.

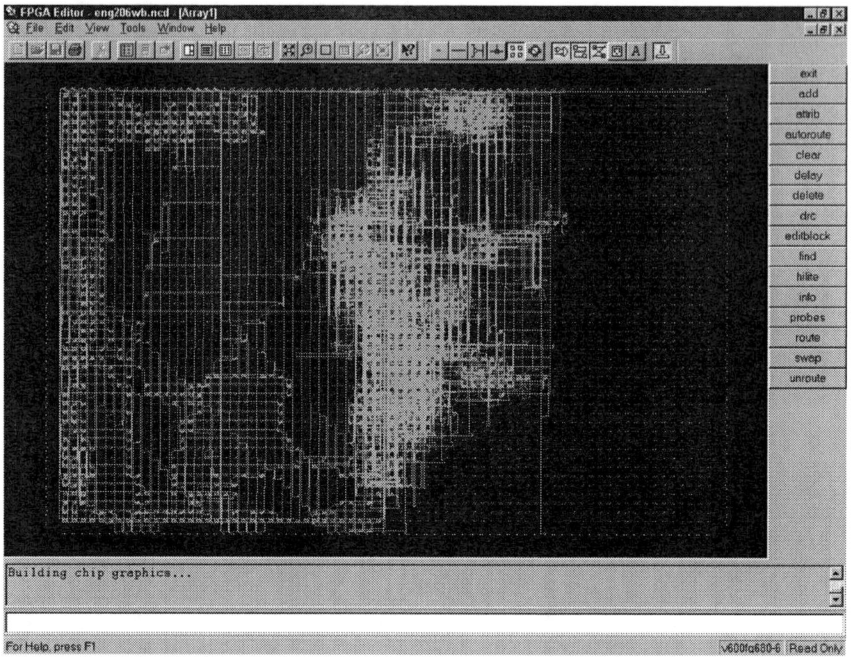

Fig. 5. FPGA layout RS(63, 59) Decoder.

7 Conclusions

The VHDL implementation of the Welch Berlekamp algorithm to decode RS code has been presented. A VHDL design RS(63, 59) has been successfully synthesized on a XILINX FPGA. The RS(63, 59) decoder has been simulated using Modelsim Altera software, and also tested for a number of error patterns. The simulation results show that the decoder works as an error only decoder and can correct up to two errors.

8 References

1. A. Mahmudi. *The investigation into generic VHDL implementation of generalised minimum distance decoding for Reed Solomon codes.* [Thesis]. University of Huddersfield, UK (2005). pp. 48–53. http://ethos.bl.uk/OrderDetails.do?uin=uk.bl.ethos.417302
2. A. Singh, M. Kaur. *International Journal of Innovative Research in Computer and Communication Engineering*, **1**,2:190–192 (2013). http://www.rroij.com/open-access/study-of-reed-solomon-encoder-.php?aid=42686
3. S. Czynszak. *Decoding algorithms of Reed Solomon code.* [Thesis]. Blekinge Institute of Technology, Sweden (2011). pp. 40-47. https://www.diva-portal.org/smash/get/diva2:833161/FULLTEXT01.pdf
4. P. Shrivastava, U.P. Singh. *International Journal of Advanced Research in Computer Science and Software Engineering*, **3**,8:965-969 (2013). https://pdfs.semanticscholar.org/7e94/64b704a9f4b59f9d7df9b437e1b8366b8912.pdf.
5. A.J. Han Vinck. *Coding concepts and Reed Solomon codes.* [Online] from www.martinvinck.com/page3/assets/bookHan.pdf (2013) [Accessed on 10 July 2017].
6. L.R. Welch, E.R. Berlekamp. *Error correction for algebraic block codes.* [Online] from https://www.google.com/patents/US4633470 (1986) [Accessed on 10 July 2017].
7. I.E. Richardson, *The H.264 Advanced Video Compression Standard.* 2nd Edition. UK :

Wiley Publication (2010). pp. 279. *https://books.google.co.id/books?id=k7nOAiIUo9IC&printsec=frontcover&dq=The+H.264+Advanced+Video+Compression+Standard&hl=en&sa=X&ved=0ahUKEwjix_nbz5jYAhWKYo8KHajEB54Q6AEIKDAA#v=onepage&q=The%20H.264%20Advanced%20Video%20Compression%20Standard&f=false*
8. J.P. Nguyen. *Applications of Reed Solomon codes on optical media storage.* [Thesis]. San Diego State University, California (2011). pp. 13–20. http://sdsu-dspace.calstate.edu/bitstream/handle/10211.10/1743/Nguyen_Johnny.pdf;sequence=1.
9. I. Diop, S.M. Farssi, O. Khouma, H.B. Diouf, K. Sylla. *International Journal of Distributed and Parallel Systems*, **3** (2012). https://pdfs.semanticscholar.org/b41c/9cbb3b3c13bee0d0f21c71a841271689f6da.pdf.
10. F.R. Ishengoma. *International Journal of Computer Applications*, **106**:28–31 (2014). https://arxiv.org/abs/1411.4790
11. A.N.U. Husain, Suwadi, G. Hendrantoro. *Jurnal Teknik POMITS*, **2**: A33–A38 (2013). http://ejurnal.its.ac.id/index.php/teknik/article/view/2319 [in Bahasa Indonesia]
12. J. Bhaumik, A.S. Das, J. Samanta. *International Journal of Soft Computing and Engineering*, **2**:395–399 (2013). http://citeseerx.ist.psu.edu/viewdoc/download;jsessionid=119E40402BD90D53B1B3EF68C680DC28?doi=10.1.1.301.6529&rep=rep1&type=pdf.
13. P. Sunitha, G.V. Ujwala. *International Research Journal of Engineering and Technology*, **2**:476–480 (2015). https://www.irjet.net/archives/V2/i6/IRJET-V2I676.pdf.

Big Data Analytics: Towards a Model to Understand Development Equity for Villages in Indonesia

Annas Vijaya[1,*], *Linda Salma* Angreani[2], and *Mokhamad Amin* Hariyadi[2]

[1]Information System Department, Faculty of Science and Technology, Universitas Ma Chung Malang, Villa Puncak Tidar N-01, Karangwidoro, Dau, Malang, East Java, 65151, Indonesia
[2]Informatics Department, Faculty of Science and Technology, Universitas Islam Negeri Maulana Malik Ibrahim Malang, Jl. Gajayana 50, Malang, East Java, 65144, Indonesia

Abstract. The aim of this paper is to design a prototype model that can be used to better understand development equity for villages in terms of public monitoring and evaluation. In designing the model, the research has reviewed several techniques of big data analytics as well as alignment of business strategic objectives and technology. The prototype model also tested using several types of data. Although some obstacles have found, as it also found in the reviewed literature, a prototype model which can guide researchers and practitioners to understand ways to capture public monitoring is presented in this paper. Furthermore, Information systems researchers could use this prototype model for further research to get a deeper understanding of big data analytics roles for development, particularly in developing countries.

Key words: Big data analytics, big data for development, developing countries, villages.

1 Introduction

The village government in Indonesia is a nearest unit to society and involved directly in government programs for several basic development areas. Because of its importance, the Indonesian government has established a specific regulation through the Act. No. 6, 2014 [1] about village governance. Nevertheless, there are issues in order to control village developments which was managed by village government. Reports of village misappropriation, including corruptions in the use of village funds are still occurred [2]. By using IT as an enabler, public control of village development, particularly from the village community over their own village, is expected to create a positive contribution to village development in Indonesia. A technology that have potentials to meet this expectation is big data analytics.

Despite big data analytics perceived have strategic potential benefits for developing countries [3], there are some challenges in implementation phase, such as data access and privacy, human resource capacity, IT infrastructure, IT management, and financial capabilities [4–7]. Furthermore, some developing countries are facing issues in digital divide and analytical processes such as methodology, interpretation accuracy, analytical methods and anomaly detection [6, 7]. This has motivated this study to further explore the creation of the prototype model to address those challenges.

In the attempt to address the situation, this paper is constructed in several sections as follows. Section 1 described background and issues related to the topic. Section 2 represented several related studies which highlight possible technologies related to big data for development and techniques of big data analytics. Next section, Section 3, described a way to address those problems by designing a prototype model that captured specific public information, and as a tool to support public control over village development. Before developing a model, in order to create alignment between strategic objectives and technology, we mapped several strategic objectives as stated in the Act (Act. No. 6, 2014) to technology, in this case is big data analytics [8]. This process included mapping the objectives to critical success factors, critical information, and solutions of big data analytics. The model presented in Section 3 is tested using several types of data which are call data record (CDR) and Twitter data. From several previous studies, the use of this service model could gain more benefits by presenting real-time information [3, 9]. Following this section, Section 4, results from the study to address the challenges is presented and discussed. Finally, a summary will ends this paper as a final section.

*Corresponding author: annas.vijaya@machung.ac.id

2 Literature review

The use of big data analytics has several potential areas for development in the developing world. Refer to results of Bellagio big data workshop in 2014, which consist of several activists, researchers and data expert; those potential areas including advocating and facilitating; describing and predicting; facilitating information exchange and promoting accountability and transparency [3]. Later, the term used for these purposes is big data for development which coined by UN Global Pulse [7].

Recently there are several research and applications related to big data for development using various data sources such as social media [9], cell phone usage [10–12], digital transactions [13], online news media [9, 14], and administrative records [15]. Some of these applications are using public datasets which were become critical elements of big data for development [7]. The combination of data capture process and information management on those studies are used in the prototype model.

The data analysis used in this paper refers to big data analytics as part of business intelligence and analytics (BIA) which become an important part for researchers and industries in more than two decades [16–18]. Big data analytics is described as in-app analysis techniques with a large and complex set of data sets that require unique data storage, management, analysis, and visualization technologies [3, 17, 19], which also used in the prototype model in this paper.

3 Prototype design

Figure 1 shows the design of prototype model. As previously mentioned, there are two types of data used, which are short message system (SMS) data from CDR and Twitter data. There are several reasons to use these types of data. Firstly, the biggest active Twitter users from developing countries is came from Indonesia [20]. This fact shows that netizens in Indonesia are often express their opinions and critiques on actual issues including those related to village development using social media. Secondly, although social networking can be used as a source of data, there are issues related to digital divide in Indonesia, and the evidence shows that Twitter data are only valid in major cities. Therefore, we used SMS data from CDR as second sources of data as it used more widely in rural areas in Indonesia. Finally, these two types of data are considered quite representative for the prototype model, however, it is possible to use other types of data as long as it already filtered as a clean data.

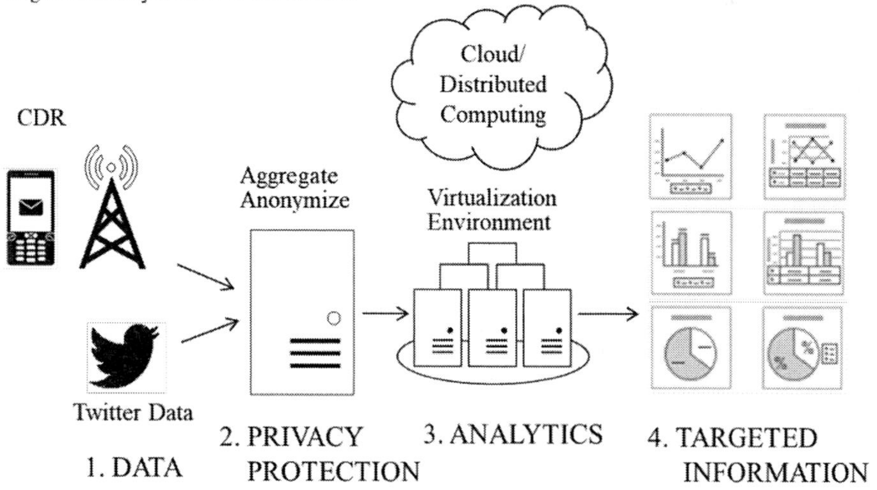

Fig. 1. Steps of prototype design.

After retrieving those type of data, next process is anonymize process as part of privacy protection process. Anonymizing CDR data is done by deleting cellular ID, while user ID was erased in the Twitter data. Following this step is the analysis process as shown in Figure 2, which includes information analysis and topic models. There are at least two experimental environment models with different methods for testing which are virtualization and physical cluster. However, in real situation there will be a third environment which is cloud computing using the same technical methods as in the physical cluster model. Figure 3 shows these three models.

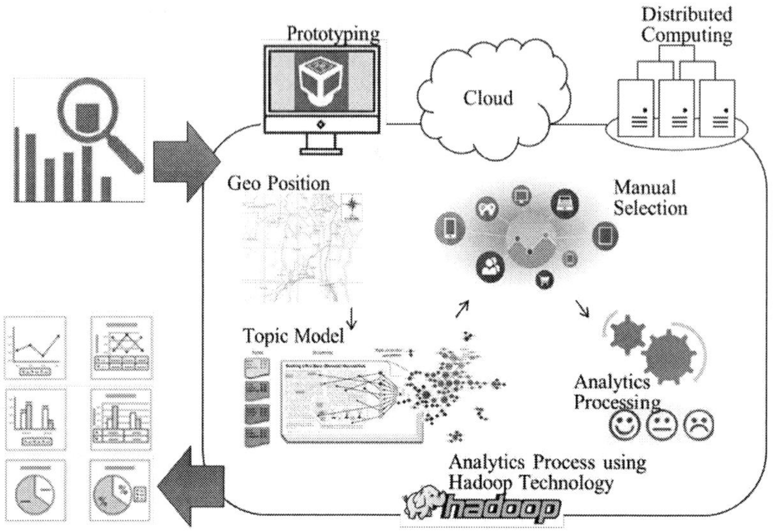

Fig. 2. Steps of big data analytics.

4 Results

As mentioned before, we have done the mapping process of business objectives to technology we used. Table 1 shows the results of this mapping process. After getting the result, we made a classification of needs of big data analytics. The classification result shows that prototype model is directed to provide the following information:

(i) Information related to the management of village government, which includes:

- i). Monitoring and reporting of village existence (1A);
- ii). Transparency of village government monitoring and reporting, including village development activities, development of village potentials, economic activities, and use of village funds (1B);
- iii). Monitoring and reporting of village public service (1C).

(ii) Information of village community activities, including:

- i). Social and cultural, such as conservation and promotion of village customs, traditions, and culture (2A);
- ii). Activities of village resilience and village politics (2B)

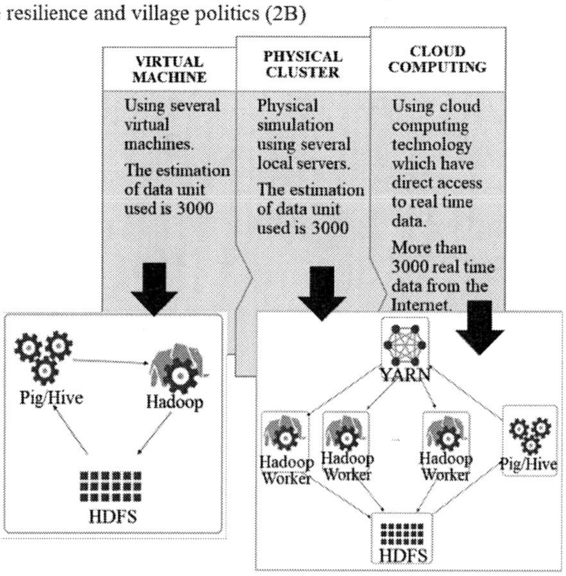

Fig. 3. Experimental environment model for the prototype.

Table 1. Mapping the objectives to achieve the alignment of technology.

Objectives of Village Management based on Government Regulation (UU No.6, 2014)	CSF on IS/IT Domain	Solution of Big Data Analytics
i). Provide recognition and respect for existing villages with their diversity before and after the establishment of the Archipelagic State of The Republic of Indonesia;	The existence of the village is recognized	Availability of information on monitoring and reporting of village existence
ii). To provide clarity on the status and legal certainty of the village in the constitutional system of the Republic of Indonesia in order to realize justice for all Indonesian people;	Clarity of legal status of the village	Availability of information on monitoring and reporting of village existence
iii). Preserve and promote the customs, traditions and culture of the village society;	The existence of efforts to preserve and promote the customs, traditions and culture of village communities	Monitoring and reporting activities for the preservation and promotion of customs, traditions and culture of village society
iv). Encourage initiatives, and participation of village societies for the development of village potentials and assets for mutual prosperity;	The existence of village community activities for the development of village potential and assets	System of monitoring and reporting of potential village development activities
v). Establishing a professional, efficient and effective, open and accountable village government;	The development of a professional, efficient, effective, open and accountable village government	A transparent village government monitoring and reporting system
vi). Improving public services for village societies to accelerate the realization of general welfare;	Achievement of accountable public services in the village	Monitoring and reporting system of public services in the village
vii). Improve socio-cultural resilience of village communities in order to realize village communities that are able to maintain social unity as part of national security;	The existence of activities to improve the social resilience of village culture	Monitoring and reporting system improving village resilience
viii). Promote the economy of rural communities and overcome the national development gap; and	The existence of activities that can promote the economy of rural communities	System of monitoring and reporting of economic activities and or use of village funds for village development
ix). Strengthen the village society as the subject of development.	The existence of activities that make village society as the subject of development	System of monitoring and reporting of village development activities

Based on the analysis and design results, data capture process from data source began. Initial data capture from Twitter are done for 5 d with the initial query word 'desa' (which means village). Total initial data obtained from Twitter with geo-location Indonesia is 28 000 units. On the contrary, we have difficulties to access CDR data from telco operators. The cellular service providers who owned the data were bound by the government policy that the data access was prohibited. So we only get five different types of CDR data including calling and SMS data. We utilized those data to extract the structure and create a model of data filters on the prototype model.

Testing process shows us that process of anonymize data from Twitter takes up to 180 min. We also found that during data capture process, particularly in rural area, there is a possibility of lack of connection to the Internet. This indicates that infrastructure availability and reliability become crucial in the actual implementation. After finishing the anonymized data process, result data are converted into text form for classification of information using topic models based on latent dirichlet allocation (LDA) [21], and the functions we used is based on online learning for latent dirichlet allocation [22]. Some modifications are made in order to make this functions suitable for the research purpose.

Result of LDA shows that several topics are match to the information classification in analytics process. Figure 4 shows percentage of topics that fit to the result of Table 1. Nevertheless, 32 % of data were not relevant to the strategic objectives. Therefore, carefulness in work while filtering the data is consider necessary. The final results of the information from prototype model can then be directed to specific information needs, such as public sentiment on village development as those undertaken by UN Global Pulse to understand food price crises [9], as well as other purposes summarized in the Bellagio big data workshop [3].

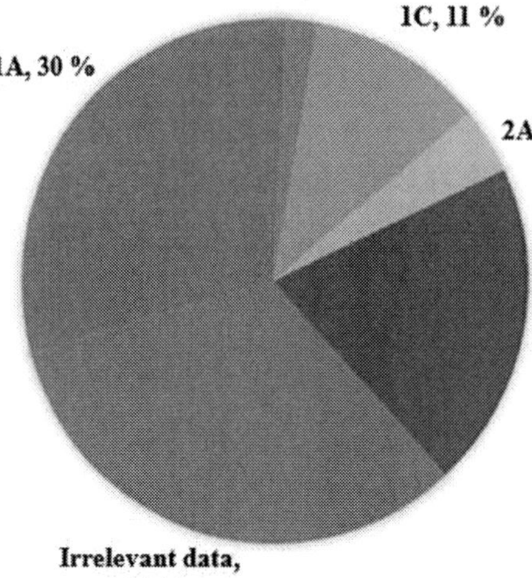

Fig. 4. Percentage of topics that fit to the result of the mapping objectives.

5 Conclusion and future work

Research conducted as described in this paper shows that there are obstacles in using big data analytics for villages in Indonesia such as data access, data privacy, IT infrastructure, digital divide, and anomaly detection. In spite of those obstacles, we found a relation between village management objectives as regulated by the Government of Indonesia and the topic of public discussion in the Internet as we captured the data. It shows us that big data analytics solution could be set as a tool to understand development equity for villages which provide public control and evaluation functions. However, it is important to note that another future work of big data analytics for villages in Indonesia will need higher-level exploration and longer research periods to obtain stronger evidence in terms of validity and effectiveness. The prototype model can also compare and combine with current model of monitoring and reporting of village government. For instance, the Government of Indonesia has provided a model of manual reporting system. By comparing and combining both, analytics result and reporting information, we can get a new perspective of the report in terms of public monitoring and evaluations. It would be easier if the adoption of domain: desa.id (a domain type for village in Indonesia) was utilized for both model. This may lead to another model to get deeper understanding of equitable development for villages.

References

1. Ministry of Justice and Human Rights of Republic of Indonesia. *Undang-undang nomor 6 tahun 2014 tentang desa*. [Law Number 6 Year 2014 About Villages]. Kementerian Hukum dan Hak Asasi Manusia Republik Indonesia, Jakarta, 2014. [in Bahasa Indonesia]. http://www.jdih.kemenkeu.go.id/fullText/2014/6TAHUN2014UU.HTM
2. M.P. Istman, I. Maulidar. *Gawat, penyelewengan dana desa makin berjibun*. [Disastrous, the misuse of village funds has become more and more overwhelming]. [Online] from https://fokus.tempo.co/read/1000406/gawat-penyelewengan-dana-desa-makin-berjibun (2017). [Accessed on 23 August 2017]. [in Bahasa Indonesia].
3. Bellagio Big Data Workshop Participants. *Big data and positive social change in the developing world: A white paper for practitioners and researchers*. Oxford: Oxford Internet Institute (2014).

https://assets.rockefellerfoundation.org/app/uploads/20140507222100/Big-Data-and-Positive-Social-Change-in-the-Developing-World.pdf

4. J. Piotrowski. *Big obstacles ahead for big data for development*. [Online] from http://www.scidev.net/global/data/feature/obstacles-big-data-development.html (2014). [Accessed on 23 December 2015].
5. UN Global Pulse. *Agile Global Development: Harnessing The Power of Real-time Information*. New York: UN Global Pulse (2011). https://www.hashdoc.com/documents/2018/agile-global-development.
6. ECOSOC. *Big data and modernization of statistical systems, report of the secretary-general*. United Nations, Economic and Social Council, Statistical Commission (2014). https://unstats.un.org/unsd/statcom/doc14/2014-11-BigData-E.pdf
7. United Nations Global Pulse. *Big data for development: A primer*. [Online]. From http://www.unglobalpulse.org/sites/default/files/Primer%202013_FINAL%20FOR%20PRINT.pdf (2013). [Accessed on 24 January 2016]
8. J. Ward, J. Peppard. *Strategic planning for information system, 3rd ed*. New York: John Willey & Sons (2002). https://www.wiley.com/en-us/Strategic+Planning+for+Information+Systems%2C+3rd+Edition-p-9781118585252
9. UN Global Pulse. *Mining Indonesian tweets to understand food price crises*. Jakarta: Pulse Lab Jakarta (2014). http://www.unglobalpulse.org/sites/default/files/Global-Pulse-Mining-Indonesian-Tweets-Food-Price-Crises%20copy.pdf
10. D. Talbot. *10 breakthrough technologies 2013: Mobile data from cheap phones*. [Online]. From http://www.technologyreview.com/featuredstory/513721/big-data-from-cheap-phones/ (2013). [Accessed on 5 December 2016].
11. X. Song, Q. Zhang, Y. Sekimoto, R. Shibasaki. *Prediction of human emergency behavior and their mobility following large-scale disaster*. Proceedings of the 20th ACM SIGKDD international conference on Knowledge discovery and data mining, 24–27 August (New York, USA, 2014). pp. 5–14. https://dl.acm.org/citation.cfm?id=2623628
12. L. Bengtsson, X. Lu, A. Thorson, R. Garfield, J. von Schreeb. PLoS Medicine **8**(8):1–9 (2011). http://journals.plos.org/plosmedicine/article?id=10.1371/journal.pmed.1001083
13. World Economic Forum. *Big data, big impact: New possibilities for international development*. Geneva: The World Economic Forum (2012). http://www3.weforum.org/docs/WEF_TC_MFS_BigDataBigImpact_Briefing_2012.pdf
14. USAID Development Credit Authority, UN Global Pulse. *Feasibility study on the potential to gain insights on Kenyans' access to finance through analysis of big data*. New York: United Nations Global Pulse (2013). https://usaidlearninglab.org/sites/default/files/resource/files/UNGlobalPulse-USAID-DCA-FeasStudyFinalReport-27Sept2013.pdf
15. United Nations Global Pulse. *Annual Report 2013*. New York: UN Global Pulse (2014). http://www.unglobalpulse.org/sites/default/files/GP%20Annual%20Report_2013.pdf
16. E.-P. Lim, H. Chen, G. Chen. ACM Transactions on Management Information Systems, **3**(4):1–10 (2013). http://ink.library.smu.edu.sg/cgi/viewcontent.cgi?article=2965&context=sis_research
17. H. Chen, R.H.L. Chiang, V.C. Storey. MIS Quarterly, **36**(4):1165–1188 (2012). https://ai.arizona.edu/sites/ai/files/MIS611D/chen-bi-december-2012.pdf
18. T.H. Davenport. *Competing on analytics*. Harvard Business Review, **84**(1):98–107 (2006). https://hbr.org/2006/01/competing-on-analytics
19. P.B. Goes. *Big Data and IS Research*. MIS Quarterly, Editor's Comments, **38**(3):iii–viii (2014). https://misq.org/misq/downloads/download/editorial/603/
20. V. Lipman. The world's most active twitter city? you won't guess it. [Online]. from http://www.forbes.com/sites/victorlipman/2012/12/30/the-worlds-most-active-twitter-city-you-wont-guess-it/ (2012). [Accessed on 1 April 2016].
21. M.D. Blei. *Probabilistic topic models*. Communication of The ACM, **55**(4):77–84 (2012). https://dl.acm.org/citation.cfm?id=2133826
22. M. D. Hoffman, F. R. Bach and D. M. Blei, "Online Learning for Latent Dirichlet Allocation," in Neural Information Processing Systems 23, New York, (2010). https://papers.nips.cc/paper/3902-online-learning-for-latent-dirichlet-allocation.pdf

Design and Development of RunForFun Mobile Application

Anthony Anci[*], and *Trianggoro* Wiradinata

Universitas Ciputra, Information and Multimedia Technology, UC Town Citraland, Made, Sambikerep, Surabaya 60219, Indonesia

Abstract. Race run for 5 km or 10 km has been trending recently in many places in Indonesia, especially in Surabaya where there were at least 11 events of race run. The participant's number also increased significantly compared to years before. However, among several race run events, it was seen that some events tended to be replicative and monotone, while among the participants recently were identified the need for increasing the fun factor. RunForFun is a mobile application which designed for participants to reach new experience when participating in a race run event. The mobile application will run on Android OS. The development method of this mobile application would use Reverse Waterfall method. The development of this mobile application uses Ionic Framework which utilizes Cordova as its base to deploy to smartphone devices. Subsequently, RunForRun was tested on 10 participants, and the test shows a significant increase in the fun factor from run race participants.

Key words: Android, mobile, RunForRun

1 Introduction

Daily exercise is one of many ways to maintain health. One kind of exercise that can be used to maintain our health is with running. Race run is so popular lately in Indonesia, especially in Surabaya. In 2016, there is 11 race run that being held in Surabaya registered to www.ayolari.in. The enthusiasm of the participant can be seen on MayBank Bali Marathon 2016 that the participants have increased by 40 % from 2015. But if it was looking closely at the inside of the race run, it is found that replicative and tends to be monotone. The participants participating in race run because it is a lifestyle, they want to look for fun, and they want to socialize with other people. Those race run is lack of variation factor and its fun factor.

[*] Corresponding author: anthony_anci@hotmail.com

2 Theoretical basis

2.1 HTML5

HTML5 is a markup language to structure and show the content on a website. The main purpose of the HTML5 development is to repair the technology from HTML so the HTML can be connected with the latest multimedia. With the HTML5 then the third party plugin is optional to run an application in a browser [1].

2.2 SDLC: reverse waterfall model

Waterfall model is a classic model that is systematic and sequential in building software [2]. But the Reverse Waterfall Model was developed again by Manand D. Shah who is an assistant professor of Information Technology Department at Charusat University. The reverse waterfall gives more flexibility when done with one phase; it allows going back to the previous phase if there is modification needed. Figure 1 illustrates the Reverse Waterfall Model architecture.

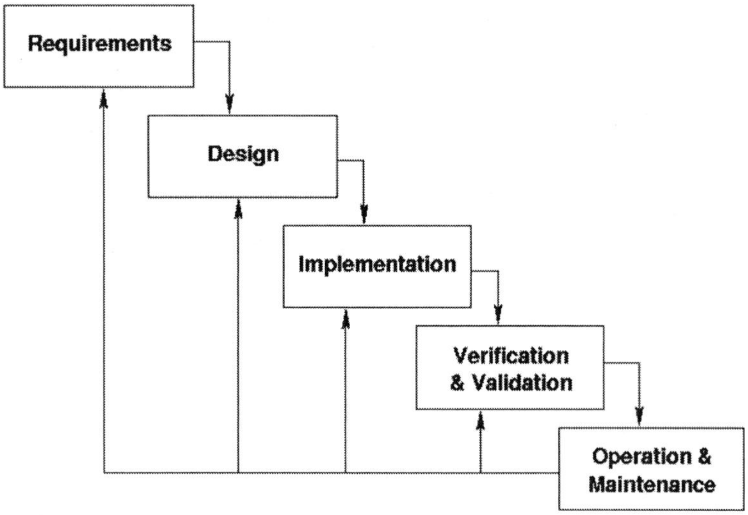

Fig. 1. Reverse Waterfall Model architecture.

2.3 Apache Cordova

Apache Cordova is an open source framework to build a mobile application using HTML5 which multiplatform. The founder of Apache Cordova builds this with the purpose that people can make mobile application multiplatform more simple and can be implemented as a combination of native mobile application technology and web application technology. In the making process of an application using Apache Cordova, this research needs a website application. After that it has to wrap it in a native container, testing that application and need to debug the application. Afterward, it can distribute to the user. That wrapping process of the website application is using Apache Cordova [3].

2.4 Android

Google, Inc. developed Android as a mobile operating system, based on the Linux kernel and designed predominantly for touchscreen devices such as phones, watches, and tablets.

Android's interface is primarily controlled based on direct operation, using touch movements that imitate natural human actions, such as hand swiping, tapping, dragging, and grasping, to manipulate objects displayed on-screen, along with software generated virtual keyboard for input. Android is an open source software toolkit for future mobile devices; the Android was created by Google partnering with Open Handset Alliance [4]. The architecture diagram of Android mobile operating system can be seen in Figure 2 below.

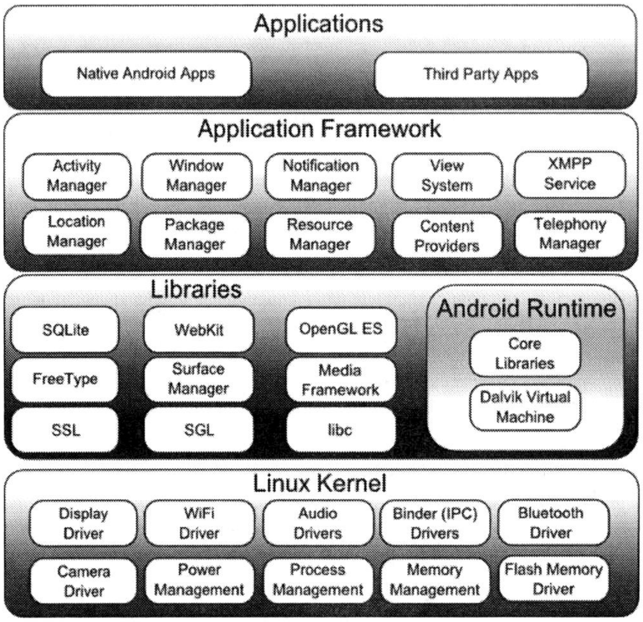

Fig. 2. Architecture diagram of Android OS

2.4.2 Application framework

The application framework was code using Java Programming Language which is tools that used by all of the application. Android offers the ability to build an application with more innovative to the developer. The developer is free to take the advantages of the hardware, access location information, run the background services, set the alarm, add a reminder to the status bar, etc. The developer has the full access to the framework API that used by the main application.

2.4.3 Libraries

Android has some library C/C++ which is used by a various component of the Android system. This ability can be seen by the developer via application framework.

2.4.4 Android runtime

Android Runtime is a location where the main component of DVM placed. DVM is specially designed for Android where it is run in the limited environment, where the battery is limited, CPU, memory and the storage is the main focus. Core libraries were code in Java and contain class, I/O, and other tools.

2.4.5 Linux kernel

Android architecture in Linux 2.6 kernel which can be used to set the security, memory management, process management, network stack and driver model. The kernel also acts as an abstract layer between hardware and the entire software stack.

3 Requirement analysis and design

3.1 Requirement analysis

3.1.1 Race run these days

Race run recently in Indonesia if used to compare with the past is already have developed much better. There are many physical variations, but they have not used technology as their variation. The physical variation is namely zombie chase, glow stick run, wet run, and many others. The variations are just thematic and add no significant value. Based on the observation, list requirement analysis can be list as listed below:
i) The participant can be categorized into two categories namely competitive and non-competitive participant.
ii) The competitive participant is a serious participant that participate in challenging himself/herself to run as fast as he/she can and usually they have some target.
iii) The competitive participant usually is a professional or amateur, usually in group or individual.
iv) The non-competitive participant is a non-serious participant, usually participate to have fun or lifestyle, they have no target or pressure.
v) The non-competitive participant is usually participating in family, moms, students, etc.
vi) The race run for the non-competitive participant based on observation is lack of fun factor and lacks variation.

3.1.2 The solution

The needs were as an opportunity that can be modified and added variation to race run utilizing technology, and the segment of a participant may be targeted to those who are participating because it is a lifestyle for them. That segment was known as a non-competitive participant. They were chosen as the target of mobile application users because it can be seen when these people running in a race run they habitually bring their phone with them. Some of them use a running application, and some of them bring their smartphone just because they want to take some photos or anything else. The fun factor and the variation will be in the form of mini-games and mapping feature.

3.1.3 Application requirement analysis

This application can be installed on Android OS min. Jelly Bean 4.1 to latest and the mobile must have the internet connection. The mobile devices must have GPS Tracker, Back Camera, Touchscreen and minimum 3G connection to support the real-time geolocation.

3.2 System design

3.2.1 Architecture design

The mobile application will be using client-server architecture. Where the client layer will be running on the user smartphone and the server layer is using firebase. The architecture design of Mobile Application RunForFun was shown in Figure 3.

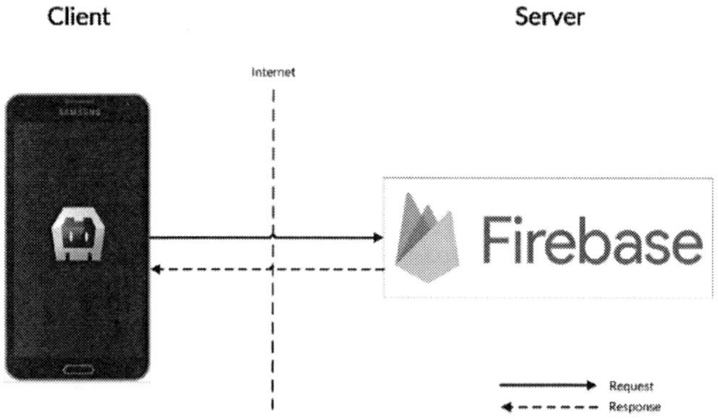

Fig. 3. Architecture Design of RunForFun.

In Figure 3, the client is the user's smartphone, and with the internet connection, they have to request to the server that in this case handled by Google Firebase. After the request success than the server response to the user's smartphone.

3.2.2 Design of database

In mobile application RunForFun, the database will be using real-time database from Firebase. Firebase is using JSON Tree as the base of their real-time database. The mechanism is all the data will be stored as a JSON object. Based on an article from www.json.org, JSON is a text format that is completely language independent but uses conventions that are familiar to programmers of the C-family of languages, including C, C++, C#, Java, JavaScript, Perl, Python, and many others. These properties make JSON an ideal data-interchange language. That database will be considered as a JSON tree which hosted in a cloud. This is not like an SQL database; there is no table or any recorded data else. Because there is no table in JSON tree, hence entity relationship diagram cannot be made. Moreover, the structure has no relationship between the references, consequently cannot force to make the ER-Diagram.

When designing database, the concept of a relational database is referenced but cannot be drawn due to its abstract nature. There will be user reference, location reference, scoreboard reference and game data reference. The inside reference to the four main reference will be decided in the process of development.

3.2.3 Use case diagram

A use case diagram is a graphic depiction of the interactions among the elements of a system. A use case is a methodology used in system analysis to identify, clarify, and organize system requirements. Use case diagram was used to illustrate the functionality that will be implemented to the RunForFun mobile application. In this application there are some features like Register, Login with Email, Login with Google, Scan QR Code, Play Games, Change User Data, Change Avatar, See Map and Logout. Figure 4 shows the use case diagram of RunForFun.

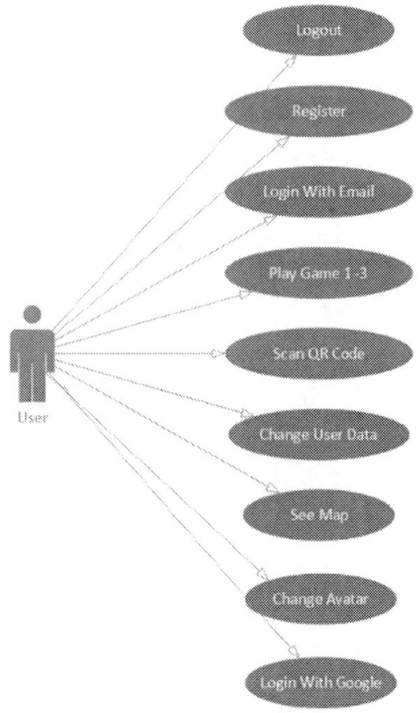

Fig. 4. Use case diagram of RunForFun.

3.2.4 User interface design

The user interfaces mockup design was done using JustInMind desktop application that has many great features and free to use. There is eight user interface which has been designed in the process of development; there is Login Screen, Register Screen, Account Screen, Scanner Screen, Game 1: Multiple Choice Screen, Game 2: Sliding Puzzle 3x3 Screen, Game 3: Guess Word Screen and the last is See Map Screen.

4 Implementation/development

4.1 Feature implementation

The Ionic Version 1 framework was used for implementing the feature. There is 11 feature referring to the use case diagram in Figure 3.

4.1.1 Register with email

This feature will be used by the user to register himself or herself as a user in RunForFun using their email.

4.1.2 Login with email

This feature will be used by the user to login himself or herself after his/her registered as a user.

4.1.3 Login with Google

This feature will be used by a user who has a google account, so they won't have to do the registration process.

4.1.4 Change user data

This feature will be used by the user to change their basic data include their password.

4.1.5 Change avatar

This feature will be used by the user to change their profile photo.

4.1.6 Scan QR code

This feature will be used by the user to scan the QR code to play the mini-games.

4.1.7 Game 1: multiple choice

This feature will be appeared after the user success to scan the QR code. This feature contains the game 1 which is a multiple choice question game.

4.1.8 Game 2: sliding puzzle 3 × 3

This feature will be appeared after the user success to scan the QR code. This feature contains the game 2 which is a sliding puzzle 3 × 3 game.

4.1.9 Game 3: guess word

This feature will be appeared after the user success to scan the QR code. This feature contains the game 3 which is a guess word game.

4.1.10 See map

This feature will be used by the user to see the map where is his/her position right now.

4.1.11 Logout

This feature will be used by the user to logout from their account.

4.2 Database implementation

The database of RunForFun is using real-time database from Firebase that using JSON Tree as the basis. The parent of the database is "runforfun-a01dd" and have four reference which is a user, game, location, and scoreboard. The database implementation can be seen in Figure 5.

```
|
'---runforfun-a01dd
    |---game
    |    |---game 1
    |    |    |--- answer
    |    |    |    '---- n: value
    |    |    '--- question
    |    |         '---- n: value
    |    '---Game 3
    |         |--- answer
    |         |    '---- n: value
    |         '--- clue
    |              '----n: value
    |---location
    |    '----userID
    |         |---lat: value
    |         '---long: value
    |---scoreboard
    |    '----userID
    |         '----totalPoint: value
    '---user
         '----userID
              |---email: value
              |---gender: value
              |---image: value
              '--- username: value
```

Fig. 5. Database implementation of RunForFun.

4.2.1 Game reference

In this reference, there is Game 1 and Game 3 reference. The Game 1 have two references there is answer and question which is the amount of the data depends on how much the organizer of the race run want to fill. The same goes for the Game 3 reference but the difference is in the name of the reference which is in Game 3 the name of reference is answer and clue.

4.2.2 Location reference

The location reference has reference name userID. The userID is based on the userID of the registered user. In every reference userID, there is two reference that has a value which is lat and long that the value is got by the geolocation of the user's smartphone.

4.2.3 Scoreboard reference

The scoreboard reference is like the location reference, they both have the same type reference that is userID. But in the scoreboard reference, the userID have the total Point reference, and it has value based on whether the user success to playing the game or not.

4.2.4 User reference

In this reference have the same type again as the two references before which is userID. But in every userID reference, there is email, gender, image and username that have value based on the field that user have filled.

4.3 User interface implementation

Based on the design user interface before, this research has implemented all of the design. Besides that, one more user interface which is Splash Screen was added when the user opens the application.

4.3.1 Splash screen

In this page, the logo of RunForFun will be shown. This page will remain until the resources of the apps is successfully loaded from the database. From this page, the next page is between login screen or direct to account screen depends on user whether the user already login or not.

4.3.2 Login screen

The login screen is the next page after the splash screen where the user can do the login feature here. There are three buttons which are to login, register, and login to Google. When the user presses the register button, the user will be redirected to register screen. When the user presses the login with Google button, then the user will be redirected to the login with google account using the in-app browser or the main browser on their smartphone.

4.3.3 Register screen

Register screen is the page that user can do the register feature. When the user already filled all the field and pressed the register button, they will be redirected back to the login screen to do the login process.

4.3.4 Account screen

Account screen will be shown if the user has already login. This is the main screen of this application. In this page, the user can do the change user data and change avatar feature. But if the user login with google they can't change the password and can't change the avatar. They can't change avatar because the avatar will be the same with their avatar on their Google account.

4.3.5 Scanner screen

This page will be shown when the user presses the scanner tab, and this page will show the preview of their smartphone's main camera to do the scan QR code feature.

4.3.6 Game 1: multiple choice screen

This page will be shown to the user that successfully scan the QR Code for Game 1. The user has 30 s to answer the question. The user just has one chance to answer the question. When the user press the answer the screen will be closed and back to the scanner screen.

4.3.7 Game 2: sliding puzzle 3 × 3 screen

This page will be shown to the user that successfully scan the QR Code for Game 2. The user just has 45 s to solve the sliding puzzle 3 × 3. When the user success the screen will be closed and back to the scanner screen, but if the user failed and the time is on the screen will be closed and back to the scanner screen too.

4.3.8 Game 3: guess the word

This page will be shown to the user that successfully scan the QR Code for Game 3. The user has 30 s to answer the question. The user have to complete the answer, they just have one clue, and they have to guess the word and answer letter by letter. If the letter is wrong, the points will be decreased. When the user success to complete the word, the screen will be closed and back to the scanner screen. The same condition will happen if they can't guess the word and the time is up.

4.3.9 Map screen

This page will be open when the user press the Map Tab. The map screen will show the position of the user and the other user. The user itself will be shown with the blue run icon and the other user will be shown as the black run icon.

5 Test result

Mobile application RunForFun is tested using two methods, first method is using the user acceptance test (UAT) to test the feature that already implemented in this application. The second is to test the benefit of the application.

5.1 Functional testing

The UAT is done to test all the feature in this application. The scenario was design for the user from the pre-condition until the post condition with the description. This is the result of the UAT.

Fig. 6. Login screen.

5.1.1 Register with email (Gmail)

As seen in Figure 6 above, login process can be done using email (Gmail). The functional test result of this feature can be seen at Table 1 below.

Table 1. UAT register with an email.

Use Case	Register With Email
Actor	User
Pre-Condition	The user is on the register page
Post-Condition	User success to do the registration process and being redirect to the login page
Description	The user has to fill all the data field and press the register button after that

5.1.2 Login with email

The result of this feature can be seen in Table 2.

Table 2. UAT login with email.

Use Case	Login with Email
Actor	User
Pre-Condition	The user is on Login Page
Post-Condition	User Success to Login and redirected to Account Page
Description	The user has to fill the login field and press the Login button

5.1.3 Login with Google

The result of this feature can be seen in Table 3.

Table 3. UAT login with Google.

Use Case	Login to Google
Actor	User
Pre-Condition	The user is on Login Page
Post-Condition	User Success to Login and redirected to Account Page
Description	The user has to press the Login with Google Button

5.1.4 Change user data

The result of this feature can be seen in Table 4.

Table 4. UAT change user data.

Use Case	Change User Data
Actor	User
Pre-Condition	The user is on Account Page
Post-Condition	Change User Data is success
Description	The user must fill all the data field and press the Save Button

5.1.5 Change avatar

The result of this feature can be seen in Table 5.

Table 5. UAT change avatar

Use Case	Change Avatar
Actor	User
Pre-Condition	The user is in Account Page
Post-Condition	Change Avatar is success
Description	The user has to press the Change Avatar button and choose the picture that the user want to and wait 'till the upload is done and finish

5.1.6 Scan QR code

The result of this feature can be seen in table 6.

Table 6. UAT scan QR code.

Use Case	*Scan QR Code to Play Game*
Actor	User
Pre-Condition	The user is in Scan Page
Post-Condition	The alert box is pop-up on the screen
Description	User have to aim the camera to the QR Code

5.1.7 Game 1: Multiple choices

The result of this feature can be seen in Table 7.

Table 7. UAT Game 1: multiple choice.

Use Case	Game 1: *Multiple Choice*
Actor	User
Pre-Condition	The user is in Scan Page
Post-Condition	User play the game 1
Description	User success to scan the QR Code of Game 1 and play the game

5.1.8 Game 2: sliding puzzle 3 × 3

The result of this feature can be seen in Table 8.

Table 8. UAT Game 2: sliding puzzle 3×3.

Use Case	Game 2: *Sliding Puzzle* 3×3
Actor	User
Pre-Condition	The user is in Scan Page
Post-Condition	User play the game 2
Description	User success to scan the QR Code of Game 2 and play the game

5.1.9 Game 3: guess word

The result of this feature can be seen in Table 9.

Table 9. UAT Game 3: guess word.

Use Case	Game 3: *Guess Word*
Actor	User
Pre-Condition	The user is in Scan Page
Post-Condition	User play the game 3
Description	User success to scan the QR Code of Game 3 and play the game

5.1.10 See map

The result of this feature can be seen in Table 10.

Table 10. UAT see map.

Use Case	See Map
Actor	User
Pre-Condition	The user is in Account Page
Post-Condition	The user can see his/her position on the map
Description	The user has to press the Map Tab to see the map

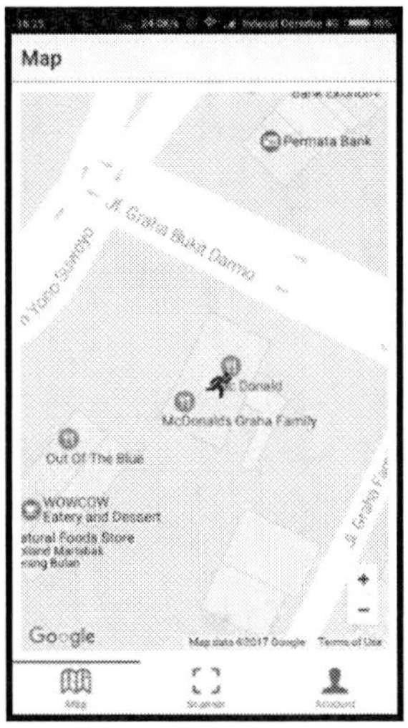

Fig. 6. Map screen.

5.1.11 Logout

The result of this Feature can be seen in Table 11.

Table 11. UAT logout

Use Case	Logout
Actor	User
Pre-Condition	The user is in Account Page
Post-Condition	User success to logout
Description	The user has to press the Logout Button

5.2 Benefit testing

The benefit testing is using the Perceived Playfulness principle to testing whether using this mobile application RunForFun can make a race run more varieties and more fun. There is three indicators which were made based on this principle which is:
i) I can enjoy the race run in general.
ii) Race run which I participate is enjoyable and interesting.
iii) I do not feel bored when I just run in a race run.

The benefit testing of this application involves ten samples of respondents and using convenience sampling [6]. The respondent will answer the question using a Likert scale from 1 to 5. After the test, data was a recap, and the recap will be processed to find the significance using Paired-samples t-test method. The result can be seen in Table 12.

Based on the result, the value of the sig is 0.001 which is based on the probability value sig $\leq$ 0.05, it can be concluded that the hypothesis that mobile application RunForFun has a significant effect on adding the fun factor in the race run is acceptable. The benefit testing is using the Perceived Playfulness principle to testing whether using this mobile application RunForFun can make a race run more varieties and more fun. Three indicators were made based on this principle which is:
i) I can enjoy the race run in general.
ii) Race run which I participate is enjoyable and interesting.
iii) I do not feel bored when I just run in a race run.

The benefit testing of this application involves ten samples of respondents and using convenience sampling [6]. The respondent will answer the question using a Likert scale from 1 to 5. After the test, data was a recap, and the recap will be processed to find the significance using Paired-samples t-test method. The result can be seen in Table 12.

Table 12. Benefit Testing Result

		Paired Differences							
					95 % Confidence Interval of the Difference				
		Mean	**Std. Deviation**	**Std. Error Mean**	**Lower**	**Upper**	**t**	**df**	**Sig. (2-tailed)**
Pair 1	Before-After	−1.53333	.91894	.29059	−2.19070	−.87597	−5.277	9	.001

Based on the result, the value of the significant is 0.001 which is based on the probability value sig $\leq$ 0.05, it can be concluded that the hypothesis that mobile application RunForFun has a significant effect on adding the fun factor in the race run is acceptable.

6 Conclusion

The conclusion of design and development of mobile application RunForFun is design and develop this mobile app can be done with the help of these tools: Trello, JustInMind, Ionic Framework Version One, Cordova, Chrome, Firefox, Smartphone Xiaomi Mi4i, Google Firebase, Atom, SPSS, Google Maps API and the QR Scanner plugin. The other conclusion is based on the benefit testing that this mobile application is useful to increase the fun factor in the race run when the participant is running. There are some recommendations based on the experience of designing and developing this project. This research recommends to use the latest version of Ionic Framework, using SASS and deploy it to smartwatch which has higher mobility than a smartphone.

References

1. J. Osborn, HTML5 (John Wiley & Sons, Inc, 2011).
2. R.S. Pressman, *Software Engineering: A Practitioner's Approach 7th Edition*. New York: McGraw-Hill Education (2010). https://books.google.co.id/books?id=y4k_AQAAIAAJ&q=Software+Engineering+:+a+practitioner%E2%80%99s+approach+7th&dq=Software+Engineering+:+a+practitioner%E2%80%99s+approach+7th&hl=en&sa=X&ved=0ahUKEwiZ5vnv36LYAhUM448KHQCSB2wQ6AEILjAB
3. J.M. Wargo. *Apache Cordova 3 Programming*. USA: Addison-Wesley Professional (2013). pp. 1–5. https://books.google.co.id/books?id=u3JVAgAAQBAJ&dq=Apache+Cordova+3+Programming&hl=en&sa=X&ved=0ahUKEwiqwbTe4KLYAhUJR48KHQhwAJsQ6AEIKDAA
4. E. Brunette. *Hello, Android: Introducing Google's Mobile Development Platform*. USA: Pragmatic Bookshelf (2009). pp. https://books.google.co.id/books?id=mJRKQQAACAAJ&dq=Android%3A%20Introducing%20Google%27s%20Mobile%20Development%20Platform&source=gbs_book_other_versions
5. Google. *Firebase App Success Made Simple.* [Online] from https://firebase.google.com/ (2012) [Accesed on 5 April 2016]

6. D. Cooper, P. Shindler, *Business Research Methods*. New York: The McGraw-Hill Companies, Inc. (2015). p. 359. https://books.google.co.id/books?id=l7u6BwAAQBAJ&printsec=frontcover&dq=Business+Research+Methods&hl=en&sa=X&ved=0ahUKEwjzwuP54aLYAhXJLo8KHWJWDewQ6AEIKDAA#v=onepage&q=Business%20Research%20Methods&f=false

Information System User Interface Design in Software Services Organization: A Small-Clan Case Study

Boonchoo Jitnupong*, and *Waraporn* Jirachiefpattana

Graduate School of Applied Statistics, National Institute of Development Administration, Bangkok 10240, Thailand

Abstract. A user interface (UI) is one of the most significant parts of an information system (IS). A user-friendly UI helps users to carry out their tasks with efficiency, effectiveness, and satisfaction. UI consists of five elements: metaphor, mental model, navigation, interaction, and appearance. Based on these, the designer must carefully select and design each element to be appropriate for the users. This research examines the influential process named user-centered design (UCD), a well-known process to raise product quality. Furthermore, the roles UI elements in IS development by observing it in a small family software services company in Thailand. The findings of this study show small family team is proper with UI design that concern in usability for user. Even though some UCD processes or UI elements are quite unclear, the clan culture helps team to design UI with flexibility, and unbiassed obtain comments from user.

Key words: Clan organizational culture, user-centered design, user interface design, information system development

1 Introduction

The purpose of any product development is to create tools that enable users to carry out their jobs accurately and easily, and should be fun to interact with. Such is the definition of usability as is clearly laid out in the ISO9241-11 standard: "The extent to which a product can be used by specified users to achieves goals with effectiveness, efficiency, and satisfaction in a specific of use" [1]. In the same manner, a usable product helps users to be more productive by reducing human error and the learning curve. Moreover, usability helps to reduce user resistance by encouraging positive user, and client interaction.

In terms of an information system (IS), usability reflects the quality of its user interface (UI) [2], which is a significant component of an IS with the duty of being a translator between users, and the system. A UI provides the look (presentation) and feel (interaction) of a system [3], and a good UI will help users to carry out their tasks with satisfaction and productively [4]. To help develop an appropriate UI for user not for designer, User-centered design (UCD) has been recognized as a process that can help create an appropriate UI [5],

* Corresponding author: boonchoo.jit@stu.nida.ac.th

hence it is a development process that designers should follow. Moreover, when taking UI elements into consideration, it is important to mix the use of individual components to enable the designer to create a usable UI.

The characteristics of UCD, and UI elements design in small family software services firm are studied in this paper. To comprehend how a small-sized software services company designs appropriate UIs for its clients. The paper is ordered as follow. Next piece presents the knowledge background of the case study. The main concept are user interface design, and collaborative culture. The third section describes the case study methodology. In the following section is the results of findings. Last section is the conclusion that summarizes the result, and suggest the future research.

2 User interface design

To develop a usable UI, an IS development team should realize that users are a vital part of the team, and multi-disciplinary design team members are likely to raise useful ideas from many points of view. Clarifying UI requirements helps a team to understand what the system should be like in detail using design guidelines and standards that are trustworthy and easy to follow. UI and usability design can be separated into two styles: process-oriented and product-oriented [6, 7], and software design tools assist development teams as well as UI evaluation by users and UI experts [8].

In this study, there are two parts in UI design: (i) the UI design process; (ii) the UI product characteristics.

2.1 UI Design process

From its beginning as an iterative and prototyping UI design approach, UCD has been developed to become a design method which ensures that the final product is developed from the users' standpoint and achieves the users' requirements; it is a method combining four main steps (see Figure 1).

First, understand and specify the context of use - this process is important towards understanding the range of physical, task social, organizational, and environmental aspects of the users. Systems analysts have a number of techniques to help understand the context of use, such as surveys, observation, task analysis, and interviewing. Second, specify the user and organizational requirements - designers and users must consider what the attributes of the UI requirements are, then the goals of each attribute, and finally the evaluation method for each attribute. The output of this stage is the UI requirements specifications - the combination of requirements and measuring the quality of the UI. Third, produce design solutions - the designers and users create a UI together that meets the requirements. Finally, evaluate the design against the requirements - this process will compare the quality of the UI with the original UI requirements to determine whether the latter have been met. If the results of the prototype evaluation meet the goals, the prototype can be used as the final product. On the other hand, if the prototype is not satisfactory, then the process must be started again.

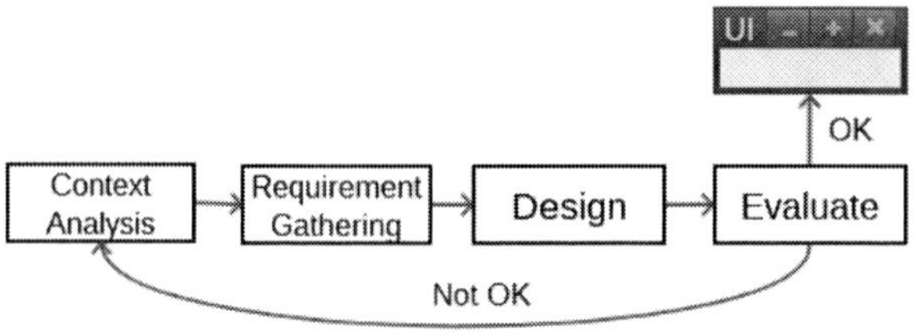

Fig. 1. The UCD process.

This study, an in-depth understanding of each step in this process was acquired from the case.

2.2 UI design product characteristics

In Marcus [9] provided the meaning of a user interface: "A computer-mediated means to facilitate communication between human beings or between a human being and an artifact. The user interface embodies both physical and communicative aspects of input and output, or interactive activity". Additionally, the UI consists of metaphors, mental models, navigation, interaction and appearance [9].

UI metaphors are computer-related elements that help users to understand, remember, and enjoy a UI. This means that the designer understands the users' needs and system objectives. Mental models are the scope of data, function, tasks, roles, and people. Navigation aids such as menus, windows, dialogue, or icons help movement through the mental model. Interactions include the techniques to receive input from the user and return the output to the user. Appearance or surface includes all perceptual attributes: visual, sound, colors, fonts, and animation (see Figure 2).

The objective of data gathering is to understand how a designer designs or selects each UI element on the basis of information from the users.

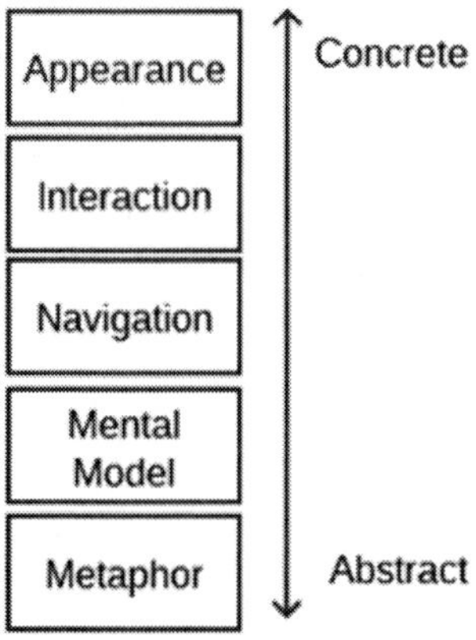

Fig. 2. Elements of UI

3 UI design in small clan company

3.1 Method

The major data collection method in this research was by interview. During the interviews, the interviewer has two tasks: (i) to obtain answer from the previously prepared questions and (ii) ask the actual questions without bias [10]. At the same time, the data of the case is observed. Background sources of information such as an organizational chart, visions, mission, and samples of technical documents were also obtained from the respondents. Unfortunately, at this company, the work place was not static since employees also work from home or at client sites, and so data on their office working environment was not available. Moreover, by the nature of Startup Company, this company does not have a concrete visions or missions statement. So, these official evidences do not gather to analysis.

In order to understand the UI design in this company, the semi-structure questions were developed to interview the respondents. These questions are separated into two parts. The first part contained design process questions in order to understand their approach to UI design, and the second part was made up of questions on UI elements. If the interviewees were finding it difficult to understand parts of the process, the UI components examples were prepared to help identify their design preferences and to distinguish how they visualize UI elements.

The researcher interviewed with two team members. One man (Member-A), who is the team member and one woman (Member-B) who not only declared herself as a team member, but she is Project Manager also. In terms of experience, Member-B works in I.T. industries more than 10 yr. While, Member-A was work in another industry before (he worked in I.T. department). The researcher makes a contact them to make appointments and met them in February 2017.

3.2 Case background

The main mission of software services is to create tailor-made products for their clients, and, to carry this out well, software service consultants need to come up with useful ideas that help them create quality products for their clients. Service quality might affect company liquidity and enable it to operate in a market where competition is high. In the case of Thailand, in 2015, the Development Business Department, Ministry of Commerce, showed that software services industries (packages, consultants, and development) still comprised of more than 2 500 firms [11]. Of these, almost all companies who are still operating are small- to medium-sized enterprises, and only a few have more than 200 employees.

The firm in this study has just recently been launched and thinks of itself as a Startup company. They do not have a physical workplace but instead use electronic communication tools such as collaborative software, instant messaging services, and/or email to brainstorm, work track, and talk within the team. IT consultancy is the key services of this team, and they organize exclusive software services development to serve clients' requirements. In terms of experience, their projects vary from ISs that assist governmental agencies, state enterprises, and private sector companies as well. Besides being expert in ISs, they are also skilled in web content systems. The predominant platform is web technology, both of fully open source and licensed. Even though today is the smartphone era, most ISs are still designed for the web platform. From the organizational culture theory, software development organization often be an adhocracy culture. The organizational culture which concern about innovative technology [12]. However, in this case, it is not follow these rules.

The design team at the company consisted of three members (two men and one woman) who are at least graduates with a Bachelor's degree in an IT field. Each of them is able to organize all of the IS tasks in the development process: analysis, design, coding, and testing. When designing, they apply their UI/UX (user experience) knowledge obtained from some of the classes when they studied, but most of their expertise comes from ten years or so of commercial experience. The team is small and very informal but its characteristics are diverse. Regardless of gender, personal feedback from these individuals concerning a UI design will probably result in a better design. Nevertheless, there is the risk that they might be similar in terms of knowledge because they graduated in the same or similar fields, but, more than anything, they are together as a family, like brothers and sisters.

A team characterized as "family" tends to share more than a job, and even without tradition, it is usually well consolidated. This behavior can contribute towards helping them share opinions openly. With regard to interactions between them and their customers, they will explicitly share knowledge together, which will aid in discovering techniques or tools that they think are good for the both the team and the users. The team are able to perform analyses in which the gained information can be presented to the users and applied to a project (this research must not effect to the main task). Therefore, they do not have a clear working framework. This characteristic alike with the group (family or clan) culture which the employees are concern about team relations and team spirits. They are less formal-structure control but love to decentralize the decision-making. They choose to push participation in team. So, everyone in the team are open-minded for others opinion. Moreover, the group culture often threat customer as an important part in team [12, 13].

"Personally, I think this situation is better (than my last organization). The formal framework should not become too habitual for an IT person." Member B said

Organizational size reflects upon the nature of the projects conceived by employees in the organization. Moreover, this might include the clients' network who are primarily concerned with the reliability of a service and/or product delivery. In contrast, working in a small team is more beneficial in terms of flexibility of service quality with more of an "as you like" attitude than big companies, which tend to be unwieldy.

Because users provide feedback about a UI at the same level as a core function, to design or rectify a UI is not easy and takes time. As a result, a design team should realize the importance of the UI design, and every member should agree that the UI is a vital part of the system that affects the success of the IS at the same level as a core system function.

3.3 UI design process

When applying UCD, the UI design process consists of four processes: users' context analysis, along with UI requirements development, prototyping, and evaluation. However, from the preliminary interviews, all four processes may not be clearly defined since they are blended into the UI design process by the design team, but not explicitly specified. An overview of the UI design process is shown in Figure 3.

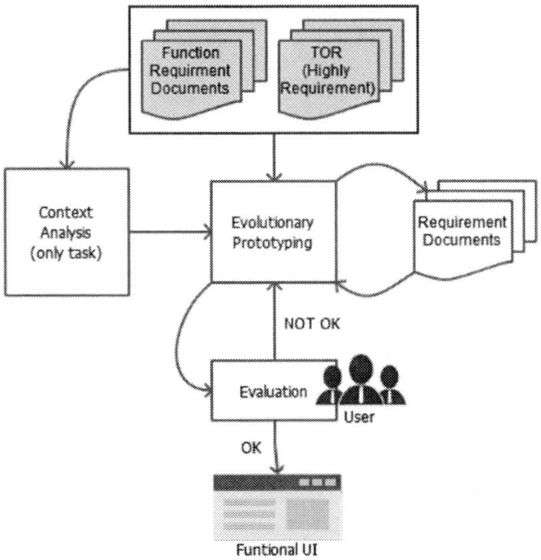

Fig. 3. UI design process.

3.3.1 Understanding the users and their tasks

During the process of context analysis, the team needs to analyze various aspects involving the users, tasks, and environment. In our case, the team surmised that they were to develop an IS for office use only, so they realized that the system should perform well in an office environment. However, they also took into account that the system should display correctly on any monitor size.

The characteristics of the users, such as gender and age, along with individual and cultural experience and knowledge affect user preferences, hence UI design. As a result, UI designers collect and analyze these factors in order to match the users' characteristics with the UI as closely as possible.

Unfortunately, as actually happened with this team, these data were not collected and analyzed clearly because user characteristics were estimated "by sight" during the requirements gathering process. Apparently, this oversight was not planned, but, in this case, the designers thought that the design was self-evident.

"We always do the task analysis." Member B said.

Task analysis is the process during which the team attempts to realize the business process or working steps involved in building the system, and the results of this process assist the designer to understand the data flow and structure of the system. Input-output of the system affects the navigation and interaction of the UI, and knowledge of this process can be translated into a diagrammatic view such as use case, data flow diagram, which describes the user interactions with the system and can be included in the system requirements.

From the above, both data on the user characteristics and task analysis can be used to create UI requirements. However, the team did not create a specific UI requirements document, but instead use the collected data to design a prototype which was then modified on the basis of the responses of the users in terms of primary need and aesthetics.

3.3.2 Make it clear with a prototype

"First impression of a user to the UI prototype will increase involvement, ownership, and satisfaction. As a result, the team can receive feedback on the pros/cons of the system easier and faster than just by talking or writing something down." They said in the same manner. This sentence tells the importance of a prototype to this team.

UI requirements development is a process that the team and users commit to with a UI prototype. If the users cannot see the system, it is not easy for them to give useful feedback, and so the prototype is a useful tool that helps in this endeavour. In this company, the UI requirements and prototype development are part of the same process. The prototype is an important part in identifying the system requirements. Creating a UI prototype as part of the requirements gathering process means that the team did not need to create a UI/usability requirements document, the creation of which they considered to be an inconvenience. Moreover, they preferred the development of the prototype as a means of identifying UI requirements so that they were not only generated from user supplied information. In addition, deliberation by the design team towards offering solutions might also help the users to accomplish their work more easily than at the present time. The team along with the clients committed to the UI theme together, where this theme provides the essentials of the prototype used in the design. Moreover, the users were able to interact with some parts of the system rather than trying to interpret its design from documents and/or drawings only.

"Prototyping takes a major role in every project since we have never built a system that fits with user requirements using analysis and design within a single iteration. The created prototype has usually become part of the real system," Member B said.

3.3.3 Evaluation with the users

The evaluation process during UI construction was not clearly methodologically determined for a person to perform. The team and the users enacted the UI evaluation together by the system testing process during unit testing, a test that the system meets with the requirements. During integration testing, the UI was evaluated by the design team from a technical perspective. Consequently, success during this process determined whether to commit to the UI design once more together with the users.

The participation of the users was important to the team, and the team requested that a user representatives participated in every UI prototype review. During each iteration, especially to provide feedback on the prototype, priority was given to users' feedback since they were the ones to determine whether a system is good or not.

One difficult problem that can occur is access to the actual users, which is something that is out of the team's control and might require a formal request to the owner of the project. It is important to have access to the real business users because trying to determine the nature of the user tasks should be a directed by their experience, and in order to understanding the importance of the system, they need to have enough knowledge about it.

As always, feedback is a shared process driven by the users' perspective. After the team obtain feedback, the development can be iterated, and so on. The completed UI needs to be equipped with the abilities of the final configuration, which is usually determined by a lot more variables than just the users, and so other people in the meeting room may be important too.

3.4 UI design product characteristics

In the case of UI characteristics, the design team predominantly work towards understanding the users' needs, designing a UI that helps them navigate the IS to carry out their business tasks, examining how the system "converses" with them, and determining the look and feel of the UI. Figure 4 shows the big picture of UI design product characteristics, and illustrates the design process from the bottom (abstract) to the top (concrete). In addition, Table 1 shows the method that this team used at each layer of the design process.

3.4.1 Metaphors and user needs

"A metaphor is a relation between language as an abstract system, individual language users, and cultural knowledge". When users encounter a user-interface metaphor, they bring their own context to the understanding and decoding of that metaphor. This context involves their culture, work, education, and all the qualities that identify them as an individual. Clearly, this is a major undertaking for the designer of a UI.

3.4.2 Navigation design

System navigation is guidance that helps user. A satisfactory system should guide the user from start to finish, which means that the team needed to understand each user task involved in the business processes in order to accomplish it. The information that describes the details of the users' business processes comes from work-flow analysis, and navigation of the processes is reflected in the structure of the system in terms of layout: template, position of buttons, system hierarchy, content organization, tabs, menu, and border in each UI.

A UI prototype contains the structure of the system, both the whole system shown on a sitemap or structure of the system and page structures or wireframes showing the structure of each page. Visualizing the system structure helps users to understand where they interact in the system - the places that they can go to and places that they already know. The wireframe is an useful tool if it makes sense, and can helps users to understand what they are currently doing and what are they should do next within the page.

Work-flow analysis helps design teams to separate main tasks from subtasks which the user must carry out to complete a main task. The design team designs a system so that the user carries out only one subtask at a time by ensuring that the UI guides the user to carry it out and either finish it or cancel it. This approach helps the users to be more productive than if trying to carry out more than one task at a time.

3.4.3 Interaction design

Interaction is communication through dialogue between the system and the users. Dialogue should be formal when used for input data validation messages so that error messages are straightforward and offer encouragement to solve the problem.

A good UI is to fully support users to complete their tasks in a short time with no crash," The interviewees said.

Additionally, interaction reflects the support level of the system and often depends on user expertise. Therefore, support level needs to be fully explained in the system requirements. In some systems, users need full support and need to perceive that the system politely informs them of any mistakes they make. On the other hand, users may require less support built in to the system because they think they are the skillful users. Usually, the design team constructs interactions along the middle path and tries to help the users by preventing, correcting, and recovering information when an error has occurred.

In term of language level, that reflects via wording in the system (dialog box, warning, validation message, system status bar etc.). The design team often use polite and formal word. In case of warning or validation message, dialog should show detail in passive way (the system have some mistakes). They think user will be more satisfactorily than aggressive system.

Table 1. Summary of activities, method in UI design product characteristics.

UI	Activities	Input	Method	Output
Metaphor	Understanding Product Goal (user needs)	-Product objective -TOR -Use Case	- Group Interviewing - Document Analysis - Business Process Analysis	-Strategic Document - Use Case Diagram
Mental Model	Understanding Users	-User Characteris-ics -User Tasks -User Environment	- Group Interview -Task Analysis -Document Analysis -Observation	-Personas -Use Case Diagram - Usage Scenario
Naviga-tion	Information Design	Use Case Diagram Usage Scenarios	- Group Interview - Document Analysis	-System Structure/ -Site Map -Wireframe
Interac-tion	User-system Dialogue Design	Personas Usage Scenarios	- User-System Sequence Analysis	-System-user Dialogue Structure
	Error Handling Design	-Personas -Function Requirement -Usage Scenarios	-Brainstorming -Observation	-Prevention Message -Correction Message -Recovery Message
	Language Usage	-Personas -Usage Scenarios	-Brainstorming -Observation	-Level of Language (Language Theme)
Appearance	Apppearance Design	-Theme (Color, Fonts) -Design Guidelines -Wireframe -Prototype -System-user Dialogue Structure -Existing System	-Observation -Brainstorming -Exist System Analysis -Design and Technology Research	-UI theme

3.4.4 Appearance and visual design

An UI usually consists of many pages and it is important to keep a consistent style for each page. Therefore, the design team usually develop a template that every page will use. To this end, a wireframe is developed in the navigation design used. In addition, the design team usually choose consistent appearance elements such as background color, color palette, typography, and icon set appropriate for the users.

A designer's experience and knowledge appears on the prototype at the beginning of the design process because they bring their own experience to the table when creating a prototype. Comments from meetings between the team and the users is used to adjust it during the next design cycle.

"The team has experience of different types of users in different organizations, but the design during the first stage will be similar." Member B said

To select each appearance element, the design team first carries out research on the existing system and selects a theme that will become the basis for the new UI. Second, they use the successful structure to become the theme for headers, footers, left menu, and so on. Next, the color palette that they use is typically chosen from a theme from the user's organization. If the organization does not have one, the designers will probably use a bright color theme that is easy on the eye via a monitor.

Designers prefer to one icon set for menus and/or buttons because they think it increases a user's enjoyment when using the system as well as sets text and images to a good size for the current display. A point to be aware of during icon set selection is it must follow the chosen theme and be well conveyed. When selecting font size and typeface style, designers should be aware that most developed systems do not require formal fonts. However, text must be clear and legible. Official fonts are likely to be present in systems used by government agencies, as is usually clearly defined at the project start, but beyond that, needs to be clear and easy to read. Moreover, it is often the case that these attributes do not need to be changed at all.

Finally, the theme will be separate from other parts of the system, so if the design team need to change it, it only needs to be modified once for the entire system.

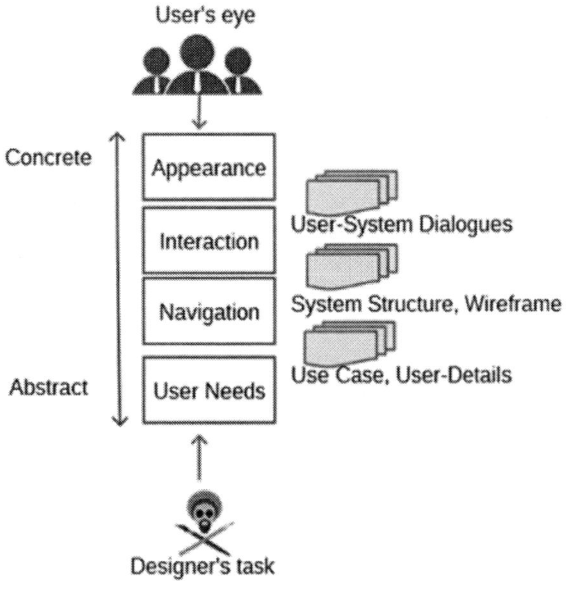

Fig. 4. UI design product characteristics.

4 Conclusion

From the UCD approach and using UI elements, the design team carried out these tasks at a level that appropriate with the team for this specific project. Their main goals were to complete the project with quality and on-time. Initially, they may not have known what design the UIs should take and how to use UCD, but they understood that important contributions and positive responses from the users were crucial in this approach. Therefore, they paid special attention to the users as well as providing their prior knowledge and experience towards designing the system.

The characteristics of the organization and value supplied by the design team helped to optimize client satisfaction, and it is worth considering that survival of a business may be affected by the way the team designs the UIs. They perhaps tried to create the product too quickly by bypassing some of the traditional steps of systems analysis by using UCD. However, in their opinion, some parts of the UCD process, especially in environments with apparently clear UI requirements, can often be overlooked. In this case, it is possible that some important organizational information which might have influenced system usage, such as culture, behavior and business type were not included in the initial UI design analysis. These data may be very useful when they have to design a system for users in organizations where the UI design is not obvious. Nevertheless, small-clan teams are more flexible and suitable for UI designs that incorporate user values than big teams. They share techniques and are open-minded when receiving feedback within the team and especially from the users.

The key lesson from this study is partial UCD and some UI elements, already recognized by software services teams, were an excellent approach in this case since the design team understood that the UI is a vital part of a successful IS. In addition, the design team understood that activities, input, output and how to query data affected the design of usable UIs. However, some user information was not properly gathered prior to the analysis and design phase and so the design team might have been better off employing UI design guidelines to help them clarify the activities and characteristics of the UI design. Consequently, they seem to be need the combinations of methods which not only UCD with abstract UI elements but also another accepted IS development process.

The researcher would like to thank Khun Kanyanut Homsapaya and Siriwatthapurich Co.,Ltd. with their useful information and comments that were used in this article.

References

1. ISO 9241-210. *Ergonomics of human-system interaction - Part 210: Human-centered design for interactive systems* [Online] from https://www.iso.org/standard/52075.html (2010). [Accessed on 12 August 2017]
2. J.R. Lewis. *Int J Hum Comput Interact.*, **30**,9:663-684 (2012). http://www.tandfonline.com/doi/abs/10.1080/10447318.2014.930311
3. E. Callahan. *Annu. Rev. Inf. Sci. Technol.*, **39**,1:255–310 (2005). https://kinasevych.ca/2010/04/28/callahan-2005-interface-design-and-culture/
4. J. Nielsen. *Usability 101: introduction to usability* [Online] from https://www.nngroup.com/articles/usability-101-introduction-to-usability/ (2012). [Accessed on 12 August 2017]
5. H. Kikuchi, S. Kimura, S. Ohkubo, H. Inamura, A. Takeshia. *NTT DOCOMO Tech. J.*, **12**,3:33–41 (2010). https://www.nttdocomo.co.jp/english/binary/pdf/corporate/technology/rd/technical_journal/bn/vol12_3/vol12_3_033en.pdf

6. E. Folmer, J. Bosch. *J. Syst. Softw.*, **70**,1-2:61–78 (2004). https://dl.acm.org/citation.cfm?id=2305799
7. T. Keinonen. *One-dimensional usability influence of usability on consumers' product preference*. Helsinki: University of Art and Design (1998). p. 311 https://books.google.co.id/books/about/One_dimensional_Usability.html?id=q7ZuAAAACAAJ&redir_esc=y
8. B. Shneiderman, C. Plaisant. *Designing the user interface: strategies for effective human-computer interaction*. 5th edition. USA: Addison-Wesley (2010). p.121 https://www.amazon.com/Designing-User-Interface-Human-Computer-Interaction/dp/0321537351
9. A. Marcus. *Interactions*, **9**,5:19–24 (2002). https://dl.acm.org/citation.cfm?id=566992
10. R.K. Yin. *Case study research: design and method*. USA: SAGE Publications (2013). P.110 https://www.amazon.com/Case-Study-Research-Methods-Applied/dp/1452242569
11. Department of Business Development. *Business Data Warehouse* [Online] from http://datawarehouse.dbd.go.th/bdw/business/index.html (2016). [Accessed on 5 December 2016]
12. K.S. Cameron, R.E. Quinn. *Diagnosing and changing organizational culture: based on the competing values framework*. USA: Jossey-Bass (2011). p. 49 https://www.amazon.com/Diagnosing-Changing-Organizational-Culture-Competing/dp/0470650265
13. J. Suderman. *J Pract Consult.*, **4**,1:52-58 (2012). https://www.regent.edu/acad/global/publications/jpc/vol4iss1/JPC_Vol4Iss1.pdf#page=59

Energy Saving Potential from Shading Design for Residential House in Rural Area

Dany Perwita Sari[1,2,*], and *Yun-shang* Chiou[1]

[1]NTUST, Architecture Department, Keelung Rd., Taipei 106, Taiwan
[2]LIPI, Research Center for Biomaterials, Jl. Raya Bogor, Cibinong 16911, Indonesia

Abstract. There are some architectural factors in the energy saving design of residential houses in Taiwan. In addition, in rural area, window glazing is a key factor to reducing electricity. For these purposes, a simulation model of exterior shading has been done in this study. Various types of shading devices have been analysed and compared in terms of energy savings. Simulation analysis by DesignBuilder reveals that shading devices has substantial impact to minimizing energy consumption. The results derived in this paper could provide useful suggestions for the shading design of residential buildings at rural area in Taiwan.

Key words: Energy saving potential, residential house, rural area, shading devices, subtropical climate

1 Introduction

Buildings sector contributed CO_2 emissions around the world. This results of high construction rates and the long lifespans of buildings [1]. It is clear seen that residential sector is one of the largest energy consumption sector in Taiwan, approximately 19 % in 2016 [2]. In other hand, Taiwan is lack of energy and more than 98.1 % of total energy supply is imported [3]. To meet the challenge of carbon reduction, conserving energy and energy efficient building design has been a concern for governments in Taiwan. They promoted green building in 1995, green building materials in 2004, and intelligent green building in 2010 [4]. By transforming the built environment to be more energy-efficient and climate-friendly, the building sector can play a major role in reducing climate change [1].

However, most of residential building in Taiwan is not designed by this regulation, especially in rural area (Figure 1). There are huge gap between urban and rural area for energy consumption because Government usually focused on newly building construction rather than conventional building. The conventional residential buildings in this subtropical climate of Taipei are normally focused on natural ventilation and solar shading. The numerous studies done on shading devices shows the importance of their usage in buildings [5, 6]. There are two location for shade in window, interior and exterior shading. Occupants tend to use blind to block the glare. Yun-shang Chiou and Yi-de Lin [7] introduced an experimental research using a portable testbed. The result indicate that blind system is only reduce the glare but not decrease the energy consumption. In another hand, the application

* Corresponding author: dany.perwitasari@gmail.com

of exterior shading devices are an essential issue for decreasing the cooling loads of building in hot climatic regions [8–10].

Fig. 1. Residential house at rural area in Taiwan. Left to right: house in Yilan, house in Guanshan.

Recently, building energy simulation has been developed as a new technique to predicted building energy consumption in early stages. The energy simulation engine will calculates the energy performance of several designs with faster and accurate. However, there is still a lack of studies analysing the impact of a shading design on the building energy consumption, especially in conventional residential building. Usually researcher only focused on newly building design. It is necessary to find optimal shading design solutions for conventional residential buildings considering both decreasing energy consumption and increasing indoor thermal comfort. In addition, designing and optimizing shadings is a complicated task. New strategy is needed to provide integrated software which can ease the design decision, modeling and solving problem.

This study makes an analysis a various shading design by using DesignBuilder. DesignBuilder allows the energy performance of a residential building. It also visualizes solar shading and investigates design alternatives to maximize thermal comfort, benefits of daylight and natural ventilation. To make the results more accurate, we used real occupant behaviour using Time Use Survey (TUS). Building simulation programs were used to demonstrate possible method of combining design and energy simulation with promises accuracy and appropriate data visualization technique [11]. This method allows architects to rely on an accurate analysis rather than on their intuition to make decisions. Therefore, designer and occupant will be easier to make decision which is the best shading design for conventional residential building in Taiwan.

2 Methodology and simulation set-up

Taiwan is classified as a subtropical area, which is characterized by hot and dry summers and cold winters. The hottest months are from June to August with the highest temperature reaching up to around 38 °C (100 °F). The average temperature of the rest of the months is around 25 °C (77 °F).

A whole building simulation using DesignBuilder was a suitable method that provides a valid decisions tool that use as shading analysis in conventional residential building. The digital model that DesignBuilder shows the user is similar to the original building. The important information that applies to the energy model has more to do with the building's construction, operations, and settings of HVAC systems. Moreover, DesignBuilder is working with a standard weather data.

In this study, simulations and analysis were made with DesignBuilder. With the aim to achieve correct and assessable data and results, the compliance of simulations with standard calculation methods is fundamental. TUS was chosen as an input variable in DesignBuilder.

TUS was record information about individual's activities during a 24 h period and personal information such as the individual's occupation and demographic background [12]. TUS data was used to establish a more reliable causal relationship between Taiwanese behaviour and residential energy use.

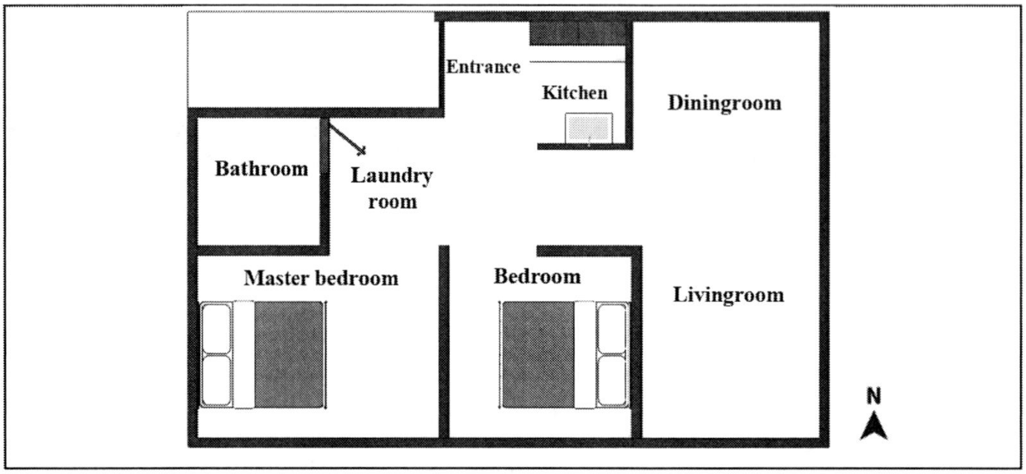

Fig. 2. Layout of space of residential building in rural area in Taiwan.

For the purpose of estimating the cooling load with various shading device, a prototype single house residential building has been established. The general configuration of the conventional residential building in Taiwan is one storey with four persons in one family. The total area of the house is 70 m^2. The whole bedroom and living room are oriented to the south (Figure 2). Designing external shading devices in existing buildings requires many design considerations, like aesthetics and integration with existing building style. This study proposes a simulation analysis of external shading devices that can be applied in conventional buildings. The current study deals with four different types of the shading device as shown in Figure 3: (i) overhang, which can control sunlight and not block the view; (ii) the horizontal louvers but they block most of the view; (iii) combined between overhang and side fin, this design can control sunlight in three sides and not block the view; (iv) mixed between overhang, side fin and horizontal louvers, which block most of the view to outside.

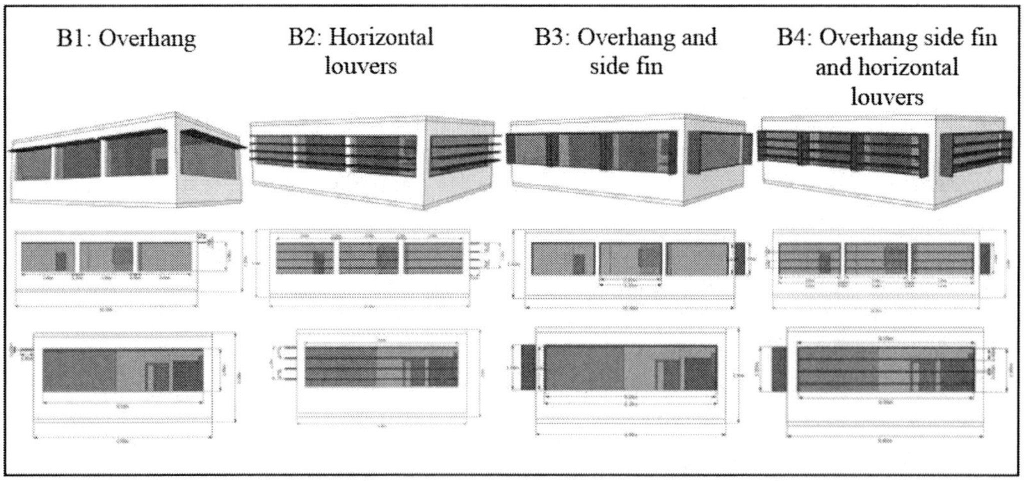

Fig. 3. Different types of window shading device for residential housing.

A whole building simulation using DesignBuilder was a suitable method that provides valid decisions tools to analysis shading devices. Figure 4 illustrates the flow of the proposed work flow methodology. The digital model that DesignBuilder shows the user is similar to the typical rural house in Taiwan. DesignBuilder is working with a standard weather data and occupant activity (TUS). Table 1 and Table 2 were shown the input data and material properties that have been applied to the energy simulation. The main purpose of analysis the shading devices is to control direct sunlight and to maintain thermal comfort, therefore can reduce the energy consumption. Another factor need to be taken into consideration in designing shading devices aside from blocking direct sun light and improve daylight quality is how to maintain a minimum level of contract with environment outside [10]. Contact with outside is an important factor to be anlyze in this research.

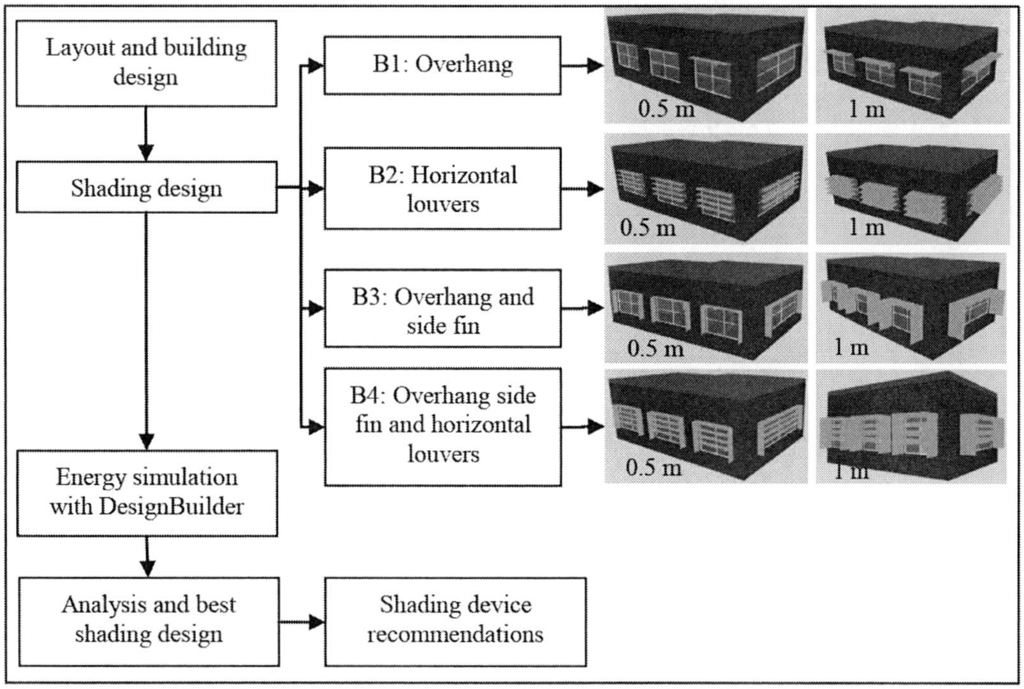

Fig. 4. Flowchart for conventional residential building with several shading devices.

Table 1. DesignBuilder simulation input data.

Variables	Values	
Design temperature	Cooling set-point	27 °C
Target luminance	-	150 lux
Minimum fresh air	Living room	7.5 (l/s-person)
	Bathroom	10 (l/s-person)
	Kitchen	12 (l/s-person)
Natural ventilation	-	27 °C
Weather data	Taiwan	-

Table 2. Material properties of building element.

Element	Construction	U-value (W/m^2K)
Wall	Concrete + ceramic tile	0.351
Foundation	Concrete	0.351
Floor	Ceramic	0.434
Roof	Flat roof	0.252
Internal partition	-	4.730
Windows	Clear glass	6.257

3. Results and Discussion

Results indicate a major influence of shading on solar gains, cooling load and visual environment of occupants. All shading devices helped reduce total electricity (Figure 5) all months in one year. It is clear that from May to September all shading devices reduce electricity higher than other months.

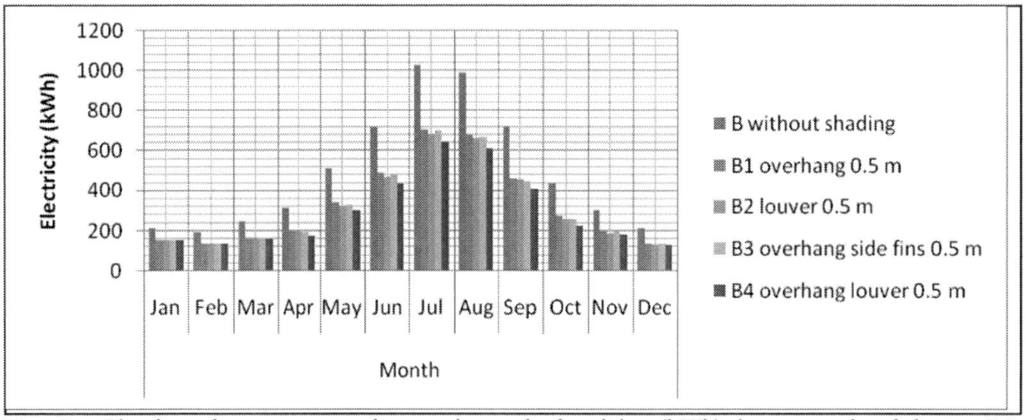

Fig. 5. The bar chart compare changes in total electricity (kWh) in conventional house B1 (overhang), B2 (louvers), B3 (overhang and side fins), B4 (overhang and louvers) compared to B (without shading).

It shows from Figure 6 that all shading devices in different size (0.5 m and 1 m) reduced the electricity by approximately the same rate. Moreover, B4, overhang and louvers design performed better than other shading devices. B1 and B3 shading devices has similar performance to lower the energy consumption rate. Graphically analysis (Figure 7) on solar gain exterior from window shows how each type of shading devices perform. Figure 7 show how the shading devices will perform all the time according to solar angel, altitude and azimuth.

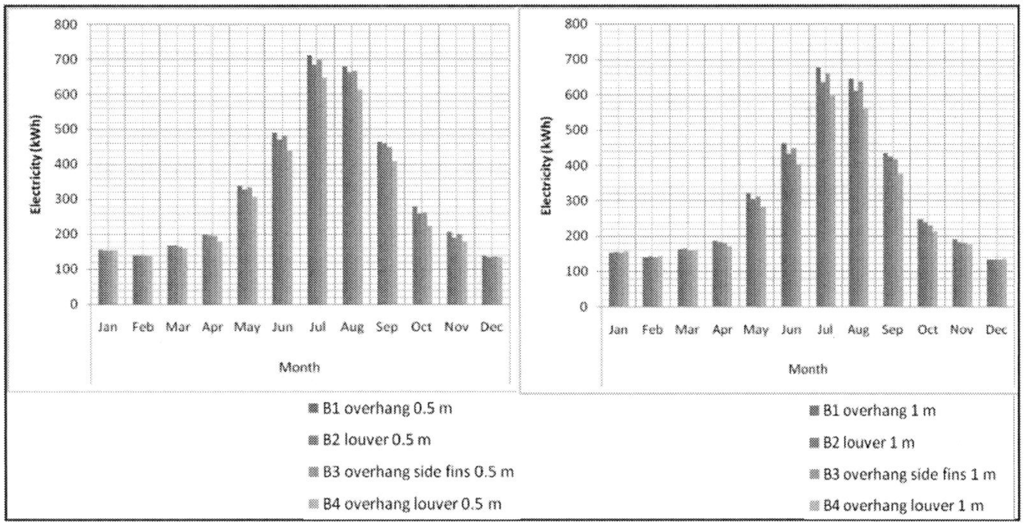

Fig. 6. The graphic was display comparison between shading devices (B1, B2, B3, B4) in different sizes (0.5 m and 1 m)

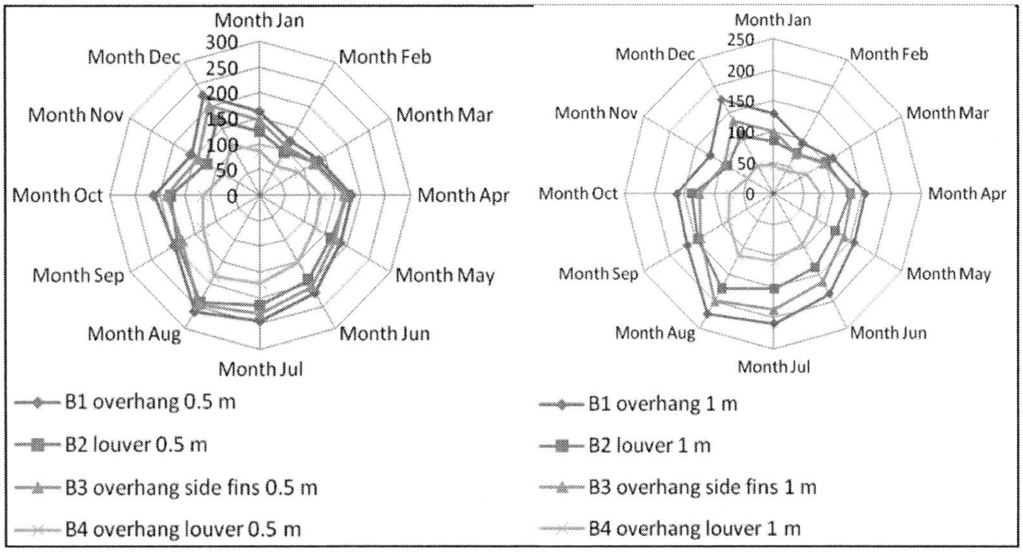

Fig. 7. Graphically analysis on solar gain exterior from window shows how B1, B2, B3, and B4 perform.

Figure 8 was display changes in electricity. Shading devices reduced electricity by up to 250 % in December, January and February respectively. In March the percentage difference in electricity consumption was around 200 %, while the difference starts to increase gradually as the increase amount of daylight in Taiwan latitude in April to November, with minimum reduction of 106 % in October. B1, overhang, as seen in Figure 8 was growth slowly from 259 % to 262 % from January to February. By contrast, electricity dropped sharply to 171 % in April, while from April to July electricity rose slowly to 222 %. Moreover, there was a fluctuated from August to December approximately 180 %.

B2 and B3 model showed a similar trend. This begin at slightly around 250 % in January also decreased at April at 160 % respectively, finishing the period at 170 %. However, the most significant was B4. Start in the same level like B1, B2 and B3 at January and February, and then B4 gradually decreased.

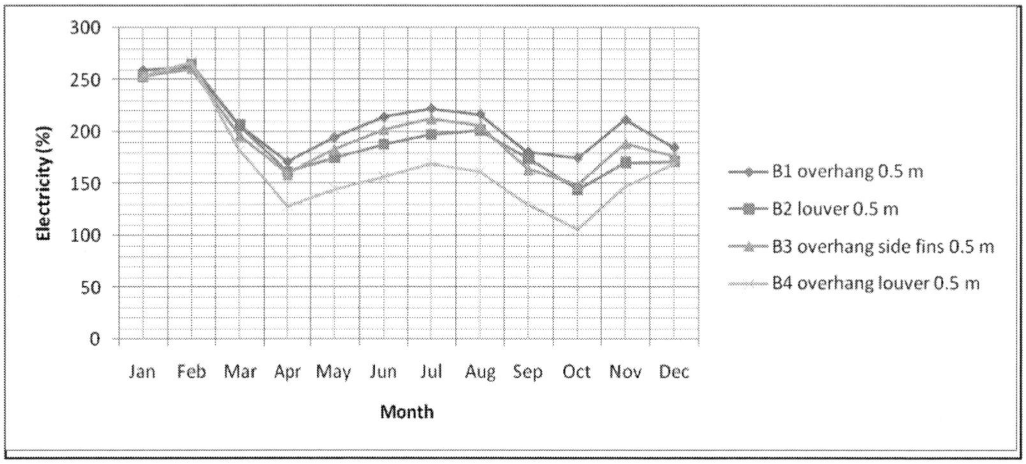

Fig. 8. Percentage results comparison between window without and with shading device. Model B4 was the best performance.

4. Conclusion

This paper discusses the simulation results of various shading devices for conventional house in rural area, Taiwan. In general, all shading devices helped to control the excessive daylight level and reduce glare. There was clear that all shading devices reduced the solar gain by approximately the same rate in December, January and February. By contrast in other months, each shading devices show different results. Moreover model B2 and B3 has similar trend almost in all months. However B3 was higher than B2. In addition, B4 was the best reduced the solar gain, whilst B1 was the least result of the four.

On top of this overhang and louver design could perform well around the year as reduced the electricity by whole simulation, while on the other hand this design will block most of the view to environment. In fact, overhang and side fin design was not perform as well as overhang and louver design or louver design, whereas occupant might have direct contact with outside.

This study provides a clear methodology for optimizing shading design for conventional residential building in rural area with the aim of minimizing the energy consumption while maximizing daylight and occupant comfort. Exterior shading devices in residential building demonstrated good improvement both in visual environment and energy-saving strategies.

This study is a part of an on-going PhD research conducted by the first author in National Taiwan University of Science and Technology. This is performed with the support of Indonesia Endowment Fund for Education (LPDP)-Ministry of Finance, Indonesia.

References

1. IPCC Summary for Policymakers. *Summary for Policymakers.* In: *Climate Change 2014: Mitigation of Climate Change.* O. Edenhofer, R. Pichs-Madruga, Y. Sokona, E. Farahani, S. Kadner, K. Seyboth, et al. (Eds). Cambridge and New York: Cambridge University Press (2014). pp. 9–23. https://www.ipcc.ch/pdf/assessment-report/ar5/wg3/ipcc_wg3_ar5_summary-for-policymakers.pdf

2. Bureau of Energy, Ministry of Economic Affairs, Taiwan. *Energy Statistics Handbook 2016*. [Online] from https://web3.moeaboe.gov.tw/ecw/english/content/ContentDesc.aspx?menu_id=1539 (2017). [Accessed on December 2017].
3. J.J. Hwang. Renew. *Sust. Energ. Rev*, **15**,2:1392–1402 (2011). https://www.sciencedirect.com/science/article/pii/S1364032110002625
4. C.F.J. Kuo, C.H. Lin, M.W. Hsu. *Energy Policy*, **95**,C:291–303 (2016). https://econpapers.repec.org/article/eeeenepol/v_3a95_3ay_3a2016_3ai_3ac_3ap_3a291-303.htm
5. L. Baumgärtner, R.A. Krasovsky, J. Stopper, J.V. Grabe. *Energy Procedia*, **122**: 211–216 (2017). https://www.sciencedirect.com/science/article/pii/S187661021732951X
6. A.K.K. Lau, E. Salleh, C.H. Lim, M.Y. Sulaiman. *Int. J. Sust. Built Environment*, **5**, 2:387–399 (2016). https://www.sciencedirect.com/science/article/pii/S2212609016300176
7. Y. S. Chiou, Y. D. Lin, *A Portable Testbed for Integrative Daylighting Design*. Paper presented in 36th International Conference on Passive and Low Energy Architecture. (Los Angeles, United States of America, 2016). http://plea2016.uscarch.com/index.php/pleapapers/fullpapers/paper/view/1195
8. M. Konstantoglou, A. Tsangrassoulis. *Renew. Sust. Energ. Rev*, **60**:268–283 (2016). https://www.sciencedirect.com/science/article/pii/S1364032115016299.
9. A. A. Y. Freewan. *Solar Energy*, **102**:14–30 (2014). https://www.sciencedirect.com/science/article/pii/S0038092X14000279
10. G. Kim, H.S. Lim, T.S. Lim, L. Schaefer, J.T. Kim. *Energy and Buildings*, **46**:105–111 (2012). https://www.sciencedirect.com/science/article/pii/S0378778811005032
11. E. Elbeltagi, H. Wefki, S. Abdrabou, M. Dawood, A. Ramzy. *J. Build. Eng*, **13**:127–136 (2017). https://www.sciencedirect.com/science/article/pii/S2352710217302711
12. Y.S. Chiou, K.M. Carley, C.I. Davidson, M.P. Johnson. *Energy and Buildings*, **43**, 12: 3528–3538 (2011). https://www.sciencedirect.com/science/article/pii/S0378778811004087

Congestion Mitigation Scenario through Public Transportation Improvement

Erma Suryani[1,*], *Rully* Agus Hendrawan[1], *Phillip* Fasrter Eka Adipraja[2], and *Lily* Puspa Dewi[3]

[1]Information Systems, Institut Teknologi Sepuluh Nopember, Kampus ITS, Jalan Raya ITS- Sukolilo-Surabaya, 60111, Indonesia
[2]STMIK Asia Malang, Jl. Soekarno Hatta - Rembuksari 1A Malang, 61234, Indonesia
[3]Informatics Engineering, Petra Christian University, Jalan Siwalankerto 121-131 Surabaya , 60236, Indonesia

Abstract. Congestion can be recognized through roads filled with cars, trucks, buses and sidewalks filled with pedestrians. It usually relates to an excess of vehicles at a particular time resulting in lower speeds, sometimes much slower than normal speeds. Public transportation is a vital element in solving the congestion problem in the city. In Indonesia, currently, safe and convenient transportation modes to move from one point to another still rarely found. Therefore, the growth rate of personal vehicles soaring from year to year. Therefore, in this research a set of simulation models have been developed to mitigate congestion through the improvement of public transportation. As a method used to develop the model, system dynamics is utilized based on consideration that the method can accommodate nonlinear relationships between factors that have significant contribution to mitigate the traffic congestion. Research results show that the improvement of public transportation through comfort, safety, reliability and affordable cost can mitigate the traffic congestion.

Keywords: Model, simulation, system dynamics, transportation mode choice.

1 Introduction

Transportation has an important role in supporting economic development and social development for the welfare of society [1]. Generally, safe and convenient transportation modes to move from one point to another still rarely found. Therefore, the growth rate of personal vehicles soaring from year to year.

Congestion can be recognized through roads filled with cars, trucks, buses and sidewalks filled with pedestrians. Congestion usually relates to an excess of vehicles on a portion of roadway at a particular time resulting in speeds that are slower—sometimes much slower—than normal or "free flow" speeds [2]. Several sources of congestion are: (i) Traffic-Influencing Events such traffic incident, work zones, and weather; (ii) Traffic Demand that includes special events and fluctuations in normal traffic, (iii) Physical Highway Features such as traffic control devices and road capacity.

Public transport that exists today, some of its forms are less feasible and less secure, the fleet of trains is still minimum so crowded and often there is interference. Based on this condition, a transportation revolution in Indonesia is required. The existence of easy, safe and convenient public transportation is very important not only to congestion mitigation, but also to reduce fuel consumption, as well as to improve the efficiency in mobility. The primary survey has been conducted to collect the data for identifying public preferences for public transport characteristics under four criteria, those are reliability, comfort, safety and cost [3].

Motorcycles in developing countries are a major cause of traffic congestion, accidents, environmental pollution and other social tensions, it is required to plan an appropriate transport system. Although bus service constitutes a small part towards several trips, they are still regarded as an alternative to motorcycle [4]. Previous study has developed a "web based monitoring traffic system". This system is useful in terms of providing surveillance, control and road network

*Corresponding author: erma.suryani@gmail.com

monitoring services. The system can integrate complex components in a modular, flexible and open structure to validate models and includes tools to simulate various traffic scenarios and communication technologies [5]. Other study has exploited the emergence of new technologies such as the Internet, to design an intelligent Traffic Management System (TMS) that can monitor traffic and control network traffic located in different locations [6]. The system utilizes a Web-based Embedded Web Server (EWS). Therefore, in this research, a system dynamics simulation model has been utilized to mitigate traffic congestion as a solution to transportation management in urban area.

2 Literature review

2.1 Transportation mode choice

According to research that have been conducted by Corpuz [7] and Buehler [8], key factors of transportation mode choice are accessibility, waiting time, transportation availability, pleasure, safety, privacy, travel time, distance, price, and fare as seen in Figure 1.

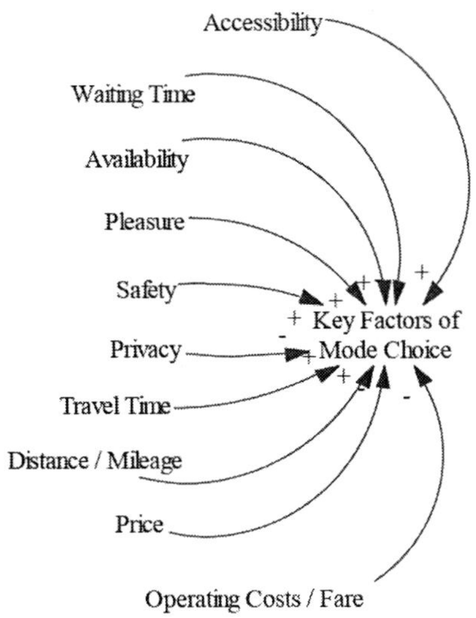

Fig. 1. Key factor of transportation mode choice.

According to Jain et al. [3], there are several factors effecting the choice of public transportation mode, as seen in Table 1. The weights of sub-criteria for global priority and sub criteria can be seen in Table 2. These weights are gathered by conducting questionnaire to people who select public transportation such as metro that is a successful example in terms of offering a comfortable, reliable and safe mode of public transport. Metro is more reliable and comfortable due to its frequency and adherence to schedule, as well as less travel time with air-conditioning facility at most of the metro stations and metro coaches.

Table 1. Factors affecting public transportation system [3].

Factors affecting Public Transportation System	Sub-factors
Comfort	Cleanliness
	Air conditioning
	Seating
	Availability
	Low floor
	Not crowded
	Accessibility
	Less travel time
Safety	Lesser accident
	Personal safety
	Staff behaviour and attitude
Reliability	Good frequency
	Adherence to schedule
Cost	Cost of travel

Table 2. The weights of sub-criteria of public transportation mode choice [3].

Sub-criteria	Global Priority Weights	Sub Criteria Percentage
Comfort		
Cleanliness	0.02	0.12
Air conditioning	0.01	0.05
Seating availability	0.02	0.12
Low floor	0.01	0.08
Not crowded	0.03	0.16
Accessibility	0.04	0.25
Less travel time	0.04	0.25
Reliability		
Good frequency	0.16	0.61
Adherence to schedule	0.11	0.39
Safety		
Lesser accident	0.12	0.33
Personal safety	0.15	0.42
Staff behaviour and attitude	0.09	0.25

2.2 System dynamic simulation

Dynamic simulation model demonstrates a system as it evolves over time, for example conveyor system in a factory [9]. It is a technique to mimic operations or processes that occur in a system with the help of computer devices so that the system can be learned scientifically. Simulation is an appropriate tool to use, especially if it is required to conduct experiments in order to find the best comments from system components. By conducting a simulation, the study can be conducted in a short time and can provide the right decision, because everything is done with the computer. This system dynamics approach begins with the development of a real system model. The model should be able to show how the various components in the system are interacting so as to truly describe the behaviour of the system. Once the model is created, then the model is transformed into a computer program. System dynamics simulation is a tool for analysing and developing policies. System dynamics is very suitable to be used in handling complex system problem, which is a combination of qualitative and quantitative analysis and based on system thinking and general reasoning. According to Sterman [10], there are five steps in developing a dynamic system model as shown in Figure 2.

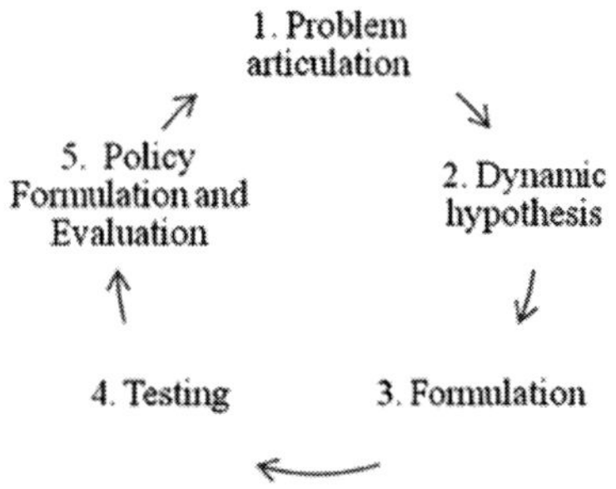

Fig. 2. Steps in developing system dynamics simulation [10].

(i) Problem articulation: In this stage the modeller need to find the problem, determine the significant variables, determine the time period of the simulation, and identify the problem dynamically to provide a basic understanding in designing the policy to solve problems.

(ii) Dynamics hypothesis: In this stage, the development a theory of how the problem arises, creating a causal loop diagram (CLD) that explains the causal relationship between variables, and converts the CLD to the level and rate (Stock and Flow) diagram.

(iii) Formulation: In this stage the modeller needs to define equations that describes the relationship between the variables, estimates the parameters, as well as determine the initial condition.

(iv) Testing: This stage is required to check the model validity, identify the model behaviour, as well as to check whether it can represent the behaviour of real systems.

(v) Policy formulation and evaluation: This stage is the formulation and evaluation of the policy that is proposed. If the structure and model behaviour are in accordance with the actual system, then the model can be utilized to design and evaluate the policy by changing the parameter values or redesigning the new structure to improve the system performance.

3 Model development

This model was developed to perform congestion analysis caused by the internal and external factors. The congestion analysis model consisted of two submodels, those are average daily traffic (ADT) and traffic congestion.

3.1 Average daily traffic submodel

Figure 3 shows the average daily traffic volume flow diagram. From Figure 3, it can be seen that the average daily traffic can be grouped into three categories, those are non-passenger, public and private transportation. Public transportation mode choice is one of several factors that influences the volume of private vehicle transportation.

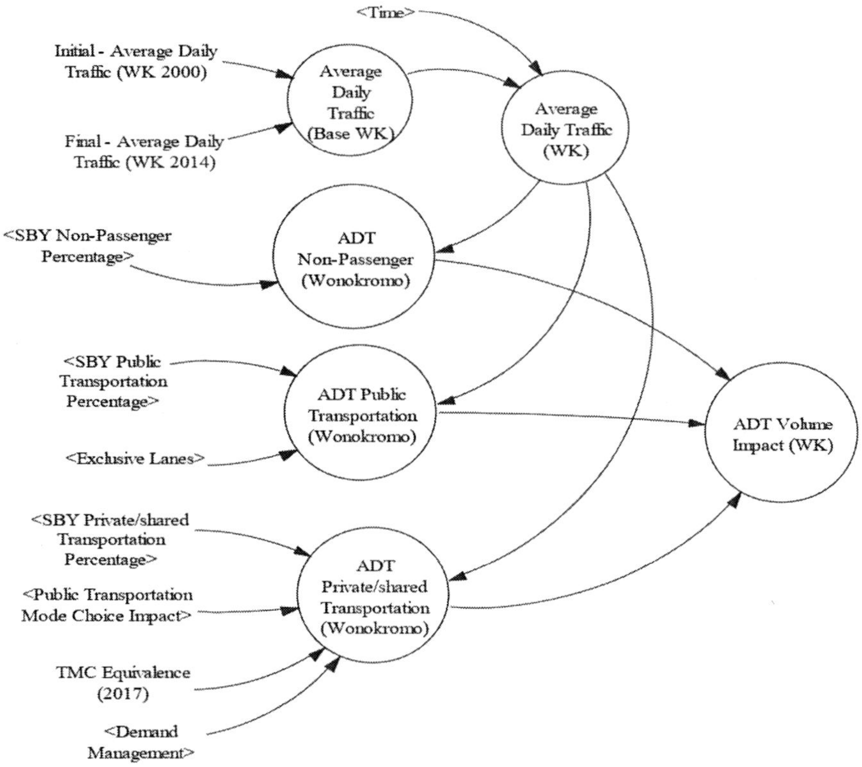

Fig. 3. Flow diagram for Average Daily Traffic (ADT).

From the simulation result, average daily traffic on Wonokromo Road has reached 594 985 vehicles per day as seen on Figure 4. Meanwhile, public transportation mode choice has an impact of around 40 % to the number of private transportation, as seen in Figure 5.

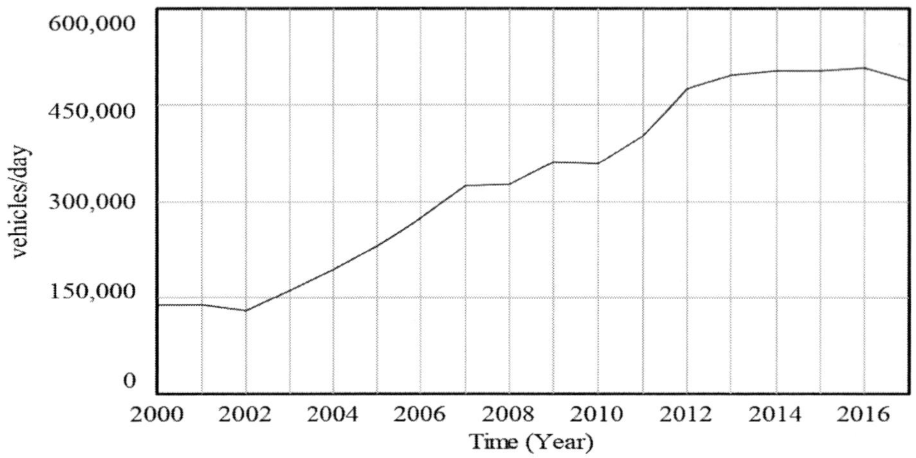

Fig. 4. Average Daily Traffic (ADT) in Wonokromo Street.

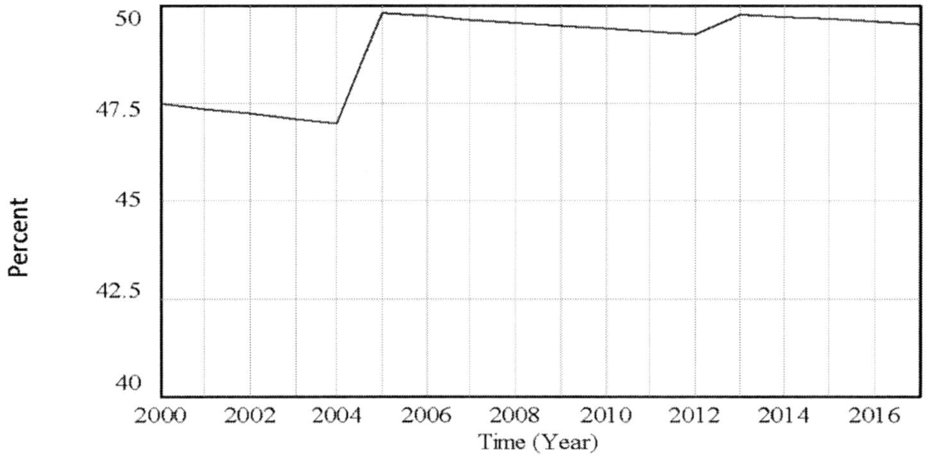

Fig. 5. Public transportation mode choice impact.

3.2 Traffic congestion submodel

The flow diagram of the traffic congestion model can be seen in Figure 6. This flow diagram is developed by considering several research results that have been done by Jain [3], Corpuz [7], and Buehler [8].

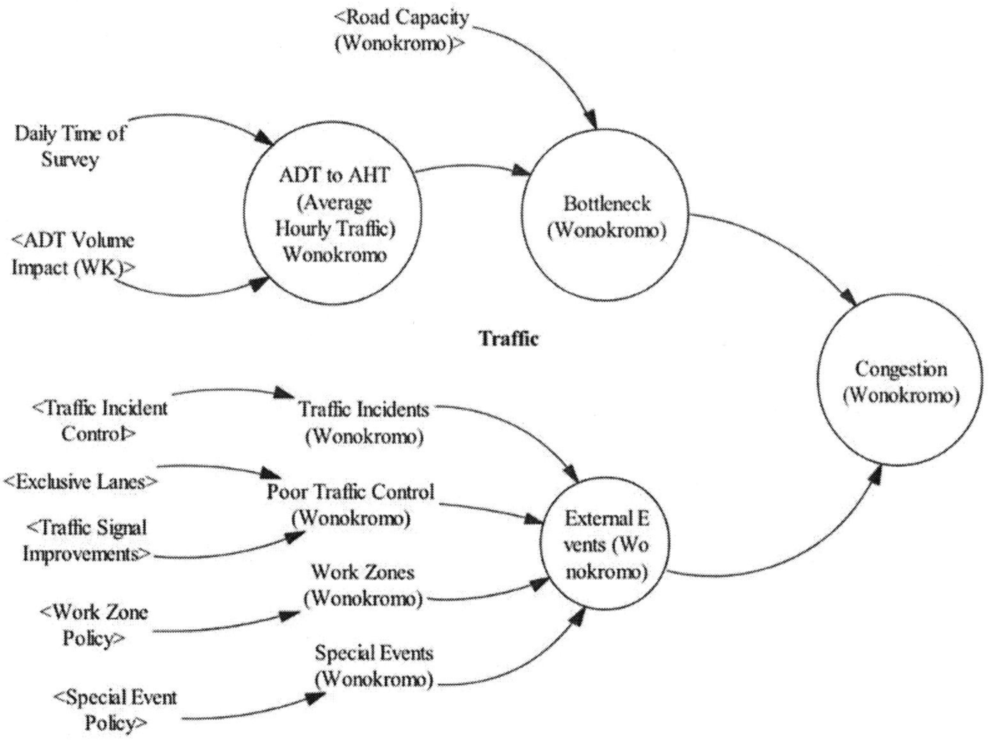

Fig. 6. Traffic congestion flow diagram.

Form Figure 6, it can be seen that traffic congestion depends on the bottleneck (internal factors) and external events (external factors). Some internal factors that affect the bottleneck include road capacity and average daily traffic (ADT). While internal factors are influenced by several factors such as traffic incidents, exclusive lanes, work zones, and special events. Simulation result shows traffic congestion in Wonokromo Road was around 184 % in 2016 as seen in Figure 7.

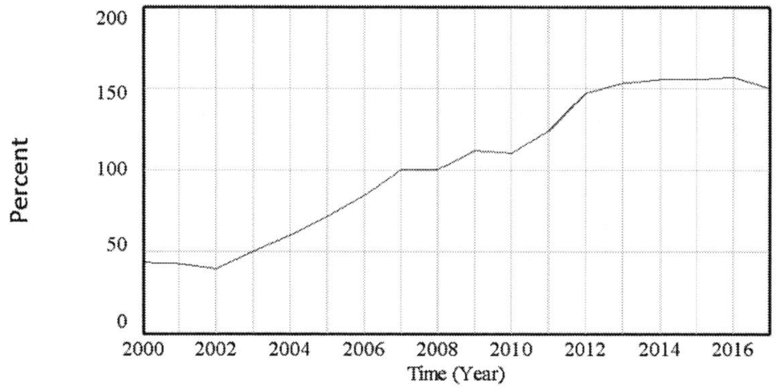

Fig. 7. Simulation result of traffic congestion in Wonokromo Street.

4 Model validation

Model validation is required to check the model accuracy. A model will be valid if the error rate is less than 5 % and error variance is less than 30 % [11]. The validation processed has been conducted to check the accuracy of average daily traffic by utilizing the error rate and error variance formulation as defined in Eq. (1) and Eq. (2).

$$ErrorRate = \frac{\left[\bar{S} - \bar{A}\right]}{\bar{A}} \quad (1)$$

$$ErrorVariance = \frac{|Ss - Sa|}{Sa} \quad (2)$$

Where:
$\bar{S}$ = The average rate of simulation
$\bar{A}$ = The average rate of data
S_s = The standard deviation of simulation
S_a = The standard deviation of data

Data use in this research is obtained from city transportation office in Surabaya. Error rate of some variables of daily traffic volume in Wonokromo and A. Yani Street are as follows:

Error rate of "daily traffic volume in Wonokromo Road"
$$= \frac{[467\,763 - 425\,968]}{425\,968} = 0.027$$

Error rate of "daily traffic volume in A. Yani Road"
$$= \frac{[381172 - 363\,339]}{363\,339} = 0.04$$

Error variance of some variables of daily traffic volume in Wonokromo and A. Yani Street are as follows:
Error variance "daily traffic volume in Wonokromo Road"
$$= \frac{[63\,565 - 89\,009]}{89\,009} = 0.28$$

Error variance of "daily traffic volume in A Yani Road"
$$= \frac{[76\,045 - 74095]}{74\,095} = 0.026$$

Based on the above calculation, all the error rates are less than 5 %, and error of variance are less than 30 % which means that our model is valid.

4 Scenario development

This scenario is developed to mitigate traffic congestion through the improvement of public transportation. Several efforts need to be conducted such as increasing comfort, reliability, safety and affordable cost [3] as seen in Figure 8. Those factors will determine the level of user satisfaction in selecting public transport and will have to be raised a shifting from private vehicles to public transport. This is because user would only be willing to shift to transportation modes with greater comfort, reliability and safety.

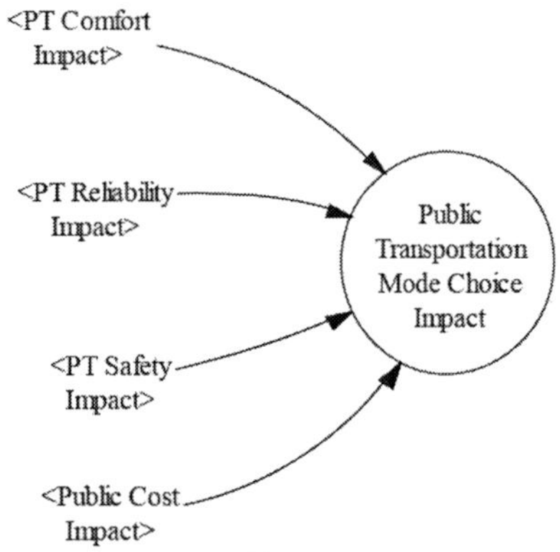

Fig. 8. Scenario of public transportation improvement.

Public transportation reliability can be done through more frequent of public transport and integrating the scheduling systems [3] as seen in Figure 9.

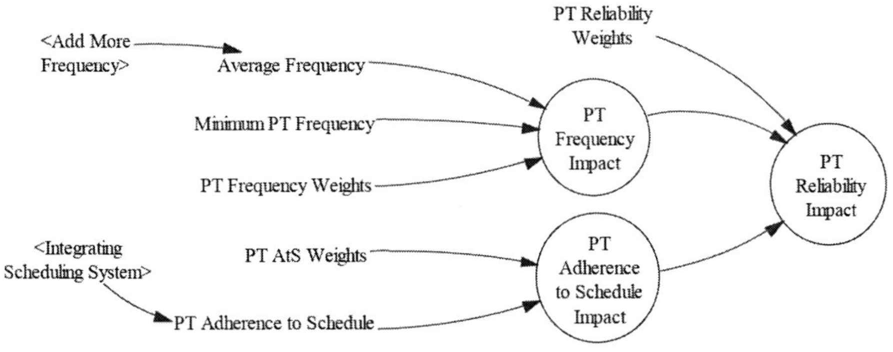

Fig. 9. Reliability improvement.

Safety can be improved through the improvement of cautions, car personal safety, as well as staff behavior and attitude [3] as seen in Figure 10.

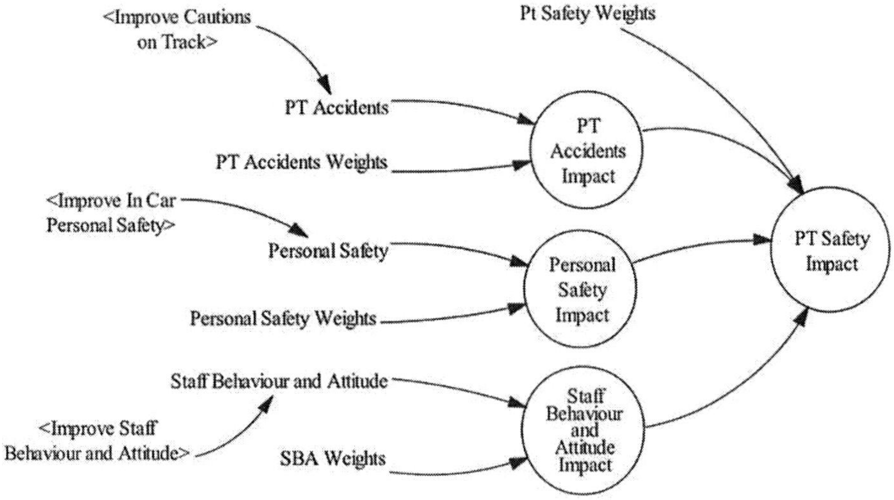

Fig. 10. Safety improvement

Comfort can be improved through the improvement of cleanliness, air conditioning, seat availability, floor level, level of cored accessibility, travel time [3] as seen in Figure 11.

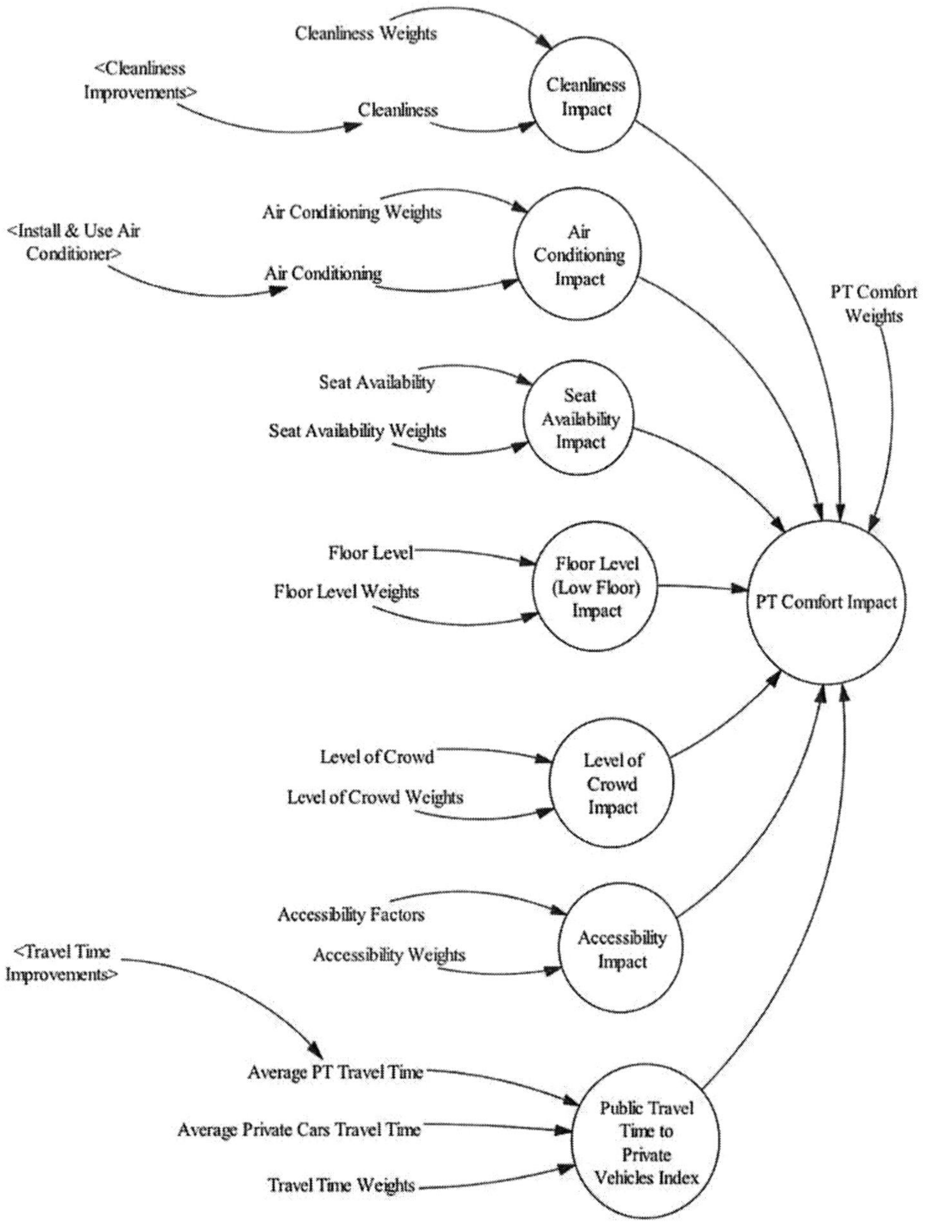

Fig. 11. Comfort improvement

Affordable cost improvement can be done through the increase in parking cost for private transportation, increase Pertamax price, and increase yearly tax of private transportation [12] as seen in Figure 12. Passenger cars and freight cars with an allowable amount of weight of less than or equal to 3 500 kg, including: (i) mini truck vehicle or other similar vehicle, imposed retribution of IDR 5 000; (ii) Sedan vehicle, pickup car or other vehicle some kind of levy is IDR 3 000. Passenger cars and freight cars with an allowable amount of weight of more than 3 500 kg, including: (i) truck vehicle with trailer, trailer or vehicle other similar type, imposed a levy of IDR 8 000; (ii) vehicle truck, bus or other large/heavy equipment similar type, charged IDR 7 000.

Fig. 12. Cost improvement.

Simulation result of traffic congestion mitigation can be seen in Figure 13. From Figure 13, it can be seen that traffic congestion after the improvement of public transportation such as the improvement of comfort, safety, and reliabilty, as well as the decrease in cost, congestion can be reduced to be around 62 %. The congestion mitigation is due to the decrease in traffic volume as many users choose public vehicles and the decrease in the impact of external events that can be done through the control of incident traffic, exclusive lanes, traffic signal improvements, as well as work zones and special event policies.

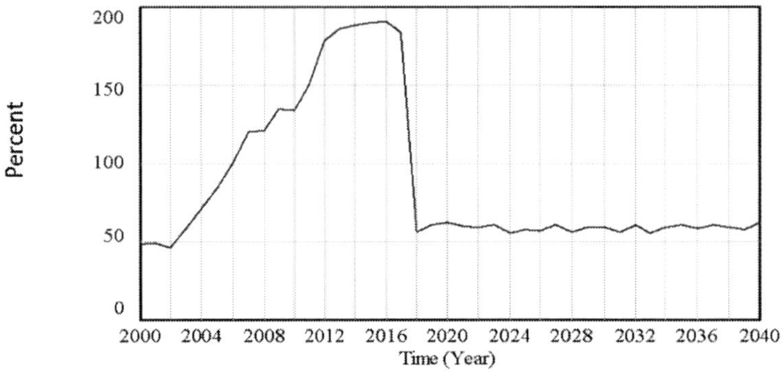

Fig. 13. Congestion mitigation after the improvement of public transportation.

6 Conclusion

In developing system dynamics model, system understanding is required as the basic building block for the model development. Traffic congestion depends on the bottleneck (internal factors) and external events (external factors). Some internal factors that affect the bottleneck include road capacity and average daily traffic (ADT). While external factors are influenced by several factors such as traffic incidents, exclusive lanes, work zones and special events. Traffic congestion mitigation can be done through the improvement of public transportation. Several efforts need to be conducted such as increasing comfort, reliability, safety and affordable cost. Traffic congestion mitigation after the improvement of public transportation can be reduced to be around 62 %.

This research is a collaboration research supported by ITS Research Center and Ministry of Research, Technology, and Higher Education.

References

1. Bappenas. *Kajian pembangunan transportasi dan perubahan iklim dalam mendukung konektivitas dan pembangunan berkelanjutan*. [Study of transportation and climate change in supporting sustainable connectivity and development] Executive Summary. [Online] from https://www.bappenas.go.id/index.php/download_file/.../8581/ (2013). [Accessed on 10 March 2017]. [in Bahasa Indonesia].
2. US Department of Transportation, *Traffic congestion and reliability: trends and advanced strategies for congestion mitigation*. [Online] from https://ops.fhwa.dot.gov/congestion_report/ (2005). [Accessed on 12 May 2017].
3. S. Jain, P. Aggarwal, P. Kumar, S. Singhal, P. Sharma. Transp Res Part F: Traffic Psychol Behav **24**:60–70 (2014). https://www.sciencedirect.com/science/article/pii/S1369847814000382.
4. T.P.L. Lea, T.U. Trinh. Proceedia Engineering **142**:236–243 (2016). https://www.sciencedirect.com/science/article/pii/S187770581600401X.
5. C. Avram, A. Astilean, R. Miron. Adv. Eng. Forum, **8-9**:3–12 (2013). https://www.scientific.net/AEF.8-9.3.
6. R.A. Alawi. Proceedings of the World Congress on Engineering and Computer Science (San Francisco, USA 2009). WCECS **1**:1–4 (2009). http://www.iaeng.org/publication/WCECS2009/WCECS2009_pp504-507.pdf.
7. G. Corpuz. *Public transport or private vehicle: factors that impact on mode choice*. 30th Australasian Transport Research Forum (Melbourne, 2007). https://scu.rl.talis.com/items/16858C50-C9C3-7E12-65E3-0026D5CFDF72.html.
8. R. Buehler. J. Trans. Geo. **19**(4):644–657 (2011). http://www.sciencedirect.com/science/article/pii/S0966692310001171.
9. A.M. Law. *Simulation modeling and analysis 5th edition*. New York: McGraw-Hill Education (2014). pp. 5. https://www.amazon.com/Simulation-Mcgraw-hill-Industrial-Engineering-Management/dp/0073401323.
10. J. Sterman, J.D. Sterman. *Business dynamics: Systems thinking and modeling for a complex world*. Boston: McGraw-Hill (2000). pp. 87. https://www.amazon.com/Business-Dynamics-Systems-Thinking-Modeling/dp/007238915X.
11. Y. Barlas. Syst. Dyn. Rev. **12**(3):183–210 (1996). http://onlinelibrary.wiley.com/doi/10.1002/(SICI)1099-1727(199623)12:3%3C183::AID-SDR103%3E3.0.CO;2-4/abstract.
12. Department of Surabaya City Transportation. *Perubahan tarif retribusi pelayanan parkir di jalan umum, Peraturan Walikota Surabaya no. 36*. [Change of parking services tariff at the right of public road, Surabaya

Mayor's Regulation no. 36]. Surabaya: Department of Surabaya City Transportation (2015). [in Bahasa Indonesia]. http://dishub.surabaya.go.id/backend/upload/files/peraturan/PERDA/perwali_1675.pdf.

Partial-factor Energy Efficiency Model of Indonesia

Fathul Nugroho[1] , and *Noor* Syaifudin[2,3,*]

[1]The Future Institute, Jl. Dukuh Patra V No.48, Kuningan, Jakarta 12950, Indonesia
[2]UWA Business School, Business School Building, Crawley Campus The University of Western Australia, 35 Stirling Highway Crawley WA 6009 Perth, Australia
[3]Fiscal Policy Agency, Ministry of Finance of Republic of Indonesia,Notohamiprodjo Building, 1st Floor, Jl. Wahidin No 1, Senen, Jakarta, 10710, Indonesia

Abstract. This study employs the partial-factor energy efficiency to reveal the relationships between energy efficiency and the consumption of both, the renewable energy and non-renewable energy in Indonesia. The findings confirm that consumption of non-renewable energy will increase the inefficiency in energy consumption. On the other side, the use of renewable energy will increase the energy efficiency in Indonesia. As the result, the Government of Indonesia may address this issue by providing more support to the development and the consumption of renewable energy in order to increase the energy efficiency and vise versa.

Key words: Energy efficiency, renewable energy, partial effect model

1 Introduction

There are several literatures and studies on the energy efficiency in Indonesia. Among others, the study by Syaifudin et al. revealed that the fiscal transfer signals a positive impact to the energy efficiency in Indonesia [1]. Setyawan viewed that revolving fund scheme is necessary to improve energy efficiency projects in Indonesia [2]. Moreover, Rajbhandari and Zhang argued that energy efficiency may significantly improve the economic growth of a country [3]. They summarized that in the middle-income countries, there was a long-run bidirectional causality between lower energy intensity and higher economic growth.

Thus, the Government of Indonesia (GOI) should adopt some policies to increase its energy efficiency. Domac et al. argued that bio-energy could contribute to the improvement of energy efficiency [4]. They further argued that the production and the use of bio-energy will create employment and economic return in most economies. In the macro-economic level, the production and the use of renewable energy such as bio-fuels, geothermal, solar, etc. to replace fossil fuels will contribute to all important elements of the economy. Generally, the increasing use of renewable energy will result in improvement in regional productivity, enhanced competitiveness, as well as further investment in resources to accommodate the economic development.

* Corresponding author: soib2007@gmail.com

According to the Ministry of Energy and Mineral Resources, in 2015, renewable energy was ranked fourth source in terms of power generation capacity in Indonesia. The proportion of oil as an energy source was accounted for 43 %, followed by natural gas at 22 %, coal at 28.7 %, and renewable energy at 6.2 % (Figure 1). It was targeted that by 2025 the proportion of the new and renewable energy will be increased to 23 % while the energy from oil is expected to reduce by 35 % (Figure 2).

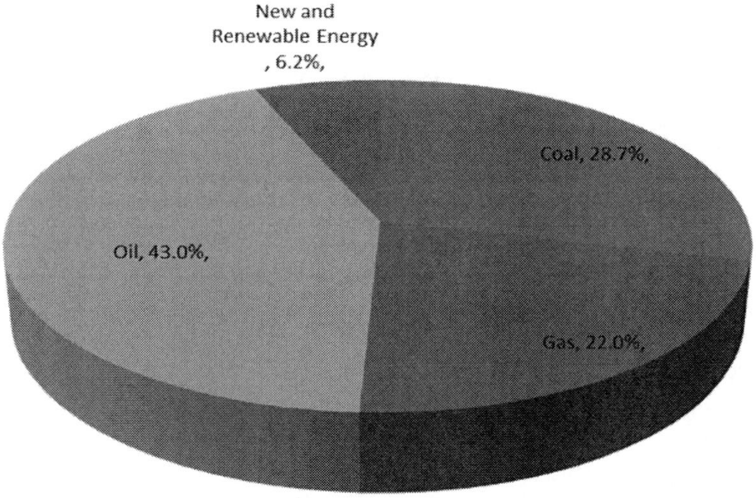

Fig. 1. Primary energy mix in 2015 [5].

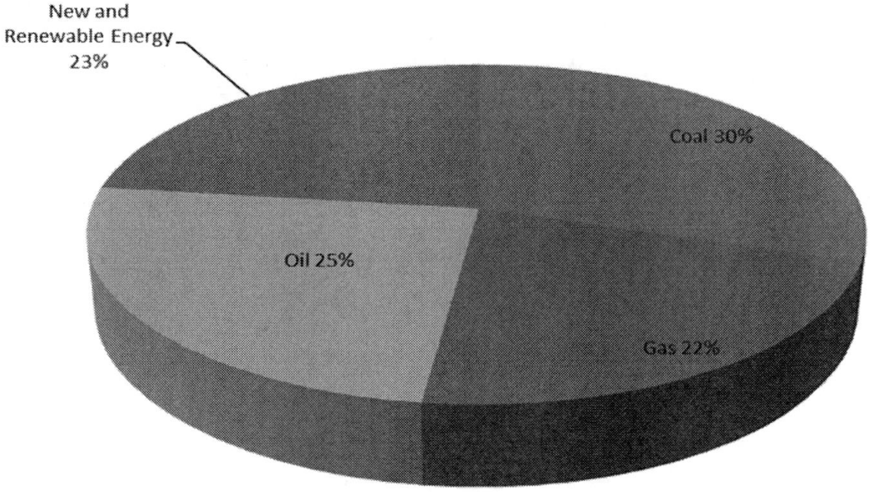

Fig. 2. Targeted primary energy mix in 2025 [6].

Chien and Hu have found a direct linkage between renewable energy and energy efficiency [7]. They verified that an increase in the percentage of renewable energy among total primary energy supply (TPES) improves energy efficiency. It is worth noting that increasing the input of renewable energy increases energy efficiency. In addition, renewable energy also has a great prospect to be a part of global energy sustainability. Currently, renewable energy is promoted to play a greater role in addressing climate change and increasing energy demand. Many nations are adopting policies to promote the use of renewable energy. Therefore, it is important for Indonesia to improve its energy efficiency by substituting fossil fuels energy with renewable energy.

Studies on energy efficiency are quite compelling among scholars nowadays. Among others are Krarti et al. who found that a large-scale energy efficiency program on buildings in Qatar may reduce about 11 000 GWh per y of the energy consumption [8]. Moreover, if the energy efficiency program is applied for more than 10 y, it can be potentially reducing more than 5.4 Mt of carbon emissions annually and may creates over 4 000 jobs yearly. While the similar program is implemented in Egypt, the program can enhance the energy efficiency by 33 % on average [9]. Li and Lin revealed that energy price reforms will lead to energy efficiency in China [10]. One of such technology that may be adopted is the capital embodied technological progress.

Otherwise, Trotta [11] and Ahmed and Stater [12] recommended stricter low energy regulation which may leads households energy efficiency as the result of the changing in the dwellers' behaviour towards the energy consumption. In the application in UK and Wales, Wang and Wang suggested that instead of reducing the energy consumption by 10 %, the energy efficiency application also supports the water sustainability [13]. The program will save the freshwater withdrawals by 0.43 % of total public water supply and may supports around 138 460 households.

However, improving energy efficiency by substituting primary energy sources with renewable energy alone will be not enough. Since energy consumption is a substantial input for economic growth, it is also important to adjust energy consumption to maximize efficiency. As a result, it is desirable for the Indonesian economy to increase its GDP and to decrease its inputs in order to maximize its macro-economic efficiency.

According to Çelen, total factor productivity (TFP) determines the improvement of energy efficiency in Turkey [14]. The energy efficiency (EE) index is calculated as a proxy for analyzing energy efficiency of Indonesia's economy. The EE index comprises of labor, capital stock, energy (fossil fuels), and renewable energy which is as inputs and GDP as the output of production function. One of the aims of this study is to verify whether renewable energy contributes to energy efficiency improvement using a regression analysis with empirical data from 1980 to 2005. The TE data is computed using data envelopment analysis (DEA) that currently has been widely used by many academics and researchers.

2 Energy efficiency issue

The first important thing to do in discussing energy efficiency issue is to have a clear definition on the term of energy efficiency. Many scholars and institutions provide the definition of energy efficiency. The most well-known term of energy efficiency is the technical definition of it, which is the ratio of energy output over energy input. The technical definition of energy efficiency often uses to describe the efficiency of engines, machineries, or power plants. The European Parliament provided a general definition of energy efficiency, which is a ratio between an output of performance, service, goods or energy, and an input of energy [15]. Indeed, it is very difficult to have a single definition of energy efficiency across the world. However, this study uses the definitions of energy efficiency in terms of economic view. That is, energy efficiency is GDP divided by total primary energy supply and the efficiency of energy use to produce economic outputs [15].

Indeed, energy efficiency improvement becomes a major global issue currently, in particular among developed nations. Most developed countries have been focusing their energy sector development for improving energy efficiency and developing renewable energy. A study by Geller et al. shows that industrialized nations have become more energy efficient than it was 30 yr ago [16]. These countries were successful in adopting several policies for improving the efficiency of their energy sectors. Empirically, they started to improve their energy efficiency since the oil price shock in the 1970s in order to reduce their dependence to oil supply. By adopting several energy efficiency policies, their energy intensity significantly was declining to an efficient level.

In over last three decades, major Organisation for Economic Co-operation and Development (OECD) countries like Japan, United Kingdom, United States, and Australia have cut their demand for energy significantly. These countries were able to cut their energy consumption as much as 49 % than it was actually consumed in 1998. Their total primary energy supply (TPES) per unit of GDP has declined sharply as well. In other words, energy intensity in major OECD countries has significantly declined, it is worth nothing, but OECD countries could produce a unit of GDP with less primary energy supply compares to in 1970s. The implementation of high-energy efficient products, energy mix, and behavioral change has contributed to the decline of energy intensity of major OECD countries [16].

There are at least two motives for developed countries to start improving their energy efficiency. First, developed countries target to improve their energy security. Since the oil price shock in 1970s, developed nations were much more aware to secure their supply of energy. In that time, most of industrialized economies relied on oil supply from the *Organization of the Petroleum Exporting Countries* (OPEC) countries, in particular from the Middle East countries. Thus, in order to reduce their dependence on oil supply from the Middle East, they responded in various ways: from conserving energy use, reducing the demand for oil, searching for alternatives energy, and restructuring their oil-intensive industry to more energy efficient industry.

In conserving energy, developed countries had promoted some policies that change their behavior and economic activities [16]. For instance, in the US, the Federal government enacted policies that limit the speed of automobiles at 24.5 m/s and enforce daylight saving time. The Federal government also implemented Corporate Average Fuels Economy (CAFE) policy that imposed automakers to produce more fuel-efficient vehicles that should meet the standard of fuel consumption at 8.55 L/(100 km). Developed nations also paid more attention to the invention and adoption of alternative energy sources such as solar, wind, and nuclear energy.

Second, developed countries intend to improve their macroeconomic efficiency. Through the implementation of energy efficient technology, developed economies have been reducing the amount of energy as input of economic production, while maximizing GDP as the output of the economy. They moved from energy-intensive industries to more efficient and productive industries such Japan that invests much on high-tech industries such electronics and automobiles.

Nowadays, energy efficiency improvement continues to become a central issue of energy sector development in developed countries. Huge investments have been allocated to promote further energy efficiency research and development. This initiative was also involving many experts and scholars to invent new efficient technologies, mostly in developed countries.

However, energy efficiency improvement has not become a crucial issue in many developing countries. They only focus to achieve high economic growth, without pay much attention to further develops their energy sector. That is why the demand for energy is increasing as their economies grow. In most cases, developing nations have used intensive input of energy, but produced less units of GDP. One plausible factor is that developing countries are still relying on energy-intensive industries. Most of industries in developing nations are using primary energy sources rather than secondary sources of energy. In addition, most of these industries are producing low value-added products.

China, however, has set an ambitious target to cut down its energy intensity by 20 % or 4.36 % per annum between 2006 and 2010 with 2005 data as the basis. Even though in 2006 China has failed to achieve this target, they continue to implement their energy efficiency programs [17]. Chinese government is trying to achieve high-energy efficiency target through implementation several policies such as: i) restructuring the current energy intensive mode to a non-energy intensive mode, ii) using more high quality sources of energy, iii) improving its current technologies, iv) using high quality raw materials, and 5) improving energy system management. The Chinese government is very strict in implementing those policies. For instance, Chinese government enacted a special policy to force the shutdown several energy-intensive industries [17].

3 Energy efficiency and macroeconomic productivity

A common indicator to measure the relationship between energy and economy is energy intensity. This indicator simply meant a ratio of the TPES and GDP annually. Energy intensity data can be easily downloaded and computed from various energy agencies such as EIA and IEA. World Development Indicators from the World Bank also provide statistical data on energy consumption and production of various sources of energy and economic indicators data that can be used to calculate energy intensity or efficiency.

Recently, however, more researchers and energy agencies are using energy efficiency indicator instead of energy intensity to measure and compare countries economic performance. As noted before, energy efficiency is nothing but an inverse measurement of energy intensity. Energy efficiency is useful to measure how efficient such an economy in using primary energy as inputs of production, the less input of energy and the high economic output the better is the economy. Hence, a country with high energy efficiency will experience some socio-economic and environmental benefits. Logically, this country could reduce its energy inputs in order to minimize total production costs. As a result, its output products will be more competitive in the global market.

For a fuel importer country, high energy efficiency level will minimize its cost for importing fuels as well as reduce its consumption and thus improve its net trade balance. High energy efficiency also indicates that a particular country is using advanced technologies for exploitation, production, and distribution [18]. Thus, it is desirable for a country to have high energy efficiency, since this will bring positive impacts to the economy and the environment as a whole. By setting high target of an improvement in energy efficiency, an economy starts to reduce its energy use through adopting highly efficient technologies, mixing its input of energy with clean and renewable energy, and cutting down current high fossil fuel consumptions by changing its behavior and economic structure.

4 Energy efficiency data

A study by Wei [18] applied Cobb-Douglas production function to analyze the impact of energy efficiency gains on economic output. The study counted energy, labor, and capital stock as inputs of production function and found that energy the energy efficiency gains always lead to higher output. Thus, the impact of energy efficiency on total output in the long term almost doubles than that in the short term. Hu and Kao [19] also mentioned that energy, labor, and capital stock are the key inputs to produce the economic output.

Data envelopment analysis (DEA) is employed to measure an efficiency frontier for Indonesian economy in each year. The macroeconomic energy efficiency is to seek how far the economy of Indonesia is from its efficiency frontier in that year. Currently, the DEA method has been widely used for measuring energy efficiency among scholars [7][14][21]. A key benefit of DEA method over other models is that this method takes into account the dynamic efficiency of multiple inputs and multiple outputs. This method is the best fit to measure the energy efficiency frontier of an economy by combining multiple inputs and outputs. This type of linear programming allows the user to choose between input orientation and output orientation methods. Input orientation method calculates energy efficiency by combining the multiple inputs while holding constant the multiple outputs. Meanwhile, the output orientation computes the variables by combining the multiple outputs while holding constant the multiple inputs.

There are some scholars who have been using the DEA methods in their study on energy efficiency such as Chien and Hu employed the DEA to measure macroeconomic productivity [7]. Zhou and Ang employed the DEA method to calculate energy efficiency by considering the undesirable output of the economy [20]. That is, they take into account CO2 emissions as the undesirable output within the framework of production function. They also employed several DEA type linear programming models for calculating macroeconomic energy efficiency. In addition, their models treat different energy sources as different inputs so that changes in energy mix could be accounted for evaluating energy efficiency.

This study applies output orientation DEA, with the aim of this orientation is to determine a potential GDP output with given capital stock, labor force, fossil fuel, renewable energy, and clean energy as its inputs if it operated efficiently as economy along the best practice frontier. Output orientation model is in line with neo-classical production functions defined as the maximum achievable output given input quantities [20].

5 Partial-factor energy efficiency model

This study employs double-log regression analysis model. This model is used due to the preliminary estimation suggests the logistic function would be the appropriate model. The double-log form is the common model to be used for analyzing such a functional form, which is non-linear in the variables, but linear in the coefficients. The regression equations are as follow:

First model:

$$LnEE = \beta 0 + \beta 1 LnGDP + \beta 2 LnPC + \beta 3 LnNGC + \beta 4 LnCC + \beta 5 \backslash LnREC + \beta 6 LnCF + \beta 7 LnLF \quad (1)$$

Second model:

$$LnEE = \beta 0 + \beta 1 LnGDP + \beta 2 LnPC + \beta 3 LnNGC + \beta 4 LnCC + \beta 5 LnREC + \beta 6 LnCF \quad (2)$$

Third model:

$$LnEE = \beta 0 + \beta 1LnGDP + \beta 2LnPC + \beta 3LnNGC + \beta 4LnCC + \beta 5LnREC \quad (3)$$

Where EE is energy efficiency, GDP gross domestic products, PC petroleum consumption, NGC natural gas consumption, CC coal consumption, REC renewable energy consumption, CF capital formation, and LF labor force.

The energy efficiency data in this section is calculated by dividing GDP over total primary energy supply data obtained from IEA statistics. The renewable energy data is the sum up of all kinds of renewable energy. By the definition of IEA, renewable energy is divided into the three categories of: i) hydro fuel; ii) geothermal, solar, tide and wind fuel; and iii) combustible renewable energy and waste.

6 Findings and analysis

Results of Model 1 show that renewable energy variable has unexpected sign and does not significantly affect energy efficiency; this could be caused by such a multicollinearity with other variables. When the labor force is dropped from Model 1, as Model 2 shows renewable energy variable does affect energy efficiency. There is a positive relationship between renewable energy and energy efficiency. However, the renewable energy and GDP variables are still not statistically significant. Results of Model 3 show a better explanation of GDP, fossil fuel and renewable energy consumptions in relation with energy efficiency.

Table 5. Results of regressions of the contribution of renewable energy on energy efficiency using Partial-factor Energy Efficiency Model.

Dependent Variable: Energy Efficiency (WDI)			
Regressor	Model 1	Model 2	Model 3
Intercept	-1.527 (1.986)	0.845 (1.315)	1.304 (1.231)
Ln GDP	0.061 (0.334)	0.208 (0.332)	0.516*** (0.117)
Ln Petroleum consumption	-0.414*** (0.143)	-0.325** (0.136)	-0.429*** (0.087)
Ln Natural gas consumption	0.145* (0.069)	0.128* (0.071)	0.078 (0.050)
Ln Coal consumption	-0.076** (0.030)	-0.061* (0.030)	-0.066** (0.029)
Ln Renewable energy consumption	-0.025 (0.055)	0.013 (0.051)	0.003 (0.049)
Ln Capital formation	0.168 (0.109)	0.104 (0.105)	
Ln Labor force	0.487 (0.314)		
Summary Statistics			
Adjusted R2	0.770	0.753	0.753
F-statistic	12.938***	13.667***	16.228***

Table 5. Continue in the next page

Table 5. Results of regressions of the contribution of renewable energy on energy efficiency using Partial-factor Energy Efficiency Model (continue).

Dependent Variable: Energy Efficiency (WDI)			
Regressor	Model 1	Model 2	Model 3
DW-statistic	2.3	1.811	1.779

Remark: Standard errors are given in parentheses under the coefficients. The individual coefficient and F-statistic are statistically significant at the *10 %, **5 %, ***1 % significant level using a one-sided test.

In Model 3, both coefficients of petroleum (-0.429) and coal (- 0.066) consumptions have negative sign and significant at 1 % and 5 % level respectively. Thus, this means that for every increase in petroleum consumption by 1 %, Indonesia energy's efficiency will drop by 0.429 %, while, for every increase in domestic coal consumption, Indonesia's energy efficiency will decrease by 0.066 %, holding other independent variable constant. It is worth noting that the increase in petroleum and coal consumptions decreases Indonesia energy efficiency. In addition, other coefficients in Model 3, GDP, natural gas and renewable energy consumptions are having positive sign. It means that for every increase in those variables by 1 %, Indonesia's energy efficiency will increase by 0.516 %, 0.078 %, and 0.003 % respectively. Consequently, it is important for Indonesian economy not to increase petroleum and coal consumptions in order to improve its energy efficiency. In addition, it is recommended to substitute petroleum and coal as primary energy sources with renewable energy.

7 Conclusion

The challenges from the decreasing trend in energy efficiency must be addressed by the Government of Indonesia. Several policy options were proposed by scholars. The policy options are including the production and uses of renewable energy are expected to improve the energy efficiency and may enhance the economic performance.

This study was employing partial factor energy efficiency model to find the relationships between energy efficiency and renewable energy. On the other side, the model is also able to explore the connection between energy efficiency and consumption of non-renewable energy.

The findings confirm the negative relationship between energy efficiency and consumption of non-renewable energy. However, the other finding revealed the positive impact of energy efficiency to the renewable energy. Those findings provide baselines to the Government of Indonesia to support the development of renewable energy and apply the policy to reduce the non-renewable energy consumption.

References

1. N. Syaifudin, A. Sutrisno, A.D. Setiawan. *Energy Procedia* **65**, 239-247 (2015). https://www.sciencedirect.com/science/article/pii/S1876610215000387
2. D. Setyawan. *Energy Procedia* **47**, 37-46 (2014). https://www.sciencedirect.com/science/article/pii/S1876610214002100
3. A. Rajbhandari, F. Zhang. Energy Economics. 128-139 (2018). https://www.sciencedirect.com/science/article/pii/S0140988317303882
4. J. Domac, K. Richards, S. Risovic. *Biomass and Bioenergy*, **28**, 2:97–106 (2005).

5. Direktorat Jenderal Energi Baru, Terbarukan dan Konservasi Energi. *Buku statistik EBTKE 2016* [Statistic book of new, renewable energy and energy conservation 2016]. Direktorat Jenderal Energi Baru, Terbarukan dan Konservasi Energi: Jakarta (2016). p. viii. [in Bahasa Indonesia] http://ebtke.esdm.go.id/post/2017/03/07/1583/statistik.ebtke.2016
6. Government of Indonesia. *Government Regulation No. 79/2014 on National Energy Policy* [Peraturan Pemerintah No. 79/2014 tentang Kebijakan Energi Nasional] (2014).
7. T. Chien, J.L. Hu. *Energy Policy*, **35**, 7:3606–3615 (2007). https://www.sciencedirect.com/science/article/pii/S0301421507000092
8. M. Krarti, F. Ali, A. Alaidroos, M. Houchati. *International Journal of Sustainable Built Environment* (2017). DOI: 10.1016/j.ijsbe.2017.12.006. https://www.sciencedirect.com/science/article/pii/S2212609017301061
9. I.E. Darwish, M Gomaa. *Alexandria Engineering Journal*, **56**, 4:579–589 (2017). https://www.sciencedirect.com/science/article/pii/S1110016817301734
10. K. Li, B. Lin. *Energy*, **143**, 812-821 (2018). https://www.sciencedirect.com/science/article/pii/S0360544217318960
11. G. Trotta. *Energy Policy*, **114**, 529–539 (2018). https://www.sciencedirect.com/science/article/pii/S0301421517308686
12. R. Ahmed, M. Stater. *Resource and Energy Economics*, **49**, 132–149, (2017). https://www.sciencedirect.com/science/article/pii/S0928765516300537
13. S. Wang, S. Wang. Energy, **140**, 1:922–928 (2017). https://www.sciencedirect.com/science/article/pii/S0360544217315207
14. A. Çelen. *Energy Policy* **63**, 300-310 (2013). https://www.sciencedirect.com/science/article/pii/S0301421513009580
15. The European Parliament. *Understanding Energy Efficiency*. Briefing October 2015 (2015) http://www.europarl.europa.eu/RegData/etudes/BRIE/2015/568361/EPRS_BRI(2015)568361_EN.pdf (last accesed 17 February 2018).
16. H. Geller, P. Harrington, A.H. Rosenfeld, S. Tanishima, F. Unander. *Energy Policy* **34**, 5:556-573 (2006). https://www.sciencedirect.com/science/article/pii/S0301421505003113
17. M. Yang. *Energy Policy* **36**, 2:561–570 (2008). https://www.sciencedirect.com/science/article/pii/S0301421507004302
18. T. Wei. *Energy Policy* **35**, 4:2023–2030 (2007). https://www.sciencedirect.com/science/article/pii/S0301421506003272
19. J.L. Hu, C.H. Kao. *Energy Policy* **35**, 1: 373–382 (2007). https://www.sciencedirect.com/science/article/pii/S0301421505003290
20. P. Zhou, B.W. Ang. *Energy Policy* **36**, 8:2911–2916 (2008). https://www.sciencedirect.com/science/article/pii/S0301421508001638

Green Industrial System in Indonesia

Fourry Handoko[1,*], *Ellysa* Nursanti[1], Gatot[1], *Martinus* Edwin Tjahjadi[2], *Julianus* Hutabarat[1], *Lalu* Mulyadi[3], and Kustamar[4]

[1]Industrial Engineering Department, National Institute of Technology (ITN), Jl. Raya Karanglo Km. 2, Malang, 65145, Indonesia
[2]Geomatics Engineering Department, National Institute of Technology (ITN), Jl. Bendungan Sigura-gura No.2, Malang, 65145, Indonesia
[3]Architecture Engineering Department, National Institute of Technology (ITN), Jl. Bendungan Sigura-gura No.2, Malang, 65145, Indonesia
[4]Civil Engineering Department, National Institute of Technology (ITN), Jl. Bendungan Sigura-gura No.2, Malang, 65145, Indonesia

Abstract. The environmentally friendly manufacturing influences the worldwide community both private and public to run the concept of green productivity. The concept of green productivity drives the organisation to seek integration of sustainable environmental management and environmentally friendly production system design. The lack of green and sustainable concept have reduced the competitiveness of the organisation due to the low capability to meet the international standard of ISO 14000. One of the important thing of being 'green' is our capability to deal with the pollution. Continuous improvement approach to achieve green productivity is an effort to increase sustainable competitiveness by maintaining green product and reducing the pollution. The continuous improvement to achieve the capability to overcome the pollution problem will lead into tangible and intangible benefit. It is therefore the green productivity is crucial. In this research, the concept of green produtivity and continuous improvement approah are utilised to overcome the problems of pollution in manufacturing industries.

Key words: Continuous improvement, green industrial system, policy, production

1 Introduction

Numerous organisations worldwide have been involved in green environment programs. Regulation and ratification of environmentally friendly product have been constructed by both develop and developing countries [1]. The growing awareness of international communities about environmentally friendly product and also 'save our earth' jargon has been elevating the imperative of the pollution free environment programs [2, 3], since our environment has suffered from un-controlled and massive exploitation of natural resources; indecomposable waste; and environmental pollution, resulting significant damage such as environmental degradation, global warming and ozone hole [4, 5].

In response, the government, businesses and universities began to campaign for environmentally friendly and energy saving products approach [2, 4, 6–10]. This approach is imperative since the capability of the organisation to deal with the environmental issues have been considered as a mean to improve organisation's competitiveness in both regional and international business environment. Furthermore, the current international policies have been maintaining the issues of the environment friendly product through the international standard series of ISO 14000 certification and other eco-labelling programs [11–15]. The Indonesian government has also initiated programs of green environment in the form of cleaner production programs [14], but this program has not been well delivered to business owners in Indonesia. To response for this issue, this study is needed to discover the implementation of green productivity in Indonesia. This study was conducted to find the way of implementation green industrial system in manufacturing industries.

*Corresponding author: fourry@lecturer.itn.ac.id

2 Green productivity

The application of Green Productivity through non-product output (NPO) is the appropriate technique, technology, and management system to produce environmentally friendly products and services [16]. Green Productivity (GP) uses the concept of environmentally friendly production yet minimum energy without disturbing productivity or also known as green industry. This environmentally friendly and energy efficient approach influences the worldwide community both private and public. GP is a concept that involves management decision, environmental programs and technologies that lead to environmentally friendly product [1, 15–18]. The concept of green productivity drives the organisation to seek integration of sustainable environmental management and environmentally friendly production system design. Continuous improvement to achieve GP is an effort to increase sustainable competitiveness by maintaining green product and reducing the pollution [16].

2.1 GP as a competitive strategy

Organisations worldwide are under regulatory pressure to be eco-efficient [19]. Therefore, the competitive strategy trough continuous improvement is a must. GP approach should be applied to achieve the competitiveness goal. Validation regarding tools and techniques application of GP is a part of organisation's continuous improvement efforts to get green product. The responsibility of the GP taskforce is to provide tools and technologies for implementing 'green' programs, including reduce, reuse and recycle (3R)[18]; and also internal audit for green, and implementing continuous improvement program (Plan, Do, Check and Action) GP to achieve sustainable competitiveness, from product design up-to final product stage [8, 20].

3 Methodology

This study identified the factors that could interfere the GP, and provide suggestions for improvement based on the external and internal regulations such as ISO 14000 and government regulation. Cause and effect approach were applied to seek the gap between available process and the regulation, followed by Quality Function Deployment (QFD) approach to determine the improvement needed. However, in conducting the research, it was necessary to resolve several issues that potentially disturb the result of the research. These included: determine the research domain, level of analysis and selecting suitable respondents.

3.1 Research domain

The subject of the research was a chemical company in East Java, Indonesia. This domain was chosen based on its potential role in GP practices, especially in reducing pollution. This company significantly applied GP approach. As this organisation has a strong commitment in GP approach and also developed knowledge regarding environmentally friendly product, the organisation was deemed as appropriate subject of this study.

3.2 Level of analysis

The issue related to the level of analysis was the persons in the organisation who were directly selected as a respondent. Ideally, the questionnaires should be completed by number of people in each part of an organisation. This approach was applied to obtain the sufficient information from the organisations, and to minimise the response bias of the respondents [21–26]. In this survey, people who were selected to be respondents were the employees whom are responsible (in-charge) for the GP program of the organisation.

3.3 Sample selection

For data sampling, more than 30 respondents were selected. The respondents were checked to ensure that respondents only belong to departments, which were responsible for GP program.

3.4 Research sequences

The research consists of four phases. The details are presented as follows:

Phase I: Assessment of instrument for green approach. This phase involved the preliminary studies; literature and regulations review. Reviewing includes the review on the Green Standard of ISO 14001, Decree No. 3 Year 2006 about 'Green Indonesia' and regulation of the Minister of Environment no. 18 year 2010 about program of companies rating performance (PROPER). The purpose of this phase was to collect information and data to construct the instruments that will be applied to assess GP based on the selected criteria of ISO 14000 clauses and government regulation. The instruments then were distributed to 33 respondents.

Table 1. ISO 14001 clauses.

Clause	Audit Clause
4.2	Environmental policy
4.3.1	Identification of environmental aspects and impacts
4.3.2	Identification of legal regulations and other requirements
4.3.3	Objectives, targets and programs
4.4.1	Resources, roles, responsibility and authority
4.4.2	Training, awareness, competence
4.4.3	Communication
4.4.4	Documentation
4.4.5	Control of documents
4.4.6	Operational control; Purchasing; Handling, Storage, Packaging, Delivery; Environmental control
4.4.7	Preparing and emergency response
4.5.1	Monitoring and measurement
4.5.2	Evaluation of conformity
4.5.3	Nonconformity, corrective action, and preventive
	Corrective Action
	Precautions
4.5.4	Control of records
4.5.5	Internal environmental audits
4.6	Overview of management

Sources: ISO 14000 Clauses

Phase II: Assessment. At this phase, the activity of the business process of the organisation and the information process associated with the activities of the GP were recorded. The area of production process control was selected to be a subject of this research. The area was chosen because this department has a significant role in controlling the pollutant. The assessment of the level of adoption of GP in that area was conducted based on the instruments of ISO 14001 clauses that have been constructed in the previous stage. Assessment phase aims to determine the remaining gap/problem between the application of GP and the ISO 14000 clauses. Based on the assessment result, the current position of the GP application was analysed to find the main factors that produce the gap/problem.

Phase III: Identification of gap/problem. This third phase was to review the main causes of the gap/problem between the implementation of GP and ISO 14000 clauses. The findings of the gap/problems were tabulated. The cause and effect diagram then was applied to identify the root of the problems. The brainstorming technique was utilise to analyse the problem based on 4M (Man Machine, Method dan material) approach. The main causes of the problem and then transformed into GP standard.

Phase IV: Strategy development. The fourth phase aimed to provide alternative solutions regarding the causes of the problems of the gap. Brainstorming and Quality Function Deployment (QFD) were applied to obtain the proposed solution for the company improvement of GP. QFD is a tool to design and develop methods.

QFD is capable in diffusing the quality into a design. In this study, new policies to improve GP were translated into a technical response. By QFD, The assessment results form previous phase were summarised into a house of quality matrix, containing the matrix relationship, technical correlation, and technical matrix. Prior to the strategy development, QFD approach was applied to produce questionnaires for respondents. The 33 respondents were selected. Questionnaires distribution was conducted carefully to meet the adequacy of the data, validity and reliability. The results of the questionnaires were utilised as attributes to assess whether GP standard in the organisation meets the ISO 14000 clauses or not. The results were also employed to determine the particular part of the GP application in production process that needs improvement. So the organisation could develop the future strategy of GP.

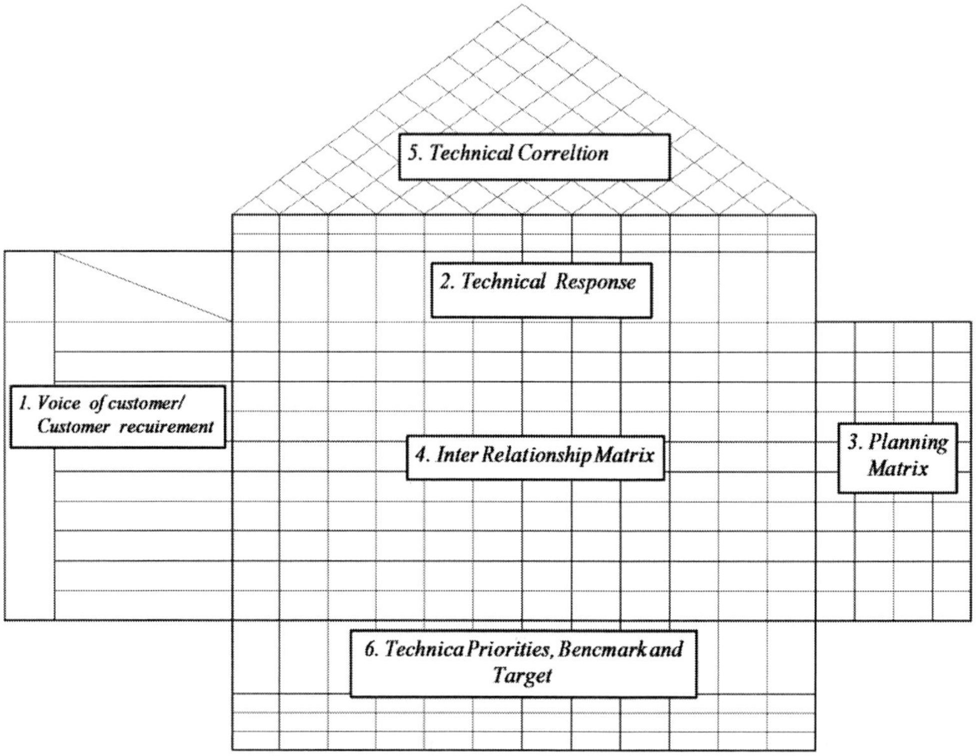

Fig. 1. House of quality (HoQ).

4 Results and discussion

Reliability and validity tests were conducted to verify the reliability and validity of the instruments.

4.1 Reliability and validity test

Before validity test, the test of the adequacy of the data was performed based on the formula [26]. If the specified confidence interval (CI) of 95 % the value of $Z = 1.645$. While the error of 5 %, $\sigma 2 = 0.891$ then the minimum number of samples needed are 32 respondents. The numbers of questionnaires distributed were 40, and the responses are up to 33 respondents. Nevertheless, the number of respondents meets the minimum requirement (33 respondents > 32 respondents). Statistical measurement was conducted to test the reliability and validity of the measurement instrument. Pearson correlation and Cronbach's alpha coefficient were applied to measure the validity and reliability of the instrument. This approach was taken to ensure that the measurement instrument was capable of measuring what was intended to be measured. For all items, Cronbach's alpha coefficient values were greater than the acceptable value of 0.6 [24-26], indicating that the items assigned to the constructs were reliable.

4.2 Assessment result based on the ISO 14000 clauses requirement

The target score of the assessment is between 155 and 165 that indicates a good score. The assessment results of the GP application based on the ISO 14000 requirement, the lowest score was 151 (Clause 4.4.6 (ISO 14000) operation control). The result indicates that the application of GP is still unacceptable.

The descriptions of operation control clauses are as follows:

Operational Control clause ISO 14000, question no. 45. 'Does the company have a method to ensure the activities, services, or products that may have an impact on the environment has been adequately controlled?' (Score: 149). Question 45: Whether the procedure has been covering all the activities of the company, since the beginning of the raw material or other additional material up to the utilised of those raw material delivered from the company? (Score: 153). Based on the data evaluation using the assessment instruments it was discovered that the green productivity deficiencies control is associated with ISO 14000 clause 4.4.6 about operation control question no. 45, especially in the treatment process.

Based on the assessment results, 'the lack of method regarding to ISO 14000 clause 4.4.6 about operation control question no. 45', particularly regarding to waste treatment method/procedure, the evaluation to find the gap was conducted using cause and effect (Fishbone) diagram. The results of the identification of causes variables the failure of waste treatment using fishbone diagrams and brainstorming are presented as follows:

(i) No suitable method
(ii) No measurement standard
(iii) No method improvement
(iv) Inappropriate waste treatment unit (WTU)
(v) Hazardous chemical for bacteria in WTU

Using fishbone diagrams and brainstorming technique, the causes variables were analysed to obtain the attribute of production operation control. The attributes were the representative of customer needs. There were 19 attributes. The attributes and then were translated into 19 technical responses (TRs) scheme and seek the problem solving to achieve GP strategies by using QFD.

The 19 attributes TRs were put into the planning matrix of HoQ. The matrix of HoQ transformed the attributes into survey instruments that were distributed to get the respond from the respondents. The respondents were asked to determine the priority for the future improvement from the available list of the attributes, based on Improvement ratio, interest level (Improvement ratio and interest level were obtained to determine the raw weight). The result shows that the highest weighted of technical response from the attributes are instrument 16 (Equipment to reduce odor), 17 (methods to prevent odor) and 18 (monitoring for water pollution).

Based on that result, the solution was implemented with PDCA method by simultaneously installing the new equipment and arranging the particular method to overcome the odor pollution. Further, the monitoring was conducted to guarantee that the problem solving is consistently conducted. The waste-processing unit to eliminate the cause of odor originating from ammonia by building the Stripping Ammonia unit PDCA is presented in Table 2.

Table 2. PDCA implementation.

Plan	**Check**	**Action**
Reduce Nitrogen with new equipment	Nitrogen content reduction ≤ 50 %	Optimisation
Do	**Task force**	
i.Splitting the waste with high loading ammonia i. Installation of ammonia Stripping Equipment ii. Splitting between Low ammonia and High ammonia in waste treatment installation	WWT and refinery Engineering and Refinery Refinery and WWT	

The principle of ammonia stripping is to drive the ammonia into the evaporated effluent and then be condensed. The result of the condensation can be utilised as elusion washing at the ionic separation stage of ammonia (using NH3 0.8 N). The (before and after) tests of the impact of Ammonia Stripping Installation were conducted. The result is presented below.

Table 3. Before and after tests result

Parameter	Unit	Before	After
BOD (Biochemical Oxygen Demand)	$uL\ L^{-1}$	77	75
COD (Chemical Oxygen Demand)	$uL\ L^{-1}$	134	121
NH3 (ammonia)	$uL\ L^{-1}$	298	105

The installation of the ammonia stripping has impacted significantly on the GP improvement. By Two samples t-test the P-value = 0.000 indicates significant ($P < 0.05$ significant).

Table 4. Two-Sample t-test and CI.

Two-sample t-test for data AN				
Subject	N	Mean	SD	SE Mean
1	19	299.7	48.6	11
2	28	104.9	17.4	3.3

Difference = mu (1) - mu (2), Estimate for difference: 194.797
95 % CI for difference: (174.705; 214.889)
t-test of difference = 0
t-value = 19.53; P-Value = 0.000; DF = 45
Both use Pooled StDev = 33.5624

Table 5. Investment cost and benefit.

Name	Unit	Need	Price (USD)	(USD)/yr
Steam/h	t	6.1	15.94	851 769.84
Electricity	Kw h	22	0.062	11 948.64
Cooling water/h	kL	80	0.02	14 016
Investment/ fixed cost	USD	400.000	400.000	452 000
Total investment				1 329 734.48
Ammonia recovery benefit/d	t	4.984	686	3 419 024

Table 5 shows that the ammonia recovery also gives a significant financial benefit. The Break Event Point (BEP) of the investment is about 5 mo.

4.3 Continuous improvement

The learning process will sharp the capability to solve the problem [27-29]. The capability improvement will ease the process of continuous improvement. Based on the direction of the QFD solution, the management, monitoring and treatment plant improvement to eliminate the problem were upgraded. The recommendation, as a result of the QFD to overcome the problems, was implemented. After the implementation of treatment plant, the analysis to find the effect of before and after was conducted. The result was applied as a standard for upcoming improvements. The result shows a significant improvement, especially the decrease of up to 65 % of the pollutant.

5 Conclusion

This research was conducted through theoretical and empirical studies to review the variables and attributes that can be developed as a strategy to deal with the waste in department of production. The application of continuous improvement is capable of locating, measuring, and overcoming the gaps/problems regarding green productivity application. This method delivers a comprehensive improvement in green-based production process application. The finding shows that even the respondents' organisation has recognised the green-based production process particularly in production division, but there are still some gaps/problems that could be found. These deficiencies regarding the GP can be overcome with the improvement of a strategy, tool, checking, monitoring and supervision to prevent pollution based on the recommendation that involve the employees that involve in that area. The application of the continuous improvement leads the decrease of environment pollutants up to 65 % pollutant. The ammonia recovery also gives a significant financial benefit. The Break Event Point (BEP) of the investment is about 5 months.

References

1. O. Boiral. Organ. Sci. **18**:127–146 (2007). https://pubsonline.informs.org/doi/abs/10.1287/orsc.1060.0224
2. T.B. Chen, L.T. Chai. Journal of Management Science and Engineering, **4**(2):27–39 (2010). http://cscanada.net/index.php/mse/article/view/j.mse.1913035X20100402.002
3. J. Dedrick. Communications of the Association for Information Systems, **27**(11):173–184 (2010). http://citeseerx.ist.psu.edu/viewdoc/download?doi=10.1.1.186.7721&rep=rep1&type=pdf
4. P.K. Ip. J. Bus. Ethics **88**(1):211–224 (2009). https://link.springer.com/article/10.1007/s10551-008-9820-2
5. C.Y. Lin, Y.H. Ho. J. Bus. Ethics **98**(1):67–83 (2011). https://link.springer.com/article/10.1007/s10551-010-0535-9
6. F. Handoko, IJPTE, **1**(2):93–107 (2017). https://jurnal.uns.ac.id/ijpte/article/view/15124/12410
7. S. Brammer, H. Walker. IJOPM, **31**(4):452–476 (2011). http://www.emeraldinsight.com/doi/abs/10.1108/01443571111119551
8. A.M. Deif. APEM. **6**(1):27–36 (2011). http://apem-journal.org/Archives/2011/APEM6-1_027-036.pdf
9. D. Etzion. J. Manag. **33**(4):637–664 (2007). http://journals.sagepub.com/doi/abs/10.1177/0149206307302553
10. J. Liu, H. Viney, D. Holt. European Business Journal **16**(2)59–69 (2004). http://oro.open.ac.uk/1898/

11. R.B. Clements. *Complete guide to ISO 14000*. Upper Saddle River: Prentice Hall (1996). pp. 78–95. https://www.amazon.com/Complete-Guide-Richard-Barrett-Clements/dp/0132429756
12. F. Wiengarten, M. Pagell, B. Fynes. J. Clean. Prod. **56**:18–28 (2012). https://www.sciencedirect.com/science/article/pii/S0959652612000339
13. Q. Wang, F. Lai, X. Zhao. Supply Chain Management: An International Journal, **13**(2):138–150 (2008). http://www.emeraldinsight.com/doi/abs/10.1108/13598540810860976
14. Ministry of Environmental. *Peraturan menteri negara lingkungan hidup nomor 31 tahun 2009*. [The ministry of environmental decree no.31, 2009]. Jakarta: Ministry of Environmental (2009). [in Bahasa Indonesia]. http://puu-pi.menlh.go.id/pdf/ind/IND-PUU-7-2009-Permen%20No.%2031Thn%202009-Ekolabel%20Stantek.pdf
15. UNEP. Emerging issues in our global environment. United Nation: UNEP Year Book (2011). pp. 33–38. http://wedocs.unep.org/handle/20.500.11822/8276?show=full
16. H. Widyantoro, F. Handoko, E. Nursanti. *Pengendalian biaya manufaktur berbasis environment oriented costmanagement (EOCM)*. [Manufacturing cost control based on environment oriented costmanagement (EOCM)]. SENIATI (Malang, Indonesia, 2016). [in Bahasa Indonesia]. http://ejournal.itn.ac.id/index.php/seniati/article/view/107/100
17. M. Atlas, R. Florida, Green manufacturing. In: *Handbook of technology management*. R.C Dorf (Ed.). America: CRC Press. (1998). pp. 25–33. https://books.google.co.id/books?id=C2u8I0DFo4IC&dq=M.+Atlas,+R.+Florida.+Handbook+of+Technology+Management&source=gbs_navlinks_s
18. C. Paula, F. Handoko, *Implementasi reduce, reuse, recycle (3R) untuk memenuhi kebutuhan palet pada PT. X*. [Implementation Reduce, Reuse, Recycle (3R) to Meet the Needs Palette at PT. X]. SENIATI (Malang, 2016). [in Bahasa Indonesia]. http://ejournal.itn.ac.id/index.php/seniati/article/view/97/90
19. W. R. Scholz, A. Wiek. J. Ind. Ecol. **9**(4):155–170 (2005). http://onlinelibrary.wiley.com/doi/10.1162/108819805775247963/abstract
20. K.D. Kalla, A. Brown. Infusing a sustainable green manufacturing course into manufacturing/mechanical engineering technology program. Washington DC: American Society for Engineering Education (2012). https://www.google.co.id/url?sa=t&rct=j&q=&esrc=s&source=web&cd=1&cad=rja&uact=8&ved=0ahUKEwjPtbuemtrYAhUKI5QKHcpJBJ8QFggoMAA&url=http%3A%2F%2Fwww.asee.org%2Fpublic%2Fconferences%2F8%2Fpapers%2F5384%2Fdownload&usg=AOvVaw05mI7xTiGekGtp7hYGhDqm
21. P.J. Singh, A.J.R. Smith. Journal of Manufacturing Technology Management, **15**(5):394–401 (2004). https://www.scopus.com/record/display.uri?eid=2-s2.0-4143087474&origin=resultslist&sort=plf-f&src=s&sid=b23964dce27a670f6f999a52f20ea666&sot=autdocs&sdt=autdocs&sl=18&s=AU-ID%2855498580900%29&relpos=17&citeCnt=87&searchTerm=
22. B.B. Flyn, R.G. Shroeder, S. Sakakibara. Journal of Operations Management, **11**(4):339–366 (1994). https://www.sciencedirect.com/science/article/pii/S0272696397900048
23. P.J. Singh. A *study of theoretical and empirical bases of operationalising popular quality management approaches in manufacturing organizations in Australia*. [Thesis]. University of Melbourne, Australia (2002). https://www.researchgate.net/publication/260908699_A_Study_of_Theoretical_and_Empirical_Bases_of_Operationalising_Popular_Quality_Management_Approaches_in_Manufacturing_Organizations_in_Australia
24. J.F. Hair Jr, W.C. Black, B.J. Babin, R. E. Anderson. *Multivariate data analysis*. (7 ed.). New Jersey: Prentice-Hall. (2014). https://www.amazon.com/Multivariate-Data-Analysis-Joseph-Hair/dp/0138132631
25. F. Handoko, A. Smith, C. Burvill. JCEBS, **12**(2):171–180 (2014). http://www.tandfonline.com/doi/abs/10.1080/14765284.2014.900968
26. F. Handoko, E. Nursanti, D. Harmanto, Sutriyono, ARPN JEAS, **11**(8):5275–5282 (2016). http://www.arpnjournals.org/jeas/research_papers/rp_2016/jeas_0416_4105.pdf
27. M.E. Tjahjadi, F. Handoko, S.S. Sai. IJECE, **7**(3):1188–1196 (2017). http://iaesjournal.com/online/index.php/IJECE/article/view/14794
28. S. Mahanal, S. Zubaidah, A. Bahri, M.S. Dinnurriya. Asia-Pacific Forum on Science Learning and Teaching, **17**(2): art. no. 21 (2016). https://eric.ed.gov/?q=thinking+skills&id=EJ1145728
29. B.A. Prayitno, D. Corebima, H. Zubaidah, M. Ramli. JBSE, **16**(2):266–277 (2007). http://www.scientiasocialis.lt/jbse/?q=node/564

Geometric Development of Point Absorber Wave Energy Conventer

Heri Saptono Warpindyasmoro[1,*],and *Kartika* Gunadi[2]

[1]Electrical Engineering Department, Petra Christian University, Jl. Siwalankerto 121-131, Surabaya, 60234, Indonesia
[2]Informatics Engineering Department, Petra Christian University, Jl. Siwalankerto 121-131, Surabaya, 60234, Indonesia

Abstract. This paper describes how to design the shape of a floating object that will be used as a point absorber on wave energy converster. The buoyant shape to be analyzed is a tube has a flat top plane with varying bottom plane, i.e cylinder, hemisphare and cone. The analysis was conducted on the diameter of the object and the influence of the ocean wave period on the area where the apparatus was later applied in the southern coast of East Java. Using Moses's software, it is found that the diameter of the body is proportional to the period in which the maximum of Response Amplitude Operator floating object. The object with a flat bottom field (cylinder) produces the largest period, which is 10 s, followed by a curve shape of a hemisphere with a period of 9 s and last with a cone shape cone with a period of at least 8 s. This shows that the curvature of the bottom of the buoyancy can be adjusted according to the wave period to obtain maximum Response Amplitude Operator.

Key words: Point absorber, wave energy conventer.

1 Introduction

The need for electrical energy always increase along with economic growth and population growth. Energy demand in Indonesia has increased by 6 % per year. In 2025 it takes an additional energy of 180 % of the present. This means that energy demand will increase from 3 000 000 BOEPD (Barrels Of Oil Equivalent Per Day) to 8 300 000 BOEPD. Of the current electrical energy needs obtained from new renewable energy sources 5.7 %. Indonesia has an ocean of 5 800 000 km^2 or 70 % of the total territory of Indonesia, this is a huge potential as a source of renewable energy from ocean energy. The government has targeted to start building a ocean energy power plant with a capacity of 3 MW of the type of ocean currents, and 10 MW of the type of ocean heat. The potential of ocean energy in Indonesia is still not utilized, so there needs to be a study related to the potential of ocean energy in Indonesia. Ocean energy has been the concern of researchers, both in Indonesia and in other countries. Studies of wind, ocean currents and waves in the Sunda Strait as an alternative energy have been made [1]. From this research, it is found that in Sunda Strait have wave energy potential with maximum wave height 3.2 m with period 17 s with electric energy potential 92 kW m^{-1}. Ocean waves caused by wind. The relationship between the wind and the waves, especially the wave period on the south coast of West Java [2]. In this study it is found that wind and wave patterns vary greatly according to seasonal pattern (quarter). Tide modeling has been done in the Alas Strait (between Lombok Island and Sumbawa), the estimated energy obtained in one year is 330 GWh [3].

The potential of ocean energy is quite large, therefore it is necessary equipment that can convert the ocean energy into electrical energy. To convert wave energy into electrical energy required a floating object (point absorber) that can move vertically in accordance with the waveform that comes to it. Before the shape of the floating object is implemented, a simulation is needed to estimate the energy produced. One of the wave energy conversion simulators is WEC-Sim developed by The National Renewable Energy Laboratory (NREL) and Sandia National Laboratories (SNL). This simulator has successfully simulated several forms such as flap [4], applying a buoyancy force and non-linear excitation forces [5], and arbitrary geometric [6]. Several studies have been conducted to study the effect of the shape of buoyancy on the energy produced [7–10]. In this papaer presented the results of research related to the influence of the form of objects with variations in diameter to produce maximum energy.

2 Mass-spring-damper system linear model

In general, floating objects move in six degrees of freedom. That is, the translational motion in the direction of the x, y, and z axes, each of which is called: surge, swey and heave, and rotational motion against the x, y and z axes respectively are called roll, pitch and yaw, as seen in Figure 1.

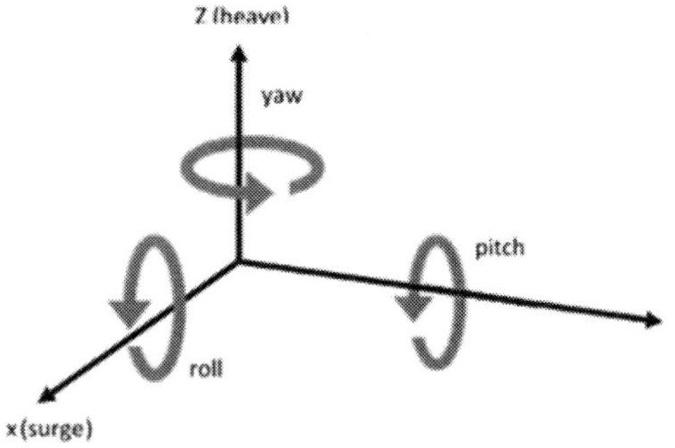

Fig. 1. Motion of buoyancy in 6 degrees freedom.

In the subsequent discussion of motion floating objects only reviewed in 1 dimension only the motion towards the z axis (heave). This is due to the motion of a buoyancy object connected with Power Take Off (PTO) equipment in the form of a linear generaor where the translator moves toward the z axis as shown in Figure 2.

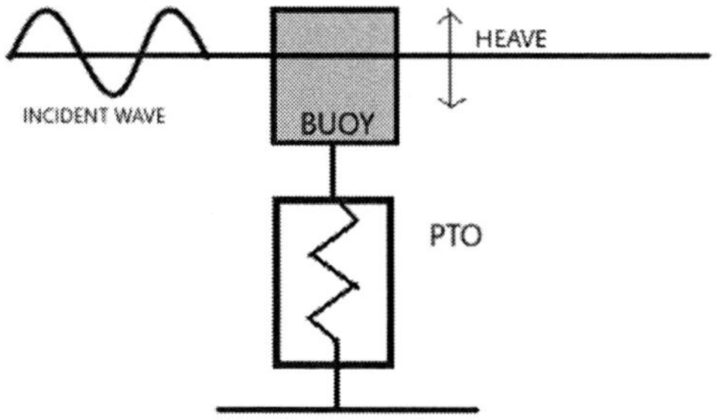

Fig. 2. Linear Mass-Spring-Damped model.

2.1 Forces on floating objects

One method for analyzing float motion is the Linear Model Mass-Spring-Damper System [11]. The forces in floating objects are:

2.1.1 Floating force (FA)

The floating force is an Archimedes force equal to the weight of the liquid removed by the floating object. This buoyant force will be a restoring force that will bring objects back to a point of equilibrium. This buoyancy force or restoring force is:

$$F_A = -C_A z \quad (1)$$

Where:

C_A : restoring constant (N m^{-1}), $C_A = \rho g A_{wl}$
ρ : density of ocean water
g : the acceleration of gravity
A_{wl} : The cross section of the floating object on the surface of the water.
z : displacement toward z axis

A negative sign to indicate that the F_A direction is always opposite to the direction of the object motion.

2.1.2 Mass addition force (Fm)

At the moment the floating object oscillates there will be an increase in the water mass as it exits and enters the water surface. This water mass will increase the mass of a floating object as m_a. So will contribute force for:

$$F_m = m_a\ddot{z} \tag{2}$$

Where:

m_a : addition of mass (kg)

z : acceleration of vertical motion of buoyancy (m dt^{-2})

2.1.3 Damping force

Damping force as a result when the floating object is moving against the water. Due to this damping force there will be a force radiated out by the system. Therefore this damping force is also called the radiation force (Frad). Thus the magnitude of this radiation force is:

$$F_{rad} = -b\,\dot{z} \tag{3}$$

Where:

b = damping constant (kg dt^{-1})

z = vertical velocity of the object (m dt^{-1})

2.1.4 PTO force

If the floating object is connected to the PTO equipment, then there will be energy released/transferred to be converted into electrical energy. This PTO force is also viewed as a damping force, so the magnitude of the PTO force is:

$$F_{PTO} = -\beta\dot{z} \tag{4}$$

Where:

β = PTO damping constant,

$$\beta = \sqrt{b(\omega_p)^2 + \frac{1}{\omega_p^2}(-(m - m_a(\omega_p))\omega_p^2 + C_A + k_p)^2}$$

z = vertical velocity of the object (m / dt)

2.1.5 Excitation force

Excitation Force is the influence of waves that result in pressure changes in the fluid on the surface of floating objects. This excitation force is obtained from a non-hydrostatic state, because the hydrostatic is said to be a buoyant force or restoring force. This excitation force is Froude-Krylov force and Diffraction force.

2.1.6 Spring force.

This spring force is a mechanical force connecting floating objects and PTO equipment. This force is equivalent to a restoring force called Fp.

$$F_p = k_p z \tag{5}$$

Where:

kp = the spring constant

$k_p = \omega_p[m + ma(w_p)] - C_A$

z = position of floating objects.

From Newton's law, it is related to the forces acting on a floating object are obtained

$$F = m\ddot{z} \tag{6}$$

$$F_A + F_m + F_{rad} + F_{PTO} + F_{Eks} + F_p = m\ddot{z}$$

$$-C_A z + m_a\ddot{z} - b\dot{z} - \beta\dot{z} + Feks - k_z z = m\ddot{z}$$

$$(m + ma)\ddot{z} + (b + \beta)\dot{z} + (C_A + k) = f_{eks} \tag{7}$$

3 Result and discussion

3.1 Determination of geometric point absorber

This research begins by determining the shape of a floating object. The selected floating object is an object with a top surface in the form of a circular plane with diameter D, whereas the lower plane has different shape: cylinder, hemisphare and cone with length respectively is L = 1,5 D. The shape of the object as in Figure 3.

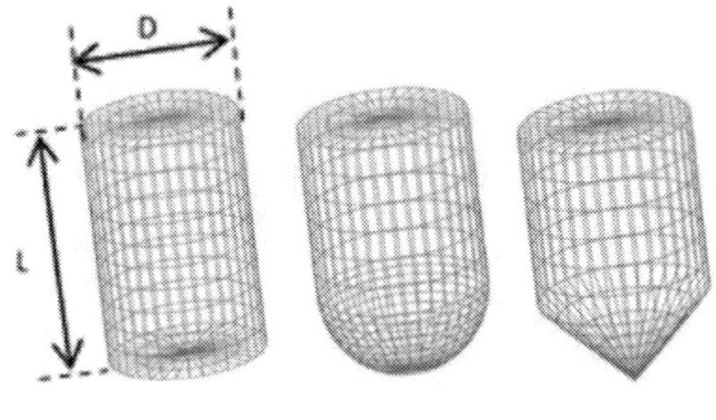

Fig. 3. The shape and dimensions of objects.

3.2 Effect of diameter floating object on response amplitude operation (RAO)

Using the MOSES simulation software, the diameter of a floating object varies with D = 6 m, 9 m, 12 m, 15 m and 18 m with floating material length L = 1.5 D. The simulation results can be seen in Figure 4 for the cylinder, Figure 5 for the hemisphere and Figure 6 for cone.

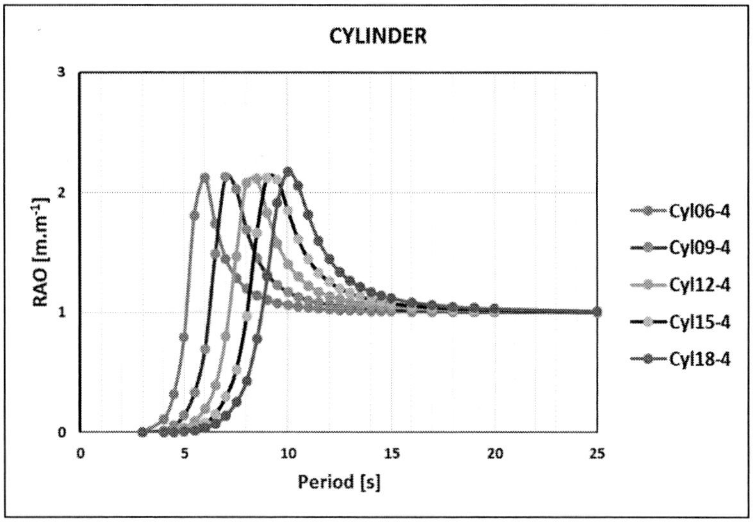

Fig. 4. RAO for cylinder with variation of diameter cylinder.

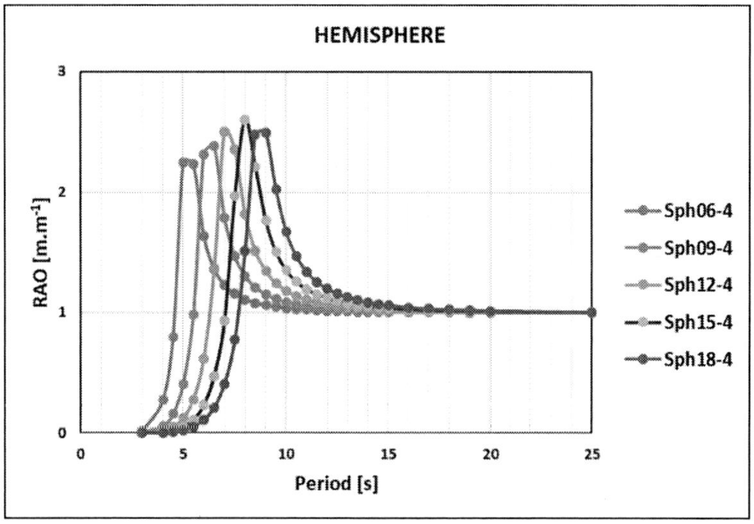

Fig. 5. RAO for a hemisphere with variations of diameter hemisphere.

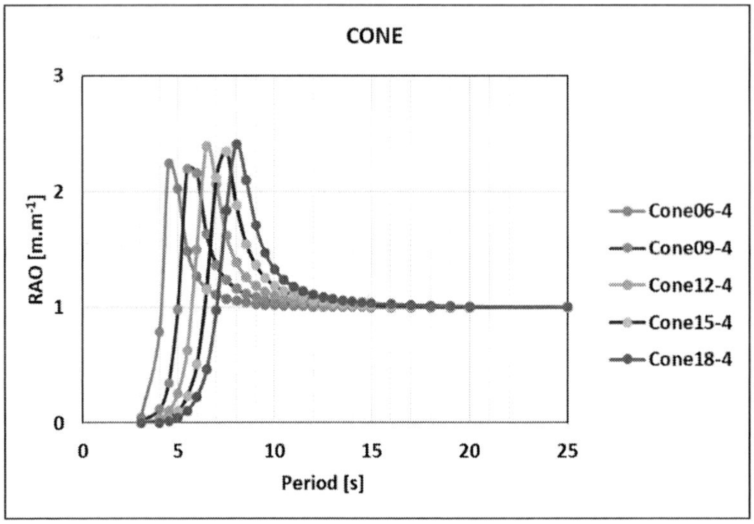

Fig. 6. RAO for cones with variations of diameter cone.

From the RAO simulation results in Figure 4 to Figure 6, the diameter of the object is proportional with the period at which the maximum RAO occurs. To determine the effect of the shape of the object on the period in which the maximum RAO is generated, it is simulated for all three objects with the same diameter (D = 18 m) and the same draft (T = 4 m). The simulation results are shown in Figure 7.

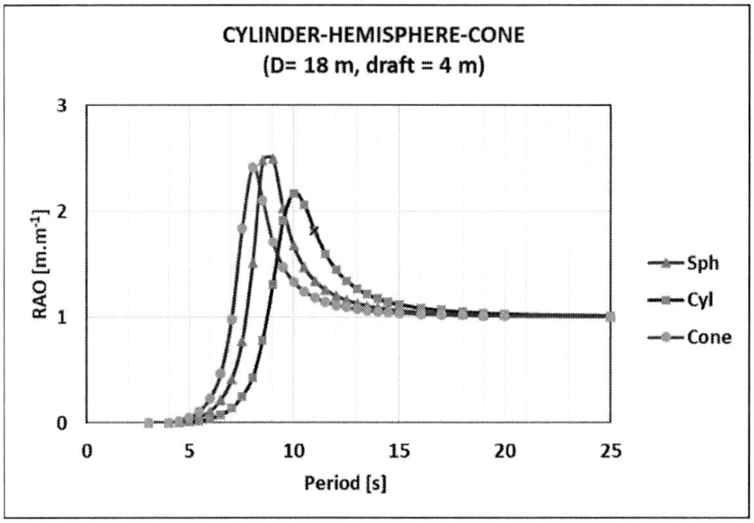

Fig. 7. Comparison of maximum RAO on cylinder, hemisphere and cone forms.

From Figure 7 it appears that the period for generating maximum RAO is different for each object. The object with a flat bottom field (cylinder) produces the largest period, which is 10 s, followed by a curve shape of a hemisphere with a period of 9 s and last with a cone shape cone with a period of at least 8 s. This shows that the curvature of the bottom of the buoyancy can be adjusted according to the wave period so as to obtain maximum RAO.

4 Conclusions

From the simulation results of the three forms of floating objects obtained that the greater the diameter of the object will produce maximum RAO in the larger period. The shape of the bottom of the floating object affects the period to produce the maximum RAO. The period will be smaller when the bottom shape is changed from the flat (cylinder), curve (hemisphere) and tilt (cone).

This research is funded by a grant from the Ministry of Research, Technology and Higher Education of the Republic of Indonesia

References

[1] R. Sandro, Arnudin, A. Tussadiah, R.M. Utamy, N. Pridina, L.N. Afifah. Energy Procedia **47**:242–249 (2014). https://www.sciencedirect.com/science/article/pii/S1876610214002367
[2] N.P. Purba. Jurnal Akuatikan **5**(1):8–15 (2014). [in Bahasa Indonesia]. http://jurnal.unpad.ac.id/akuatika/article/view/3699
[3] L.S. Blunden, A.S. Bahaj, N.S. Aziz. Renewable Energy **49**(January):137–142 (2013). https://www.sciencedirect.com/science/article/pii/S0960148112000572
[4] Y.-H. Yu, Y. Li, K. Hallett, C. Hotimsky. *Design and analysis for a floating oscillating surge wave energy converter*. The 33rd International Conference on Ocean, Offshore and Arctic Engineering. pp. 1–10 (San Francisco, CA, 2014). https://www.nrel.gov/docs/fy14osti/61283.pdf
[5] K. Ruehl, C. Michelen, S. Kanner, M. Lawson, Y. H. Yu. *Preliminary Verification and Validation of WEC-Sim, an Open-Source Wave Energy Converter Design Tool*. The 33rd International Conference on Ocean, Offshore and Arctic Engineering. pp. 1–8 (San Francisco, California, 2014). https://www.nrel.gov/docs/fy14osti/61531.pdf
[6] K. Ruehl, R. Paasch, T. K. A. Brekken, and B. Bosma. *Wave energy converter design tool for point absorbers with arbitrary device geometry*. The Twenty-third International Offshore and Polar Engineering Conference. pp. 538–545 (Anchorage, Alaska, 2013). https://www.onepetro.org/conference-paper/ISOPE-I-13-193
[7] P.J.B.F.N. Beirão, C.M.S.P. Malça. International Journal of Energy and Environmental Engineering, **5**(91):1–11 (2014). https://link.springer.com/article/10.1007/s40095-014-0091-7
[8] J. Kim, H. Kweon, W. Jeong, I. Cho, and H. Cho. Int. J. Nav. Archit. Ocean Eng., **7**(4):739–749 (2015). https://www.sciencedirect.com/science/article/pii/S2092678216300450
[9] H. Gao. B. L i. Polish Maritime Research, **22**(1):106–111 (2015). https://www.degruyter.com/view/j/pomr.2015.22.issue-s1/pomr-2015-0041/pomr-2015-0041.xml
[10] J. Orszaghova, A. Rafiee, H. Wolgamot, S. Draper, and P.H. Taylor. *Experimental study of extreme responses of a point absorber wave energy converter*. 20th Australasian Fluid Mechanics Conference. pp. 2–5 (Perth, Australia, 2016). http://people.eng.unimelb.edu.au/imarusic/proceedings/20/753%20Paper.pdf
[11] F. Kalofotias. *Study for the hull shape of a wave energy converter-point absorber*. [Thesis] Master of Science, Water Enggineering and Management, University of Twente (2016). pp. 16–19. https://www.utwente.nl/en/et/wem/education/msc-thesis/2016/kalofotias.pdf

Turbine Design for Low Heat Organic Rankine Cycle Power Generation using Renewable Energy Sources

Herry Susanto[1], *Kamaruddin* Abdullah[1,*], *Aep* Saepul Uyun[1], *Syukri* Muhammad Nur[1], and *Teuku* Meurah Indra Mahlia[2,3]

[1]Program Study of Renewable Energy, Graduate School, Darma Persada University, Jl. Radin Inten II, Pondok Kelapa 13450, East Jakarta, Indonesia
[2]Department of Mechanical Engineering, Universiti Tenaga Nasional, 43000 Kajang, Selangor, Malaysia
[3]School of Systems, Management and Leadership, Faculty of Engineering and Information Technology, University of Technology Sydney, 81 Broadway, Ultimo, NSW 2007, Australia

Abstract. In recent years, due to its feasibility and reliability, the organic rankine cycle has become a widespread concern and is the subject of research. In the organic rankine cycle system, the radial turbine component is a highly influential component of the high low performance resulting. This paper discusses the design of radial turbines for organic rankine cycle systems. The design stage consists of preliminary design and detail design with parametric methods on the working fluid R22 to determine the geometry and initial estimation of the performance of the radial turbine. After that, a numerical study of the fluid flow region in the radial turbine with R22 as the working fluid was performed. The analysis was performed using computational fluid dynamics of Autodesk Computational Fluid Dynamics Motion software on two models of real gas, k-epsilon and shear stress transport. From the results of this analysis, there is pressure, velocity and temperature distribution along the radial turbine blades and estimated performance under various operating conditions. Comparison between parametric and computational fluid dynamics analysis results show different performance. The difference is due to the computational fluid dynamics analysis already involving the real gas shear stress transport model.

Key words: Computational fluid dynamics, finite element analysis, k-epsilon, organic rankine cycle, shear stress transport.

1 Introduction

Interest in the utilization of low grade heat recovery has increased dramatically in the past decade as it increases environmental issues such as air pollution, global warming, ozone layer depletion and acid rain caused by the acceleration of fossil fuel consumption [1–3]. A number of new solutions have been proposed to produce heat-generated plants at low temperature and pressure, and has been proven to be applied in various fields such as solar thermal power, biological waste heat, engine exhaust gases, domestic boilers and so forth [3–11]. Among the solutions offered, for now the Organic Rankine Cycle (ORC) system is the most widely studied. ORC has at least two advantages, namely as a power generation system, ORC has simple components and the availability of components that are quite a lot in the market. Furthermore, ORC also uses organic working fluids that perform better than water as a working fluid at low temperature and pressure [12–18]. Various ORC applications have been reported in previous studies. As in the utilization of waste heat recovery, solar energy, a combination of heat and power (CHP), geothermal and heat utilization of the exhaust from the engine. From the results of the experimental study it is seen that on small scale units of ORC showed promising performance, especially in remote areas, because ORC has reliability, wide output power range, wide component parts availability and reduced number of rotating components so that the ORC construction can be more compact and smaller than that of conventional power plants. Many researchers have focused on the thermodynamic studies of the ORC cycle, and the selection of working fluids, with particular attention to the efficiency of power generation. On the other hand, relatively little writing is published on the design and optimization of turbomachinery

*Corresponding author: kamaruddinabd@gmail.com, smt.eng77@gmail.com

equipment. Basically, within the relevant power range (5 kW to 5 000 kW) two options can be proposed: that is, axial turbine or radial turbine. This last option is considered more attractive, as it allows better performance on a lower scale. Therefore knowledge of radial turbines on ORC systems requires further study [19–29].

Organic Rankine Cycle (ORC) cycle is one form of Rankine cycle that utilizes organic refrigerant as a working fluid. In general, the ideal ORC has four process stages: isentropic compression at the pump, isobaric evaporation of the boiler, isentropic expansion on the turbine, and isobaric condensation on the condenser. The advantage of this cycle is to use a refrigerant with boiling point and condensation point lower than the water used in the regular Rankine cycle. The impact of using the refrigerant is that the cycle can utilize a heat source whose temperature is lower than the boiling temperature of water. Here is the entalpy-entropy diagram and temperature on ORC [12]. Simple Organic Rankine Cycle (ORC) and the Organic Rankine Cycle P-h diagram shown in Figure 1.

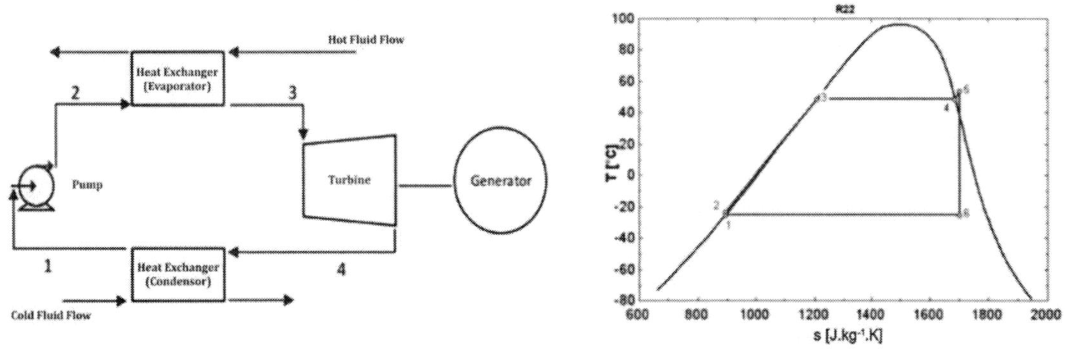

Fig. 1. Simple Organic Rankine Cycle (ORC) (left) and The Organic Rankine Cycle P-h diagram (right).

Working fluids have an important role in ORC as working conditions vary. There are also many number of compounds that can be used as a choice of working fluids including hydrocarbons refrigerants, alcohols and others [12]. Working fluids can be categorized into three types: dry, wet and isentropic fluid. The fundamental difference between the three types of refrigerant is the dT ds^{-1} slope of the fluid vapor curve in the temperature-entropy diagram. Dry fluid has a positive dT ds^{-1} slope, wet fluid has a negative dT ds^{-1} slope, and isentropic fluid categorized if dT ds^{-1} has a zero value [12]. As shown in Figure 2, there are generally three types of saturated steam curves in the T-s (Temperature-entropy) diagram. Dry fluid with positive slope, wet fluid with negative slope, and isentropic fluid.

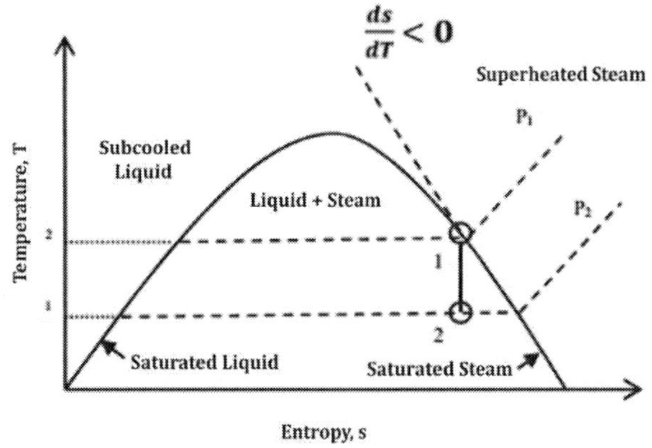

(a)

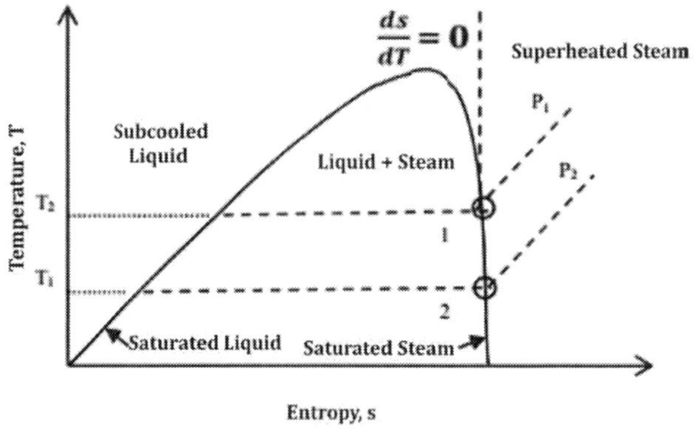

(b)

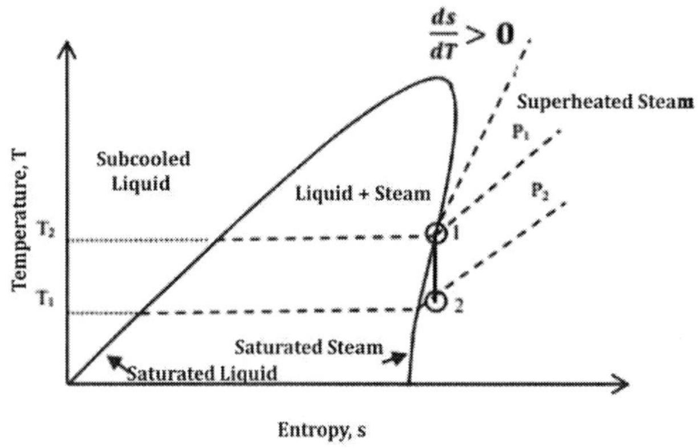

(c)

Fig. 2. T-s diagram for fluid (a) wet, (b) isentropic, and (c) dry.

The choice of working fluid should pay attention to the heat source to be used, the optimum criteria of thermodynamic properties, and meet various criteria such as non-toxic, non-flammable, and environmentally friendly. Currently, a system of power plants is being developed using renewable energy. The power plant system used is a power plant system using ORC (Organic Rankine Cycle) technology. This system generates electricity from renewable energy sources by utilizing low-temperature and low-pressure heat sources [21]. The advantage of using the ORC power plant system is simpler than through biomass gasification processes plus gas/diesel fuel engines when fueled by biomass. The cost required is about five times less than the utilization of other renewable energy. In addition, efficiency rises about three times as large as over-wasted capture [21]. Figure 3, shows the following components in an ORC (Organic Rankine Cycle) power plant:

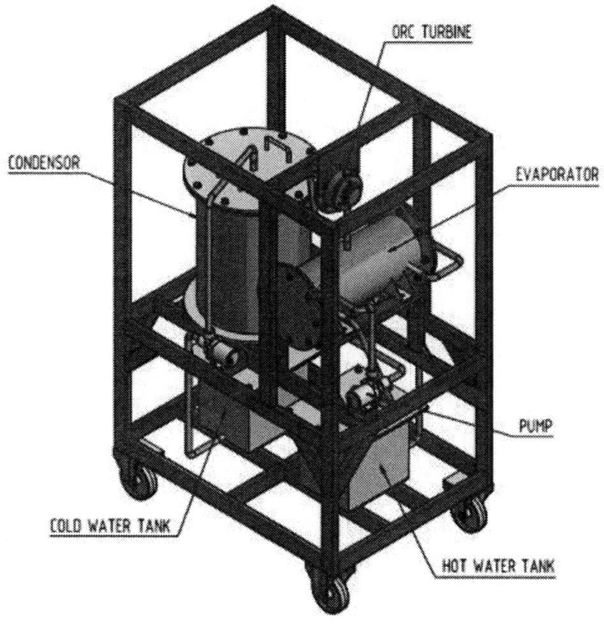

Fig. 3. ORC (Organic Rankine Cycle) power plant.

The above-mentioned ORC power plant can be developed as a substitute for generators in rural areas or areas where electricity supply is not available. In addition, the design of the ORC power plant can also be applied to power generation from other renewable energy sources, such as ocean thermal energy (OTEC), solar thermal, biological waste heat, engine exhaust gas, geothermal, biomass and other sources. By utilizing exhaust heat that is still hot and below 100 °C (range 65 °C to 80 °C), it is connected to an ORC generator engine evaporator, and by heat transfer process will evaporate the organic working fluid inside the evaporator and increase the pressure inside the evaporator chamber. Furthermore, the flow of the working fluid will flow into the turbine that will turn the turbine runner as well as rotate the generator so that it can generate electricity.

In this turbine chamber begin to decrease the pressure of organic working fluid. Furthermore, the organic working fluid will flow into the condenser and there will be again the process of heat transfer so that the remaining heat in the working fluid will be absorbed by cold water taken from the cooling tower or other cold water source. As the organic working fluid is in the condenser and cools down, the working fluid pressure will be at the lowest point in the system requiring the pumping aid to suck up the organic working fluid and flush it back into the evaporator to continue the working cycle. Utilization of ORC power plant in renewable energy sources is shown in Figure 4 below:

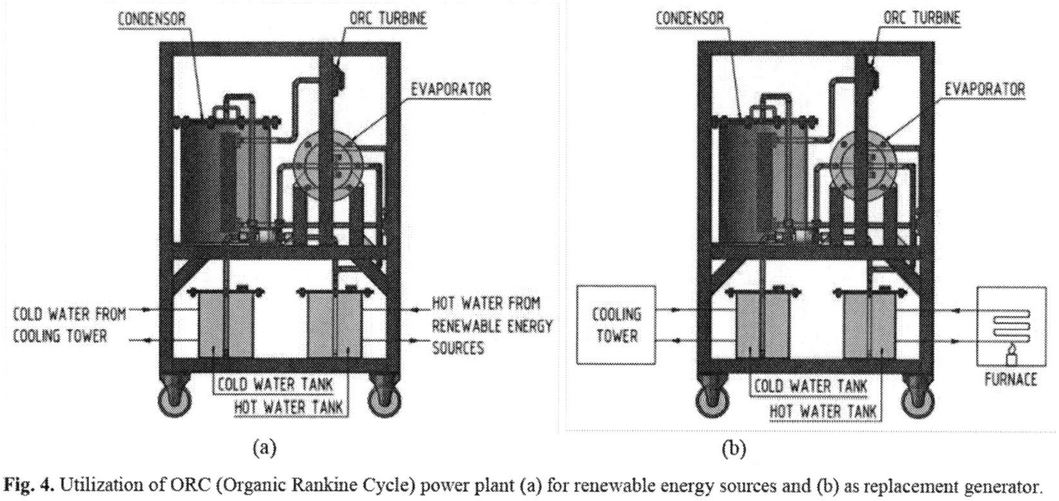

Fig. 4. Utilization of ORC (Organic Rankine Cycle) power plant (a) for renewable energy sources and (b) as replacement generator.

2 Research methodology

2.1 Research flow diagram

In this paper, the research steps are shown in the following Research Flow Diagram in Figure 5 below:

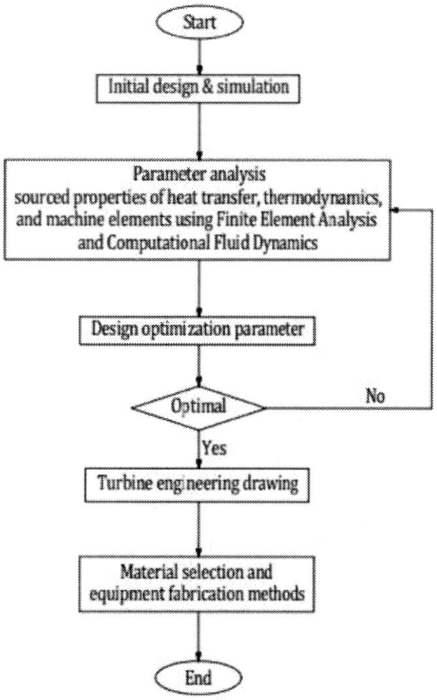

Fig. 5. Research flow diagram.

2.2.ORC (Organic Rankine Cycle) turbine design

The ORC turbine design to be studied can be seen in Figure 6, below:

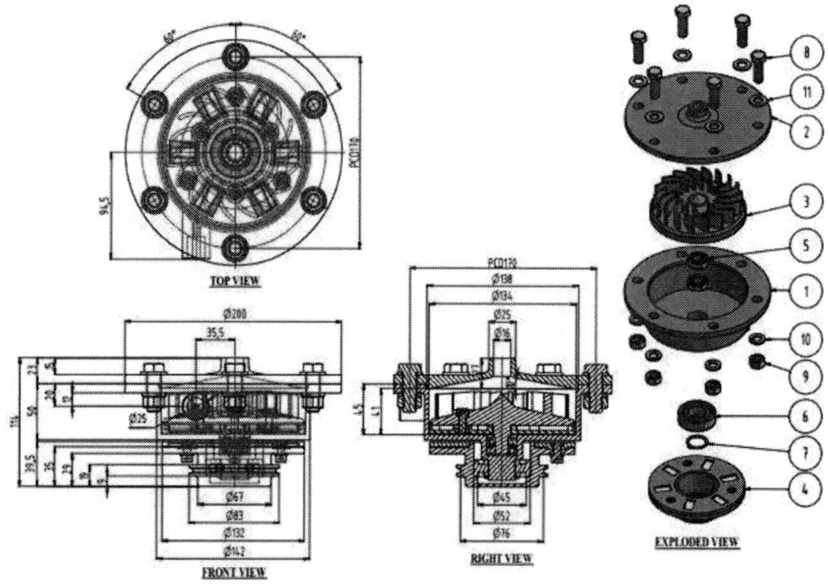

Fig. 6. ORC turbine components.

The explanations of these components are as follows:

(i). Housing, is a major component of the ORC turbine, which houses the turbine runner and generator runner components as well as an inlet hole. In this paper research, housing component is designed using SUS 304 material. Selection of the material to optimize the use of magnets mounted on the turbine runner and generator runner, so it will not interfere with the magnetic pull force that occurs on both components. The housing component is shown in Figure 7, below:

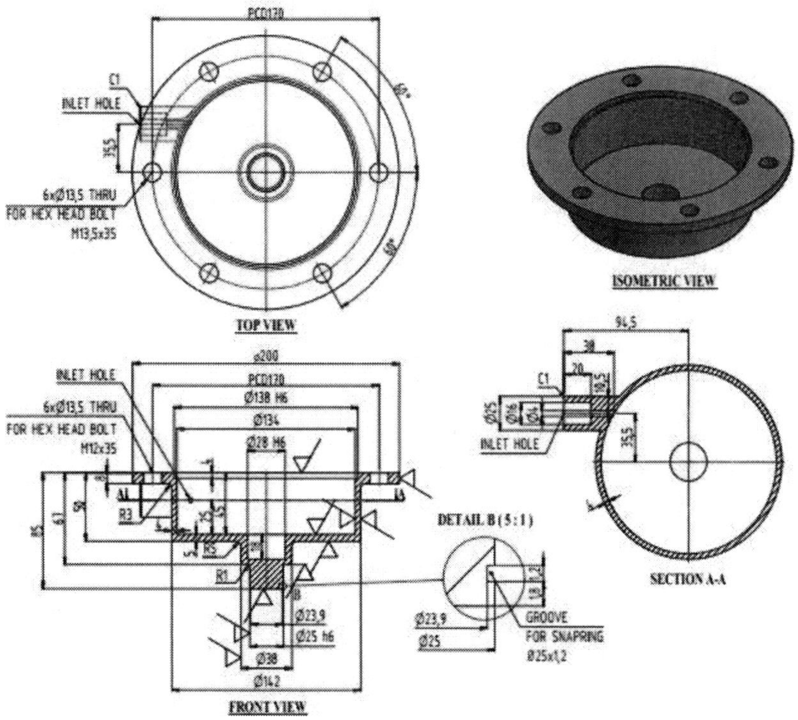

Fig. 7. Housing component on ORC turbine.

(ii). Housing cover, is a major component of the ORC turbine which is the closing component of housing. In the housing cover component there is an outlet hole and the design is also made using SUS 304 material. The housing cover component is shown in Figure 8, below:

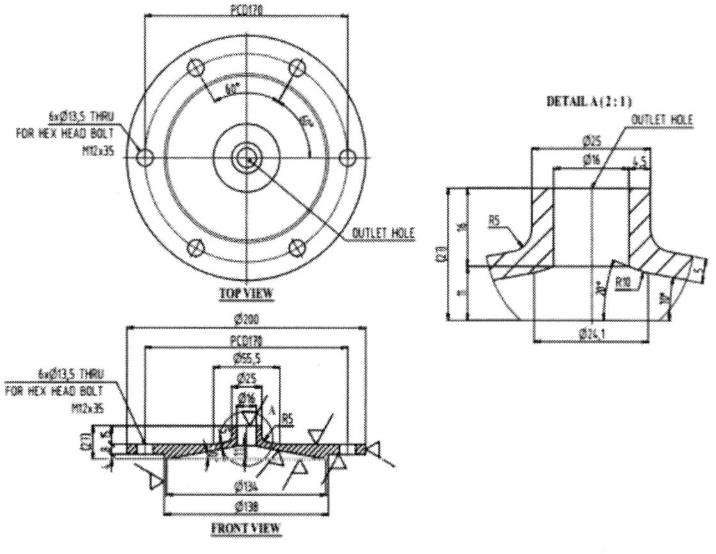

Fig. 8. Housing cover component on ORC turbine.

(iii). Turbine runner, is a component of ORC turbine residing in the housing component. This component will rotate when receiving fluid pressure into the housing chamber. The greater the fluid pressure that goes in, the rotation on the turbine runner will also accelerate. While the magnet attached to the turbine runner will draw the magnet attached to the generator runner, so that when the turbine runner rotates due to the inlet working fluid pressure, it will cause the generator runner to rotates also in the direction of the turbine runner. The turbine runner component is shown in Figure 9, below:

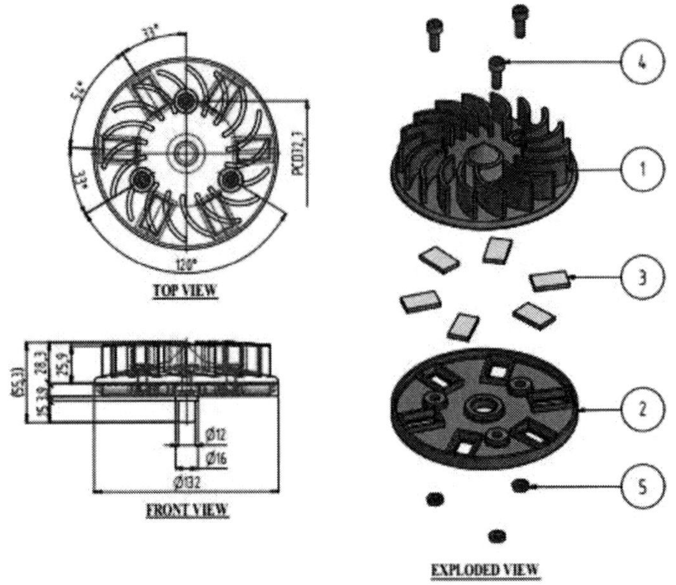

Fig. 9. Turbine runner component on ORC turbine.

(iv). Generator runner, is a component of the ORC turbine that is outside the housing component. This component will rotate along with turbine runner's spin, because the magnets attached to the two components will attract each other. Furthermore, the generator runner component will be connected to the generator using the V-Belt component, so that from the rotation that occurs in the generator will be converted into electrical energy. The generator runner component is shown in Figure 10, below:

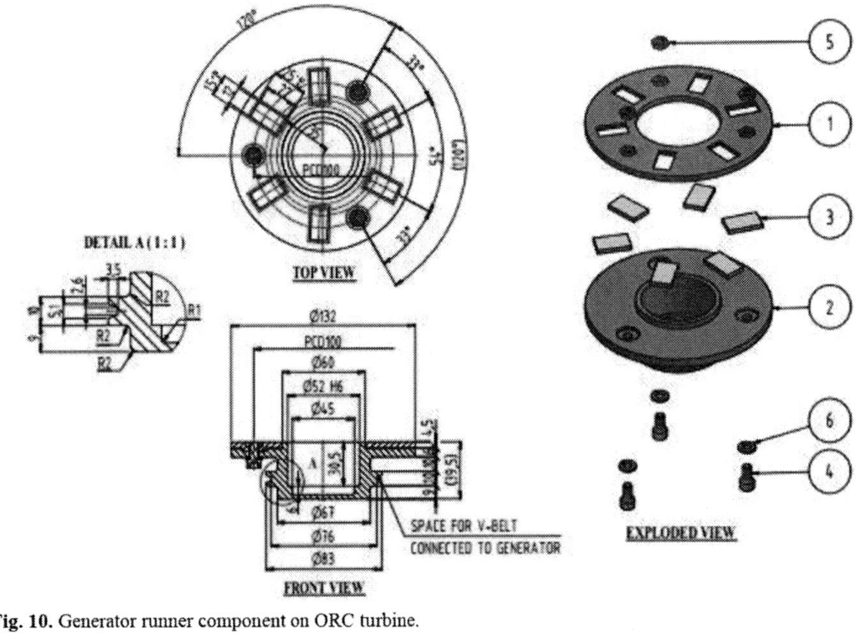

Fig. 10. Generator runner component on ORC turbine.

2.2 Research stages

The research activity is planned to be divided into two stages as follows:

i). The initial stage is the initial design of ORC turbine.

ii). ORC turbine movement simulation, fluid distribution inside the ORC turbine chamber, analysis of design parameters and analytical optimization.

3 Mathematical modeling

ORC (Organic Rankine Cycle) turbine has two main components groups which become the most important part of turbine system performance optimization, that is :

(i). Housing & housing cover, both of these components are the main components to which the turbine runner and generator runner components are installed. Both of these components must also be able to withstand internal pressure that occurs due to the working fluid that flowed into the turbine chamber. The first step that we must do to make the design housing and housing cover is to determine its dimensions. Since housing and housing cover must be able to withstand internal pressure, it must be designed following the pressure vessel rules according to ASME Section VIII Division 1 standard.

(ii). Turbine runner, this component is a component that will rotate due to the pressure effect of the working fluid being fed into the turbine chamber. Therefore, this turbine runner needs to be designed by taking into account the pressure, velocity, temperature and density of the working fluid used. Although on this turbine runner installed magnets which will pull each other with magnets attached to the generator runner, but we will not analyze specifically the magnetic flux that occurs in the magnets attached to the turbine runner and generator runner. Design modeling and velocity triangle of turbine runner can be seen in Figure 11, below:

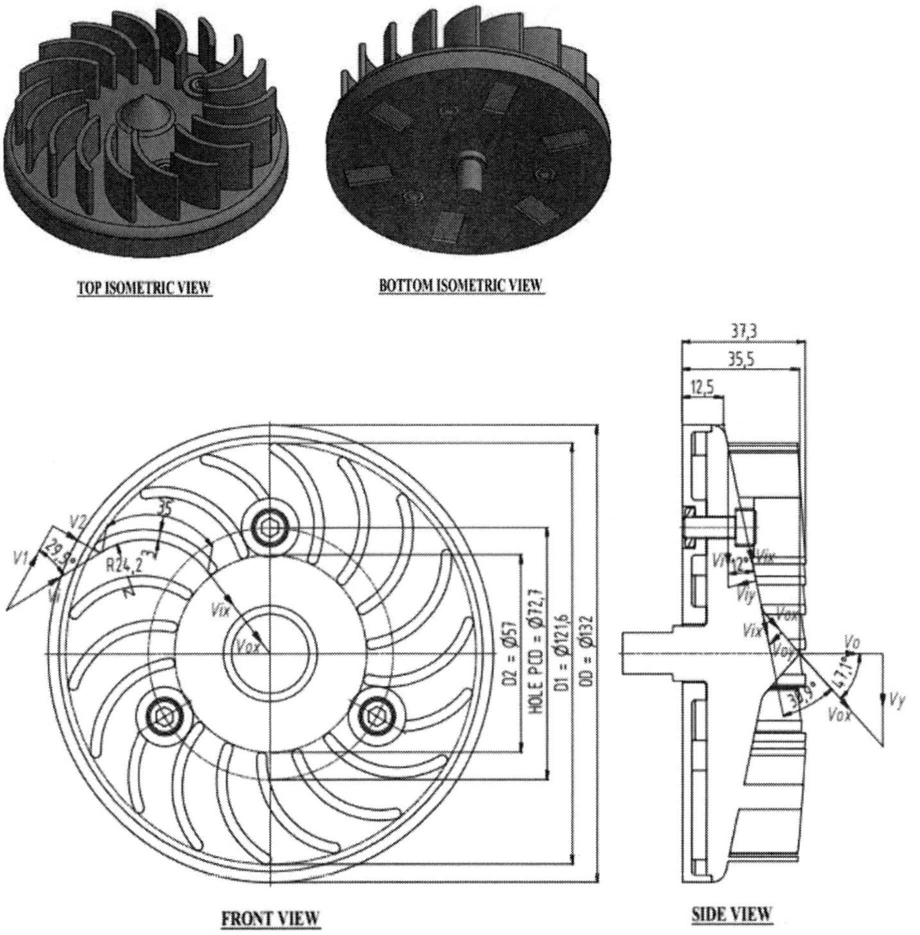

Fig. 11. Modeling and velocity triangle of turbine runner.

Mathematical modeling to calculate the amount of power generated, seen in the following Equation:

i). Turbine power (P_T)

The turbine power (P_T), can be calculated using the following Equation [21]:

$$P_T = \frac{T\, 2\, \pi\, n}{60} \tag{1}$$

ii). Electrical power (P_L)

The electrical power (P_L), can be calculated using the following Equation [21]:

$$P_L = P_T\, \eta_g \tag{2}$$

Where : P_L = Electrical power (W)
P_T = Turbine power (W)
T = Turbine torque (N m)
n = Turbine rotation (rpm)
η_g = Generator efficiency = 82 % = 0.82

4 Turbine modeling and simulation

4.1 Turbine Design Parameters

Table 1. Initial design parameter of housing and housing cover.

No	Input Parameters	Value	Unit
1	Material	SUS 304	
2	Design Pressure (P)	0.8	MPa
3	Design Temperature (T)	80	°C
4	Material Strength Value (S)	215	MPa
5	Joint Efficiency (E)	1	
6	Shell Inner Diameter (Ds)	134	mm
7	Inlet Nozzle Inner Diameter (Di)	4	mm
8	Outlet Nozzle Inner Diameter (Do)	16	mm
9	Corrosion Allowance (C.A.)	1	mm

Table 2. Initial design parameter of turbine runner.

No	Input Parameters	Value	Unit
1	Material	PLASTIC	
2	Design Pressure (P)	0.1 to 0.8	MPa
3	Design Temperature (T)	80	°C
4	Density of R22 Fluid (ρf)	1 330	kg m^{-3}
5	Viscosity of R22 Fluid (υf)	0.000 263	Pa s
6	Gravity (g)	9.81	m s^{-2}
7	Turbine Chamber Diameter (D)	0.134	m
8	Turbine Chamber Height (h)	0.045	m
9	Inlet Nozzle Diameter (di)	0.004	m
10	Inlet Nozzle Length (Li)	0.038	m
11	Outlet Nozzle Diameter (do)	0.016	m
12	Outlet Nozzle Length (Lo)	0.016	m
13	Turbine Blade Outer Diameter (D1)	0.122	m
14	Turbine Blade Inner Diameter (D2)	0.057	m
15	Turbine Blade Area (As)	0.000 672	m^2
16	Turbine Blade Quantity (NST)	18	pcs
17	Turbine Runner Mass (mT)	0.32	kg
18	First Uphill Angle (α1)	12	°
19	Top Angle (α2)	30.9	°
20	Outlet Angle (α3)	47.1	°
21	Generator Efficiency (ηg)	82	%

ORC (Organic Rankine Cycle) Turbine has two main components groups which become the most important part of turbine system performance optimization. Therefore, the initial turbine design parameters discussed will also be divided into two groups of parameters, that is (1) the initial design parameters in housing and housing cover and (2) the initial design parameters on the turbine runner. The initial design parameters can be seen in Table 1 and Table 2.

4.2 Turbine design calculation using mathematical modeling

Calculations using this mathematical modeling will be divided into two groups, that is (i) Calculations on housing and housing cover design and (ii) Calculation on turbine runner design. The results of calculations are shown in Table 3, Table 4, and Table 5. Graphs of inlet nozzle diameter vs turbine rotation and inlet nozzle diameter vs turbine torque at pressure of 0.8 MPa presented in Figure 12. Graphs of inlet nozzle diameter vs power at pressure of 0.8 MPa and turbine head vs volume flow Rate at constant turbine rotation of 4 918 rpm (1 rpm = 1/60 Hz) shown in Figure 13.

Table 3. Calculation results of thickness on housing and housing cover.

Part Name	P (MPa)	t_s (mm)	t_{si} (mm)	t_n (mm)	t_{ni} (mm)	t_{min} (mm)	t_{nom} (mm)	Design Status
Shell Housing	0.8	0.25	1.25	0.00	0.00	1.25	4	OK
Bottom Head Housing	0.8	2.95	3.95	0.00	0.00	3.95	5	OK
Housing Cover	0.8	2.95	3.95	0.00	0.00	3.95	5	OK
Inlet Nozzle	0.8	0.25	1.25	0.011	1.01	1.13	10.5	OK
Outlet Nozzle	0.8	0.25	1.25	0.034	1.03	1.14	4.5	OK

Table 4. Calculation results at constant pressure of 0.8 mpa.

P_i (MPa)	d_i (mm)	A_i (m^2)	F_i (N)	v_T (m s^{-1})	H (m)	n (rpm)	T (N m)	P_T (kW)	P_L (kW)
0.8	4	1.26e-05	10.05	31.4	61.3	4,918	0.61	0.3	0.3
0.8	5	1.96e-05	15.71	49.1	61.3	7,684	0.96	0.8	0.6
0.8	6	2.83e-05	22.62	70.7	61.3	11,066	1.38	1.6	1.3
0.8	7	3.85e-05	30.79	96.2	61.3	15,061	1.88	3.0	2.4
0.8	8	5.03e-05	40.21	125.7	61.3	19,672	2.45	5.1	4.1
0.8	9	6.36e-05	50.89	159.0	61.3	24,898	3.10	8.1	6.6
0.8	10	7.85e-05	62.83	196.3	61.3	30,738	3.83	12.3	10.1

Table 5. Calculation results of head (h) and volume flow rate (q) at constant turbine rotation of 4 918 rpm.

n (rpm)	di (mm)	Ai (m^2)	Q (m)	H (m)
4,918	4.0	1.26e-05	0.2	61.3
4,918	5.0	1.96e-05	0.3	39.2
4,918	6.0	2.83e-05	0.4	27.3
4,918	7.0	3.85e-05	0.6	20.0
4,918	8.0	5.03e-05	0.8	15.3
4,918	9.0	6.36e-05	1.0	12.1
4,918	10.0	7.85e-05	1.2	9.8
4,918	11.0	9.5e-05	1.5	8.1

The graphs below are graphs of calculation results:

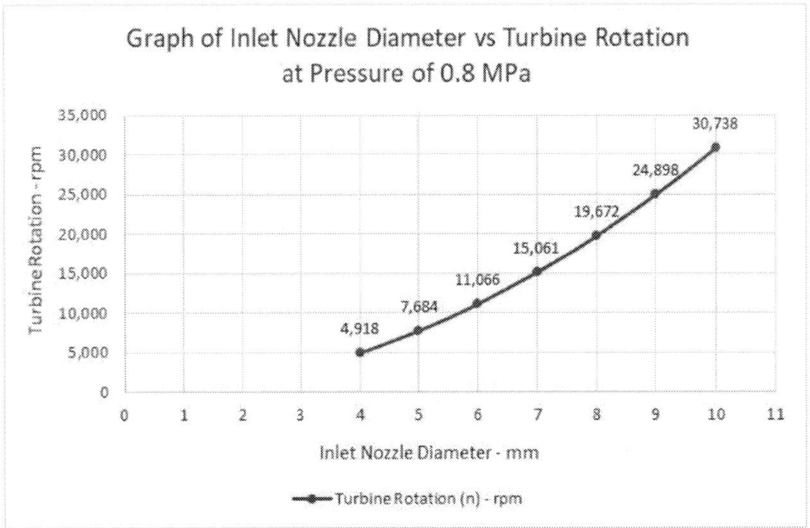

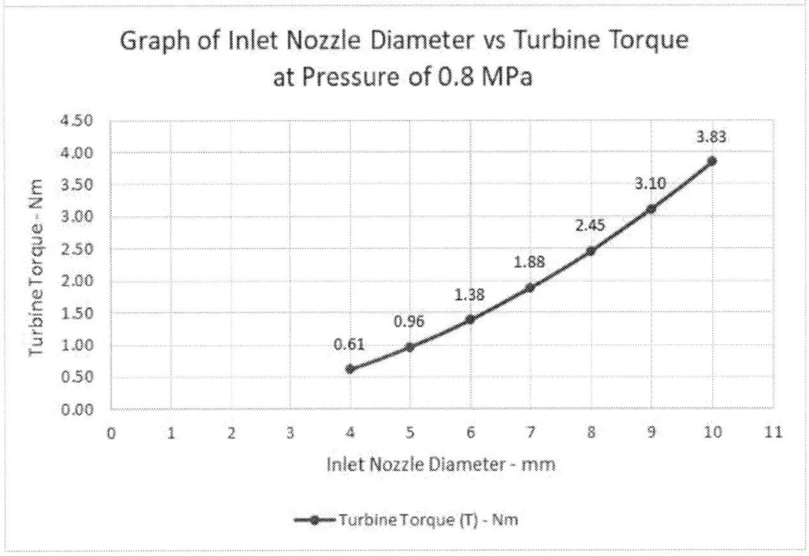

Fig. 12. Graphs of inlet nozzle diameter vs turbine rotation (top) and inlet nozzle diameter vs turbine torque at pressure of 0.8 MPa (bottom).

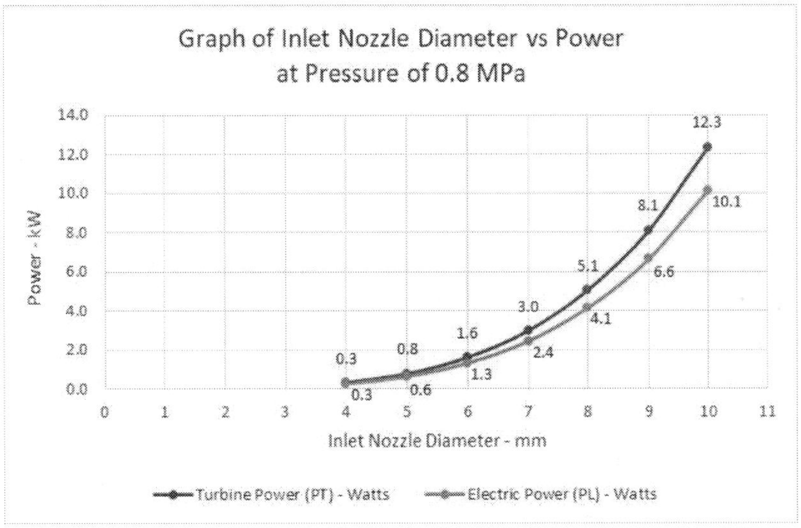

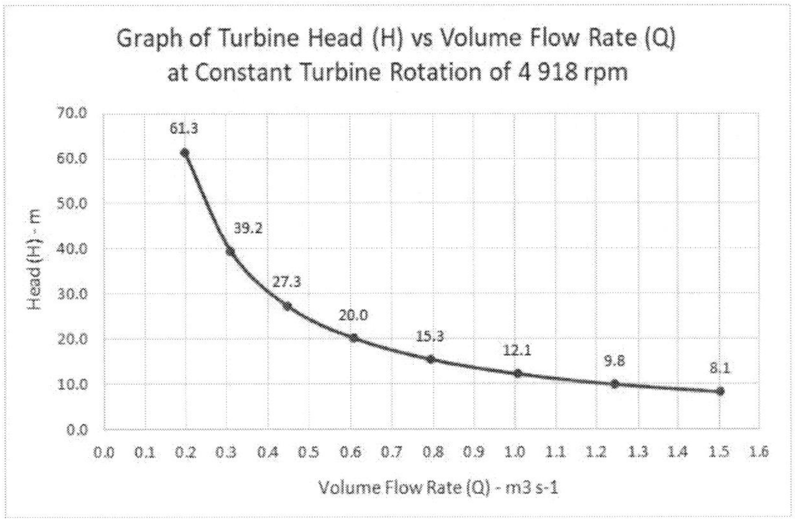

Fig. 13. Graphs of inlet nozzle diameter vs power at pressure of 0.8 MPa (top) and turbine head vs volume flow rate at constant turbine rotation of 4 918 rpm (bottom).

4.3 Turbine design and simulation using fea

In the simulation of turbine design using FEA, simulation will be done testing the strength of materials from housing and housing cover components. The analysis report of the FEA simulation is shown in Figure 14:

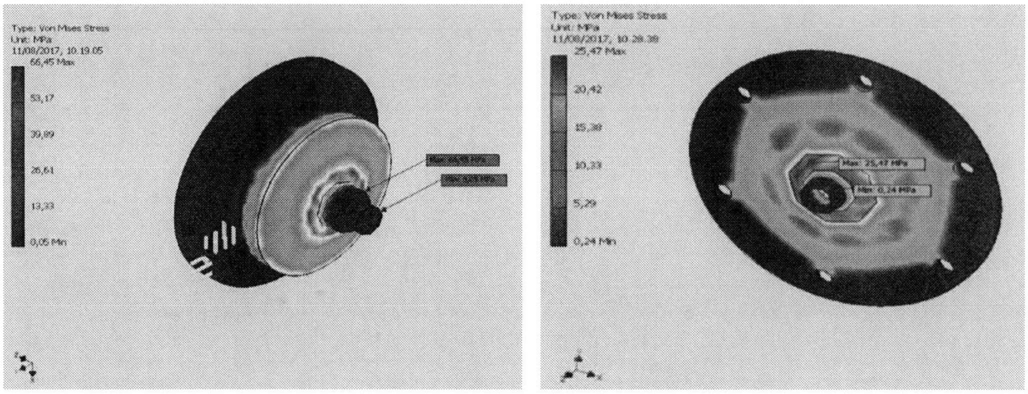

Fig. 14. Distribution of Von Mises Stress on housing (left) and housing cover (right).

From the FEA simulation result, the maximum Von Mises Stress that happened at housing was 66.45 MPa and at housing cover was 25.47 MPa. This value is smaller than the yield strength value of the material, which is 215 MPa. Displacement and safety factor that occurred in housing and housing cover shown in Figure 15.

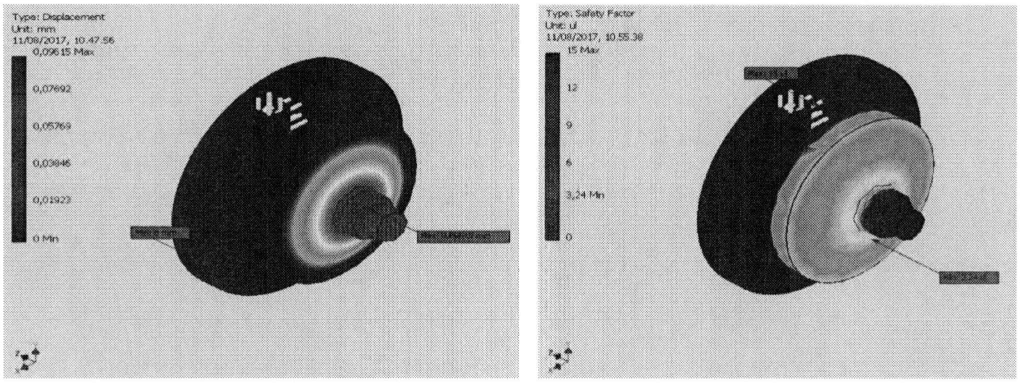

Fig. 15. Displacement (left) and safety factor (right) that occurred in housing and housing cover.

From the FEA simulation result, the maximum displacement that occurred in housing and housing cover is 0.09 615 mm. This value is less than 1 mm. And the minimum Safety Factor that occurred in housing and housing cover was 3.24. Whereas according to the calculation rules of pressure vessel, the minimum permissible safety factor value of 3.

4.4 Turbine design simulation using CFD

In the simulation of the turbine design using this CFD, simulation will be performed on the working fluid movement inside the turbine chamber and rotate the turbine runner. This simulation aims to find out some important design parameters, such as working fluid flow velocity at inlet and outlet nozzles, working fluid pressure, working fluid volume flow rate, turbine runner, turbine torque and generated power. Report analysis of the CFD simulation is presented in Figure 16 to Figure 19.

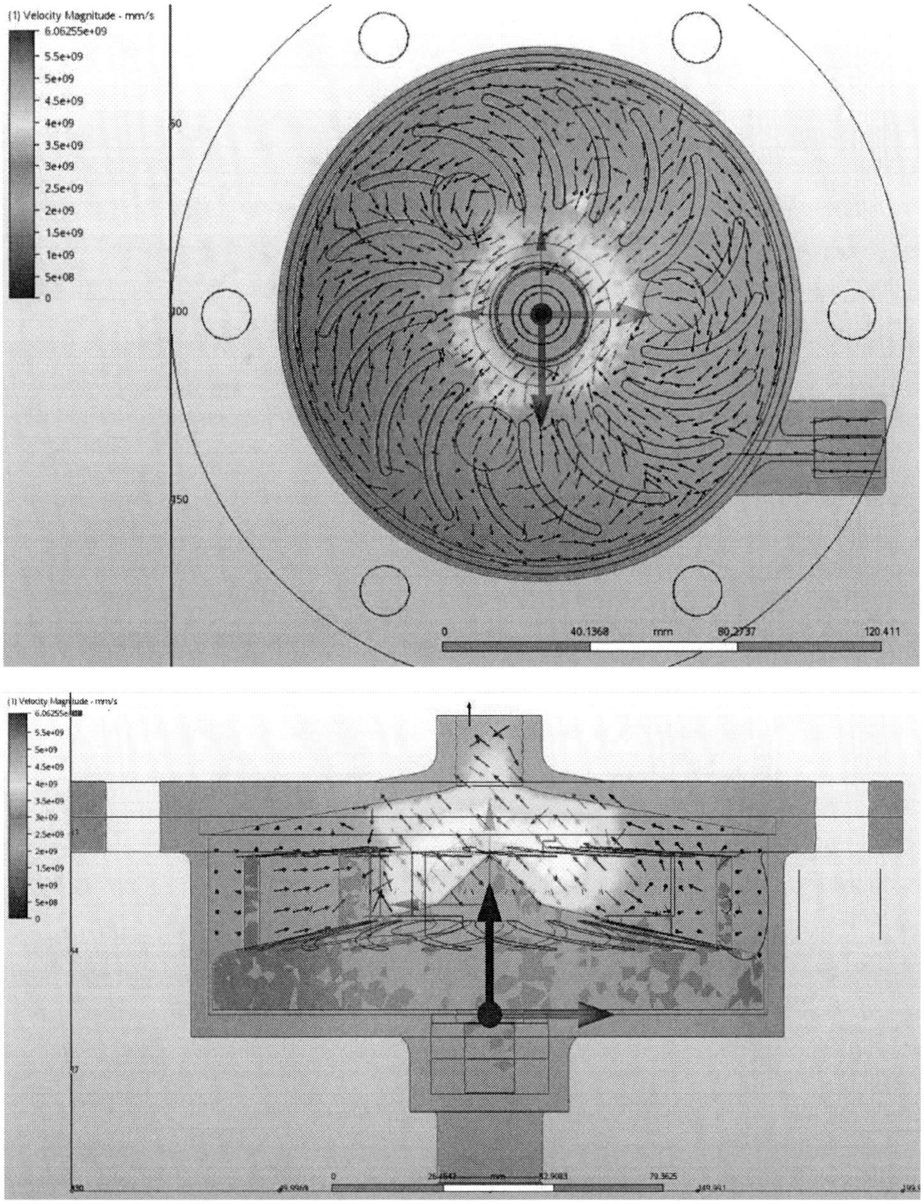

Fig. 16. CFD simulation results—Inlet (top) and outlet (bottom) working fluid velocity.

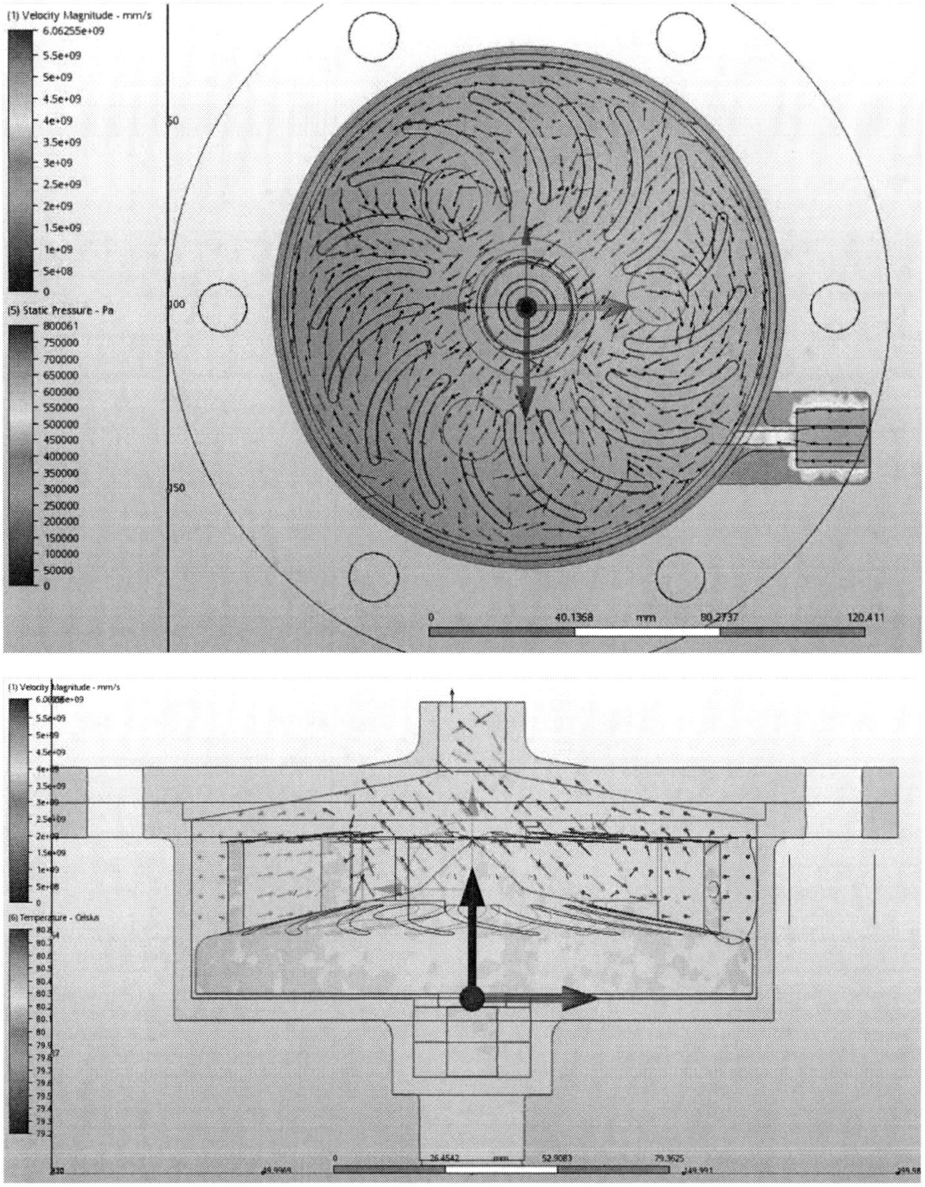

Fig. 18. CFD simulation results—Inlet (top) & outlet (bottom) working fluid temperature.

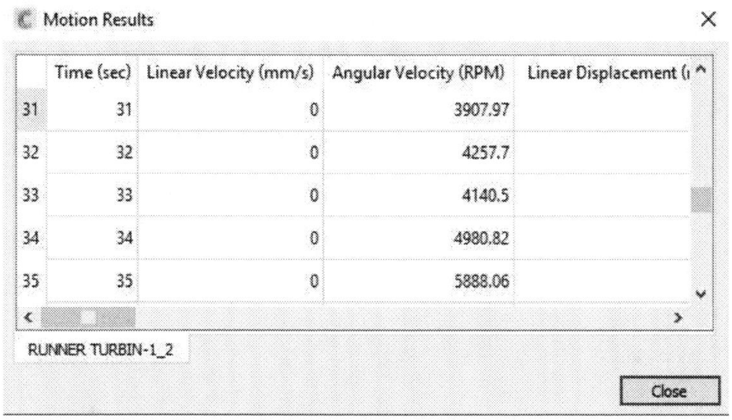

	Time (sec)	Linear Velocity (mm/s)	Angular Velocity (RPM)	Linear Displacement ((
31	31	0	3907.97	
32	32	0	4257.7	
33	33	0	4140.5	
34	34	0	4980.82	
35	35	0	5888.06	

Fig. 19. CFD simulation results—Turbine runner rotation.

(i). Turbine power.

It can be seen the amount of Turbine Power as follows:

$$P_T = T\,2\,\pi\,n\,/\,60 = (0.61) \times 2 \times (3.14) \times (5{,}888)\,/\,60 = 376 \text{ W} \quad (3)$$

(ii). Electrical power.

Once turbine power is known, electrical power can be calculated using the Equations as follows:

$$P_L = P_T\,\eta_g = 376 \times 0.82 = 308.32 \text{ W} \quad (4)$$

So the amount of turbine power is 376 W and the amount of electrical power is 308.32 W.

4 Conclusion

From the calculation using mathematical modeling, it can be seen that when the fluid pressure is constant at 0.8 MPa and the inlet nozzle dimension varies, the magnitude of the turbine rotation speed, turbine rotation, turbine torque, turbine power and electrical power will be getting bigger as the inlet nozzle dimension. From the simulation result using FEA (Finite Element Analysis), it can be seen that housing and housing cover design for ORC turbine, safe and feasible to make. From the simulation results using CFD (Computational Fluid Dynamics), it can be seen that the turbine runner design for ORC turbine, at inlet working fluid pressure of 0.8 MPa and 4 mm inlet nozzle dimension, produces a good working fluid flow distribution and turbine rotation, and is estimated to produce electrical power approximately 308.32 W.

References

1. L. Aditya, T.M.I. Mahlia, B. Rismanchi, H.M. Ng, M.H. Hasan, H.S.C. Metselaar, et al. Renew. Sust. Energ. Rev., **73**(2017):1352–1365 (2017). https://www.sciencedirect.com/science/article/pii/S1364032117302484
2. M. Amin, N. Putra, E.A. Kosasih, E. Prawiro, R.A. Luanto, T.M.I. Mahlia. Appl. Therm. Eng., **112**(2017):273–280 (2017). https://www.sciencedirect.com/science/article/pii/S1359431116323845
3. T.M.I. Mahlia, J.Y. Lim, L. Aditya, T.M.I. Riayatsyah, A.E. Pg Abas, Nasruddin. *Methodology for implementing power plant efficiency standards for power generation: potential emission reduction.* Clean Tech n Environ Policy. Berlin: Springer (2017). pp. 1–19. https://link.springer.com/article/10.1007/s10098-017-1473-3
4. M. Hanif, T.M.I. Mahlia, H.B. Aditiya, M.S.A. Bakar. Biofuel Research Journal, **4**(1):537–544 (2017). https://www.biofueljournal.com/article_43430.html
5. N. Hossain, J.H. Zaini, T.M.I. Mahlia. International Journal of Technology, **8**(1):5–18 (2017). http://www.ijtech.eng.ui.ac.id/old/index.php/journal/article/view/3948
6. Nasruddin, M.I. Alhamid, Y. Daud, A. Surachman, A. Sugiyono, H.B. Aditya, et al. Renew. Sust. Energ. Rev., **53**(2016):733–740 (2016). https://www.sciencedirect.com/science/article/pii/S1364032115010023
7. A.S. Silitonga, H.H. Masjuki, H.C. Ong, T. Yusaf, F. Kusumo, T.M.I. Mahlia. Industrial Crops and Products. **85**(2016):274–286 (2016). https://www.cabdirect.org/cabdirect/abstract/20163129770

8. T.M.I. Mahlia. Renewable Energy. **27**(2):293–300 (2002). https://www.sciencedirect.com/science/article/pii/S096014810100177X
9. T.M.I. Mahlia. Energy Conversion and Management. **44**(5):723–730 (2003). https://www.sciencedirect.com/science/article/pii/S0196890402000857
10. T.M.I. Mahlia, M.Z. Abdulmuin, T.M.I. Alamsyah, D. Mukhlishien. Renewable Energy. **28**(8):1235–1256 (2003). https://www.sciencedirect.com/science/article/pii/S0960148102002185
11. H.H. Masjuki, T.M.I. Mahlia, I.A. Choudhury, R. Saidur. Energy Conversion and Management. **43**(6):763–770 (2002). https://www.sciencedirect.com/science/article/pii/S0196890401000747
12. P. Prasetyo. *Studi penentuan geometri turbin radial aliran masuk pada siklus rankine organik dengan fluida kerja R134a*. [Determination study of radial turbine inlet flow geometry in organic rankine cycle with R134a working fluid]. [Undergraduate Thesis]. Fakultas Teknik Mesin dan Dirgantara. Institut Teknologi Bandung (2015). [in Bahasa Indonesia]. https://slides.tips/studi-penentuan-geometri-turbin-radial-aliran-masuk-pada-siklus-rankine-organik.html#
13. E. Bellos, C. Tzivanidis. Energy Convers. Manag. **156**:427–439 (2018). https://www.sciencedirect.com/science/article/pii/S019689041731110X
14. O. Dumont, R. Dickes, M. De Rosa, R. Douglas, V. Lemort. Energy Convers. Manag. **157**:294–306 (2018). https://www.sciencedirect.com/science/article/pii/S0196890417311731
15. A. Sadreddini, M. Fani, M. Ashjari Aghdam, A. Mohammadi. Energy Convers. Manag. **157**:111–122 (2018). https://www.sciencedirect.com/science/article/pii/S019689041731107X
16. E. Saloux, M. Sorin, H. Nesreddine, A. Teyssedou. Appl. Therm. Eng. **129**:628-635 (2018). https://www.sciencedirect.com/science/article/pii/S135943111734591X
17. D. Vera, F. Jurado, J. Carpio, S. Kamel. Energy. **144**:41–53 (2018). https://www.sciencedirect.com/science/article/pii/S0360544217320108
18. M. Yari, L. Ariyanfar, E.A. Aghdam. Renewable Energy. **119**:262–281 (2018). https://www.sciencedirect.com/science/article/pii/S096014811731217X
19. M. Arifin. *Penentuan geometri rotor dan analisis parameter kinerja turbo-expander radial untuk sistem siklus rankine organik*. [Determination of rotor geometry and performance parameters analysis of radial turbo-expander for organic rankine cycle system]. [Thesis]. Program Studi Teknik Mesin, Institut Teknologi Bandung (2014). [in Bahasa Indonesia]. https://www.researchgate.net/profile/Maulana_Arifin/publication/272623129_Determination_Rotor_Geometry_And_Analysis_Performance_Parameters_Of_Turbo-Expander_Radial_For_Organic_Rankine_Cycle_System/links/54f68d470cf21d8b8a5cc6d7/Determination-Rotor-Geometry-And-Analysis-Performance-Parameters-Of-Turbo-Expander-Radial-For-Organic-Rankine-Cycle-System.pdf
20. A.D. Yunus. *Mesin konversi energi*. [Machine of energy conversion]. Jakarta: Darma Persada University (2012). [in Bahasa Indonesia]. http://ft.unsada.ac.id/wp-content/uploads/2012/06/bab_1-2_mke.pdf
21. A.N. Firdaus. *Variasi laju pendinginan cooling tower terhadap sistem ORC (organic rankine cycle) dengan fluida kerja R-123*. [Cooling rate variation of cooling tower on ORC (organic rankine cycle) system with R-123 working fluid]. [thesis]. Fakultas Teknik Industri. Institut Teknologi Sepuluh Nopember (2014). [in Bahasa Indonesia]. http://docplayer.info/43753875-Studi-variasi-laju-pendinginan-cooling-tower-terhadap-sistem-orc-organic-rankine-cycle-dengan-fluida-kerja-r-123.html
22. S. Quoilin, V. Lemort. *The organic rankine cycle: Thermodynamics application and optimization*. UNESCO: Encyclopedia of Life Support System (2014). pp. 1–12. https://www.eolss.net/sample-chapters/C05/E6-35-43-00.pdf
23. L.D. Lio, G. Manente, A. Lazzaretto. Applied Energy. **205**:187–209 (2017). https://www.sciencedirect.com/science/article/pii/S0306261917309959
24. L. Guillaume, A. Legros, A. Desideri, V. Lemort. Applied Energy. **186**(3):408–422 (2017). https://www.sciencedirect.com/science/article/pii/S0306261916303233
25. Z. Han, W. Fan, R. Zhao. Energy Conversion and Management. **150**:259–268 (2017). https://www.sciencedirect.com/science/article/pii/S0196890417307379
26. J. Song, C.W. Gu, X. Ren. Energy Convers. Manag. **123**:308–316 (2016). https://www.sciencedirect.com/science/article/pii/S019689041630512X
27. Z. Wang, L. Yin. Dongli Gongcheng Xuebao/Journal of Chinese Society of Power Engineering. **37**(5):367–372 (2017). https://www.researchgate.net/publication/320144727_Effects_of_Impeller_Twisting_Law_on_Performance_of_the_ORC_Radial_Inflow_Turbine
28. Z. Wang, L. Yin, Y. Liu, Q. Jiao, H. Qu. Dongli Gongcheng Xuebao/Journal of Chinese Society of Power Engineering. **37**(10):801–807 (2017). https://www.researchgate.net/publication/321888652_Analysis_on_Structure_and_Loss_of_Secondary_Flow_in_Stator_Cascades_of_an_ORC_Radial_Inflow_Turbine

The Role of Tangible Interfaces in Enhancing Children's Engagement in Learning

Hestiasari Rante[1,2*], *Michael* Lund[2], and *Doris* Caliz[3]

[1]Department of Computer Science, University of Bremen, Bibliothekstraße 1, 28359 Bremen, Germany
[2]Department of Creative Multimedia, Electronics Engineering Polytechnic Institute of Surabaya, Jl. Raya ITS-Sukolilo, Surabaya 60111, Indonesia
[3]Department of Pervasive Computing Systems, Karlsruhe Institute of Technology, Vincenz-Prießnitz-Straße 1, 76131 Karlsruhe, Germany

Abstract. This paper presents the results of an exploratory study in which the authors investigated the impact of tangible interface used by children at the elementary school level. Exploration of the viability of graphics tablet and the pen tool was conducted by investigating the children's ease in acclimating to the technology and the effectiveness in engaging them to complete some tasks. Several children were invited to a workshop where they learned and played BatiKids, a game-based learning developed to support children in learning the process of making Indonesian hand-written batik. The qualitative analysis based on the notes and video recording taken on the field observational, and the responses to interview questions to the participants. The results show the main findings and discuss the design implications for a tangible interface in the context of BatiKids.

Keywords: BatiKids, children, tangible interface, user interface

1 Introduction

Xie et al. [1] mentioned that tangible interfaces and tangible interaction are terms that nowadays progressively increasing within the Human-Computer Interaction community [2]. The last decade has shown a wave of new research concerned with the coupling of the physical and digital worlds [1]. Marshall [3] stated that tangible interfaces are reflecting a greater emphasis on the role of the physical body and environment in embodied interaction [2, 4, 5]. Many different research projects have studied enabling technologies, usability aspects and various applications of tangible user interfaces [2, 6, 7].

The authors' interest in repurposing a device such as a graphic and pen tablet for media control stems from the authors' dissatisfaction when children using the mouse, either with cable or wireless, in completing the tasks on BatiKids. BatiKids is a game-based learning designed to support children in learning the process of making Indonesian hand-written batik [8–10]. The hand-written batik is a traditional way of producing batik using canting, a tool like a pen that holds a small reservoir of hot wax applied on a fabric [11].

* Corresponding author: rante@uni-bremen.de, hestiasari@pens.ac.id

BatiKids has two levels. In the Level 1, children have to do some tasks including selecting a batik pattern, drawing the pattern following dots, then coloring the pattern by choosing one color or they can also mix two or three different colors, and the last is multiplying the pattern. Level 2 has the same structure as Level 1 with additional features such as resizing, rotating, and flipping the pattern [8, 9]. Initially, a mouse was used as the media to control and to complete all the tasks. After some trials, it was noticed that children had difficulty using the mouse particularly when it came to the phase of drawing. In addition, it was also noted that they lost the enjoyment that supposed to be gained when playing BatiKids.

For the above reasons, a decision was made to use a graphics and pen tablet as a media control to replace the mouse. In the next sections, there is a justification that the graphic and pen tablet is not only useful to facilitate children in drawing, but it also enhances children's engagement in learning the process of making batik as if they were using the real canting.

2 Tangible interfaces for Learning

Can tangible interface enhance children's engagement in learning?

Xu [12] argued that historically children have played with physical objects to learn various skills. Therefore, a tangible interface would appear as a 'natural' form to them. She gave an example of the museum project 'Everyday Technology' launched by the University of Limerick museum projects [13], where paper, books, and other physical displays have been augmented digitally. In one spot they provided an antique desk with a projection on the book. As the user turns the page to reveal the marker they will see an image overlaid onto the page of the book. The exhibitions like this create a unique museum visiting environment. It may appear to children as 'magical', interesting, and unforgettable experience [12].

There are a number of reasons why using tangible interfaces may be of particular benefit for learning [3]. Both theoretical and exploratory work on tangible interfaces has suggested that they could be particularly suitable for engaging children in playful learning [e.g. 14]. Furthermore, Marshall [3] described that novel links between physical activity and digital effects might lead to increased engagement and reflection in learning [15]. As interaction with tangible interfaces is assumed to be more natural or familiar than with other types of interface [4, 16], they might be more accessible to young children, to people with learning disabilities, and to novices [17], they lowering the threshold of participation [2].

Xu [12] even explained the benefits in more detailed. Tangible interfaces can benefit children's learning from many ways. The interface requires little time to learn how to use it as if it is a natural interface which requires little cognitive effort to learn. Therefore, children can concentrate more on the task rather than how to use the computer or software. The tangible interface can offer a variety of interactions; it allows user to solve problems with concrete physical objects and physical activity when they fail using more abstract representations and complex syntax. Therefore, the interface can empower children with the control of the computing environment; they will feel and 'own' the environment and will be actively engaged and not lose their interest easily. The tangible interface supports trial-and-error activity as it gives a continuous presentation of the object of interest. It uses rapid incremental and reversible actions whose impact on the object of interest is immediately visible. Another advantage of using a tangible is that it is no longer restricted to a single user, children can sit down and collaborate with their friends face to face in an entirely natural way. It can provide children with a social experience. Also, research shows that children are more productive when they cooperate. Therefore, compared to a single child a group of children may be able to do a task more efficiently and benefit more from the experience. Furthermore, the benefits of tangible interfaces in learning have been already well demonstrated by many researchers [14, 18, 19].

In addition, from psychologist and educationist point of view [20], tangibles are beneficial for learning because the following reasons; i) physical activity is important in learning; ii) concrete objects are important in learning; iii) physical materials give rise to mental images which can then guide and constrain future problem-solving in the absence of the physical materials; iv) learners can abstract symbolic relations from a variety of concrete instances; and v) physical objects that are familiar are more easily understood by children than more symbolic entities [12].

2.1 Graphic and pen tablet

Felton [21] defined that a graphics tablet–also called drawing tablet or digitizer–is an input device with the pen tool or stylus used primarily by digital artists, although many non-artists use it as well. These graphics tablets have a hard plastic, touch-sensitive drawing surface that delivers pen stylus, whose function as a mouse, movements to a monitor or screen. The position of the stylus is correlated directly to the cursor position of on the screen. For some people, it takes a while to get used to drawing on the tablet surface, but once the learning curve is overcome, it will be as natural as using a pen or pencil on paper.

After the authors found out that children had difficulty in doing a particular task on BatiKids using a mouse, it was then decided to replace the mouse with a graphic and pen tablet. In particular, Intuos Creative Pen Tablet from Wacom was chosen. The tablet surface is designed super slim and compact, but it is still as durable and powerful as ever. Whilst the pen tool is designed ergonomic and lightweight, make it sit comfortably in hand, allowing user to experience both precision and control (https://www.wacom.com/en-us/products/pen-tablets/wacom-intuos#Features). These features make this selected graphics and pen tablet ideal for children.

2.2 Pen tablet as canting

Canting is one of the main tool required to produce batik. Holding canting filled with hot melted wax and moving it carefully to make a pattern on the white fabric is not easy. It is not only about the skill, but also considerable patience and concentration to fully control the flow of the wax in the canting.

Using a graphics tablet and the stylus while learning and playing on BatiKids is a way to translate the physical batik processing and the environments into digital space. The pen tool will teach user's hand movements in relation to the use of canting in the real process. By using the tool, children will get the sense of moving canting on fabric [10]. This function justified the benefit of using a stylus instead of a mouse, in the context of BatiKids.

3 Workshop

As the main part of the research, a two-day workshop was conducted in an elementary school, International School of Bremen. Eight international students from the different country and diverse cultural background were involved in the workshop. Their ages range from 10 yr old to 11 yr old. The objective of the workshop was to examine children's ease in acclimating to the technology of graphic and pen tablet and the effectiveness in engaging them to complete several tasks provided on BatiKids.

A set of pre-test and post-test questionnaires were prepared, also a camera and video camera as well to record the whole activity. When doing the interviews in the workshop, it is very important to watch and listen to children carefully in order to collect relevant data of their difficulties and successes along the test. Recording the children while interacting with the system is also very relevant because recordings can be useful for perceiving events and behaviours not noticed during the test. From the video recordings, it could be identified which of the tasks children had more difficulties with, and how well they successfully completed them. This observation helped the authors to think of alternative designs that better supported the application's workflow [22].

Before started the workshop, the authors carefully set up and planned the environment so that children would feel comfortable when performing the test. A computer and the graphics and pen tablet were placed on the desk that children used every day in the class. The authors also prepared a scenario for running the tests and divided the workshop into four phases: introduction, pre-test questionnaire, usability test, and post-test questionnaire. BatiKids stickers were brought into the workshop, to be given as complimentary for the participants.

In the introduction phase of the workshop, a close relationship with children was established in order to make them feel more comfortable. Introduction of the authors was necessary along with delivering an overview of the application, the tasks, and the learning objectives. As none of the children have ever used graphics and the pen tablet, it was essential to give them a brief information about the function.

BatiKids has four main learning objectives: i) to motivate children to learn the real process of making batik; ii) to understand the philosophy of the batik patterns; iii) to teach how to mix colors, and iv) to teach hand movements in relation to the use of canting in the real process. Due to the limited time, it was not possible to talk deeper to find out more about the children. If more time were available, the authors would have tried to engage children in evoking joyful memories in order to make them feel more comfortable [23].

Fig.1. A child using the graphic and pen tablet.

Figure 1 shows a child playing BatiKids using the graphic and pen tablet in the workshop. This set of interface enabled children to see what they draw directly on the screen. The graphics tablet with pen immediately provided handwritten input to the screen of the computer. Observation showed that, somehow, this interaction was not easy due to the separation between the eye reference and hand movements. Children had to move their hand on the tablet while keeping their eyes on the screen. Sometimes, they lose the sight of the cursor on the screen and consequently had to try harder to coordinate their movements with the pen [10]. But the more they moved pen tablet, the more they got used to it. Some interesting comments from the participants were noted.

"Oh, this is the first time I use this kind of tool ..."
"It's not easy using this pen ..."
"Interesting pen, I like it even it's sometimes not easy to drag it".
"In the beginning, it was hard ... But I'm getting used to it".

The last phase of the workshop was a post-test questionnaire. A list of questions delivered to each participant. In general, children were satisfied with BatiKids; they enjoyed it and got the benefits. They also agreed that the tangible interface used to complete the tasks was helpful. Figure 2 presents an author interviewed a child and helped him to answer the questions.

The issues, indeed, arose mainly came from the application BatiKids itself. Some instructions were unclear for children. Therefore, during the workshop, it is necessary that an author sat next to the children and assisted them when they encountered any issues.

Fig. 2. An interview with a child after the workshop.

Another thing that has to be taken into consideration is there was no information on what user has to do when they made a mistake and needed to recover their work. This matter happened particularly when it came to the task of colouring the pattern. Some children got into trouble and had to start from the beginning because they did not know how to remove the wrong colour and change it to the new one. In fact, they could simply choose the new colour and cover it on the wrong colour; it will automatically alter the colour to the new one. For this reason, it was considered that more information should be added to BatiKids, either as text narrative or voice-over.

"I made mistakes and I did not know how to fix it, so I clicked BACK button, but then I lose all the colours".
"I made two-times mistakes ..."
"Why there is no DELETE button here?"

4 Results

The result of eight children interacting with BatiKids through the graphics tablet with the pen is shown in Figure 3. The task of creating or drawing the pattern was the most difficult part for children in this group. Half of the children in this group had to spend more time to complete this task. Hand movements with pen on the tablet required patience and concentration from children.

When the children working with the pen on a graphics tablet, some of them had to struggle when moving the pen of tablet surface. It was clearly seen that many of them had to try several times to get the right point where the pen connected to the point on the screen.

This issue decreased the concentration and some of the children even lose their patient when facing this matter. This even looked worse to left-handed students. Since the graphics tablet was installed to be used with the right hand, then it became harder for the left-handed to move the pen.

However, by the end of the workshop, all children were conscious and got the point of the importance of canting in making hand-written Indonesian batik. Nevertheless, in order to allow a more tangible experience, the employment of the graphics tablet with the pen is essential, because it drives the children to perform similar hand movements as if they were using canting. Using tangible interfaces can also be more engaging and keep children interested in using the application [12].

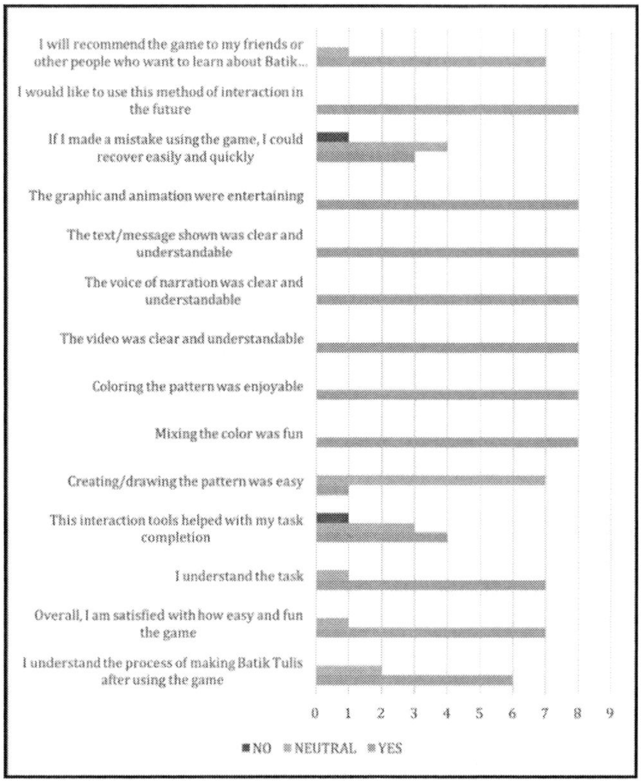

Fig. 3. Results of the interview after the workshop.

At the end of this section, some drawing results designed by the participants at the workshop is attached. Their drawing is shown in Figure 4.

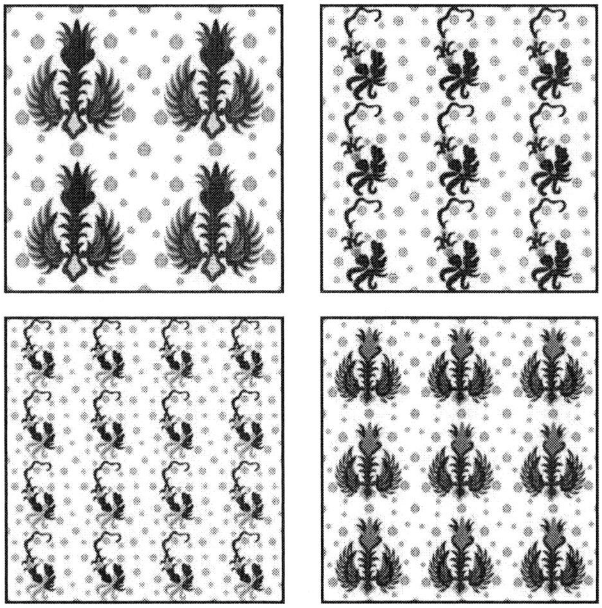

Fig. 4. Drawing results of the workshop.

5 Summary

As mentioned in the Results section, one of the problems with the graphics tablet with the pen is the dissociation between the movements performed with the pen and the generated images as a result of this movement. The visuals are displayed on an ordinary monitor far from the pen. The authors believe that better results can be achieved with the use of smart tablets that allow drawings to be created through direct contact of a stylus against a screen. The child, therefore, would be able to see the drawings as a result of the path through which the pen touches the monitor. In this way, the canting process can be represented with a higher degree of likeliness [10].

Likeliness between action and representation is an important factor especially for children in the phase of concrete operations, as they would experience the application with a better understanding of the overall batik process, which is mainly manual. The application would neither be oversimplified by touch user interfaces nor too confusing because of dissociation generated by pen tablets [10].

From the experiments with BatiKids, it is summarized that tangible interface is a natural interface, due to its role that gives user the chance to be more explorative and expressive. The pen tablet used to complete the tasks has successfully given the children the sense of using canting as if they were making batik in the real process. The results of the workshop lead us to further improvement on BatiKids.

In general, Xu [12] also concluded that the tangible interface supports a better collaborative work compared to others. The tangible interface even has greater potential, if there is enough technology support. In many ways, the tangible interface can be beneficial to children in learning.

Research in a relatively new area raises more questions than it answers, and this work is no exception. For further works in the field of Computer Science, there is a multitude of applications in the general area of Ubiquitous Computing and Tangible User Interface to be discovered [12].

References

1. L. Xie, A.N. Antle, N. Motamedi. *Are tangibles more fun? Comparing children's enjoyment and engagement using physical, graphical and tangible user interfaces*. Proceedings of the Second International Conference on Tangible and Embedded Interaction (TEI'08) (Bonn, Germany, 2008). Tangible and Embedded Interaction:191–198. http://citeseerx.ist.psu.edu/viewdoc/download?doi=10.1.1.518.5338&rep=rep1&type=pdf.
2. E. Hornecker, J. Buur. *Getting a grip on tangible interaction: A framework on physical space and social interaction*. Proceedings of CHI 2006 (Montreal, Canada, 2006). Proceedings of CHI 2006:437–446. (2006). http://citeseerx.ist.psu.edu/viewdoc/download?doi=10.1.1.122.9553&rep=rep1&type=pdf.
3. P. Marshall. *Do tangible interfaces enhance learning?* Proceedings of the First International Conference on Tangible and Embedded Interaction TEI'07 (Baton Rouge, USA, 2007). Tangible and Embedded Interaction:163–170. https://dl.acm.org/citation.cfm?id=1227004
4. P. Dourish. *Where the action is: The foundations of embodied interaction*. USA: MIT Press, 50–53 (2001). https://mitpress.mit.edu/books/where-action
5. S.R. Klemmer, B. Hartmann, L. Takayama. *How bodies matter: Five themes for interaction design*. Proceedings of the Sixth Conference on Designing Interactive Systems (DIS '06) (University Park, USA, 2006). Proceedings of the Sixth Conference on Designing Interactive Systems (DIS'06):140–149. (2006). https://dl.acm.org/citation.cfm?id=1142429
6. L. Holmquist, A. Schmidt, and B. Ullmer. Personal and Ubiquitous Computing, **8**, 5:291–293 (2004). https://dl.acm.org/citation.cfm?id=1023814
7. Y. Rogers and H. Muller. Journal of Human Computer Studies, **64**, 1:1–14 (2006) https://www.sciencedirect.com/science/article/pii/S1071581905001126
8. H. Rante, H. Schelhowe, M. Lund. International Journal of Information and Education Technology, **6**, 7:580–583 (2016). http://www.ijiet.org/vol6/755-T061.pdf.
9. H. Rante, H. Schelhowe, M. Lund. *Paper prototyping for BatiKids: A technique to examine children's interaction and feedback in designing a game-based learning*. Proceedings of Second International Conference on Electrical Systems, Technology and Information 2015 (ICESTI 2015). F. Pasila, Y. Tanoto, R. Lim, M. Santoso, N. Pah (Eds). Singapore: Springer (2016). pp. 447–455. https://link.springer.com/chapter/10.1007/978-981-287-988-2_49
10. H. Rante, L. de Araújo, H. Schelhowe. International Journal of Educational and Pedagogical Sciences, **10**, 10:3500–3504 (2016). https://waset.org/publications/10005779/usability-testing-with-children-batikids-case-study.
11. H. Rante, M. Lund, and H. Schelhowe. International Journal of Multidisciplinary Education and Research–IJMER, **1**, 2:50–54 (2014). https://www.researchgate.net/publication/283349024_A_Digital_Batik_Tool_Supporting_children_in_understanding_and_constructing_traditional_batik_patterns_within_a_museum_context
12. D. Xu. Tangible user interface for children – An overview [Online] from http://www.chici.org/references/tangible_user_interface.pdf. (2005). [Accessed on 15 March 2018]
13. K. Ferris, L. Bannon, L. Ciolfi, P. Gallagher, T. Hall, M. Lenno. *Shaping experiences in the Hunt Museum: A design case study*. Proceedings of the Fifth Conference on

Designing Interactive Systems (DIS'04) (Cambridge, USA, 2004). Proceedings of the Fifth Conference on Designing Interactive Systems (DIS'04):205–214 (2004). https://dl.acm.org/citation.cfm?id=1013115.1013144&coll=DL&dl=ACM
14. S. Price, Y. Rogers, M. Scaife, D. Stanton, H. Neale. Interacting with Computers, **15**, 2:169–185 (2003). https://www.sciencedirect.com/science/article/pii/S0953543803000067
15. Y. Rogers, M. Scaife, S. Gabrielli, H. Smith, E. Harris. Presence: Teleoperators & Virtual Environments, **11**, 6:677–686 (2002). http://ieeexplore.ieee.org/document/6791104/
16. R.J.K. Jacob, H. Ishii, G. Pangaro, J. Patten. *A tangible interface for organizing information using a grid*. Proceedings of the SIGCHI Conference on Human Factors in Computing Systems (CHI'02) (Minneapolis, USA, 2002). Proceedings of the SIGCHI Conference on Human Factors in Computing Systems (CHI'02):339–346 (2002). https://dl.acm.org/citation.cfm?id=503437
17. O. Zuckerman, S. Arida, M. Resnick. *Extending tangible interfaces for education: Digital Montessori inspired manipulatives*. Proceedings of the SIGCHI Conference on Human Factors in Computing Systems (CHI'05) (Portland, USA, 2005). Proceedings of the SIGCHI Conference on Human Factors in Computing Systems (CHI'05):859–868. (2005). https://dl.acm.org/citation.cfm?id=1055093
18. N. Ditter. TechSportiv: Constructing objects-to-think-with for physical education. Proceedings of the 8th Nordic Conference on Human-Computer Interaction: Fun, Fast, Foundational (NordiCHI '14) (Helsinki, Finland, 2014). Proceedings of the 8th Nordic Conference on Human-Computer Interaction: Fun, Fast, Foundational (NordiCHI '14): 569–577 (2014). https://dl.acm.org/citation.cfm?id=2639202&dl=ACM&coll=DL
19. K. Lee, D. Jeong, R.C. Schindler, E.J. Short. Computers in Human Behaviour, **65**:163–175 (2016). https://www.sciencedirect.com/science/article/pii/S0747563216305878
20. C. O'Malley, D.S. Fraser. Literature review in learning with tangible technologies [Online] from https://www.nfer.ac.uk/publications/FUTL69 (2004). [Accessed on 15 March 2018]
21. J. Felton. Do you need a graphics tablet? Find out what you need to know [Online] from https://design.tutsplus.com/articles/do-you-need-a-graphics-tablet-find-out-what-you-need-to-know--vector-13586 (2013). [Accessed on 16 March 2018]
22. J. Rubin, D. Chisnell. *Handbook of usability testing: How to plan, design and conduct effective tests*. 2nd edition. USA: Wiley Publishing, Inc. (2008). pp. 54–57 https://www.amazon.com/Handbook-Usability-Testing-Conduct-Effective/dp/0470185481
23. L. Hanna, K. Risden, and K. Alexander. Guidelines for usability testing with children: Methods & Tools [Online] from https://www.microsoft.com/usability/UEPostings/p9-hanna.pdf. (1997). [Accessed on 16 March 2018]

Uniform and Non-Uniform Image Enlargement Based on the Window Kernel

I Komang Somawirata*, *Bambang* Prio Hartono, *Teguh* Herbasuki, and *Aryuato* Soetedjo

Electrical Engineering, Faculty of Industrial Technology, National Institute of Technology (ITN Malang), Karanglo km 2, Malang 65145 Indonesia.

Abstract. Several different of image resizing methods have been proposed. However, resizing image in different ratio produces non proportional feature image enlarged and the enlarged image in different ratio with retaining the salient content is limited. This paper proposes an image enlargement method with edge improvement and inpainting method. This method consists of two steps. First, the image enlargement method is used for enlarging an image to the minimum size of the target image. Second, image inpainting method is used for obtaining the full-size image. We have evaluated the proposed method for enlarging an image uniformly and it compares with the typical of image enlargement methods. The uniform image enlarged and image enlarged in different ratio using the proposed method have been presented.

Key words: Image enlargement, inpainting, window kernel

1 Introduction

Image enlargement is changing small size image to bigger size. Image enlargement can be done in two ways. There are using hardware or optical zoom-in and software or digital zoom-in. Image enlargement using hardware is a lot more expensive than using software. Image enlargement has been applied to numerous fields such as medical photo results, photo satellite, digital TV, digital camera etc. Currently, many sizes and ratios of display have been presented. The ratios of display size are ranging from 3:2, 4:3, 5:4, 16:9, 16:10, 17:9 and 21:9 respectively for the width and height. So that, the image enlargement method for enlarging images in uniform and non-uniform is needed.

There are several methods that have been developed to refine the performance of classic methods such as, image enlargement methods in [1–5]. The method [1] proposed image enlargement using weighing method known as WLE method. This interpolation method explains interpolation in three different conditions: interpolation between two horizontal pixels, interpolation between two vertical pixels, and interpolation among four pixels. WLE method does not provide good result especially in enlarging images whose scale factor is bigger than two. However, WLE method can be easily computed so it is very convenient to apply to hardware. The image enlargement method using edge-direction has been proposed in [2, 3]. The recovery of sharp edges on high-resolution (HR) image using reverse diffusion interpolation (RDI) [2] is capable for reducing blurred edge image. The blur edges

* Corresponding author: kmgsomawirata@lecturer.itn.ac.id

image is caused by low frequency. It could happen during the application of low-pass-filter during the data-acquisition process. RDI uses nine pixels-samples with 3×3 windows. Elements of matrix 3×3 windows are ordered using rank-order-statistic. Partial differential equation is used to obtain the value of the highest gradient direction to produce the reverse diffusion process. RDI method is no filtering in homogeneous regions, and no extra parameter is needed to characterize an edge. The image enlargement based on regularity on the geometric is presented by [3]. This method is called by new edge-directed interpolation (NEDI). NEDI method uses covariance-based adaptive interpolation especially in edge and pixels near of edge. They use bilinear interpolation for non-edge pixels. So that, the scale factor for NEDI method is only for even value. The method [4] proposes a frequency domain method which based on low frequency aliasing-free part. This method is called by frequency domain approach (FDA). FDA uses bicubic interpolation for image reconstruction. The low-frequency aliasing-free part of the image is used to estimate planar rotation and translation parameters. Image enlargement based on windows kernel by applying the pyramid method has been done in [5]. This method is called with PWK. The PWK method is also easy to be implemented on image retargeting. Target image size is not only in the same ratio, but also in the different ratio can be handled. In addition, PWK can be implemented in the variety of shapes and sizes of the target image. However, the methods [1–5] are only good for uniform enlarging. When the scaling factor for high and width are different, then non proportional salient features are obtained.

Recently, many researchers especially down-scale on image retargeting start to focus on dealing the visual salience, while suppressing non-salient regions [6]. Seam carving method [7] is a novel content-aware resizing scheme. This method uses gradient magnitude for measuring the image importance. However, the visual distortions often occur when it is used to up-scale image.

Fig. 1. The combination of image enlargement and inpainting methods. (a) Source image size. (b) Source image is enlarged to the minimum size of target image. (c) Full size image is obtained by inpainting method.

Currently, many researcher adopt the seam carving method for image scaling which retains the salient features of the image. The method [8] improves the warping-based image retargeting by adding the line constraints after applying original retargeting process. Image enlargement which is only based on seam carving that results the same size of the salient feature with the salient feature in the source image. So that, the combination of seam carving with image enlargement method [9] has resulted proportional salient feature image enlarged. This method requires iterations until the target size image is obtained. The method [9] is improved by [10], which is without iteration process. However, the energy gradient is not optimal for guiding the slicing process. The energy gradient is improved by salient feature energy which is adopted from [11]. The method [12] uses salient feature energy for guiding the slicing process. So, the slicing process is optimal for selecting the non-salient feature.

Image enlargement based on seam carving and slicing fail for enlarging an image, if the salient feature in an image is connecting from left to right sides of image. To overcome the limitation of existing methods, we propose the image retargeting especially for image enlarging based on the uniform image enlargement and image in painting methods. The image upscaling method uses the image enlargement method based on window kernel with edge improvement.

2 Proposed method

Our method is a combination between image enlargement and image inpainting methods. The image enlargement method is based on window kernel method with edge improvement, and inpainting method is also using window kernel method. Detailed explanation about these methods will be explained in the following subsection.

2.1 Image enlargement based on window kernel and edge improvement

The source image or low-resolution (LR) image is symbolized by **I** with the size $N \times M$ (N and M are height and width of LR image). The size of an image enlarged ($\hat{\mathbf{I}}$) is obtained by multiplying the size of the LR image (**I**) with scale factor (S). In this case, the image $\hat{\mathbf{I}}$ is still empty (no pixel), then we fill each coordinate in image $\hat{\mathbf{I}}$ by pixels which is calculated by Equation 1.

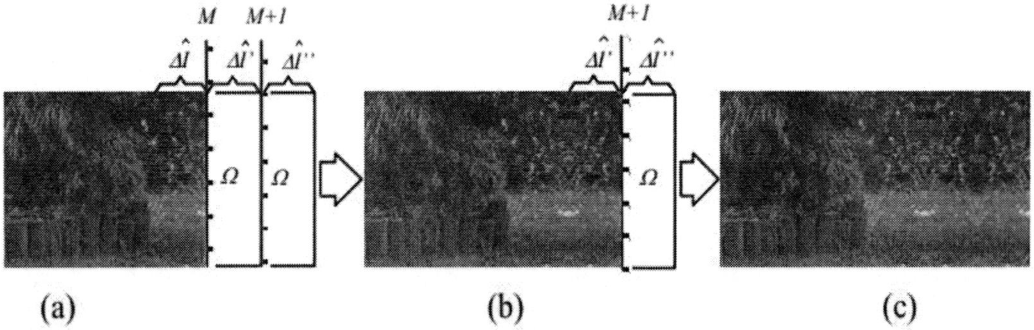

Fig. 2. Image enlarged based on inpainting with multi-mirroring method. (a) Source image that will be enlarged by multi-mirroring method (M and $M+1$). (b) The first mirroring has done. (c) The second mirroring has done

Equation 1 is adopted from bilinear interpolation formula. However, the weight window is not only in linear weighting, but also with weighting which is based on edge direction. An image $\hat{\mathbf{I}}$ is uniformly image enlarged with $\hat{N} \times \hat{M}$ ($\hat{N} = NS$ and $\hat{M} = MS$).

$$\hat{\mathbf{I}}_{\hat{x}\hat{y}} = \sum_{j=1}^{2}\sum_{i=1}^{2} W_{ij}^{P} W_{ij}^{W} \tag{1}$$

W_{ij}^{P} is the element of sample pixel window $\mathbf{W^P}$ and W_{ij}^{W} is the element of weight window $\mathbf{W^W}$. $\hat{I}_{\hat{x}\hat{y}}$ is element of HR image. $\hat{x}$ and $\hat{y}$ are height and width coordinates of HR image.

2.2 Image inpainting

As in Figure 1(b), inpainting method is used for completing the red areas in the left side (Ω^L) and right side (Ω^R) of target image. We use an inpainting method like a multi-mirroring process. The Ω^L and Ω^R are element of image $\hat{\mathbf{I}} \notin \hat{\Omega}$, where $\hat{\Omega}$ is blocking area in image $\hat{\mathbf{I}}$.

However, the $\hat{\Omega}$ can be manually or automatically selected. The mirroring process just as wide $\Delta\hat{\mathbf{I}}$, and it is continuing to repeat mirroring the $\Delta\hat{\mathbf{I}}$ until the full size of target image obtained. $\Delta\hat{\mathbf{I}}$ is the width size of mirroring process. If in the mirroring process contains a region of $\hat{\Omega}$, then we will change it with a pixel which is obtained from the close area of $\hat{\Omega}$.

The multi-mirroring method can also be implemented for inpainting an image as in the inpainting section on Figure 3. The multi-mirroring method is used for completing the big hole or blank area in the image.

2.3 Proportional salient feature image enlarged

Proportional salient features image enlargement is obtained, if only the scale factor for the height and width in the same value. While the salient features will not be proportional, if the scale factor for the height and width are not equal. To solve the problem of magnification image at the different ratio, we do it with two stages, such as illustrated in Figure 1. First, source image (Figure 1(a)) is enlarged uniformly to the smallest size of the target image as in Figure 1(b). Second, the inpainting method is applied to get the full size image as in Figure 1(c).

In this paper, we explain two solutions for obtaining an enlarged image in the different ratio. First, Enlarge an image in Figure 1(b) uses multi-mirroring method as illustrated in Figure 2. In this example, an image is mirrored to right side by two times $\Delta\hat{I}$. The first and second mirroring results are shown in Figure 2(b) and Figure 2(c), respectively. The second solution of image enlarged in different ratio uses a method that is illustrated in Figure 3. In this method, we separate the region of interest (ROI) in an image. For automatically ROI selected, we use saliency image detection that has been proposed in [11], and we symbolize the saliency image with $\mathbf{I}_s$. However, the saliency detection in $\mathbf{I}_s$ is not covering full region of ROI. So that, we are convolving (*) the $\mathbf{I}_s$ with a circular averaging filter ($\mathbf{H}_c$) with radius equal to ten as in Equation 2. By this solution, we can increase the region of ROI.

$$\hat{\mathbf{I}}_s = \mathbf{I}_s * \mathbf{H}_c \tag{2}$$

So that, the salient feature map ($\mathbf{F}_s$) is obtained by threshold (τ) the value of feature image $\hat{\mathbf{I}}_s$, as in Equation 3. We set the threshold value slightly bigger than zero.

$$\mathbf{F}_s = \begin{cases} 1 & \text{if } \hat{\mathbf{I}}_s > \tau \\ 0 & \text{others} \end{cases} \tag{3}$$

The salient feature map ($\mathbf{F}_s$) is a binary image with high-intensity values equal to 1 and low intensity value equal to 0, where 1 and 0 represent salient and a non salient feature of image as shown in Figs. 6(e) and (g). The ROI is separated by multiplying the salient feature map and image $\hat{\mathbf{I}}$, as in Equation 4, while the non-ROI is obtained by multiplying the complement of the salient feature map with image $\hat{\mathbf{I}}$, as in Equation 5.

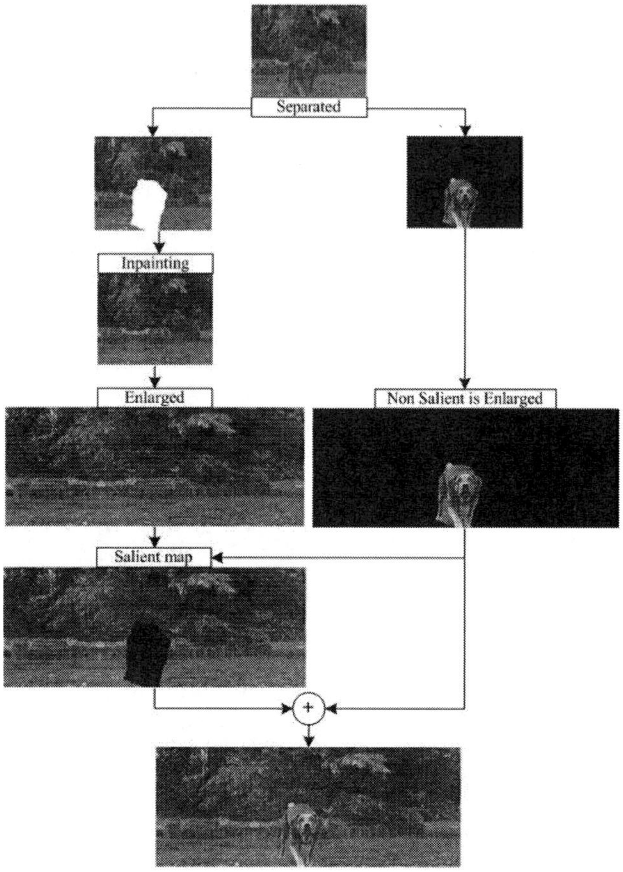

Fig. 3. Flow diagram of image enlargement in different ratio.

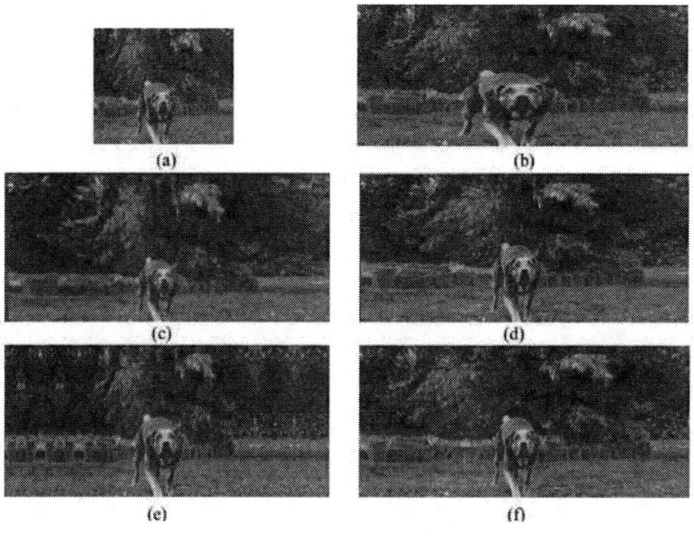

Fig. 4. Image enlargement in different ratio. (a) Source image. (b) The result of image enlargement based on window kernel and edge improvement. (c) The result of seam-carving method [7]. (d) The result of method [12]. (e) The result of multi-mirroring method. (f) Proposed method.

$$\mathbf{F}_{\mathbf{I}}^{\mathbf{s}} = \hat{\mathbf{I}} \times \mathbf{F}_{\mathbf{s}} \tag{4}$$

$$\mathbf{F}_{\mathbf{I}}^{\mathbf{n}} = \hat{\mathbf{I}} \times \overline{\mathbf{F}_{\mathbf{s}}} \tag{5}$$

where, $\mathbf{F}_{\mathbf{I}}^{\mathbf{s}}$ and $\mathbf{F}_{\mathbf{I}}^{\mathbf{n}}$ are ROI and non-ROI image respectively. Overline ($\bar{\ }$) is NOT operator.

As in Figure 3, an image without ROI (the blank region) is inpainted by using the multi-mirroring method. The blank area is filled with pixels based on multi mirroring process start from left to right and right to left, until all empty areas filled with pixels. After the blank area is filled with pixels, this image is enlarged to different ratio, and then it is continued to make the ROI map. Finally, the image enlarged with maintained ROI is obtained by summing two images, there are an enlarged image with ROI map and an image which only contains ROI, as shown in Figure 3.

3 Experimental result

In this experiment, the proposed method is tested for uniform and nonuniform image enlargement. For uniform image enlargement, we evaluate the image enlargement result using PSNR and we use seven samples image such as baboon, boat, buterfly, clown, lena, peppers and parrot. These image resize to smaller size using nearest-neighbor method. The sizes of images which would be enlarged were quarter of the standard image size. After that, we enlarge the small image size using all methods by the scale factor equal to four to become the standard image size. We use four comparison methods such as bi-linear interpolation (BLI), NEDI [3], RDI [2] and WLE [1].

Table 1 shows the image quality evaluation using PSNR by a scale factor equal to four. The PSNR values of proposed method show bigger than the comparison method. This means that our method is better than the comparison method.

For non-uniform image enlarged, Figure 4 shows the comparison results of five kind image enlargement method. Figure 4 (a) is source image that will be enlarged to different ratio, and the target ratio is 21:9.

Table 1 PSNR result of four times image enlarged.

Methods	Image samples						
	Baboon	Boat	Buterfly	Clown	Lena	Peppers	Parrot
BLI	18.42	21.90	16.81	19.53	23.66	25.66	21.32
NEDI [3]	17.54	19.57	15.12	16.90	20.73	21.96	19.00
RDI [2]	18.30	21.74	16.70	19.30	23.41	25.43	21.09
WLE [1]	18.4	22.25	16.72	19.67	24.41	26.66	21.58
Proposed Method	20.14	24.34	18.87	22.60	27.20	29.85	23.99

Figure 4(b) show the result of image enlarged using the image enlargement method based on window kernel and edge improvement. Figure 4(c) shows the image enlarged using a seam carving method that has been improved, Figure 4(d) the results of method [12], Figure 4(e) the results of multi-mirroring method and Figure 4(f) the result of the proposed method with a combination between "image enlargement method based on window kernel and edge improvement" and an image inpainting method based on multi-mirroring process.

Image enlargement in different ratio using scaling method produces non-proportional feature enlarged compared with their original image feature as in Figure 4(b). While, the seam carving method on Figure 4(c) produces the same size of the salient feature with the salient feature in the source image and it produces non-proportional feature enlarged, especially on the background of the image. Figure 4(d) shows a result of method [12]. In this result, only the slice region on left and right sides of ROI are enlarged to target image size. The image slicing direction is guided by feature energy of the image and the image slicing starts from top to bottom. So, the non ROI image is not uniformly enlarged to the wide size of the target image.

4 Conclusion

In this paper, we have proposed an image enlargement method for uniform and non-uniform image enlarging. The method is a combination between image enlargement method with edge direction based on the window kernel and image inpainting method. For uniform image enlarged, we only use image enlargement method with edge direction based on the window kernel, while for enlarging an image in different ratio (non-uniform enlarged), we combine it with image inpainting method, as in the following steps: first, the source image is enlarged to the minimum size of the target image. Second, the inpainting method is used for completing the empty areas. The proposed method has been tested for enlarging an image in uniform and non-uniform image enlarged. We have evaluated the uniform image enlarged result using PSR and The PSNR value of proposed method always bigger than the comparison method. The image enlarged in different ratio has been presented.

For the next research, we have plans to solve the problem of image enlargement, especially for different ratios. We will improve the inpainting method and salient feature detection.

References

1. T. Aso, N. Sutake, T. Yamakau. *A Fast and Accurate Image Enlargement Algorithm Employing a Weighted Sum of Linear Extrapolations*. Proceedings World Automation Congress 2004, (Seville, Spain, 2004). IEEE Automation Congress, Proceedings, **18**:251–258 (2004). http://ieeexplore.ieee.org/document/1441050/
2. O. Salvado, C.M. Hillenbrand, D.L Wilson. *Int J Biomed* Imaging, **2006** (2006). https://www.ncbi.nlm.nih.gov/pmc/articles/PMC2324046/
3. X. Li, M.P. Orchard. *IEEE Trans. on Image Processing*, **10**,10:1521–1527 (2001). http://ieeexplore.ieee.org/document/951537/
4. P. Vandewalle, S. Süsstrunk, M. Vetterli. *EURASIP J. Adv. Signal Process*, **2006** (2006). https://link.springer.com/article/10.1155/ASP/2006/71459
5. I.K. Somawirata, K. Uchimura, G. Koutaki. *IJICIC*, **9**, 12:4863–4873 (2013). http://www.ijicic.org/ijicic-12-12035.pdf.
6. W. Kim, C. Kim. *IEEE Signal Processing Letters*, **18**, 11:631–634 (2011). http://ieeexplore.ieee.org/document/5986690/?denied
7. S. Avidan, A. Shamir. *ACM Trans. Graph.*, **26**,3:267-276, (2007). http://citeseerx.ist.psu.edu/viewdoc/summary?doi=10.1.1.117.7257

8. S.F. Wang, S.H. Lai. Fast structure-preserving image retargeting, 2009 IEEE International Conference on Acoustics, Speech and Signal Processing, (Taipei, Taiwan, 2009). IEEE ICASSP:1049–1052 (2009). http://ieeexplore.ieee.org/document/4959767/
9. I.K. Somawirata, K. Uchimura, G. Koutaki. *Proportional image enlargement using combinations of scaling and carving method*, Internationl conference on Signal Image Technology and Internet based System (SITIS), (Kyoto, Japan, 2013). SITIS (2013). http://ieeexplore.ieee.org/document/6727177/
10. I.K. Somawirata, K. Uchimura, G. Koutaki. *Image enlargement based on the different scale factors for slice region*, The 1st IEEE/ IIAE International Conference on Intelligent Systems and Image Processing (ICISIP), (Kitakyushu, Japan, 2013). ICISIP:119–123 (2013). https://www.researchgate.net/publication/269061963_Image_Enlargement_Based_on_the_Different_Scale_Factors_for_Slice_Region
11. S. Goferman, L.Z. Manor, A. Tal. *EEE Trans. on Pattern Analysis and Machine Intelligence*, **34**, 10:1915–1926 (2012). http://ieeexplore.ieee.org/document/6112774/
12. I.K. Somawirata, K. Uchimura, G. Koutaki. *Image enlargement in different ratio based on the non salient feature enlarged*, International Workshop Advanced Image Technology (IWAIT), (Nagoya, Japan, 2013), IWAIT:579–584 (2013). https://scholar.google.co.id/citations?user=c5DnN88AAAAJ&hl=id

Understanding a Deep Learning Technique through a Neuromorphic System a Case Study with SpiNNaker Neuromorphic Platform

Indar Sugiarto[1,2], *and Felix* Pasila[2,*]

[1]School of Computer Science, University of Manchester, Manchester M13 9PL, United Kingdom
[2]Department of Electrical Engineering, Petra Christian University, Jawa Timur 60236, Indonesia

Abstract. Deep learning (DL) has been considered as a breakthrough technique in the field of artificial intelligence and machine learning. Conceptually, it relies on a many-layer network that exhibits a hierarchically non-linear processing capability. Some DL architectures such as deep neural networks, deep belief networks and recurrent neural networks have been developed and applied to many fields with incredible results, even comparable to human intelligence. However, many researchers are still sceptical about its true capability: can the intelligence demonstrated by deep learning technique be applied for general tasks? This question motivates the emergence of another research discipline: neuromorphic computing (NC). In NC, researchers try to identify the most fundamental ingredients that construct intelligence behaviour produced by the brain itself. To achieve this, neuromorphic systems are developed to mimic the brain functionality down to cellular level. In this paper, a neuromorphic platform called SpiNNaker is described and evaluated in order to understand its potential use as a platform for a deep learning approach. This paper is a literature review that contains comparative study on algorithms that have been implemented in SpiNNaker.

Key words: Deep learning technique, neuromorphic system, SpiNNaker

1 Introduction

In recent years, researches on artificial neural networks (ANNs) become a hype again, especially with the rise of learning engines equipped with "deep" learning capability. Many researchers, especially in the machine learning com-munity, consider deep learning (DL) as a second break-through for ANNs after many years of "silence" (not much progresses). The first breakthrough is attributed to the application of backpropagation (BP) algorithm for ANNs [1, 2]. Since then, no further significant progress on ANNs has been reported until recently.

Generally speaking, GP is a gradient-based approach applied as a means of learning for an ANN [3]. This is done by transforming the learning process into an optimization problem. In the optimization theory, gradient-based methods are well-known approaches to

* Corresponding author: indar@ieee.org, indar.sugiarto@manchester.ac.uk, felix@petra.ac.id

find a global optimum of a function. This is why the activation function of neurons in ANNs are expected to be di erentiable functions.

Since early 1970, GP has been used as a prominent tool for learning in ANNs. Both shallow and deep ANNs can be trained by using GP. However, due to computer hard-ware limitation at that time, only shallow ANNs were actively explored and deployed in real world applications. Only recently, when the computing power of computers becomes dramatically increased, especially with the advent of GPGPU (general purpose graphical processing unit) computing, deep ANNs are actively being explored [4]. This leads to the advancement of DL for practical pur-poses.

DL is a machine learning algorithm that relies on a many-layer network which exhibits a hierarchically non-linear processing capability. The idea of DL can be traced back from the work of Ivakhnenko [5] that produced a general learning algorithm for supervised feedforward Multi-layer Perceptrons (MLPs). It is commonly used by many layer networks, such as deep neural network (DNN), deep belief network (DBN), recurrent neural network (RNN), generative adversarial network (GAN), and convolutional neural network (CNN) [6–10]. Conceptually, DL is a generic technique and can be applied on other graphical models, for example deep reinforcement learning [11]. However, in this paper we focus on DL for ANNs, including spiking neural network (SNN) model.

DL is closely related to a class of theories of brain development, specifically neocortical development [12, 13]. Marblestone et. al. hypothesize that the brain optimizes cost functions, in which the cost functions are diverse and di er across brain locations and over development [12]. In this circumstance, the impressive performance demonstrated by DL as a credit assignment through multiple layers of neurons is in fact a manifesto of an optimization operation within a pre-structured architecture matched to the computational problems for specific classes. However, such interpretation does not show a direct relation between learn-ing mechanism in DL and in the brain. In particular, DL mechanism does not reflect brain dynamics even though its structure resembles the hierarchical neuronal circuitry of the brain cortex [14].

2 Overview of deep learning architectures

In this section, we describe some prominent ANN architectures where DL can be applied. These are architectures used by the second generation of ANN.

2.1 Deep neural network

Deep Neural Network (DNN) is a generalized feedforward neural network with several (hidden) layers. It is an advanced extension of the first generation of ANN, which was developed by Rosenblatt based on a single thresh-old logic unit neural network proposed by McCulloch and Pitts in 1943 [15]. This early simple ANN, known as "Perceptron", soon became a larger network by adding more neurons and layers; thus creating a Multilayer Perceptron (MLP) [16, 17].

The structure of MLP is similar to DNN, and the application domains of MLP is as diverse as DNN. The most distinguishable feature of DNN from MLP is the learning process, especially during the initialization. Instead of using random number for initialising the weights, DNN can use other technique such as restricted Boltzmann machine (RBM) to find initial weight values that close to optimal. With this approach, vanishing/exploding gradients problem, which is common in "deeper" MLPs, can be avoided [18–20].

DNN learns to map a fixed-size input (e.g, images) to a fixed-size output (e.g, a probability for each of several categories). Currently, the rectified linear unit (ReLU) is the most popular non-linear activation function used in DNNs. It is much faster than conventional but smoother activation functions such as tanh or sigmoid. Within the hidden layers, ReLU creates distortion to the input in a non-linear way, making categories linearly separable at the output layer [21]. Figure 1 shows typical structure of a DNN for image recognition.

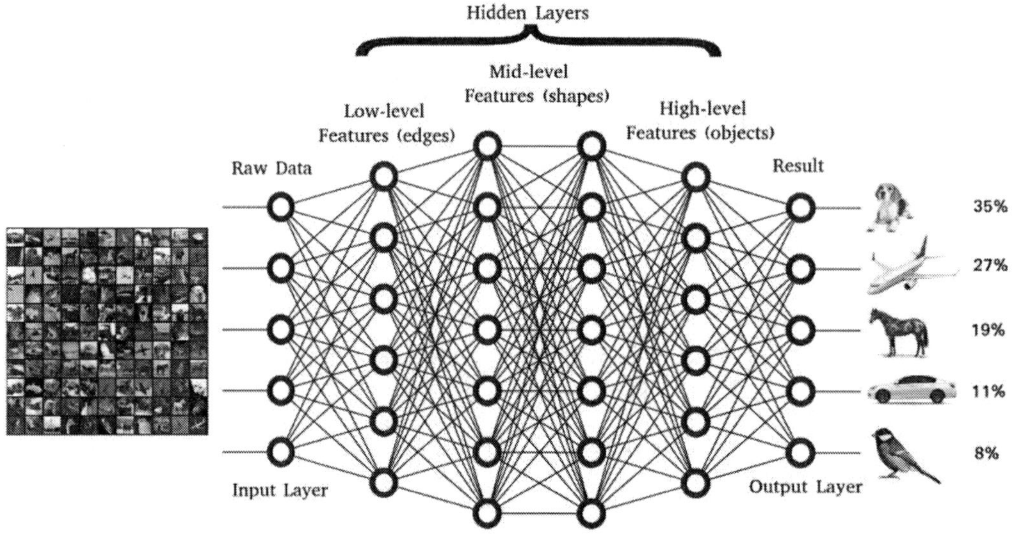

Fig. 1. A typical DNN structure for image/object recognition.

2.2 Deep recurrent neural network

Similar to DNN, a deep recurrent neural networks (DRNN) has several layers between its input and output layer. Conceptually, a DRNN is an extension to the standard recurrent neural network (RNN), whose neurons send feedback signals to each other exhibiting dynamic temporal behaviour. This feedback loop mechanism includes a huge number of possibilities, but conceptually can be classified into two classes: loops within a single layer, and loops between multiple layers. From these, several RNN structures have been proposed, such as fully recur-rent, recursive, Hopfield, Elman, echo state, long short-term memory, etc.

The temporal dynamic exhibited by RNNs leads into the memory capability that can be classified as short-term memory (STM), medium-term memory (MTM), or long-term memory (LTM) [22, 23]. These create the foundation of Adaptive Resonance Theory, which is the most advanced cognitive and RNN theory of how the brain autonomously learns to categorize, recognize, and predict objects and events [24].

A more practical example of DRNN is the long short-term memory (LSTM), which were invented by Hochreiter and Schmidhuber in 1997 [25]. This LSTM can have a very deep structure, allowing it to perform excellently in tasks such as speech recognition, handwritten recognition, and multilingual language processing [26].

An LSTM has several "gates" that control the feedback flow of information. A special "forget" gate which deletes the information in the self-recurrent unit without releasing the information into the network whilst making room for a new memory. An example structure of an LSTM is shown in Figure 2; it consists of four input weights (from the data to the input and three gates) and four recurrent weights (from the output to the input and the three gates). Occasionally, peepholes are added as extra connections between the memory cell and the gates.

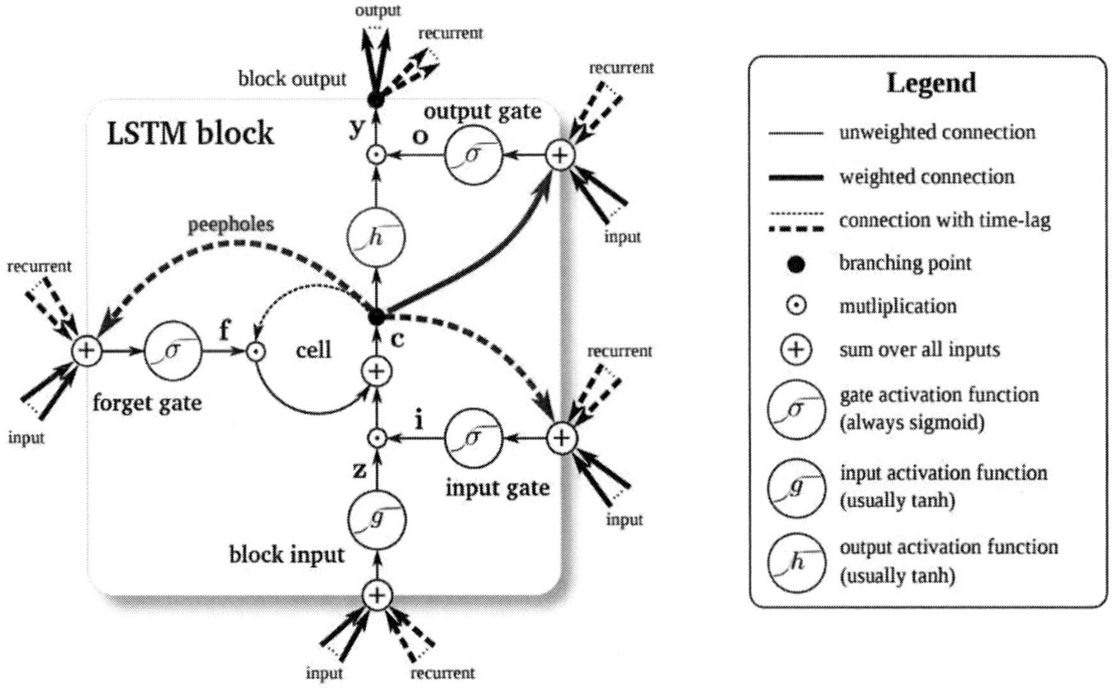

Fig. 2. An example of LSTM structure (modified from [27]).

2.3 Deep convolutional neural netword

Another form of ANN that can have a deep structure is the Convolutional Neural Network (CNN). Basically, it is a feed-forward network that is designed to require minimal pre-processing [9, 28, 29]. A CNN consists of an input and an output layer, as well as multiple hidden layers. The hidden layers are either convolutional, pooling or fully connected.

CNNs were inspired by biological processes in which the connectivity pattern between neurons is inspired by the organization of visual cortex [30]. Individual cortical neurons respond to stimuli only in a restricted region of the visual field known as the receptive field. The receptive fields of different neurons partially overlap such that they cover the entire visual field. This mechanism underlies the convolutional layer - the core building block of a CNN.

The convolutional layer has a set of kernels that operates as a small receptive field. Each kernel is convolved across the width and height of the input data, computing the dot product between them and resulting in two dimensional activation map of that kernel. As a result, the network learns kernels that activate when it detects some specific type of feature at some spatial position in the in-put. Stacking the activation maps for all kernels along the depth dimension forms the full output of the convolution layer, which can be interpreted as an output of a neuron that looks at a small region in the input and shares parameters with neurons in the same activation map.

Another important layer in CNNs is the pooling layer. Basically it performs a non-linear down-sampling to reduce the spatial size of the representation as well as to reduce the number of parameters and amount of computation in the network. This way the network can avoid overfitting. The pooling layers are periodically inserted between successive convolutional layers.

Finally, after a series of several convolutional and pooling layers, a fully connected layer is added at the final stage that is responsible for the high-level reasoning. Neurons in this final layer have connections to all activations in the previous layer. Fig. 3 shows the general structure of a DCNN.

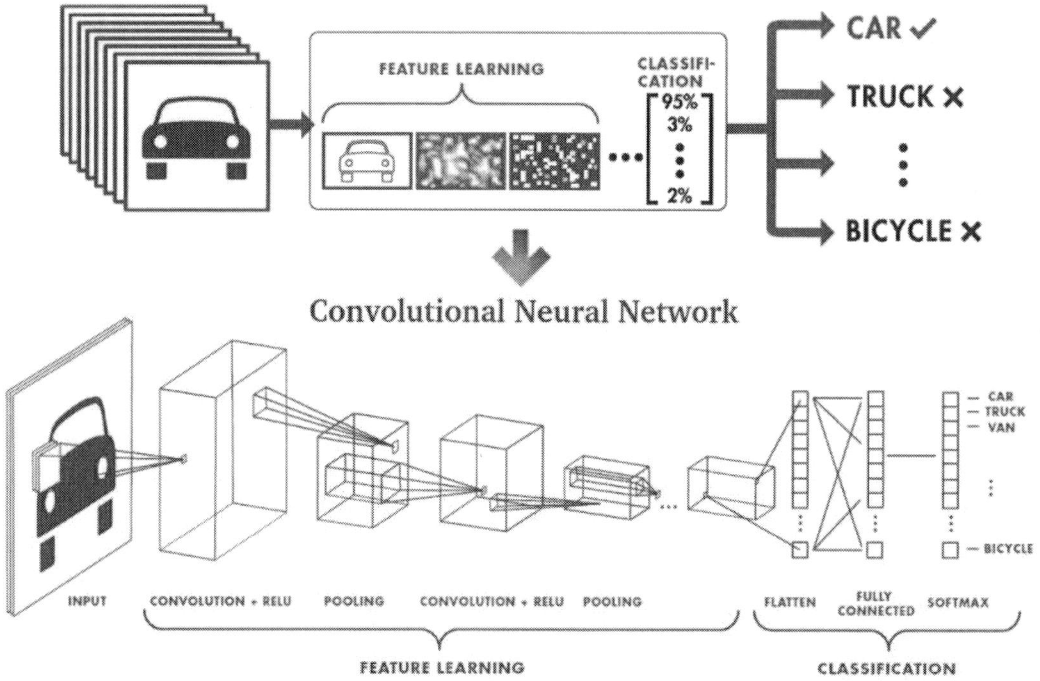

Fig. 3. The general structure of a DCNN (adopted from [31].

2.4 Deep belief network

Deep Belief Networks (DBNs) are another example of networks with a deep structure. They are composed of stacked smaller networks called restricted Boltzmann ma-chines (RBMs). RBMs are different to the standard ANNs; whereas ANNs use real scalar values for the weights, RBMs use probabilistic functions (usually in the form of conditional probability) for the weights [32]. The term "belief" is usually associated with the concept of generative model of the RBM, very similar to the Bayesian net-work in stochastic modelling [33].

Instead of using a stochastic ANN, a DBN can also be constructed by using a rather conventional network called autoencoder. Basically, an autoencoder is an MLP or feed-forward net with input and output tied together. This way, an autoencoder is supposed to be able to learn a representation (encoding) for a set of data, typically for the purpose of dimensionality reduction [34].

Either using RBMs or autoencoder, a DBN presents a hierarchical network where each sub-network's hidden layer serves as the visible layer for the next [7]. The learning mechanism of a DBN is performed layer-by-layer top-down with one layer at a time by treating the values of the latent variables in one layer, as the data for training the next layer.

DBNs have been used successfully in many applications such as in EEG (electroencephalography) analysis [35], generating and recognizing images [7, 36, 37], video sequences [38], and motion-capture data [39].

2.5 Deep generative adversarial

Generative Adversarial Network (GAN) is a neural net-work model for estimating generative models via an adversarial process. There are two models in the network contesting with each other in a zero-sum game framework: a generative model G that captures the data distribution, and a discriminative model D that estimates the probability that a sample came from the training data rather than G. In his paper (see [10]), Goodfellow et.al use this technique to generate synthetic photographs that look authentic to human observers. In his GAN, the G model creates natural looking images that are similar to the original data distribution, whereas the D model determines whether the given image looks natural or looks like it has been artificially created. Here, the generator is trying to fool the discriminator while the discriminator is trying to not get fooled by the generator. As the models train through alternating optimization, both methods are improved until a convergence has been achieved (i.e., a point where the synthetic image is indistinguishable from the genuine one).

For some test cases, such as images of number or face, GAN produces good quality synthetic images. But for other test cases, such as natural scenes, GAN does not work well. To overcome this, GAN can be combined with other technique such as CNN to produce a deeper network [40], such as Laplacian Pyramid of Adversarial Network (LAPGAN) [41].

Even though the combination of CNN and GAN pro-duces higher accuracy than the original GAN, however, it still su ers from scaling problem: it does not work well to recover the finer texture details when using a large up-scaling factors. To overcome this problem, Ledig et.al proposes to uses an adversarial loss function in their Su-per Resolution Generative Adversarial Network (SRGAN) [42]. Figure 4 shows the deep structure of a GAN as used in [42].

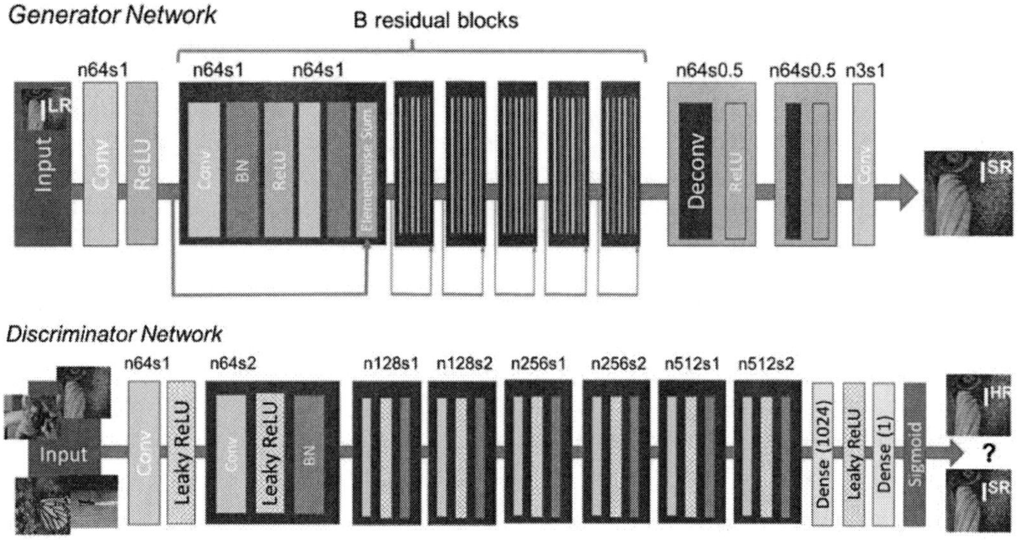

Fig. 4. SRGAN structure with corresponding number of fea-ture maps (n) and stride (s) indicated for each convolutional layer. (adopted from [42])

3 Overview of neuromorphic systems

This section focus on the implementation of the third generation of ANN known as the spiking neural net-work (SNN) [43]. SNNs leads into the development of neuromorphic computing, which tries to mimic neurobiological architectures present in the nervous system (i.e., the brain).

3.1 Connection with neuroscience

The first generation of ANN started with the work of Mc-Culloch and Pitts in 1943 on a computational model for neural networks based on threshold logic units. Since then, newer and more complex (and "deeper") networks have been proposed/implemented. However, those ANN models are more into mathematical models rather than biologically realistic models.

Neuroscientists argue that a more flexible and general AI could be built based on biologically plausible ANNs [44].Furthermore, in order to obtain more reciprocal benefits between neuroscience and machine learning, the integration of DL and neuroscience should be explored further [12]. For this reason, the third generation, spiking based, ANNs have been proposed.

In SNNs, the concept of time has been incorporated inherently, allowing them to produce a dynamic ANN model. Neurons will only generate out-put (i.e. "spike") when they have collected enough pre-information to surpass the internal threshold; hence, they do not "fire" at each propagation cycle as it hap-pens with conventional ANNs (e.g., MLP, DNN, etc.) /citemaass1997networks,gerstner1998spiking.

Maass shows that SNNs, with regard to the number of neurons that are needed, are computationally more pow-erful than conventional second generation of ANNs [43]. He shows that a single spiking neuron exhibits a biologically relevant function, which requires hundreds of hidden units on a sigmoidal-based ANN. Also, any function that can be computed by a small sigmoidal ANN can also be computed by a small SNN.

Prior to 1980s, most of ANNs and SNNs were conceptualized and implemented as software on computers, either on standard PCs or mainframes. With the advancement in chip fabrication technologies, researchers have a new option to implement ANNs and SNNs on dedicated hard-ware. In the late 1980s, Carver Mead started to look into neural-inspired hardware implementation [45] and coined the term neuromorphic. Neuromorphic systems strive to mimic neurobiological architectures present in the brain. Using analog VLSI technology in his work, Carver Mead demonstrated that biological solutions are many orders of magnitude more e ective than those that have been implemented using digital methods.

In recent years, however, the term neuromorphic has been used not only for describing analog-based neural-inspired hardware, but also for digital, mixed ana-log/digital VLSI, and even software systems that implement broader spectrum models of neural systems (from sensory level to cognitive processing) [46–48]. In this pa-per, we particularly describe scalable neuromorphic plat-forms.

3.2 Scalable neuromorphic platform

Taking advantage of chip fabrication technology, a number of large-scale neuromorphic systems have been developed recently, ranging from a single chip form to a full silicon wafer. Those systems are designed with scalability feature to make them able to support a large scale neural network model with millions of neurons along with their tremendous and complex synaptic connectivity [49]. This feature is inherently required in order to build a massive network for emulating a whole brain of animals ranging from nematode species (such as *Caenorhabditis elegans*, or C. *elegans*) up to smaller mammals [50, 51]. The scalability is also one of the main requirements to develop a framework with cognitive architecture. The ultimate goal of such plat-forms is to model a complete human brain [52]. However, this is a long-term goal and is treated with cautious optimism by scientific community, since the full potential of those neuromorphic systems has yet to be realized.

Four of the most prominent scalable neuromorphic platforms to date are: the IBM TrueNorth chip, the Stan-ford Neurogrid, the Heidelberg BrainScaleS system, and the Manchester SpiNNaker machine [53–56]. These plat-forms are built with complementary approaches and diver-gent intermediate goals. Table 1 summarizes some of the main features of these neuromorphic platforms.

3.3 SpiNNaker many-core platform

SpiNNaker (Spiking Neural Network Architecture) is a many-core neuromorphic platform built on top of commercial general purpose ARM microprocessor. At the lowest level, it is a multi-core system-on-chip (SoC) composed of 18 ARM968 processors and equipped with 128 MB low-power SDRAM mounted on top of the processor die.

Table 1. Main features of four large-scale neuromorphic platforms.

Platform	Mode	Chip Fabrication	Power per Chip	Neuron Model	Synapse Model	Plasticity
IBM TrueNorth	Digital	28nm	72 mW	LIF	Binary	No
Neurogrid	Analog	180nm	150 mW	IF	Shared dendrite	No
BrainScaleS	Analog	180nm	1.3 W	IF	4-bit Digital	STDP
SpiNNaker	Digital	130nm	1W	Programmable	Programmable	Programmable

The chip incorporates various digital elements for con-trolling the processors as well as for providing neurally-inspired communication infrastructure. The SpiNNaker uses small size data packets in various protocols, such as multicast, point-to-point, and nearest-neighbourhood. Multicast is the most used communication protocol in SpiNNaker for propagating neuron spikes in neural net-work models. It uses a packet switched network to emu-late the very high connectivity of biological systems. The packets are source-routed, i.e., they only carry information about the issuer and the network infrastructure is responsible for delivering them to their destinations.

Each SpiNNaker chip has six bidirectional links that can be connected to other chips. The links incorporate asynchronous digital circuitry to achieve the optimal band-width whilst maintaining the lowest power consumption. Using these links, 2D triangular mesh topology can be created by connecting several SpiNNaker chips. If the number of chips is su cient enough (at least 144 chips) and full-links connection is employed, then a 3D torus net-work will be created (see Figure 5(a)). Currently, the complete SpiNNaker system development is underway; when it is complete, it will have 50k chips, in which 1 million ARM cores are available for neuromorphic computing, as well as 7 Tera bytes of memory needed for simulating a massive neural network in biological real-time.

From SpiNNaker chips, several type of SpiNNaker machines are constructed. For the sake of naming simplic-ity, SpiNNaker machines are classified by the approximate number of processor cores in the format of 10x, where x is the power number for the base 10. For example, the 102 and 103 machines, which are single printed circuit boards, actually contains 72 cores and 864 cores respec-tively. The final 106 machine, will have 1036800 proces-sor cores. Figure 5(b) shows the physical appearance of several SpiNNaker machines.

SpiNNaker uses a simple event-driven model program-ming model. Since SpiNNaker is developed for a specific application (e.g. SNN), it does not require any general pur-pose operating system to be run on the platform. Instead, it only has a small dedicated run-time kernel to manage the entire operation of the machine. The SpiNNaker Application Run-time Kernel (SARK) controls the flow of exe-cution and schedules/dispatches application callback functions. Applications do not control execution flow, they can only indicate the functions, referred to as callbacks, to be executed when specific events occur, such as the arrival of a neural packet, the completion of a Direct Memory Access (DMA) transfer or the lapse of a periodic time interval.

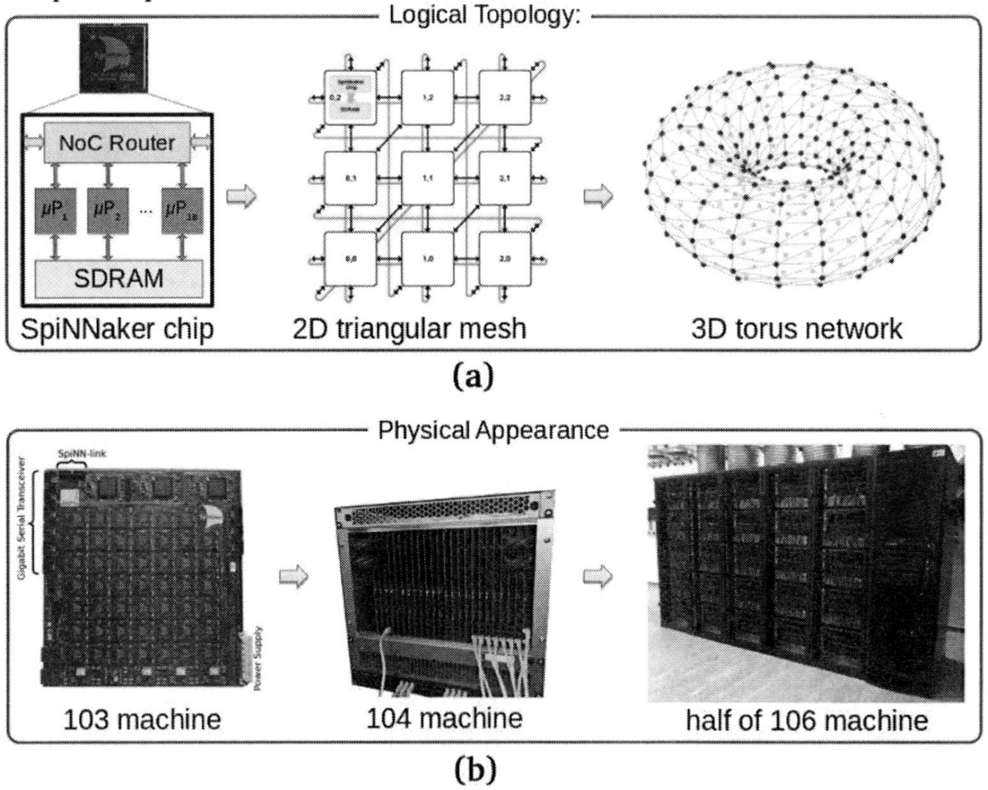

Fig. 5. SpiNNaker architecture in (a) logical topology, and (b) physical appearance.

4 Case study with SpiNNaker

In this paper, several experiments on SpiNNaker are studied. The publications related to those experiments are explored in order to understand how SpiNNaker can be used to implement DL concepts as well as to gain some insight on problems faced during SpiNNaker implementation of the corresponding aspect.

The main issue a network modeller instantly faces when using SpiNNaker is the fact that SpiNNaker runs on the basis of spiking neuron model; whereas common DL algorithms assume that the network falls into the category of second generation ANN. However, since SpiNNaker machines are built on top of a general purpose processor, it is still possible, using the direct programming approach on SpiNNaker, to implement a DL concept on SpiNNaker. This approach proves that SpiNNaker can also be used for general purpose computing, even in a domain far from spiking neural network, such as in image process-ing [57]. The following sub-sections provide examples of applications that are closely related to the concept of DL.

4.1 DNN on SpiNNaker

The vast amount of processor in SpiNNaker is definitely an attractive resources for implementing a DNN. As de-scribed in Section 2.2, basically a DNN is a feed forward ANN with many layers. Like SNNs, connections between neurons are through adaptable synapses (or "weights"). DNN models, however, have important di erences. Typically weights are only plastic for a certain time, that is during the "training phase", and then are fixed afterwards (or during the "test phase"). Each phase consists of some number of examples, individual data items presented to the network. This in turn implies that the DNN has no time model, or to be exact, a discrete-time model. Contrasting strongly with SNNs: the DNN model thus has a synchronous dataflow. In addition, the most popular learning technique is backpropagation, a method that involves propagating errors from output units backwards through the network to update the weights. Both of these proper-ties present challenges to the SpiNNaker architecture.

To solve the synchronous dataflow problem, a new technique called "update-on-demand" was proposed [58]. In this technique, partial results are computed and for-warded on through the network as soon as they are avail-able. The backpropagation algorithm, which presents challenges for the source-routed SpiNNaker topology be-cause it is e ectively bidirectional, is solved using a matrix remapping method that distributes the processing between cores.

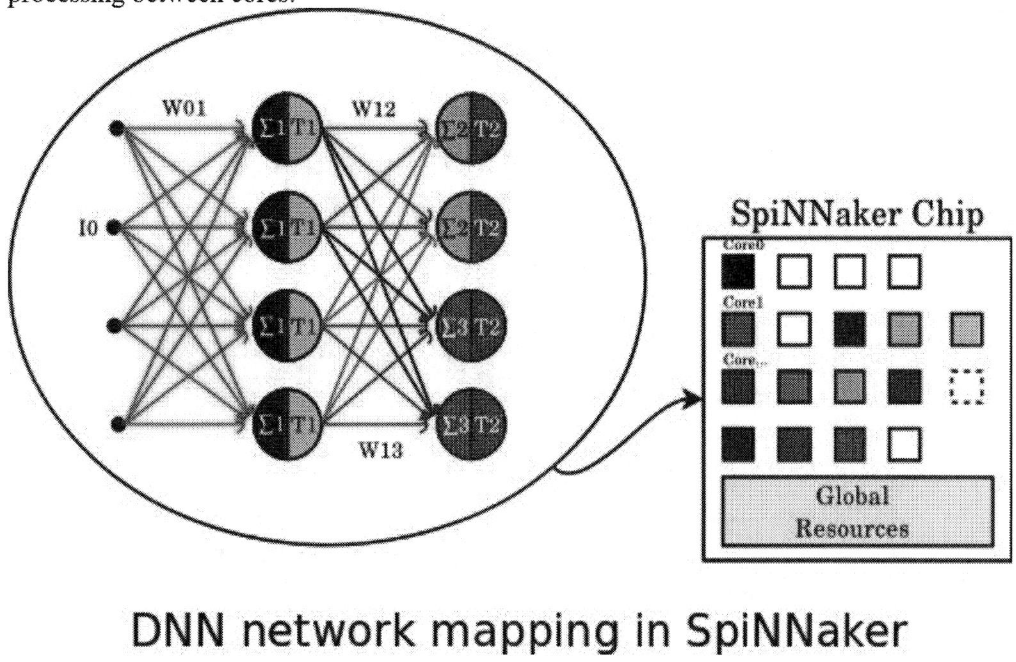

Fig. 6. Implementing a DNN on SpiNNaker. At each stage the unit sums the contributions from the previous stage. One processor may implement the input path for more than one final output neuron (shown here for the threshold stage).

The processing in a DNN model remains event-driven. Each processor in the DNN responds to a single hardware event (packet-received) and schedules software-generated events to complete processing. The packet-received event performs only 2 tasks: i) it places the packet into an internal service queue; ii) it schedules a deferred event to dequeue and process the packet. The dequeue software event, having retrieved the packet, performs the address decode and data processing required, as per each stage.

The SpiNNaker implementation models DNN networks using the Lens (http://tedlab.mit.edu/dr/Lens) specification and provides support for both feed forward and re-current networks. Initial support is provided for networks defined at a Group level; future plans may include sup-port for Unit-level definitions. Full support is provided for Group-to-Unit and Unit-to-Unit connectivity. A SpiNNaker package plugin for Lens allows Lens scripts to be implemented directly on SpiNNaker using the SpiNNaker software tool-chain.

4.2 CNN on SpiNNaker

Conventional CNNs as described in Section 2.3 work in a frame-based fashion, where the data (e.g., image) is acquired and presented to the network at a given frame rate (at about 30ms to 40ms). Each frame is processed sequentially by the different convolution layers and it must be completely finished before the processing of the next layer can be started. However, this is not how the brain works. In the brain, when a pixel in the retina is stimulated, it emits a spike with a very small propagation delay to neurons of the next layers. Neurons in the next layer will emit an-other spike when they have received enough spikes from the previous layer. This process continues up to the higher recognition layer levels.
To implement such a more biologically plausible CNNs on SpiNNaker, an event-based CNN for poker card symbol classification has been proposed [59], which is based on the work in [60]. It consists of four convolution layers (C1-C3-C5-C6) interleaved with two subsampling stages (S2-S4). Figure 7 shows the architecture of the event-based CNN.

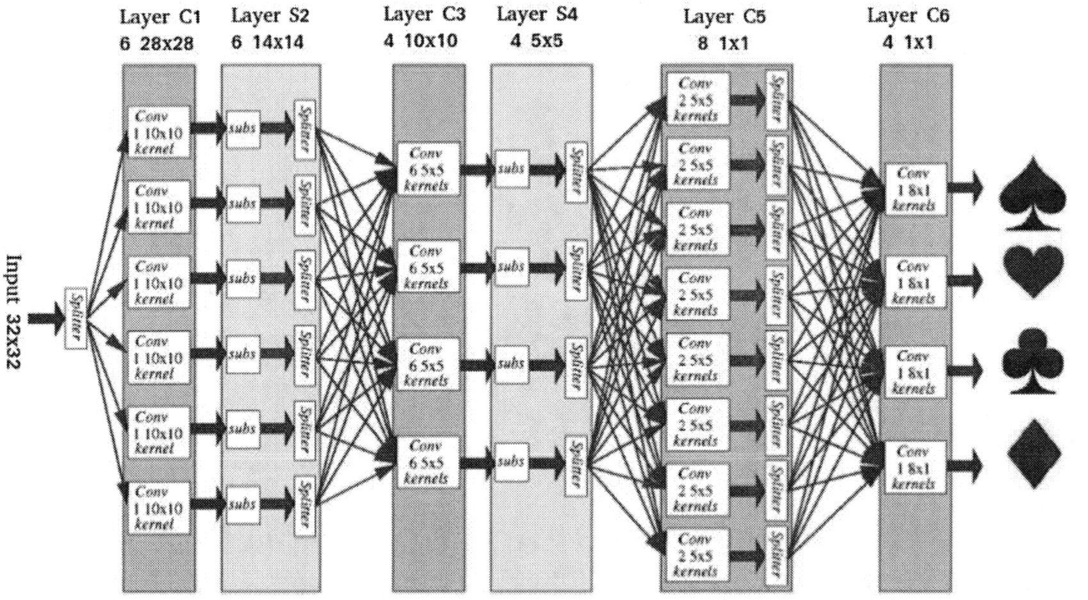

Fig. 7. The architecture of a CNN for the poker card symbol classification in [59].

The first convolution layer implements Gabor filters at three different orientations and two spatial scales (their weights were not trained). The rest of the network weights were obtained by backpropagation, training a frame-driven CNN version and afterwards applying a conversion method to obtain the corresponding parameters for the event-driven CNN [60].

One important element of a CNN is the kernel. The kernels possess the "weight sharing" property, where the weights of the kernels that connect neurons in two consecutive feature maps do not depend on the particular neuron positions but just on the relative positions of the two neurons in the origin and destination feature maps. To optimize the processing speed, the author in [59] introduced a special "convolution connector" to the SpiNNaker soft-ware tool. The convolution connector contains the kernel weights which are stored in the processor's local memory of the corresponding neuron population.

To test the recognition success rate, the author used a test sequence of 40 32×32 tracked symbols obtained from a very high speed event-driven camera. In a slow-mode experiment, a total of 189 category output events were generated, and the recognition success rate was 97.5 %. How-ever, when the processing speed was increased by using a slowdown factor of 10 for the same input stimulus event sequence, the success recognition rate decreases to 80 % and the total number of output events generated by the net-work has also decreased to 121 events.

Another finding by the authors was the source of the bottleneck in the processing flow that limits the maximum event throughput. The bottleneck happens in the first layer which employs the Gabor filters. Each Gabor filter receives all the events from the input stimulus, while generating each a significant number of events, which need to be transmitted and processed by the second layer. Unfortunately, there is no solution for this problem yet, which leaves a future work for those who are interested on this topic.

4.3 DBN on SpiNNaker

DBNs, as described in Section 2.4, can be implemented in several fashions. One of them that has been implemented on SpiNNaker is the model using RBM [61], which basically implements a spike-based DBN proposed by [62]. Since RBM is a stochastic model, the most convenient method to approach it in a spiking neuron models is by using firing rate. In this model, the Siegert approximation was used for the activation function of neurons. The Siegert function (see for detail in [63]) produces firing rate of a neuron given input firing rates and input weights for certain neuron parameters. For representing the weight, the author used 16 bits for the fractional part and 6 bit for the integer part (i.e., using the format Q6.16).

For testing, the MNIST dataset [28] was used as a classification benchmark. The MNIST dataset consists of 28×28 grey-scale pixel images of handwritten digits and is divided into a training set, which comprises 60 000 digits, and a test set, which consists of 10 000 digits. The network that consists of 4 layers were used: one input layer with 784 neurons, two hidden layers with 500 neurons each, and a 10 neuron output layer (see Figure 8(b)).

Static images are transformed into spike trains by converting each pixel of an MNIST image into a Poisson spike-train with a rate proportional to its intensity, while all firing rates are scaled such that the total firing rate of the population is constant [62]. The firing rate of neuron populations are depicted in Figure 8(c).

For the evaluation purpose, the authors used the classification accuracy and the latency as performance metrics. Regarding the classification result, their model achieved 95.01 % accuracy when using Q6.16 format for the weight values. When measuring the real-time performance of their model, the author found a mean classification latency of 20 ms. This was expected since the timing used for solving neuron equations in SpiNNaker was set to 1 ms, which is the default value in SpiNNaker configuration. The experiment also showed that increasing the number of input spikes reduces the mean classification latency, and has a positive e ect on the classification accuracy. The latency of the hidden layers also varies with the number of input spikes. For the MNIST test set encoded with 2 000 spikes per second, the mean spike latency between the hid-den layers is 2.3 ms; whereas in 500 spikes per second ex-periment, the mean latency per hidden layer rises to 6.22 ms.

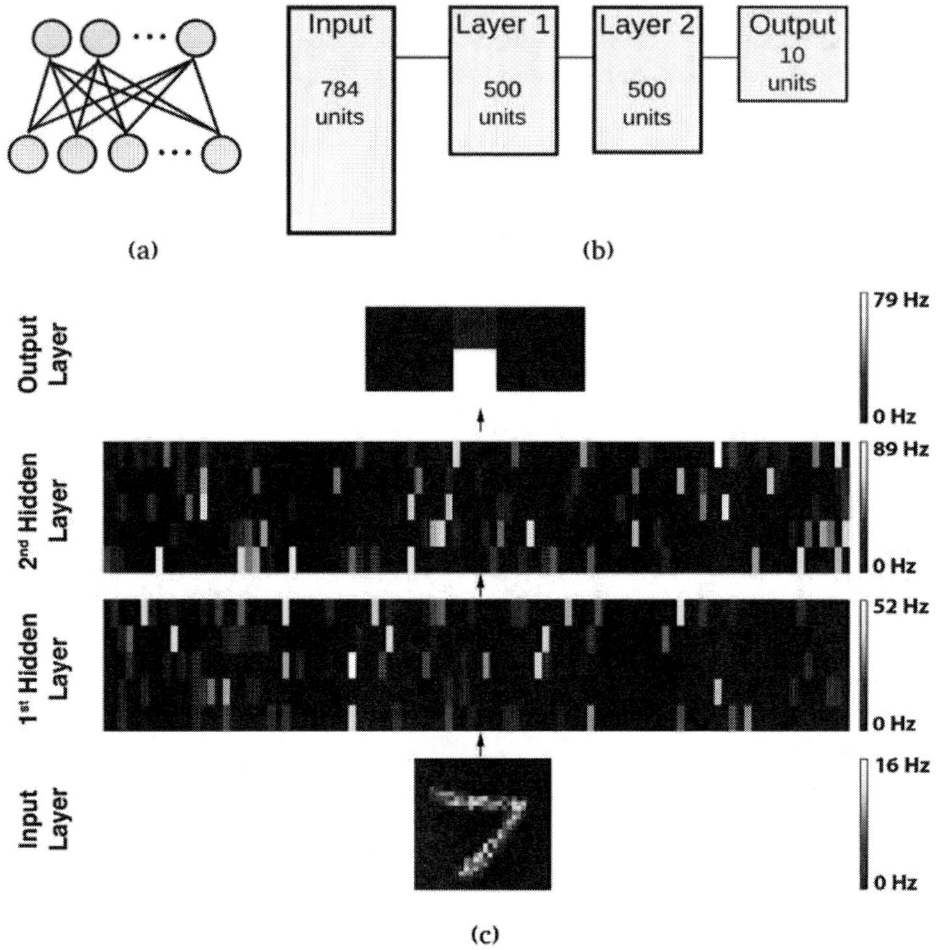

Fig. 8. DBN experiment on SpiNNaker as reported in [61]. In (a), a general architecture of RBM used as a layer for DBN. In (b), a topology of DBN in 784-500-500-10 structure used as a MNIST classification network. In (c), the firing rates of the network was under investigation for a single input MNIST digit. The bottom plot shows firing rates of the 28×28 neurons in the input population. The next two rows of 5×100 show the firing rates of the neurons in the first and second hidden layer (500 neurons each), and finally the top plot shows the firing rates of the 10 neurons in the output population, one for each digit from 0 to 9.

5 Discussion

From the study in the previous section, we gain several in-sight on how useful and challenging is the SpiNNaker for application in the domain of machine learning and artificial intelligence. As described in Section 4.1, it is fairly straight forward to implement feed-forward DNNs. The current SpiNNaker software tool-chain supports, at some degrees, modelling of general purpose DNNs. If specific application constraints are needed, however, users need to go a bit deeper by modifying the software tool-chain flow. Fortunately, SpiNNaker is programmed using stan-dard C/C++ and Python, which are common language pro-gramming known by most users.

In Section 4.2, we have described how the SpiNNaker platform can be used to implement a CNN. As proposed by its developer, a special "weight sharing" mechanism can be implemented e ciently in SpiNNaker by storing all synaptic weights on local memory called DTCM (data-tightly-coupled-memory) at each processor core [59]. This way, the memory access efficiency is increased consider-ably that leads into the increasing processing speed of the CNN.

Even though SpiNNaker provides a convenience way for handling the CNN parameters, overall, the efficiency of implemented CNN model is determined by the maxi-mum number of addressable neurons, limited by the implemented routing scheme of the current SpiNNaker soft-ware tool-chain. Currently, for small size CNNs, this limitation is not a problem. But for larger networks, this might impose reduced performance. Hence, in the future, the SpiNNaker developer needs to develop a more flexible neural addressing routing scheme.

As emphasized by authors in [59], the SpiNNaker architecture is very flexible and it allows to trade o maximum number of neurons per core versus maximum event processing throughput. By eventually reducing the maximum number of neurons per core, one effectively achieves parallelization of event processing, and the system would be capable of handling higher input event rates. This suggests that in the future SpiNNaker software release, the trade-o between maximum neurons per core and maxi-mum event throughput should be optimized according to the given desired parameters by the SpiNNaker user.

In Section 4.3, we describe how SpiNNaker was used to implement an event-driven DBN. There is an issue regarding the implementation of DBNs on SpiNNaker: both training and execution of large-scale DBN require vast computing resources, leading to high power requirements and communication overheads. To overcome this problem, authors in [61] proposed to limit bit precision during execution and training. Even though this idea sounds contra-intuitive, the experiment showed that the spiking DBNs can tolerate very low levels of hardware bit precision down to almost two bits. By limiting the bit precision, the performance of spiking DBNs can be improved by at least 30 %.

In addition to the improved performance, the authors also noticed the very promising feature of SpiNNaker with regard to scalability issue. It is well known that adding more layers to DBNs can improve performance. With the SpiNNaker architecture it becomes possible to create very large DBNs by adding additional layers, running on different cores or chips, without significantly increasing the latency of the system, and at reasonable power dissipation. This suggests that future work on DBNs should explore the implementation of larger DBN networks on bigger SpiNNaker machines. While the SpiNNaker hard-ware might not achieve the energy performance of dedicated neuromorphic hardware, the programmability of its architecture makes it an excellent exploration platform for event-based computing [61].

Finally, as shown in Table 1, some features of SpiNNaker are identified as "programmable". This has consequences of bringing both cons and pros upon the SpiNNaker system. The most obvious advantage of being programmable is the high degree of flexibility in terms of novel modelling purpose. For example, modellers can specify what kind of neurons they want to use in the model, simply by modifying the neuron parameters. Or, changing the synapse behaviour by specifying the plasticity rule. As mentioned by its developer [56], the SpiNNaker is meant to be a generic neuromorphic platform for novel research in neuroscience and it's following application domains (such as artificial intelligence). With this idea in mind, the SpiNNaker provides a very interesting alternative to the existing neuromorphic technology.

6 Conclusion

In recent years, Deep Learning (DL) has been considered as a breakthrough technique in the field of artificial intelligence and machine learning. Conceptually, it relies on a many layer network that exhibits a hierarchically non-linear processing capability; hence mimicking the underlying topology of human brains. However, this claim needs to be clarified since there are some degree of incompatibility between DL and cognitive feature of the brain.

In this paper, we are aiming to understand better how actually DL techniques fit our current knowledge of how the brain works. To achieve the goal, we are looking into the direct implementation of cognitive machine in a form of neuromorphic systems. For the study, we use SpiNNaker references that have close relationship with the DL techniques. SpiNNaker is a neuromorphic platform for simulation of a massive spiking neural network. After exploring several references, we confirm that to use it for general purpose applications in deep learning frame-works, software and hardware adaptation is needed. Some DL-based architectures have been implemented on SpiNNaker: DNN, CNN and DBN. Indeed, the results from those implementations show some promising features in terms of performance and scalability.

The authors would like to thank the Institute of Research and Community Development, Petra Christian University, Indonesia, for supporting our work through the project grant 02/LPPM/V/2017. The authors also would like to thank the Advanced Processor Technology (APT) group of the School of Computer Science at the University of Manchester, United Kingdom, for the opportunity to conduct the study and the discussion with the SpiNNaker team as well as with the experts in the field of neuromorphic technology.

References

1. P.J. Werbos, The roots of backpropagation: from ordered derivatives to neural networks and political forecasting. 1st Edition. John Wiley & Sons, Inc.: USA (1994). https://www.amazon.com/Roots-Backpropagation-Derivatives-Forecasting-Communications/dp/0471598976
2. D.E. Rumelhart, G.E. Hinton, R.J. Williams, Tech. rep., California Univ San Diego La Jolla Inst for Cognitive Science (1985)
3. S. Dreyfus. *Journal of Mathematical Analysis and Applications* **5**, 1:30–45 (1962). https://www.sciencedirect.com/science/article/pii/0022247X62900045
4. K.S. Oh, K. Jung. *Pattern Recognition* **37**, 6:1311–1314 (2004). https://www.sciencedirect.com/science/article/pii/S0031320304000524
5. A.G. Ivakhnenko, V.G. Lapa, Tech. rep., *Purdue Univ Lafayette Ind School Of Electri-Cal Engineering* (1966)
6. D.C. Ciresan, U. Meier, L.M. Gambardella, J. Schmidhuber, Neural computation **22**, 12:3207–3220 (2010). https://www.mitpressjournals.org/doi/full/10.1162/NECO_a_00052
7. G.E. Hinton, S. Osindero, Y.W. Teh, *Neural computation* **18**:1527–1554 (2006). http://www.cs.toronto.edu/~fritz/absps/ncfast.pdf.
8. A. Graves, A. Mohamed, G. Hinton. *Speech recognition with deep recurrent neural networks*. International Conference on Acoustics, Speech and Signal Processing (ICASSP) (Vancouver, Canada, 2013). ICASSP: 6645– 6649 (2013. http://ieeexplore.ieee.org/document/6638947/
9. A. Krizhevsky, I. Sutskever, G.E. Hinton. *Imagenet classification with deep convolutional neural networks*. Advances in Neural Information Processing Systems 25 (Lake Tahoe, Nevada, 2012). NIPS:1097–1105 (2012). https://papers.nips.cc/paper/4824-imagenet-classification-with-deep-convolutional-neural-networks

10. I. Goodfellow, J. Pouget-Abadie, M. Mirza, B. Xu, D. Warde-Farley, S. Ozair, A. Courville, Y. Bengio. *Generative adversarial nets*. Advances in Neural Information Processing Systems 27 (Montreal, Canada, 2014). NIPS:2672–2680 (2014). https://papers.nips.cc/paper/5423-generative-adversarial-nets
11. M. Hutter. *Universal artificial intelligence: sequential decisions based on algorithmic probability*. Springer: Berlin (2005). https://www.amazon.com/Universal-Artificial-Intelligence-Algorithmic-Probability/dp/3540221395
12. A.H. Marblestone, G. Wayne, K.P. Kording, *Front. Comput. Neurosci.* **10**, 94 (2016). https://www.ncbi.nlm.nih.gov/pmc/articles/PMC5021692/
13. J.L. Elman, Rethinking Innateness: A Connectionist Perspective on Development (MIT Press, 1998). https://mitpress.mit.edu/books/rethinking-innateness
14. R.J. Douglas, K.A. Martin. *Annu. Rev. Neurosci.* **27**, 419–451 (2004). http://www.allpsych.uni-giessen.de/rauisch/readings/Douglas&Martin_2004.pdf.
15. M. Anthony. *Discrete mathematics of neural networks: selected topics*. SIAM: USA (2001). https://books.google.co.id/books?id=qOy4yLBqhFcC&printsec=frontcover&dq=Discrete+Mathematics+of+Neural+Networks:+Selected+Topics&hl=en&sa=X&ved=0ahUKEwjtlfj3mp7ZAhVGQY8KHfK2BscQ6AEIKDAA#v=onepage&q=Discrete%20Mathematics%20of%20Neural%20Networks%3A%20Selected%20Topics&f=false
16. P. Auer, H. Burgsteiner, W. Maass. *Neural Networks* **21**, 786–795 (2008). https://igi-web.tugraz.at/people/maass/psfiles/126.pdf.
17. B. Widrow, M.A. Lehr. *Proceedings of the IEEE* **78**, 9:1415–1442 (1990). http://ieeexplore.ieee.org/document/58323/
18. S. Hochreiter, Y. Bengio, P. Frasconi, J. Schmidhuber. Gradient flow in recurrent nets: the di culty of learning long-term dependencies [Online] from https://pdfs.semanticscholar.org/aed0/54834e2c696807cc8b227ac7a4197196e211.pdf. (2001). [Accessed on]
19. J. Schmidhuber, Learning 4 (2008)
20. G.E. Hinton. *What kind of a graphical model is the brain?*. The 19th Proceeding International Joint Conference on Artificial Intelligence (Edinburgh, Scotland, 2005). IJCAI'05:1765–1775. https://www.semanticscholar.org/paper/What-kind-of-graphical-model-is-the-brain-Hinton/a4a5bef06587350604c7a9857ca09d91bd95763e
21. Y. LeCun, Y. Bengio, G. Hinton. *Nature* 521:436–444 (2015). Nature 521, 436
22. I. Boardman, D. Bullock. *A neural network model of serial order recall from short-term memory*. IJCNN-91-Seattle International Joint Conference on Neural Networks (Seattle, USA, 1991). IJCNN-91-Seattle International Joint Conference on Neural Networks, **2**:879– 884 (1991). http://ieeexplore.ieee.org/document/155450/
23. S. Grossberg. *Proc. Natl. Acad. Sci. U.S.A.* **60**, 3:758–765 (1968). https://www.ncbi.nlm.nih.gov/pubmed/5243922
24. S. Grossberg. *Neural Networks* 37:1–47 (2013). https://www.sciencedirect.com/science/article/pii/S0893608012002584
25. S. Hochreiter, J. Schmidhuber. *Neural Computation* **9**, 8:1735–1780 (1997). https://dl.acm.org/citation.cfm?id=1246450
26. J. Schmidhuber. *J Neural Networks* **61**:85–117 (2015). https://arxiv.org/abs/1404.7828
27. K. Gre , R.K. Srivastava, J. Koutník, B.R. Ste-unebrink, J. Schmidhuber, CoRR abs/1503.04069 (2015)

28. Y. LeCun, L. Bottou, Y. Bengio, P. Haffner. *Proceedings of the IEEE* **86**, 11:2278–2324 (1998). http://ieeexplore.ieee.org/document/726791/
29. P.Y. Simard, D. Steinkraus, J.C. Platt. *Best practices for convolutional neural networks applied to visual document analysis*, Seventh International Conference on Document Analysis and Recognition (Edinburgh, UK, 2003). ICDAR **3**:958–962 (2003). http://ieeexplore.ieee.org/document/1227801/?denied
30. M. Matsugu, K. Mori, Y. Mitari, Y. Kaneda. Subject independent facial expression recognition with robust face detection using a convolutional neural network. International Joint Conference on Neural Networks, (Portland, Oregon 2003). Neural Networks **16**:555–559(2003) https://pdfs.semanticscholar.org/6dd4/40eec6718f29a35b464345df2c77a4f0e085.pdf
31. The MathWorks, Convolutional neural network, [Online] from https://uk.mathworks.com/discovery/convolutional-neural-network.html. [Accessed September 30th 2017].
32. A. Fischer, C. Igel. Pattern Recognition **47**,1:25–39(2014) https://www.sciencedirect.com/science/article/pii/S0031320313002495
33. I. Sugiarto, J. Conradt. Discrete belief propagation network using population coding and factor graph for kinematic control of a mobile robot. IEEE International Conference on Computational Intelligence and Cybernetics (CYBERNETICSCOM), (Yogyakarta, Indonesia 2013). IEEE Xplore:136–140(2014). http://ieeexplore.ieee.org/document/6865797/
34. C.Y. Liou, W.C. Cheng, J.W. Liou, D.R. *Liou. Neurocomputing*, **139**:84–96 (2014) https://www.sciencedirect.com/science/article/pii/S0925231214003658?via%3Dihub
35. F. Movahedi, J.L. Coyle, E. Sejdic. IEEE Journal of Biomedical and Health Informatics, PP,99:1(2017) http://ieeexplore.ieee.org/document/7981315/
36. M. Ranzato, F.J. Huang, Y.L. Boureau, Y. LeCun. Unsupervised learning of invariant feature hier-archies with applications to object recognition. IEEE Conference on Computer Vision and Pattern Recognition, (Minneapolis, USA 2007). IEEE Xplore:1–8(2007). http://ieeexplore.ieee.org/document/4270182/?part=1
37. Q.V. Le, R. Monga, M. Devin, G. Corrado, K. Chen, M. Ranzato, J. Dean, A.Y. Ng, Building high-level features using large scale unsupervised learning. Appearing in Proceeding of the 29th International Conference on Machine Learning (Scotland, UK 2012). https://arxiv.org/pdf/1112.6209.pdf
38. I. Sutskever, G. Hinton. Learning multilevel dis-tributed representations for high-dimensional se-quences. In Proceedings of the Eleventh International Conference on Artificial Intelligence and Statistics, (San Juan, Puerto Rico 2007). PMLR 2:548-555, 2007. http://proceedings.mlr.press/v2/sutskever07a.html
39. G.W. Taylor, G.E. Hinton, S.T. Roweis. Modeling human motion using binary latent variables. In Neural Information Processing Systems Conference on Advances in Neural Information Processing Systems, (Vancouver, Canada 2006). p.1345–1352(2006). https://papers.nips.cc/paper/3078-modeling-human-motion-using-binary-latent-variables.pdf
40. A. Radford, L. Metz, S. Chintala. Unsupervised representation learning with deep convolutional generative adversarial networks. In International Conference on Learning Representations, (San Juan, Puerto Rico 2016). https://arxiv.org/pdf/1511.06434.pdf
41. E.L. Denton, S. Chintala, A. Szlam, R. Fergus. Deep Generative Image Models using a Laplacian Pyramid of Adversarial Networks. Advances in Neural Information

Processing Systems 28 (Montreal, Canada, 2015). NIPS:1486–1494. https://dl.acm.org/citation.cfm?id=2969405

42. C. Ledig, L. Theis, F. Huszár, J. Caballero, A. Cun-ningham, A. Acosta, et al. [Online] from https://arxiv.org/abs/1609.04802 (2016). [Accessed on]
43. W. Maass. *Neural networks* **10**, 9:1659–1671 (1997). https://www.sciencedirect.com/science/article/pii/S0893608097000117
44. A.J. Bell, Philosophical Transactions of the Royal Society of London B: Biological Sciences 354, 2013 (1999)
45. C. Mead. *Proceedings of the IEEE* **78**, 10:1629–1636 (1990). http://ieeexplore.ieee.org/document/58356/
46. R.J. Douglas, M.A. Mahowald, K.A.C. Martin. *Hybrid analog-digital architectures for neuromorphic systems*. Proceeding IEEE Conference on Neural Networks (Orlando, USA, 1994). Proceeding IEEE Conference on Neural Networks **3**:1848–1853. http://ieeexplore.ieee.org/abstract/document/374439/
47. E. Chicca, F. Stefanini, C. Bartolozzi, G. Indiveri. *Proceedings of the IEEE* **102**, 9:1367–1388 (2014). http://ieeexplore.ieee.org/document/6809149/
48. S.C. Liu, T. Delbruck, G. Indiveri, A. Whatley, R. Douglas. Event-based neuromorphic systems. John Wiley & Sons: India, (2015)
49. E.M. Izhikevich. *IEEE Transactions on Neural Networks* **15**, 5:1063–1070 (2004). http://ieeexplore.ieee.org/document/1333071/
50. B. Szigeti, P. Gleeson, M. Vella, S. Khayrulin, A. Palyanov, J. Hokanson, et al. *Front Comput Neurosci* **8**, 137 (2014). https://www.ncbi.nlm.nih.gov/pmc/articles/PMC4217485/
51. E.M. Izhikevich, G.M. Edelman. *PNAS* **105**, 9:3593–3598 (2008). http://www.pnas.org/content/105/9/3593
52. K. Amunts, C. Ebell, J. Muller, M. Telefont, A. Knoll, T. Lippert. *Neuron* **92**, 3:574–581 (2016). https://www.ncbi.nlm.nih.gov/labs/articles/27809997/
53. P.A. Merolla, J.V. Arthur, R. Alvarez-Icaza, A.S. Cassidy, J. Sawada, F. Akopyan, et al., *Science* **345**, 6197:668–673 (2014). http://science.sciencemag.org/content/345/6197/668
54. B.V. Benjamin, P. Gao, E. McQuinn, S. Choudhary, A.R. Chandrasekaran, J.M. Bussat, et al. *Proceedings of the IEEE* **102**, 5:699–716 (2014). http://ieeexplore.ieee.org/document/6805187/
55. J. Schemmel, D. Briiderle, A. Griibl, M. Hock, K. Meier, S. Millner. *A wafer-scale neuromorphic hardware system for large-scale neural modelling*. 2010 IEEE International Symposium on Circuits and Systems (Paris, France, 2010). ISCAS:1947–1950. http://ieeexplore.ieee.org/document/5536970/
56. S.B. Furber, F. Galluppi, S. Temple, L.A. Plana. *Proceedings of the IEEE* **102**, 5:652–665 (2014). http://ieeexplore.ieee.org/document/6750072/
57. I. Sugiarto, G. Liu, S. Davidson, L.A. Plana, S.B. Furber. *High performance computing on SpiNNaker neuromorphic platform: a case study for energy efficient image processing*, 2016 IEEE 35th International Performance Computing and Communications Conference. IPCCC:1–8. http://ieeexplore.ieee.org/document/7820645/
58. X. Jin, M. Luján, L.A. Plana, A.D. Rast, S.R. Welbourne, S.B. Furber. *Effcient parallel implemen-tation of multilayer backpropagation networks on SpiNNaker*. Proceedings of the 7th ACM International Conference on Computing Frontiers (Bertinoro, Italy,

2010 Proceedings of the 7th ACM International Conference on Computing Frontiers :89–90. https://dl.acm.org/citation.cfm?id=1787297

59. T. Serrano-Gotarredona, B. Linares-Barranco, F. Galluppi, L. Plana, S. Furber. *ConvNets experiments on SpiNNaker*. 2015 IEEE International Symposium on Circuits and Systems (Lisbon, Portugal, 2015). ISCAS:2405–2408. http://ieeexplore.ieee.org/document/7169169/
60. J.A. Pérez-Carrasco, B. Zhao, C. Serrano, B. Acha, T. Serrano-Gotarredona, S. Chen, et al. *IEEE Transactions on Pattern Analysis and Machine Intelligence* **35**, 11:2706–2719 (2013). http://ieeexplore.ieee.org/document/6497055/
61. E. Stromatias, D. Neil, F. Galluppi, M. Pfeiffer, S.C. Liu, S. Furber. Scalable energy-effcient, low-latency implementations of trained spiking deep belief networks on SpiNNaker. 2015 International Joint Conference on Neural Networks (Killarney, Ireland, 2015). IJCNN:1–8. http://ieeexplore.ieee.org/document/7280625/
62. P. O'Connor, D. Neil, S.C. Liu, T. Delbruck, M. Pfeiffer. *Front Neurosci* **7**, 178 (2013). https://www.ncbi.nlm.nih.gov/pubmed/24115919
63. F. Jug, J. Lengler, C. Krautz, A. Steger, Swiss Society for Neuroscience (2012)

Optimization Twist Angle of *Darrius* Wind Turbine with Computational Fluid Dynamics (CFD) Simulation for Highway Area Application

Ismail[*], *Erlanda* Augupta Pane, and *Soleh*

Department of Mechanical Engineering, Universitas Pancasila, Jl. Raya Lenteng Agung Timur No. 56–80, Jakarta, 12640, Indonesia

Abstract. The research conducted to analyze and optimization of *Darrius* wind turbine based on air velocity and twist angle blade which can influence of turbine torque, turbine rotation speed and turbine power capacity. The method of research uses three steps that is the air velocity observation, wind turbine design, and simulation of wind turbine design. The twist angle as a variable parameter has degree angle of 0° and 30°. The result showed that the *Darrius* wind turbine with the twist angle of 30° which has chosen has the torque value is 0.285 N m that capable to increase the rotation speed is 6.42 rpm, and generate the turbine power capacity is 0.221 W. The research will be continuing to data validation with the result of pilot scale experiment.

Key words: *Darrius* wind turbine, power capacity, rotation speed, torque, twist angle.

1 Introduction

The street lighting is an important factor to help the transportation activity in the night-time, where it has the primary function that is to keep the person safety, and reduce hazards by illuminating objects in the roadway [1]. Today, street lighting uses solar cell technology that can absorb solar radiation by utilizing silicon materials that can transform solar radiation into electrical energy that is generally applied in highways area. Unfortunately, solar cells still have a weakness factor that is the increase of solar radiation absorbed by solar cells requires more silicon thickness, and silicon purity processes still have a high price [2]. The wind energy can be an alternative energy to complement solar energy, where wind energy has a high potential to be utilized, especially in highway areas. Highway wind energy potential of the high-speed vehicle movement produces strong disturbance to the air

[*] Corresponding author: ismail2k7@gmail.com

and transmits its energy to local wind energy form [3]. Highway wind energy potential depends on large mileage and high traffic flow [4].

Research on the utilization of wind energy using wind turbines has been previously done [3–6]. In previous research, wind energy is managed by vertical axis wind turbines (VAWT), where the VWAT working principle is based on the drag force in appropriate with high-speed vehicles movement that produces high torque in the wind turbines [7]. The VAWT has two types turbine that is *Darrius* wind turbine and *Savonius* wind turbine [8]. *Darrius* wind turbine type have power coefficient and minimum velocity flow greater than the *Savonius* wind turbine, where have the power coefficient (Cp) between 0.2 to 0.4; while the minimum wind velocity to rotate of wind turbine between (3 to 7.5) m s^{-1} [6]. This research conducted to analyze and optimization of *Darrius* wind turbine which produce the turbine torque that can influence of power capacity and rotation speed. The basic parameters that influence *Darrius* turbine performance are air velocity, turbine blade numbers, twist angle of turbine blade, and air density. The analyze of basic parameters use the Computational Fluid Dynamics (CFD) simulations has the aims to produce the optimal of *Darrius* turbine performance with generate the turbine torque to influence the rise of power capacity, which can influence the high of electric energy production that transform from wind energy that collected in the turbine blade.

2 Method

This research conducted to analyze and optimization of *Darrius* wind turbine use Computational Fluid Dynamics (CFD) simulations. This research has the three steps that is the observation of air velocity, create of wind turbine design, and wind turbine simulation. Air velocity, air density, turbine blade numbers, and the twist angle of wind turbine can be the basic parameters to simulate of wind turbine. The observation of air velocity and design *Darrius* wind turbine has been done [9].

2.1 Observation of air velocity

The observation of air velocity has been held in the daytime and nighttime, where the nighttime air velocity has a greater value rather than air velocity in the daytime that caused by the rises of air to take the high temperature [10], beside the high transportation activity in the nighttime. The result of air velocity and air direction also depended by the height of rotor turbine that has four position areas based on the standard point [650 mm (1st position), 1 000 mm (2nd position), 1 350 mm (3th position), and 1 700 mm (4th position)], where the position can be shown in Figure 1. The results of observation can be shown in Table 1.

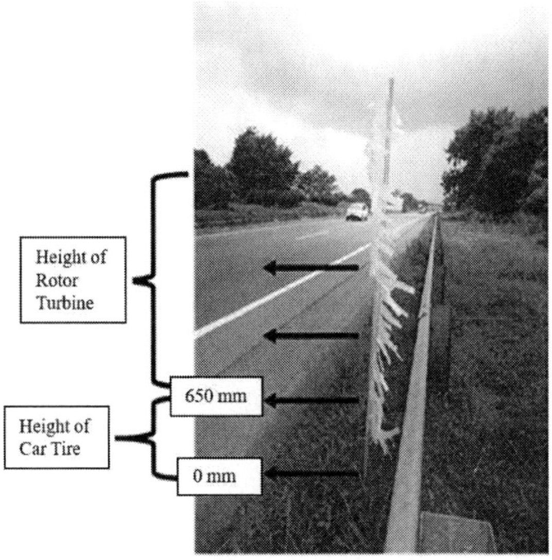

Fig.1. The height of rotor turbine [9].

Table 1. Air velocity [9].

No	Variable	Value
1	Data total	80
2	Score range	2.87
3	Class number	7
4	Class length	0.41
5	Average of air velocity with the high-speed vehicle	2.10 m
6	Average of air velocity without the high-speed vehicle	0.95 m s^{-1}
7	Deviation Standard	0.909
8	Minimum frequency distribution	1.7 m s^{-1}
9	Maximum frequency distribution	3.43 m s^{-1}

2.2 Wind turbine design

Based on the observation results [9] can be seen that the average of air velocity with the high-speed vehicle is 2.10 m s^{-1}, and the great value of air velocity has been occur in the height of 1 700 mm (4th position). The results can be basic parameter to design of *Darrius* wind turbine. The design results can be shown in the Table 2.

Table 2. Design of *Darrius* Wind Turbine [9].

Parameters	Symbol	Value	Units
Average of air velocity	v	2.10	m s^{-1}
Air density	ρ	1.225	Kg m^{-3}
Power Capacity	C_p	0.4	-
Blade numbers	B	2	-
Tip Speed Ratio (TSR)	λ	5	-
Height of rotor turbine	h	1 700	Mm
Rotor diameter	D	700	Mm
Chord width	C	488	Mm
Attack of angle	α	8	degree
Reynolds number	Re	71 143.219	-
Airfoil type		NACA 4412	
Material		Aluminum and fiber reinforced plastic	

2.3 Wind turbine simulation

Darrius wind turbine simulations use the continuity and momentum equation to control volume based on discrete integration equation and to reach the conversion value with the smallest error. The continuity and momentum equation can be shown in Equation 1, Eq. 2, Eq. 3, and Eq. 4 [12].

Continuity Equation:

$$\frac{\partial \rho}{\partial t}+\frac{\partial(\rho U)}{\partial x}+\frac{\partial(\rho v)}{\partial y}+\frac{\partial(\rho W)}{\partial z}=0 \quad (1)$$

X- Momentum equation:

$$\rho\left(u\frac{\partial u}{\partial x}+v\frac{\partial u}{\partial y}+W\frac{\partial u}{\partial z}\right)=$$

$$\rho gx-\frac{\partial P}{\partial x}+\frac{\partial}{\partial x}\left(2\mu\frac{\partial u}{\partial x}+\lambda\vec{V}.\vec{V}\right)+\frac{\partial}{\partial y}\left[\mu\left(\frac{\partial u}{\partial y}+\frac{\partial v}{\partial x}\right)\right]+\frac{\partial}{\partial z}\left[\mu\left(\frac{\partial w}{\partial x}+\frac{\partial u}{\partial z}\right)\right] \quad (2)$$

Y- Momentum equation:

$$\rho\left(u\frac{\partial u}{\partial x}+v\frac{\partial u}{\partial y}+W\frac{\partial u}{\partial z}\right)=$$

$$\rho gy-\frac{\partial p}{\partial y}+\frac{\partial}{\partial x}\left[\mu\left(\frac{\partial v}{\partial x}+\frac{\partial u}{\partial y}\right)\right]+\frac{\partial}{\partial y}\left[2\mu\frac{\partial v}{\partial y}+\lambda\vec{V}.\vec{V}\right]+\frac{\partial}{\partial z}\left[\mu\left(\frac{\partial v}{\partial z}+\frac{\partial w}{\partial y}\right)\right] \quad (3)$$

Z – Momentum equation:

$$\rho\left(u\frac{\partial u}{\partial x}+v\frac{\partial u}{\partial y}+W\frac{\partial u}{\partial z}\right)=$$

$$\rho gz-\frac{\partial p}{\partial z}+\frac{\partial}{\partial x}\left[\mu\left(\frac{\partial w}{\partial x}+\frac{\partial u}{\partial z}\right)\right]+\frac{\partial}{\partial y}\left[\mu\left(\frac{\partial v}{\partial z}+\frac{\partial w}{\partial y}\right)\right]+\frac{\partial}{\partial z}\left(2\mu\frac{\partial w}{\partial z}+\lambda\vec{V}.\vec{V}\right) \quad (4)$$

The *Darrius* wind turbine model use the twist angle as a variable parameter to simulate, which the result of simulation can describe that the *Darrius* wind turbine performance can collect the maximum of wind energy to convert to electrical energy, which can indicated by power capacity. The twist angle was determined by normalization power turbine graph with *Qblade* simulation. The result can be described that the twist angle can determine the estimation result of power capacity and the air flow numbers collecting. The result can be shown in Figure 2. Based on Figure 2 can be described that the twist angle of 30° has the more collect of air flow based on the surface of area blade, where the rise of air flow collected can increase the power capacity [9].

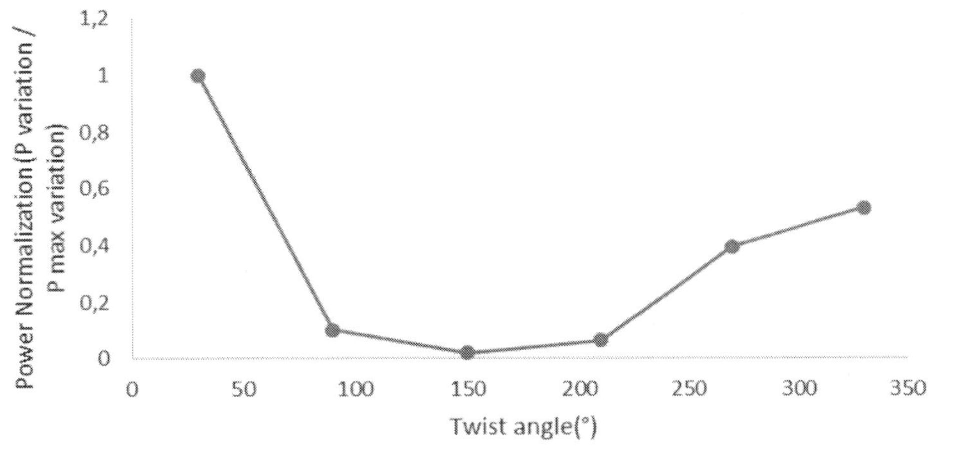

Fig.2. Correlation between twist angle and power normalization [9].

The twist angle that used as a variable parameter in simulation is 0°, and 30° as a result of *Qblade* simulation, where the twist angle is divided into two variants [9]. The first variant can be shown in Figure 3a, while second variant can be shown in Figure 3b. The first variant described that the *Darrius* wind turbine model has the twist angle with the value of 0°, while the second variant described that *Darrius* wind turbine model has and the twist angle with the value of 30°. The condition between the both of them has the similarity condition, where air velocity that passed of blade turbine is 2.1 m s^{-1}.

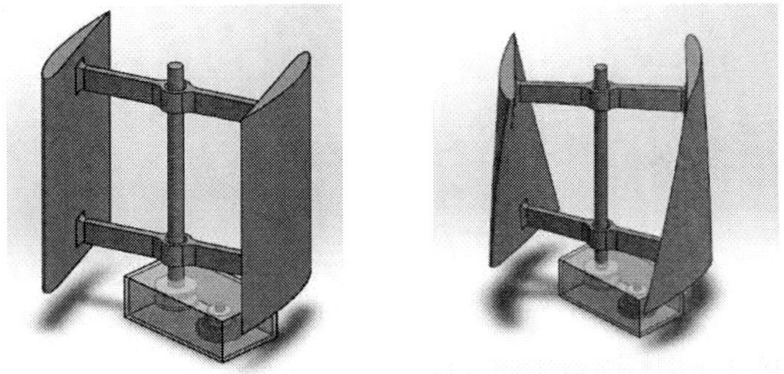

(a) (b)

Fig.3. Variant twist angle of *Darrius* wind turbine model: a) 0° and b) 30°.

3 Results and ddiscussion

The simulation of *Darrius* wind turbine based on twist angle variant as a variable parameter can determine the air flow collected which carry out of energy to being convert to electrical energy pass the torque of wind turbine and power capacity of wind turbine. The results simulation divide into two variant, where the first variant use the twist angle of 0°, the second variant use the twist angle of 30°, and the basic parameters simulation based on the data in Table 2. The simulation can be describe how the air flow pass of the turbine blade that can be seen in the front, side, and upper views, and giving the effect to determine the air flow type. The air flow also can determine the turbine blade rotation speed that influence of turbine torque. The result simulation of the variant of twist angle 0° and 30° can be shown in Figure 4. Based on Figure 4a which have the twist angle of 0° can be describe that the maximum air flow pass the turbine blade from front side of wind turbine that can be known with the red color has the value maximum of air velocity is 2.9 m s^{-1}. The second variant of *Darrius* wind turbine simulation use the twist angle of 30°, where the rise of twist angle can increase of power capacity. The result of second variant simulation can be shown in Figure 4b.

The air flow that has pass wind turbine will be generating the decrease of air velocity, caused by the collision between air flow and surface of blade area. The collision between surface of blade area and air velocity can rotate the rotor turbine that continue to being converted to electrical energy. The electrical energy can be recognized by the power capacity of wind turbine. Based on Figure 4b can described that the Figure 4b has the different view with the Figure 4a, which can be known from the different color of simulations. The wide side in Figure 4b can be described that the air flow collection that passed the surface area of turbine blade has the maximum value, when the air velocity the turbine blade is 2.9 m s^{-1} and has different value with the wide side in Figure 4a where the collected of air flow in the turbine blade has the great losses. The great losses of air velocity can be known by the air velocity has been pass the turbine blade still has the high value which approach to maximum air velocity value that is 2.9 m s^{-1}.

A. Twist angle of 0°

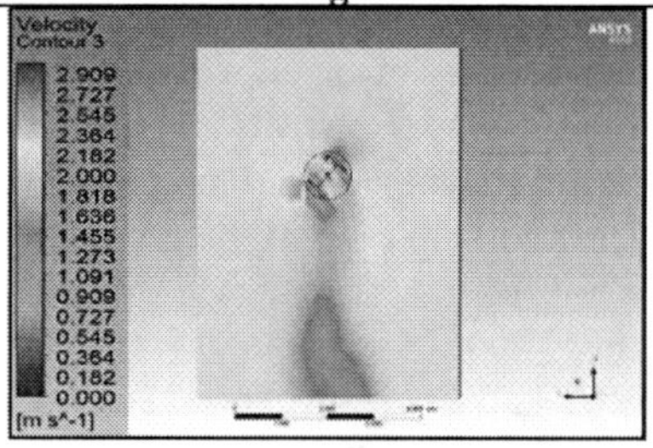

(a) Upper side

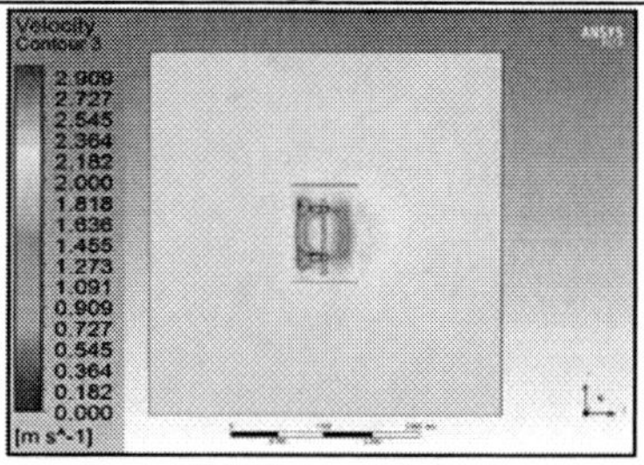

(b) Front side

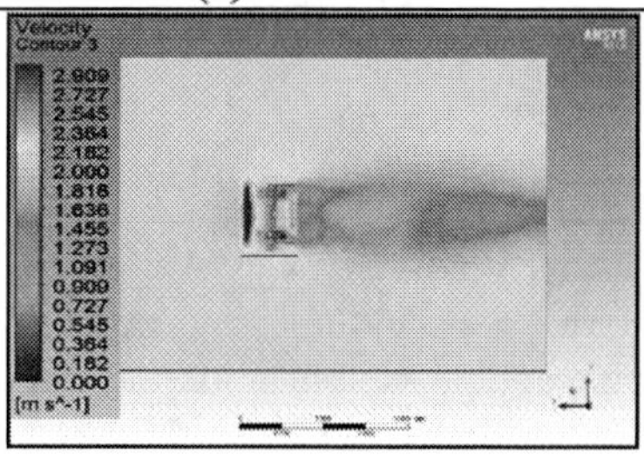

(c) Wide side

B. Twist angle of 30°

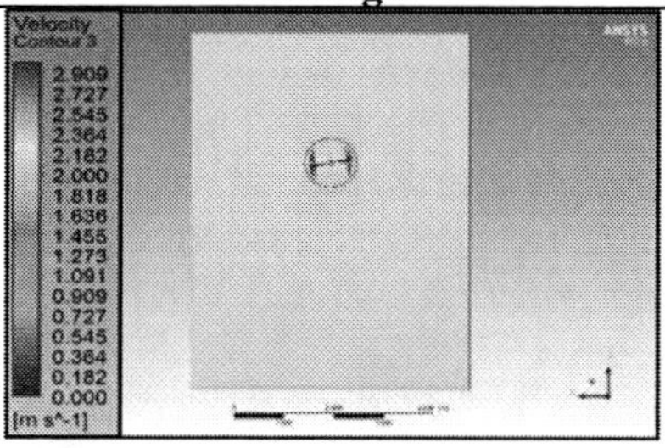

(a) Upper side

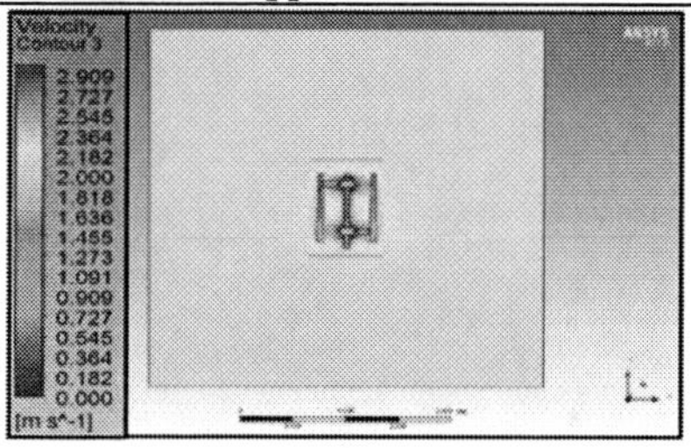

(b) Front side

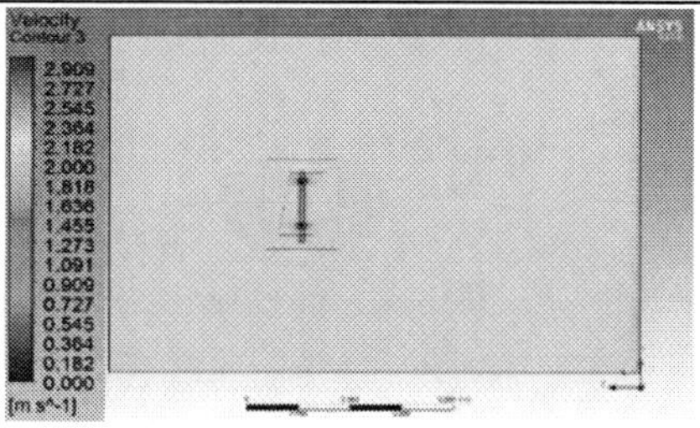

(c) Wide side

Fig.4. Simulation of air velocity in the *Darrius* wind turbine.

The results of data simulations also can be shown in the Table 3.

Table 3. Torque, rotation speed, and power capacity of *Darrius* wind turbine.

No	Parameters	Value		Units
		0°	30°	
1	Maximum rotation speed	234.01	366.46	rpm*
2	Maximum torque	1.21	0.673	N m
3	Maximum power	12.49	22.2	W
4	Minimum rotation speed	0.05	0.018	rpm*
5	Minimum torque	0.001	0.000 45	N m
6	Minimum power	0.000 3	0.000 3	W
7	Average of rotation speed	9.77	6.42	rpm*
8	Average of torque	0.319	0.285	N m
9	Average of power	0.357	0.221	W

*) 1 rpm = 1/60 Hz

The Table 3 the *Darrius* wind turbine simulation with the twist angle of 0° has the maximum torque is 1.21 N m and the maximum rotation speed is 234.1 rpm (1 rpm = 1/60 Hz), whereas the twist angle of 30° has the maximum torque is 0.673 N m and the maximum rotation speed is 366.46 rpm. The result can obtain that the maximum of air velocity 2.9 m s^{-1} has been passing the blade turbine. Based on Table 3 also can be described that the different data between the twist angle of 0°, and 30° can be described that the increase of rotation speed turbine blade can decrease of torque and increase the power capacity, and the second variant with the twist angle of 30° has been chosen as a blade of *Darrius* wind turbine.

4 Conclusions

The results of *Darrius* wind turbine simulations can be concluded that the second variant with the value of twist angle is 30° have the optimum power capacity rather than the first variant with the value of twist angle is 0°. The result torque of second variant is 0.285 N m, with the rotor turbine rotation speed is 6.42 rpm can produce the power capacity is 0.221 W. The research will be continued to data validation process with the result of pilot scale experiment.

The authors are grateful to the laboratories product of mechanical engineering, Universitas Pancasila.

References

1. A. Ekrias, M. Eloholma, L. Halonen, X.J. Song, X. Zhang, Y. Wen. Journal of Building and Environment, **43**(4):530–536 (2008). https://www.sciencedirect.com/science/article/pii/S0360132307000157
2. P. Yu, J. Wu, S. Liu, J. Xiong, C. Jagadish, Z.M. Wang. Journal of Nano Today **11**(6):704–737 (2016). https://www.sciencedirect.com/science/article/pii/S1748013216302110
3. C. Lapointe, H. Gopalan. Journal of Solar Energy Engineering, **138**(2):1–4 (2016). http://solarenergyengineering.asmedigitalcollection.asme.org/article.aspx?articleid=2481137
4. W. Tian, Z. Mao, X. An, B. Zhang, H. Wen. Energy. **141**:715–728 (2017). https://www.sciencedirect.com/science/article/pii/S036054421731366X
5. A. Zarkesh, M. Heidari. *Developing a new application for wind generators in highways*. The Fifth International Conference on Computational Intelligence,

Communication Systems and Network, 5–7 June (Madrid, Spain, 2013). http://ieeexplore.ieee.org/document/6571379/
6. C. Promdee, C. Photong. Procedia Computer Science, **86**: 401-404 (2016). https://www.sciencedirect.com/science/article/pii/S1877050916303805
7. S.C. Goh, S.R. Boopathy, C. Krishnaswami, J.U. Schulter. Journal of Renewable Energy, **87**(1):332–345 (2016). https://www.sciencedirect.com/science/article/pii/S0960148115303682
8. M. D'ambrosio, M. Medaglia. *Vertical axis wind turbines: History, technology and applications*. [Thesis Master]. Hogskolan Halmstad University, Halmstad, Sweden (2010). pp. 91. http://windharvest.com/wp-content/uploads/2018/02/Vertical-Axis-Wind-Turbines-History-Technology-and-Applications.pdf
9. Ismail, Erlanda Pane, Triyanti. *Optimasi perancangan turbin angin vertikal tipe Darrieus untuk penerangan di jalan tol*. [Optimization of *Darrius* Wind Turbine Design To Applicate in The Highways Area]. Prosiding Seminar Nasional Sains dan Teknologi (SEMNASTEK) Fakultas Teknik Universitas Muhammadiyah (Jakarta, Indonesia, 2017). pp. 1–12. https://jurnal.umj.ac.id/index.php/semnastek/article/view/1965
10. Y.M. Kim, K.P. You, J.Y. You. The Scientific World Journal, **2014**:1–12 (2014). https://www.ncbi.nlm.nih.gov/pubmed/25136681
11. J. McCosker. *Design and optimization of a small wind turbine*. [Thesis Master]. Renssalaer Polytechnic Institute, New York, United States of America (2012). pp. 56. http://www.scirp.org/(S(lz5mqp453edsnp55rrgjct55))/reference/ReferencesPapers.aspx?ReferenceID=1306595
12. S.N. Saleh, A.A. Mohammed, F.K. Al-Jubory, S. Barghi. Journal of Petroleum Science and Engineering **161** (2017). https://www.researchgate.net/publication/320979271_CFD_assesment_of_uniform_bubbly_flow_in_a_bubble_column

Design of Monitoring Tool Heartbeat Rate and Human Body Temperature Based on WEB

Jalinas[1], *Wahyu* Kusuma Raharja[2], and *Bobby* Putra Emas Wijaya[2,*]
[1] Department of Computer System, Gunadarma University, Jl. Margonda Raya No.100, Pondok Cina, Beji, Kota Depok, Jawa Barat 16424
[2] Department of Electrical Engineering, Gunadarma University, Jl. Margonda Raya No.100, Pondok Cina, Beji, Kota Depok, Jawa Barat 16424

Abstract. The heart is one of the most important organs in the human body. One way to know heart health is to measure the number of heart beats per minute and body temperature also shows health, many heart rate and body temperature devices but can only be accessed offline. This research aims to design a heart rate detector and human body temperature that the measurement results can be accessed via web pages anywhere and anytime. This device can be used by many users by entering different ID numbers. The design consists of input blocks: pulse sensor, DS18B20 sensor and 3x4 keypad button. Process blocks: Arduino Mega 2560 Microcontroller, Ethernet Shield, router and USB modem. And output block: 16x2 LCD and mobile phone or PC to access web page. Based on the test results, this tool successfully measures the heart rate with an average error percentage of 2.702 % when compared with the oxymeter tool. On the measurement of body temperature get the result of the average error percentage of 2.18 %.

Key words: Heartbeat rate, temperature, WEB

1 Introduction

Health is a very important aspects in life, one of them is heart health. The heart is a vital organ in the human body who have a function to pump blood throughout the body. Pumping activity of the heart can be measured using equipment called an electrocardiograph or ECG. Many factors that makes heart are not working normally, one of which is temperature, body temperature or environment temperature, based on a journal written in [1]. In the study said by Waterman, which claimed that in environments with high temperature will increase the metabolism in the body, then will leads to increased respiration rate and also have an impact on increased heart rate [1].

Human body temperature also important aspects in human life, too warm human bodies have mean that our health was interfere. The earth's temperature continues to rise due to several factors such as the greenhouse effect that makes global warming. Increasingly hot environment temperature around us, one of our body will dehydration and lack of water, this can make an increase in body temperature because the body fails to cool its own body, hot

* Corresponding author: bobbyhoult@gmail.com

temperatures also makes emotional unstable and heart health was impaired, as written by Ananya Mandal in his article in news-medical.net [2]. With these conditions, the authors created a tool to detect the human heart rate and body temperature, because in order to know whether at a certain temperature conditions a person's heartbeat is still in the normal range is 60 bpm to 100 bpm for adult (bpm = beats per minute).

Research has been carried by [3, 4], has made a heart rate monitoring devices. In that studies, a tool designed just for a heartbeat, and there is a WiFi communication to sent the result data but that communication there are to much weakness like limited distance because that things the authors created a tool that monitoring heart rate and body temperature with WEB or internet connection. Then creating a circuit which use a pulse sensor component as the detection of the heartbeat by placing one finger to the pulse sensor will be detected, the heart rate and blood volume is synchronous to the heart beat, this technique can be used to calculate the heart rate, and sensor DS18B20 as the temperature gauge body Because DS18B20 sensor accurate body temperature reading. This tool is certainly very useful, because we can check the state of the heart and body temperature anywhere, with pulse sensor and a temperature sensor which is accurate enough.

Rapid development of information technology, one that is internet technology. Internet is a technology that uses an electronic device to exchange data wirelessly with easy installation and cost, that the technology is in great demand by the public. Because of that the author wants to make the heartbeat detection device and the body temperature automatic calculation process works with the results displayed on a 16×2 LCD which also results can be accessed via the WEB with the internet on a PC or a smartphone with a internet connection, the author choose internet because it was very easy to use, and whoever can be access. When someone check them heart and temperature condition, the result can be seen leter because the result saved by internet and can be accessed.

2 Literature Review

2.1 Heart rate

Heart rate, or heart pulse, is the speed of the heartbeat measured by the number of poundings of the heart per unit of time, typically beats per minute (bpm). The heart rate can vary according to the body's physical needs, including the need to absorb oxygen and excrete carbon dioxide. Activities that can provoke change include physical exercise, sleep, anxiety, stress, illness, ingesting, and drugs. The resting heart rate of a newborn can be 120 bpm and this gradually decreases until maturity and then gradually increases again with age. The normal resting adult human heart rate ranges from 60 bpm to 80 bpm. Bradycardia is a slow heart rate, defined as below 60 bpm. Tachycardia is a fast heart rate, defined as above 100 bpm at rest. When the heart is not beating in a regular pattern, this is referred to as an arrhythmia. These abnormalities of heart rate sometimes indicate disease [5].

2.2 Photoplethysmography (PPG)

Photoelectric plethysmography, also known as photoplethysmography and its acronym in some literature, is (PTG/PPG) and when it is called digital volume pulse, the acronym is (DVP). PPG is easy to set up, convenient, simple and economically efficient. Moreover, it does not need direct contact with the skin surface. It uses a probe which contains a light source and a detector to detect cardio-vascular pulse wave that propagates through the body. The PPG signal reflects the blood movement in the vessel, which goes from the heart to the fingertips and toes through the blood vessels in a wave-like motion. It is an optical measurement technique that uses an invisible infrared light sent into the tissue and the amount of the backscattered light corresponds with the variation of the blood volume. The low-cost and simplicity of this optical based technology could offer significant benefits to healthcare (e.g. in primary care where non-invasive, accurate and simple-to-use diagnostic techniques are desirable). Further development of PPG could place this methodology among other tools used in the management of vascular disease [6].

2.3 Body temperature

Temperature is a magnitude that states the degree of cold or heat of an object and a tool used to measure the temperature is a thermometer. In daily life people measure temperature using the sense of touch. But with the development of technology that was created a thermometer to measure the temperature with a thermometer with valid result. First pioneered who making the thermometer is Galileo Galilei (1564–1642) at 1595. The tool is called the termoskop in the shaped of empty flask equipped with a long pipe with end of the pipe opened. At first, the air in the flask was heated so that it expands. End of the pipe that open is then dipped into a colorless liquid. When the air inside flask is shrinking, the liquid into the pipe, but not until the flask. That's how termoscop work. For different temperatures, a high column of liquid in the pipeline are also different. The height column is used to determine the temperature. The working principle of artificial Galileo thermometer based on changes in the volume of gas in the flask. But now the thermometer that often used are made of liquid mercury and alkhohol. The principle used is thermal expansion of liquids when an increase in temperature of the object [7].

3 System Design

3.1 Detailed circuit design

Figure 1 shows block diagram Monitoring Tool Heartbeat Rate and Human Body Temperature system design. There are three blocks were used that block pulse sensor [7], temperature sensor DS18B20 [8] and 3×4 keypad. The output of this sensor will go to block the process. Block process consists of three distinct blocks namely Arduino Mega 2560 Microcontroller block [9] and block Ethernet Shield TL-MR3020 router [10]. At the output blocks are also composed of three different blocks that block LCD Display, PC block, and block the smartphone. So pulse sensor and a temperature sensor results will be processed by a microcontroller Arduino Mega 2560 is then displayed on the LCD display, and can be displayed via the WEB on smartphones and PC but the result of a block of microcontroller Arduino Mega 2560 is passed to block the Ethernet Shield and then to the router.

 https://doi.org/10.1051/matecconf/201816401017

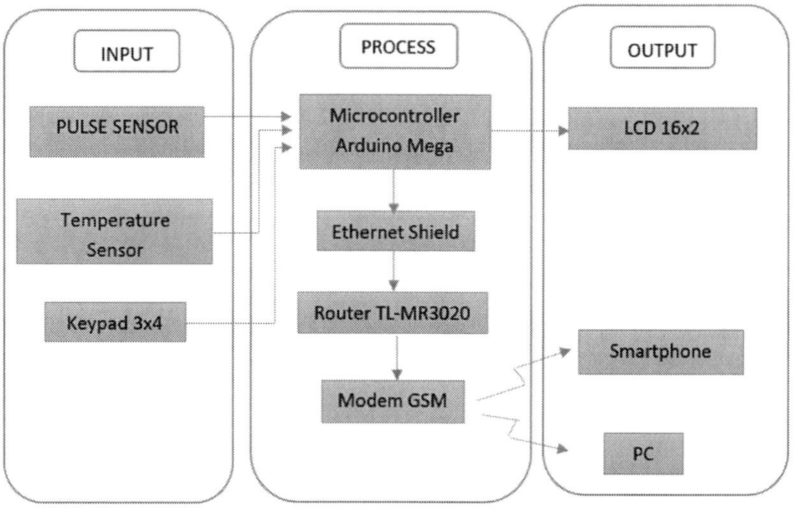

Fig. 1. Block diagram of monitoring tool heartbeat rate and human body temperature system design.

Figure 2 shows schematic of monitoring tool heartbeat rate and human body temperature. The circuit using a voltage of 5V of Arduino Mega or ethernet, because in terms of the hardware installation of ethernet is take below the Arduino Mega, but used by ethernet Circuit below using a voltage of 5V of Arduino Mega or ethernet, because in terms of the hardware installation of ethernet is below the Arduino Mega, but used by ethernet only four pins of arduino mega i.e. pin 50 MISO, pin 51 MOSI, pin 52 SCK, pin 53 ETH CS, next to the LCD side.

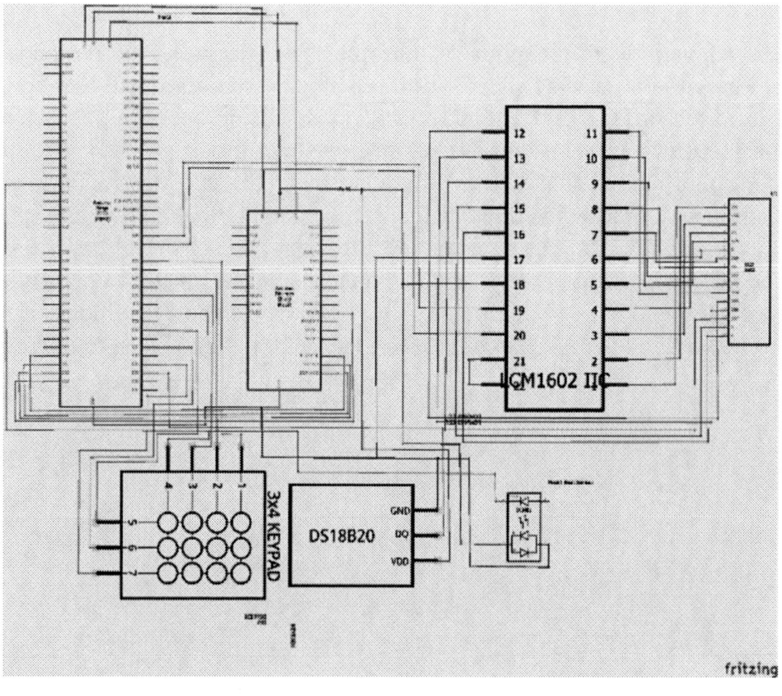

Fig. 2. Schematic of monitoring tool heartbeat rate and human body temperature .

On the circuit using 16×2 LCD is connected to the I2C LCD so that the pins are used less, with explanations pin 1 to 16 LCD connected to pins 1 to 16 on I2C, pin 1 connected to pin 1 following pin 2 connected with pin 2 and up to 16 pins, and the pins 21 and 22 on the I2C on a direct dial aim to make the brightness on and pin 17 I2C connected to ground, pin 18 connected to VCC, pin 19 is connected to pin 20 arduino that the SDA and the pin 21 arduino which is connected to the SDL. Next to the keypad, the keypad using 7 pins connected to digital pin arduino mega namely digital pins 1 to 7, pins 1 keypad is connected to the pin 22 follows the pin 2 connected to pin 24 and until 7 pin keypad. Then the temperature sensor DS18B20 on the circuit above using 3 pin them vcc, ground and data, VCC is connected to the voltage arduino 5V following with the ground, then pin of data from the sensors connected to the pin 35 digital arduino, then to the heart beat sensor.

3.2 Software design

Software design shown in Figure 3, Figure 4, Figure 5 and Figure 6 describes a program that is used to operate the device. In this section consists of a flowchart and explain how the device works.

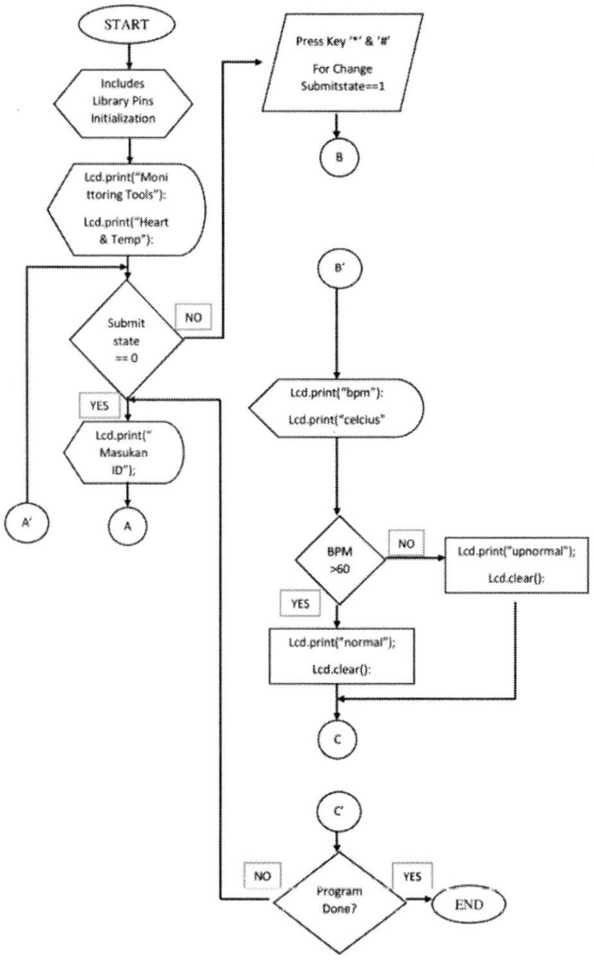

Fig. 3. System flowchart.

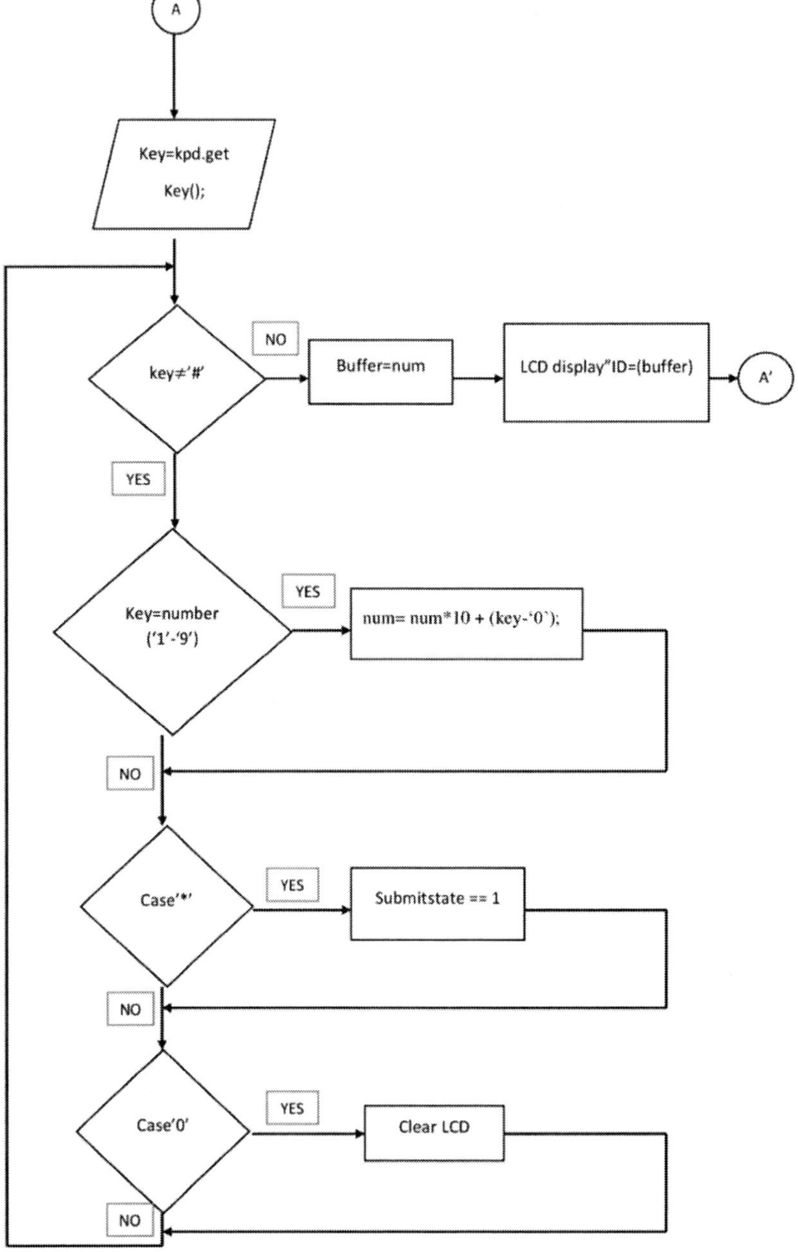

Fig. 4. Keypad system flowchart.

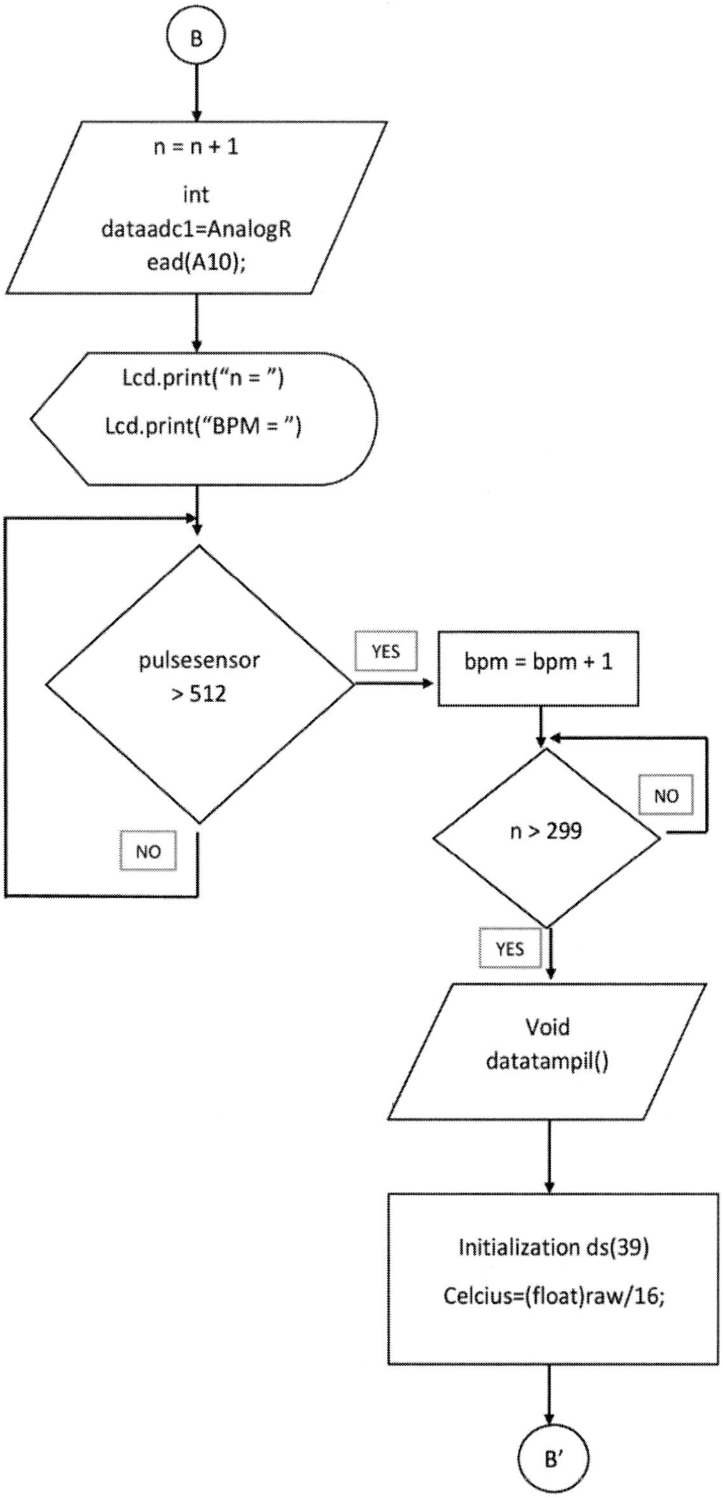

Fig. 5. Sensoring system flowchart.

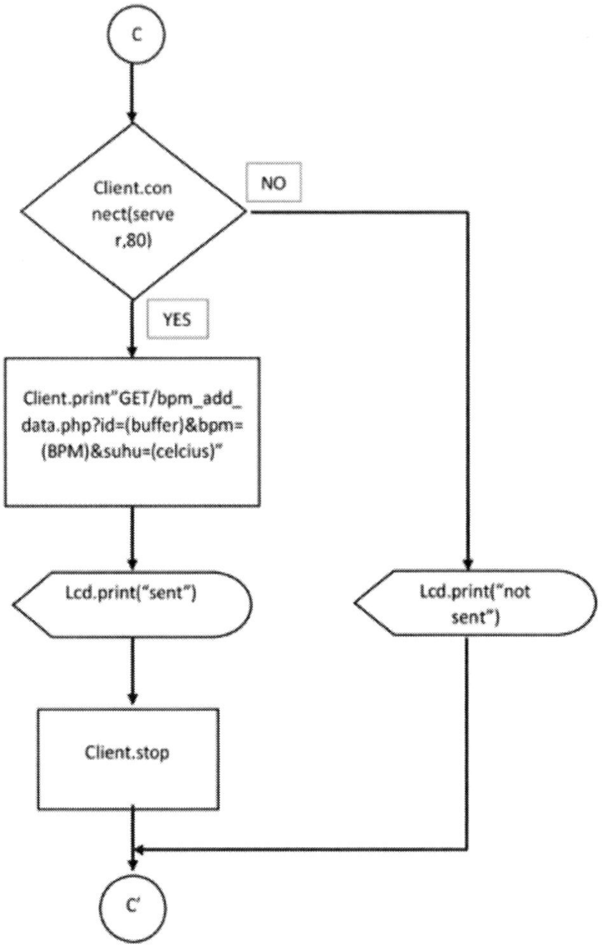

Fig. 6. Internet system flowchart.

4 Device testing and analysis

4.1 Pulse sensor and DS18B20 testing

Figure 7 shows the results from the heartbeat sensor output waveform of pulse sensor when it is not detected and detected.

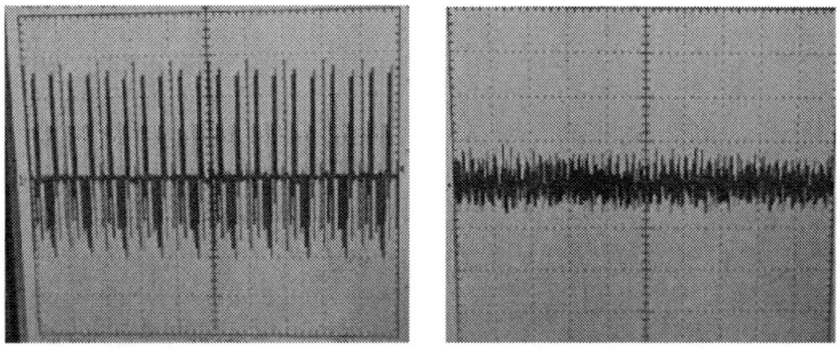

(a) (b)

Fig. 7. (a) When sensor detected, (b) when sensor not detected.

The image shown in Figure 8 result of body temperature sensor output waveform DS18B20

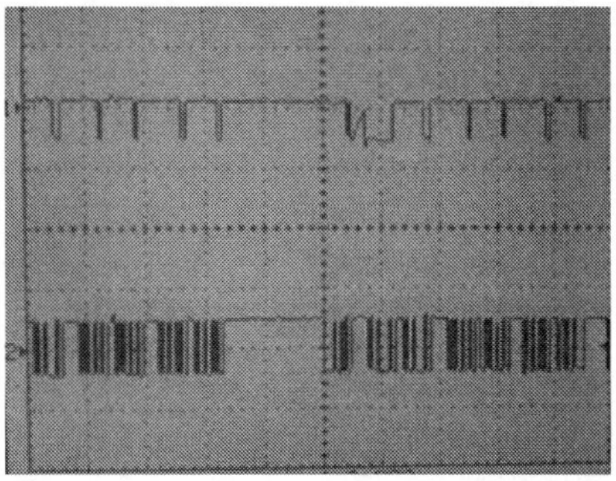

Fig. 8. DS18B20 sensor signal.

In Figure 7 shows a wave when the sensor is detected and not, the pulse sensor obtained output voltage of 2.44 v, and in Figure 8. The results obtained from the temperature sensor ds18b20 with two different temperature sensor conditions, the first when the sensor detects a temperature of 28 degrees (first wave), and the second when the sensor detects a temperature of 34 degrees (second wave), based on the first wave of the resulting output voltage 4.41 v and the second is 4.66 v, the measurement can be inaccurate because of the condition of the measuring instrument is not good.

4.2 SPI pins testing

Figure 9 shows the observed results on serial communication output waveform between the arduino and ethernet shield:

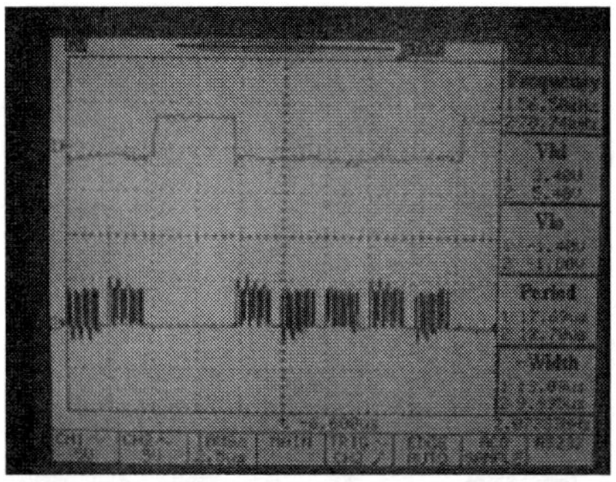

Fig. 9. Osciloscope display of pin SS and SCK signals.

Pin SS is a pin that have function to activate the slave so that data transmission can only be done if the slave is active (active low) and PIN SCK have functions as clock. To avoid communication errors, synchronization is required, Synchronization is done by using the SCK path (or called as SCLK, Serial CLOCK). Data (MISO and MOSI) will be considered valid only when SCK high state. Figure 10 shows the observed results on SS pin waves against MISO and MOSI.

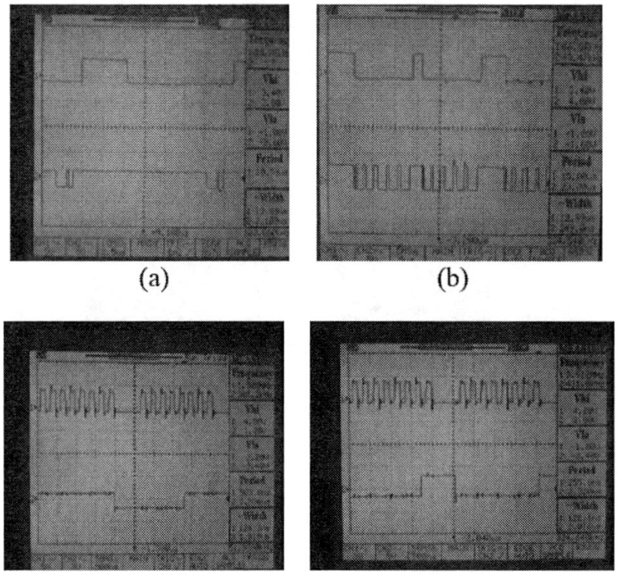

(a) (b)

(c) (d)

Fig. 10. (a) SS and MISO Pin, (b) SS and MOSI Pin, (c) SCK and MISO Pin, (d) SCK and MOSI Pin.

MISO (Master In Slave Out) & MOSI (Master Out Slave In) is the data path for communication between master (programmer /downloader, USBAsp) and Slave (microcontoller IC). As the name implies, MISO is the path used to download or receive data, then MOSI is downloader path sending data to IC microcontroller.

4.3 Overall device testing

This test aims to determine whether the overall design is working properly or not. This test is done by assembling all parts of the device and then testing the device. Not only on assembly, in this testing described the working order of tools, ranging from hardware to the order of how to access data on the website The entire section of the device that has been assembled can be seen in Figure 11.

Fig. 11. Overall device.

Testing is done by following steps:

1. Type in browser:
   http://heartbeattemperature.890m.com.

2. Login form will appear. Then enter the correct name and password and then click login, then "Daftar Pasien" will appear.
3. Then add new data to the database by clicking the "Tambah Pasien" button on the "Daftar Pasien" page and then fill in the required information. Here we fill in the name as "Pasien Baru", date of birth January 4, 1995 and gender is male.

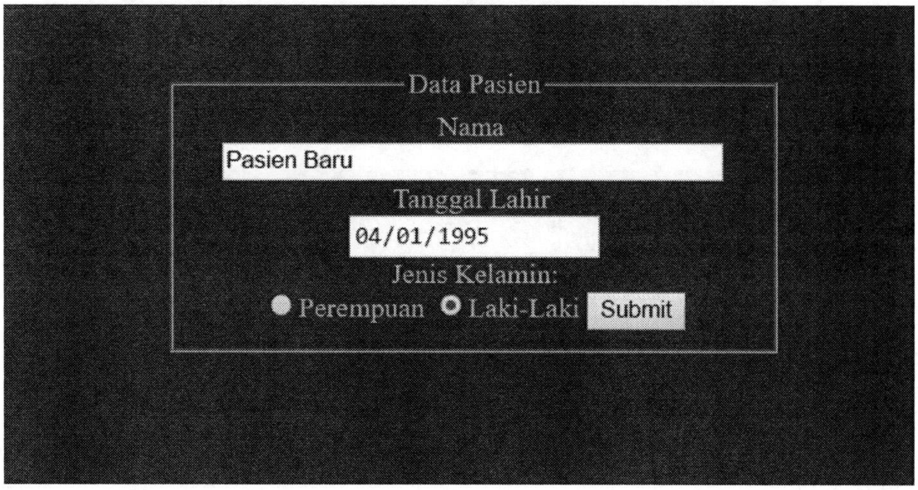

Fig. 12. Adding new data display.

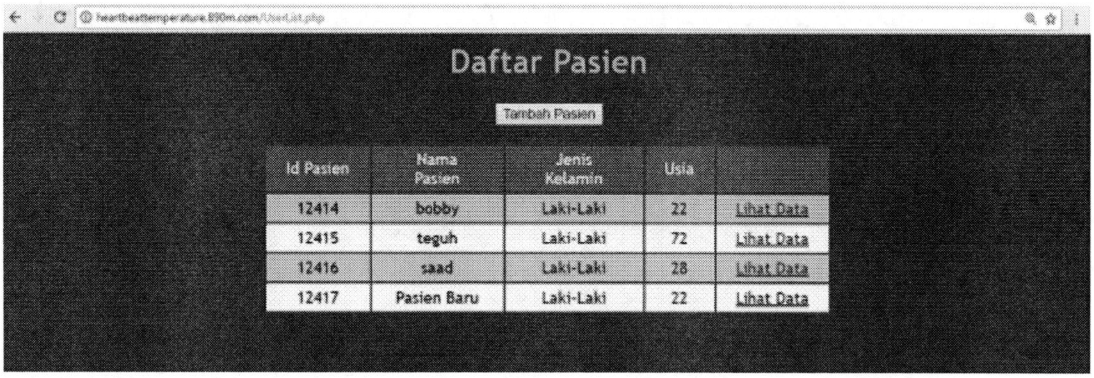

Fig. 13. New data already added.

As we can see in Figure 13, "New Patients" data has been added.

4. Measure the heart rate by using the device, enter the ID number and upload the result to the web server.

Fig. 14. New patient input ID number.

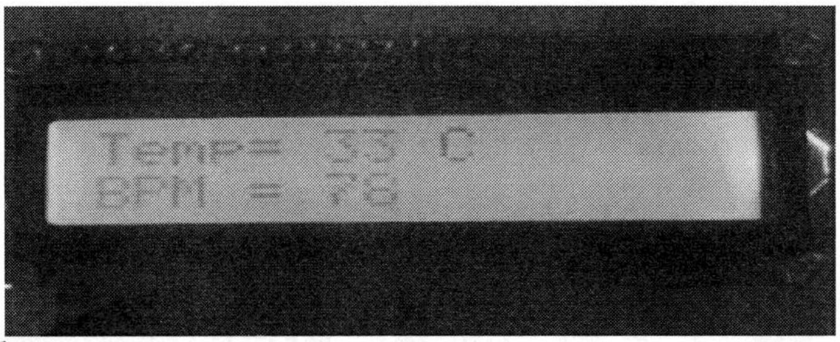

Fig. 15. New patient measures.

Fig. 16. Measurement result has sent to database.

5. Check whether the results have been uploaded by clicking "Lihat Data" on the "Patient List" page.

Fig. 17. Data before measurement.

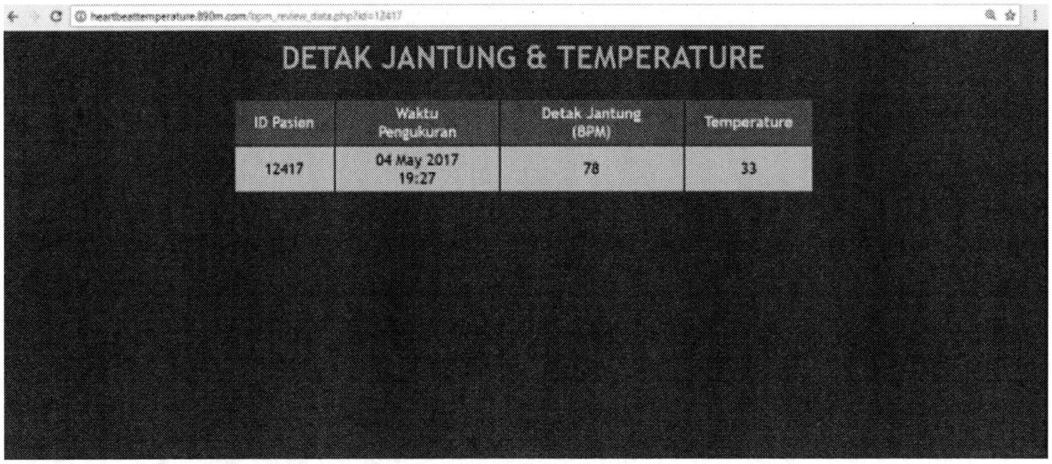

Fig. 18. Data after measurement.

4.4 Testing accuracy of heartbeat counter

The test aims to determine the accuracy value of the tool by comparing the measurement results of devices that have been made with Oxymeter Elitech Mobile Fox 1 and Smartphone Iphone 7 that supports the calculation of the human heart rate also compares the body temperature gauge with digital thermometer innate magic star. The comparison will be displayed as a percentage error by comparing different measurements (Δbpm) with BPM measurements in oxymeter (oxbpm), smartphone (pbpm) as shown in the following formula:

$$\%error = \left(\frac{\Delta bpm}{oxbpm}\right) \times 100\% \quad (1)$$

$$\%error = \left(\frac{\Delta bpm}{pbpm}\right) \times 100\% \quad (2)$$

The results of the test are written in the table below:

Table 1. Heartbeat rate measurment result with oxymeter.

NO	Name	Gender/ Age	BPM Tool Value	BPM Oxymeter Value	Error Rate (%)
1	Bobby	Male/22	80	79	1.27
2	April	Female/23	81	82	1.22
3	Yanti	Female/50	76	76	0
4	Saad	Male/22	97	95	2.11
5	Nayla	Female/12	80	80	0
6	Daniel	Male/22	112	105	6.67
7	Cheril	Female/6	73	77	5.19
8	Edy	Male/58	80	77	3.89
9	Aji	Male/22	98	98	0
10	Inggri	Female/22	70	75	6.67
Average Error Rate (%)					2.702

Table 1 summarizes the results of measurements to ten respondents. The results are different for each person because of the condition and age. Based on the table data, the results of comparison between heartbeat sensors and oxymeter measurements have an average error rate of 2.702 %. The test results of compare tools made with smartphone applications are written in the Table 2.

Table 2. Heartbeat rate measurement result with smartphone.

NO	Name	Gender/ Age	BPM Tool Value	BPM Smartphone Value	Error Rate (%)
1	Bobby	Male/22	80	81	1.23
2	April	Female/23	81	84	3.57
3	Yanti	Female/50	76	76	0
4	Saad	Male/22	97	97	0
5	Nayla	Female/12	80	73	9.59
6	Daniel	Male/22	112	117	4.27
7	Cheril	Female/6	73	74	1.35
8	Edy	Male/58	80	80	0
9	Aji	Male/22	98	101	2.97
10	Inggri	Female/22	70	73	4.11
Average Error Rate (%)					2.709

Table 2 summarizes the comparison between heartbeat sensors and smartphone measurements has an average error rate of 2.709 %. Several levels of error respondents is quite high because the measurement under different conditions, especially the condition of the sensor there is gross error, systematic or random error.

4.5 Testing accuracy of temperature

Testing aims to determine the value of the accuracy of the tool by comparing the measurement results of devices that have been made with the body temperature thermometer digital thermometer congenital magic star. The comparison will be displayed as a percentage error by comparing the different temperature measurements (Δcel) with the measurement of a digital thermometer (tcel) as shown in the following formula:

$$\%error = \left(\frac{\Delta cel}{tcel}\right) \times 100\% \tag{3}$$

In testing tools made and compared with a digital thermometer is written in the table below:

Table 3. Temperature measurment result of ten respondents.

No	Name	Gender/ Age	Tool Value (°C)	Public Termo Digital (°C)	Error Rate (%)
1	Bobby	Male/22	36	36.6	1.64
2	April	Female/23	35	35.6	1.69
3	Yanti	Female/50	34	35.2	3.43
4	Saad	Male/22	36	36.6	1.64
5	Nayla	Female/12	37	36.3	3.58
6	Daniel	Male/22	37	38	2.63
7	Cheril	Female/6	36	36.1	0.28
8	Edy	Male/58	36	36.4	1.1
9	Aji	Male/22	36	37.4	3.74
10	Inggri	Female/22	34	34.7	2.02
Average Error Rate (%)					2.18

Table 3 summarizes the results of measurements to ten respondents. The results are different for each person because of the condition and age. Based on the table data, the result of comparison between sensor temperature and digital thermometer measurement has an average error rate of 2.18 %.

4.6 Testing precision of heartbeat counter

This test aims to determine the precision value of the tool made. In the first precision test, the test was performed for three people tested by doing 10 times with the same tool and finger location then tested for five different fingers for five times. Besides, it is also tested the precision of thermometer made on 10 people tested as much as five times the test. The precision value of each finger measurement can be obtained using the relative standard equation (RSD) is a statistical measurement that describes the distribution of data to the mean and the result is expressed as a percentage.

$$s = \sqrt{\frac{1}{N}\sum_{i=1}^{N}\left(xi - \bar{x}\right)^2} \quad (4)$$

$$RSD = \frac{s}{\bar{x}} \times 100\% \quad (5)$$

Where:

s : Standard Deviation
xi : Observed value
$\bar{x}$: Mean of observed value
N : size of sample
RSD : Relative Standard Deviation

4.7 Precision for one finger

The Table 4 summarizes the results of the test with one finger of the same but performed for 10 times:

Table 4. Result of one finger measurement.

TESTING	Heartbeat Result (BPM)		
	Responden 1	Responden 2	Responden 3
1	81	88	82
2	82	85	82
3	78	87	84
4	81	84	86
5	81	84	84
6	86	86	83
7	82	90	83
8	83	92	86
9	84	86	84
10	81	84	83
RSD(%)	2.60	3.14	1.69
Average RSD (%)	2.48		

Table 4 shows the measurements of 3 tested people who are tested in ten times to get value of precision. The first tested person obtained RSD value 2.60 %, for the second 3.14 %, for the third 1.69 %, so the average RSD yield is 2.48 %. In this study, the smaller the RSD value the better the precision value.

4.8 Precision for all finger

Table 5 and Table 6 shows the measurements of five joint human fingers and test in five times to get the value of precision, first tested is the thumb, index finger to little which is distinguished based on the right and left hands. In Table 5 the five right hand fingers have an average RSD value of 1.48 % or an average BPM of 83.9 with a tolerance of 1.48 %. In Table 6 the five left hand fingers have an average RSD value of 1.80 % or an average BPM of 88.44 with a tolerance of 1.80 %.

Table 5. Right hand fingers measurement result.

Heart Beat Result (BPM)							
Right Finger	RESPONDEN					STDEV	RSD (%)
	1	2	3	4	5		
Thumb	90	87	88	87	90	1.52	1.72
Index	93	90	90	93	91	1.52	1.66
Middle	88	87	84	88	85	1.82	2.10
Ring	89	88	87	90	88	1.14	1.29
Little	85	90	89	87	87	1.95	2.23
AVERAGE						1.59	1.80

Table 6. Left hand fingers measurement result.

Heart Beat Result (BPM)							
Left Finger	RESPONDEN					STDEV	RSD (%)
	1	2	3	4	5		
Thumb	81	84	85	82	82	1.64	1.98
Index	88	87	88	84	87	1.64	1,89
Middle	84	84	84	85	84	0.45	0.53
Ring	81	82	83	82	84	1.14	1.38
Little	84	84	85	82	82	1.34	1.61
AVERAGE						1.24	1.48

4.9 Testing precision of temperature

This test aims to determine the precision value of the tool made. Precision test is done by counting body temperature 10 respondents with each responder counted five times, as shown in Table 7.

Table 7 shows the measurements of 10 tested people who are tested five times to get the value of precision, for first to ten respondents have an average average RSD 1.77 % or an average BPM of 35.56 with a tolerance of 1.77 %. The smaller value of RSD then too greater precision value of a tool.

Table 7. Temperature measurement result table.

Temperature Testing (°C)							
RESPONDEN	TESTING					STDEV	RSD (%)
	1	2	3	4	5		
1	36	36	36	35	36	0.45	1.25
2	35	36	35	35	36	0.55	1.55
3	37	35	34	36	36	1.14	3.20
4	37	37	37	37	37	0.00	0.00
5	36	36	35	36	36	0.45	1.25
6	34	34	35	35	34	0.55	1.59
7	36	35	34	35	34	0.84	2.40
8	36	36	36	37	37	0.55	1.50
9	35	34	34	37	36	1.30	3.70
10	35	35	36	35	35	0.45	1.27
AVERAGE						0.63	1.77

5 Conclusion

This research has succeeded in designing heart rate control device and human body temperature which result can be accessed on web page with internet. This research consists of input blocks are Pulse sensors, DS18B20 sensors and 3×4 keypad buttons, process blocks: Microcontroller, Ethernet Shield, Router and USB Modem, and output blocks: 16×2 LCD and smartphone or PC to access web pages.

The measurement did at 60 s time for pulse sensor and temperature sensor DS18B20. Based on the tests that have been done to all correspondents, the heartbeat rate test with the device made has an error rate of 2.702 % compared to the mobile for 1 pulse oxymeter, and when compared to the measurement in the smartphone application the device is made to have an error rate of 2.709 %. Then on the test of human body temperature measurement, the device made has an error rate of 2.18 % compared to digital thermometer that is already common or sold in the market.

Based on the tool's precision test, the test on the respondent's one point finger has an average precision value of RSD 2.48 %. In addition, for measurements of right and left correspondent point fingers, right hand measurements have an average precision value of RSD 1.48 % and for the left hand is RSD 1.80 %. Then for the device precision test on the body temperature measurement has an average precisiom value of RSD 1.77 %. Based on the measurements of three tested people who are tested in ten times, the average RSD yield is 2.48 %.

7 References

1. D.O.L Sihombing, L. Lubis, N. Setiowati, S. Sophiana. *Pengaruh suhu terhadap denyut jantung* [temperature effect to heartbeat]. [Online] from https://www.scribd.com/doc/245978378/Pengaruh-Suhu-Ter hadap-Denyut-Jantung (2016). [Accessed 12 July 2017]. [In Bahasa Indonesia]

2. A. Mandal. *Penyebab stroke panas* [cause of heat stroke]. [Online] from http://www.news-medical.net/health/Causes-of-heat-stroke-(Indonesian).aspx (2016). [Accessed 12 July 2017].
3. W.K. Raharja, S. Frandika. *Alat pengukur jumlah detak jantung berdasarkan aliran darah ujung kiri* [hearbeat measurement tool based on left blood flow]. Prosiding Seminar Ilmiah Nasional Komputer dan Sistem Intelijen (Jakarta, Indonesia 2014). KOMMIT 2014, **8**:425–431(2014). [in Bahasa Indonesia]. http://ejournal.gunadarma.ac.id/index.php/kommit/article/view/1060/922
4. Jalinas, W.K. Raharja, F. Permana, Y. Rianto. *Rancang bangun alat pemonitor detak jantung berbasis koneksi WIFI* [Heartbeat monitoring tool's plan based on WIFI connection]. *Prosiding Seminar Nasional Aplikasi Sains & Teknologi,* (Yogyakarta, Indonesia 2016). Prosiding SNAST: 275–281. [in Bahasa Indonesia]. http://journal.akprind.ac.id/index.php/snast/article/view/786 [Accessed 12 July 2017].
5. InnerBody. *Human heart - diagram and anatomy of the heart*. [Online] from http://www.innerbody.com/image/card01.html (2016) [Accessed 12 July 2017].
6. M. Elgendy. *Current Cardiology Reviews*, **8**(1):14–25 (2012) [Accessed 12 July 2017].
7. Pulse Sensor. *Pulse Sensor Open Hardware*. [Online] from https://pulsesensor.com/pages/open-hardware (2016). [Accessed 18 July 2017].
8. Arduino. Arduino *DS18B20 Temperature Sensor*. [Online] from https://www.tweaking4all.com/hardware/arduino/arduino-ds18b20-temperature-sensor (2016). [Accessed 12 July 2017].
9. Arduino. *Arduino Mega 2560 REV3*. [Online] from http://www.arduino.cc/en/Main/ArduinoBoardMega2560 (2016). [Accessed 18 July 2017].
10. TP-Link. *Portable 3G/4G Wireless N Router TL-MR3020*. [Online] from http://www.tp-link.com/en/products/details/cat-4691_TL-MR3020.html (2016). [Accessed 18 July 2017].

Information System Strategic Planning for Department of Housing and Settlement Region in the Jakarta Provincial Government - Indonesia

Jarot Sembodo Suroso, *Harisno*, *Tuga* Mauritsius*, and *Agung* Setyawan

Information Systems Management Department, Bina Nusantara Graduate Program, Master of Information Systems Management, Bina Nusantara University, Jl. Syahdan No. 9, Jakarta 11480, Indonesia

Abstract. This research was conducted in the *Unit Pengelola Rumah Susun*—UPRS (Flats Manager Unit) in Jakarta Provincial Government and based on the existence of problems strategic planning of information systems. The purpose of this study is to provide a proposal of Information System Strategy and Management Information System for UPRS. The strategic planning of the information systems on research was conducted using the method of Ward and Peppard. The IS strategic planning in the UPRS which is proposed in this research is hope to be used to integrate each business process and IS system which is connected to the Jakarta Smart City. IS is needed with the competent human resources to manage the IS/IT of the UPRS to increase the service quality to the flat occupants and to increase the employees productivity in implementing their job functions.

Key words: E-government, information system strategic planning, ward and peppard framework.

1 Introduction

With the development of the world of Information Technology, both Information System (IS) and Information Technology (IT) play an important role in improving organization's strategic advantages/competitiveness. The management of IT is greatly needed to increase the success in achieving organization's objectives and to ensure the safety and accuracy of strategic information effectively by managing IT assets [1]. Managing the IS technology is not only done by private company, but public company also needs to manage their IS technology asset to ensure that their vision and mission is achieved effectively and efficiently, hence increasing their service to the community.

Unit Pengelola Rumah Susun—UPRS (Flats Manager Unit) is a unit under the *Unit Kerja Perangkat Daerah*—UKPD (Regional Area Work Unit) in Jakarta Provincial Government based on the Regulation of the Regional Special Province of Jakarta No. 5/2016 on the Establishment and Composition of the Region Special Province of Jakarta. Their main task and function is managing public residential flats based on the Governor of the Province of Jakarta Capital Special Region's Regulation No. 351/2016 on the Establishment, Organization and Work Flow management Unit Housing Project.

UPRS has the function to provide housing for low income people and relocated program people. Housing which is manage by the UPRS are public residential flats which are build by the Department of Housing and Settlement Region of the Jakarta Provincial Government using the Local Government Budget (APBD-*Anggaran Pendapatan dan Belanja Daerah*) or from the Corporate Social Responsibility (CSR) activities. The management of each inhabited public residential flats is conducted by the UPRS according to the Jakarta Provincial Governor's Regulation No. 351/2016 regarding the formation, organization and work procedure of the public residential flat's management.

The UPRS public residential flat service business process consist of the registration process, occupant candidate's requirement validation, placement of prospective occupants to flat unit, services, data collection and financial administration of flat occupants, policing flat occupants and report preparation. The current IS utilization in the UPRS is only used to increase the effectiveness and efficiency of UPRS's operational activities but is not yet used to upgrade the

*Corresponding author: tmauritsus@binus.edu

services to the Jakarta Provincial people. The IS in the UPRS is not integrated to one another. Each of the 13 location of public residential flats has their own IS to provide services to their own occupants. Therefore this condition is not effective and efficient to the provision of service to the occupants. Databases which are not yet integrated can cause inconsistency of data, which can lead to problems in the data making process and reporting. The current IS condition in the UPRS is not yet used maximally and there is no planning for the development of IS in the UPRS.

The IS strategic planning in the UPRS which is proposed in this research is hope to be used to integrate each business process and IS system which is connected to the Jakarta Smart City application manage by the Department of Communication, Information and Statistic of the Jakarta Provincial Government. It is hoped that data will be more consistent and the operational activities in the UPRS will be more effective and efficient and hence providing disclosure of information to the public of Jakarta.

Identification of the problems that occur in UPRS based on previous research is as follows:

(i). Strategic planning of information systems is needed in an organization to support and assist the implementation of the tasks, responsibilities and functions as well as to achieve their goals. With the absence of information systems strategic, an organization will have difficulties in achieving their objectives. UPRS currently does not have an information systems strategic planning portfolio, and based on previous research this will make UPRS difficult in achieving their objectives [2–4].

(ii). Strategic planning is required to design and improve information systems in the future, so that organization can have a proper information system to help the organization achieve its objectives. UPRS currently does not have information system applications that can be used by UPRS to support the implementation of UPRS's duties. The application of information systems is required to support UPRS in carrying out the duties and achieve its objectives [2].

(iii). A division is needed in an organization that specializes on IS/IT, so that the development of IS/IT in an organization can be organized and developed properly. UPRS currently does not have a special division that deals with the development of IS/IT hence the IS/IT needs in UPRS is not available [4].

2 Literature review

Strategic planning based on the Ward and Peppard method is divided into two stages, input stage and output stage. Input stage contains the identification and analysis of internal and external conditions and the condition of IS internal and external to the organization where the input stages will be taken into consideration in determining the strategic plan of IS. Output stages produces physical documents based on the results of the strategic plan of IS input stages. Physical Document Management Strategies strategic plan in the form of IS, Business Strategy, and evaluation of business strategy and management.

2.1 PEST analysis

This analysis is used to identify the general environmental conditions of the organization. This identification is carried out from the aspects of the Political, Economic, Social and Technological.

(i) Political

Analysing the political factors which can affect the organization.

(ii) Economy

Analysing the current and upcoming economical condition factors which can affect the progress and the strategy of the organization.

(iii). Social

Analysing the social factors which focus on the occupants' and employees' appraisal which can affect the strategy of the organization.

(iv).Technology

Technological changing factors that can affect the strategy of the organization.

2.2 SWOT analysis

SWOT analysis is an analysis environment based on four aspects: Strengths, Weaknesses, Opportunities and Threats.

(i). Strengths

Strength is the quality owned by the organization in obtaining their objectives. Strength can be tangible or intangible. It can be the expertise, quality and the loyalty of employee, high financial resources, free from any kind of debt and so forth.

(ii). Weaknesses

Weakness is something that prevents an organization in obtaining their objectives. Weakness can decrease the chance of organization's success. Weaknesses can be in the form of low quality of employees, low financial ability and so forth.

(iii). Opportunities

Opportunities comes from the external environment's condition that be optimized by the organization in planning and doing their strategy in obtaining their objectives. Organization can achieve competitive advantage by utilizing the opportunities available. Opportunities can arise from competitiveness, the industries, government and technology.

(iv). Threats

Threat comes from the external environment's condition that threatened the reliability and advantages of an organization's business. Threats can affect the livelihood of an organization. For example uncomfortable working atmosphere, technological changes, and so forth.

2.3 Critical Success Factor (CSF)

CSF analyses the main factors that determine the organization's business development. It is very important for a thorough understanding of the business. CSF aims to attain the objectives and strategies and to emphasize the priority activities [5].

2.4 Value Chain Analysis

Value Chain is carried out to map the entire work process within the organization. It is mapped into two categories of activity, namely primary activities and support activities. An example of the value chain analysis can be seen in Fig. 1.

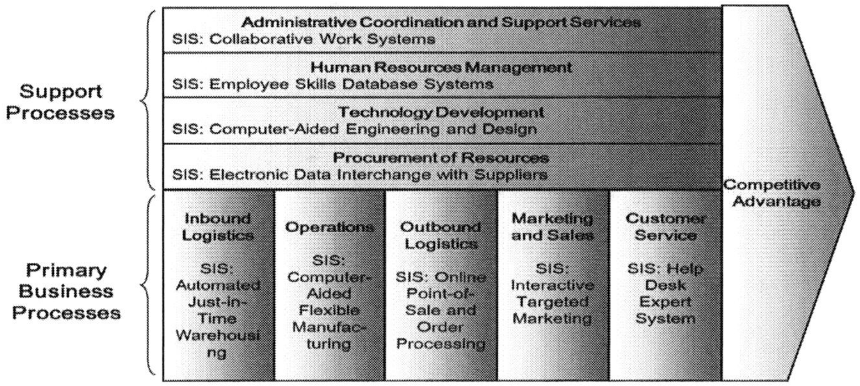

Fig. 1. Value Chain Analysis.

McFarlan Strategic Grid is used to map IS applications based on its contribution to the organization. Mapping is done in four quadrants (strategic, high potential, key operation, and support). The result obtained shows the role of each IS application is the organization and its future development [6]. An example of the McFarlan Strategic Grid can be seen in Figure 2.

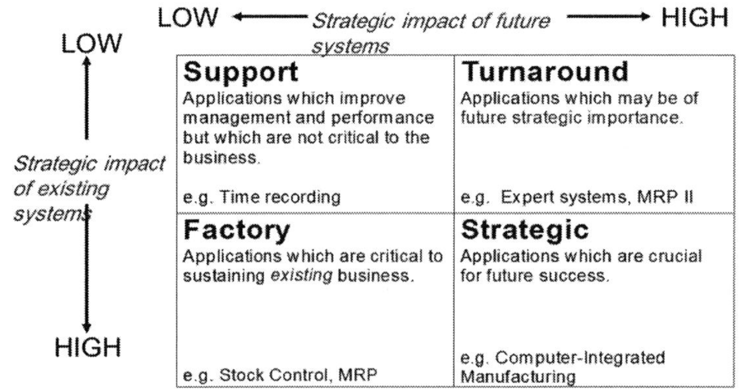

Fig. 2. McFarlan Strategic Grid.

3 Method

The case study begins with an overview of formulation and identification of internal and external business environment and the environment of internal and external information systems of UPRS. An analysis of the IS needs in UPRS is then conducted through the IS strategic planning using the Ward and Peppard method's framework [2] which can be seen in Figure 3. Data are collected through literature study available from books and journals, interviews with the leader in UPRS, observation, documentation and the distributions of questionnaires to the UPRS employees.

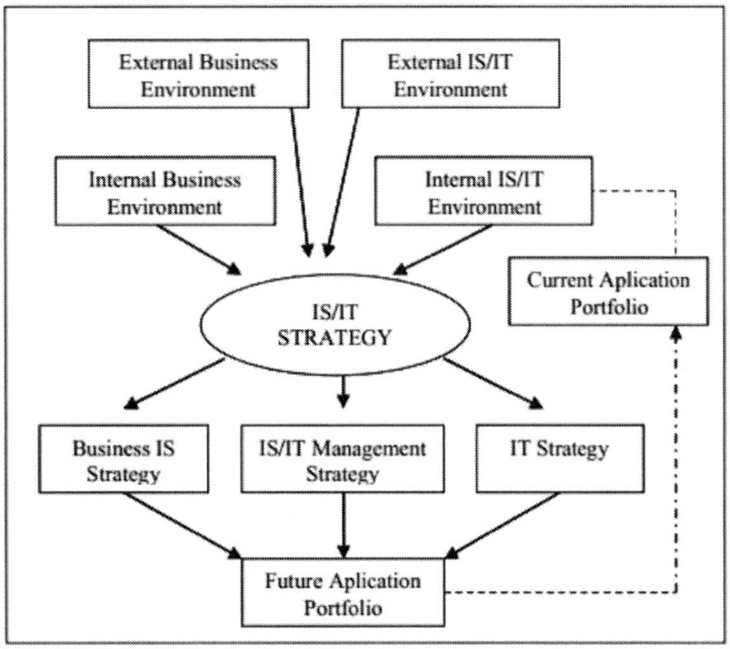

Fig. 3. Ward & Peppard method's framework [2].

4 Results and discussion

4.1 PEST analysis

(i). Political factors

As one of the Regional Working Unit (UKPD) in the Provincial Government of Jakarta, UPRS have a regulatory basis as a reference in implementing their function. Regulations related to UPRS are as follows:

- Jakarta Governor Regulation number 111/2014 concerning the Mechanism Occupancy of Public Residential Flats' rents. These regulations govern the management of public residential flats, specify the tenants, manage kiosk on the ground floor and to curb residential area that is not in accordance with regulations. This regulation requires UPRS to work professionally so that the need for a system that helps UPRS in managing their modest public residential flats rental in a professional manner so that public residential flats' management can be effective, efficient and accountable.

- Regulation of the Governor of the Province of Jakarta Capital Special Region number 351/2016 on the Establishment, Organization and Work Flow Management Unit Housing Project. This regulation specifies the duties of employees in UPRS Cipinang. Given these rules, the scope of work of employees UPRS Cipinang are regulated and restricted in accordance within the rules. These regulations should be used by the UPRS's employees as much as possible. By limiting the scope of the job function of the employee, it will maximize their job function to achieve UPRS's vision and mission.

- Jakarta Governor Instruction number 131/2016 on Optimizing the Management of Public Residential Flat in Jakarta. This instruction instructs other agencies to participate in the management of Public Residential Flat Rent. UPRS cannot manage their own subsidized Public Residential Flat because of the complex problems in Public Residential Flat, either from residents or the infrastructure's quality of the Public Residential Flat. Therefore, this instruction instructed the relevant agencies to participate and manage subsidized Public Residential Flat.

UPRS should be able to maximize the Governor Instruction because with the involvement of other agencies the management of Public Residential Flat can be optimized.

(ii). Economic Factors
Having a large amount of Local Government Budget (APBD), the UPRS can plan their budget of maximally. The increase in prices can not affect the UPRS in providing the management needs and public residential flat repairmen budget due to the fact that Jakarta Provincial Budget can become self-sufficient for the UKPD.

(iii). Social Factors
The occupants of public residential flat are mostly relocated/slum realignment residents which needs different treatments for each residents. The occupants also need assistance and empowerment because most of them have lost their jobs due to the relocation, while living in public residential flat needs rent money.

(iv). Technological factors
The current information system used in UPRS is only Microsoft office applications. With the increase in number of public residential flats, an integrated information system is needed. An integrated information system will support the management of public residential flats with the increase of amount of work load.

4.2 SWOT Analysis

(i). Improve the facilities subsidized apartment units
(ii). Improve the quality of service to the community
(iii). Develop Information Systems needed by Public Residential Flat
(iv). Marketing Public Residential Flat dwelling units for common low income people.
(v). Increase cooperation with other agencies and the private sector to empower citizens Public Residential Flat.

4.3 CSF Analysis

The CSF analysis can be seen in Table 1.

Table 1. CSF Analysis

Objecti ves	Critical Success Factors	Indicators	Strategy	Needs SI
Occupants towers serve citizens well	Increased citizen satisfaction occupants towers	The level of citizen satisfaction ≥ 80 %	Facilitate access to services citizens	*E-Service*
			Improve communication with citizens	*E-News*
			Streamline the handling of complaints of citizens	*E-Disposition*
Having data processing with IS	Increased data processing functions with IS	Data processing functions IS ≥ 50 %	Developing applications IS	E-Rusunawa *HRIS* *E-Assets*
Provides information for prospective residents rusunawa	The increasing interest in prospective residents rusunawa	The number of applicants ≥ 50 %	To develop means and complete information to prospective rusu nawa residents	Website Rusunawa
Reducing the number of violations	Minimi zing abuses rusunawa	The number of violations of ≤ 50 %	Provide means to media reports of citizens	*E-Aduan*

4.4 Value Chain Analysis

Based on interviews with informants, the main activities to value chain UPRS are as follows:

(i). Inbound Logistics: Selection Apparatus State Civil Servants (ASN-*Aparatur Sipil Negara*) and Other Services Provider Individual (PJLP).
(ii). Operations: Service Flats, Flats Management.
(iii). Outbound Logistics: Disposition of UPRS employees to follow up flat occupants' complaints, demography services, repair services unit, Security Services and Sanitary Service.
(iv). Sales and Marketing: Facility received by the flat occupants.
(v). Services: The rental payment, settlement, security, cleanliness, orderliness and repair unit.

As for the supporting activities consist of:

(i). Infrastructure: Organizational Structure, Local Government Budget (APBD) of Jakarta Province and Flats.
(ii).Human-Resource Management Training, the State Civil Apparatus (ASN), Other Services Provider Individual (PJLP) Administration, PJLP Technician, PJLP Safety and Hygiene.
(iii). Technology Development: The Internet and Wifi.
(iv).Procurement: Tools hygiene, electronics & mechanics tools, security tools, stationery office (ATK-*Alat Tulis Kantor*), office facilities and means of enforcement.

4.5 McFarlan strategic grid

Based on discussions with sources and analysis, the application portfolio of future IS UPRS can be seen in Table 2.

Table 2. IS application portfolio for UPRS in the future.

High	***Strategic***	***High Potential***
	e-News e-Service e-Rusunawa	e-Assets e-Aduan Website Rusunawa
	Key Operational	***Support***
Low	e-Disposition	HRIS MS Office
	Low	*High*

The proposed information system for UPRS can be seen in Table 3.

Table 3. The proposed IS application for UPRS

No.	Information Systems	Year Of Develop	Category
1	*Website* Rusunawa	2018	*High potential*
2	e-Rusunawa	2018	*Strategic*
3	HRIS	2019	*Support*
4	*e-Assets*	2019	*High potential*
5	*e-Service*	2020	*Strategic*
6	*e-News*	2020	*Strategic*
7	*e-Disposition*	2021	*Key operational*
8	e-Aduan	2021	*High potential*

To evaluate the acceptance of the proposed IS strategies; questionnaires were given out using the Technology Acceptance Model (TAM). The TAM model consist of four dimensions which are perceived ease of use, perceive usefulness, attitude towards using and behavioural intention to use. Questionnaires were given out to 28 samples, where only 24 respondents responded to the questionnaires. The respondents were UPRS employees that will use the proposed IS in the future.

Based on the questionnaire result, it can be concluded that the proposed IS is well accepted by the respondents. Most respondents responded positively to the proposed IS. These are the following explanations:

(i). Perceived ease of use
In the perceived eased of use dimension most of the respondents responded "agree" and "strongly agree" to the questions given. This means that the respondents realize that the IS proposed is easy to use and can help UPRS employees in doing their functions.

(ii).Perceived usefulness

In the perceived usefulness dimension, most of the respondents responded "strongly agree" to the questions given. This proves that the proposed IS is believed to be useful in providing services to the flat occupants and in increasing the productivities of UPRS employees.

(iii).Attitude toward using

In the attitude toward using dimension most of the respondents responded "agree" that the use of IS is a good idea and accepted the proposed IS.

(iv).Behavioural intention to use

In the behavioural intention to use dimension, most of the respondents responded "agree" in utilizing the IS proposed and will use the IS proposed to support their function in the UPRS.

5 Conclusion

Based on the analysis and business IS strategic planning in the UPRS of Department of Housing and Settlement Region of Jakarta Province, it can be concluded that: There are some obstacles in the UPRS regarding the IS such as UPRS does not have an IS which can help UPRS to do their job functions, the absence of IS that can present data that is integrated and accurate, the absence of automatic dissemination of information to the flat occupants, such as information regarding rent and arrears, and other important information available, the absence of IS strategic planning that can be used as guidance for future IS development in the UPRS and the absence of a specific human resource which is assigned to manage IS and IT in the UPRS. Therefore IS is needed with the competent human resources to manage the IS/IT of the UPRS to increase the service quality to the flat occupants and to increase the employees productivity in implementing their job functions. Supports area also needed from the board of managers in the Department of Housing and Settlement Region of Jakarta Province to support in terms of policy and budget making so that the development of IS in the UPRS becomes a priority. This is due to the fact that IS is needed to accommodate the increase number of public residential flats and the flat occupants due to the on going relocation program.

References

1. L. M. Applegate, R. D. Austin, D. L. Soule. *Corporate information strategy and management*. Pennsylvania: Mc-Graw Hill (2009). pp. 41–207 https://books.google.co.id/books/about/Corporate_Information_Strategy_and_Manag.html?id=DWfbGAAACAAJ&redir_esc=y
2. J. Ward, J. Peppard, *Strategic planning for information systems*. New Jersey: Wiley (2002). pp. 1–573 https://www.amazon.com/Strategic-Planning-Information-Systems-John/dp/0470841478
3. C. Slamet. *Analysis of information security audit using iso 27001:2013 & iso 27002:2013 at it division - x company, in Bandung, Indonesia*. [Online] from http://www.insikapub.com/index.php/vol01-no01-july-2012?id=26 (2012). [Accessed on July 30 2017]
4. A. Cassidy. *A practical guide to information systems strategic planning*. Florida: Auerbach Publications (2005). pp. 1–22, https://www.amazon.com/Practical-Information-Systems-Strategic-Planning/dp/0849350735
5. K. C. Laudon, J. P. Laudon. *Sistem informasi manajemen, mengelola perusahaan digital*. [Management information systems, managing the digital firm]. Jakarta: Salemba Empat (2004). pp. 45–52. [in Bahasa Indonesia]. http://library.um.ac.id/free-contents/index.php/buku/detail/sistem-informasi-manajemen-mengelola-perusahaan-digital-buku-1-kenneth-c-laudon-jane-p-laudon-38239.html
6. J. M. Bryson. *Strategic planning for public and non-profit organization*. NewYork: John Wiley & Son (2011). pp. 81–317 https://www.wiley.com/en-us/Strategic+Planning+for+Public+and+Nonprofit+Organizations%3A+A+Guide+to+Strengthening+and+Sustaining+Organizational+Achievement%2C+4th+Edition-p-9780470392515
7. K. E. Pearlson, I. C. S. Saunders. *Strategic of management information system*. Fourth Edition. New York: John Wiley & Sons (2009). pp. 19–32. https://books.google.co.id/books/about/Strategic_Management_of_Information_Syst.html?id=Zfw8nwEACAAJ&redir_esc=y
8. E. Turban, R. K. Rainer, R. E. Potter. *Introduction to information technology (8th ed.)*. New York: John Wiley & Sons (2003). pp. 1–56. https://www.amazon.com/Introduction-Information-Technology-Efraim-Turban/dp/0471347809
9. H. M. Jogiyanto. *Sistem informasi strategik untuk keunggulan kompetitif* [Strategic information system for competitive advantages]. Yogyakarta: Andi (2005). pp. 50–65. [in Bahasa Indonesia]. https://openlibrary.telkomuniversity.ac.id/pustaka/18833/sistem-informasi-strategik-untuk-keunggulan-kompetitif.html

10. D. Urumsah. Jurnal Siasat Bisnis, **1**,10: 123–140 (2005). [in Bahasa Indonesia]. http://journal.uii.ac.id/index.php/JSB/article/view/996/927
11. A. Peter. *High, implementing world class IT strategy: How IT can drive organizational innovation*. San Fransisco: Josey-Bass (2014) pp. 91–135. https://www.amazon.com/Implementing-World-Class-Strategy-Organizational/dp/111863411X

Data Mining Application using Association Rule Mining ECLAT Algorithm Based on SPMF

Jason Reynaldo*, and *David* Boy Tonara

Management Information System, Ciputra University, UC Town, Citraland, Made, Sambikerep, Surabaya 60219, East Java, Indonesia

Abstract. Data mining is an important research domain that currently focused on knowledge discovery database. Where data from the database are mined so that information can be generated and used effectively and efficiently by humans. Mining can be applied to the market analysis. Association Rule Mining (ARM) has become the core of data mining. The search space is exponential in the number of database attributes and with millions of database objects the problem of I/O minimization becomes paramount. To get the information and the data such as, observation of the master data storage systems and interviews were done. Then, ECLAT algorithm is applied to the open-source library SPMF. In this project, this application can perform data mining assisted by open source SPMF with determined writing format of transaction data. It successfully displayed data with 100 % success rate. The application can generate a new easier knowledge which can be used for marketing the product.

Key words: Association rule mining, data mining, ECLAT, mining library, SPMF

1 Introduction

Data mining is an important research domain is currently focused on knowledge discovery in databases. Where data from the database are mined so that information can be generated and used effectively and efficiently by humans. Its objective is prediction and description. One of the aspects of data mining is the Association Rule mining. It consists of two procedures: first, finding the frequent item set in the database using a minimum support and constructing the association rule from the frequent item set with specified confidence. It relates to the association of items wherein for every occurrence of A, there exists an occurrence of B. This mining is more applicable in the market basket analysis. That application is helpful to the customers that buy certain items. That for every item that they bought, what would be the possible item/s coupled with the purchased item [1].

Association Rule Mining (ARM) has become the core data mining tasks and has attracted remarkable attention among researcher data mining. ARM is a data mining without direction or without supervision is a technique that works on a long variable data, and produce results that are clear and easy to understand [2].

* Corresponding author: jreynaldo@student.ciputra.ac.id

A new algorithm for ARM combine features item sets, depending on the format of the database, decomposition techniques, and procedures used search. One of them is ECLAT (Equivalence Class Transformation). The algorithm which was found by Zaki, not only minimize the cost of I/O by simply making a small number of database scans, but also minimize the cost calculations with efficient search schemes. This algorithm is very effective when used for small to medium item set [3].

This study uses ECLAT algorithm which is applied to the open-source library SPMF. SPMF will be used to run the algorithm ECLAT on restaurant xyz sales data as a case study. Therefore, researchers are interested in discussing about ECLAT Algorithm Implementation on sales data with xyz restaurant case studies using a program embed with open-source SPMF.

2 Related

The task of discovering all frequent associations in very large databases is quite challenging. The search space is exponential in the number of database attributes and with millions of database objects the problem of I/O minimization becomes paramount. However, most current approaches are literative in nature, requiring multiple database scans, which is clearly very expensive. Some of the methods, especially those using some form of sampling, can be sensitive to the data-skew which can adversely affect performance. Furthermore, most approaches use very complicated internal data structures which have poor locality and add additional space and computation over- heads [3].

3 Analysis and design

To get the information and the data, there are some important things such as, observation of how the xyz restaurant run the master data storage systems and for every transaction that occurs at xyz restaurant, as well as conducting interviews to the xyz restaurant manager. Interview was conducted on Friday, December 16th, 2016 at xyz restaurant and below are the results obtained by the author.

3.1 Result interview

(i) For each sales transaction in the xyz restaurant was already systemized, so every number of transactions, the customer, total payment and others are already recorded in the system, so it is very easy to pick and process the data using the application.

(ii) For each transaction data processing that are very private for xyz restaurant, system must go through the authorities of the restaurant manager.

3.2 Result interview

In the project, the authors use the attributes of the data that collected by the authors to learn the sale of the food menu in the xyz restaurant. So it is easier for the application to analyze the data and the ease of use for the data mining application, it can be very helpful for manager or anyone on the part of the restaurant to be able to use the application easily and its main purpose is to make it easier for the sales promotion through data mining analysis application which the authors designed and built.

3.3 Data source

The data that used for this project is the data from the xyz restaurant that located in Surabaya, Indonesia. The data was taken from the xyz restaurant system for 12 months data transactions, it started from January 2016 until December 2016. With the Excel type data, the data obtained about 40 876 rows with eight data attributes columns and had 364 food menu data. The data was reduced to two columns of attributes. The attributes are:

Table 1. Attributes table.

No	Attributes	Explanation
1	Transaction ID	Transaction Id for each transaction.
2	Item Name	Name of goods in accordance with the master data.

3.4 System architecture design

Before getting the output from the analysis results that obtained from the application, there are several stages before preprocessing until post processing, which of these steps will be detailed in several segments below:

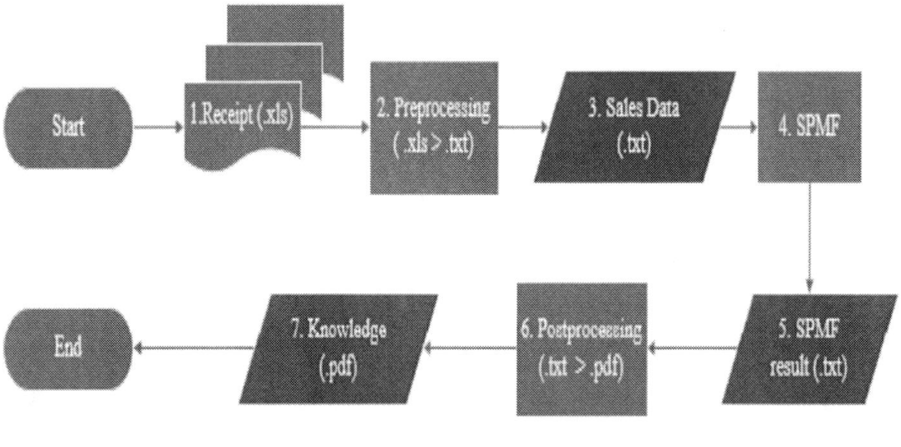

Fig. 1. System architecture design.

3.4.1 Collecting transaction receipts

First of all, researcher collect all data that start from interview from restaurant manager to get the transaction data starting from January 2016 until December 2016 with data format of Excel type (.xls) with 40 876 rows with eight columns of data attributes.

3.4.2 Preprocessing (.xls > .txt)

- Data reduction

Data reduction is to reduce the attributes used before entering into the preprocessing application manually by reducing the eight columns attribute into two columns attribute. There are transaction id and item name [4].

- Data transformation

Data Transformation is performed when data is converted into a text file, because SPMF can only read a text file [4].

The purpose of the transformation are: for each name of the menu in the Excel file will be converted into number of codes, the use of the transaction id is used as a separator for each new transaction that has transformed in vertical line and entered for each new transaction id.

- Data integration

Integration of data that occurs in sub preprocessing is to combine the data from January to December 2016 by inputting data per month one by one in the application and put together into a whole data which will be processed by SPMF and produce a result of information [4].

3.4.3 Sales data (.txt)

At the end of the preprocessing, the files format is changed to text files. And the form of numbers as a substitute of the name of the goods in the database used as a code of the food menu.

3.4.4 SPMF process

The output generated from the preprocessing stage above will be processed using open source data mining program that called SPMF. In the program we have chosen the ECLAT algorithm and then run the program to generate the text into the SPMF, so the SPMF can generate all the data based on ECLAT algorithm. The author will explain how ECLAT works on open source data mining SPMF, here is a flowchart drawing to explain how the ECLAT algorithm works.

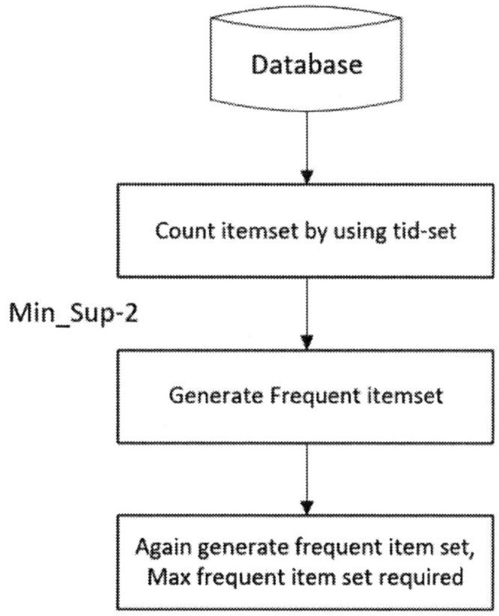

Fig. 2. Flowchart of ECLAT algorithm [2].

Inputs for this ECLAT algorithm include a database of transactions and a threshold named minimum support (which is filled between 0 % and 100 %).

The transaction database is a set of transactions. For each transaction is a set of items, for example consider the following transaction database. There are five sample transactions (t1, t2, ..., t5) and 5 items (1, 2, 3, 4, 5). For example, the first transaction represents the set items 1, 3, and 4. It is important to note that items are not allowed to appear twice in the same transaction and that items are assumed to be sorted by lexicographical order in transaction.

Table 2. Attributes table.

No	Transaction ID	Items
1	t1	{1, 3, 4}
2	t2	{2, 3, 5}
3	t3	{1, 2, 3, 5}
4	t4	{2, 5}
5	t5	{1, 2, 3, 5}

ECLAT is an algorithm for discovering item sets (group of items) which occurs frequently in a transaction database. A frequent item sets is an item set appearing in at least minimum support transactions from the transaction database, where minimum support is a parameter given by the user.

For example, if ECLAT is run on the previous transaction database with minimum support of 40 % , ECLAT produces the following result:

Table 3. Examples of SPMF output.

No	Transaction ID	Items
1	{1}	3
2	{2}	4
3	{3}	4
4	{5}	4
5	{1,2}	2
6	{1,3}	3
7	{1,5}	2
8	{2,3}	3
9	{2,5}	4
10	{3,5}	3
11	{1,2,3}	2
12	{1,2,5}	2
13	{1,3,5}	2
14	{2,3,5}	3
15	{1,2,3,5}	2

Each frequent item set is annotated with its support. The support of an item set is how many times the item set appears in the transaction database. For example, the item set

{2,3,5} has support of 3 because it appears in transaction t2, t3, and t5. It is a frequent item set because its support is higher or equal to the minimum support parameter [3].

The input file format used by ECLAT is defined as follows. It is a text file. An item is represented by a positive integer. A transaction is a line in the text file. In each line (transaction), items are separated by a single space. It is assumed that all items within a same transaction (line) are sorted according to a total order and that no item can appear twice within the same line [5].

3.4.5 SPMF result

The output of the SPMF program is a file that contain the total number of transactions per set item that has been analyzed in accordance with the support or parameters.

3.4.6 Post processing (.txt > .pdf)

This stage is very important in this application because, at this stage, the data that initially on the preprocessing number of code which is an item of the transaction will be changed and put together into a sentence and paragraph which allows users to read the results of analysis that has been in data mining. In this post processing the author uses iTextsharp in visual studio plug-in which is used to assist in generating a new files with portable document format (.pdf) file format. Which is very easy and flexible for users in reading the results.

3.4.7. Knowledge (.pdf)

At this stage, knowledge is generated from the stages before, knowledge is generated in accordance with the result of SPMF. The purpose of the SPMF data changed to a sentence in the PDF is to make it easier for the novice user, because not everyone can read from the results that is generated by SPMF because SPMF does not provide the data extract directly into an easily understood result. Knowledge that can be used by ordinary users to facilitate in learning what food menu most often appear in every transactions in the restaurant and can be used as a reference promotion menu according to the number of transactions that occur as in the example.

SPMF Result

The result of the SPMF analysis with Eclat algorithm declare that :

Total number of sales items 2 :

Item "Teh manis (ES) " and Item "Nasi putih" has the highest number of transaction data 1038 from 40864 (2,54 %) transactions. Item "Teh manis (ES) " with the number 1232 from 40864 (3,01 %) and Item "Nasi putih" with the number 4168 from 40864 (10,20 %).

Item "Sayur asem" and Item "Nasi putih" has the highest number of transaction data 916 from 40864 (2,24 %) transactions. Item "Sayur asem" with the number 1447 from 40864 (3,54 %) and Item "Nasi putih" with the number 4168 from 40864 (10,20 %).

Item "Air mineral 600 ml" and Item "Nasi putih" has the highest number of transaction data 813 from 40864 (1,99 %) transactions. Item "Air mineral 600 ml" with the number 951 from 40864 (2,33 %) and Item "Nasi putih" with the number 4168 from 40864 (10,20 %).

Fig. 3. Generated knowledge.

3.5 Database design

Here is a database design that will be used to perform some data storage on the application, the author uses MySQL as a database.

1. For temporary transactions storage

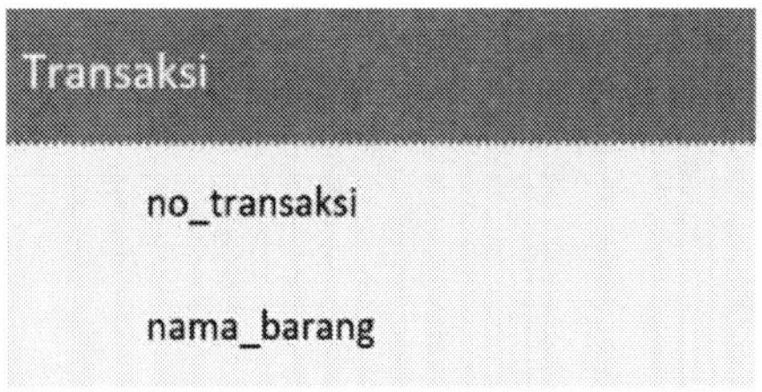

Fig. 4. Transaction database.

•no_transaksi: Varchar (50)
•nama_barang: Varchar(45)

2. Master database for items that converted into a number of code

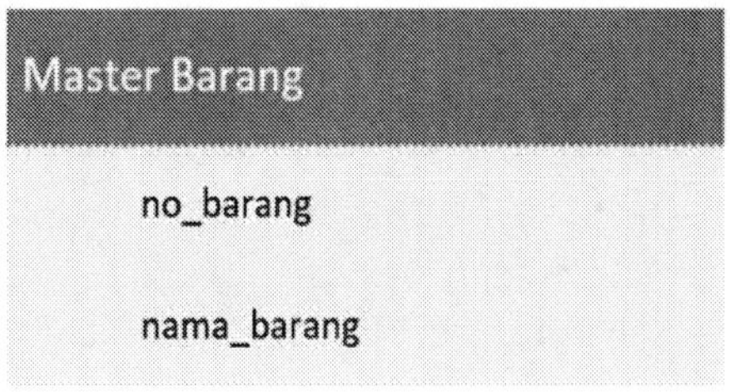

Fig. 5. Master item database.

•no_barang: Integer
•nama_barang: Varchar(100)

3. For temporary files result from SPMF

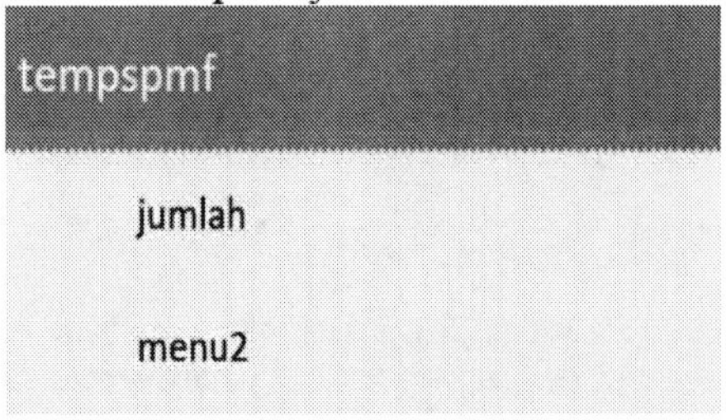

Fig. 6. Temporary database for SPMF result.

•jumlah: Integer
•menu2: Varchar (45)

4 Results and discussions

After the design and implementation have been done in the previous chapter, then will be proceed some test about data mining algorithm and application, which will be explained in this chapter.

4.1 Data accuracy test in preprocessing

4.1.1 Writing test for transactional data

Before transactional data test is done in preprocessing data process, each food menu in transactional data of restaurant xyz is stored one by one in the database and then transformed into numeric code which describe the names of the food and if there is new name in the transaction, a new code in the database will be generated. The stored data thus will be useful to help SPMF working with ECLAT algorithm. The sum of food menu in the previous 12 months that successfully get in the database are 364 menus (which means the code for each menu is filled until 364), and the data which failed to get in is zero, thus the food menu percentages that is already transformed is 100 % from all the transactional data in the last 12 months.

4.1.2 Preprocessing performance test

In this sub-chapter will be shown the results of performance test when the preprocessing is done. Here is the PC (personal computer)/laptop specification that was used in the performance test:

PC/laptop type	: Lenovo G400s
Display size	: 14 inch TFT LCD
Resolution	: 1366 ×768 px
Aspect ratio	: 16:9
Graphics Card	: Nvidia GeForce GT 720M
Graphics Memory	: 2 GB
Processor	: Intel(R) Core(TM) i5-3230M
Processor Speed	: 2.60 GHz (4 CPUs)
Memory	: 4 GB RAM
Storage	: 500 GB HDD

In this sub chapter will be shown the result of previous preprocessing with writing format and file in PDF, with the sentence structure and passages which make the user feel easier to read the application results and analysis, which designed for data mining.

There are the three biggest item sets that shown in final result. The final result of the application is a form of sentences and the order of biggest item set is on the top of the list, and is getting smaller in the third item set. The order in Figure 7 is matched with the order of code in item master database.

Table 4. Performance test result.

Month	*Total Rows*	*Time Passed*
January	3716	1 min 59 s
February	3436	1 min 51 s
March	2918	1 min 33 s
April	3419	1 min 40 s
May	3122	1 min 36 s
June	3003	1 min 31 s
July	4892	2 min 32 s
August	3263	1 min 40 s
September	3293	1 min 46 s
October	3113	1 min 37 s
November	3315	1 min 44 s
December	3656	1 min 53 s

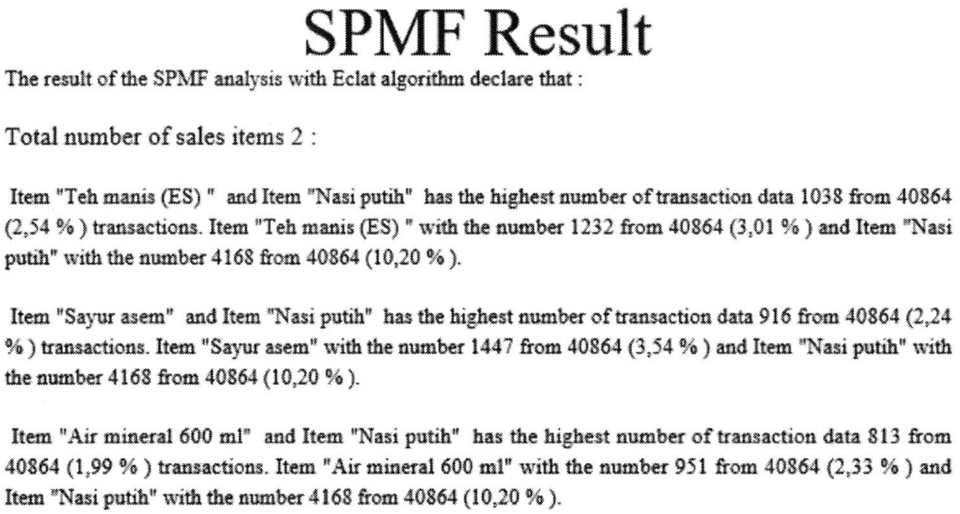

Fig. 7. Final result of the application.

5 Conclusion

In this chapter will be described and explained about the conclusions of the results from the project. This application can successfully changed all data from the sales transactions. It can perform ECLAT data mining assisted by open source SPMF with determined writing format of transaction data. It successfully displayed data with 100 % success rate according to the highest amount of sales in transaction.The application can generate a new easier knowledge in PDF file format which can be used for marketing the product.

Reference

1. S. A. Abaya. *IJSER,* **3**,7 (2012). http://citeseerx.ist.psu.edu/viewdoc/summary?doi=10.1.1.302.2946
2. M.J. Zaki. *IEEE Transactions on Knowledge and Data Engineering,* **12**,3:372-390 (2010). https://dl.acm.org/citation.cfm?id=628066
3. Philippe Fournier. *Philippe-fournier-viger* [Online] from http://www.philippe-fournier-viger.com/spmf/index.php?link=documentation.php#e1 (2017) [Accessed on 16 March 2017].
4. J.J. Davis, A.J. Clark. *Computers & Security,* **30**, 6-7:353-375 (2011). https://www.sciencedirect.com/science/article/pii/S0167404811000691
5. S. Paul. *IJCSIT,* **2**,2:88–101 (2010). http://airccse.org/journal/jcsit/0202csit8.pdf.
6. E.J. Gardiner, V.J. Gillet. *J. Chem. Inf. Model.*, **55**, 9 :1781–1803 (2015). http://pubs.acs.org/doi/abs/10.1021/acs.jcim.5b00198
7. Z. Ma, J. Yang, T. Zhang, F. Liu. IJDTA, **9**, 5:251–266 (2016). http://www.sersc.org/journals/IJDTA/vol9_no5/26.pdf.
8. S. Paul. IJCSIT, **2**,2 :88–101 (2010). https://www.researchgate.net/publication/43121793_An_Optimized_Distributed_Association_Rule_Mining_Algorithm_in_Parallel_and_Distributed_Data_Mining_with_XML_Data_for_Improved_Response_Time
9. S.P. Ye, J.L. Ding. *Applied Mechanics and Materials,* **488-489** :961–965 (2014). https://www.scientific.net/AMM.488-489.961
10. I. Bruha, A. Famili. *ACM SIGKDD Explorations Newsletter-Special issue on "Scalable data mining Algorithms"*, **2**, 2:110–114 (2000). https://dl.acm.org/citation.cfm?id=381059

RFID and IOT for Attendance Monitoring System

Joseph Dedy Irawan [1,*], *Emmalia* Adriantantri [2], and *Akh* Farid[1]

[1] Informatics, National Institute of Technology, Raya Karanglo Km.2 Malang 65153, Indonesia
[2] Industrial Engineering, National Institute of Technology, Raya Karanglo Km.2 Malang 65153, Indonesia

Abstract. In recent years, RFID technology has been widely used in various sectors, such as in-education, transportation, agriculture, animal husbandry, store sales and other sectors. RFID utilization in education is student attendance monitoring system, by using Internet of Things (IoT) and Cloud technology, it will produce a real time attendance monitoring system that can be accessed by various parties, such as lecturer, campus administration and parents. With this monitoring system if there are students who are not present can be immediately discovered and can be taken immediate action and the learning process can run smoothly.

Key words: Attendance monitoring system, internet of things, RFID

1 Introduction

One of the factors that support the success of the learning system is the presence of students, because if students are often absent then the material they received becomes less and can't understand the material that has been taught, one that causes the absence of students is they ditch, so the attendance monitoring system becomes very important because with this process the attendance of students can be monitored properly.

Various kinds of presences can be used from manual way to automatic way using electronic equipment, if the monitoring system attendance using electronic equipment so the recording of attendance data becomes easier, fast and accurate. In this research, attendance monitoring system using RFID technology and with the application of Internet of Things (IoT) and cloud technology will be obtained a presence system that can run and monitored in real time, so that all parties who need information such as lecturers, parents, and energy the administration can immediately find out if there are students who skip classroom, it can immediately be prevented so that the next meeting does not ditch again.

* Corresponding author: joseph@lecturer.itn.ac.id

2 Materials and methodology

2.1 Radio-frequency identification (RFID)

RFID has grown rapidly in recent decades [1] along with the demand from modern industry where data accuracy is required and efficiency improvements of a system, the supporting components of this electronic equipment are RFID reader and RFID Tags, where many kinds of tags have been manufactured according to industry needs. This technology has been applied to various sectors such as industry [2], airports [3], attendance monitoring systems [4–8], and with the use of IoT will be able to make this system more optimal [9–11].

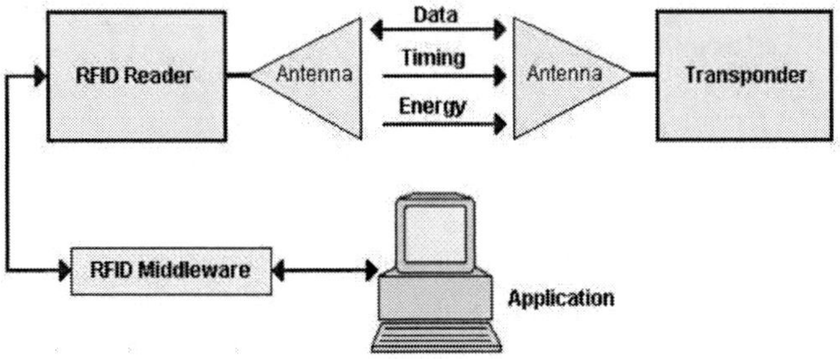

Fig. 1. Components of an RFID system [1].

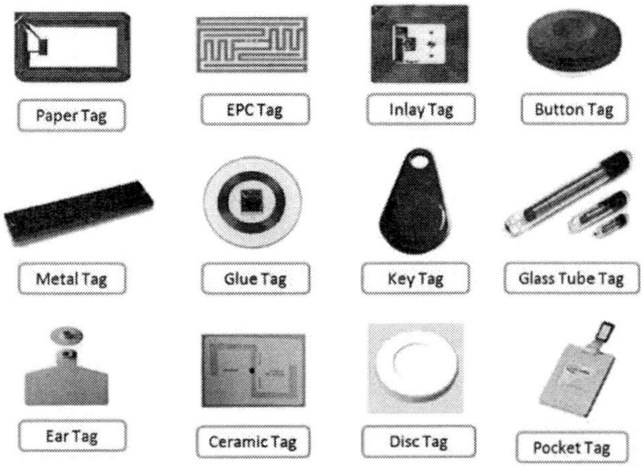

Fig. 2. Type of an RFID tags.

2.2 Attendance technology

2.3.1 Barcode

In this technology, students carry barcodes printed on their student cards, which at the time of presenting barcodes read using barcode reader, this presence is fast enough and does not cost a fortune, but this system has a drawback where barcodes can be easily duplicated by printed using a regular printer.

2.3.2 Magnetic Stripe

The use of magnetic strips can eliminate the deficiencies of barcodes, because in this technology magnetic card is required as an ID for each student, in the duplication of the magnetic card cannot be done easily because it requires a magnetic card reader and magnetic card writer, which because of the price quite expensive so it cannot be easily owned by students.

2.3.3 Biometric

The use of presences using biometric is an excellent solution, because as the ID of each student can be a finger print, retina, or face recognition. However, it has to consider the price of this equipment is very expensive.

Radio Frequency Identification (RFID) attendance monitoring system using RFID is highly recommended, because the required equipment is relatively cheap and the attendance process is very fast, so to make a monitoring system presence with this equipment can save time and budged.

2.3 Attendance monitoring system with RFID

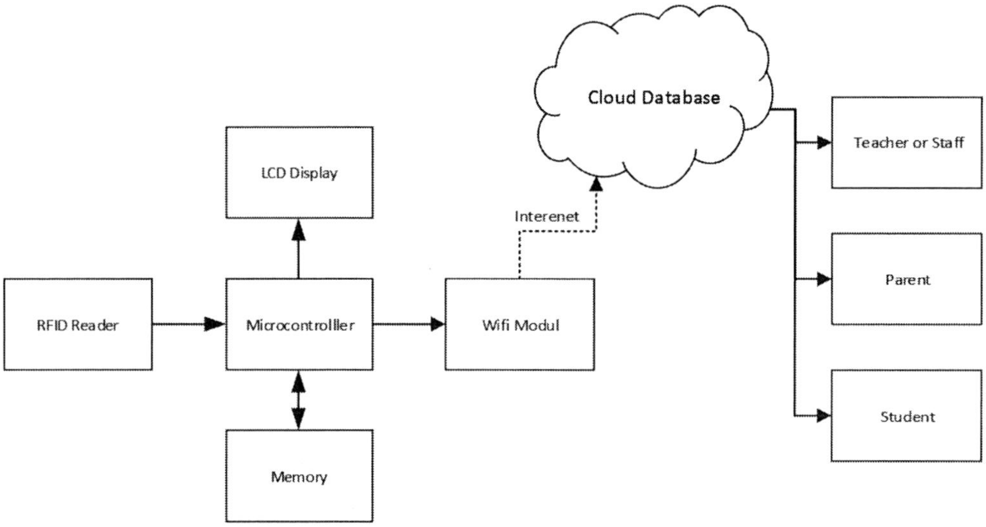

Fig. 3. Block diagram of attendance monitoring system.

Block diagram in Figure 3. Show that the process of attendance is done by using RFID technology, in this system each student has an RFID Tag to do presence, student put RFID Tag near RFID Reader, then ID result from RFID reader will be sent to microcontroller and compare it with the student data stored in memory, memory serves to store the data of the student's name of the course, if the data ID is a lecture participant then the student's name will be displayed on the LCD Display as well if the student data is not listed it will be informed through LCD Display that the student unregistered, using Wi-Fi module microcontroller can send student attendance data to cloud database by using internet network, data already accommodated in cloud database can be seen in real time by teacher, student and even parent, so that student presences can be monitored from anywhere in real time using Internet of Things (IoT).

2.4 Flowchart presence using IoT-based RFID

Presence process as illustrated in the flowchart in Figure 4 starting from the RFID Tag scanning process using RFID Reader, the data obtained will be compared to the database, if the data match the database then the presence data will be stored in the cloud database, but if the data is not suitable then will be asked to scanning again RFID Tags, data stored in the cloud database is Student ID data, date and time of attendance, courses and on what week of attendance.

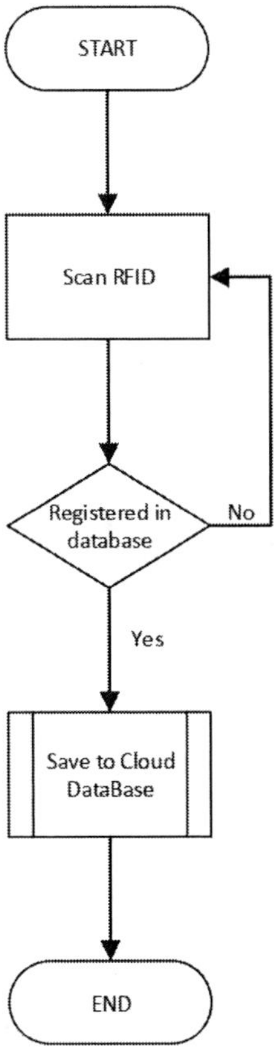

Fig. 4. Flowchart of RFID scan.

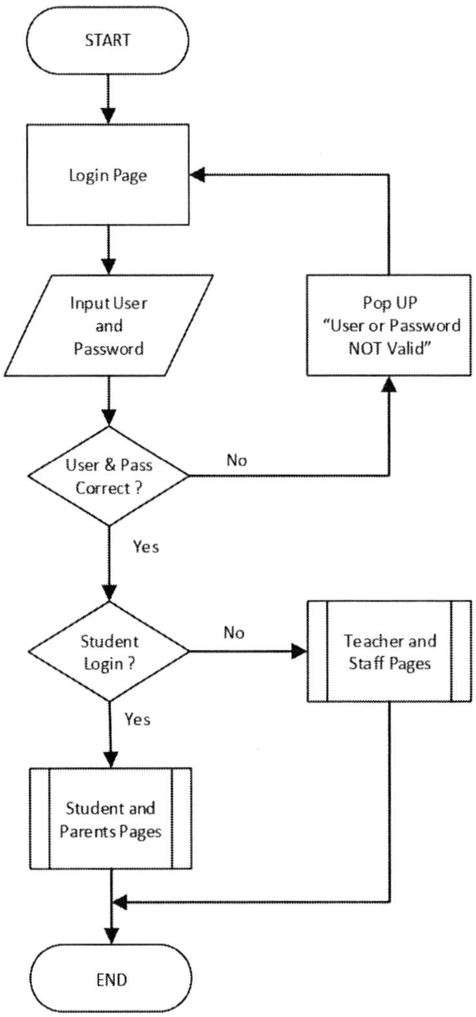

Fig. 5. Flowchart system

To display the results of presence data the user must login first, the login process determines the view that can be seen later, the user is divided into two kinds of login as a teacher or administration, and login as a student or parent, attendance data that has been stored in the cloud database can be displayed through two types of users, in Figure 6 is the output display for teachers and administration, where in this view attendance data from students are grouped by subject and class, while in Figure 7 is the output display for students and parents, it only displays data from students who login only, the name of the students displayed depending on the user's students and parents, so that each student and parents can only see their own presence data only. Figure 8 shows that the presence with RFID is faster than manual

3 Implementation and results

In Figure 6, a list of students on a particular course for one semester is shown. From the list, the presence and absence of a student can be observed. For instance, the student at the top of the list is shown to be absent at the second week of computer networking courses.

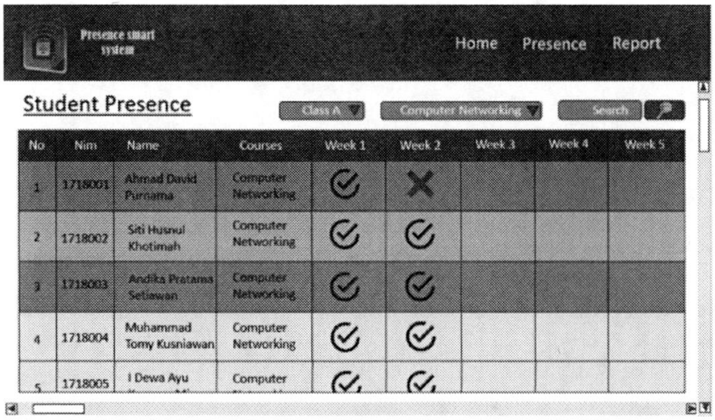

Fig. 6. Attendance list each subject and class for lecturer.

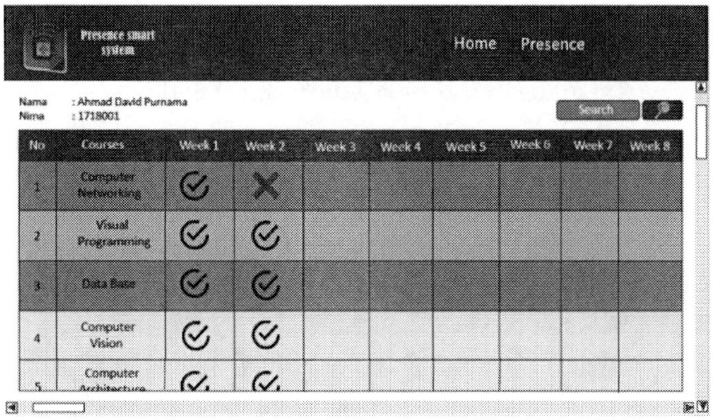

Fig. 7. Attendance list each student for student and parents.

Figure 7 displays a list of courses taken by a student along with his attendance for one semester. Through the list, the student's presence or absence can be observed on all courses he took. As shown in Figure 7, the student is absent during the second week of computer networking course. As for Visual Programming, Data Base and Computer Vision courses he is present in both, the first and second week.

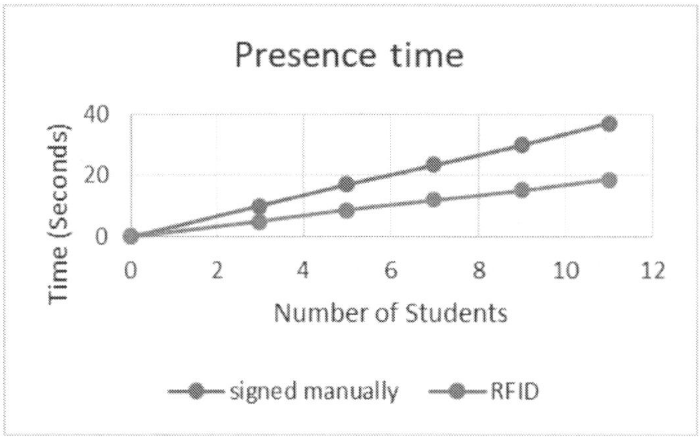

Fig. 8. Comparison of time attendance.

In Figure 8, it shows the comparison between the listing attendance manually and using RFID. The figure represents that using RFID, listing the attendance of 11 students took only 20 s, whereas the manual method takes twice as long which is 40 s.

4 Conclusion

From the test results can be concluded that the presence by using RFID faster than the traditional way and the implementation of the Internet system of things and data storage cloud enables the system to run in real time with accurate data.

References

1. S. Nainan, R. Parekh, T. Shah. *IJCSI*, **10**,1(2013). https://arxiv.org/abs/1306.5381
2. K. Ding, P. Jiang. *IEEE/CAA Journal of Automatica Sinica*, **5**,1 :128–138(2017). http://ieeexplore.ieee.org/document/7833265/
3. A. Singh, S. Meshram, T. Gujar, P.R. Wankhede. *Baggage tracing and handling system using RFID and IoT for airports*. International Conference on Computing, Analytics and Security Trends (CAST), (Pune, India, 2016). http://ieeexplore.ieee.org/document/7915014/
4. T. Sharma, S.L. Aarthy. *An automatic attendance monitoring system using RFID and IOT using Cloud*. 2016 Online International Conference on Green Engineering and Technologies (IC-GET), (Coimbatore, India, 2016). http://ieeexplore.ieee.org/document/7916851/
5. O.T. Arulogun, A. Olatunbosun, O.A. Fakolujo, O.M. Olaniyi. *IJSER*, **4**,2:1–9(2013). https://www.ijser.org/researchpaper/rfid-based-students-attendance-management-system.pdf.
6. O.G., Chiagozie, O.G. Nwaji. *Academic Research International*, **2**,2:168–183 (2012). https://www.researchgate.net/publication/280558358_RADIO_FREQUENCY_IDENTIFICATION_RFID_BASED_ATTENDANCE_SYSTEM_WITH_AUTOMATIC_DOOR_UNIT
7. M. Kassim, H. Mazlan, N. Zaini, M.K. Salleh. *Web-based student attendance system using RFID technology*. IEEE Control and System Graduate Research Colloquium,

(Selangor, Malaysia, 2012). ICSGRC:213-218(2012). http://ieeexplore.ieee.org/document/6287164/

8. N. Saparkhojayev, S. Guvercin, *IJCSI*, **9**,3:227–230(2012). http://citeseerx.ist.psu.edu/viewdoc/download?doi=10.1.1.401.8786&rep=rep1&type=pdf.
9. J.D. Irawan, S. Prasetio, S.A. Wibowo. IP based module for building automation system. In: *Proceedings of second international conference on electrical systems, technology and information 2015 (ICESTI 2015)*. F. Pasila, Y. Tanoto, R. Lim, M. Santoso, N. Pah (Eds), Singapore: Springer (2016). pp. 337–343). https://link.springer.com/chapter/10.1007/978-981-287-988-2_36
10. H.M. Nguyen, S.H. Kim, D.T. Le, S. Heo, J. Im, D. Kim. *Optimizations for RFID-based IoT applications on the Cloud*. 5th International Conference on the Internet of Things, (Seoul, South Korea, 2015). http://ieeexplore.ieee.org/document/7356551/
11. Z. Singhal, R.K. Gujral, *International Journal of Computer Applications*, **39**,3:37–41 (2012). http://citeseerx.ist.psu.edu/viewdoc/download?doi=10.1.1.259.3846&rep=rep1&type=pdf

Investigation on Voltage Quality Problems on the Process of Cement Industry Production in Indonesia: A Case Study of Cement Kupang Factory - Indonesia

Julius Sentosa Setiadji*, *Daniel* Rohi, and *Yoanne* Flantine Mozes

Electrical Engineering Department, Petra Christian University, Jl. Siwalakerto 121-131, Surabaya, Indonesia, 60236

Abstract. The decline in the quality of electric power becomes a serious problem in the industrial sector and affects a significant cost loss. One of the dominant power quality problems is the voltage dip. The use of electric motors in an industry becomes one of the main causes. This paper discusses the investigation on voltage dip problems at a cement factory at Kupang,, Indonesia. The cement factory uses an induction motor as the prime mover and is proven to trigger a voltage dip because of its high starting current. Based on the observed data of the disturbance, a single line diagram was created. The single line diagram was analyzed using an equivalent circuit. It was found out that as the induction motor was started, it created a very significant voltage drop as of 20.43 % to 62.26 %. The voltage dip correlated to the capacity of the induction motor used. The larger the capacity of the induction motor, the larger the voltage dip occured.

Key words: Induction motor, power quality, voltage dip.

1 Introduction

The availability of qualified electrical energy is one of the important factors for the sustainability of the operation of an industrial estate. The quality of electrical energy is determined by two main factors: The availability of continuous energy or minimal power outages and electrical energy characteristic. The characteristics of the electrical energy volumes are guaranteed in accordance with the minimum requirements for the equipments to work securely and efficiently. The existence of continual electrical power distribution in and industrial area is of utmost important. The poor quality of the electric power, can stop the production process, especially in industries using sensitive loads such as control equipments. If this problem is not handled properly, a significant financial loss will be resulted.

The problems faced by a power system in the supply of electrical energy need to be investigated thoroughly and continuously. Then the main cause of the disturbance that occurs, will be obtained. One of the most common disruptions to power systems is the blurring of the voltage. This disturbance is a transient disturbance in the electric power system, ie a momentary voltage drop in the power system network. Cement Industry is one of the industries requiring considerable electric power from the power system network. In the production process of the cement industry, electric motors both large and small are used greatly.

The use of electric motors is causing the problem of decreasing quality of voltage in the electrical system of factories. The problem often arises is the voltage dip. Based on the observed disturbance data on a regular basis, the cause and effect of the voltage dip was identified. These data were used as parameters in the designated equivalent circuit. Then the data was analyzed to give recommendations as a corrective action. Voltage sags is one of the major problems in the industry and has provided significant financial losses [1, 2].

*Corresponding author: julius@petra.ac.id

2 Voltage dip problems

The definition of a voltage dip according to IEC (International Electrotechnical Commission) is a brief interruption of a sudden termination of voltage at all phases at a certain point in the power supply system below the threshold disturbance (usually 10 % of nominal voltage) followed by restoration after a short time interval. In other words, a sudden voltage reduction at some point in the power supply system is below the dip limit (typically 90 % of nominal voltage) followed by recovery after a short interval. The above definition is shown in Figure 1 [1]. Voltage is a phenomenon of decreasing the voltage amplitudes (ΔV) to its nominal price over the time interval t. This phenomenon is usually caused by a sudden disturbance or change in load [3, 4].

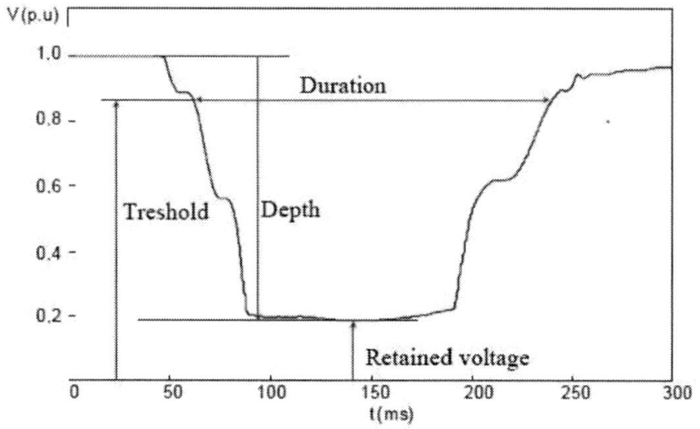

Fig. 1. The basic concept of a voltage dip [1].

When an induction motor is started directly at full voltage then the induction motor will draw a start current of 5 to 7 times the full load current. A high start current is required for the induction motor to obtain sufficient torque to start rotating. The presence of a large start current which is suddenly withdrawn from the power system can cause a voltage dip. The voltage dip induced by the induction motor start current depends on the motor capacity, the motor power factor, the system impedance and the starting method [4, 5, 7].

Table 1. Sensitivity of equipment to voltage dip [4].

Type of Equipment	Remaining Voltage (%)	Time Duration Max (ms)
Motor starter	50	40
Variable speed motor with electronics	85	10
Programable Logic Control	50 to 90	8 to 20
Frequency Inverter	82	1.5
Variable speed drive rectifier	50 to 80	2 to 3
Process controller	70	< 8
Direct current drive controller	88	< 8
Personal Computer	50 to 70	60 to 160

3 Results and discussion

Observations were conducted and the data were recorded periodically to the operation of three large induction motors. The characteristics of the three motors are as follows: The first condition is one piece of motor with the power of 1 000 kW (120 A). This motor is used as the Cement Mill Motor. The second condition is two pieces of motors with the power 460 kW (55 A). This motor is used as the Raw Mill Motor and Ventilator Motor. The motors in the Cement Factory operate non-stop during the production process. The configuration of the distribution chain and the extent of each piece of the equipment are shown in Figure 1. Based on the data in Figure 1, a series of substitute drawings were made for further analysis [8–10].

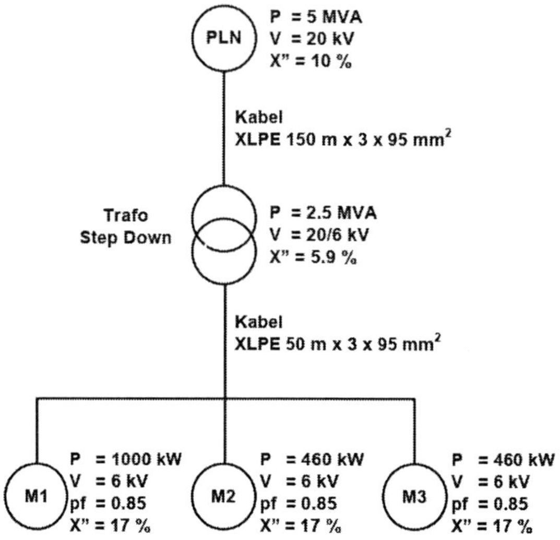

Fig. 2. Schematic of distribution circuit impedance.

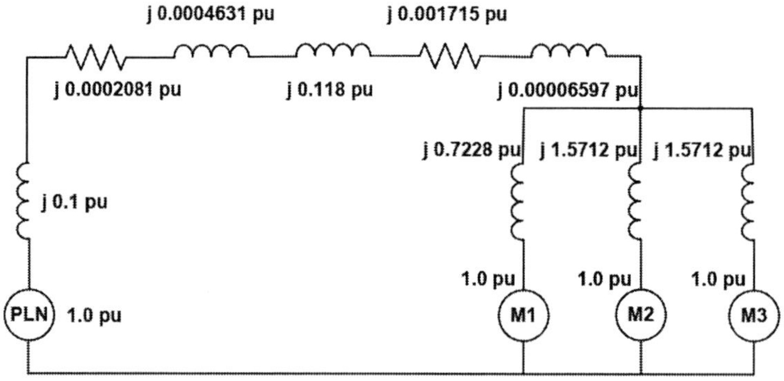

Fig. 3. Equivalent circuits of distribution networks.

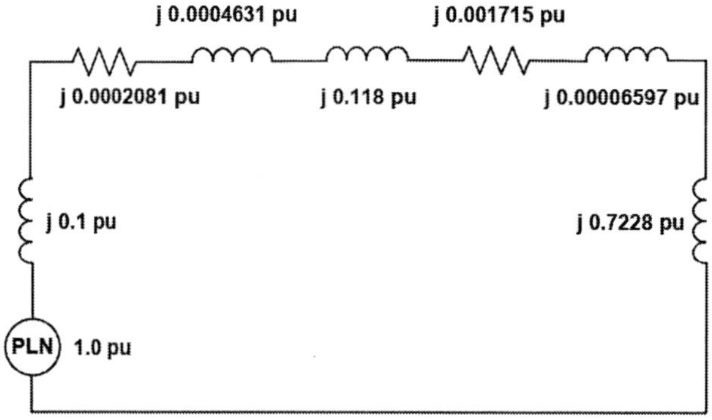

Fig. 4. The equivalent circuit at M1 start with the condition of M2 and M3 has not been activated.

Based on the sequence mentioned above, the voltage dip, occuring when the motor starts, can be calculated by the following Equation (1):

$$V = [Xpln + Z1 + Xtrafo + Z2] \times [6 \times I\ pu1] \quad (1)$$

$$V = [0.1 + (0.0002081 + j\ 0.0004631) + 0.118 + (0.001715 + j\ 0.00006597)] \times [6 \times 0.24317]$$
$$V = [0.219923 + j\ 0.00052907] \times 1.45902$$
$$V = 0.32087 + j\ 0.0007720 = 0.32087 \angle 0.1°$$

$$\Delta V = \frac{0.32087}{1.0} \times 100\,\% = 32.8\,\%$$

The possibility of the operation of the three motors is presented in Table 2. Based on the data on the equivalent circuits, calculations and analysis were performed as described above. The calculation results are presented in Table 3.

Table 2. Possible operating conditions of motor and equivalent circuit.

No.	Conditions	Equivalent Circuit
1.	If M2 starts with active M1 and M3 is not activated	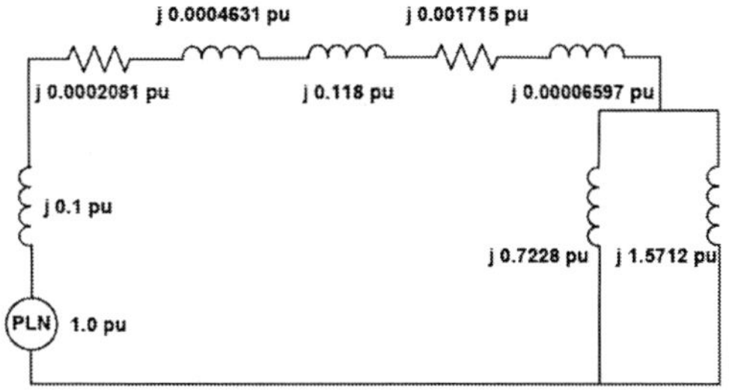
2.	If M3 starts with the condition of M1 and M2 is active	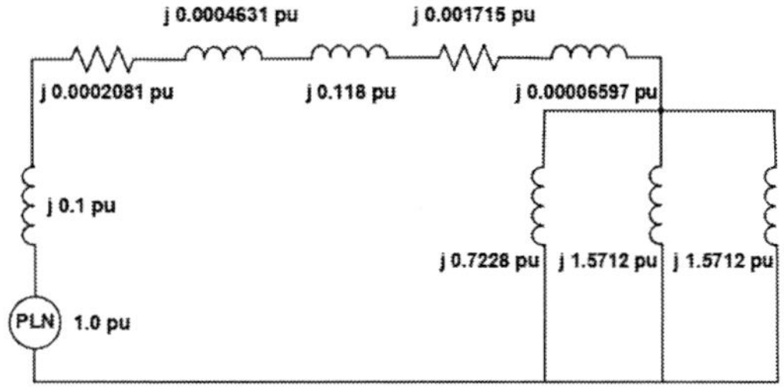
3.	If M1, M2 and M3 are mutually active	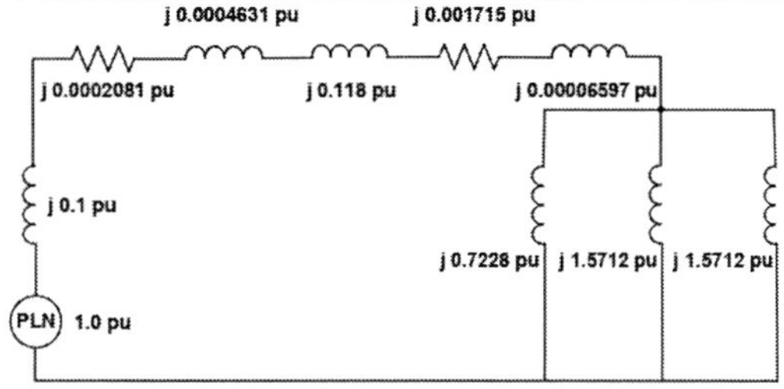

Table 3. Voltage dip that occurs when the motor starts

Condition	Dip Voltage (%)	Duration (s)	Standar IEEE 1159-1995	
			Range Voltage + (%)	Duration (second)
M1 starts, M2 and M3 (off)	32.08	0.6	10 to 90	0.01 s to 1 min
M2 starts, M1(on), M3 (off)	20.43			
M3 starts, M1 and M2 (on)	23.00			
M1, M2 and M3 start together	62.26			

Based on the data in Table 3, the dip voltage occurred when the motor was starting on all conditions with the magnitude ranges from 20.43 % to 62.26 %. The greater the capacity of the motor, the dip voltage that occurred on the channel was also greater. M1 with the starting condition (32.08 %) or all three starting motors together (62.26 %) was not ideal because it could cause other problems in power system network, such as the inability of sensitive electrical load, disruption of function of equipment motor control and others. The voltage dip values that occured in all conditions are seen to exceed the standard limits based on IEEE (Institute of Electrical and Electronics Engineers) Std.1159-1995.

4 Conclusion

The magnitude of a dip voltage at the motor starting in any condition was ranging from 20.43 % to 62.26 %. This condition proved to have exceeded the permitted standard that exceeds 10 %. It is a condition that can cause problems in the electrical system. The proposed solution is to use an inverter as a great starting motor method considering the possibility of current and voltage harmonics due to the use of inverter.

References

[1] P.K. Lim, D.S. Dorr. *Understanding and resolving voltage sag related problems for sensitive industrial customers*. Power Engineering Society Winter Meeting, 23–27 January (Singapore, 2000). IEEE **4**:2886–2890(2002). http://ieeexplore.ieee.org/document/847343/authors?ctx=authors

[2] G. Ranko, M. Eugen, L. Marko. *Voltage dips influence zone and propagation through the industrial facility*. Power Tech, 27–30 June (St. Petersburg, Russia, 2005). http://ieeexplore.ieee.org/document/4524585/

[3] R.C. Dugan, M.F. McGranaghan, S. Santoso, H.W. Beaty. *Electrical power systems quality*. New York: McGraw-Hill (2002). pp. 79–81. https://www.amazon.com/Electrical-Power-Systems-Quality-Santoso/dp/007138622X

[4] A.C. Wang, J.H. Teng, C.C. Shen, C.N. Lu, Y.T. Chen, C.Y. Huang, E. Liu. *Voltage sag vulnerability study in power system planning*. Power Engineering Society General Meeting, 16 June (San Francisco, 2005). IEEE, pp. 383–388(2005). http://ieeexplore.ieee.org/abstract/document/1489434/

[5] L. Luna, L. Gallego, M. Romero. *Evaluation and identification of critical zones due to sag activity*. The 14th International Conference on Harmonics and Quality of Power (ICHQP), 26–29 September (Bergamo, Italy, 2010). IEEE, pp. 1–5(2010). http://ieeexplore.ieee.org/document/5625312/

[6] M. Bollen, M. Häger, C. Roxenius. Voltage dips in distribution systems: Load effects, measurements and theory. The 17th International Conference on Electricity Distribution, 12–15 May (Barcelona, 2003). CIRED **2**(47):1–5(2003).
https://www.researchgate.net/publication/229005708_Voltage_dips_in_distribution_systems_Load_effects_measurements_and_theory

[7] R.C. Seebald. IEEE Power Engineering Review **PER-5**(9):61–62
http://ieeexplore.ieee.org/document/5526472/

[8] J.C. Das. *Power system harmonics and passive filter designs*. New Jersey: John Wiley & Sons. (2015). pp. 332–334. https://www.wiley.com/en-us/Power+System+Harmonics+and+Passive+Filter+Designs-p-9781118861622

[9] W.D. Stevenson. *Elements of power system analysis*. 4th edition. Singapore: MC-Hill Internasional Book Company (1982). pp. 133–136. https://www.amazon.com/Elements-Analysis-ELECTRICAL-COMPUTER-ENGINEERING/dp/0070612781

[10] IEEE Power & Energy Society. *IEEE recommended practice for monitoring electric power quality*. New York: IEEE (2009). pp. 46–51. http://ieeexplore.ieee.org/document/5154067/

Experimental Investigation of Air Conditioner using the Desiccant Cooling System in Equatorial Climates

Kamaruddin Abdullah[1,*], *Aep* Saepul Uyun[1], *Syukri* Muhammad Nur[1], *Alie* Bamahry[1], *Rino* Imanda[1], and *Teuku* Meurah Indra Mahlia[2,3]

[1]The Graduate School, Renewable Energy Program of Study, Darma Persada University, Jl.Radin Inten II, Pondok Kelapa-East Jakarta, 13450, Indonesia
[2]Department of Mechanical Engineering, Universiti Tenaga Nasional, Jl. Ikram-Uniten, 43000 Kajang, Selangor, Malaysia
[3]School of Systems, Management and Leadership, Faculty of Engineering and Information Technology, University of Technology Sydney, 81 Broadway, Ultimo NSW 2007, Australia

Abstract. Indonesia lies in the tropical climate which requires air conditioning to increase working productivity of the people. Up to now people are still using the compressive cooling system which uses Freon as the refrigerant, which have been known to have a negative environmental impact. Therefore, new cooling system which is environmentally friendly is now needed. Desiccant cooling system manipulates the humidity condition of outside air in such a way so that the final temperature should become at 25 °C and RH of 65 %. Since it does not require refrigerant, a desiccant cooling has the potential to be developed in a tropical country like Indonesia. In this study an experimental desiccant cooling system has been designed and constructed and tested under laboratory condition. Experimental results have shown that the resulting air temperature was 26.1 °C with RH of 55.6 %, and average cooling capacity was 0.425 kW. The COP was found to be 0.44.

Key words: Air conditioning, desiccant cooling, desiccant wheel, evaporative cooling, sensible heat exchanger.

1 Introduction

Indonesia economic growth rapidly for last two decades, this economic growth subsequently increases the energy demand in the country. The pattern of energy consumption, energy scenario and sustainable energy in the country discussed deeply by Hasan et al. [1, 2]. Due to this reason the country trying to develop alternative energy sources for every sector in the country such as geothermal [3], bioenergy [4], biodiesel [5–8] bioethanol [9–11]. The country also actively promotes energy efficiency and sustainable energy program as to counter global warming [12–15]. This research a part of improving human comfort in the tropical climates indirectly also will contribute to energy conservation program in the country.

Indonesia lies on the equator with an average temperature of 30 °C and RH of above 80 % [16]. Under this weather condition it is not fit for people to work in the office or stay at home. Therefore, there is an urgent need for air conditioning facilities in order to be able to live in a better condition. There is also need for industry to increase their productivity by creating a better working environment. Heretofore, people have been using the compressive cooling system which Freon as the refrigerant. As we know Freon having a bad impact on ozone depletion has been prohibited its use, according to the Montreal protocol [17]. In this study a desiccant cooling system was selected, due to its environmentally friendly nature. This cooling system does not emit greenhouse gasses since the working principle is on how to manipulate the condition of the air so that a pleasant air condition can be achieved. This can be obtained by first heating the desiccant wheel with solar collector to get rid of moisture from the desiccant. Later within the evaporative component of the desiccant cooling system, the air temperature will be cooled down by the evaporation of cooling water of the evaporative cooling while its relative humidity will increase from the moisture added from the evaporative cooling water [18–21]. For the purpose of this study a laboratory scale desiccant cooling system was designed and

*Corresponding author: kamaruddinabd@gmail.com

constructed and later a series of test was conducted to obtain the performance of the system. The current heater of the system used electric power, but later it will be replaced by a solar collector.

2 Literature study

Research on the desiccant cooling system is quite new in Indonesia and very rare if any attempt to apply the system in Indonesia. Research by Maalouf [23] indicated that the use of solar energy they were capable to construct adsorption cooling system for application in several city in France. Daou et al. [24] have conducted research to determine the performance of an adsorption cooling machine using silica gel the Pennington cycle. Mavroudaki et al. [25] reported two studies related to the feasibility of adsorption cooling machine using solar energy Pennington cycle in South Europe and in England. Davangere et al. [26] had applied a desiccant cooling system with capacity 10 kW (2.85 t refrigeration) assisted by vapor compression machine. The resulting room temperature 26.7 °C with humidity ratio of W = 0.01183 kg kg^{-1} dry air for the condition Florida which have outside air of 36 °C. They conducted an analysis using a psychometric chart and the result of their simulation works were applied to four cities in the USA. Bellia et al. [22] had studied several hybrids cooling system using various desiccant wheels and using DesiCalcTM computer program and applied to four cities in Italy. They concluded that the maximum saving in cost was 22 %, and for the theater the saving was greater from 23 % to 38 % with electricity saving of up to 55 %. Pesaran,et al. [27] had studied experimental dessicant cooling operated in ventilation mode and the rusults were presented in Psychrometric chart. A heat supply was needed in the system to regenerate the desiccant (natural Zeolite) and a low-grade heat at a temperature of about 60.95 °C was used. Parametric studies are performed to investigate the effects of ambient temperature and relative humidity on the various COP terms and cooling load.

2.1 Working principle of the desiccant cooling system.

Figure 1 shows the major component of a desiccant cooling system which comprises of a desiccant wheel (DW) containing natural Zeolite or silicagel, sensible heat exchanger wheel (rotary heat exchanger), an electric heater which can be substituted with hot water supplied from solar collectors, two evaporative coolers (EC1 and EC2). Outside air is introduced through point (1) passing the hot desiccant wheel where the humidity is reduced to the point (2). The air will further pass through the sensible heat exchanger (point 3) where its temperature will be reduced while keeping its RH constant. From the sensible heat exchanger, the air will be introduced into the evaporative cooling chamber where its temperature will be reduced due to evaporative cooling action while its RH will be increased (point 4). When entering the room, the temperature and RH will reach 25 °C and 65 %, respectively, a comfortable condition for air conditioning. The air condition in the desiccant cooling system can also be traced using the Psychometric chart in Figure 2. When the air is leaving the air condition room under condition of point (5) the air will be passed again through the evaporative cooling unit which will reduce its temperature and increase its RH (point 6). After passing through the sensible heat exchanger, its temperature will increase while its RH is kept constant as in point (7). After passing through the evaporative cooler (point 6), the tempeature the air silgthly is decreased while its RH is increased. After passing through the sensible heat exchanger, its temperature will increase while its RH is kept constant as in point (7). After this the air will pass the solar air heater where the air temperature increases again heating the desiccant within the desiccant wheel to make moisture from silica gel evaporated, the air than become as the condition of point (8). After passing the desiccant wheel the air will be exhausted to the environment at a lower temperature (point 9).

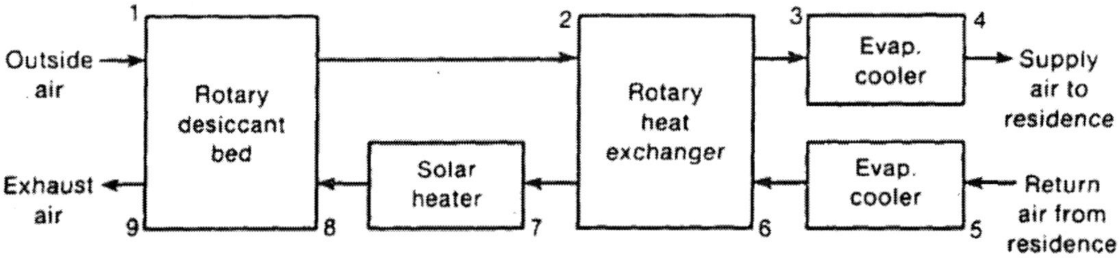

Fig. 1. Main component of desiccant cooling system [27].

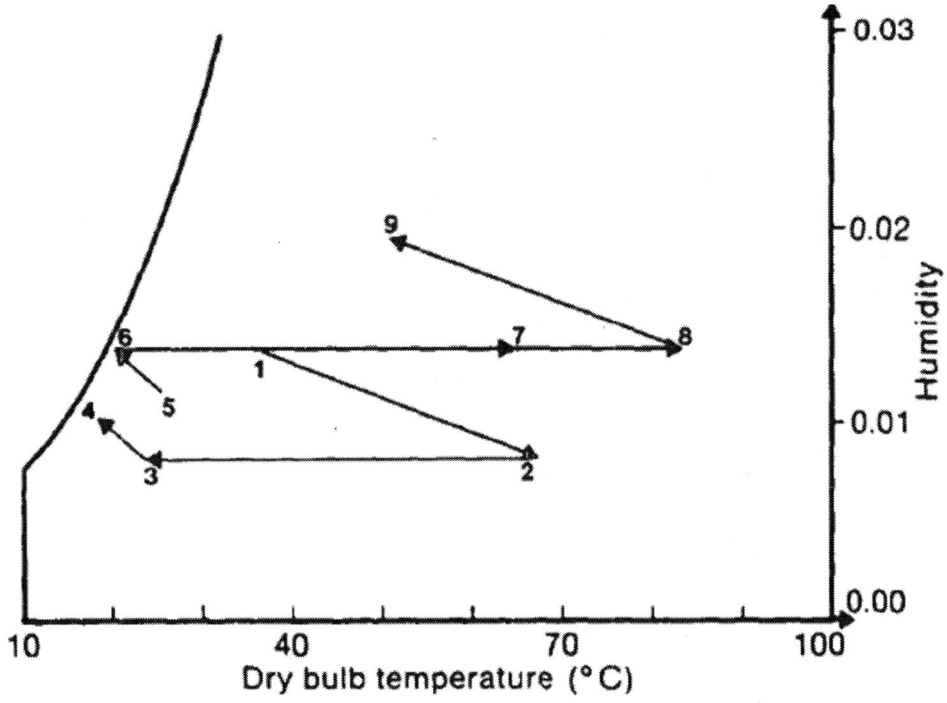

Fig. 2. The condition of the air as represented by a psychometric chart [27].

3 Experiment setup

3.1 The apparatus and instruments

The apparatus used in the experiment is as shown in Figure 3. It consisted of a desiccant wheel (2) equipped with a motor to turn it, a blower with the heater (3) to function as a solar collector, a sensible heat exchanger (4) and an evaporative cooling system (5). In addition, there was a blower located in front of the desiccant wheel to draw outside air into the four 50 mm ID PVC piping and length of 0.46 m. In addition there was one blower located in front of desiccant wheel (1). During the test all components of the system were started simultaneously and the outside air was introduced through the duct inlet and passing through the desiccant wheel. The condition of the air will change as it passed through each component of the system as explained in the section 2.1. on working principle of the desiccant cooling system. For measuring each data an Automatic data acquisition system shown in Figure 4 was used. Several DHT 11 sensors for measuring both temperature and RH were placed according to the number point in Figure 3 and then all connected to the Arduino UNO microcontroller, shown in Figure 4 and then to the computer. For measuring air flow rate an electronic anemometer was used while for measuring water flow rate in the evaporative cooling system an electronic sensor was used. For measuring the RPM of the desiccant wheel and sensible heat exchanger a Laser & Touch Tachometer DT-2236B a tachometer was used.

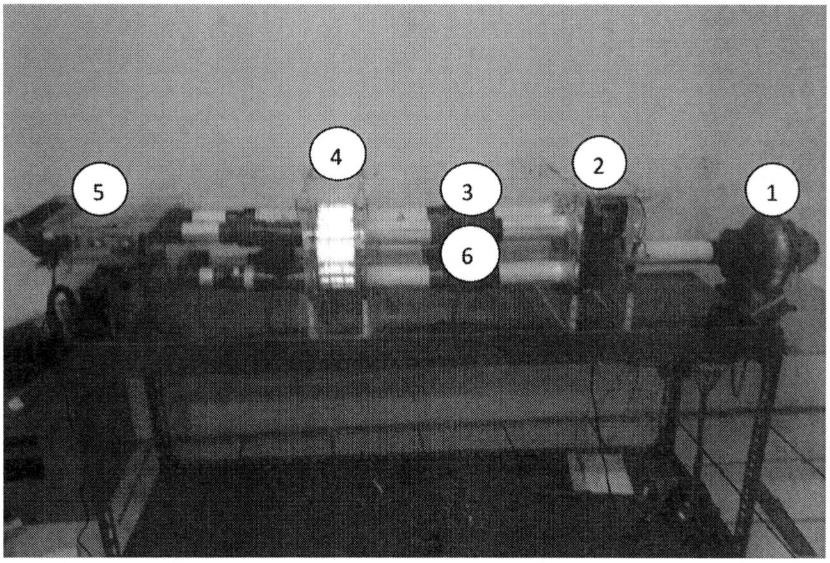

Fig. 3. Experimental apparatus.

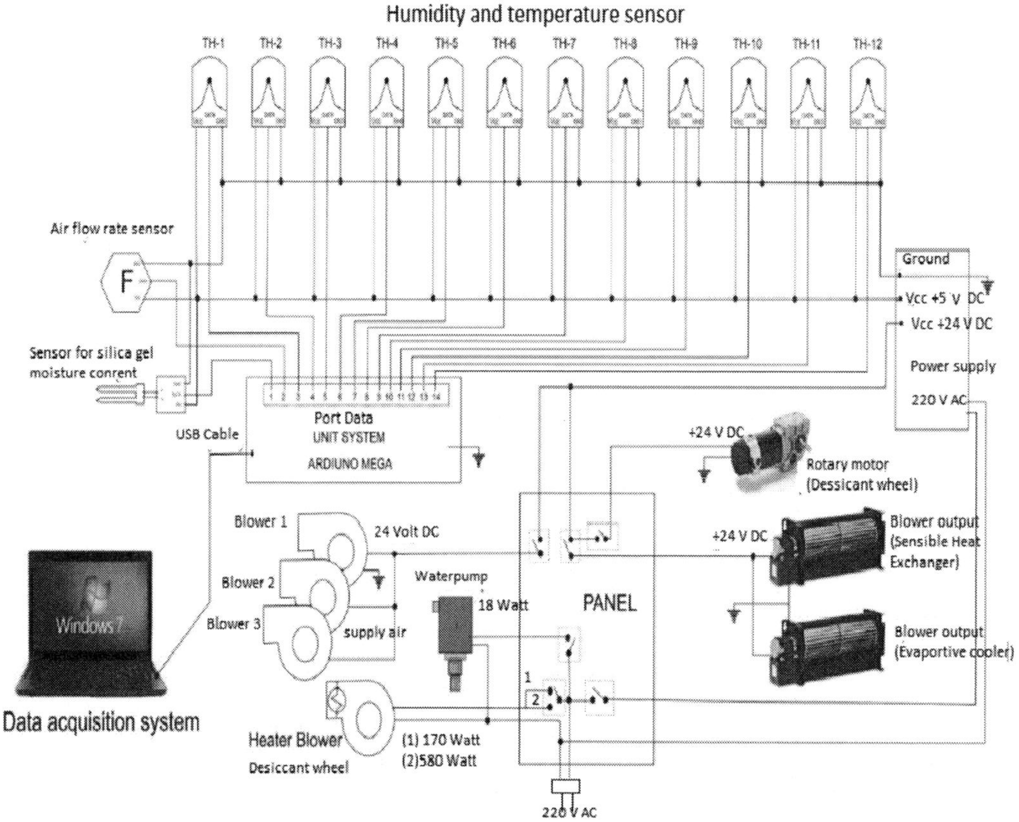

Fig. 4. Automatic data acquisition system.

3.2 Experimental procedure

First, it was necessary to fill the desiccant wheel with adequate amount of silica gel. The silica gel, then was spread and glued on both sides of aluminum plates arranged in such a way to give an ample way of the air passing through the desiccant wheel and the silica gel. The desiccant wheel was put on a steel bar axis rotated together with the sensible heat exchanger by means of a 24 V DC electrical motor. Several aluminum plates were placed in the sensible heat exchanger to cool the air ling the desiccant wheel and heating the air coming from the evaporative cooler. The evaporative cooler consisted of porous pad above which spray nozzles were placed to spray cool water to the pad. There were two evaporative coolers provided one before entering the air-conditioned space and after the air return from the air-conditioned space. At the outlet before the desiccant wheel a 580 W electric heater was placed to provide heat to evaporate moisture from the desiccant wheel. Four blowers were provided one in front of the desiccant wheel to switch the air and discharged to the surrounding environment, one after the desiccant wheel in front of the sensible heat exchanger and one each at the evaporative cooler inlet. After putting all the sensors at the specified location as given in Figure 3, the desiccant cooling system was operated and data were taken automatically by means of a laptop computer.

4 Results and discussions

Typical experimental results indicated that the temperature of air leaving the sensible heat exchanger was at 33.5 °C while the air temperature leaving the evaporative cooling system was at 26.1 °C, while the RH was at 55.6 %. As the air flow rate passing through the evaporative cooling system was at 5 m s^{-1} then the calculated cooling power of the system was 0.425 kW (see Table 1). When the heat input from the heater was used the COP was found to be 0.44 which was lower than the recorded data by Davangere et al. [27] which was 0.66. Table 1, shows the results of experimental run for the temperature difference between the sensible heat exchanger exit and the evaporative cooling exits from this data together with air flow rate the cooling capacity could be calculated as shown in the 5th column of Table 1, and in Figure 6. While, Figure 5 shows the variation in outlet temperature leaving the sensible heat exchanger and that leaving the evaporative cooler. It was found that the heating power was inadequate to heat the desiccant wheel so that the air temperatures were still low while the air RH was low. The evaporation of cooling water in evaporative cooler was inadequate to increase air RH so that the cooling effect was not adequate to cool the coming air from the sensible heat exchanger. Therefore, the heating capacity of the electric heater should be increased while the spray water flow rate with the evaporative cooler should be reduced.

Table 1. Experimental results from temperature differences between sensible heat exchanger exit, evaporative cooling exit, cooling capacity and air RH at the evaporative cooler outlet.

Run	T3 (°C) (Evaporative cooling exit)	T4 (°C) (sensible heat exit)	Air flow rate (m s^{-1})	Cooling capacity kW	RH (%) after evap cooling
1	24.6	33.15	5	0.336	58.9
2	25.2	33.5		0.326	53.3
3	25.2	33.8		0.338	52.3
4	24.9	33.1		0.322	52
4	25.7	35.2		0.373	55.4
5	26.3	39		0.499	57
6	26.8	39		0.479	51.9
7	27.3	40.2		0.507	51.9
8	27.5	41		0.530	62.2
9	27.2	41		0.542	61
Ave.	26.07	36.9		0.425	55.59

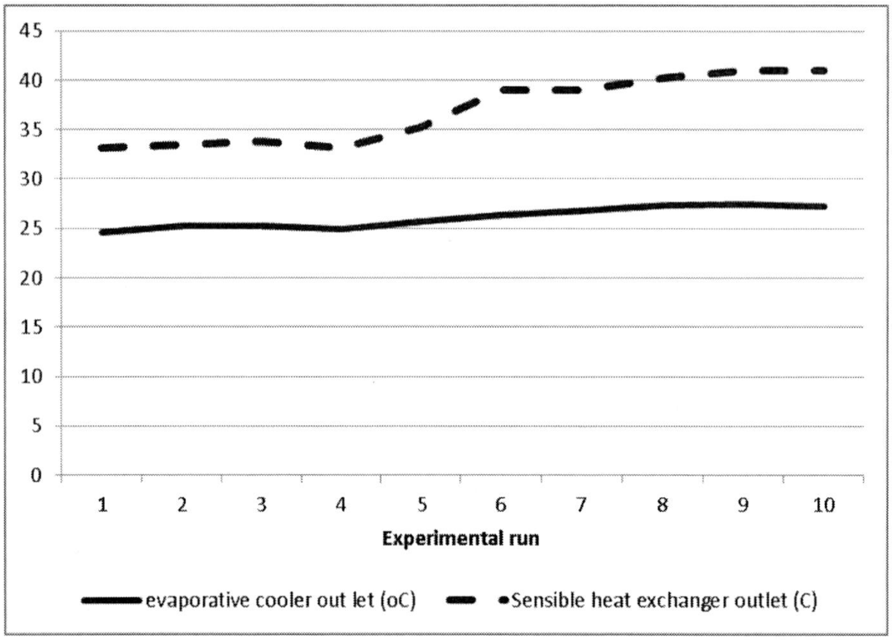

Fig. 5. Air temperature difference between sensible heat exchanger outlet and that of evaporative cooler outlet.

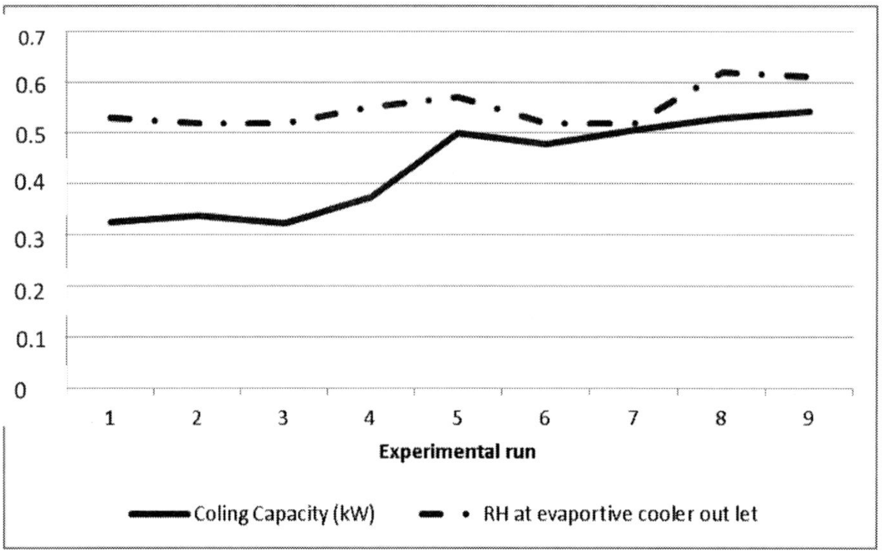

Fig. 6. Cooling capacity of the experimental desiccant cooling system and the air RH at the evaporative cooler outlet.

5 Conclusions

From experimental results, it was found that the average cooling capacity of the system achieved was 0.425 kW.The final temperature and RH leaving the air duct was 26.1 °C and 55.59 %, respectively. The COP of the system was found to be 0.44.It was recommended that the evaporative cooling water flow rate should be reduced to allow good contact with the coming air while heating power should be increased so that it could create standard comfort where a temperature of 25 °C and RH of 65 % can be created.

The authors wish to thank the Directorate General of Research and Technology and Higher Education for providing us research grant through contract No.104/K3/KM/2015, February 23, 2015.

REFERENCES

1. M.H. Hasan, T.M.I. Mahlia, H. Nur. Renew. Sust. Energ. Rev., **16**(4):2316–2328 (2012). https://www.sciencedirect.com/science/article/pii/S1364032111005995
2. M.H. Hasan, W.K. Muzammil, T.M.I. Mahlia, A. Jannifar, I. Hasanuddin. Renew. Sust. Energ. Rev., **16**(5):3206–3219. https://www.sciencedirect.com/science/article/pii/S1364032112000871
3. Nasruddin, M.I. Alhamid, Y. Daud, A. Surachman, A. Sugiyono, H.B. Aditya, T.M.I. Mahlia. Renew. Sust. Energ. Rev., **53**:733–740 (2016). https://www.sciencedirect.com/science/article/pii/S1364032115010023
4. T.M.I. Mahlia, M.Z. Abdulmuin, T.M.I. Alamsyah, D. Mukhlishien. Energy Convers. Manag., **42**(18):2109–2118 (2001). https://www.sciencedirect.com/science/article/pii/S0196890400001667
5. F. Kusumo, A.S. Silitonga, H.H. Masjuki, H.C. Ong, J. Siswantoro, T.M.I. Mahlia. Energy, **134**:24–34 (2017). https://www.sciencedirect.com/science/article/pii/S0360544217309921
6. F. Kusumo, A.S. Silitonga, H.C. Ong, H.H. Masjuki, T.M.I. Mahlia. Energy Sources, Part A: Recovery, Utilization and Environmental Effects, **39**(13):1339–1346 (2017). http://www.tandfonline.com/doi/abs/10.1080/15567036.2017.1328003
7. M.H. Jayed, H.H. Masjuki, M.A. Kalam, T.M.I. Mahlia, M. Husnawan, A.M. Liaquat. Renew. Sust. Energ. Rev., **15**(1):220–235 (2011). https://www.sciencedirect.com/science/article/pii/S1364032110002893
8. A.S. Silitonga, A.E. Atabani, T.M.I. Mahlia, H.H. Masjuki, I.A. Badruddin, S. Mekhilef. Renew. Sust. Energ. Rev., **15**(8):3733–3756 (2011). https://www.sciencedirect.com/science/article/pii/S1364032111002462
9. H.B. Aditiya, W.T. Chong, T.M.I. Mahlia, A.H. Sebayang, M.A. Berawi, H. Nur. Waste Management, **47**:46–61 (2016). https://www.ncbi.nlm.nih.gov/pubmed/26253329
10. H.B. Aditiya, T.M.I. Mahlia, W.T. Chong, H. Nur, A.H. Sebayang. Renew. Sust. Energ. Rev., **66**:631–653 (2016). https://www.sciencedirect.com/science/article/pii/S1364032116303434
11. N. Hossain, J.H. Zaini, T.M.I. Mahlia. International Journal of Technology, **8**(1):5–18 (2017). http://www.ijtech.eng.ui.ac.id/old/index.php/journal/article/view/3948
12. L. Aditya, T.M.I. Mahlia, B. Rismanchi, H.M. Ng, M.H. Hasan, H.S.C. Metselaar, et al. Renew. Sust. Energ. Rev., **73**:1352–1365 (2017). https://www.sciencedirect.com/science/article/pii/S1364032117302484
13. M. Amin, N. Putra, E.A. Kosasih, E. Prawiro, R.A. Luanto, T.M.I. Mahlia. Appl. Therm. Eng., **112**:273–280 (2017). https://www.sciencedirect.com/science/article/pii/S1359431116323845
14. A.E. Atabani, A.S. Silitonga, T.M.I. Mahlia, Renew. Sust. Energ. Rev., **16**(5):3547–3558 (2012). https://www.researchgate.net/publication/236853970_Cost_benefit_analysis_and_environmental_impact_of_fuel_economy_standards_for_passenger_cars_in_Indonesia
15. A.S. Silitonga, A.E. Atabani, T.M.I. Mahlia, A.H. Sebayang. Renew. Sust. Energ. Rev., **15**(9):5212–5217 (2011). https://www.sciencedirect.com/science/article/pii/S1364032111001407
16. T. Uno, S. Hokoi, E.S. Nastiti. Journal of Asian Architecture and Building Engineering, **2**(2):15–21 (2003). https://www.jstage.jst.go.jp/article/jaabe/2/2/2_2_b15/_pdf
17. M.W. Roberts. Review of European, Comparative and International Environmental Law, **26**(3): 220–230 (2017). http://onlinelibrary.wiley.com/doi/10.1111/reel.12225/full
18. S. Khosravi, T.M.I. Mahlia, Y.H. Yau. *Feasibility study of hybrid wheel desiccant dehumidification cooling systems in Malaysia*. ASHRAE Transactions, 2010 Winter Conference, **116**:392–397. (Orlando, 2010). https://www.thefreelibrary.com/Feasibility+study+of+hybrid+wheel+desiccant+dehumidification+cooling...-a0227975407
19. S. Khosravi, Y.H. Yau, T.M.I. Mahlia, M.H. Saidi, *A new approach to exergy analyses of a hybrid desiccant cooling system compares to a vapor compression system*. International Conference on Mechanical and Aerospace Engineering (ICMAE) (Venice, Italy, 2011). Applied Mechanics and Materials, **110–116**:2163–2169 (2012). https://www.scientific.net/AMM.110-116.2163
20. M.A. Fazilati, A.A. Alemrajabi, A. Sedaghat. Heat and Mass Transfer, **54**(3):903–913 (2018). https://link.springer.com/article/10.1007/s00231-017-2191-4
21. F. Zhang, Y. Yin, X. Zhang. Building and Environment, **117**:218–229 (2017). https://www.sciencedirect.com/science/article/pii/S0360132317301130
22. L. Bellia, P. Mazzei, F. Minichiello, and D. Palma, “Air conditioning systems with desiccant wheel foritalian climates,” International Journal on Architectural Science, vol. 1, no. 4, pp. 193-213, 2000.
23. C. Maalouf, E. Wurtz, F. Allard. *Evaluation of the cooling potential of a desiccant evaporative cooling system using the SimSPARK environment*. UTAP, University of Reims, Campus du Moulin de la Housse. [online] from http://citeseerx.ist.psu.edu/viewdoc/download?doi=10.1.1.576.6438&rep=rep1&type=pdf (2006). [Accessed on 18 February 2018].
24. K. Daou, R.Z. Wang, Z.Z. Xia. Renew. Sust. Energ. Rev., **10**(2):55–77 (2006). https://www.sciencedirect.com/science/article/pii/S1364032104001200
25. P. Mavroudaki, C.B. Beggs, P.A. Sleigh, S.P. Halliday. Appl. Therm. Eng. **22**(10):1129-1140 (2002). https://www.sciencedirect.com/science/article/pii/S1359431102000340
26. B.S. Davanagere, S.A. Sherif, D.Y. Goswami. International Journal of Energy Research, **23**(1):7–21 (1999). http://onlinelibrary.wiley.com/doi/10.1002/(SICI)1099-114X(199901)23:1%3C7::AID-ER439%3E3.0.CO;2-U/abstract

27. A.A. Pesaran, T.R. Penney, A.W. Czanderna. *Desiccant cooling: State-of-the art asessement*. Washington: National Renewable Energy Laboratory A, Division of Midwest Research Institute, operated for the US Department of Energy Under Contract No DE-AC02-83CH10093, (1992). https://www.osti.gov/biblio/6925169

Modified Floating Search Feature Selection Based on Genetic Algorithm

Kanyanut Homsapaya*, and *Ohm* Sornil

Graduate School of Applied Statistics National Institute of Development Administration, 118 Serithai Rd., Bangkapi, Bangkok, 10240, Thailand

Abstract. Classification performance is adversely impacted by noisy data .Selecting features relevant to the problem is thus a critical step in classification and difficult to achieve accurate solution, especially when applied to a large data set. In this article, we propose a novel filter-based floating search technique for feature selection to select an optimal set of features for classification purposes. A genetic algorithm is utilized to increase the quality of features selected at each iteration. A criterion function is applied to choose relevant and high-quality features which can improve classification accuracy. The method is evaluated using 20 standard machine learning datasets of various sizes and complexities. Experimental results with the datasets show that the proposed method is effective and performs well in comparison with previously reported techniques.

Key words: Feature selection, floating search, genetic algorithm.

1 Introduction

Classification, a process for predicting a class of a given input data, is one of the most fundamental tasks in data mining. A number of methods are commonly used for data classification, such as decision trees; rule-based, probabilistic and instance-based methods; support vector machines (SVMs); and neural networks. Noisy and irrelevant data are major obstacles to data mining.

Selecting features relevant to the problem is a critical first step in classification, especially when applied to a large dataset. The aim is to select a representative subset of highly relevant dimensions while removing irrelevant and redundant ones [1]. Feature selection can significantly improve the running time of a machine learning algorithm as well as improve the quality of the model.

Consequently, Bins and Draper [2] proposed a technique to reduce a large set of features (1 000) to a much smaller subset without removing any highly important features or decreasing classification accuracy. There are three steps in the algorithm: first, irrelevant features are removed using a modified form of the relief algorithm [3]; second, redundant features are eliminated using K-means clustering [4]; and, lastly, a combinatorial feature selection algorithm is employed to the current feature subsets using the sequential floating backward selection (SFBS) algorithm. The basic concept is to filter feature subsets on each step until the smallest possible one is obtained. In this article, we propose a technique to improve the effectiveness of the floating search feature selection method which leads to a higher classification rate. Our method employs a genetic algorithm to enrich and improve the resultant features after each iteration of the sequential forward feature search (SFFS) process.

2 Backgrounds

2.1. Feature selection

Two important components of the feature selection process: subset generation and subset evaluation are shown in Figure 1. The subset generation engine identifies feature subset candidates and subset evaluation measures the quality of the subsets. Lastly, in order to terminate the process, a stopping criterion is tested at every iteration.

There are three main types of feature selection method: filter, wrapper and hybrid. Wrapper methods rely on a classification algorithm employed as the subset evaluation process for feature subsets [5]. Maroño et al. [6] proposed a wrapper method by applying ANOVA. In general, the wrapper approach gives a higher performance than the filter approach since the feature selection process is optimized for the specific classification algorithm. Nevertheless, when wrapper methods are applied to huge dimensional datasets, they will incur high computational cost and may become unfeasible.

Filter methods use an independent criterion which relies on general characteristics of the data to evaluate and select feature subsets without involving a classification algorithm. Common evaluation functions usually are measures such as distance, mutual information (MI), dependency or entropy, calculated directly from the training data. Karegowda et al. [7] developed a filter-based technique in a cascade fashion with a genetic algorithm (GA) using a correlation-based criterion. Dash and Liu [1] proposed Hybrid methods exploit the positive aspects of both wrapper and filter methods. It utilizes a filter-based technique to select highly representative features and applies a wrapper-based technique to add candidate features and evaluate the candidate subsets in order to select the best ones.

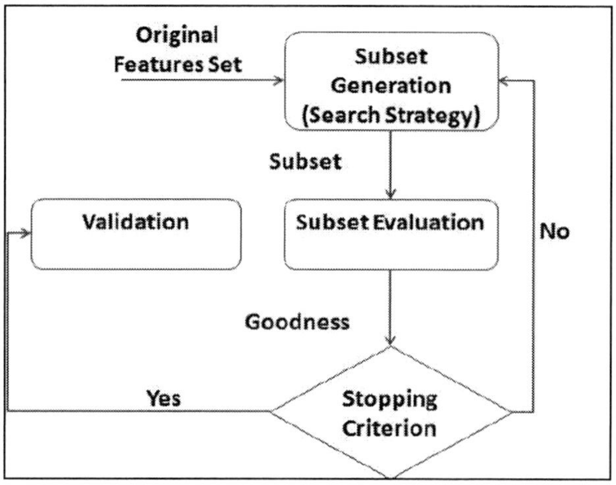

Fig. 1. The feature selection process.

The sequential forward search (SFS) method operates in a forward search manner starting with an empty set and adds one feature subset during each round until a new feature subset that maximizes the criterion function value is found, whereas the sequential backward search (SBS) method starts with a full feature subset and eliminates a feature on each iteration until a predetermined criterion is satisfied. A drawback of both methods is that they have a nesting effect problem, which means that the features discarded cannot be re-selected, and the features selected cannot be removed later. Since these algorithms do not examine all possible feature subsets, they are not guaranteed to produce an optimal result. Generalized forms GSFS and GSBS based on group collection feature testing are better solutions, but at the cost of increased computational time. The plus l take away r (PTA) method was proposed to take care of the nesting problem [8].

2.2 Floating search method

Pudil et al. [9] proposed "floating" search methods based on two main categories: the search process in a forward direction (SFFS) and the process in a backward direction (SBFS). These methods use a criterion function to select a feature and compare candidate subsets. SFFS and SBFS can be classified as a wrapper or a filter approach depending on the criterion function used. They perform well but the computational time is long, especially with large datasets. The floating search methods can be viewed as predictive text algorithms (PTAs) without the use of a fixed parameter. They have been shown to give very good performance (close to optimum results) and to overcome the nesting problem. SFFS, SBFS, and bidirectional selection as a combination of both are greedy search algorithms that add or discard features one at a time [9]. The floating search method consists of two phases: forward and backward. SFFS starts with an empty set and sequentially adds one feature at a time. The structure of the floating search algorithm is shown in Figure 2.

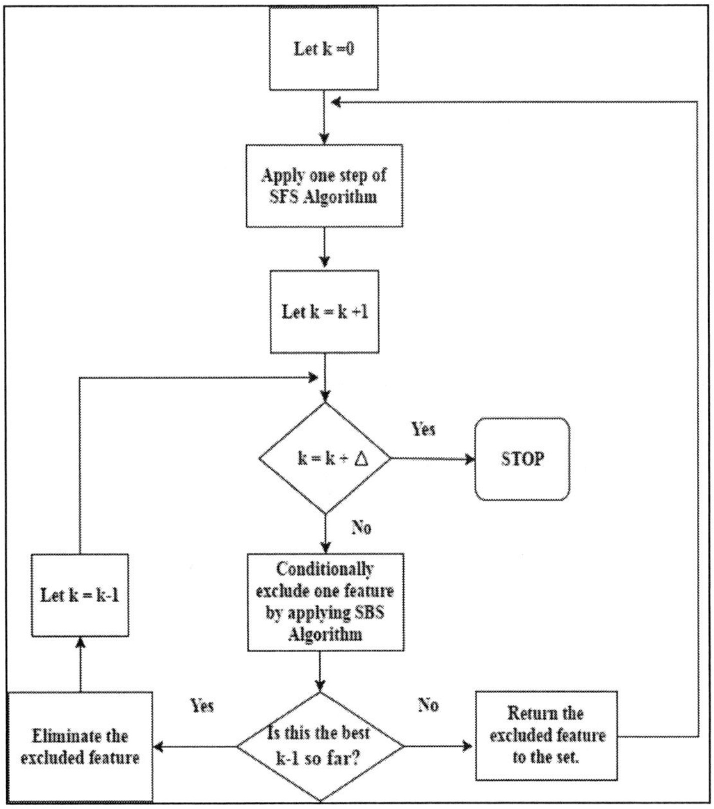

Fig. 2. The structure of a floating search algorithm.

SBFS, the counterpart of the forward search, is initialized with a full set and sequentially eliminates one feature at a time after execution of SFFS. An SFFS search selects the best unselected feature according to a criterion function to form a new feature subset, and an SBFS search iteratively determines which members of the selected subset are to be removed if the remaining set improves performance according to the same criterion function in the forward search. The algorithm loops back to a forward search until the stopping condition is reached. There are disadvantages when using either algorithm. With SFFS, it is not possible to succeed in eliminating redundant features generated in the search process, whereas SBFS cannot re-calculate evaluation feature usefulness together with other features at the same time.
Improved versions of SFFS have been proposed in many researches to obtain better performance. Somol et al. [10] presented the adaptive sequential forward floating selection (ASFFS) algorithm with a parameter "r" which specifies the number of features to be added in the inclusion phase calculated dynamically. Parameter "o" is used in the exclusion phase to remove the maximum number of features if it improves performance. Nakariyakul and Casasent [11] came up with an improved forward floating search algorithm, which has a new search step to check whether to replace a weak feature and remove it again until the replacement can no longer improve the criterion function. They found that this method obtained optimal solutions for many feature subsets and was less computationally intensive than exhaustive search optimal feature selection algorithms. Chaiyakarn and Sornil [12] proposed a filter-based method to return a small subset of features for classification by employing two different criterion functions in the forward and backward steps. The functions helped remove redundant features, maximize inter-class distances, and minimize intra-class distances.

2.3 Feature subset evaluation

In order to perform feature selection with the filter approach, a measure is needed to evaluate the relevance of the subset to the classification process.

2.3.1 Mahalanobis distance

The Mahalanobis distance is very helpful solution of determining the "similarity" of a set of values from an "unknown" sample to a set of values measured from a collection of "known" samples. Yongli [13] used the Mahalanobis of candidate feature subsets and selected the best quality subset to be used as input data. One of the main reasons the Mahalanobis distance method is used is that it is very sensitive to inter-variable changes in the training data. The Mahalanobis distance between two points $x = (x_1,...,x_p)^t$ and $y = (y_1,...,y_p)^t$ in the p-dimensional space R_p is defined as:

$$d_S(x,y) = \sqrt{(x-y)^t S^{-1}(x-y)} \tag{1}$$

and $d_S(x,0) = \|x\|_S = \sqrt{x^t S^{-1} x}$ is the norm of x.

2.3.2 Mutual information

In order to perform feature selection with the filter approach, measures are needed to evaluate the relevance of the subset to the classification process. MI is a widely used measure to evaluate candidate feature subsets. Battiti [14] used MI on candidate feature subsets to select a quality subset to be used as input data for a neural network classifier. MI measures absolute dependencies between random variables and can be calculated as follows:

$$I(X,Y) = H(X) + H(Y) - H(X,Y) \tag{2}$$

Where H is an entropy function, Y is a class attribute, and X is the feature to select. Given a random variable X such that:

$X = 0$ with probability p

$X = 1$ with probability $1 - p$

$$H(X) = -p \log p - (1-p)\log(1-p) = H(p) \tag{3}$$

A genetic algorithm (GA), introduced by John Holland in 1975 [15], is an adaptive optimization search algorithm to find an optimal solution inspired by natural selection in biological systems. The genes of an organism are gathered into structures called chromosomes, and a set of chromosomes is referred to as a population. In general, there are three operations employed in GAs. First, selection is an operator for selecting potentially useful solutions for recombination, and is achieved by either tournament or roulette wheel selection. Second, crossover refers to the process of producing an offspring chromosome from two matching parent chromosomes. Third, mutation causes genetic diversity of chromosomes by making random binary changes in a chromosome, thus adversely affecting their fitness value. These principles have led to new solutions in the pursuit of better search solutions.

2.4 Genetic algorithm

GAs have been successfully applied to feature selection [16] with the objective to save on computational time without processing in an exhaustive fashion, which is achieved by finding promising regions and selecting quality feature subsets. Furthermore, hybrid GAs [17] are involved in a new search method that includes local search operators to improve the fine-tuning quality of a simple GA search.

The fitness function, based on the principle of survival of the fittest, is the process whereby a GA evaluates each individual's fitness and obtains the optimal solution after applying the genetic operators. This process is repeated many times and over many generations until the stopping criterion is satisfied. For feature selection, the feature subsets are represented as a binary; a feature is either included or not included in the feature subset.

3 The proposed algorithm

We now discuss our algorithm to select the best subset of size d of the total of D features. The inclusion step using MI as the criterion function (J) is executed to create a set of candidates for inclusion. In the exclusion step, a candidate feature subset is used to generate smaller subsets from the result of the inclusion step by removing one feature and re-evaluating them. A selection subset of size k + 1 is generated and compared to the previously best subset of size k + 1

from the inclusion part. If evaluation of the new subset is more qualified than the formerly selected set, the exclusion step retains the better one and iterates to smaller subsets, or else the algorithm goes back to the inclusion step.
Our feature improvement step based on GA is included after the exclusion step at each iteration. The chromosome structure consists of binary genes, corresponding to individual features. The value of 1 at the *i*th gene means that the *i*th feature is selected; otherwise it is 0.

The initial population is generated from the resulted subsets of size k + 1 from the exclusion step by first removing the weakest features from the best subset resulting in a subset of size k. Each remaining feature is thus added to that subset generating the niched initial population for GA. The fitness function used in this study is MI. Then, a new population is created by selection, crossover and mutation operations. The process is terminated when the current feature set reaches the size of D-2 features. We now provide an illustrative example of how the proposed algorithm works and how it improves SFFS. Assume that the first five feature sets selected by the SFS method at each size are {f1}, {f1, f4}, {f1, f4, f5}, {f1, f4, f5, f7} with the corresponding J values of 4.1, 6.2, 9.1 and 10.2, respectively, and the next iteration is to determine subsets with five features.

3.1 Step 1: Inclusion

A feature is added to the feature subset. The SFS method adds a feature to the subset up to a total of five: J (f1, f4, f5, f7, f6) = 13. Assume that feature f6 is chosen using the SFS method and J for the 5th features is 14.

3.2 Step 2: Exclusion

A feature is removed from the feature subset. The SBS method is applied in this step by backtracking and conditionally removing one feature from the subset selected in Step 1 and returning an improved subset, e.g. (f1, f5, f6, f7) J value = 11; (f1, f4, f5, f7) J value = 9; (f1, f4, f7, f6) J value = 9.5; and (f4, f5, f7, f6) J value = 10. In this case, the best feature subset of size 4 is (f1, f5, f6, f7).

3.3 Step 3: Feature improvement

The weakest feature is removed from the subset from of size k the previous step which is (f1, f5, f6, f7) by iteratively evaluating the smaller subsets: (f1, f5, f7), (f1, f5, f6), (f5, f6, f7) and (f1, f7, f6). In this case, we assume that the best performance subset of size 3 is (f5, f7, f6). Then, each feature is added to each subset of (f5, f7, f6) in order to find the best four feature subset, either (f5, f7, f6, f1), (f5, f7, f6, f2), (f5, f7, f6, f3), (f5, f7, f6, f4), (f5, f7, f6, f8), or (f5, f7, f6, f9). Top n chromosomes is selected as the initial population for GA and passed through the crossover and mutation operations.

3.3.1 Step 3.1: Crossover operation

Once a pair of chromosomes has been selected, crossover can take place to produce child chromosomes. A crossover point is randomly chosen from two randomly selected individuals (parents). This point occurs between two bits and divides each individual into left and right sections. Crossover then swaps the left (or the right) section of the two individuals thus (Figure 3):

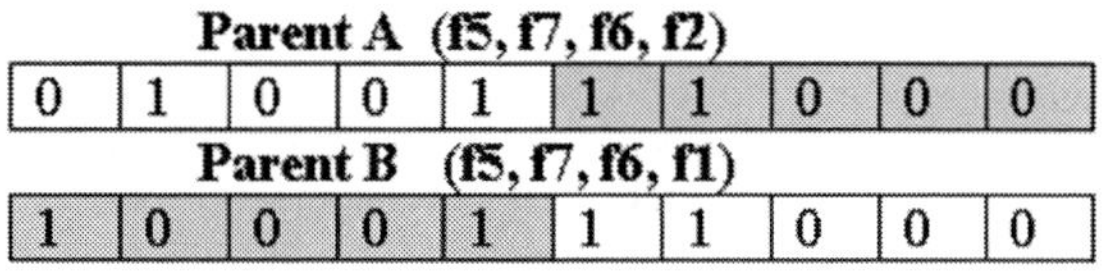

Fig. 3. Crossover operation.

Suppose the crossover point randomly occurs after the sixth bit, then each new child receives one half of each parent's bits (Figure 4):

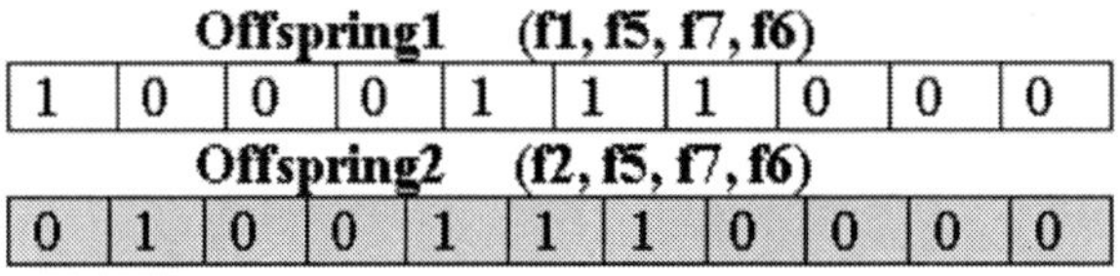

Fig. 4. Child chromosome.

This algorithm continues to select parental chromosomes to apply the crossover operation. Child chromosomes may have one bit more than the current size of k features subset. In this case, a random bit is automatically flipped to preserve the size of the chromosome (i.e. current feature set size).

3.3.2 Step 3.2: Mutation operation

The mutation operation (Figure 5) is applied to all of the offspring chromosomes from the crossover step. Mutation operates at the bit level by randomly flipping bits in the new chromosome within the current population (turning a '0' into '1', and vice versa).

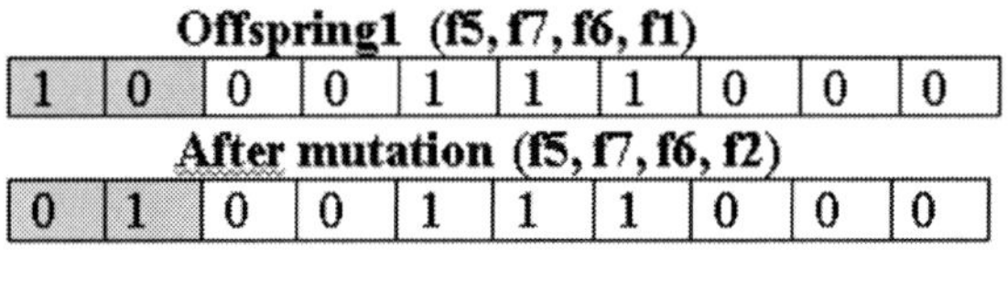

Fig. 5. Mutation operation.

After all child chromosomes have passed through the mutation operator, the resultant chromosomes are evaluated by the fitness function. After this, we can discover the best performing features subset, which is (f5, f7, f6, f2). We assume that J ({f5, f7, f6}) = 8.35, and that J ({f5, f7, f6, f2}) = 12, which is larger than the prior largest value for four features, J = 11 Thus, the best 4-feature subset becomes {f5, f7, f6, f2} with J = 12, whereas the best 3-feature subset remains {f1, f4, f5} since J ({f1, f4, f5}) = 9.1 > J ({f5, f7, f6}) = 8.35.

The improvement step helps discover subsets not discoverable by the greedy nature of SFFS. From the above example, the SFFS algorithm is not able to produce this best 4-feature four subset because it cannot backtrack to the set {f5, f7, f6}, thus could not add feature f2 to subset {f5, f7, f6}. The example above demonstrates the advantage of our proposed algorithm. The algorithm replaces the weak feature (feature f1 in our example) in the feature set {f1, f5, f7, f6} with feature 2, which results in a new set of four features {f5, f7, f6, f2} which has a larger J value. Therefore, the search strategy of our proposed algorithm is more thorough than the SFFS algorithm, so it is more effective.

3.4 Step 4: Terminating condition

After each iteration, the selection/crossover per mutation cycle continues until all possible combinations of chromosomes in the population have been evaluated. The higher the fitness value, the higher the probability of that chromosome being selected for reproduction. This generational process is repeated until a pre-determined termination condition has been reached. We terminate the algorithm when the current feature set reaches $d < D$ features, where D is the total number of features in the dataset). The pseudo-code is depicted in Figure 6.

A fitness function is commonly needed in GAs to evaluate a candidate chromosome of an individual to assess whether the latter should survive or not. At each iteration, calculation of the fitness function is processed repeatedly, which, because of its simplicity, is a fast process, although it still impacts performance. In our model, we use the Mahalanobis criterion as a fitness function.

Input: Y_m is a feature set, m is a predefined number of selected features, J is a criterion function. P_c is probability of crossover, P_m is probability of mutation, Population is set of individuals, max_generation is the maximum number of generations, and Fitness is a function which determines quality of individuals. Output: The best solution in all generation.

```
(1) Inclusion
    Initialize: Y0 = {Ø}; m = 0
    Find the best feature and update Ym
    x = +arg max [J(Ym − x)]
              x/∈Ym
    Ym = Ym + x+; m = m + 1
(2) Conditional Exclusion
    Find the worst feature
    x = −arg max [J(Ym − x)]
              x/∈Ym
    If J (Ym − x (−> J (Ym ) then
           Ym+1 = Ym − x,
    Go to Step 3 Else Go to Step1
(3) Feature Improvement Step.
      Repeat
       population ← SBFS feature subsets Ym
       generation = 0;
       loop for i from 1 to size Population(do)
       s1 ← selection (Population, Fitness)
       s2 ← selection (Population, Fitness)
    child ← crossover (s1, s2) with pc and check feasibility of n element
    child ← mutate (child) with pm and check feasibility of n element
          Fitness (child)
             Generation = generation +1
       until generation < max_generation
     m = m + 1
    return the best individual solution Ym
```

Fig. 6. Pseudo-code of the proposed algorithm.

4 Experimental evaluation

To evaluate the proposed feature selection algorithm, 20 standard datasets of various sizes and complexities from the UCI machine learning repository [18] are used in the experiments. These datasets have been frequently used as a benchmark to compare the performance of classification methods and consist of a mixture of numeric, real and categorical attributes. Details of the datasets are shown in Table 1.

Three classification modeling techniques are used in the experiments which consist of Classification and Regression Tree (CART), Support Vector Machine (SVM), and Naïve Bayes. Training and testing data is used as provided in the datasets. For those not providing separate testing data, a 5-fold cross validation is applied. To evaluate a feature subset, MI is applied as the criterion function.

4.1 The classifiers

CART is a well-known decision tree algorithm for supervised machine learning that is applied to both classification and regression problems. It was first introduced by Brieman et al. [19]. A decision tree represents a series of decisions. The key components of the tree are a set of rules for splitting each node in the tree, and assigning a class outcome to each terminal node.

The Naïve Bayes algorithm is a statistical classifier for supervised learning [19], and is based on the principle of conditional probability. It can predict class membership probabilities, such as the probability that a given sample belongs to a particular class, and its performance has been shown to be excellent in some domains but poor on specific domains, e.g. those with correlated features. The classification system is based on Bayes 'rule under the assumption that the effect of an attribute on a given class is independent from the other attributes. This assumption is called the class conditional independence which makes computation simple.

SVMs, originally proposed by Cortes and Vapnik [20], have become important in many classification problems for a variety of reasons, such as their flexibility, computational efficiency, and capacity to handle high dimensional data. They are a recent method to extract information from a dataset. Classification is achieved by a linear or nonlinear separating surface in the input space of the dataset. SVMs have been applied to a number of applications, such as bioinformatics, face recognition, text categorization, handwritten digit recognition, and so forth. SVM is a binary classifier assigning a new data to a class by minimizing the probability of error

4.2 Performance of the proposed techniques using classifiers

We studied the effectiveness of the proposed feature selection using three different classification methods: CART, SVM and Naïve Bayes on 20 standard UCI datasets. The results in Table 1 show that, in 97.7 % of the cases, the proposed technique improved classification effectiveness and greatly reduced the number of features selected, thus increasing classification efficiency, for all of the classification methods. We actually achieved 100 % selection accuracy from four datasets with the proposed method. In a comparison of the classification methods, SVM yielded the highest classification accuracy in 65 % of the datasets while CART gave the highest accuracy in 35 % of the datasets.

Table 1. Classification effectiveness.

Dataset	Original Datasets	No. of Attributes	PM* CART	PM* SVM	PM* Naïve Bayes
Wine	88.87	13	100.00 (7)	100.00 (7)	96.43 (7)
Breast Cancer (Original)	93.13	10	97.42 (5)	97.55 (5)	92.12 (5)
Breast Cancer (WDBC)	92.23	32	95.5 (5)	96.10 (8)	91.00 (8)
Breast Cancer (WPBC)	72.00	34	84.23 (6)	86.36 (6)	79.00 (6)
Iris	94.00	4	98.95 (3)	100.00 (3)	94.60 (3)
Pima -Indian Diabetes	72.51	8	74.38 (4)	77.00 (4)	71.89 (4)
Abalone	49.07	8	55.00 (4)	58.50 (4)	50.00 (4)
Dermatology	95.08	34	98.03 (26)	97.5 (26)	94.15 (26)
Heart	76.67	13	82.00 (6)	84.00 (6)	79.00 (6)
German	68.50	20	73.00 (6)	72.5 (6)	70.00 (6)
Lung cancer	59.67	56	78.00 (21)	85.33 (21)	72.00 (21)
Soy bean	85.00	35	100.00 (22)	100.00 (22)	98.28 (22)
Spambase	93.26	57	96.00 (26)	93.00 (26)	91.76 (26)
Glass Identification	62.00	10	63.13 (5)	67.00 (5)	65.00 (5)
Teaching Assistant	54.92	5	60.03 (2)	61.86 (2)	62.00 (5)
Contact Lens	76.00	4	80.00 (2)	100.00 (2)	85.00 (2)
Sonar	69.50	60	84.00 (18)	85.70 (18)	75.00 (7)
Statlog (Australian)	65.45	14	75.30 (7)	80.00 (7)	75.24 (7)
Ionosphere	84.00	34	91.00 (6)	92.62 (7)	90.10 (5)
Image Segmentation	85.00	19	92.00 (14)	90.57 (14)	84.10 (14)

*Proposed Method
Note. Results expressed as percentages.

Table 2. Comparison with other previously reported methods on common datasets [21–27].

Dataset	PM* CART	PM* SVM	[Liu, 2004]	[Ratanamahatana, 2003]	[Anwar, 2014]	[Yang, 2010]	[Gupta, 2015]	[Tsai, 2011]	[Lavanya, 2011]
Breast Cancer (Original)	97.42	97.55	-	97.4	94.4	96.5	-	-	94.8
Breast Cancer (WDBC)	95.5	96.1	95.4	-	-	-	-	-	93.0
Iris	98.95	100	97.3		-	97.3	96.7	96.6	-
Pima Indian Diabetes	74.38	77.0	73.8	79.9	76.0	73.2	-	-	-
German	73.0	72.5	72.6	76.2	-	74.5	-	69.9	-
Soybean	100	100	-	88.3	-	97.8	-	-	-
Wine	100	100	-	-	91.6	98.3	-	-	-
Heart	82.0	84.0	-	-	61.1	84.8	87.1	-	-
Sonar	84.0	84.7	-	-	83.7	-	-	-	-
Abalone	55.0	58.5	54.5	-	-	-	30.0	25.7	-
Dermatology	98.03	97.5	-	-	-	95.4	-	-	-
Contact Lenses	80.0	100	-	-	-	-	75.0	-	-

*Proposed Method
Note. Results expressed as percentages.

5 Conclusion

Feature selection is critical to the performance of classification. We propose a feature selection algorithm that improves the performance of SFFS by incorporating a feature improvement step based on a genetic algorithm. This step helps discover important subsets that are not possible using SFFS alone. The algorithm employs mutual information as the feature subset evaluation function. The proposed technique was evaluated using 20 standard datasets from the UCI repository using three different classification methods. The results show that the proposed feature selection technique significantly improves classification accuracy and gives a much smaller feature set, thus improves efficiency. In addition, it performed very well in comparison with other previously reported studies.

References

1. M. Dash, H. Liu. Intelligent Data Analysis, **1**(1-4):131–156 (1997). https://www.sciencedirect.com/science/article/pii/S1088467X97000085
2. J. Bins, B. Draper. *Feature selection from huge feature sets*. Proceedings on Eighth IEEE International Conference on Computer Vision (Vancouver, Canada, 2001). http://ieeexplore.ieee.org/document/937619/
3. K. Kira, L. Rendell. *The Feature Selection Problem: Traditional Methods and a New Algorithm*, AAAI-92 Proceedings, pp .129-134, (San Jose, California, 1992) https://www.aaai.org/Papers/AAAI/1992/AAAI92-020.pdf
4. MacQueen, J., *Some Methods for Classification and Analysis of Multivariate Observations*, Proceedings of the Fifth Berkley Symposium on Mathematics, Statistics and Probability, pp. 281-297, 1967.
5. I. Guyon, A. Elisseeff. J. Mach. Learn. Res. **3**:1157–1182 (2003). http://www.jmlr.org/papers/volume3/guyon03a/guyon03a.pdf
6. Maroño, N.S., Betanzos, A. & Castillo, E., *A new wrapper method for feature subset selection*. Proceedings European Symposium on Artificial Neural Networks, pp. 515–520. (Belgium, 2005). https://www.elen.ucl.ac.be/Proceedings/esann/esannpdf/es2005-106.pdf
7. A.G. Karegowda, M.A. Jayaram, A.S. Manjunath. IJCA, **23**(2):1–10 (2011). http://www.ijcaonline.org/archives/volume23/number2/2865-3711
8. H. Zhang, G. Sun. Pattern Recognit. **35**(3):701-711 (2002). https://www.sciencedirect.com/science/article/pii/S0031320301000462
9. P. Pudil, J. Novovicova, J. Kittler. Pattern Recognit. Lett. **15**(11):1119–1125 (1994). https://www.sciencedirect.com/science/article/pii/0167865594901279
10. P. Somol, P. Pudil, J. Novovicova. *Flexible hybrid sequential floating search in statistical feature selection*. Structural, Syntactic, and Statistical Pattern Recognition, Lecture Notes in Computer Science. A. Fred, T. Caelli, R.P.W. Duin, A. Campilho, D. Ridder (eds.), Springer, **4109**:632–639 (2006). https://link.springer.com/chapter/10.1007/11815921_69
11. S. Nakariyakul, D.P. Casasent. Pattern Recognit. **41**(9):1932–1940 (2009). https://www.sciencedirect.com/science/article/pii/S0031320308004937
12. O. Sornil. *Filter-based feature selection using two criterion functions and evolutionary fuzzification*. International Workshop on Multi-disciplinary Trends in Artificial Intelligence. Springer International Publishing. (Chiang Mai, Thailand, 2016). https://link.springer.com/chapter/10.1007/978-3-319-49397-8_15
13. Z. Yongli, Z. Yungui, T. Weiming, C. Hongzhi. *An improved feature selection algorithm based on MAHALANOBIS distance for network intrusion detection*. International Conference on Sensor Network Security Technology and Privacy Communication System (SNS & PCS), IEEE (Nangan, China, 2013). http://ieeexplore.ieee.org/document/6553837/
14. R. Battiti. IEEE Transactions on Neural Networks, **5**(4):537–550 (1994). http://ieeexplore.ieee.org/document/298224/
15. D. Goldberg. *Genetic algorithms in search, optimization, and machine learning*. Boston: Addison Wesley (1989). https://dl.acm.org/citation.cfm?id=534133
16. F. Brill, D. Brown, W. Martin. IEEE Transactions: Neural Networks, **3**(2):324–328 (1992). http://ieeexplore.ieee.org/document/125874/
17. I.S. Oh, J.S. Lee, B.R. Moon. IEEE Transactions: Pattern Analysis and Machine Intelligence, **26**(11):1424–1437 (2004). http://ieeexplore.ieee.org/document/1335448/
18. A. Asuncion, D.J. Newman. *UCI machine learning repository*. University of California, Department of Information and Computer Science. [Online] from http://archive.ics.uci.edu/ml/index.php
19. L. Brieman, J. Friedman, R. Olshen, C. Stone. *Classification of regression trees*. Routledge: Wadsworth Inc. (1984). https://books.google.co.id/books?id=gLs6DwAAQBAJ
20. C. Cortes, V. Vapnik. Machine Learning, 20(3):273–297 (1995). https://link.springer.com/article/10.1007/BF00994018
21. Ratanamahatana, C. & Gunopulos, D. Appl. Artif. Intell., 17(5-6):475–487 (2003). http://www.tandfonline.com/doi/abs/10.1080/713827175
22. H. Liu, H. Motoda, L. Yu. Artificial Intelligence, **159**(1–2):49–74 (2004). https://www.sciencedirect.com/science/article/pii/S0004370204000980
23. H. Anwar, U. Qamar, A.W.M. Qureshi. Sci. World J. **2014**(Article ID 313164):1–9 (2014). https://www.hindawi.com/journals/tswj/2014/313164/

24. T. Yang, L. Cao, C. Zhang. *A novel prototype reduction method for the K-nearest neighbor algorithm with K ≥ 1.* Pacific-Asia Conference on Knowledge Discovery and Data Mining **Part II**:89–100 (Hyderabad, India, 2010). https://link.springer.com/chapter/10.1007/978-3-642-13672-6_10
25. A. Gupta. IJSTR, **4**(5):85–94 (2015). http://www.ijstr.org/final-print/may2015/Classification-Of-Complex-Uci-Datasets-Using-Machine-Learning-And-Evolutionary-Algorithms.pdf
26. C.F. Tsai, W.Y. Lin, Z.F. Hong, C.Y. Hsieh. EURASIP Journal on Advances in Signal Processing, **2011**(62):2–11 (2011). https://link.springer.com/article/10.1186/1687-6180-2011-62
27. D. Lavanya, D. K.U. Rani. IJCSE **2**(5):756–763 (2011). http://www.ijcse.com/docs/INDJCSE11-02-05-167.pdf

The Integration of Gasification Systems with Gas Engine by Developing Wet Tar Scrubbers and Gas Filter to Produce Electrical Energy from Biomass

Kiman Siregar[1,*], *Rizal* Alamsyah[2] , Ichwana[1], Sholihati[3], *Saminuddin* Tou[4] , and *Nobel* Cristian Siregar[2]

[1]Department of Agricultural Engineering, Syiah Kuala University, Jl. Teuku Nyak Arief, Darussalam Banda Aceh, 23111, Indonesia
[2]Center for Agro-Based Industry, Ministry of Industry, Jl. Ir. H. Juanda No. 11, Bogor, 16122, Indonesia
[3]Departement of Agricultural Industry Technology, Serambi Mekkah University, Jl. Unmuha, Batoh, Lueng Bata, Banda Aceh, 23245 Indonesia
[4]Ministry of Forestry and Environment, Aceh Province, Jl. Jenderal Sudirman No 21, Banda Aceh, 23239, Indonesia

Abstract. The need for energy especially biomass-based renewable energy continues to increase in Indonesia. The objective of this research was to design downdraft gasifier machine with high content of combustible gas on gas engine. Downdraft gasifier machine was adjusted with the synthetic gas produced from biomass. Besides that, the net energy ratio, net energy balance, renewable index, economic analysis and impact assessment also been conducted. Gas engine that was designed in this research had been installed with capacity of 25 kW with diameter and height of reactorwere 900 mm and 1 000 mm respectively. The method used here werethe design the Detailed Engineering Design, assembly, and performance test of gas engine. The result showed that gas engine for biomass can be operated for 8 h with performance engine of 84 % and capacity of 25 kW. Net energy balance, net energy ratio, and renewable index was 30 MJ/kW h electric; 0.89; 0.76 respectively. The value of GHG emission of Biomass Power Generation is 0.03 kg-CO_2 eq per MJ. Electrical production cost for Biomass Power Generation is about IDR 1 500 per kW h which is cheaper than solar power generation which is about of IDR 3 300 per kW h.

Key words: Biomass power plant, renewable energy, wet tar scrubber.

* Corresponding author: ksiregar.tep@unsyiah.ac.id

1 Introduction

In 2015, Indonesia set a target to realize 23 % of primary energy supply from modern renewable energy by 2025 [1]. Indonesia is the largest country in ASEAN, so the need for energy continues to increase. The role of renewable energy is needed to meet the growth of energy demand. There is a large difference in the ratio of electrification throughout Indonesia, where for Papua the electricity ratio is less than 40 % while in the Jakarta is close to 100 %. The Indonesian state electricity company PT PLN (Persero) is seeking to increase the electricity ratio by 98 % in 2022 [2]. The ratio of electricity in Indonesia is only around 80 % on a national scale. For several regions lagging the ratio of the electricity is still 60 %, as in the area which isolated from electricity network system PT.PLN (Persero). At this region, electricity only life at night. One solution that can be done is use renewable energy sources [3].

The government has committed to realize 35 000 MW of electricity supply within 5 yr (2014 to 2019). The contribution of new and renewable energy-based power plants is still quite low, i.e. 9.9 % Hydropower (PLTA), Geothermal Power Plant (PLTP) of 2.6 % and other renewable energy (EBT) below 0.5 %. The process of gasification consists of four stages of the process based on the difference of temperature range, which are drying (T > 150 °C), pyrolysis (150 °C < T < 700 °C), oxidation (700 °C < T < 1 500 °C), and the reduction (800 °C < T < 1 000 °C) [4, 5]. The results of this system produce combustible gases (CO, H_2, CH_4, etc). Gasification technology is suitablefor the area which has large quantities of biomass, which currently have not been yet traversed by electrical network system such as PT.PLN (Persero) and private companies. In this area the price of diesel fuel is very expensive with price is about IDR 50 000 per liter. This condition caused the price of electrical energy per hours would be very expensive for all of them e.g. in the Island of Papua.

The gasification is designed to produce combustible gas (CO, H_2, CH_4) [4–9]. These combustible gas are produced to replace fossil fuel as engine fuel to generate electricity. However, the properties and characteristics of these combustible gas should meet the characteristic of the engine as every engine has its own specific characteristic. Some engines are designed working more properly with methane gas (CH_4) but some work more properly with carbon monoxide gas (CO) [10]. Biomass Power Generation (BPG) designed in this research adjusted with combustible gas produced that is CO and H_2. Therefore the objective was to design biomass gasification system that suits the dominant gas produced from biomass. High level of tar contained in produced combustible gas contaminates the engine filter rapidly. Therefore, the machine cannot be operated at a longer time. The objectives of this research is to design gasification system with high content of combustible gases (CO, H_2, CH_4, etc). The gasification system will be connected to gas engineto produce electrical energy from biomass. Besides that, the net energy ratio, net energy balance, renewable index, economic analysis, and impact assessment also been conducted.

2 Method

2..1 Tools and materials research

The biomass power generation (BPG) consists of biomass tank, reactor, cyclone, tar wet scrubber, gas filter and gas engine. Gasification engine was made using downdraft type in order to produce fewer tar values. The specifications of materials, materials and gasification machine capacity produced are shown in Table 1.

Table 1. Specification gasification engine/Biomass power plant

No	Description	Technical specifications	Quantity
1	Gasification type	*Downdraft* gasifier	1 set
2	*Carbon steel of* tube reactor	OD (3.81 to 5.08) m × 0.001 m thickness	1 pcs
3	*Engine*	25 kW	1 pcs
4	*Blower*	Daya ¼ - ½ HP	1 pcs
5	*H-Beam*	Steel, (0.508 to 1.016) m	20 m
6	*Steel plat*	0.05 m width x 0.005 m thickness	20 m
7	*Pipe from carbon steel*	OD (0.254 to 0.508) m, 0.001 m thickness	30 m
8	Power cable	Merk ETERNA	50 m
9	Temperature indicator	Merk SIKA	6 pcs
10	*Pressure indicator*	Merk SIKA	4 pcs
11	*Control panel*	ASTM Standard	1 set
12	Portable temperature	Thermometer laser and digital	1 pcs
14	Heast resistant hoses	Material tahanpanas, ±100 °C	5 m

2.2 Research method

2.2.1 Analysis of synthetic gases

The method used in this research was to analyze the gases produced from the downdraft gasifier system which was designed and made. The biomass utilized in this research was wood. Wood was fed on the top of downdraft gasifier and then enters biomass storage in gasifier. The biomass would enter pyrolysis phase about 200 °C to 700 °C, and then combustion and reduction phase about 1 000 °C to 1 400 °C. The gases produced passed the wet tar scrubber and gas filter to ensure the tar limit meet the requirement and clean gases was used to run the gas engine. Engine performance was measured by test the effectiveness power produced for specific time given.

2.2.2 Analysis of energy, econonmy, and life cycle assessment

The important parameter regarding analysis of energy is Net Energy Ratio (NER), Net Energy Balance (NEB), and Renewable Index (RI). It can be stated as formula as below:

$$NER = \frac{E_o}{E_i} \tag{1}$$

$$NEB = E_o - E_{pr} \tag{2}$$

$$RI = \frac{E_{rn}}{E_{pr}} \leq 1 \tag{3}$$

The determination of the value of Input Energy (E_i), Process Energy (E_{pr}), Renewable Energy (E_{rn}), Output Energy (E_o) are shown onequations 4, 5, 6 and 7.

$$E_i = E_{bm} \tag{4}$$

$$E_{rn} = E_{bm} \tag{5}$$

$$E_{pr} = E_f + E_{bm} + E_{el} \tag{6}$$

$$E_o = E_{ge} \tag{7}$$

Where E_i is input energy of biomass (E_{bm}); E_{rn} is renewable energy of biomass (E_{bm}); E_{pr} is process energy which is the sum of fossil energy (E_f), biomass energy (E_{bm}), and electrical energy (E_{el}), while E_o is output energy of electric power generated by gas engine (E_{ge}). Impact Assessment was measured by using Life Cycle Assessment (LCA) method which is described below:

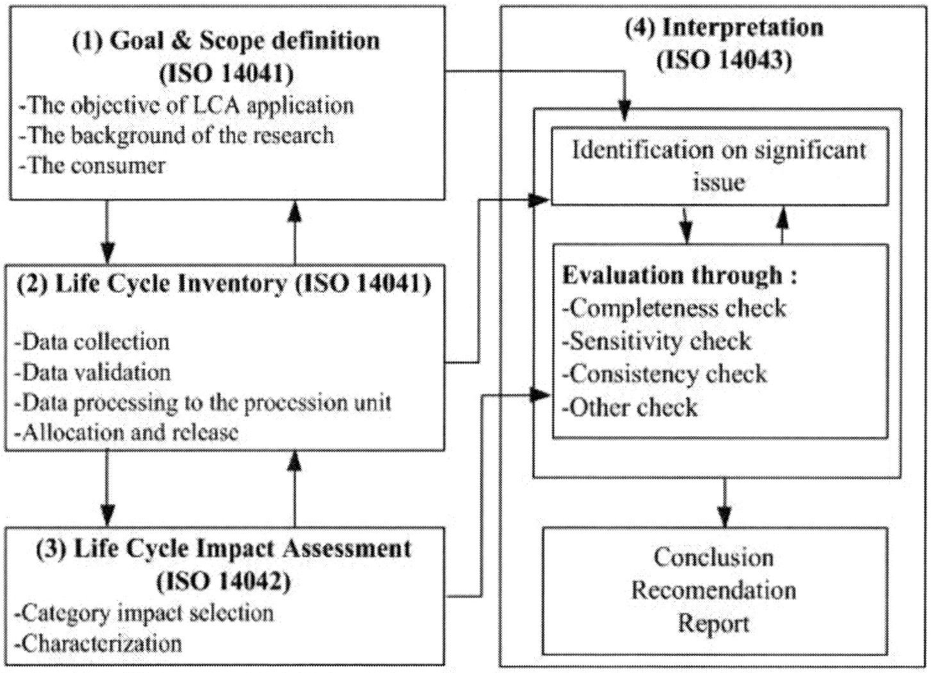

Fig. 1. Impact assessment by Life Cycle Assessment (LCA) method [11, 12]

To estimate the economic feasibility, the parameter used is to compare electrical production cost frrom Biomass Power Generation and Diesel Power Generation in IDR per kW h unit.

3 Result

3.1 Biomass power generation

The biomass power plant produced has been connected to the gas engine which in its series already uses tar wet scrubber and gas filter. Overall the biomass power generation engine consists of tanks of biomass, reactor, cooler, cyclone, tar wet scrubber, gas filter, blower, and valve system control. The series of BPG engines generated in this study are shown in Figure 2. This gasification technology was aimed to produce combustible gas (CO, H_2, CH_4). This combustible gas is used to replace fossil fuel as an engine fuel used to generate electricity. The biomass fuel used in the research is wood. With relatively uniform shape and size, congestion can be avoided [5], so in this study,woodchopper was also used as a cutting tool that can produce uniformity of biomass sizes.

The type of downdraft gasifier designed in this study is a fixed bed downdraft gasifier with a direction of air flow from the bottom up as shown in Figure 3a and Figure 3b. The advantages of this type of downdraft are it is not too sensitive to tar and can easily adapt to the amount of biomass feed. Another advantage was that it appears to be cleaner because the tar and oil will burn. This is reinforced by the tar data generated from the various types of gasifiers produced as shown in Table 2.

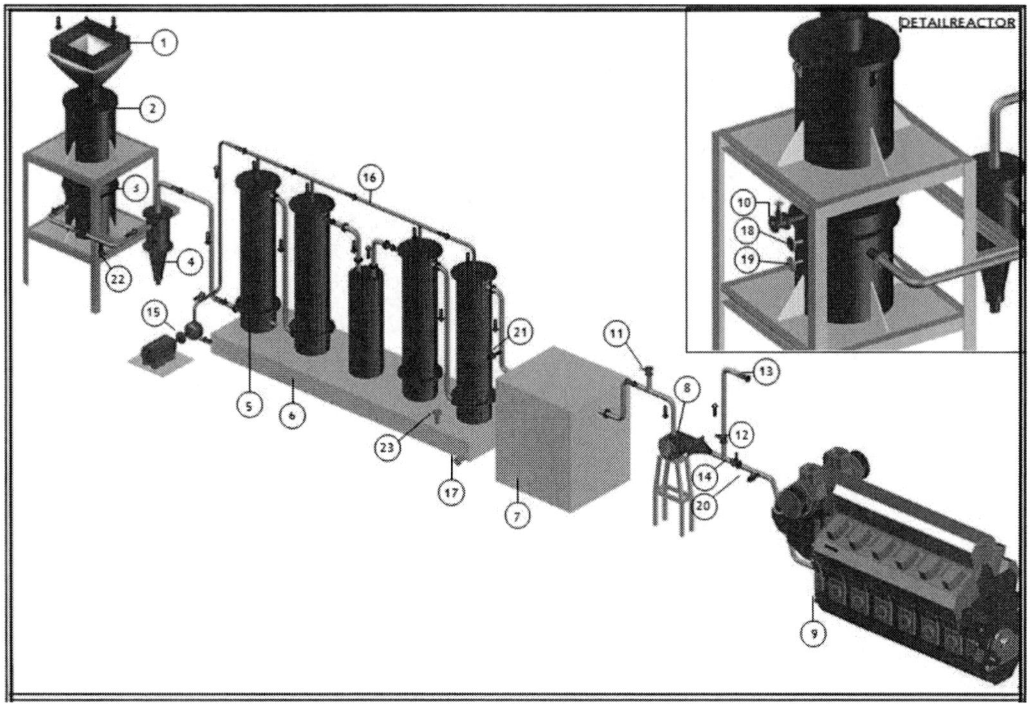

Remarks : (1)Hopper input for biomass, (2)Biomass tank, (3)Reactor, (4)Cyclon, (5)Wet tar scrubber, (6)Water tank, (7)Gas filter, (8)Blower, (9)Gas engine, (10)Air inlet nozzle (Valve 1), (11)Valve 2, (12)Valve 3, (13)Exhaust gas, (14)Valve 4, (15)Circulating water pump, (16)Nozzle spray, (17)Nozzle drain, (18)Pressure gauge, (19)Thermometer gauge, (20)Sample gas nozzle 3, (21)Sample gas nozzle 2, (22)Sample gas nozzle 1, (23)Nozzle filling water

Fig. 2. A system gasification type downdraft and gas engine capacity of 25 kW.

Table 2. Tar content resulting from various types of gasification produced [7].

Type of gasification	The average fuel gas concentrations in the tar is produced (g Nm^{-3})	Tar percentage of biomass used
Downdraft	< 1	< 2
Fluidized bed	10	1 to 5
Updraft	50	10 to 20
Entrained flow	ignored	

Fig. 3a. Gasifier type downdraft designed and used in this research.

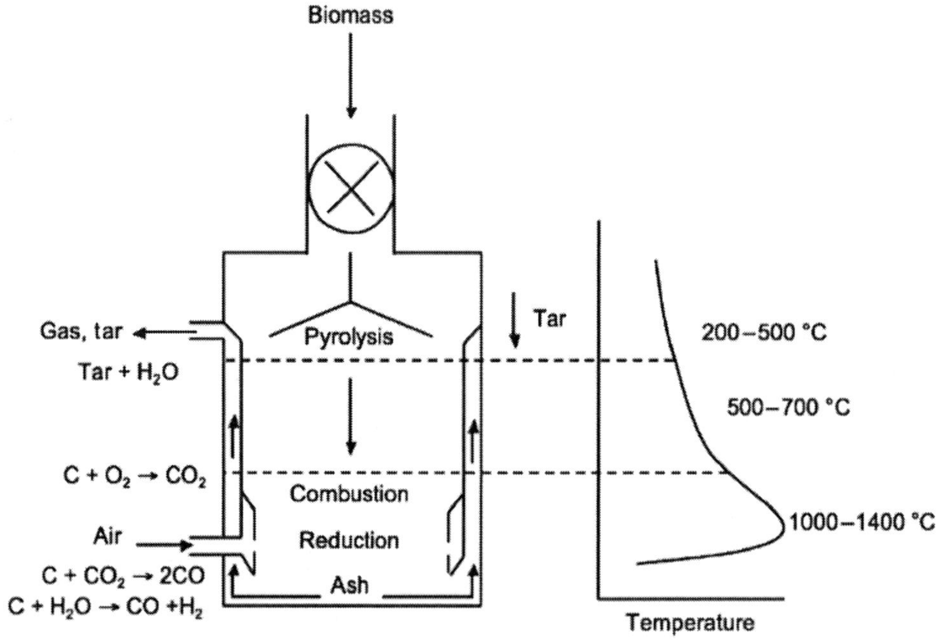

Fig. 3b. Commonly phase on Gasifier type downdraft [4].

3.2 Design and main components of biomass power generation with capacity of 25 kW

The gasifier used in this study has a total dimension of 1 340 mm diameter and a height of 2 455 mm as shown in Figure 3 above. Cyclon has a length of 580 mm, a width of 426 mm with a height of 1 766 mm. Gas filter has a length of 700 mm, a height of 700 mm and a width of 700 mm. Tar wet scrubber consists of five tubes (300 mm tube diameter) which are strung together with the aim of capturing the tar still contained in the combustible gas produced from the gasification reactor. Gasification reactor itself has total dimensions of 1 750 mm width and 1 300 mm height. The design has considered resident time of biomass in gasifier reactor in order to produce synthetic gas optimally. The comparison of height to diameter of 1.8 has been chosen. Overall this series of Biomass Power Plant with Engines is shown in Figures 4 and Figure 5.

Fig. 4. Biomass power generation with capacity of 25 kW.

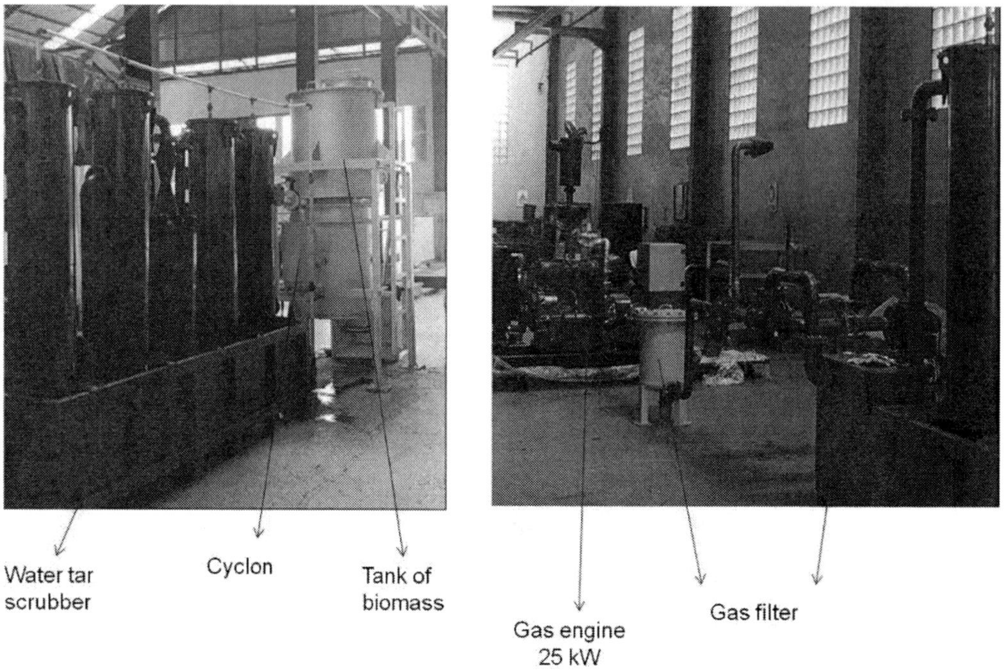

Fig. 5. Biomass power generation with capacity of 25 kW.

3.3 Engine performance test

To ensure the composition of the fuel gas content, the laboratory testing was carried out and the results is shown on Table 3. Laboratory test result that the gases produced contained combustible gas those are CO and H_2 in sufficient concentration. In case of biogas in which dominant gas was CH_4, then the gas engine designed is which is suitable for CH_4.

Table 3. The average composition of the combustible gases.

No	Component name	Concentration (% vol)	Normalization 100 %
1	Hydrogen (H_2)	11.22	11.43
2	Nitrogen (N_2)	48.23	51.45
3	Carbon monoxide (CO)	23.16	24.86
4	Methane (CH_4)	1.72	1.85
5	Carbon dioxide (CO_2)	10.26	11.02

The gas engine with capacity of 25 kW was operated in specified operating condition and run for 8 h. The result was that gas engine from biomass-based gas (synthetic gas) can give power with effectiveness of 84 %. The net energy ratio obtained in this research was 0.89. This value less than 1 because much of energy losses into the environment because the material of reactor body and gas piping have not been coated with insulators.

The renewable index (RI) on this research was 0.76 which is close to 1. The closer the value to 1 the better the renewable index is. This value assumed that the use of unrenewable fuel on this research was very little. The use of diesel/kerosene is only on the starting point, so are the electricity on blower as the initial trigger to pull the combustible gas from the reactor. Net energy balance on this research was 30 MJ/kW h of electric.

3.4 Economic feasibility

Economic feasibility studies has been conducted. The assumption used was the average price of biomass about IDR 700 per kg and the rate of biomass use on electricity production about (1.4 to 2) kg (kW h)$^{-1}$ of electrical. Therefore, the cost of electricity producedabout IDR 1 650 per kW h. This cost is cheaper than electrical production cost from Diesel Power Generation which is about IDR 3 300 per kW h.

3.5 Analysis of impact assessment

The calculation of greenhouse gas emission (ERK) was approached using Life Cycle Life Assessment Method ISO 14040. The GHG emission value for biomass power plant is 0.04 kg CO_2 eq per MJ, and the diesel power plant engine is 0.111 kg-CO_2 eq per MJ or in the other words the PLTBm GHG emission value was almost three times lower than the Diesel Power Plant. Siregar et al. [13] states that the production of biodiesel in catalyst can reduce global warming emissions 37,83 % compared to fuel oil (diesel). In the national arena this activity will support the government target to reach renewable energy mix up to 23 % by 2025. This activity is also in line with the achievement of 35 000 MW electricity production until 2019.

4 Conclusion

The conclusion of this research was that the Biomass Power Generation with capacity of 25 kW has already been designed and operated with performance test of 84 % from installed capacity. It resulted net energy balance, net energy ratio, and renewable index was 30 MJ/kW h of electric; 0.89; 0.76 respectively. The value of GHG emission of Biomass Power Generation is 0.03 kg-CO_2eq per MJ.Electrical production cost for Biomass Power Generation is about IDR 1 500 per kW h, whereas electrical production cost for Solar Power Generation is about IDR 3 300 per kW h.

The authors say thank you to KEMRISTEKDIKTI for its support under joint research INSINAS RISET PRATAMA KEMITRAAN 2017, No. 136/UN11.2/PP/SP3/2017.

References

[1] Department of Energy and Mineral Resources (DESDM). *Blueprint blueprint pengelolaan energi nasional pengelolaan energi nasional 2005–2025*. [Blueprint of National Energy Management 2005–2025]. Workshop Sosialisasi Blue Print Pengelolaan Energi Nasional 28–29 June (2005). [in Bahasa Indonesia]. http://psdg.bgl.esdm.go.id/kepmen_pp_uu/blueprint_PEN.pdf

[2] IRENA. *Renewable energy prospects: Indonesia*. A REmap analysis, Abu Dhabi: International Renewable Energy Agency (IRENA) (2017). pp. 213–217. https://www.irena.org/-/media/Files/IRENA/Agency/Publication/2017/Mar/IRENA_REmap_Indonesia_report_2017.pdf.

[3] PT. PLN (Persero). *Statistic of electricity Indonesia at PT.PLN (Persero)*. Jakarta (2011).

[4] T.B. Reed, A. Das. *Handbook of biomass downdraft gasifier engine systems*. Colorado: Solar Energy Research Institute (1988). pp. 113–116 https://www.nrel.gov/docs/legosti/old/3022.pdf

[5] C. Higman, M. van der Berg. *Gasification*. Amsterdam: Elsevier Science (2003). pp. 45–56. https://www.elsevier.com/books/gasification/higman/978-0-7506-7707-3 .

[6] H. Pranolo. The Potential of aplicationtechnolgy gasification with corn biomass as energy alternative in the village. *Seminar Nasional of Renewable Energy in Indonesia* (Jendral Sudirman of University, Purwekerto, Indonesia, 2013).

[7] T.A. Milne, R.J. Evans. *Biomass Gasifier "Tars": Their Nature, Formation, and Conversion National*. Missouri: Midwest Research Institute (1998). pp. 320–323. https://www.nrel.gov/docs/fy99osti/25357.pdf .

[8] Y.A. Cengel Y.A., and Boles M.A. *Themodynamics an enginering approach*. Singapore: McGraw Hill (2006.). https://www.amazon.com/Thermodynamics-Engineering-Yunus-Cengel-Dr/dp/0073398179

[9] Siregar, K., Sholihati, Syafriandi. International Journal of Engineering Research and Application. **6**(1):9–16 (2016). https://issuu.com/www.ijera.com/docs/b61040916

[10] Weifang Naipute Gas Genset Co.Ltd. *Operation and maintanance manual for NPT brand gas generating sets*. China: Weifang Naipute Gas Genset Co.Ltd. (2013.).

[11] S.J. Cowell. 1999. *Use of environmental life cycle assessment to evaluate alternatif agricultural production systems*. Proceeding 52nd Plant Protection Conference (New Zealand, 1999). pp. 40–44. http://agrienvarchive.ca/bioenergy/download/lca_alt_ag_production_nz.pdf

[12] C. Searcy. 2000. *An introduction to life cycle assessment*. [Online] from http://www.i-clps.com/lca/. [Accessed on 20 January 2018].

[13] K. Siregar, A.H. Tambunan, A.K. Irwanto, S.S. Wirawan, A. Tetsuya. *Comparison of emission and energy for biodiesel production from oil palm (Elaeis guineensis) and Jatropha Curcas (Jatropha curcas L.) based on life cycle assessment (LCA) in Indonesia*. [Dissertation] Bogor Agricultural University, Indonesia (2013). https://www.researchgate.net/publication/317171762_COMPARISON_OF_EMISSION_AND_ENERGY_FOR_BIODIESEL_PRODUCTION_FROM_OIL_PALM_Elaeis_guineensis_AND_JATROPHA_CURCAS_Jatropha_curcas_L_BASED_ON_LIFE_CYCLE_ASSESSMENT_LCA_IN_INDONESIA

The Encyclopedia of Virtual Art Carving Toraja - Indonesia

Lande Sudianto[1,*], and *Petrus* Simon[2]

[1]Program Study of Electrical Engineering, Paulus Chrystian University of Indonesia, Jl. Perintis Kemerdekaan Km. 13, Makassar, 90243, Indonesia
[2]Program Study of Management, Paulus Chrystian University of Indonesia, Jl. Perintis Kemerdekaan Km. 13, Makassar, 90243, Indonesia

Abstract. The unity of local culture in Indonesia is the national culture which represented the identity of Indonesia. There are many cultural resources of our nation which needs to preserved and improved to maintain the national identity of Indonesia. The art of crafting from Toraja contains value and philosophy which based on the values of local wisdom as the part of Toraja and national culture. The application of Virtual Encyclopedia of Toraja Crafting Art which based on information and communication technology (ICT) is developed in order to integrate the culture in education for preservation, improvement, and education of cultural noble values for Indonesia especially the culture of crafting art in Toraja. There are 128 kinds of Toraja crafting which are divided into four groups: i) *Garontok Passuraq*; ii) *Passuraq iii) Todolo*; iv) *Passuraq Malollek*; v) *Passuraq Pakbarean*. Toraja crafting has denotative and connotative meaning. The explicit and implicit meanings in Toraja cultural make the Toraja culture become very interesting and challenging. The explicit meaning of Toraja crafting is called denotative meaning which is objective. Meanwhile, the implicit meaning of Toraja crafting is called connotative meaning which is subjective.

Key words: Carving, encyclopedia, ICT, Toraja, virtual.

1 Introduction

Indonesia has a local cultural diversity that can be used as an asset that cannot be equated with the local culture of other countries. Indonesia's local cultures vary in each region. Each region has its typical culture, such as traditional houses, traditional clothes, traditional dance, music, art carving/sculpture and others. All that can be used as a power to be able to strengthen the resilience of the nation's culture in the eyes of the International. Local cultural distinctiveness is often interesting views of other countries. Proven many foreign tourists trying to learn Indonesian culture such as learning a dance typical of a region or looking for craft items to be used as a souvenir. This proves that the culture of Indonesia has a unique characteristic. Local cultural unity that Indonesia is a nation's culture that represents the identity of the Indonesian state. To that end, local culture should be maintained and inherited properly to the nation's culture remained firm. Public awareness to keep local cultures today still fairly minimal [1, 2].

Integration of culture in the learning values is one of the themes discussed by the commission VIII in National Consultation, Ministry of Education and Culture in 2012 were held in Sawangan, Depok-West Java, Indonesia on 26 to 28 February 2012. One of the issues that need attention in the current era of globalization is a matter of national identity. Swift influence of foreign culture in the era of globalization is a threat to national security. Many of our cultural values are very high value but not recognized, let alone implemented. If this is allowed to continue, the next generation would lose its identity as a nation of Indonesia. Cultural wealth of the nation very much needs to be preserved and developed with the aim to strengthen the national identity (national identity), maintaining the philosophy of the nation *Pancasila* and the motto 'unity in diversity (cultural diversity), to strengthen the community (social cohesion), fostering a culture of peace (culture of peace), forming a national character (character building) and make

*Corresponding author: sudianto@ukipaulus.ac.id

referrals culture (standard setting) [3]. Awareness of culture gave way to the realization of national identity in accordance with the noble values of national culture and creates a climate conducive and harmonious so that the values of local wisdom will be able to respond in a positive and productive modernization in line with national values. In line with this is the problem of culture in re-emphasized in the discussion of the theme "Preserve and Strengthen Cultural Indonesia" by commission IV on the National Ministry of Education and Culture 2013 held in Sawangan on 10 to 13 February 2013.

In the Strategic Plan 2010 to 2014 of the Ministry of Culture and Tourism has registered two nominations culture of the region as a world cultural heritage, namely: "The Cultural Landscape of Bali Province" (a temporary number 1194C) and "Tana Toraja Traditional Settlement" (a temporary number 1038C), so that the necessary efforts to preserve and develop the cultural arts [4–7]. Traditional decoration is a source of cultural information, because it can be used to determine the background of the cultural and natural history of the public mind of the wearer. Decorative arts, also expressed the values espoused and nurtured and procedures applicable in community life [8]. Similarly, the decorative carvings Toraja that are well known to foreign countries. Not only the beauty of the motifs, but also the culture behind them. Decorative arts Toraja is one embodiment of the values of trust *Todolo*. To the Toraja people will never lose its culture during the traditions and values of the old custom (*Todolo*) maintained in public life. In addition, the process of cultural inheritance that has lasted for centuries is always rooted in the culture of the past grandeur. Tana Toraja is expected to overcome the transition period by means of an inventory of cultural and learn about the richness of the traditional culture, dwindling resources. Therefore we need a culture of Toraja conservation efforts in the form of decorative carving Toraja documentation contained therein wisdom values and its existence.

2 Literature review

On 26 to 28 February 2012, the Ministry of Education and Culture held a national consultation as the first step in formulating policies in the development of education and culture in Indonesia, in the national consultation, the commission VIII discusses the integration of culture in education. The discussion stated that the rationale of integration of culture in education, among others [3]:

(i). Many of the values of our culture are very high value but not recognized, let alone implemented;
(ii). If this is allowed to continue, the next generation would lose its identity as a nation of Indonesia;
(iii). Cultural wealth of the nation very much needs to be taught (integrated) in units of subjects ranging from early childhood, basic education, high school and universities;
(iv). Integration of the wealth of cultural values can be implemented in the form of games and performances are played directly by learners.

With the problems and obstacles encountered are:

(i). Uncharted cultural values that originate from local wisdom.
(ii). Has not formulated values that need to be internalized;
(iii). Charge of cultural values in the curriculum has not been adequate;
(iv). The swift influence of foreign culture in the era of globalization.

The opportunities and potential are:

(i). Many cultural values that originate from local wisdom
(ii). Every ethnic indigenous knowledge which has noble values;
(iii). There is a similarity in meaning between one region to another;
(iv). Internalization of cultural values can enrich the curriculum based on local content;

Based on the results of the national consultation, the commission 8 provide solutions and recommendations as follows:

(i). Urgent need mapping noble values that exist in each ethnic/regional
(ii). Formulate the noble values of each ethnic/areas that can be lifted into a noble cultural values of national culture
(iii). Incorporate cultural values noble nation Indonesia in the education curriculum from primary to higher levels, as well as non-formal education.

Encyclopedia is one of the media education are quite popular among people who are reliable accuracy, some types of encyclopedias such as books and electronic media available. But in Indonesia is less socialized and perhaps the cost is quite expensive, so this encyclopedia is rarely used and there were only a few fruits. With the virtual encyclopedia software can help develop interest in learning to use the educational tools [9–11]. The word encyclopedia is derived from the Greek, namely *enkyklios* and *peideia*, which means a work that contains information on all branches of science or explanation comprehensive of branches of science, usually in the form of articles are arranged alphabetically and sometimes by subject [12]. Encyclopedia system is processed to meet the information needs of the general and complex nature, the information obtained can be ensured accuracy. Globally result of information obtained from the encyclopedia would be support in the learning process to achieve a form of active learning pattern.

Some kinds of encyclopedia have specific objectives, but basically an encyclopedia aims to provide information in the form of data that has been processed in such a way so as to include a field of science in depth. For example, cultural encyclopedia aims to provide detailed and complete information about the entire cultural diversity based on the group and nail-values of local wisdom that contained in it. In general encyclopedia published more in the form of a book (hard cover), so the lack of appeal in addition to the sale price is relatively expensive (Figure 1).

Fig. 1. Books encyclopedia culture.

Virtual encyclopedia is innovative blend of multimedia-based encyclopedia with utilization of ICT technology. By utilizing the Internet network so that the content encyclopedia can be stored and accessed by users. With multimedia-based encyclopedia will culture and more attractive, inexpensive, and informative as in use can interactively with users.

3 Research method

Stages of development of the system was made with the approach of the paradigm of the System Development Life Cycle (SDLC) which includes five phases: (i) identification of the needs of the system; (ii) analysis and modeling system; (iii) creation of the system; (iv) testing and improvement of the system; and (v) implementation (Figure 2) [13, 14].

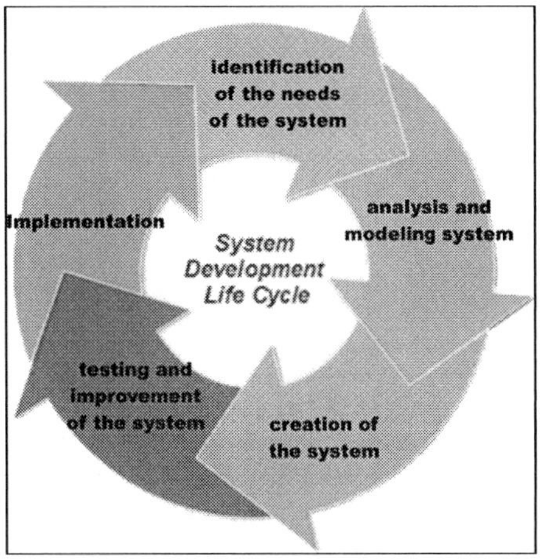

Fig. 2. Paradigm system development life cycle.

Phase identification of the needs of the system, beginning with the preparation of the instruments in the form of research: interview guidelines and support tools such as tape recording, digital cameras, camcorders (video recording), transport equipment and supporting software. Further data collection directly or indirectly. Directly in the form of a survey to study sites for inventory types of existing motif and interviews with relevant parties, among others: craftsmen carving, indigenous stakeholders, government and manager's museum/cultural heritage. Indirectly in the form of literature through literature books and the internet. Data were obtained at this stage in the form of documentation and information about the various types, meaning and purpose, the rules of the use of carving Toraja. Surveys will be conducted in two districts of Tana Toraja and North Toraja district.

Phase analysis and modeling systems, performed analysis and modeling systems with flow map to determine the functions or activities that will be implemented in the system. Flow system folder is created in the form of context diagrams, data flow diagrams, entity relationship diagram, relationships between files, the file structure, the structure of the program, the menu structure, the input format and output format. Analysis and modeling of the system is based on quantitative data and attributes of each motif carving Toraja. Stage of the manufacturing system, the process of making software systems Encyclopedia of Virtual Art Carving Toraja in full using the techniques of the Unified Modeling

Language (UML), the choice of program packages that are suitable to establish the feasibility of the analysis system. UML techniques used by the technology used. Stage testing and repair systems, testing systems Encyclopedia of Virtual Art Carving Toraja is based on WEB technology.

4 Results and analysis

As one of the largest ethnic groups in South Sulawesi, Toraja have a culture in the form of art carvings are beautiful and full of philosophy. Art carved carving Toraja is typical Malay tribes Toraja in South Sulawesi. This engraving printed using special carving tools on a wooden plank, pole traditional house, window or door. Carving Toraja is one of the national cultural wealth it contains a lot of values and philosophy Toraja culture rooted in the values of local wisdom. Toraja motif inspired by a variety of things, such as folklore, objects in the sky, the sacred buffalo, pigs, household appliances, plants and others. These things by the Toraja indeed sacred [15].

Carving Toraja also called *passuraq* by the Toraja people is a form of sculpture that is printed with a special carving tool on a wooden plank, pole house, window or door. Carving Toraja not only as an image which was created to adorn a form or object or *Tongkonan* (Toraja traditional house), all kinds of engraving was born out of the sense of a matter of life or social life as well as the ideals of community life, so the entire carving present has meaning in [6, 16]. Carving Toraja contains values, among others:

(i). Economy, some kind of carving Toraja also used as a commodity that bring economic benefit to society;
(ii). Preservation of tradition, carving Toraja is a valuable ancestral heritage which has an important role in the execution of traditional ceremonies.
(iii). Symbol, this value is reflected in the use of decoration by the public for something symbolic.
(iv). Art, carving Toraja a variety of art objects beautiful views and has a sacred value.
(v). Social class, for the people of Toraja, having carved with a particular motif is a pride and express social status in life.

According to the history of engraving at first only known to four forms the base image (symbol) is the epitome of four principal human life, and than applied to *Tongkonan* home with the intention to remain a concern and always remembered by the public. Therefore installation engraving is not placed at random places on *Tongkonan* building or house, but installed in the view and philosophy of life Toraja (*aluk sanda pitunnna*). There are approximately 130 motifs *passuraq* images ever created, each of which depict the reality of life and there are 75 devoted solely to *Tongkonan* motive. Based on the results of recent research, there are approximately 67 decoratives carving Toraja of which are in the walls of the Toraja traditional house or household appliances. Nevertheless, ethnic Toraja still classify images *passuraq* into four categories based on customary provisions [4, 17, 18].

(i). *Garontok Passuraq*, the main image and is regarded as the base or foundation for understanding the culture of Toraja, among others: *Pa 'Barre' Allo*, *Pa 'Manuk Londong*, *Pa' Tedong* and *Pa 'Sussu'*.
(ii). *Passuraq Todolo*, namely engravings concerning equipment considered has merit ceremony for the wearer, among others: *Pa 'Erong, Pa' Ulu Karua, Pa 'Doti Langi' Pa 'Sometimes Pao, Pa' Barana 'Pa' Bai, Pa 'Lolo Tabang, Pa' Leaf Bolu, Pa 'Leaves of Paria, Pa' Bombo Wai, Pa 'Kapu' Baka, Pa 'Tangke Lumu' Pa 'Bungkang Lake, Pa' Lolo Paku, Pa 'Tank' Pattung, Pa 'Bulintong Pa 'katik, Pa' Talinga Tedong*, and others.
(iii). *Passuraq Malollek*, which are widely used carved carve buildings that do not have a customary role (*Tongkonan* Stone *A'riri*). This engraving is used as a symbol of the attitudes and social behavior or relationships with institutions is limited by ethical and moral. Sometimes these engravings no linkage meaning and significance by carving *Passura 'Todolo*, among others: *Pa' Sala'bi 'Pa' Horns Ra'pe*, *Pa* 'brought instantly *Pare, Pa' Flower Kaliki, Pa 'Poya Munda, Pa' Bulintong Siteba 'Pa' Bulintong Situru 'Pa' Karrang Longa, Pa 'Board Kandaure, Pa' Passulan, Pa 'Sepu' Torongkong*, and others.
(iv). *Passuraq Pakbarean*, interpreted as representing a variety of different kinds of life associated with an atmosphere of fun and excitement in childhood. *Passuraq Pakbarean* an engraving consisting of pieces of the same shape there are those that are straight and curved form, among others: *Pa 'Bannangan, Pa' Barra'-barra', Manik Bu'ku Pa' Pa 'Ara' Dena 'Pa' Komba Kalua 'Pa' Bua Kapa 'Pa' Gayang*, and others.

To carve carving Toraja using colors consisting of natural color carries meaning and significance for the people of Toraja, which is in accordance with the philosophy of life and the development of human life Toraja. Therefore, the use of color on the engraving should not be changed or altered in usage. *Passuraq* color material called litak which is the basis for the Toraja people of color are: red (*litak mararang*), white (*litak Mabusa*), yellow (*litak mariri*), black (*litak malotong*).

Red and white is the color of blood and human bones that symbolizes human life. The colors can be used anywhere in time of traditional ceremonies and in everyday life. The yellow color is the color of glory as a symbol of divinity that is used during the ceremony *Rambu Tuka'* for the sake of human salvation. Being black is a symbol of death or darkness used during the ceremony Signs Solo' (funerals). Meaning black at the base of each *passuraq* (engraving) is that the life of every human being overwhelmed by death because, according *Todolo Aluk* view that the world is only a place to sleep alone or a place to stay temporarily. All colors *Passuraq* as mentioned above is the color of nature because the material from the ground, except for the black color of charcoal taken from the pot. The use of this material is more durable against the weather and climate in comparison with the color of the synthetic material.

4.1 Motif carving Toraja

Toraja motif consisting of various types, among others: *Neq Limbongan*, Toraja people believe that the name is taken from the name of their ancestors alive *Limbongan* estimated at 3 000 yr ago. While *neq* means "lake", *Limbongan* means springs that never dry so that it becomes a source of life. This motif is interpreted that the fortune came from four corners like springs that are united in the lake and give happiness (Figure 3a). *Paqbarre allo*, *Bare* means "circle", and *allo* means "sun". This type resembles carving circle with a radiant sun rays. This engraving is defined as the knowledge and wisdom that illuminates like the sun (Figure 3b).

Fig. 3. Motif *Neq Limbongan* and *Paqbarre allo*.

4.2 Torajapedia

Torajapedia is a virtual encyclopedia of software applications built with technology web based PHP and MySql. (Figure 4 to 8).

Fig. 4. Front page view Torajapedia.

Fig. 5. The main menu display Torajapedia.

Fig.6. Display carving art encyclopedia Torajapedia.

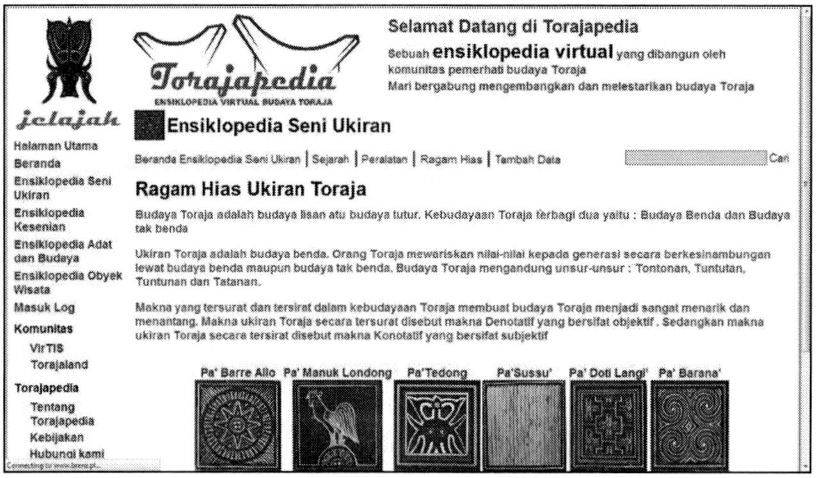

Fig. 7. Display decorative carving Toraja.

Fig. 8. Display popup_window carved image and meaning.

5 Conclusion

There are 130 decoratives carving of Toraja which are divided into four group, namely: i) *Garontok Passuraq*; ii) *Passuraq Todolo*; iii) *Passuraq Malollek*; iv) *Passuraq Pakbarean*. Toraja carvings have denotative and connotative meanings. The explicit and implicit meanings in Toraja culture make Toraja's culture become more interesting and challenging. The explicit meanings are objective and called denotative meanings while the implicit meanings are subjective and called connotative meanings. Toraja Carving Art Encyclopedia application is developed using PHP and MySQL database program which run optimally on a variety of platforms and browsers that supports multimedia applications. Toraja Carving Art Encyclopedia application helps the user to identify and understand about art and decorative Toraja carving easily.

References

1. M. Abdul. *Integrasi nilai-nilai kearifan lokal dalam pembelajaran untuk menanamkan nasionalisme di sekolah dasar*. [Integration of values of local wisdom in learning to infuse nationalism in primary schools]. Proceding Seminar Nasional Lembaga Penelitian UNY (Yogyakarta, 2010). [in Bahasa Indonesia]. p. 1–10. http://scholar.googleusercontent.com/scholar?q=cache:bmGdE6-36gIJ:scholar.google.com/&hl=en&as_sdt=0,5
2. S. Erman, H. Hasriyanti, A. Fatchan, I.K. Astina, S. Sumarmi. Journal of EFL, Linguistics, and Literature, **1**(1): 17–23 (2016). http://www.efljournal.org/index.php/efljournal/article/view/6
3. Ministry of Education and Culture Indonesia. *Rencana strategis (renstra) Kementerian Pendidikan dan Kebudayaan*. [Strategic plan Ministry of Education and Culture], Jakarta: Kementrian Pendidikan dan Kebudayaan (2010). [in Bahasa Indonesia]. pp. 83–104. https://www.kemdikbud.go.id/dokumen/Renstra%202015-19/renstra.rar
4. UNESCO, *Evaluations of cultural properties*. International Council on Monuments and Sites (ICOMOS), Paris: UNESCO (2001) pp. 87–90. http://whc.unesco.org/archive/2001/whc-01-conf205-inf4e.pdf
5. N. Sitonda. *Toraja warisan dunia*. [Toraja world heritage]. Makasar: Pustaka Refleksi (2007). [in Bahasa Indonesia]. p. 20–26. https://books.google.co.id/books/about/Toraja.html?id=7X5RIwAACAAJ&hl=en&output=html_text&redir_esc=y
6. S. Luekveerawattana. Procedia - Social and Behavioral Sciences, **65**:387–396 (2012). https://www.sciencedirect.com/science/article/pii/S1877042812051245
7. K. Matsuura, Z. Xinsheng, F. Bandarin. *The State of world heritage in the Asia-Pacific region 2003*. United Nation: UNESCO (2004). p. 17. http://whc.unesco.org/document/4968; http://whc.unesco.org/en/series/12/
8. A. Duli. The Journal of Archaeology, Consciousness and Culture **8**(1):3–20 (2015). http://www.tandfonline.com/doi/abs/10.1080/1751696X.2014.993235
9. E. Widiyantara. *Perancangan media pembelajaran berbasis multimedia pengenalan seni dan budaya Indonesia pada SD Negeri Blumbang Banjararum Kalibawang Kulon Progo*. [Design designing learning multimedia introduction to Indonesian art and culture in State Primary Schools Blumbang, Banjararum Kalibawang, Kulon Progo] [Undergraduate Thesis] Informatic, STIMIK AMIKOM, Yogyakarta, (2011). [in Bahasa Indonesia]. p. 2–10. http://docplayer.info/47548732-Perancangan-media-pembelajaran-berbasis-multimedia-pengenalan-seni-dan-budaya-indonesia-pada-sd-negeri-blumbang-banjararum-kalibawang-kulon-progo.html
10. P. Indrias. *Pembuatan CD interaktif pengenalan kebudayaan Indonesia berbasis flash*. [Making interactive CD of introduction of flash based indonesian culture]. [Thesis] Fakultas Matematika dan Ilmu Pengetahuan Alam, Universitas Sebelas Maret Surakarta, (2010). [in Bahasa Indonesia]. p. 2–4. https://eprints.uns.ac.id/346/1/161812608201009491.pdf

11. R.V. Aliniaina. *How is encyclopaedia authority established?* [PhD Thesis] University of Glasgow, (2013). p. 87–118. http://theses.gla.ac.uk/3414/1/2012RasoamampianinaPhD.pdf
12. C. Sherly. *Perancangan grafis buku wisata budaya Tana Toraja beserta media pendukungnya*. [Graphic design of Tana Toraja cultural tour book and its supporting media] [Undergraduate Thesis], Faculty of Art and Design, Universitas Kristen Petra, (2009). p. 26–34. [in Bahasa Indonesia]. http://repository.petra.ac.id/1832/
13. K. Lunn. Software Development Life Cycle. In: *Software development with UML*. London: Plagrave (2003). p. 53–68. https://link.springer.com/chapter/10.1007/978-0-230-80419-7_5
14. N. Khan, I. Yaqoob, I.A.T. Hashem, Z. Inayat, W.K.M. Ali, M. Alam, et al. Scientific World Journal, **2014**(712826):1–18 (2014). https://www.hindawi.com/journals/tswj/2014/712826/
15. R. Muslimin. Journal of Asian Architecture and Building Engineering, **16**(1):39–44 (2017). https://www.jstage.jst.go.jp/article/jaabe/16/1/16_39/_pdf
16. A. Nediari, G. Hartanti. Humaniora **5**(2):1279–1294 (2014). [in Bahasa Indonesia]. http://journal.binus.ac.id/index.php/Humaniora/article/view/3271
17. S. Salam, M.S. Husain, Tangsi. Panggun Jurnal Seni dan Budaya, **7**(4):284–292 (2017). https://simlitmas.isbi.ac.id/e-jurnal/index.php/panggung/article/view/280/pdf
18. R. Muslimin. *Decoding Passura': Representing the indigenous visual messages underlying traditional icons with descriptive grammar.* Open Systems: Proceeding of the 18th International Conference on Computer-Aided Architectural Design Research in Asia, 15–18 May. pp. 781–790 (Singapore, 2013). http://papers.cumincad.org/data/works/att/caadria2013_113.content.pdf

Production Capacity of Several Hybrid Genotypes of *Jatropha curcas* Linn. for Five Years in Pasuruan, East Java – Indonesia.

Maftuchah[1,*], *Agus* Zainudin[1], *Ali* Ikhwan[1], *Adi* Purnama[1], and *Lim* Kok Kuan[2]

[1] Faculty of Agriculture and Animal Science, University of Muhammadiyah Malang, Jl. Raya Tlogomas 246, Malang, Jawa Timur, 65144, Indonesia.
[2] Nippon Biodiesel Fuel, 655 Chiyo, Odawara-city, Kanagawa, 250-0251, Japan

Abstract. *Jatropha curcas* Linn. is one of shrubs mainly exist in tropical area. The research team has succeeded to produce several excellent hybrid genotypes which then were planted to be tested its production capacity for 5 yr. Those genotyes were: genoptype 5 (HS49 × SP34), genotype 6 (HS49 × SM35), genotype 7 (HS49 × IP1A), and genotype 18 (SP16 × SM35). This research aims at finding out the production capacity of several hybrid genotypes of *J. curcas* Linn. which was conducted for 5 yr in Kedung Pengaron, Pasuruan. The research was arranged in Randomized Complete Block Design with four repetitions. Each block contained 20 plants, with plant treatment of hybrid result of genotype 5 (JC5), 6 (JC6), 7 (JC7), 18 (JC18) and two comparators of IP3A and IP3P. Observation was conducted on the number of fruit bunches and fruit on each plant, the number of fruit per plant, seed dry weight per plant. The study showed that *J.curcas* hybrids of genotypes JC5, JC7 and JC18 had higher production capacity (in term of number of fruit per plant, seed dry weight per plant and dry weight of 100 seeds) than other genotypes (JC6, IP3A, IP3P) in environment with drought stress.

Key words: Drought stress, genotype, *Jatropha curcas*, production capacity.

1 Introduction

Jatropha curcas Linn. is a member of shrubs plant which is mainly found in tropical area and is included as an alternative plant for biodiesel [1]. *J. curcas* is including the succulent plan, its leaves close in dry season, so this plant has a very good adaptation in dry and semi-arid

* Corresponding author: maftuchah_umm@yahoo.com

regions [2]. It is also known as medicinal plant. Nowadays it also has gained more attention on its other function as biofuel source due to its seed's oild content [3].

The research and development agency has launched planting material in the form of IP1 seed with production potential of (3 to 4) t ha^{-1}, (5 to 7) t ha^{-1} [4] and IP3 of (8 to 9) t ha^{-1} [5]. During the past 5 yr, there has been a research on production capacity on several genotypes of *J. curcas* hybrid. Based on result ptential and its seed's oil content selection, there were four genotypes with higher result compared to others in drought stress condition, they were genotype number 5 (HS49 × SP34), 6 (HS49 × SM35), 7 (HS49 × IP1A) and 18 (SP16 × SM35) [6].

The production capacity of four genotypes of *J.curcas* hybrid has been conducted in Experimental Garden of Kedung Pengaron, Pasuruan, East Java, Indonesia for 5 yr. The research aimed at finding the production capacity on the plant under drought stress condition. The environmental factor referred to all factors except genetic ones, which might affect the phenotype of a certain plant characteristics [7]. The environmental factors here include not only growing environment, but also the different of weather, plant duration, harvesting time, fertilizer dosage, length or planting, planting pattern, irrigation level, drought condition and others. Plant production from time to time was varied depending on genetic stability, environment, and the interaction between genetic factors and its environment.

The initial test result showed that the seed's oil content was ranging between 27.04 % to 35.24 %. The highest oil content was gained from hybrid of SM35 × SP38 in Experimental Garden of Kedung Pengaron, Pasuruan, which was of 35.24 %. From four dry lands in the research, the highest oil content was achieved from hybrid of SM35 × SP38 with its content of 32.035 % [6].

2 Objectives

This research aimed at finding the production capacity of several hybrid genotypes of *J. curcas* Linn. within 5 yr period in Experimental Garden of Kedung Pengaron, Pasuruan, East Java, Indonesia. This research is expected to produce a *J. curcas* Linn. genotype with a high production capacity in drought stress environment.

3 Methodology

This research was conducted at Kedung Pengaron, Pasuruan, East Java. The agroecology specification of field is specified in Table 1. The *J. curcas* Linn. experiment was conducted in 5 yr, from the year 2012 to 2016 [8].

Table 1. The rainfall intensity (mm per month) at Pasuruan, East Java [8].

Month	2012	2013	2014	2015	2016
January	219	26	233	10	8
February	92	23	68	5	13
March	24	17	183	3	3
April	50	25	12	4	2
May	32	20	1	2	2
June	-	34	8	-	7
July	-	6	3	-	-
August	-	-	-	2	-
September	-	-	-	-	-
October	-	-	-	-	29
November	55	34	-	2	2
December	79	8	169	9	9

Instruments and tools applied in this research were: oven, agricultural tools, stationaries, hand sprayer, plastic, research identity board, camera, logbook, pylox, sack, mower, etc. Material used in this research were: various genotypes of *J. curcas* seeds, herbicide, urea, phonska and pesticide. The research was arranged in Randomized Complete Block Design with four repetitions. Each block's size is 10 m × 8 m with plant space of 2 m × 2 m so that each block consisted of 5 × 4 plants. Treatment being tested were hybrid genotypes of JC5, JC6, JC7, JC18 and two comparators of IP3A and IP3P [9]. Planting had plant space of 2 m × 2 m which was divided into four groups and each group consisted of 20 plant samples so that there were 480 plants material in total. There was no watering process during the observation for the research itself is aimed at producing a *J.curcas* Linn. genotype with a high production capacity in drought stress environment. The plant's water requirement merely achieved during rainy season.

Observation was conducted toward the number of plants' fruit bunches per plant,fruit per plant, seed's dry weight per plant and seed's dry weight per 100 seeds. Fruit harvesting was conducted after the seed was ripe. The characteristics of ripe seed can be viewed from its yellowish brown rind. When the rind has begun to open it means that the seed has ripen. Too early harvesting time would decrease the oil content, while the late harvesting caused ruptured fruit resulting in more lost seed. Data analysis result by F test gained 5 % and 1 %, it was proceeded by Tukey test on level 5 % by using Software Statistical Analysis System (SAS) version 9.0 Portable.

4 Results and analysis

The analysis result showed that the genotype had a significant influence toward the fruit bunch per plant. Genotype that has high production capacity does not always perform similarly in different location (specific location). Fact is in line with a statement from [10] that the level of production capacity of certain plant is greatly depended on the environment where the genotype is planted and the type of genotype itself. The genotype interaction with its environment is a result of response from each genotype being tested on each growing environment of [11]. Based on that statement, it is definite that choosing the genotype with the best fruit bunch, breeders must choose one typical genotype for each different environment.

Table 2. Average fruit bunches per plant for each genotype of *J.curcas* at Kedung Pengaron, Pasuruan, Indonesia for 5 yr.

No.	Genotype*	Pasuruan*				
		Year				
		2012	2013	2014	2015	2016
1.	JC5	12.74 ab	37.59 a	13.86 a	41.29 b	22.43 a
2.	JC6	10.93 abc	40.09 a	12.57 ab	75.24 a	14.46 bc
3.	JC7	13.90 ab	36.17 a	15.06 a	39.79 b	17.83 abc
4.	JC18	19.72 a	38.21 a	15.14 a	52.95 ab	19.98 ab
5.	IP3A	7.56 bc	20.04 ab	11.54 ab	40.00 b	17.43 abc
6.	IP3P	5.66 c	29.07 b	9.22 b	40.40 b	14.01 c

Note: (*)The number which is followed by similar alphabet in the same column is not significantly different based on Tukey test on level of 5 %.

The average of fruit bunch per plant of each genotype for 5 yr (2012 to 2016) is presented in Table 2. From six genotypes being tested, JC5, JC7 and JC18 produced consistently higher fruit bunches compared to their comparators, the genotypes IP3A and IP3P. The JC6 genotype was potentially able to produce 75.24 bunches of fruit/plant in the 4th year. Plant with high level of adaptation skill has a more stable production capacity [12]. This shows that the particular plant owns adaptation skill toward different environment [13]. A genotype with the same adaptation and productivity capacity on different environment proves a static stability, while the adaptation skill which follows environment index shows a dynamic stability [14].

An evaluation of several *J.curcas* germplasm collection at Experimental Garden of Pakuwon, East Java and at Experimental Garden of Asembagus, East Java has shown a variety of morphological characteristics and production capacity [15]. Apart from genetic factor, the different growing environment and plant age may affect the influorescent in fruit bunch production. production capacity of plant greatly depends on its genotype's growing environment and the genotype itself [10].

Table 3. Average fruit bunches/plant on each genotype of *J.curcas* in Pasuruan,Indonesia for 5 yr.

No.	Genotype*	Pasuruan*				
		Year				
		2012	2013	2014	2015	2016
1.	JC5	28.38 a	107.58 a	61.89 a	156.68 ab	114.19 a
2.	JC6	26.42 ab	116.44 a	54.53 a	75.90 c	64.96 c
3.	JC7	49.70 a	111.94 a	60.66 a	141.08 b	86.74 bc
4.	JC18	44.28 a	107.21 a	53.65 a	187.84 a	101.08 ab
5.	IP3A	18.73 ab	53.63 b	24.02 b	144.50 b	81.28 bc
6.	IP3P	11.48 b	108.00 a	26.53 b	132.58 b	63.96 c

Note: (*)The number which is followed by similar alphabet in the same column is not significantly different based on Tukey test on level of 5 %.

The average of fruit per plant of each genotype for 5 yr (2012 to 2016) is presented in Table 3. Genotype JC18 was potentially able to produce 187.84 fruit/plant in the 4th year. The rainfall intensity was the most important weather factor in growing J.curcas. Limited water affecting jatropha production [16].

Table 4. Average seed's dry weight/ plant on each genotype of *J.curcas* in Pasuruan for 5 yr.

No.	Genotype*	Pasuruan*				
		Year				
		2012	2013	2014	2015	2016
1.	JC5	46.47 a	213.94 a	133.73 a	275.00 ab	222.58 a
2.	JC6	41.50 ab	230.44 a	99.72 b	214.30 c	125.98 c
3.	JC7	41.07 ab	233.44 a	110.17 ab	221.90 ab	163.27 bc
4.	JC18	52.80 a	230.06 a	115.02 ab	629.20 a	192.25 ab
5.	IP3A	24.88 ab	106.90 b	57.69 c	217.70 ab	140.29 bc
6.	IP3P	16.20 b	214.10 a	64.38 c	202.30 b	113.25 c

Note: (*)The number which is followed by similar alphabet in the same column is not significantly different based on Tukey test on level of 5 %.

The average of seed's dry weight/plant of each *J.curcas* genotype in Pasuruan for 5 yr (2012 to 2016) is presented in Table 4. Based on observation result, in a year the plant produces twice, it is in rainy and dry seasons. Seed production during rainy season is higher than in dry season. The above data shows total production in a year, both from rainy and dry season.

Genotype had significantly affected the seed's dry weight of 100 seeds. JC5 genotype produced 100 seeds of 74.38 g on 5th year (Table 5) which is not much different with JC7 and JC8. The three genotypes produced the average of dry weight of 100 seeds higher than IP3A and IP3P. In general, the obtained data showed that the production capacity of *J. curcas* for 5 yr was not very significantly high. Yet, this plant cultivation system, as stated in research method, was conducted without any watering process (only depended on water during rainy season). This has become the advantage of tested genotype, for those genotypes have proven its potential, which is tolerant toward drought stress when compared with IP2A and IP3P. The JC5, JC7 and JC18 genotypes showed higher production capacity potential compared to the other three genotypes.

Table 5. Average seed dry weight per 100 (g) on each *J.curcas* in Pasuruan for 5 yr.

No.	Genotype*	Pasuruan*				
		Year				
		2012	2013	2014	2015	2016
1.	JC5	69.94 a	69.69 a	69.79 a	70.57 ab	74.38 a
2.	JC6	66.46 ab	70.42 a	64.17 a	69.94 ab	66.88 bc
3.	JC7	68.97 a	68.33 a	69.17 a	71.23 a	70.00 ab
4.	JC18	72.61 a	68.13 a	68.75 a	70.85 ab	70.00 ab
5.	IP3A	60.05 b	63.13 b	69.79 a	68.36 ab	61.88 c
6.	IP3P	68.22 a	63.13 b	67.50 a	67.59 b	61.25 c

Note: (*)The number which is followed by similar alphabet in the same column is not significantly different based on Tukey test on level of 5 %.

5 Conclusion and recommendation

The result of the study showed that *J. curcas* Linn. hybrids of genotypes JC5, JC7 and JC18 had higher production capacity (in term of number of fruit per plant, seed dry weight per plant and dry weight of 100 seed) than other genotypes (JC6, IP3A and IP3P) in experimental garden of Kedung Pengaron, Pasuruan in environment with drought stress.

Thanks to the Directorate of Research and Community Services, The General Directorate of High Education Republic of Indonesia, The National Department of Education Republic of Indonesia and Agriculture Department Republic of Indonesia, which have supported the research fund No. 069/SP2H/PDSTRI/K7/KL/III/2013.. Awards are also presented to the head and staff Muhammadiyah University of Malang and Crops Research Institute Sweeteners and Fiber Indonesia for all the support of research facilities.

References

[1] A. Demirbas A. biodiesel: A realistic fuel alternative for diesel engines. London: Springer (2008). pp? http://www.springer.com/gp/book/9781846289941

[2] J. Heller. Physic Nut (*Jatropha curcas* L.). Promoting the conservation and use of underutilized and neglected crops 1. Rome: IPGRI (1996). https://www.bioversityinternational.org/uploads/tx_news/Physic_nut__Jatropha_curcas_L._161.pdf

[2] G.S.A. Fatah, A.D. Hastono, Soebandi. Teknologi Pertanian Journal, **14**(2):87–94 (2013). [in Bahasa Indonesia]. http://jtp.ub.ac.id/index.php/jtp/article/view/397

[3] C. Hasnam, Syukur, R.R.S. Hartati, S. Wahyuni, D. Pranowo, S.E. Susilowati, et al. *Pengadaan bahan tanam jarak pagar (Jatropha curcas L.) di indonesia; desa mandiri energi serta strategi penelitian di masa depan*. [Supply status of physic nut (*Jatropha curcas* L.). high quality planting material, self sufficient energy village program and research strategy in the future]. Lokakarya Nasional III: Inovasi Teknologi Jarak Pagar Mendukung Desa Mandiri. 5 November 2007 (Malang, Indonesia, 2007). pp. 9–18. (2007). [in Bahasa Indonesia].

http://balittas.litbang.pertanian.go.id/images/prosiding/jp3/pengadaan%20bahan%20jp3.pdf
[4] M. Syakir. Perspektif **9**(2):55–65 (2010). [in Bahasa Indonesia]. http://perkebunan.litbang.pertanian.go.id/wp-content/uploads/2011/03/N-1-M-Syakir-Jarak-Pagar
[5] Maftuchah, A. Zainudin, H. Sudarmo. Agricultural Sciences, **4**(1):48–56 (2013). http://www.scirp.org/journal/PaperInformation.aspx?PaperID=27485
[6] D.S. Falconer, T.F.C. Mackay. *Quantitative to genetics*. London: Pearson (1996). Pp? https://www.amazon.com/Introduction-Quantitative-Genetics-Douglas-Falconer/dp/0582243025
[7] Badan Pusat Statistik Kota Pasuruan. (2017) Data Curah Hujan Kabupaten Pasuruan. https://pasuruankota.bps.go.id/statictable/2017/11/08/1644/jumlah-rata-rata-curah-hujan-bulanan-di-kota-pasuruan-mm-2009-2016.html.
[8] Maftuchah, H.A. Reswari, E. Ishartati, A. Zainudin, H. Sudarmo. Energy Procedia, **65**:186–193 (2015). https://www.sciencedirect.com/science/article/pii/S1876610215000594
[9] S. Sujiprihati, M. Syukur, R. Yunianti. Bul. Agron, **34**(2):93–97 (2006). [in Bahasa Indonesia]. http://journal.ipb.ac.id/index.php/jurnalagronomi/article/view/1285
[10] Z. Mut, A. Gülümser, A. Sirat. Afr. J. Biotechnol, **9**(11):1610–1618 (2010). https://www.ajol.info/index.php/ajb/article/view/78346/0
[11] P. Vita, A.M. Mastrangelo, L. Matteu, E. Mazzucotelli, N. Virzi, M. Palumbo, et al. Field Crop. Res., **119**(1):68–77 (2010). https://www.sciencedirect.com/science/article/pii/S0378429010001632
[12] A. Rasyad, A. Idwar. J. Agron. Indonesia, **38**(1):25–29 (2010). [in Bahasa Indonesia]. http://journal.ipb.ac.id/index.php/jurnalagronomi/issue/view/228
[13] R. Mohammadi, M. Roostaei, Y. Ansari, M. Aghaee, A. Amri. Canadian J. Plant Sci, **90**(6):819–830 (2010). http://www.nrcresearchpress.com/doi/abs/10.4141/cjps09102#.Wo1TolpubMw
[14] Hariyadi. *Sistem budidaya tanaman jarak pagar* (*Jatropha curcas* L). [The Culture Sistem of *Jatropha curcas* Linn.]. Prosiding Seminar Nasional Pengembangan Jarak Pagar (Jatropha curcas L). Untuk Biodiesel dan Minyak Bakar. 22 Desember 2005, pp. 61–67 (Bogor, Indonesia, 2005). [in Bahasa Indonesia]. http://repository.ipb.ac.id/jspui/bitstream/123456789/25139/1/prosiding_Pengembangan_Jarak_Pagar.pdf
[15] R. Ndong, M. Montrejaud-Vignoles, O.S. Girons, B. Gabrielle, R. Pirot, M. Domergue, et al. Global Change Biology Bioenergy, **1**:197–210 (2009). http://oatao.univ-toulouse.fr/3617/1/Ndong_3617.pdf

Simulation Study of Bio-Methane Conversion into Hydrogen for Generating 500 kW of Power

Maizirwan Mel[1,*], *Fouad* Riyad Hussein Abdeen[1], *Hamzah* Mohd Salleh[1], *Sany* Izan Ihsan[2], *Fazia* Adyani Ahmad Fuad[1], and *Roy* Hendroko Setyobudi[3,4]

[1]Department of Biotechnology Engineering, International Islamic University Malaysia, Jalan Gombak, Kuala Lumpur 53100, Selangor, Malaysia,
[2]Department of Mechanical Engineering, International Islamic University Malaysia, Jalan Gombak, Kuala Lumpur 53100, Selangor, Malaysia Jalan Gombak, Kuala Lumpur 53100, Selangor, Malaysia
[3)]Waste Laboratory of University Muhamadiyah of Malang, Jl. Raya Tlogomas No. 246 Malang, 65114, Indonesia
[4]Indonesia Association of Bioenergy Scientist and Technologist, BPPT Building II, 22nd Floor Jl. MH. Thamrin No. 8 Jakarta 10340, Indonesia

Abstract. Research and development sectors have made great efforts for finding cleaner and greener supplements for fossil fuels. The uses of POME (Palm oil Mill Effluent) as feedstock of biogas production has attracted many industries to produce energy because this source (waste) is abundance and not fully utilised. Methane from biogas production has shown to have a significant potential to replace the depleting sources as it can be produced from renewable feed stocks. The main objective of this study is to produce hydrogen from methane obtained by digesting of POME and to transform bio-methane into hydrogen for generating 500 kW of electric power using a simulation software of SuperPro Design.

Key words: Anaerobic digestion, bio methane, biogas upgrading, hydrogen production, electric power.

1 Introduction

Fossil fuels have been used extensively all over the world for decades [1]. Consequently, their depletion have caused a continuous increase in the price as well as a high escalation in global warming [2]. Therefore, the research and development sectors have made great efforts for finding alternative energy sources such as biomass, solar, wind, natural gas and biogas, which are cleaner supplements [3, 4]. Among these energy sources, biogas has shown a promising potential to be future energy source as it can be produced from various feed stocks including landfill material, animal manure, wastewater and organic waste from industrial activities [5–7].

The focus of this project is to produce hydrogen from methane obtained by digesting palm oil mill effluent (POME) and to transform bio-methane into hydrogen for power generation. POME is broadly available in Malaysia and the conversion of this waste into a

* Corresponding author: maizirwan@iium.edu.my

beneficial product is of great benefits in terms for economy and environment [7−11]. In addition, the conversion of bio-methane to hydrogen prior to its utilization as an energy source is believed to be an environmental friendly process [11−16]. In this study, five major processes are included namely are; biogas production, biogas upgrading, reforming, hydrogen storage and converting hydrogen to energy. The bio-methane obtained from the anaerobic digestion was used for hydrogen gas production to generate 500 kW of power.

2 Materials and Method

2.1 Feedstock selection and site location

The POME is selected as a feedstock for biogas production due to its wide availability in Malaysia. The anaerobic digestion of POME was done using closed tank digester and further upgraded using column adsorption. In order to convert the bio methane into hydrogen gas, steam reforming in catalytic bed reactor with (600 °C to 1 100 °C) was used and compression process was employed to store the hydrogen gas before the combustion process of hydrogen gas into engine.

In order to build a hydrogen production plant, the location of the plant to be built also is an important matter where the consideration of the raw materials availability, space availability, utilities availability, local community considerations, climate, political consideration and transportation. For this project, the hydrogen production plant location is decided to be near the Kempas palm oil mill and near the highway. Thus, POME can be obtained easily and can minimize the cost for transportation of materials.

2.2 Materials preparation

The different processes performed in this project are well explained by the operational diagram shown in Figure 1. The diagram in Figure 1 shows the composition at each stage for the different gas components and shows the details of each unit operation used. SuperPro Design software (v9.5) was used to simulate the overall process. The designed process is shown in Figure 2.

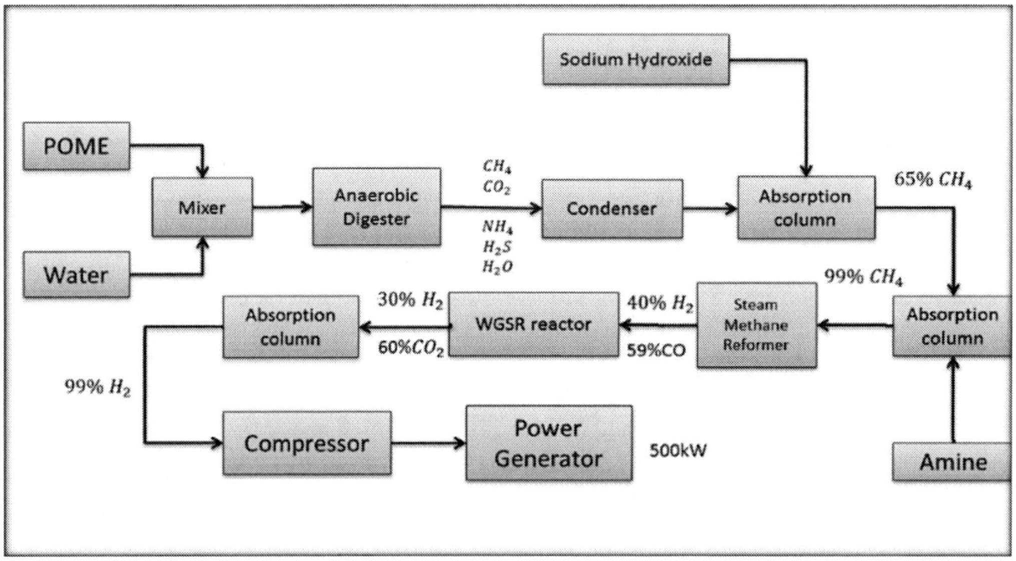

Fig. 1. Operational diagram.

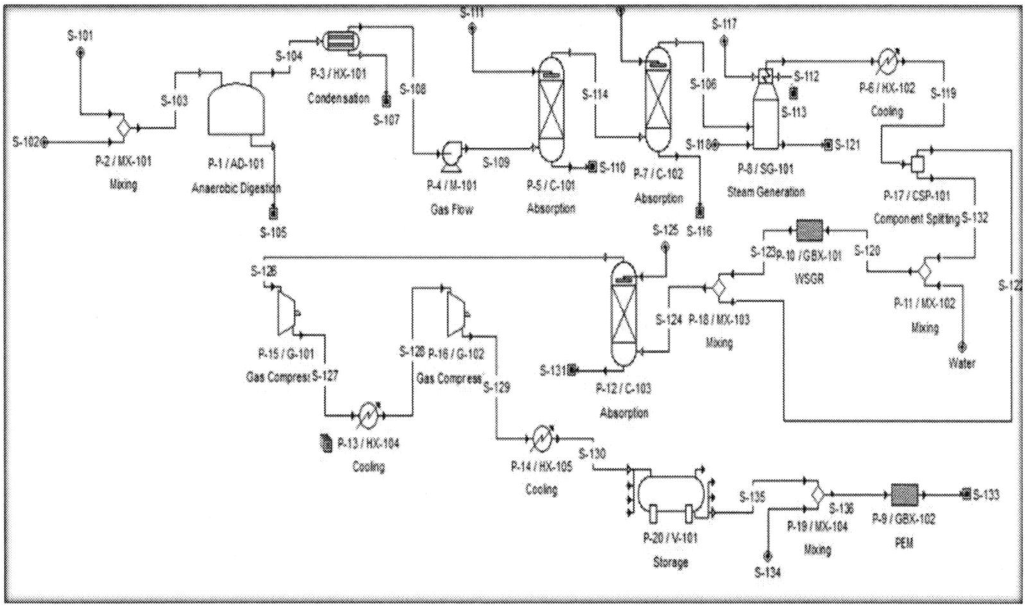

Fig. 2. Process simulation of power generation by hydrogen transformed from bio-methane.

As shown in Figure 1 and Figure 2, raw biogas exits from anaerobic digester enter the condenser to remove water content in the biogas. To make sure the water is totally condensing; flow rate leaving the condenser is monitored and controlled by the flow rate entering the condenser. Condensed water trapped in the condenser is monitored to overcome overflow.

The biogas from digester is blown into absorption column. The biogas then enters the absorption column for H_2S removal. The solvent for removing H_2S, NaOH is pumped into the system where the pump pressure is controlled by the vessel pressure. The operation condition is monitored by pressure gauge and thermocouple for high efficiency. The spent solvent goes out of the column is maintained by level controller.

The purified biogas enters the system from the absorption system where H_2S has been removed to acceptable levels. The flow rate reading in biogas vessel is transmitted to the controller whereby the flow rate of biogas entering is controlled. The solvent for removing CO_2, MEA (Methyl-Ethanolamine) solution is pumped into the system where the pump pressure is controlled by the vessel pressure. The pressure and temperature operated is monitored by pressure gauge and thermocouple to enhance the removal of CO_2. The spent solvent goes out from the column, monitored and maintained by float level sensor. The upgraded biogas leaves the column at expected concentration. Flow rate of upgraded biogas (pure methane) is being monitored and controlled before it enters the steam methane reformer to produce hydrogen. Temperature for both process in the steam methane reforming (SMR) which are steam reformer and fixed bed reactor for water steam generation reaction is being monitored to produce a high percentage of hydrogen. Accordingly, the pressure of both processes also being monitored and controlled by releasing the pressure. Product of water gas shift reactor (WSGR) is CO_2 and H_2, thus scrubber technique is required to separate them. The level of the spent MEA is being controlled and monitored.

The hydrogen enters into two compressors and two heat exchangers. The pressure of the hydrogen leaving the compressor is being monitored and controlled to reduce the storage tank. The temperature of the hydrogen is being monitored and controlled by the flow rate of the coolant.

In order to produce electricity from polymer electrolyte membrane (PEM) fuel cell, air (oxygen) is needed. Thus, flow rate of both hydrogen and air (oxygen) is being monitored and controlled to produce high electricity. Since the PEM fuel cell is operated at 50 °C, temperature is being monitored and controlled by flow rate of coolant into the PEM fuel cell. The reaction will produce water and the water level in the cell stack is monitored and controlled by the flow rate leaving the cell stack.

3 Result and discussion

The sizing of equipment is a major result obtained by this study. As shown in Table 1, the sizing of all the equipment used in this study is presented in details. It is obvious that a big digester of 202 m^3 volume is required for the purpose of generating 500 kW of power. A big digester might be very costly unless it is divided into several smaller digesters with the total volume of 202 m^3. The length of the condenser was calculated to be 16 m which is considered very long as well and needs to be replaced by shorter and more efficient condenser. Column absorption #2 size is also very huge with 263 m^3 volume, but the length to diameter ratio is still in the acceptable range.

The sizing of the other equipment (column absorption #1, fixed bed reactor for SMR, fixed bed reactor for WSGR, cooler 1, cooler 2, compressor 1 and compressor 2) has shown to be reasonable and acceptable. It is believed that the sizing of the equipment is helpful reference to be used for the design of such systems. While, the economic analysis for this study is not discussed.

Table 1. Sizing of each of equipment

Equipment	Size
Digester	Volume = 202.1 625 m^3 Height = 2.42 m Diameter = 7.28 m
Condenser	Heat Transfer Area = 0.4 m^2 Length = 16 m Diameter = 0.03 m
Column Absorption 1	Volume = 8.595 m^3 Height = 7.6 m Diameter = 0.6 m, Stages = 10
Column Absorption 2	Volume = 263.34 m^3 Height = 12.4 m Diameter = 2.6 m, Stages = 18
Fixed bed reactor (SMR)	Volume = 148.45 m^3, Height = 5.74 m, Diameter = 2.9 m, Catalyst diameter = 0.3 cm
Fixed bed reactor (WSGR)	Volume = 31.74 m^3 Height = 3.43 m Diameter = 1.72 m
Cooler 1	Heat Transfer Area = 64 m^2 Length = 3.3 m Diameter =19.4 m
Compressor 1	t = 757 min, volume = 7.6 m^3 compressor power = 373 kW
Compressor 2	t = 0.63 min, volume = 0.4 m^3 compressor power = 18.7 kW
Cooler (2 units)	Heat Transfer Area = 39.2 m^2 Length = 13 m, Diameter = 6 m

3.1 Sizing determination of SMR and WGSR

For conversion of 99 % methane into hydrogen at pressure of 15 atm and temperature of 700 °C with volume feed flow rate 296.904 $L \cdot h^{-1}$. Assuming pellet catalyst size is 0.3 cm and bed density is 0.6 $g \cdot cm^{-3}$

3.2 SMR Reactor

V= (Volume rate) (HRT)
= (296 904.759 L · h−1) (30 min × 1 h · 60 min)
= 148 452.38 L

Assume: H/D = 2, H = 2D, thus D =

$$D = \sqrt[3]{\frac{148.45\ m^3}{2\pi}}$$

D = 2.9 m, H = 5.74 m, and A= 65.51 m^2

For conversion of 40 % carbon monoxide into hydrogen at pressure of 15 atm and temperature of 250 °C with volume feed flow rate is 2 284 829 L · h−1.

3.3 WSGR Reactor

V= (π/4) D^2 H
V= (Volume rate) (HRT)
= (2 284 829.595 L/h) (50s × 1min/60s × 1h/60min)
= 31 733.74 L

$$D = \sqrt[3]{\frac{31.74\,m^3}{2\pi}}$$

D = 1.72 m, H = 3.43 m, and A= 23.18 m^2

Mass of catalysts

$$w_c = \left(950\,kg \cdot m^{-3}\right)\left(0.18\,m^3\right)$$

$$w_c = 171\,kg$$

4 Conclusion

POME is a waste produced in palm oil mill industries and if released to the environment untreated can cause major environmental pollution. It consists of large amount of volatile and suspended compounds that can be used for biomethane production. Then this biomethane can be converted into hydrogen to generate 500 kW of power. This is an ideal approach and can greatly provide green and clean sustainable energy and also lead to a considerable income for the company.

References

1. G.L. Juste. *Int. J. Hydrog. Energy* **31**, 14:2112–2121 (2006). https://www.sciencedirect.com/science/article/pii/S036031990600067X

2. S. Shahid, A. Minhans, O.C. Puan. *Jurnal Teknologi* **70**, 4 (2014). https://jurnalteknologi.utm.my/index.php/jurnalteknologi/issue/view/148
3. D. Deublein, A. Steinhauser. *Biogas from waste and renewable resources: An introduction*. Wiley-VCH: Germany (2008). http://onlinelibrary.wiley.com/book/10.1002/9783527621705
4. N.A. Azli,, A.H.M. Yatim. A modular structured multilevel inverter for fuel cell applications. Journal of Teknology 32. [Online]. Available from: http://www.researchgate.net/profile/Nik_Rumzi_Nik_ Idris/publication/224375883_The_Role_Power_Electronics_in_Future_Energy_Systems_and_Green_Industrialization/links/53e2efe00cf2b9d0d832c419.pdf#page=122 (2000). [Accessed on 20 May 2016].
5. H.K. Ahn, M.C. Smith, S.L. Kondrad, J.W. White. *Appl. Biochem. Biotechnol.* **160**, 4: 965–975 (2010). https://www.ncbi.nlm.nih.gov/pubmed/19462259
6. K. Braber. *Biomass and Bioenergy* **9**, 1–5:365–376 (1995). https://www.sciencedirect.com/science/article/pii/0961953495001034
7. M.J. Chin, P.E. Poh, B.T. Tey, E.S. Chan, K.L. Chin. *Renewable and Sustainable Energy Reviews* **26**:717–726 (2013). https://www.sciencedirect.com/science/article/pii/S1364032113003857
8. S. Tabassum, Y. Zhang, Z. Zhang. *Journal of Cleaner Production* **95**:148–155 (2015). https://www.sciencedirect.com/science/article/pii/S0959652615001699
9. P.E. Poh, M.F. Chong. *Bioresource Technology* **100**, 1: 1–9 (2009). https://www.sciencedirect.com/science/article/pii/S0960852408005427
10. A.R. Khalid, W.W. Mustafa. *Environmentalist* **12**, 4:277–285 (1992). https://link.springer.com/article/10.1007/BF01267698
11. N.H. Abdurahman, N.H. Azhari, Y.M. Rosli. *The Performance Evaluation of Anaerobic Methods for Palm Oil Mill Effluent (Pome) Treatment: A Review* [*Online*] from http://cdn.intechopen.com/pdfs/42628/InTech-The_performance_evaluation_of_anaerobic_methods_for_palm_oil_mill_effluent_pome_treatment_a_review.pdf (2013).
12. Reith, J.H., R.H. Wijffels, H. Barten. Bio-Methane and Bio-Hydrogen: Status and Perspectives of Biological Methane and Hydrogen Production. Dutch Biological Hydrogen Foundation. [Online]. Available from: http://www.cabdirect.org/ abstracts /20033182266.html (2003). [Accessed on 20 May 2016].
13. M.D. Redwood, M. Paterson-Beedle, L.E. Macaskie. *Reviews in Environmental Science and Biotechnology* **8**, 2: 149–185 (2009). http://eprints.bham.ac.uk/1007/
14. D. Liu, D. Liu, R.J. Zeng, I. Angelidaki. *Water Research* **40**, 11: 2230–2236 (2006). https://www.sciencedirect.com/science/article/pii/S0043135406002004
15. G. Kvesitadze, T. Sadunishvili, T. Dudauri, N. Zakariashvili, G. Partskhaladze, G. Ugrekhelidze, et al. *Energy* **37**, 1: 94–102 (2012). https://www.sciencedirect.com/science/article/pii/S0360544211005792
16. P.A.M. Claassen, T. De Vrije. *International Journal of Hydrogen Energy* **31**, 11: 1416–1423 (2006). https://www.sciencedirect.com/science/article/pii/S0360319906002102

Development of Presentation Model with Cloud Based Infrastructure

Maria Magdalena Widiantari[1], and *Arief* Budiman[2,*]

[1]Program Study of Communication Sciences, Merdeka University of Madiun, Jl. Serayu No. 79, Madiun, East Java, 63133, Indonesia
[2]Program Study of Informatics Management, Merdeka University of Madiun, Jl. Serayu No. 79, Madiun, East Java, 63133, Indonesia

Abstract. Computer mediated communication are the communication activities using technology which have rapidly in progress. Communication interactive activities nowadays has no longer only involving person to person but mediated by technology, and have been done in many fields including in education and teaching activity. In this study, presentation media based on cloud's infrastructure designed to replace face to face or in class lectures. In addition, the presentation will allow media data storage indefinitely, and accessible wherever and anytime. This is in line with the concept of student center learning where students were encouraged to more active in the lecture activities. The purpose of this research is making or designing a presentation model based on cloud's infrastructure. This research is using research and development method which is consists of four stages, where the first phase is composing the concept of media presentation design. The second phase are choosing the subject that will be designed as the subject of presentation. The third stage is designing presentation model. And the fourth phase is collecting materials of the subject that will be presented by each lecturer.

Key words: Cloud, internet, lecture, presentation, student center learning.

1 Background

In 2011 was the new era beginning of cloud computing technology, where there was some many providers which quite popular like dropbox, google drive, icloud dan skydrive [1]. Along with the quick progress of internet technology development, online digital storage

* Corresponding author: arief@unmer-madiun.ac.id

media known as cloud's getting more popular. The Indonesian people served well with cloud service where they could have access their data anywhere and anytime, so users could increase and decrease the use of service and the computing resources both easily and flexible. Users do not need to made a large investment for computing resources, storage media, the cost of management system maintenance, network and database [2].

It is also felt by company or agency that running their business core no longer based on a local server or long distance server. Company or agency were also have the ability to provides central data services like company internet access, so they could provide their own storage data services to meet their needs [3, 4]. On the other side, especially in the urban life, cause the changing of life behavior where pushing the community to use the cloud service to share and collaborated [6].

As the advancement of information technology and communication, media communication between faculty and students also progressively. Besides face-to-face communication, faculty and students also could interact through email, mailing list, social media, or short message service. Easy access to the internet made the communication between faculty and students can be done by internet media. So it was necessary to developed a presentation model that can be accessed wherever and anytime with the service of clud storage, that would give ease in the process of presentation material dissemination without having dependency of a limited storage medium and must always be brought and, and can be accessed anytime and wherever. This presentation model were also could replace the face-to-face lecture if there is a missed meeting that could happen at any time.

2 Literature review

2.1 Computer mediated communication

In line with the developments in communication and information technology, the context of communication between humans also developed. Consider the history of mass media, also have technology development, now with the development of digital technology especially computer, the context of communication was increasing. Now, communication activities between humans has grown in the context of computer mediated communication. The practice of computer mediated communication has been actually done in our daily life. The simplest was short message service, sending e-mail, chat through instant message or chat on facebook or tweeter, or other various forms social media.

One of the unique things going on in the computer based media communication was based on the power of text or words and non verbal symbols like emoticons, pictures and graphic. Because it was based on the strength of the text, the message displayed itself should be prepared or designed in such a way. Therefore, written communication or textual was not same with the technique of oral communication like face to face communication. However, the response delivered could be as an delayed feedback so that any response could be prepared in a more carefull.

Today the learning process in lecture, not only introduced a classic learning technique where the students seen as the object of education. Now the education forced the students to active in various kinds of other learning activities and be the subject of education itself. Effective learning will set the students on the activity that able to attract all of the optimal potention. In Nasution [6] research shown that there was a view activities of sthe students, it is:

i). Visual activities, like reading, seeing pictures, and demonstration or practice.

ii). Oral activities, like speech, to formulate, asking, giving advice, issued opinion, doing interview, discussion and interruption.

iii). Listening activities, like Listening to discussion, conversation, discussion, music and speech.
iv). Writting activities, like writing a story, a wreath, creating test report, quisionare and copying.
v). Drawing activities, like painting, create a graphics, creating map, diagram and pattern.
vi). Motor activities, like doing experiments, constructions, modeling, reparation, playing, gardening, and look after pets.
vii). Mental activities, like remembering, solving a question, analyze, seeing relationship and make decisions.
viii). Emotional activities, like put on interest, feeling bored, happy, quiet and nervous.

In the lecture activities involving communication between faculty and students, development in information technology and communication also support the activities. Easy access to the internet made the communication between faculty and students could be done in the internet media, both in the personal communications or related to lecture activities. So, every lecturers and students are required to know how to work with internet based communication media, so that it could be used more effective.

The development of information technologies and communication change the way of human life including ways to communicate. Now human lived in age where the various form of information and various accuracy levels easily obtained. In education world, so many learning material, college material, and literatures that can be easily get. Information and communication technology also allows faculty and students to sent and exchange messages each other related with lecture material and assignment easily, cheap and fast. The learning process in lecture could modified in such a way that the lecture material could be diseminated through information and communication technology, while the lecture face-to-face meeting can be used to facilitate and push the student to understand certain college material.

It is possible, because the easy access to information through the internet, students could find information or lecture material first than lecturers. In this case, lecturers become the facilitator to push students understanding to the lecture material. Or in a face-to-face meeting, the items shared through the internet could be as a discussion material so that it can be extending the perspectives and strengthen students understanding.

2.2 Multimedia based learning

In the learning and lecture process, there were many strategy that could be chosen by lectures, like talk, discussion class, working group or other learning activities. In all strategy selected, effective communication should be important factor to support the purpose of learning activities. Learning strategy through speech was a classic way of lecture activities. Seen from time perspective, this model considered efficient, to convey many information gived to students with the minimal used of media, but this learning method less effective because students act passively, just hear, noted, and less encourage activities higher learning stage like analysis, synthesis or evaluation.

Another learning model that usually used by lecturer to create active learning condition was discussion team or workgroup. In this model lecturer act as a manajer that controlling the discussion team or workgroup doing their duties, to make sure that it would be working interactively in communication and provide information needed by each group. In the lecture activities based on a learning source, lecturers can serve as coordinator and an innovator. Learning communication not only relate to the lecturer verbal communication skill, but also the ability of designing a source of learning and learning media. Other media which could be learning tools like movie, video, magazine, the internet and many of presentation media that served in multimedia based. The present of media and the learning source would facilitate lecturers in communicate the learning. So a lecturers had to master and understand the learning source and learning media effectively so the utilization would increase the quality of learning.

Multimedia based learning being one learning model that is essential to developed along with the technology development. According to Arsyad [7] in his research said that multimedia traditionally refer to the use of several media, while multimedia in nowdays refer to the use of joint several media in learning presentation through the computer. Multimedia as presentation media different from the multimedia as a learning media. Presentation media did not demand the user to have active even though there is interactivity inside the activity then it called vogue interactivity. In this case, between lecturer and student could have face-to-face meetings where lecturers use multimedia-based presentations and deepened through lectures. Or students could access presentation media without face-to-face meetings, and on the other the opportunity on face to face discussion can be done to deepen the understanding of lecture material.

While multimedia as a learning media involve users in activities that demand mental processes in learning activity. Based on this perspective, specific mental activity required in learning could be raised through the manipulation of systematic instructional events. Based on it multimedia learning was package of interactive multimedia where there was instructional steps designed to involve users actively in learning. There are several forms of multimedia based learning. According to Arsyad [7] there were four forms of multimedia learning that usually used to described ways of learning using information technology, it was:

i). Programed model tutorial, set of views whether static or dynamic that already set before.

ii). Intelligent model tutorial, different form programmed tutorial because the answer from the computer were generate artificially.

iii). Drill modelled practice, it was a model to strengthen the mastery of concept.

Simulation Model, Simulation on a computer provides an opportunity to learn in dynamic, interactive and individual, just like in the real activity.

2.3 Cloud based applications

Cloud computing was new concept in information technology implementation, where cloud computing used to provide storage and application that could accessed from computer network with central data [8]. And some big companies had develop and implemented like Amazon, Microsoft, and Google [9]. There were three models of cloud computing services, it was Infrastructure as a Service (IaaS), Platform as a Service (PaaS), and Software as a Service (SaaS) [10]. Where on those three models, users did not participate to manage and check the network infrastructure, server, operating system, storage media and application used.

There were four model implementation of cloud computing it were private cloud, community cloud, public cloud, and the hybrid cloud. When cloud infrastructure owned by an organization and limiting the user access to the application using firewall it called as a personal cloud. However when an organization provide cloud services to a community with common organization purpose and to support the achievement of organization main objective it is called as a community cloud. The cloud services provided to users in general purpose without explicit goals and managed by an organization that aims to give a good cloud service at no charge it was called as a public cloud, whereas for the combination of several service called as a hybrid cloud.

There were five major challenges and it needs special attention in the implementation of the cloud computing, it were security, interoperability, availability, performance, data and migration. Security focus on the privacy of data stored on the clouds services, secrecy, and network access. Interopability provide easy services, and offered some choice option needed by the user. The availability and performance guarantee the service were always ready to used by users. And the last was a problem in data and ability to perform data migration between cloud services, until now this would be the greatest challenges that had to be solved [8].

Multimedia based learning could be packaged to be multimedia learning presentation media. Presentation is one of communication form, as an activity to share a topic, opinion, or information to others, in presentation there were some basic elements: first, a person who do presentation, second was participants or audience, and third the presentation media or device. Learning presentation media was a tool to provide or convey message that helps lecturer in lecture, not replace the overall roles of lecturers but could convey a message effectively and efficiently.

3 Research methodology

The presentation in lecture activities using visual aids become an ordinary thing. Current lecture presentation model already using multimedia tools. Many benefits could get by using interactive multimedia learning system which more innovative and interactive, the lecture would combine between the text, pictures and video in one whole of mutual support to the achievement of learning purpose, add learner motivation during the process of learning and teaching until obtained the learning purpose desired.

Lecture presentation model that use cloud based infrastructure was designed through the following stages :

i). First step was preparing the concept of presentation model.

ii). Second, develope the application and the implementation infrastructure.

iii). Third, analyze the implementation result of presentation model based on cloud infrastructure.

For the development of application use the research and development methodology like former research by Ariesto [11] and Budiman [12]. Where this methodology had six steps, it is concept, design, collecting material, assembly, testing, and distribution.

i). Concept—at this stage arranged the development concept to performed, started by literature study from former research and later concluding problems concerned about how to build an learning application based on cloud infrastructure and multimedia learning.

ii). Design—after doing the problem analysis from the concept stage before, then arrange the design of application, infrastructure and the model implementation.

iii). Collecting material—after doing design, the next step is to do the acquisition of lecture material to upload in the application.

iv). Assembly—when design and data acquisitions completed the next step is to do a material compilation that has obtained into the application. And then it was uploaded to a server.

v). Testing—after the application had finished to built, then it tested and reviewed, testing carried out in two stages, namely alpha and beta testing testing. In the alpha phase of testing conducted feasibility validation by media experts and material expert. Validation of the application in terms of learning media performed by three experts media. Validation is done by filling out a questionnaire assessment of applications with a choice of five ratings ranging from very decent to very unfit.

4 Result and discussion

For the implementation and testing were done at Communication Department at Merdeka Madiun University. The application can be used both lecturers and students, and both could create, download, upload or read the lecture material from the application by using internet browser. All the data would save in the cloud so both wouldn't need removable storage media. User in this application divide into two diferent roles, first lecturer role and second was student role, where the differences was the size of storage permission. The storage size for students were smaller than lecturers storage size.

The user of this application could create text document, spreadsheet document, and presentation document straightly trough the application or just upload the those document from the computer. The application also had messenger fiture, where it could be use to chat personaly or create public announcement to all active users. The main page of the application shown in Figure 1.

Fig.1. Home interface of the cloud based application.

In the main page shown shortcut to every appilcation provide, like Address Book, Application, Calculator, Home Folder, and RSS Feed. On the top menu shown shortcut to Office Application like Word Processor, Spreadsheet, and Presentation shown in Figure 2 and Figure 3.

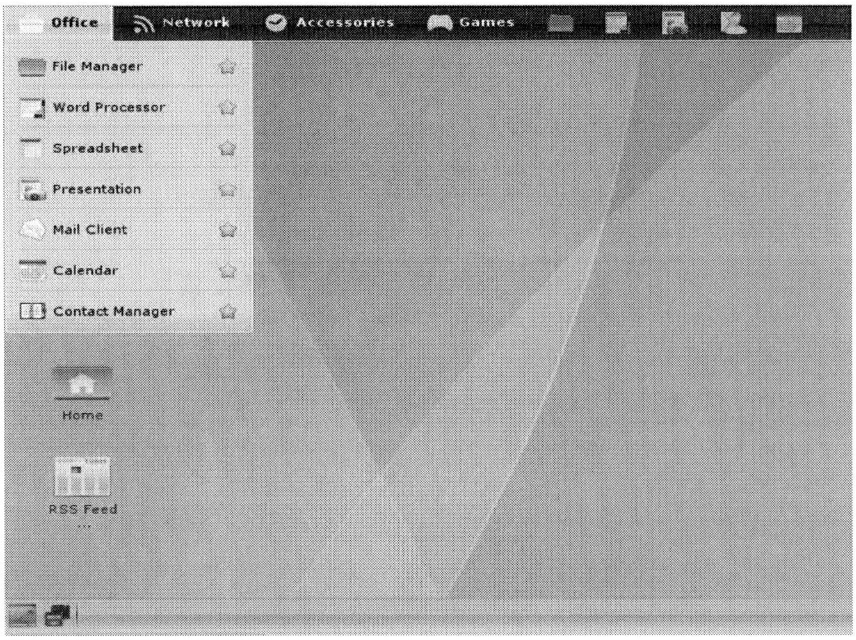

Fig.2. Taskbar menu at cloud based application.

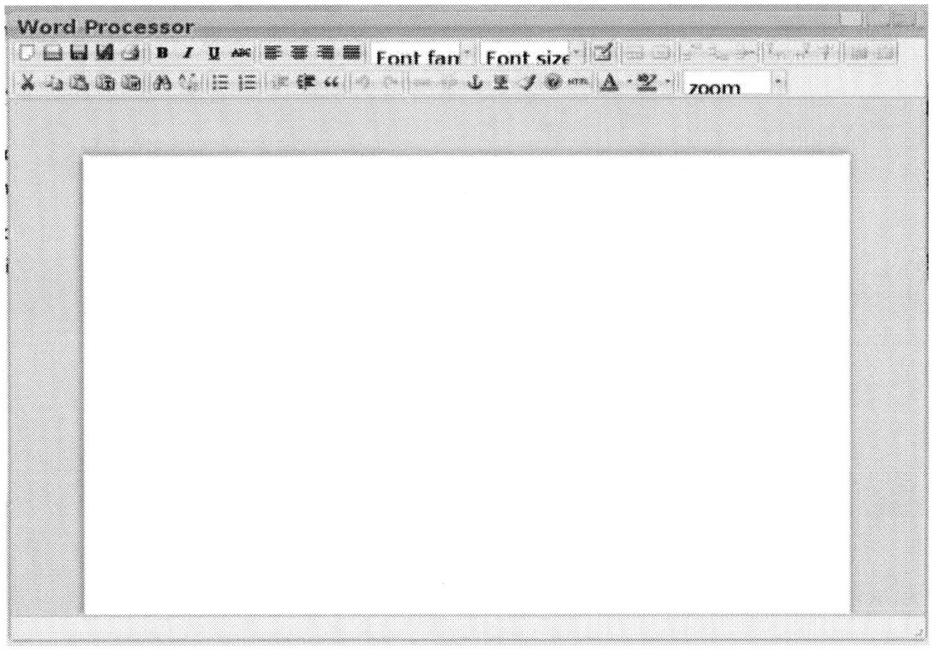

Fig.3. Word processor dan presentation application provide in cloud based application.

For the class implementation, every class would have small form factor computer using Raspberry Pi shown in Figure 4, where it's connected to the network using wireless access to access the lecture material such as word documents or presentation document. And it's also connected to the HDMI port to projector in the classroom. The student could do the same, they could access the lecture material by laptop, smartphone, or tablet through the wireless access like shown in Figure 5.

Fig.4. Raspberry Pi2 (small form computer).

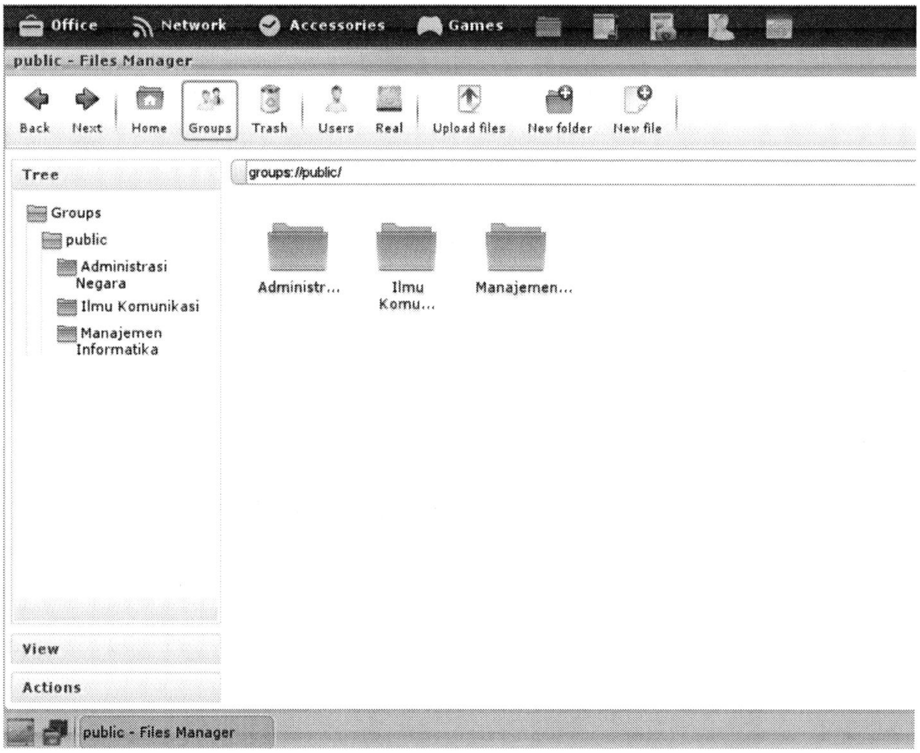

Fig.5. Accessing the lecture material.

After the implementation of the cloud application, then we do the analysis of feasibillity of the application. To measure the result of the cloud based application in this research using quantitative data obtained from feasibility assessment. There are three measurements which are eligibility assessment from media experts. Then for analysis measurement from the result of application developed, this research uses quantitative data obtained from feasibility assessment. There are three measurements which are eligibility assessment from media experts, eligibility assessment for the content material, and eligibility assessment for general public. Quantitative data derived then calculated using the formula adapted from Rizkiansyah [8] research. Then converted into qualitative value by comparing a score from the reviewer with an ideal score calculated from conversion table reference as follows:

Table 1. Scoring criteria.

Score	Category
$X > Xi + 1.80\ Sbi$	Very Feasible
$Xi + 0{,}60\ Sbi < x \leq Xi + 1.80\ Sbi$	Feasible
$Xi - 0{,}60\ Sbi < x \leq Xi + 0.60\ Sbi$	Quite Feasible
$Xi - 1{,}80\ Sbi < x \leq Xi - 0.60\ Sbi$	Not Feasible
$X \leq Xi - 1.80\ Sbi$	Very Not Feasible

where (*Xi*) was Ideal Average Score which is 1/2 x (maximum score + minimum score), (*Sbi*) was Ideal Deviation Score which is 1/6 x (maximum score - minimum score), and *X* was Average score from implementation. After we have count the quisioner result we have score as follows:

Table 2. Scoring result

No	Respondent	Score	Category
1	Media Expert	71.34	Feasible
2	Material Expert	80.67	Very Feasible
3	Students	84.67	Very Feasible

Cloud based presentation tools application are able to use as a media for creating presentation material or keeping the lecture material both for lecture and students. Testing is done with two stages of testing, namely alpha testing and beta testing. Thus based on the assessment from experts and students, this application fit for use as a new model of presentation media based on cloud infrastructure. In this research also using quisioner to measure user satisfaction, quisioner were sent into three different class, and from the result conclude as follows.

Table 3. Quisioner result.

Communication Department	Informatics Management Department
• The application were little difficult to understand. • Need high internet access. • The user interface were not too exiciting.	• The Application were average. • Need High Internet Access. • Easy to share article.

5 Conclusion

The result of this research after the first implementation of presentation model based on Cloud Infrastructure on Communication Department and Informatics Management Department at Merdeka Madiun University were conclude as follows:

i). The application for Presentation Model based on cloud infrastructure were successfully developed and implemented in lecture. Lecture and student both could access the lecture material through internet connection whether in lecture activity (face to face lecture) or outside the lecture activity.

ii). From the feasibility analysis, conclude that the developed application were feasible, so the application could support the presentation model with cloud infrastructure. So the Presentaion Model with cloud infrastructure were successfully implemented and could use for further lecture activity.

This work supported by Indonesian Research Technology and Higher Education Department and Merdeka Madiun University Research and Community Service Department.

References

1. F.P. Suprobo. International Refereed Research Journal, **IV**(3):79–86 (2013). http://www.researchersworld.com/vol4/issue3/vol4_issue3_1/Paper_08.pdf
2. W. Kim. Journal of object technology, **8**(1):65–72 (2009). https://pdfs.semanticscholar.org/6b81/d052c3a4c703e154eb6512c2ccee26076f56.pdf
3. Q. Zhang, L. Cheng, R. Boutaba. Journal of Internet Services and Applications, **1**(1):7–18 (2010). https://link.springer.com/article/10.1007/s13174-010-0007-6
4. Zhang, S. Zhang, S. Chen, X. Huo, X. *Cloud computing research and development trend*. Second International Conference on Future Network, 22–24 January 2010 (Sanya, Hainan, China, 2010). http://ieeexplore.ieee.org/document/5431874/
5. D. Apriono. Prospektus Jurnal Ilmiah Unirow Tuban, **56**(2):159–172 (2012). [in Bahasa Indonesia]. http://id.portalgaruda.org/?ref=browse&mod=viewarticle&article=105209
6. S. Nasution. *Berbagai pendekatan dalam proses belajar dan mengajar*. [A variety of approaches in the learning and teaching process]. Jakarta: Bumi Akasara (2000). pp. 7–8. [In Bahasa Indonesia]. http://library.um.ac.id/free-contents/index.php/buku/detail/berbagai-pendekatan-dalam-proses-belajar-mengajar-s-nasution-38088.html
7. A. Arsyad. *Media pembelajaran*. [Instructional Media]. Jakarta: Raja Grafindo Persada (2010). pp. 3–4. [in Bahasa Indonesia]. http://library.um.ac.id/free-contents/index.php/buku/detail/media-pembelajaran-azhar-arsyad-24788.html
8. G. Lin, D. Fu, J. Zhu, G. Dasmalchi. IT Professional, **11**(2):10–13 (2009). https://www.computer.org/csdl/mags/it/2009/02/mit2009020010.html
9. J. Cappos, I. Beschastnikh, A. Krishnamurthy, T. Anderson. *Seattle: A platform for educational cloud computing*. SIGCSE Bulletin, **41**:111–115 (2009). https://www.cs.ubc.ca/~bestchai/papers/sigcse09.pdf
10. P. Mell, T. Grance. *The NIST definition of cloud computing*. Gaithersburg: NIST (2011). http://nvlpubs.nist.gov/nistpubs/Legacy/SP/nistspecialpublication800-145.pdf
11. A.H. Sutopo. *Multimedia interaktif dengan flash*. Yogyakarta: Graha Ilmu (2003). [in Bahasa Indonesia]. http://digilib.unikom.ac.id/repo/sector/buku/view/1/key/9407/MULTIMEDIA-interaktif-dengan-flash.html
12. A. Budiman. D.N. Amadi. International Journal of Advanced Research in Computer Science, **7**(3):50–53 (2016). https://www.researchgate.net/publication/313477014_Development_of_Dhungkrek_Dance_Learning_Application_to_Preserve_Local_Culture_Existence

Broadcasting the Status of Plant Growth Chamber using Bluetooth Low Energy

Moh Noor Al-Azam[1*], *Mochamad Mizanul* Achlaq[1], *Aryo* Nugroho[1], *Adri* Gabriel Sooai[2], *Aris* Winaya[3], and *Maftuchah*[3]

[1]Faculty of Computer Science, Narotama University, Jl. Arif Rahman Hakim, Surabaya, 60111, Indonesia
[2]Faculty of Informatics Engineering, Widya Mandira Catholic University, Jl. Jend. Achmad Yani, Kupang, 85226, Indonesia
[3]Faculty of Agriculture and Animal Science, University Muhammadiyah of Malang, Jl. Raya Tlogomas 246, Malang, 65144, Indonesia

Abstract. Mobile users are getting smarter in using their phones. Many tasks are usually completed or monitored via a computer screen, nowadays can be taken anywhere with Android phones or tablets. Likewise with features in the phone is increasingly sophisticated. Currently bluetooth version 4 is almost mandatory in all phones. Even for entry level phones are now equipped with bluetooth version 4. This paper discusses the use of Bluetooth Low Energy—which is part of bluetooth version 4, in providing information about the status of plant growth chamber conditions. By using this concept, all phones or tablets that have bluetooth version 4 and there are applications in it will be able to receive the latest chamber status. The results show that this way of broadcasting is very effective. The data required to be monitored by a laboratory technician can be continuously broadcasted so that anyone on duty will get instant information at his grasp.

Key words: Bluetooth Low Energy (BLE), data transmission, growth chamber, Internet of Things (IoT), temperature and relative humidity

1 Introduction

Bluetooth Low Energy (BLE) is part of bluetooth version 4, with lower power consumption than previous bluetooth versions or classic bluetooth. BLE still utilizes the 2.4 GHz frequency which is also used by Classic Bluetooth. However, BLE does not have communications compatibility with the classic bluetooth. In contrast to the classical

* Corresponding author: noor.azam@narotama.ac.id

bluetooth that has the rule that it can connect up to seven devices, in BLE it has no limit on the number of devices that can be connected simultaneously. Therefore BLE is very suitable for use in broadcasting an information. Especially in the last few years, a device that supports BLE is more and more [1].

What also makes BLE interesting to learn is that this technology is the right technology, and by way of the right compromise and made at the right time [2]. For a relatively new standard (originally designed by Nokia as Wibree before being adopted by Bluetooth Special Interest Group—Bluetooth SIG, in 2010), BLE has been seen to have a very fast adoption rate, and with the number of "BLE enable" products ranked leading edge than any other wireless technology at the same time point in their release cycle [1, 2].

One of the famous BLE classes is iBeacon technology-introduced by Apple Inc. in 2013, which is used to broadcast unique information to nearby BLE devices [3]. Compared to traditional bluetooth technology, iBeacon signals with BLE are meant to have the same coverage area but lower power consumption. Most smartphones, like the latest iPhone, Android and Blackberry, are compatible with BLE technology that indicates they can perform collaborative operations with iBeacon [4].

BLE implementation is widely used in indoor Location Based Services (LBS) applications. The workings of this application is to calculate the Received Signal Strength Indication (RSSI) received by the BLE observer compared to the signal strength during transmission performed by BLE broadcaster [5]. The result of this RSSI measurement shows the relative distance of BLE observer to BLE broadcaster based on the calculation of RSSI in equation 1.

$$\text{RSSI (dBm)} = -10n \log_{10}(d) + A \quad (1)$$

In the implementation of BLE for indoor LBS, BLE broadcaster will continuously send the major, minor and Universal Unique Identifier (UUID) data as the identification of the broadcast location. The same way will be done in this study, only the data packet transmitted is containing data about the number of laboratory, reference chamber and the status of the plant growth chamber that will be translated by BLE observer and displayed in a visual form the report to determine the condition of the micro climate Plant Growth Chamber.

2 BLE and the hardware

BLE is designed to perform small and sparse data transfers at a simple data rate with very little energy. This design is different from the classic bluetooth design in general. Bluetooth SIG has therefore introduced two trademarks: Bluetooth Smart for single-mode devices (devices that only support BLE) and Bluetooth Smart Ready for dual-mode devices (devices that support Bluetooth Classic and BLE) to distinguish them. BLE has begun to enter in various types of accessories that collaborate with mobile devices such as mobile phones, tablets and notebook computers. Fancy devices such as smartwatches and other wearing devices are already equipped with Bluetooth 4.0 or later chipsets also have BLE functionality.

2.1 BLE stack

BLE stack has two layers that are complementary to provide maximum performance (Figure 1). We call it the lower layer and uppler layer. These two layers are separated by a control function that can be ruled from the upper layer to do something on the lower layer. Lower layer on BLE stack consists of Physical Layer (PHY), Link Layer (LL), and Direct Test Mode (DTM) for the test interface. PHY is in charge of transmitting and receiving data packets. LL is responsible for providing media access, connection establishment, error control, and data flow control. DTM is only used if required a test [6].

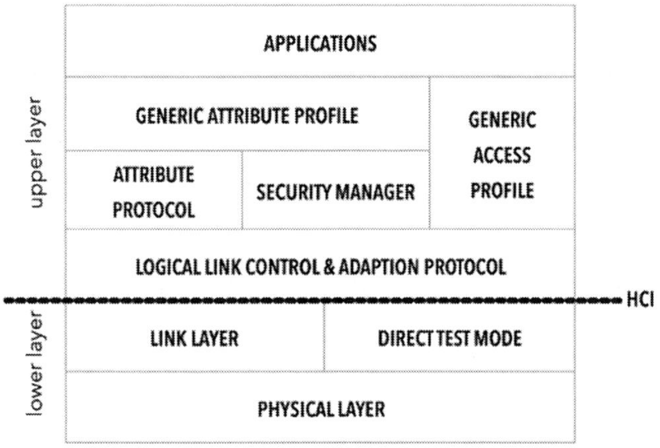

Fig. 1. BLE protocol stack [6].

The upper layer consists of Logical Link Control and Adaptation Protocol (L2CAP), Attribute Protocol (ATT), Security Manager (SM), Generic Attribute Profile (GATT), and Generic Access Profile (GAP). A Host Controller Interface (HCI) separates lower layers-often implemented for BLE controllers, while from the upper layer, often implemented as a host stack [6]. GATT and BLE profiles together make it possible for apps in standard ways without using IP Addess. While L2CAP provides multiplexing capabilities with multiplexed data channels from the above layers. L2CAP also provides fragmentation and reassembly for large data packets. Security Manager defines protocols and mechanisms for installation, distribution of keys, and security equipment boxes for BLE devices [1–4, 6].

2.2 The processing unit and sensors

A key element in a Wireless Sensor Network (WSN) is a sensor node consisting of four basic elements: the sensor unit, the processing unit, the communication unit and the power supply [7]. In this study, the processing unit uses a Raspberry Pi computer, which is reasonably priced, flexible, adaptable and programmed quite easily. One of the elements that determine Raspberry Pi's choice is Raspberry Pi version 3 which has been embedded with Bluetooth 4.0—which became the main objective in this research. In some studies, Raspberry Pi is a cheap computer whose use is very successful in the domain of sensor networks and various research applications.

Raspberry Pi is a single-board computer developed in the UK by the Raspberry Pi Foundation to promote the teaching of basic computer science in schools and developing countries [8]. Several generations of Raspberry Pi have been released. The first generation (Raspberry Pi 1) was released in February 2012 with the base model A and with higher specifications on model B. Model A+ and B+ released a year later. Raspberry Pi 2 Model B was released in February 2015 and Raspberry Pi 3 model B in February 2016.

In this study, the processing unit used a Raspberry Pi 3 model B (figure 2) equipped with Broadcom system-on-chip (SoC) system, which includes a CPU—compatible ARM unit and a VideoCore IV graphics processing unit (GPU) chip. The 1.2 GHz CPU speed has 1 GB of RAM. As storage media used SD-Card in MicroSDHC. This type of Raspberry Pi is also equipped with four USB slots, HDMI output, and 3.5 mm jack for audio. As for the purposes of digital communication provided 40 pin General-Purpse Input/Output (GPIO) that supports common protocols such as I2C and 1 Ethernet port, Wi-Fi 802.11n and Bluetooth 4.0 [9].

Fig. 1. Raspberry Pi & its's ports [5].

Meanwhile, as the main sensor to obtain the data of temperature and humidity chamber, this study uses production BME280 Bosch Sensortec, which can provide three types of information as well, such as temperature, humidity and air pressure (Figure 3). This sensor already has the ability of Inter-integrated Circuit (I2C) protocol, so in communication with Raspberry just use four wires only.

Fig. 2. BME280 presure, temperature & humidity sensor

The BME280 sensor is a temperature sensor that has a very rapid response to temperature changes, especially for environmental temperature measurements that have no physical contact on the sensor. In addition, because the packaging that already supports communication through the I2C protocol, thus making cabling between the sensor and processing unit becomes more simple [10].

3 Programming

The programming in this study is divided into two major sections. The first is the programming on the BLE broadcaster side or on the Raspberry Pi side. In this section the main program task is to read the data from the temperature and relative humidity sensor, then format the data in the 128-bit UUID form, and lastly broadcast the UUID in BLE (including major and minor data as laboratory and chamber numbers). Meanwhile the air pressure data is not included as it is not the part of the Plant Growth Chamber yet.

The second programming is on the mobile device, which in this study used an Android phone. This programming is to receive all BLE broadcast signals around the device, and sort them out specifically for the required data. The data is then interpreted into an information that will be displayed visually on the Android screen.

3.1 Broadcaster side: Operating system & programming language

The broadcaster processing unit using a Raspberry Pi 3 that is already equipped with a bluetooth 4.0. This single-board computer has several options operating system that can be used, namely Noobs, Raspbian, Ubuntu, Windows 10 IoT Core, OSMC, LibreElec and several other Linux variants. This study uses the Raspbian operating system for several reasons. The main reason for choosing Raspbian is because Raspbian is a derivative of Debian GNU/Linux ported for Raspberry, so when dependencies are needed it will be easier to get it. At least through the existing source code and then compiled in the Raspbian system. For the purposes of programming language, there are also several options. Starting from the C++ language to a lot of choice scripting language based can be done in Raspbian. In this study, will be used Python language which is the official programming language in Raspberry [8, 11].

3.2 BlueZ library

In Raspbian distribution standard, bluetooth access must go through low level language. This method of course will be difficult in doing programming and looking for errors—when something goes wrong. Therefore, to access BLE on Raspberry Pi, in this study selected using the BlueZ library [12].

To simplify the application of this research, this BlueZ library, will be executed in python application by using subprocess. This is not the best way to access bluetooth via python, but it can still be done primarily in research. BlueZ Library provides support for the bluetooth core layer and protocol. The library is also flexible, efficient and uses a modular implementation. BlueZ also has many interesting features, such as:

i). Complete modular implementation
ii). Symmetric multi processing safe
iii). Multithreaded data processing
iv). Support for multiple Bluetooth devices
v). Real hardware abstraction
vi). Standard socket interface to all layers
vii). Device and service level security support

BlueZ provides downloadable source code and must be compiled in the desired environment—in this case Raspbian. To do the BlueZ installation can be done easily, simply follow the following commands:

i). mkdir bluez
ii). cd bluez
iii). wget http://www.kernel.org/pub/linux/bluetooth/bluez-5.48.tar.gz
iv). tar xvzf bluez-5.48.tar.gz
v). cd bluez-5.48
vi). ./configure --disable-systemd
vii). make all
viii). sudo make install
ix). sudo reboot

3.3 Data format

Broadcasting chamber status data via BLE in this study, will be done through UUID-like when iBeacon broadcasts (Figure 4). This UUID contains four data fields, that is:

i). proximityUUID: a data of 32 digits hexadecimal which will be used as a place of broadcasting chamber status data.

ii). major: data with a width of four hexadecimal digits to be used as a laboratory number in which the chamber resides.

iii). minor: data with a width of four hexadecimal digits to be used as a chamber number that broadcasts.

iv). power: a data with four hexadecimal width that we do not need for temporarily, and we will fill it with 0 × 0000 values.

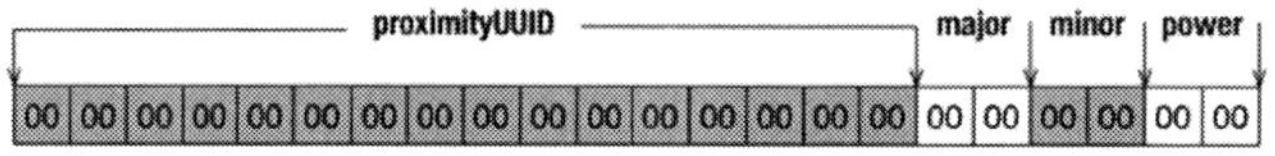

Fig. 3. BLE UUID format.

In the proximityUUID data, the first eight digits of hexadecimal will be used as the value of the measured air temperature and relative humidity. The first two digits are the air temperature and followed by the next two digits as the numbers behind the comma in hexadecimal format. So the data 20.95 °C will be written as 0 × 14 for the first byte and 0 × 5F for second. Similarly for write the relative humidity, in proximityUUID is also done in the same way on the third up to the forth byte. The full picture format for proximityUUID can be seen in Figure 5.

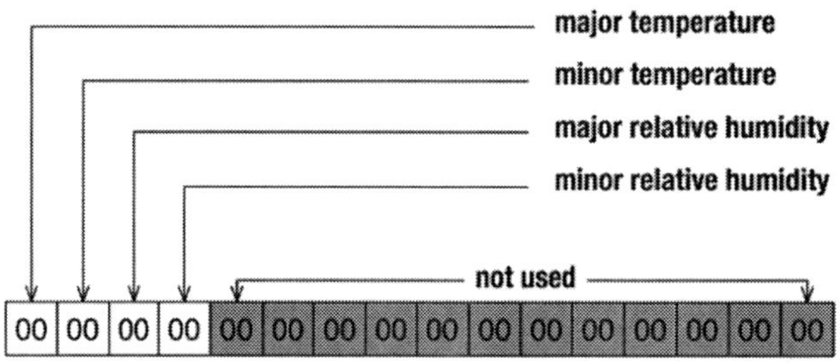

Fig. 4. The data in proximityUUID format.

Meanwhile, for major and minor BLE information, each of which has a width of four hexadecimal digits, we will use the laboratory code number and the chamber number code that does the advertising UUID. With four digits hexadecimal this will be accommodated as many as 65 656 labs and each laboratory has 65 536 pieces of chamber. The amount is very sufficient for now. For example, suppose in the measurement of chamber number 10 in laboratory no. 3 get a temperature of 21.36 °C and 78.95 % relative humidity, then complete the UUID will be like in Figure 6.

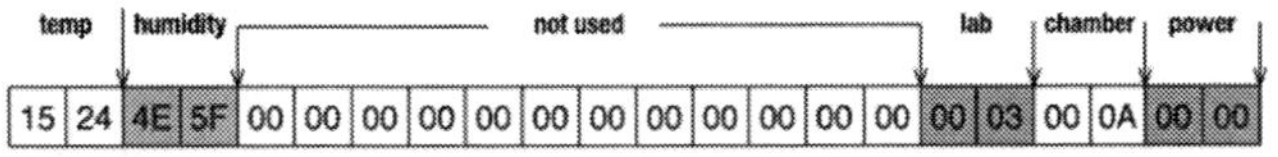

Fig. 5. Complete UUID to sent via BLE.

3.4 Flowchart

Like most applications, the Raspberry Pi application in this study will first initialize the necessary devices, the BME280 sensor and the Low Energy Bluetooth module. Flowchart application used in Raspberry Pi is like in Figure 7.

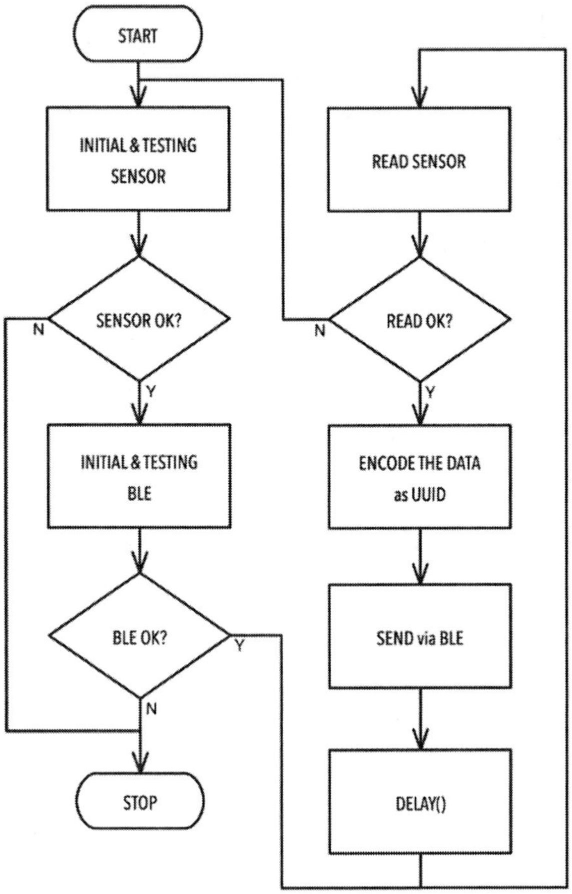

Fig. 6. Flowchart BLE broadcaster.

When executed, the first time the application will initialize and test on the sensor device (BME280 and I2C). If in this check is encountered an error, then the application will stop. If successful then it will proceed with sensor initialization and proceed with check on BLE module. After all initialization and checking are done, the application will read the data present on the sensor. The data obtained from this sensor module is numerical so it needs to be converted into hexadecimal data and placed on the first digit up to the eighth digit of proxymityUUID (the remaining digit proximityUUID will be assigned a value of 0×00).

The proximityUUID data is then added with four digits of laboratory number data as major and four digit BLE broadcasting as minor (laboratory code number and chamber code number filled in application configuration), and ending with 0 × 0000 value as calibrated power data. Once all data is ready, the data will be broadcasted via BLE with BlueZ library as a command to HCI with OGF = 0 × 08 and OCF = 0 × 0008.

This broadcaster application is an infinite loop application. Therefore the application will stop briefly according to the time specified in the configuration and will start again reading the sensor, formating it as UUID, send it to BLE and so on. The application will only stop when there is a sensor read error or force-down from the system.

3.4 Observer side

Capturing the BLE signal on the mobile device can be done quite easily. All programming applications on mobile operating system environments are equipped with modules or plugins to access BLE and perform the iBeacon data scanning. In this study we use an Android with hybrid programming using Cordova framework [13, 14].

Cordova is a development framework with open source licenses. This framework that developed by Apache Software Foundation enables the use of standard web technologies—using HTML, CSS and JavaScript, for cross-platform application development. Applications will be run in the environments targeted to specific platforms, and rely on standard APIs suitable for accessing the capabilities of individual devices such as bluetooth or BLE modules [15, 16].

By using hybrid programming, this research requires the help of plugin for applications running on the top layer (javascript) in accessing hardware (in this case BLE module) to retrieve its data. The plugin used for this purpose is cordova-plugin-ibeacon [17] which according to information on its website can run in Android and iOS environments. UUID results obtained from the plugins in applications, then we translated in decimal form and display on screen as in Figure 8 and Figure 9.

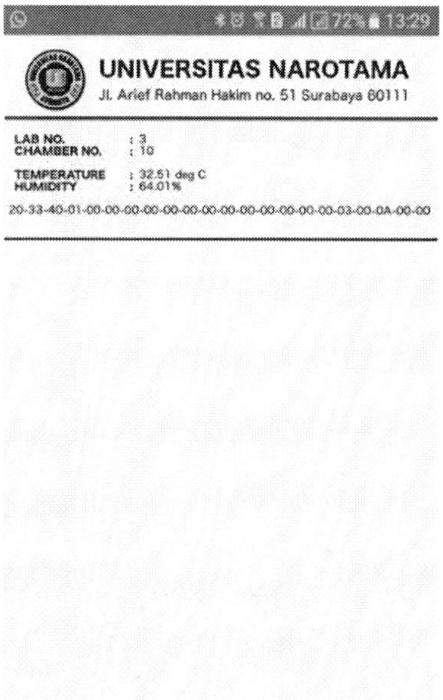

Fig. 7. Screenshot of BLE scanner application #1.

In this study, we attach broadcaster BLE delay in the amount of 10 min. So the next 10 min, the data on the sensor will be broadcasted via BLE broadcaster and received BLE observer as in Figure 9.

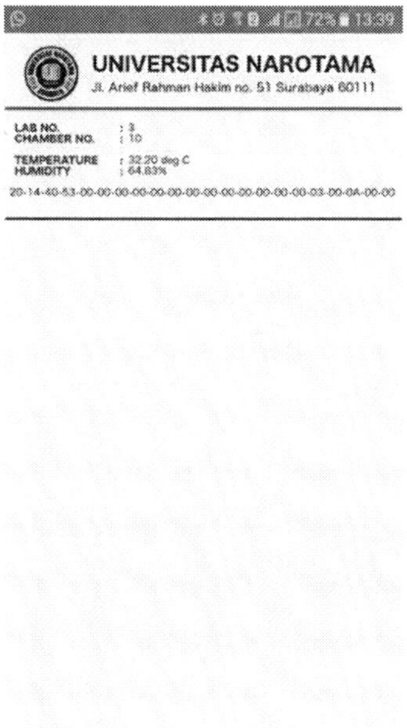

Fig. 8. Screenshot of BLE scanner application #2.

4 Conclusion and future works

By using BLE as a medium of data transmission from chamber (BLE broadcaster) to mobile device (BLE observer), we can make the data available in chamber can be sent to all mobile devices equipped with the appropriate application. Broadcast delivery mode can be read by mobile devices instantly-no waiting time. So that the changing conditions in the chamber will be directly informed to the technician on duty.

In addition, by way of broadcast also reduces power consumption of mobile devices because it does not require power to make the request so it suitable for use in moving indoors. In addition to some of the results observed above, the way we do in this study also has some disadvantages. Especially on the system developed at this time and we plan to have improvements in the mining of the system to come.

The first is the weakness of the effectiveness of UUID data format usage, that is:

i). The hexadecimal format refers directly to the numeric format of the numbers in front and behind the comma. This makes numerical handling ineffective because it can not generate code for negative numbers.

ii). The same format can make the maximum data becomes very large in a case. For example, the maximum relative humidity to 255 %, which in real conditions is not possible.

iii). Major and minor uses as laboratory code numbers and chamber number codes also tend to be overkill. There can be almost no 65 536 labs or chambers in the same location.

The next weakness is the security factor of transmitted data. Currently it is not considered if this data needs encoding, given the data that is sent is general data about the condition of a chamber. But this encoding should be thought of for the future. In addition to the BLE observer side, data received can not be checked data integrity. So that all incoming data is considered as valid data and translated directly into visual data. Integrity data checking is also required especially if it will be developed commercially. Another thing to do is to bring light intensity data, both in Red-Green-Blue and light intensity in white format. For this need will be discussed with the related science field for real needs in the field.

This research is part of Automatic Plant Acclimatization Chamber research funded by DIPA Ministry of Research, Technology and Higher Education, no. SP DIPA-042.06.1.401516/2017. Authors express appreciation and gratitude to all those who have assisted in this research activity.

References

[1] R. Tabata, A. Hayashi, S. Tokunaga, S. Saiki, M. Nakamura, S. Matsumoto. *Implementation and evaluation of BLE proximity detection mechanism for pass-by framework*. International Conference on Computer and Information Science (ICIS), 26–29 June 2016 (Okayama, Japan, 2016). IEEE, pp. 1–6 (2016). http://ieeexplore.ieee.org/document/7550872/

[2] T. Nilsson, C. Hogsden, C. Perera, S. Aghaee, D.J. Scruton, A. Lund, et al. ACM Trans. Multimed. Comput. Commun. Appl., **12**(4):1–23 (2016). https://dl.acm.org/citation.cfm?id=2962720

[3] S.M.H. Sharhan, S. Zickau. *Indoor mapping for location-based policy tooling using bluetooth low energy beacons*. Wireless and Mobile Computing, Networking and Communications (WiMob) Proceedings, 19–21 October 2015 (Abu Dhabi, United Arab Emirates, 2015). IEEE, pp. 28–36 (2015). http://ieeexplore.ieee.org/document/7347937/

[4] Y. Yang, Zhouchi Li, K. Pahlavan. *Using iBeacon for intelligent in-room presence detection*. Cognitive Methods in Situation Awareness and Decision Support (CogSIMA) Proceedings, 21–25 March 2016 (San Diego, CA, USA, 2016). IEEE, pp. 187–191 (2016). http://ieeexplore.ieee.org/document/7497808/

[5] M.N. Al-Azam, B. Anindito. *BLE observer device menggunakan raspberry Pi 3 untuk menentukan lokasi Ble broadcaster*. [BLE observer device using raspberry Pi 3 to determine the location of Ble broadcaster]. Seminar Nasional Teknologi Dan Informatika (SNATIF), Universitas Muria Kudus (Kudus, Jawa Tengah, Indonesia, 2016). pp. 181–188 (2016). [in Bahasa Indonesia]. https://jurnal.umk.ac.id/index.php/SNA/article/view/646/658

[6] J. Nieminen, T. Savolainen, M. Isomaki, B. Patil, Z. Shelby, C. Gomez. *IPv6 over BLUETOOTH(R) low energy*. Internet Engineering Task Force (IETF), RFC7668 (2015). https://tools.ietf.org/html/rfc7668

[7] V. Vujovic, M. Maksimovic. *Raspberry Pi as a wireless sensor node: Performances and constraints*. Information and Communication Technology, Electronics and Microelectronics (MIPRO) Proceedings, 26–30 May, 2014 (Opatija, Croatia, 2014). IEEE, pp. 1013–1018 (2014). http://ieeexplore.ieee.org/document/6859717/

[8] E. Upton, G. Halfacree. *Raspberry Pi user guide*. New Jersey: Willey Publishing (2014). pp. 4. https://dl.acm.org/citation.cfm?id=2721682

[9] D. Rachman, M.N. Al-Azam, B. Anindito. *Sistem pemantau & pengendalian rumah cerdas menggunakan infrastuktur internet messaging*. [Intelligent Home Monitoring and Control System Using Internet Messaging Infrastructure]. Jurnal Ilmiah Link, **26**(1):1–6 (2017). [in Bahasa Indonesia]. http://link.narotama.ac.id/files/1-SISTEM%20PEMANTAU%20&%20PENGENDALIAN%20RUMAH%20CERDAS

%20MENGGUNAKAN%20INFRASTUKTUR%20INTERNET%20MESSAGING.pdf

[10] D. Japhet, K. Ndai. Int. J. Sci. Eng. Res., **7**(10):1043–1052 (2016). https://www.ijser.org/researchpaper/COMPARISONS-OF-THERMAL-RESPONSES-OF-DIFFERENT-TEMPERATURE-SENSORS.pdf

[11] S. Monk. *Programming the Raspberry Pi: getting started with Python*. New York: McGraw Hill Education, (2016). pp. 24. https://www.amazon.com/Programming-Raspberry-Pi-Getting-Started/dp/0071807837

[12] J. Hendberg. *Release of BlueZ 5.48*. BlueZ, Official Linux Bluetooth Protocol Stack [online] from http://www.bluez.org/release-of-bluez-5-48/ (2017). [Accessed on 5 January 2018].

[13] F. E. Karuna, M.N. Al-Azam. *Pengembangan prototipe quick response code (QR Code) sebagai autentikasi keamanan login sistem dengan memanfaatkan teknologi android*. [Development of Prototype Quick Response Code (Qr Code) As Login Authentication System Security Utilizing Android Technology]. Surabaya: Sistem Komputer Universitas Narotama, (2016). [in Bahasa Indonesia]. http://sistemkomputer.narotama.ac.id/wp-content/uploads/2016/04/PENGEMBANGAN-PROTOTIPE-QUICK-RESPONSE-CODE-QR-CODE-SEBAGAI-AUTENTIKASI-KEAMANAN-LOGIN-SISTEM-DENGAN-MEMANFAATKAN-TEKNOLOGI-ANDROID.pdf

[14] C. Darujati, M. Hariadi. *Facial motion capture with 3D active appearance models*. The 3rd International Conference Instrumentation, Communications, Information Technology, and Biomedical Engineering (ICICI-BME), 7–8 November 2013 (Bandung, Indonesia, 2013). IEEE, pp. 59–64 (2014). http://ieeexplore.ieee.org/document/6698465/

[15] J. Stark, B. Jepson, B. MacDonald. *Building Android apps with HTML, CSS, and JavaScript: making native apps with standards-based web tools*. Beijing: O'Reilly Media (2010). pp. 110. https://www.amazon.com/Building-Android-Apps-HTML-JavaScript/dp/1449316417

[16] J.M. Wargo. *PhoneGap essentials: Building cross-platform mobile apps*. Boston: Addison-Wesley (2012). pp. 45. https://www.amazon.com/PhoneGap-Essentials-Building-Cross-platform-Version/dp/0321814290

[17] Cordova. *Cordova plugin for ibeacon*. Mobile apps with HTML, CSS & JS [online] from https://www.npmjs.com/package/cordova-plugin-ibeacon. [Accessed on 7 December 2017]

Design and Development of Smart Aquaculture System Based on IFTTT Model and Cloud Integration

Muhammad Iskandar Dzulqornain*, *M. Udin* Harun Al Rasyid, and *Sritrusta* Sukaridhoto

Department of Informatics and Computer Engineering, Electronic Engineering Polytechnic Institute of Surabaya, Jl. Raya ITS, Keputih, Sukolilo, Keputih, Sukolilo, Surabaya, Jawa Timur, 60111 Indonesia

Abstract. The internet of things technology (IoT) is growing very rapidly. IoT implementation has been conducted in several sectors. One of them is for aquaculture. For the traditional farmers, they face problems for monitoring water quality and the way to increase the quality of the water quickly and efficiently. This paper presents a real-time monitoring and controlling system for aquaculture based on If This Then That (IFTTT) model and cloud integration. This system was composed of smart sensor module which supports modularity, smart aeration system for controlling system, local network system, cloud computing system and client visualization data. In order to monitor the water condition, we collect the data from smart sensor module. Smart sensor module consists of sensor dissolved oxygen, potential of hydrogen, water temperature and water level. The components of smart aeration system are microcontroller NodeMCU v3, relay, power supply, and propeller that can produce oxygen. The system could set the IFTTT rules for the ideal water condition for the pond in any kinds of aquaculture based on its needs through the web and android application. The experimental result shows that use IFTTT model makes the aquaculture monitoring system more customizable, expandable and dynamic.

Key words: Cloud computing, IFTTT, IoT, smart aerator, smart aquaculture.

1 Introduction

Aquaculture is one of the vital factors to support the food needs of the world community, especially in developing countries. The total world fish production, aquaculture production accounted for 40.1 % that is 88.5 % of the world aquaculture production is contributed by Asia. Indonesia is in the 4th position of the top 20 producers in 2011 [1]. The Aquaculture land in Indonesia is about 17 300 km^2, and the utilization is only about 1 200 km^2 [2]. Utilization rate is still far from potential utilization. In the aquaculture cultivation process, water quality is crucial to the success of cultivation. Water quality monitoring can be measured by various variables including physical, chemical and biological aspects.

There are four essential water parameters for aquaculture, those are dissolved oxygen (DO), salinity, water temperature and hydrogen potential (pH). The ideal content for those parameters varies depending on the type of aquaculture and fish species that are the object of cultivation. The priority of those parameters is also different, where the dissolved oxygen (DO) is the highest priority for aquaculture that determines the growth of the fish. Increasing water temperatures can also cause the DO content to decrease as it is unable to hold O_2 [3]. However, if dissolved oxygen (DO) is too high it will cause a gas bubble disease that can kill fish. If too low, cause fish easily infected with bacteria. The Ambient temperature also affects the daily fluctuations of dissolved oxygen. The dissolved oxygen is able to be less than 3 mg L^{-1} in the morning and more than 15 mg L^{-1} in the afternoon [4]. The content of dissolved oxygen must be maintained and stable to support the success of aquaculture. In addition, neutral water also makes aquaculture more productive [5]. By increasing the dissolved oxygen content by using the aerator in water. It can purify water by absorbing pollutants, thus keeping the acidity of water in a neutral condition [6] which is necessary for increasing aquaculture productivity.

Some of the water quality monitoring systems have been conducted before [7]. And there is still no research on cloud system architecture with the If This Then That (IFTTT) [8] model and integrate with smart aerator dynamically for aquaculture. This paper proposes the idea of a real-time monitoring system of aquaculture that integrated with smart aerator using IFTTT rule based on the cloud system. This system is used by traditional farmer, who does not have ability for computer programming. IFTTT helps farmer to customize the aerator system. With IFTTT, the user can set

*Corresponding author: midzulqornain@gmail.com

time of working aerator based on his own needs for his pond condition dynamically. The sensors data will be sent to cloud system to be analyzed and processed before published to the client devices.

A further explanation of this paper will be explained as follows. Reviews for previous works from other researchers that have been conducted explained in Section 2. Section 3 presents the detail of our system design including smart sensor module, smart aeration system, local network system and cloud computing system. The result of the experimental implementation of our work will be presented in Section 4. Section 5 presents conclusion and suggest the future work that is able to be conducted for extensions.

2 Related works

Some works of IoT smart system has been developed various kinds of technology, protocol system and real-time system. This section will describe some works of popular approaches to design a smart system of Internet of Things. One application of IoT technology for broad field implementation has been done by the Italian researcher. A smart city application in the City of Padova, Italy. The application is an example of the application of a relative IoT paradigm to smart cities. The main objective of Padova Smart City is to implement open public data and provide ICT solutions for public administration. The built system works by collecting environmental data and monitoring public street illumination with various types of sensors using wireless nodes. Placement is done on street light poles and connected to the internet in real-time. In such an application, the HTTP protocol is used for communication. There are two developed, mobile and web platforms. Implementation of proxy protocols is also set up to facilitate monitoring of the network coming to IoT devices [9].

An IoT implementation has also been conducted in the fish farming sector, not just for applying in the city. In this paper [10], an IoT intelligent system for fish farming was designed using four sensors, water temperature, pH, dissolved oxygen, and water level. The MSP430 series chip was used In this system. It worked for processing of each sensing node of the core. For communication interface, ZigBee wireless sensing network interface with low-power digital radios was used. In this research, they also used four control devices, RGB light, heaters, inflator, and feeder. By using ZigBee wireless transmission, the power consumption was very significant low. The central system comes with a WIFI transmission module that is able to be used with Android mobile devices that connect directly to enhance overall system timeliness and convenience.

The result of research for big data architecture at under water for water quality monitoring has also been done in several pieces of research [11–13]. A coral monitoring system was created by having four major subsystems. Those are the underwater camera to take a picture of coral, buoy mechanics, a control unit for running image capture program and the communication unit. By using coaxial cable, signal loss problem on underwater WIFI Camera can also be resolved. For big data analytics, the comparison between Hadoop MapReduce and RDBMS is also conducted. With the use of Hadoop MapReduce proven to provide faster query time than MySQL. In addition, Hadoop distributed server also provides high scale data processing, capable to process unstructured data and high availability as well.

Another point of concern in implementation of IoT technology is a matter of protocol. A study of protocol comparisons has been performed [14]. The rapid development of internet technology must be followed by a reliable and energy-efficient communication protocol. In this study, they tested several Internet protocols on various issues, including Constrained Access Protocol (CoAP), Telemetry Transport Message Queue (MQTT) and MQTT-SN (for sensor networks). The experiment was conducted by applying KP-ABE and CP-ABE cryptography algorithms. They also described the security resilience of the schemes they posed under various attacks. In their study also showed that MQTT protocol is very good and suitable for IoT implementation.

A work on the IFTTT model system has been performed [15]. The work presented the development of a software framework for home automation systems based on the modified concept of the popular web service IFTTT. This framework consists of two software systems: A stack of software at home automation gates and web applications as a cloud service. The service handles two main functions: An API bridge for web/social network services and automated scripting repository. The simplified core scripts were integrated by the stacked software, a group of trigger and action scripts, and the features that provided by software applications. The main advantage of the framework itself is its simplified design while keeping usability and feasibility. Using IFTTT, the custom triggers can be defined to execute custom actions. From this study, we adopt the IFTTT concept and build on the architecture of IoT in aquaculture.

3 Methodology

In this work, several methods from various references are combined to design the system which has five main elements: smart sensor module, smart aeration system, local network system, cloud computing system and client visualization data.

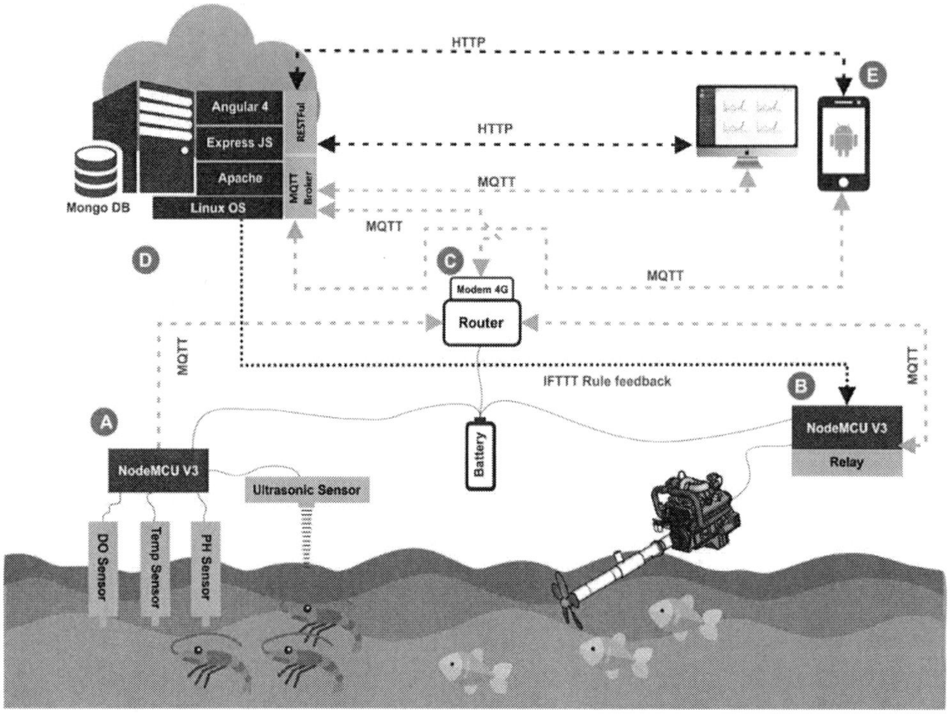

Fig. 1. System overview.

Figure 1 shows the overall system architecture overview of smart aquaculture monitoring and controlling system based on IFTTT Model. The main processing unit uses NodeMCU v3 as the microcontroller which already has the embedded wifi module. The main processor unit NodeMCU v3 collects experimental data from each sensor. The read data from all sensors will be sent using MQTT protocol to the cloud server to be analyzed before visualized it to the client devices.

3.1 Smart sensor module

Smart sensor module is a circuit consisting of water sensors, NodeMCU v3, and battery 12 V in order to read the environment data of water condition (Figure 2). The sensor data sent by NodeMCU v3 which already has wifi embedded module via MQTT protocol to the cloud server.

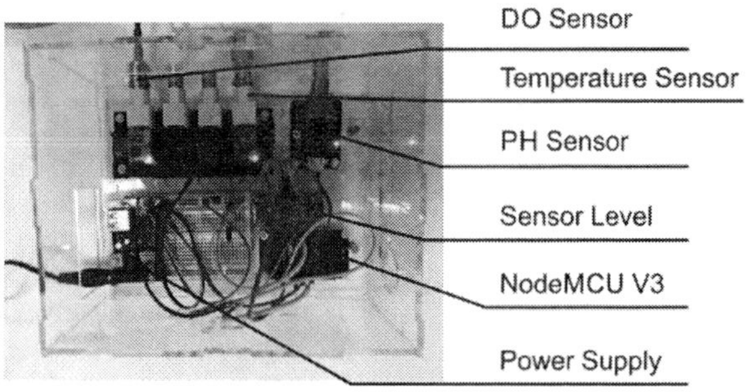

Fig. 2. Smart sensor module.

3.2 Smart aeration system

Smart aerator is modified diesel machine that gets addition of propeller, motor, battery 12 V, relay and NodeMCU v3 (Figure 3). The motor works to make aerator can be controlled by the microcontroller. There are two relays in smart aeration system. The first relay is connected to the motor. The relay works for turning on or off the motor. The motor works to trigger the diesel machine to be turned on. The second relay is connected to the diesel machine which is working for turning on or off the diesel machine especially for turning off it.

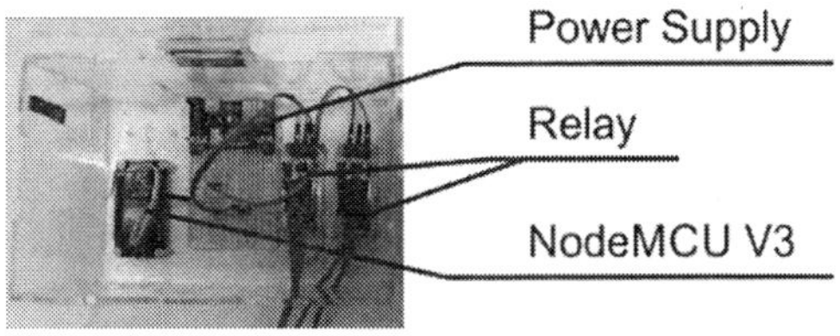

Fig. 3. Control device as part of smart aeration system.

3.3 Local network system

Local network system consist of router, modem and battery 12 V (Figure 4) which worked for sending and receiving data packets either from sensors to cloud server or from cloud server to smart aerator using MQTT protocol. MQTT allows devices to send (publish) information about a given topic to a server that functions as an MQTT message broker. The broker then pushes the information out to those clients that have previously subscribed to the client's topic.

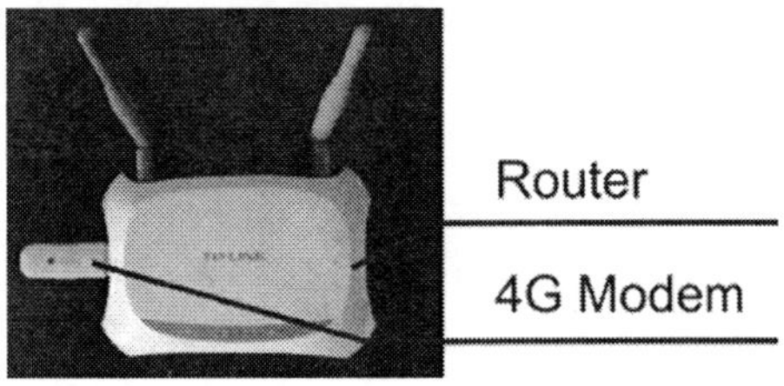

Fig. 4. Router and 4G modem as part of local network system.

3.4 Cloud computing system

In cloud computing system, we used Debian GNU/Linux with several applications installed, Mosca MQTT broker, Express JS and MongoDB. We designed a client model system separately either for web or android development. In server side, Express JS framework of Node Js was implemented for creating server application. The Express JS works for handling the RESTful API which is consumed by client devices either web or Android.

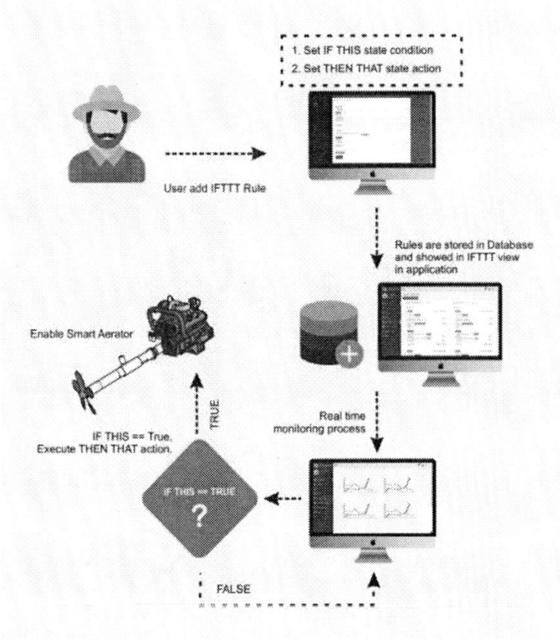

Fig. 5. Flow of IFTTT model.

IFTTT rule processing is conducted in server side (Figure 5). IFTTT is containing a set of rules that are set by the user to integrate sensor system with the aerator. IFTTT is divided into two states, IF THIS and THEN THAT. In IF THIS state, the user input the sensors condition which includes three parameters, undervalue, overvalue and time. In THEN THAT state, the user input the actions that will be executed if IF THIS rule is true. There are three parameters in THEN THAT, aerator ID, period and over value.

3.5 Client visualization data

The data published by Mosca MQTT broker is read by three clients, smart aeration system, web application and Android application (Figure 6). In web applications, Angular 4 framework is used for developing the web. It is also installed MQTT client in it in order to read data by subscribing to the certain topic or send data by publishing to the certain topic. The application has some features to optimize and support the aquaculture process, real-time statistic data, multi node supported, expandable sensors, smart control aerator and IFTTT rules.

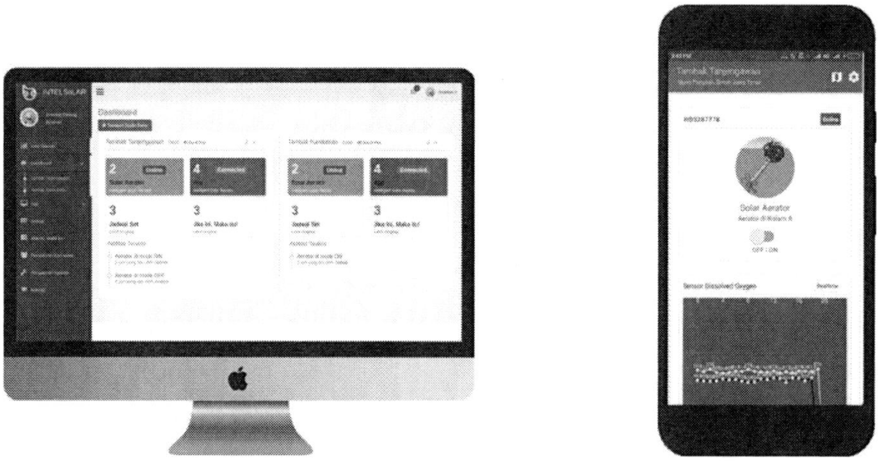

Fig. 6. Web-based and android-based platform.

4 Results and discussion

In this part, we present implementation of the development software and hardware and the results of the experiments performed as well (Figure 7). This test showed how the user can set rules of IFTTT depends on his own needs of his pond condition dynamically. This test also displayed the result of the graphics rate for dissolved oxygen (DO), potential of hydrogen (PH) and water temperature.

Fig. 7. Implementation of smart aquaculture.

4.1 Web-based application

Figure 8 is an application screenshot of web-based on the IFTTT view. The web-based application itself has seven main features. They consisted of statistics data, node dashboard, device, schedules system, IFTTT rules, user management and application setting. Statistics data provided the detail of the whole system that user has, such as node location detail, number of sensors and nodes that user have, number of schedules and IFTTT rules that user set.

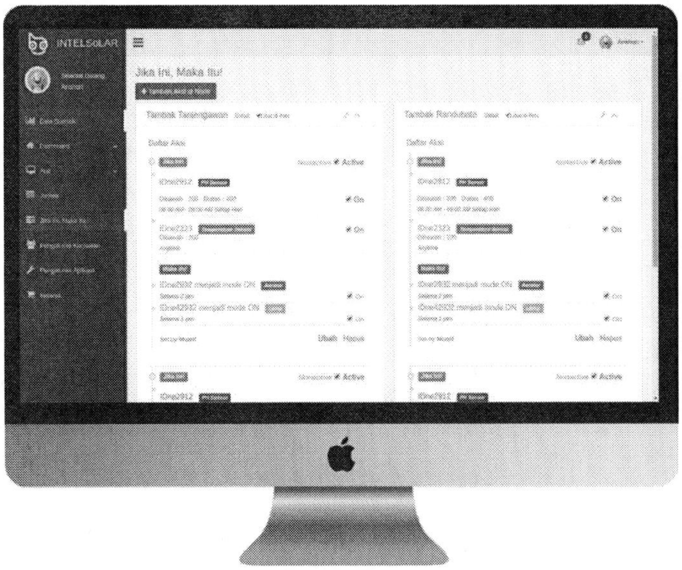

Fig. 8. Web-based platform shows the view of IFTTT service.

Schedules system provided a service for setting the schedule of working time of the aerator and the sensors. The sensors real-time data were showed on the detail of node dashboard. The sensors were composed of dissolved oxygen, potential of hydrogen, water temperature and ultrasonic sensor.

4.2 Android-based application

Beside web-based platform, Android-based platform for the system also provided. Figure 9 is an application screenshot of android-based on the node dashboard view. In user management feature, the user can add the other user that under his authority as well. The detail of devices that user have and set was showed in device feature. There two types of devices, sensor device, and smart aerator device. In Device feature, the user also can add the new device by inputting the unique ID of the device.

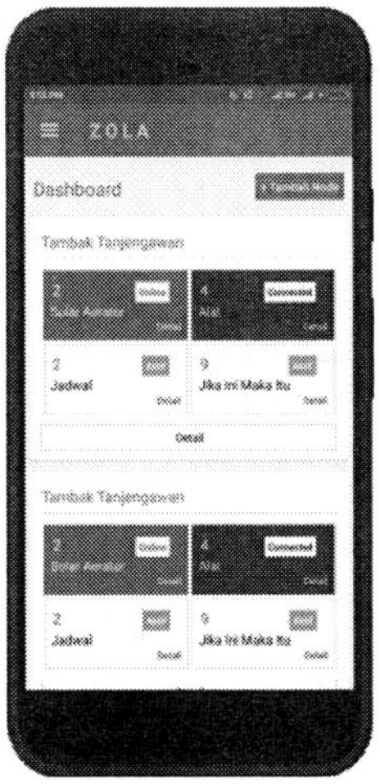

Fig. 9. Android-based platform shows the view of node dashboard.

4.3 The graphics rate of sensors with IFTTT implementation

The following are the results of the performance testing of using IFTTT model for aquaculture monitoring system that integrates with the smart aerator.

Table 1. Experimental specification.

Experiments	Testing Time	Pond Area	Aerator Power	IFTTT			
				IF THIS State		THEN THAT State	
Experiment 1	First day at 15.00 GMT +7	4 m × 5 m	2 HP	**Dissolved Oxygen**		**Enable Aerator**	
				Under value	5 mg L^{-1}	Period	Not set
				Over value	Not set	**Dissolved Oxygen**	
				Time	anytime	Over value	10 mg L^{-1}
Experiment 2	Second day at 15.30 GMT +7	4 m × 5 m	2 HP	**Dissolved Oxygen**		**Enable Aerator**	
				Under value	5 mg L^{-1}	Period	Not set
				Over value	Not set	**Dissolved Oxygen**	
				Time	anytime	Over value	10 mg L^{-1}
				Potential of Hydrogen		**Potential of Hydrogen**	
				Under value	6	Over value	7.5
				Over value	Not set		
				Time	anytime		

Table 1 shows the specification of our working for two experiments. For the first experiment, we just set up for only dissolved oxygen parameter in IF THIS state. And for THEN THAT state, the aerator would be enabled automatically when the condition of dissolved oxygen was below 5 mg L^{-1}. Due to we did not set the period of working aerator, the aerator would be automatically off when the dissolved oxygen value had been reached more than 10 mg L^{-1}.

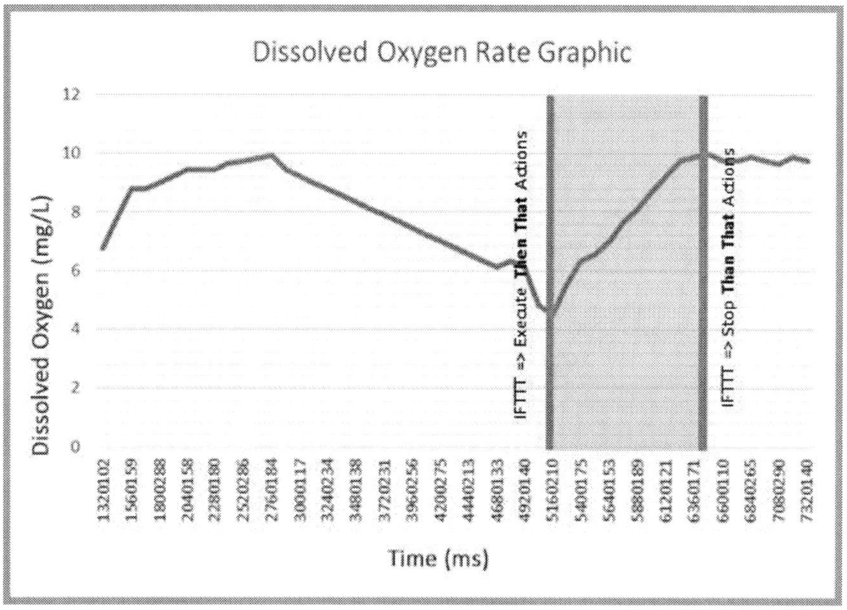

Fig. 10. Dissolved oxygen condition in Experiment 1.

Figure 10 shows that when the rate of the dissolved oxygen was under 5 mg L^{-1} which is the IF THIS state was true, needs to execute the THEN THAT actions. The dissolved oxygen rate value shows the increased data for along 1 199 961 ms or around 33 min because of aeration process.

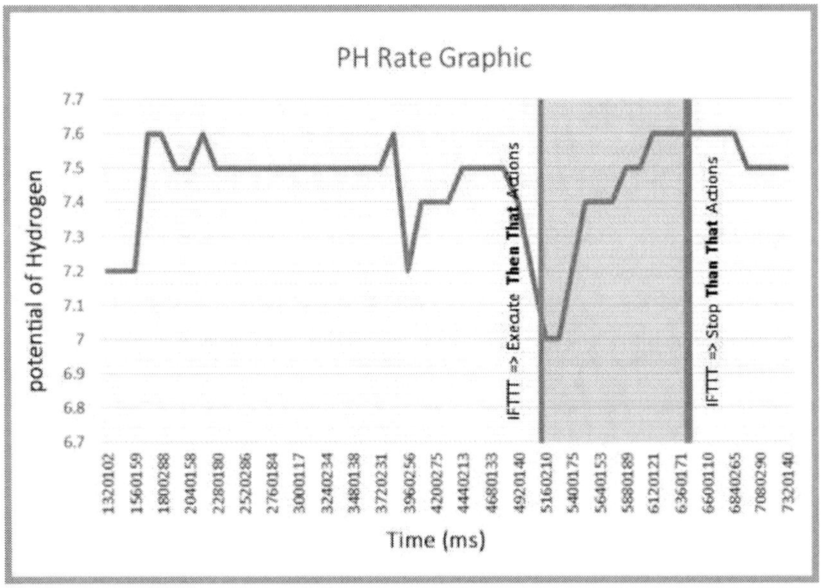

Fig. 11. Potential of hydrogen (pH) condition in Experiment 1.

Potential of hydrogen has also been increased when the aeration process was working as shown in Figure 11. Aeration process started with the value of pH was 7 and increase while the aerator worked and stopped in 7.6.

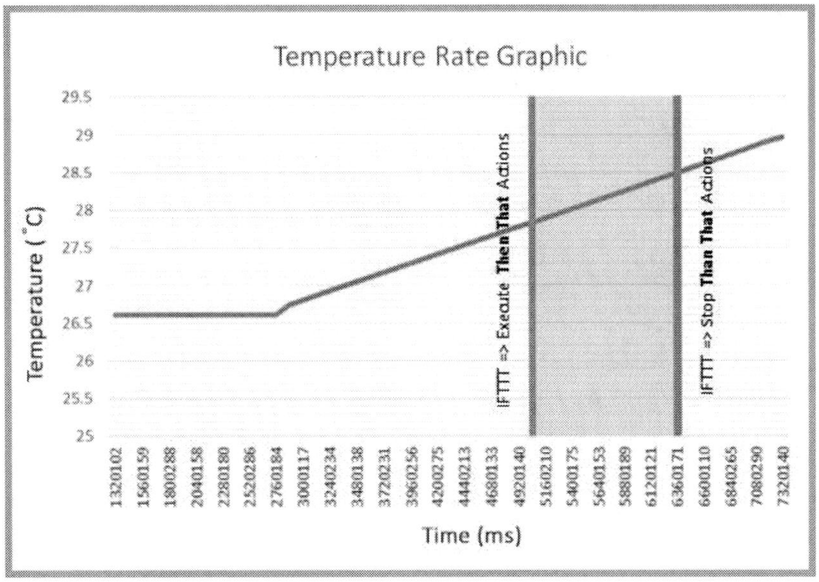

Fig. 12. Water temperature condition in Experiment 1.

Figure 12 displaying the rate of temperature in first experiment. The value of the water temperature was constantly increased before and after aeration process. The THEN THAT actions started when the value of water temperature was 27.5 and got stopped in 28.5.

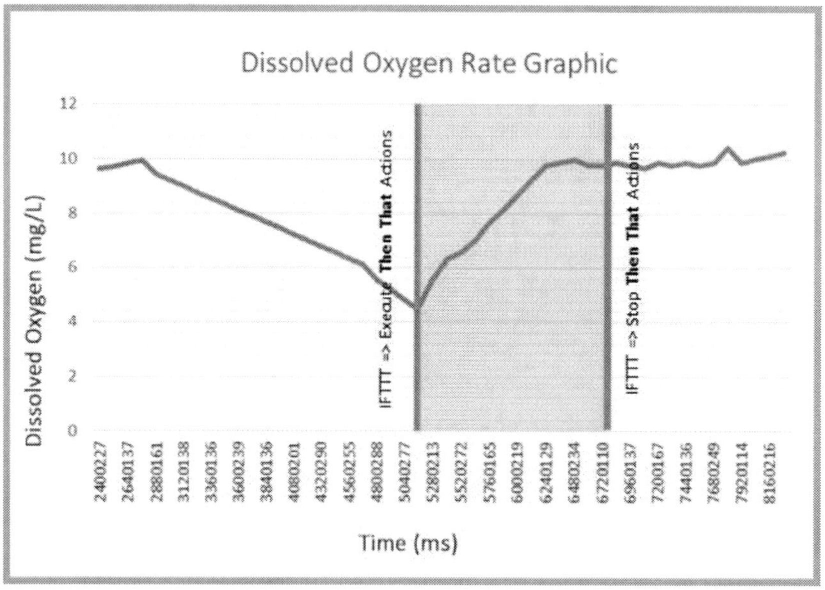

Fig. 13. Dissolved oxygen condition in Experiment 2.

In the second experiment, the IF THIS state was set with two parameters of the sensor with the same THEN THAT actions like the first experiment. The first sensor parameter was dissolved oxygen. Figure 13 shows that rate value of dissolved oxygen was increased when aeration process was conducted.

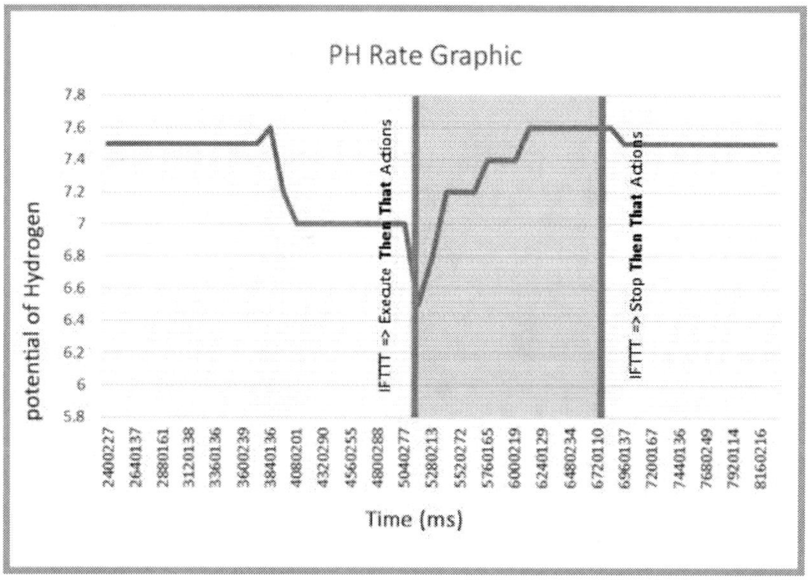

Fig. 14. Potential of Hydrogen (pH) condition in Experiment 2.

The second sensor parameter that used for IF THIS state in the second experiment was potential of Hydrogen (Figure 14). The THEN THAT actions are set with the value of pH was under 6. But it would not automatically enable aerator if the value of dissolved oxygen was not under 5 mg L^{-1}. Figure 15 shows the graphic rate of water temperature when the aeration process was conducted. The temperature was constantly increased either before the aeration or while aeration process. After the aeration process the water temperature became constant for few minutes.

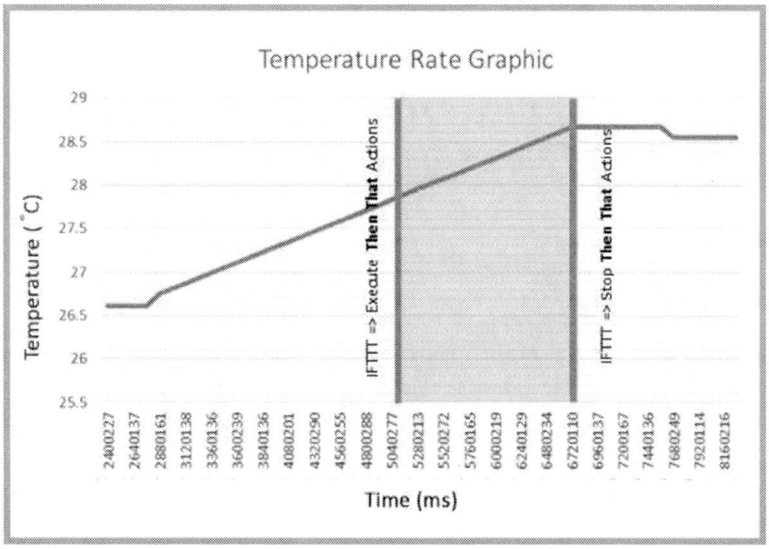

Fig. 15. Water temperature condition in Experiment 2.

4.4 The latency time between the occurrence of the event of IFTTT trigger and the starting of the smart aerator

Various experiments have been conducted to measure the latency time between the occurrence of the event of IFTTT trigger and the starting of the smart aerator.

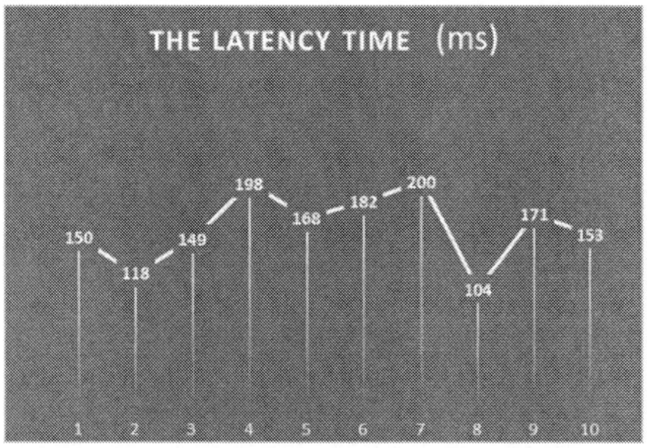

Fig. 16. Latency time between trigger of IFTTT and starting of aerator.

Figure 16 shows the result for latency time with an average value of 159 ms. From the results obtained that with only 0.15 s the aerator can work automatically if the water condition is not ideal. So it can be concluded that with these results water conditions can increase rapidly and prevent water from becoming unhealthy.

5 Conclusions

This paper propose an Internet of Things (IoT) to environment conditions monitoring for aquaculture that integrates with the smart aerator using IFTTT model. In the proposed system, the authors use sensor water temperature, dissolved oxygen (DO), potential of Hydrogen (pH) and water level for node sensors and the smart aerator for the control device. Based on the experiment results, IFTTT model makes the aquaculture monitoring system more customizable, expandable and dynamic. By using IFTTT, the user is able to set the ideal condition of water for his pond in any kinds of aquaculture based on its needs through the web or Android application. In the future, the authors want to extend the device functionality, add solar panel resource to lengthen the life of battery resource, integrate with different big data architecture and develop chat bot for the interactive monitoring and controlling system.

References

1. FAO Fisheries and Aquaculture Department, *The global aquaculture production statistics for the year 2011* [Online] from http://www.fao.org/fishery/docs/news/GlobalAquacultureProductionStatistics2011.pdf (2013). [Acessed on 16 September 2017].
2. Marine and Fisheries Ministry. *Analisis data pokok Kementerian Kelautan dan Perikanan 2015*. [Basic Data Analysis Ministry of Marine Affairs and Fisheries 2015]. Jakarta: Pusat Data Statistik dan Informasi (2015). [in Bahasa Indonesia]. http://statistik.kkp.go.id/sidatik-dev/Publikasi/src/analisisdatakkp2015.pdf
3. N.P. Mahalik and K. Kim. World Journal of Agricultural Research, **2**,4:176–182(2014). http://pubs.sciepub.com/wjar/2/4/7/index.html
4. Y. Parlaungan. Kualitas air dan hubungannya dengan penyakit ikan air tawar. [Online] from https://web.archive.org/web/20161213050336if_/http://bakorluh.riau.go.id:80/yansen_parlaungan/images/stories/perikanan/kwtairpyktikn.pdf [Acessed on 16 September 2017]. [in Bahasa Indonesia]
5. Carmudi, *Kualitas faktor kimia perairan kolam ikan*. [Quality of Chemical Factor of Fish Pond Waters]. [Online] from http://bio.unsoed.ac.id/sites/default/files/Kualitas%20Faktor%20Kimia%20Perairan%20Kolam%20Ikan-.pdf [Acessed on 16 September 2017]. [in Bahasa Indonesia]
6. H. Tsuge. *Micro- and Nanobubbles: Fundamentals and Applications*." Singapore: Pan Stanford Publishing Pte. Ltd. (2014). pp. 239–242. https://www.crcpress.com/Micro--and-Nanobubbles-Fundamentals-and-Applications/Tsuge/p/book/9789814463102
7. S. Sukaridhoto, R.W. Sudibyo, W. Sarinastiti, R. Dharmawan, A. Sasono, A.A. Saputra, S. Sasaki. *Design and development of a portable low-cost COTS-based water quality monitoring system*. International Seminar on Intelligent Technology and Its Applications (ISITIA), 28–30 July 2016 (Lombok, Indonesia, 2016). IEEE, pp. 635–640. http://ieeexplore.ieee.org/document/7828734/
8. IFTTT. *IFTTT/Connect the apps you love*. [Online] from https://ifttt.com/ (2016). [Accessed on 8 June 2017].
9. A. Zanella, N. Bui, A. Castellani, L. Vangelista, M. Zorzi. IEEE Internet of Things Journal, **1**,1:22–32(2014). http://ieeexplore.ieee.org/document/6740844/
10. J.-H. Chen, W.-T. Sung and G.-Y. Lin. *Automated monitoring system for the fish farm aquaculture environment*. International Conference on Systems, Man and Cybernetics, 9–12 October 2015 (Kowloon, China, 2015). http://ieeexplore.ieee.org/document/7379340/
11. M.H. Berlian, T.E.R. Sahputra, B.J.W. Ardi, L.W. Dzatmika, A.R.A. Besari, R.W. Sudibyo, S. Sukaridhoto. *Design and implementation of smart environment monitoring and analytics in real-time system framework based on internet of underwater things and big data*. International Electronics Symposium (IES), 29–30 September 2016 (Denpasar, Indonesia, 2016). IEEE pp. 403–408(2017). http://ieeexplore.ieee.org/document/7861040/
12. A.F. Abdillah, M.H. Berlian, Y.Y.F. Panduman, M.A.W. Akbar, M.A. Afifah, A. Tjahjono, S. Sukaridhoto, S. Sasaki. Journal of Telecommunication, Electronic and Computer Engineering, **9**,2-5:97–101(2017). http://journal.utem.edu.my/index.php/jtec/article/view/2406
13. S. Sukaridhoto, D. Pramadihanto, Taufiqurrahman, M. Alif, A. Yuwono, N. Funabiki, *A design of radio-controlled submarine modification for river water quality monitoring*. International Seminar on Intelligent Technology and Its Applications (ISITIA), 20–21 May 2015 (Surabaya, Indonesia, 2015). IEEE, pp. 75–80. http://ieeexplore.ieee.org/document/7219956/
14. M. Singh, M.A. Rajan, V.L. Shivraj, P. Balamuralidhar. *Secure MQTT for internet of things (iot)*. Fifth International Conference on Communication Systems and Network Technologies, 4–6 April, 2015 (Gwalior, India, 2015). http://ieeexplore.ieee.org/document/7280018/
15. S. Vorapojpisut. Journal of Software. **10**,12:1343–1350(2015). http://www.jsoftware.us/vol10/115-TE06.pdf

Indonesian Stock Prediction using Support Vector Machine (SVM)

Murtiyanto Santoso[1], *Raymond* Sutjiadi[2], and *Resmana* Lim[1,*]

[1]Electrical Engineering Department, Petra Christian University, Jl. Siwalan Kerto 121-131, Surabaya, Indonesia 60236
[2]Informatics Department, Institut Informatika Indonesia, Jalan Pattimura No.3, Sonokwijenan, Surabaya, Indonesia 60189

Abstract. This project is part of developing software to provide predictive information technology-based services artificial intelligence (Machine Intelligence) or Machine Learning that will be utilized in the money market community. The prediction method used in this early stages uses the combination of Gaussian Mixture Model and Support Vector Machine with Python programming. The system predicts the price of Astra International (stock code: ASII.JK) stock data. The data used was taken during 17 yr period of January 2000 until September 2017. Some data was used for training/modeling (80 % of data) and the remainder (20 %) was used for testing. An integrated model comprising Gaussian Mixture Model and Support Vector Machine system has been tested to predict stock market of ASII.JK for 1 d in advance. This model has been compared with the Market Cummulative Return. From the results, it is depicts that the Gaussian Mixture Model-Support Vector Machine based stock predicted model, offers significant improvement over the compared models resulting sharpe ratio of 3.22.

Keywords: GMM, Indonesian stock prediction, support vector machine.

1 Introduction

Recently, the Support Vector Machine (SVM) [1, 2] is a common method in stock price predictions. However, as the stock market is affected by many factors, i.e. economic, political, financial, social factors and noises, stock prices may have different pattern and behaviour over different time horizons. But few studies have introduced the price features into the SVM to make price predictions. Zhang, et. al. [3] used the Ensemble Empirical Mode Decomposition (EEMD) to analyze fundamental features of petroleum price series over different time horizons and pointed out that the decomposed terms can be introduced into the SVM to make predictions. But the EEMD has some limitations in the analysis of stock price series. The EEMD can not effectively extract noise from the price prediction, but the impact of noise is prevalent in the stock market. Therefore, the EEMD can not catpure this feature well.

To make predictions more accurate, we use the Gaussian Mixture Model (GMM) [4, 5] to decompose stock price series into the terms of trend. Then introduce these terms by combining the technical indicators data into the SVM to make price predictions. In voice recognition applications, GMM has been successfully used to mark speakers and channels using the eigenvoices and eigenchannels method [6]. They combine the latest results in the SVM method with the GMM supervisor concept. In this paper, we combine the SVM method with the GMM concept to predict stock trends.

2 Material and methods

2.1 Gaussian mixture models [5]

Gaussian Mixture Models is the type of density model with some components of Gaussian functions. This algorithm is good enough to support stock trends extraction process since it has the reliability on the existence of noise on stock data. With this algorithm, every stock value (ie. close price) in a stock data is modelled into K of Gaussian distribution. In this case, K is the number of used Gaussian distribution model from 3 to 5. Every Gaussian model represents the different of stock trends (ie. Bullish, Stong-Bullish, Bearish, Strong-Bearish, and Sideways).

*Corresponding author: resmana@petra.ac.id; murtis@petra.ac.id

The choosing on number of used model depends on the consideration of stock volatililty, the performance of computer system, and complexity of stock price movement. More number of model on every stock value can cause more adaptive trends extraction process since more trends can be modelled into every stock value. However, it must be compensated with system resource that will be used, especially when stock data is big enough. In other words, this algorithm will model every stock data at one time t {X1,..., Xt} on stock data frame that is modelled into Gaussian distribution K by using the same initialization parameter. Probability from stock value based on the previous condition can be formulated as follows [7, 8]:

$$P(X_t) = \sum_{i=1}^{K} w_{i,t} * \eta(X_t, \mu_{i,t}, \Sigma_{i,t}) \tag{1}$$

Where
$P(X_t)$ = Probability of trends value at time t.
K = Number of Gaussian distribution on every value.
$W_{i,t}$ = Estimation on weight from i-th Gaussian distribution at time t.
$\mu_{i,t}$ = Mean value from i-th Gaussian distribution at time t.
$\Sigma_{i,t}$ = Covariance matrix from i-th Gaussian at time t.
η = Function of Gaussian probability density.
With the formula of function of Gaussian probability density as follows [9]:

$$\eta(X_t, \mu, \Sigma) = \frac{1}{(2\pi)^{n/2} |\Sigma|^{1/2}} e^{-\left(\frac{1}{2}\right)\left(X_t - \mu_t\right)^T \Sigma^{-1}\left(X_t - \mu_t\right)} \tag{2}$$

And the covariance matrix is assumed in forms of [7]:

$$\Sigma_{k,t} = \sigma_k^{\ 2}I \tag{3}$$

For the next data frame, every stock value is combined with every K of of Gaussian distribution model on the same corresponding value, starting from the distribution model with the largest to the smallest probability. A stock value is determined to be suitable with one of Gaussian distribution models when it belongs to the range 2.5 of deviation standard. On the other hand, when a stock value has the value instead of 2.5 of deviation standard, it is stated to be unsuitable with that Gaussian distribution model. [7, 10].

$$\mu_k - 2.5 * \sigma_k < X_t < \mu_k + 2.5 * \sigma_k \tag{4}$$

Where
X_t = stock value (Close price) at time t.
μ_k = Vector of mean value from k-th Gaussian.
σ_k = Value of deviation standard from k-th Gaussian.

If a stock value is suitable with one of Gaussian distribution models, the parameter of Gaussian model will be updated. To update the weight value, the following formula is used [7]:

$$\omega_{k,t} = (1 - \alpha)\, \omega_{k,t-1} + \alpha\, (M_{k,t}) \tag{5}$$

Where
$\omega_{k,t}$ = Weight from k-th Gaussian at time t.
α = Learning rate.
$M_{k,t}$ = The value is 1 for the suitable model and 0 for other model.
After updating the weight value, do the normalization to make the total weight from K of Gaussian distribution model = 1.
To update the mean value, the following formula is used [7]:

$$\mu_t = (1 - \rho)\, \mu_{t-1} + \rho X_t \tag{6}$$

where $\rho = \alpha \eta\, (X_t \mid \mu_k, \sigma_k)$

The value of deviation standard needs periodic update when there is pixel value that is suitable with distribution. The following formula is used for the update [7]:

$$\sigma_t^2 = (1 - \rho)\,\sigma^2_{t-1} + \rho\,(X_t - \mu_t)^T\,(X_t - \mu_t) \qquad (7)$$

If a stock value is not suitable with all Gaussian distribution models on corresponding value, the Gaussian model with the smallest probability will be removed and replaced with Gaussian model for the new stock value. The new Gaussian model will be initialized with mean value based on the vector value, high variant value, and low weight value.

2.2 Use of technical indicators [9]

A technical indicator is a series of data points that are derived by applying a formula to the price data of a security. The combination of price data, for example open, high, low or close can be used as data point over a period of time. Some indicators may use only the opening and/or closing prices, while others incorporate several price data into their formulas. The price data is entered into the formula and a data point is produced. For example, the average of 3 closing prices is one data point ((28 700 + 27 670 + 27 560)/3 = 27 976.66). However, in most cases one data point does not offer much information. To enable better analysis, a series of data points over a period of time is required to create valid reference points.

By creating a time series of data points, a comparison can be made between present and past levels. For analysis purposes, technical indicators are usually used for smoothening the data points and shown in a graphical form above or below a security's price chart [9]. In literature many technical indicators can be found such as moving averages, price adjustments, volatility indicators, momentum indicators, trend indicators, market trend indicators, special indicators etc. For more smoothening the dataset and prediction few technical indicators such as simple moving average (SMA), exponential moving average (EMA), triangular moving average (TMA) and modified moving averages (MMA), Williams %R, true strength index (TSI), relative strength index (RSI), average true range (ATR), and volatility ratio (VR) are used in the experiement [9].

2.3 Proposed GMM-SVM stock predicting model

The proposed stock market analysis model is shown in figure 1. This model works in three phases. In phase 1, first the price trends (bullish, bearish, sideway) is evaluated using Gaussian Mixture Model, and class label is identified. Later the dimension of dataset is increased by adding technical indicators by using Close, High, Low, SMA, RSI, SAR, ADX and MFI. The combination of technical indicators being used is depending upon the requirement. After application of technical indicators data sets are regenerated and the data points are normalized and mapped within range (0 to 1). In phase 2, dataset is divided into two parts, one part is used for training (using 80 % of data) and other for testing (20 % of data). The model is trained using SVM classifier. In phase 3, testing data is classified using SVM. Output of SVM is either +1 or −1 indicated as p, which represents price-up or price-down. This value of p is compared with class label y to compute accuracy of the model. Then we accumulate the result of the predicted price-up or price-down resulting a Strategy Cummulative Return. We compute a performance indicator which is called sharpe ratio. Sharpe ratio = (Strategy Cummulative Return - Market Cummulative Return)/Strategy Cummulative Return.

3 Results and discussions

The price of Astra International Inc. (ASII.JK) stock data was modelled. The data used taken during 17 yr period of January 2000 until September 2017. Some data was used for training/modeling (80 % of data) and the remainder (20 %) was used for testing to perform strategy cummulative return.

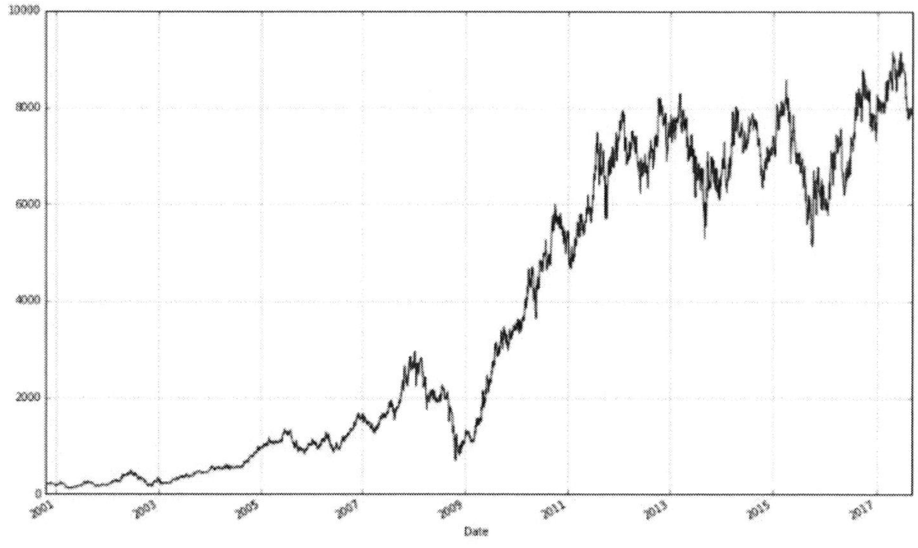

Fig. 1. The price movement of ASII.JK Astra International Inc.

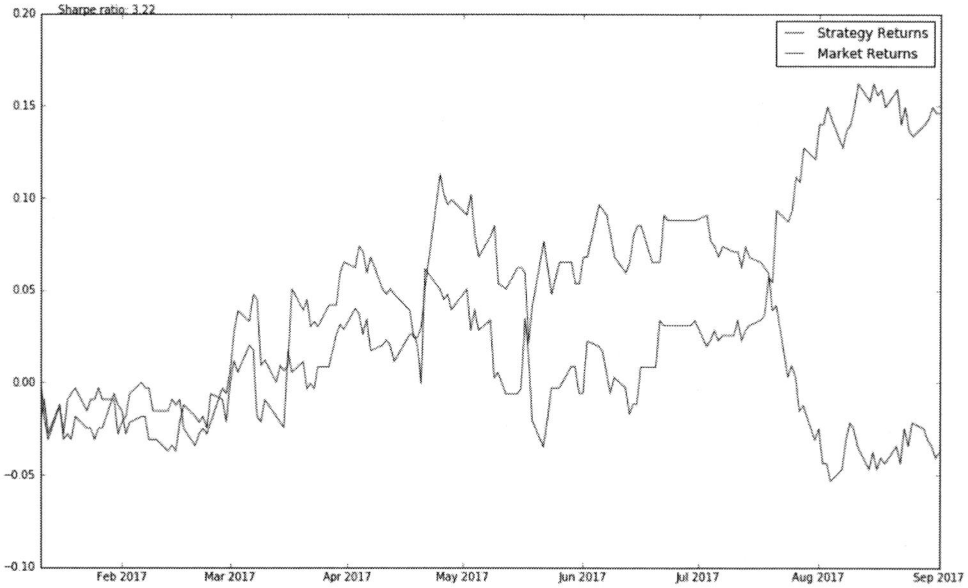

Fig. 2. The strategy cummulative return using GMM-SVM.

This strategy works on some stocks (i.e. ASII.JK—Astra International Inc. Resulting sharpe ratio of 3.22) but doesn't work on others, which is the case with most prominant other strategies. There are a few reasons why the algorithm did work consistently and the author will list some of them here: i) No autocorrelation of returns; ii) No Support Vector hyper parameter optimization; iii) No error propagation; and iv) No feature selection. The autocorrelation of the returns have not checked yet, which would have increased the predictability of the algorithm. The returns column was shifted by one and passing it as feature set. The result will increase the sharpe ration by 5 %.

4 CONCLUSION

An integrated model comprising GMM and SVM system has been proposed to predict stock market of ASII.JK for 1 d in advance. This model has been compared with the market cummulative return. From the results, it is clearly depicts that the GMM-SVM based stock analysis model, where training with SVM offers significant improvement over the compared models and also the prediction capability has been improved for Indonesian stock market datasets.

The authors would like to thank the Indonesian Directorate General of Research and Higher Education, which provided the funds (No: 08/SP2H/PDSTRL-PEN/LPPM-UKP/V/2017) for the research project.

REFERENCES

1. H. Ince, T. Trafalis. Int. J. Gen. Syst., **37**(6):677–687 (2008). http://www.tandfonline.com/doi/abs/10.1080/03081070601068595?journalCode=ggen20
2. S. Madge. Predicting Stock Price Direction using Support Vector Machines. Independent Work Report Spring. (2015). https://www.cs.princeton.edu/sites/default/files/uploads/saahil_madge.pdf
3. S. Ying, Z. Fengting, Z. Tao. China Journal of Management Science. **03**(6):35–39 (2013). http://en.oversea.cnki.net/kcms/detail/detail.aspx?QueryID=13&CurRec=6&dbCode=CJFD&filename=ZGGK201303007&dbname=CJFD2013
4. Zhang Xuegong. Acta Automatica Sinica, **01**:36–46 (2000). http://en.cnki.com.cn/Article_en/CJFDTOTAL-MOTO200001005.htm
5. S. Rostianingsih, R. Adipranata, F.S. Wibisono. Jurnal Teknik Informatika. **9**(1):68–77 (2008). [in Bahasa Indonesia]. https://media.neliti.com/media/publications/105037-ID-none.pdf
6. W.M. Campbell, D.E. Sturim, D.A. Reynolds. IEEE Signal Processing Letters, **13**(5):308–311 (2006). http://ieeexplore.ieee.org/document/1618704/
7. Y. Huang, K.B. Englehart, B. Hudgins, A.D. Chan. IEEE Transactions on Biomedical Engineering, **52**(11): 1801–1811 (2005). http://ieeexplore.ieee.org/stamp/stamp.jsp?arnumber=1519588
8. P. KaewTra Kul Pong, R. Bowden. *An improved adaptive background mixture model for real-time tracking with shadow detection*. Proc.2nd European Workshop on Advanced Video Based Surveillance Systems (September 2001). Video-Based Surveillance Systems. Boston: Springer, pp 135–144 (2002). https://link.springer.com/chapter/10.1007/978-1-4615-0913-4_11#citeas
9. E. Kristensen, S. Østergaard, M.A. Krogh, C.J. Enevoldsen. J. Dairy Sci. **91**(2):620–631 (2008). https://www.ncbi.nlm.nih.gov/pubmed/18218749
10. Nasrabadi, N. M. Journal of electronic imaging, **16**(4), 049901 (2007). https://www.spiedigitallibrary.org/journals/Journal-of-Electronic-Imaging/volume-16/issue-4/049901/Pattern-Recognition-and-Machine-Learning/10.1117/1.2819119.short?SSO=1

The Importance of Credit Program Scheme on Waste to Energy Program in Indonesia: Case Study on Tofu Industry

Noor Syaifudin[1,*], *Nurkholis*[2] , *Rangga* Handika[3] , and *Roy* Hendroko Setyobudi[4,5]

[1]Fiscal Policy Agency, Ministry of Finance of Republic of Indonesia,Notohamiprodjo Building, 1st Floor, Jl. Wahidin No 1, Senen, Jakarta, 10710, Indonesia
[2]Faculty of Economics, University of Indonesia, Economics Department Building, 1st Floor, Depok, West Java, 16424, Indonesia
[3]College of Business Administration, Abu Dhabi University, Abu Dhabi Campus, P.O Box 59911, Abu Dhabi, Uni Arab Emirates
[4] Waste Laboratory University Muhamadiyah of Malang, Jl. Raya Tlogomas No. 246 Malang, 65114, Indonesia
[5]Indonesian Association of Bioenergy Scientist and Technologist. BPPT Building II, Jakarta, 10340, Indonesia

Abstract. This study aimed to provide a basis for future policy making in supporting the waste to energy from tofu in Indonesia. The policy studied was the credit program scheme for tofu industry. The financial feasibility, as well as cost and benefit analysis, were conducted to meet the objectives. Tofu industries are mostly small-sized industry which supports people with middle-to-low incomes. On the other hand, tofu industry also contributes significant amounts of emissions. Thus this calls for government intervention to encourage tofu industries to convert their wastes to energy. The result of the study shows that the developments of biogas reactors are feasible for size 84 m^3 and 94 m^3. The study also found that for both sizes, the benefits are higher than the costs.

Key words: Tofu industry, waste to energy, credit program, feasibility study

1 Introduction

The steadily increasing price of energy has resulted in higher energy costs to industry for production and simultaneously a larger portion of household expenditures on energy. The growing energy demand and prices also affect the State Budget contributing to ever higher energy subsidies. Further, the high dependency on fossil fuel energy contributes to slowing down efforts to reduce greenhouse gas (GHG) emissions. Thus, biomass utilization by conversion from Waste to Energy (WtE) is an alternative energy source that allows reductions in GHG emissions.

* Corresponding author: soib2007@gmail.com

Utilization of agricultural and other wastes as an energy alternative provides advantages. Firstly, there is scope for overall improvement in energy efficiency because agricultural/other wastes contain large energy potential and are wasteful if not utilized. Secondly, the use of agricultural/other wastes can be very cost efficient because waste disposal is sometimes more costly than using the waste itself. Thirdly, utilization of wastes reduces needs for landfilling/piling which can generate significant costs in waste management.

A number of existing credit promotion programs have been supported by the Ministry of Finance (MoF) including the e Credit for Food and Energy Security which to date in the energy area has mainly targeted on biofuel raw materials [1–3]. Such interest subsidy programs may provide useful model for the development of WtE credit support programs but are likely to require adaptation.

Financing WtE investment through credit programs, besides of having potential benefits, has a logical consequence on the cost side. By providing the supports to the financing in the WtE, it is expected that the benefits are expected to be greater than the costs incurred. Thus, this study purposed (i) to elaborate the industry and the possibility of the financing, (ii) to provide a basis for future policy making, and (iii) provide the necessary analysis of the costs and benefits of a WtE investment financing through a credit program.

2 Objectives

This study aims to identify and to analyze the costs and benefits associated with the proposed scheme of investment financing credit program to support the development of WtE for tofu industry. The study was also supported with the financial feasibility analysis to measure the viability of the program from the financial perspective. It is expected that the results of these analysis can be used for setting policies related to WtE investment financing through credit program.

3 Methodology

The study was conducted mainly based on the financial analysis (FA), cost and benefit analysis (CBA) and literature review. The assumptions in the FA and CBA of development projects in the WtE were based on a primary survey and secondary data from the Ministry of Energy and Mineral Resources (MEMR) and the MoF. The secondary data was captured from various programs of WtE investment that has been undertaken by the MoF and the MEMR.

3.1 Financial feasibility analysis

To find the proper indicators for the study, there are several criteria to be fulfilled. The criteria were including net present value (NPV) and internal rate of return (IRR). NPV is the different between the present value from the positive cash flows and negative cash flows. On the other hand, the IRR describes the rate of return on net investment. In the project evaluation, the project is feasible when the NPV level is equal to or greater than the IRR and bigger than the discount rate.

Other financial indicators are Profitability Index (PI) and Return on Investment (ROI). PI is the comparison between net cash flow in the future with present cash flow. ROI is the ratio of net income to expenses. Investment is feasible to run when PI is greater than 1. A positive ROI shows that the investment is feasible to run.

Moreover, FA is already known and commonly used in several studies. The application of FA can be used either as a single method or combined with the other method such as technical analysis [4] as well as regional and sectoral economic approach [5]. FA was also employed in measuring the feasibility of the introduction of new energy sources including waste cooking oil [6], solar energy [4] and also for the feasibility of mass production [7].

3.2 Cost and benefit analysis

The Cost and Benefit Analysis is the process to identify, calculate, and compare the costs and the social benefits that are produced by project/investment activities. The justification for cost and benefit analysis is the limited utility of narrow financial analysis that cannot capture all the benefits and losses that have an impact on the society as a consequence of investment project. Indicators that focus only on financial analysis can be wrong if used as an indicator of social welfare because some projects/investments result in goods that cannot be sold freely in the market, such as garbage management, emission reductions, or health facility repairs.

One method of cost and benefit analysis that is commonly used are benefit-cost ratios (BCR). Benefit-cost ratios (BCR) basically are the comparison between the present values of benefit values that are being received by society to the cost that society must pay as a result of the project. Projects are judged as feasible to run if the BCR is larger than 1. Therefore the value of benefits over time are larger than estimated cost values.

$$BCR = \frac{\sum_{i=1}^{n} \frac{Bn}{(1+i)^n}}{\sum_{i=1}^{n} \frac{Cn}{(1+i)^n}} \quad (1)$$

Where
BCR = Benefit and cost ratio
Bn = benefit at the end of period
Cn = cost at the end of period
n = period of investment

There is a wide range use of BCR in measuring the feasibility of the project or program including health [8–10], natural resources management [11, 12], and renewable energy from wind power [13]. Thus, it is expected that the combination of the application FA and CBA in this study may provide comprehensive analysis and may also provide broad policy recommendation.

4 Development of biogas reactors from tofu industry waste

The tofu industry plays an important role in Indonesia. The industry is a small-sized industry which supports people with middle-to-low incomes. In Indonesia, there are 177 tofu and tempeh cooperatives in 18 provinces. There are 115 000 units of tofu makers with 1×10^6 workers being absorbed by the industry. The tofu industry depends a lot on the availability of soybean. Approximately, the tofu industry needs 132 t of soybeans per month.

The tofu industry contributes significant amounts of emissions. There are 84 000 business entities in Indonesian tofu industry. With production capacity exceeding 2 560 000 t per year, the tofu industry produces 20×10^6 m^3 of liquid emissions per year, which is equivalent to 1×10^6 t of carbon dioxide. With 80 % of the tofu industry concentrated on

Java Island, the liquid emissions from the tofu industry on Java Island may be around 800×10^9 t of carbon dioxide.

The tofu industry waste contains a high concentration of organic materials in general, such as protein, carbohydrate, fat, and oil. That high concentration of organic materials potentially emits methane. Similar to cattle farm waste, tofu industry waste can also be processed with a biogas reactor.

One type of tofu industry waste processing technology is the use of a Fix Bed Reactor which is constructed with an anaerobic system. This system needs large tracts of land and does not need energy for aeration. The advantage of this system is its good output. This system will result in a form of biogas and dregs and also water for feeding fish. Besides that, the process is more stable and creates less mud. Tofu liquid waste processing units consist of the main unit of the digester, sewage collection pipe network, gas container, trickling, filter, processed residual waste network, and processed residual water pool.

5 Existing credit programs

Among fiscal facilities that are provided by the government, there are some that are relevant to the credit programs, among others:

5.1 Interest subsidy pattern

This scheme will allow the government to provide fiscal facilities to the beneficiaries by providing a fund from the budget to pay the interest as the result of the implementation of the program. There several interest subsidy pattern and among others are: first, Credit for Food and Energy Security (Kredit Ketahanan Pangan dan Energi/KKP-E) [1] that supports the food security program and the biofuels raw materials development program and emphasizes the role of funding through the involvement of national banks with interest subsidies from the government. In addition, to ensure supply, distribution and funding accountability of the KKP-E the scheme needed to be created with an integrated credit mechanism.

Second, Credit for Bio Energy Development and Plantation Revitalization [14]. In order to accelerate the development smallholdings plantation, the Minister of Agriculture has issued Regulation of the Ministry of Agriculture [15] about Estate Development through a Plantation Revitalization Program. This program was purposed to enhance the development of estate crop plantations through expansion, regeneration and rehabilitation. This is related to the implementation of development programs for feedstock crops especially biofuels and plantation revitalization funding support which involves the national banks. Third, Credit for Businesses Program [16]. This scheme is purposed to accelerate the development of economic activities in the real sector to alleviate poverty and expand work opportunities. Four, Credit for Cattle Breeding (KUPS) [17, 18]. Under this scheme, the government committed to develop one million cows over five years period. To smooth the program, the business community were provided with adequate rate in terms of subsidized interest loans executed via an executing bank.

5.2 Assurance services pattern

The empowerment of Micro, Small, Medium Enterprises and Cooperatives (MSME) to support job creation, and poverty reduction was pursued through the issuance of a government policy package in 2007. To improve MSME access to financing sources, it was considered necessary to provide credit/bank financing with soft and affordable requirements backed by a guarantee facility from the Government.

5.3 Combination pattern program (Indonesia regional water companies)

In order to speed up the drinking water supply, the Central Government with regard to the financial capacity of the State has guaranteed the repayment of bank loans and subsidies on the interest charged by banks [19]. The guarantee is for the debt of regional (local) water (supply) companies while providing interest subsidies on loans by the banks to local water companies. This step is expected to improve the company's financial condition and ultimately facilitate the supply of clean water in the area. Credit support is given only for investment, based on the agreement between the regional water companies and the bank.

6. Credit for Food and Energy Security (KKP-E)

Below is a further description of KKP-E as the potential incentive for the WtE from tofu program.

Table 1. Description of KKP-E.

Definition	**Financing Object**	**Financing Subject**	**Credit Size**	**Interest Rate**	**Participant Interest Expense**	**Interest Subsidy**
Credit in order to improve food security and energy	Business activities that can be funded: development of food crops, horticultural crops development, plantation development, procurement of food (rice, corn, soybean and fisheries), livestock, arrests and fish farming, procurement/ rejuvenation equipment, machinery and other means to support other business activities.	Farmers/ ranchers/ growers/ fishermen and fish farmers who are members of groups and/or cooperatives	•Maximum IDR 100 million per person •Maximum IDR 500 million per farmer groups and cooperatives	• KKP-E Plantation: LPS + 5 % • KKP-E Non-Plantation: LPS + 6 %	•KKP-E Plantation: 7 % •KKP-E Non-Plantation: 6 %	•KKP-E Plantation: 5 % •KKP-E Non-Plantation: 7 %

KKP-E is purposed to improve food and energy security. The coverage is quite wide from the development of crops to the rejuvenation of equipment. This means that in the WtE from tofu program, it may be used to improve the quality of the tofu as well as increasing the machinery capacity of the conversion. The subject also covers the low-level farmers either as an individual or as a group. With the low-interest rate caused by the interest subsidy, it is expected that farmers will be interested in joining the program.

7 Result and analysis

Prior to further analysis with the feasibility of the financial support mechanism, the general assumptions were set. This was purposed to provide the basic scheme for the government to support with the financial intervention from the budget. It was also aimed to set the minimum requirement for the scheme to be financially feasible. The general assumptions were then provided in Table 2 as follows.

Table 2. General assumptions.

No	Item	Amount
1.	Loan term	5 yr
2.	Economical period	20 yr
3.	LPS interest rate/ Lending rate	7.5 %/6 % = total 13.5 %
4.	Exchange rate 1 USD	IDR 11 500
5.	SME income tax rate	1 % of the turnover
6.	Big industry income tax rate	35 % of taxable profits
7.	Substituted Gas	Subsidized LPG
8.	Diesel	Non-Subsidized Diesel
9.	No Carbon Trade	0
10.	Financial Feasibility	NPV > 0, IRR > market interest rate (12 %), ROI > 0, Profitability Index > 1
11.	Various size of biogas reactors	MEMR = 90 m^3 (without cleaner production development) MoE = 94 m^3 and 84 m^3 (with cleaner production development)

7.2 Financial feasibility analysis

In this study, the financial feasibility was determined by four categories i.e. Net Present Value, Interest Rate of Return, Return on Investment and Profitability Index. The analysis will measure whether NPV > 0, IRR > market interest rate (12 %), ROI > 0, and Profitability Index > 1, which therefore the scheme is considered to be financially feasible.

Table 3. Financial feasibility calculation.

Debtor Interest Rate	NPV (IDR million)			IRR (%)			ROI (%)			PI		
	94 m^3	84 m^3	90 m^3	94 m^3	84 m^3	90 m^3	94 m^3	84 m^3	90 m^3	94 m^3	84 m^3	90 m^3
0 %	103.65	193.7	-49.38	19.13 %	30.28 %	7.50 %	20.10 %	390.29 %	80.68 %	1.70	2.83	0.59

continue on next page

Table 3. Financial feasibility calculation (continue)

Debtor Interest Rate	NPV (IDR million)			IRR (%)			ROI (%)			PI		
	94 m³	84 m³	90 m³	94 m³	84 m³	90 m³	94 m³	84 m³	90 m³	94 m³	84 m³	90 m³
1 %	100.21	191.24	-52.18	18.83 %	29.88 %	7.29 %	19.95 %	383.05 %	78.01 %	1.68	2.81	0.57
2 %	96.77	188.79	-54.97	18.53 %	29.49 %	7.09 %	19.79 %	376.01 %	75.42 %	1.65	2.79	0.54
3 %	93.32	186.33	-57.76	18.24 %	29.11 %	6.89 %	19.64 %	369.18 %	72.90 %	1.63	2.76	0.52
4 %	89.88	183.87	-60.55	17.96 %	28.73 %	6.69 %	19.49 %	362.54 %	70.45 %	1.61	2.74	0.5
5 %	86.44	181.41	-63.34	17.67 %	28.36 %	6.50 %	19.33 %	356.09 %	68.08 %	1.58	2.72	0.47
6 %	83.00	178.95	-66.13	17.40 %	27.99 %	6.31 %	19.18 %	349.81 %	65.76 %	1.56	2.69	0.45
7 %	79.56	176.49	-68.92	17.13 %	27.63 %	6.12 %	19.03 %	343.70 %	63.51 %	1.54	2.67	0.43
8 %	76.12	174.04	-71.71	16.86 %	27.28 %	5.94 %	18.88 %	337.76 %	61.32 %	1.51	2.65	0.4
9 %	72.68	171.58	-74.50	16.60 %	26.93 %	5.76 %	18.73 %	331.97 %	59.19 %	1.49	2.62	0.38
10 %	69.23	169.12	-77.29	16.30 %	26.58 %	5.58 %	18.58 %	326.34 %	57.11 %	1.47	2.60	0.36
11 %	65.79	166.66	-80.08	16.10 %	26.25 %	5.41 %	18.43 %	320.85 %	55.09 %	1.44	2.58	0.33
12 %	62.35	164.2	-82.87	15.80 %	25.91 %	5.24 %	18.28 %	315.50 %	53.12 %	1.42	2.55	0.31
13 %	58.91	161.74	-85.66	15.60 %	25.59 %	5.07 %	18.13 %	310.29 %	51.20 %	1.40	2.53	0.29
13.5 %	57.19	160.51	-87.06	15.50 %	25.43 %	4.99 %	18.05 %	307.73 %	50.26 %	1.39	2.52	0.27

The financial feasibility analysis is in-line with the notion to support the provision of interest subsidy to the farmers. The higher burdens of the debtor results smaller level of the financial indicators means less feasible the program. Further, according to the result, bio digester with size 94 m^3 and 84 m^3 are financially feasible, whilst the 90 m^3 is not feasible.

7.3 Cost and Benefit Analysis

The cost and benefit analysis was employed by measuring the cost, the benefit and then comparing both to find the result. The project is feasible if the ratio is above 1.

Table 4. Cost and benefit analysis.

No.	Indicator	94 m³	84 m³	90 m³
1	Initial Cost (IDR)	148 000 000	105 720 000	120 000 000
2	Loan Tenure (Year)	5 yr	5 yr	5 yr
3	Lended Interest Rate	13.5 %	13.5 %	13.5 %
4	Interest Rate Borne by Beneficiaries (Scenarios)			
A.	Scenario 1: Interest Rate Borne by Beneficiaries	0.0 %	0.0 %	0.0 %
continue on next page				

Table 4. Cost and benefit analysis (continue)

No.	Indicator	94 m^3	84 m^3	90 m^3
	Interest Subsidy	13.5 %	13.5 %	13.5 %
	Cost (C) (IDR)	302 109 086	215 127 576	244 185 671
	Benefit (B) (IDR)	753 439 700	547 826 431	462 564 344
	Net Benefit (IDR)	451 330 614	332 698 855	218 378 672
	B per C Ratio (BCR)	2.49	2.55	1.89
	Feasibility (If BCR > 1)	Feasible	Feasible	Feasible
	CO2 Emission Reduction (t)	1 557	321	862
B.	Scenario 2: Interest Rate Borne by Beneficiaries	1.0 %	1.0 %	1.0 %
	Interest Subsidy	12.5 %	12.5 %	12.5 %
	Cost (C) (IDR)	302 109 086	215 127 576	244 185 671
	Benefit (B) (IDR)	753 439 700	547 826 431	462 564 344
	Net Benefit (IDR)	451 330 614	332 698 855	218 378 672
	B per C Ratio (BCR)	2.49	2.55	1.89
	Feasibility (If BCR > 1)	Feasible	Feasible	Feasible
	CO_2 Emission Reduction (t)	1 557	321	862

The above table shows that the CBA results all sizes are feasible. The ratios of BCR are more than 1 for all of the investments. The highest level comes from size 84 m^3 at 2.55, followed by 94 m^3 with 2.49 and 1.89 for 90 m^3.

Even though the financial feasibility analysis and cost and benefit analysis give a positive result to the support of the WtE program, there are several key success factors that may give impact to the success of the program i.e.:

- Fossil energy and electricity prices are high and not subsidized,
- Conducted to substitute fossil energy types,
- Sustainable availability of waste,
- Limited land for waste disposal,
- High tipping fee for disposal of garbage/waste,
- Policies for better WTE support,
- Public support.

9 Conclusion and recommendation

The result of the study shows that financially, not all development of WtE for Tofu Industry types are feasible to develop. It is only for 84 m^3, and 94 m^3 investments are financially feasible. While on the other hand, economically, all kinds development of WTE Tofu industry as a focus in this study deserves to be developed.

To make it more financially feasible, interest subsidies are needed to finance the development of WTE Tofu Industry. When using existing credit scheme, KKP-E (with revision in the regulation), WtE for biogas from tofu industry are potential, where the primary concern is the large investment required can be up to IDR 100 000 000 for individual and IDR 500 000 000 for the group (communal).

The authors gratefully acknowledge the support from Ministry of Energy and Mineral Resources and Ministry of Finance. This study was also supported by United Kingdom Climate Change Unit (UKCCU).

References

1. Ministry of Finance. *Peraturan menteri keuangan nomor 79/PMK.05/2007 tentang kredit ketahanan pangan dan energi* [minister of finance decree number 79/PMK.05/2007 on credit for food and energy security] [Online] from http://www.sjdih.depkeu.go.id/fulltext/2007/79~pmk.05~2007per.htm (2007). [Accessed on 20 May 2016]. [in Bahasa Indonesia]
2. Ministry of Finance. [Minister of Finance Decree Number 48/PMK.05/2009 on Credit for Food and Energy Security (2009) [Kredit Ketahanan Pangan dan Energi]
3. Ministry of Finance. *Peraturan menteri keuangan nomor 198/PMK.05/2010 tentang perubahan kedua atas peraturan menteri keuangan nomor 79/PMK.05/2007 tentang kredit ketahanan pangan dan energi* [minister of finance decree number 198/PMK.05/2009 on second amendment for minister of finance decree number 79/PMK.05/2007 credit on food and energy security] [Online] from https://peraturan.bkpm.go.id/jdih/userfiles/batang/Permenkeu_198_PMK05_2010.pdf. (2010). [Accessed on 20 May 2016]. [in Bahasa Indonesia]
4. C.C. Bode, T.J. Sheer. *J. energy South. Afr.* **21,** 2:2–11 (2010). http://www.scielo.org.za/scielo.php?pid=S1021-447X2010000200001&script=sci_abstract
5. I.J. Altman, T.G. Johnson, P.C. Badger, S.J. Orr. *Journal of EUEC* **1** (2007). https://www.researchgate.net/publication/258398752_Financial_Feasibility_and_Regional_Economic_Impacts_Three_Case_Studies_in_US_Biopower
6. I. Ahmad, I. Hermadi, Y. Arkeman. *TELKOMNIKA Indonesian Journal of Electrical Engineering* **13**, 3:546–554 (2015). https://pdfs.semanticscholar.org/253f/4accc17a17cb1d0757a00a4fdd7ab06dfe7e.pdf.
7. A.S. Abdelmajeed, and M. H. Aboul-Nasr. *Journal of Finance, Accounting and Management*, **4** 2:87–96 (2013). http://www.gsmi-ijgb.com/Documents/JFAM%20V4%20N2%20P06%20Suzan%20Abdelmajeed%20-Financial%20Feasibility%20Study%20of%20Bananas%20Tissue.pdf.
8. B. Z. Diomedi, L. Gunn, B. G. Corti, A. Shiell, and J. L. Veerman. *Preventive Medicine*, **106**, 224-230 (2018). https://www.sciencedirect.com/science/article/pii/S0091743517304504.
9. G. Battistoni, M. Genco, M. Marsilio, C. Pancotti, S. Rossi, and S. Vignetti. *Technological Forecasting and Social Change*, **112**, 79-91 (2016). https://www.sciencedirect.com/science/article/pii/S0040162516300233.
10. B. P. Horn, C. Crandall, A. Forcehimes, M. T. French, and M. Bogenschutz. *Journal of Substance Abuse Treatment*, **79**, 6-11 (2017). https://www.sciencedirect.com/science/article/pii/S0740547216302963.
11. S. Greenhalgh, O. Samarasinghe, F. Curran-Cournane, W. Wright, and P. Brown. *Ecosystem Services*, **27**, A: 1-14 (2017). https://www.sciencedirect.com/science/article/pii/S2212041616304715.
12. E. Ustaoglu, B. Williams, and E. Murphy. *Case Studies on Transport Policy*, **4**, 2: 104-121 (2016). https://www.sciencedirect.com/science/article/pii/S2213624X16300037.
13. A. Kumar and K. Nair. *International Journal of Energy, Information and Communications*, **4**, 1:51–62 (2013). http://repository.usp.ac.fj/5795/
14. Ministry of Finance. *Peraturan menteri keuangan nomor 117/PMK 06/2006 tentang kredit pengembangan energi nabati dan revitalisasi perkebunan* [minister of finance

decree number 117/PMK.06/2006 on credit for bio energy development and plantation revitalization] [Online] from http://www.sjdih.depkeu.go.id/fulltext/2006/117~PMK.06~2006Per.htm (2006). [Accessed on 5 April 2016]. [in Bahasa Indonesia]

15. Ministry of Agriculture. *Peraturan menteri pertanian nomor: 33/Permentan/OT.140/7/2006 tentang pengembangan perkebunan melalui program revitalisasi perkebunan* [ministry of agriculture decree number 33/Permentan/OT.140/7/2006 on estate development through plantation revitalization program] [Online] from http://www.iopri.org/wp-content/uploads/2016/10/PERMENTAN-33-2006-REVITALISASI-PERKEBUNAN.pdf (2006). [Accessed on 5 April 2016]. [in Bahasa Indonesia]
16. Ministry of Finance. *Peraturan menteri keuangan nomor 135/PMK.05/2008 tentang fasilitas penjaminan kredit usaha rakyat* [minister of finance decree number No.135/PMK.05/2008 on credit for businesses program] [Online] from http://www.jdih.kemenkeu.go.id/fullText/2008/135~PMK.05~2008Per.htm (2008). [Accessed on 5 April 2016]. [in Bahasa Indonesia]
17. Ministry of Finance. *Peraturan menteri keuangan nomor 131/PMK.05/2009 tentang kredit usaha pembibitan* sapi [minister of finance decree number No.131/PMK.05/2009 on credit for cattle breeding] [Online] from http://www.jdih.kemenkeu.go.id/fullText/2009/131~PMK.05~2009Per.htm (2009). [Accessed on 5 April 2016]. [in Bahasa Indonesia]
18. Ministry of Finance. *Peraturan menteri keuangan Republik Indonesia nomor 241/PMK.05/2011 tentang perubahan atas peraturan meteri keuangan nomor 131/PMK.05/2009 tentang kredit usahan pembibitan sapi* [minister of finance decree number No.241/PMK.05/2011 on amendment minister of finance decree number No.131/PMK.05/2009 on credit for cattle breeding] [Online] from http://ngada.org/bn906-2011.htm (2011). [Accessed on 5 April 2016]. [in Bahasa Indonesia]
19. Government of Indonesia. *Peraturan presiden Republik Indonesia nomor 29 tahun 2009 tentang pemberian jaminan dan subsidi bunga oleh pemerintah pusat dalam rangka percepatan penyediaan air minum* [presidential regulation number 29/2009 on the provision of guarantees and interest subsidies by the central government] [Online] from http://storage.jak-stik.ac.id/ProdukHukum/Sekneg/Perpres%2029%20Tahun%202009.pdf. (2009). [Accessed on 5 April 2016]. [In Bahasa Indonesia]

Formulating Interest Subsidy Program to Support the Development of Electricity Generation from Palm Oil Mill Effluent (POME) Biomass: An Indonesian Case Study

Noor Syaifudin[1,2*], *Nurkholis*[3], *Rangga* Handika[4], and *Roy* Hendroko Setyobudi[5,6]

[1]Fiscal Policy Agency, Ministry of Finance of Republic of Indonesia, Jl. Dr.Wahidin Raya No 1, Jakarta, 10710, Indonesia
[2]UWA Business School, Crawley Campus, The University of Western Australia, 35 Stirling Highway, 6009 Perth, Australia
[3]Faculty of Economics, University of Indonesia, Jl. Margonda Raya, Beji, Pondok Cina, Depok, 16424, Indonesia
[4]College of Business Administration, Abu Dhabi University, Abu Dhabi Campus, 59911, Abu Dhabi, Uni Arab Emirates
[5]Waste Laboratory University Muhamadiyah of Malang, Jl. Raya Tlogomas No. 246 Malang, 65114, Indonesia
[6]Indonesian Association of Bioenergy Scientist and Technologist. BPPT Building II, Jl. MH. Thamrin. No. 8, Jakarta, 10340, Indonesia

Abstract. This paper analyses financial feasibility and cost-benefit and formulates the relevant subsidy program that is currently implemented by the government. We find that providing interest subsidy is financially feasible only if it serves to substitute the consumption of diesel. The benefits are higher than the costs among three types (45 t, 60 t and 75 t) of the palm waste generator capacity. The paper also reveals that Credit Program is relevant with the objective, to provide interest subsidy to farmers, but certain adaptations are required.

Key words: Cost and benefit analysis, credit program, financial feasibility, interest subsidy, POME

1 Introduction

Oil palm, coconuts and sugar cane have higher levels of productivity among other plantation commodities in Indonesia. Besides their main outputs, those commodities produce huge amounts of biomass waste. There are several oil palm biomass wastes among others are midrib, oil palm shell, oilcake and fruit bunches. Coconut provides shell, sawdust, and fibre as dry biomass waste, while sugar canes biomasses are leaves and grout.

---

*Corresponding author: soib2007@gmail.com

Among these three commodities, palm oil has developed quite significantly in the last few years.

It is estimated that there are 28.7×10^6 t of palm oil mill effluent (POME) being produced in Indonesia annually [1]. POME is liquid oil palm waste which still contains dissolved solid materials. Most of these solid materials come from lignocellulosic material producing oil from palm fruit. Generally, POME is processed using a pond system, and potentially produce biogas.

Coconut, oil palm, and sugar cane are mostly spread outside Java Island. Many areas outside of Java Island are not electrified. Therefore, the development of power plants from dry biomass waste is a perfect solution to equip electricity network for people who live outside Java Island. Dry biomass waste has total potential of (2 000 to 3 000) kkal kg^{-1} of waste. Dry biomass will produce steam which able to generate electricity through a steam turbine generator. Potentials electricity from all biomasses are 49 810 MW. However, only 3 % (1 618 MW) of the biomasses are currently being utilized. Indeed, 60 % of potential electricity from biomass could be utilized as alternative energy sources as targeted by the government [2].

The Ministry of Environment (MoE) has experience in the provision of renewable energy through the development of biomass power plants from palm oil midrib. Ministry of Energy and Mineral Resources (MEMR) also has experience in developing power plants from POME. Developing a small size (200 KW) palm oil midrib biomass power plant needs funding about IDR 5×10^9. Furthermore, more than IDR 20×10^9 is needed to build one POME power plant. According to the previous experience there are at least three types of power plant from POME: (i) 45 t h^{-1} can produce 1.5 MW electricity, (ii) 60 t h^{-1} for 2 MW electricity and (iii) 75 t h^{-1} for 3.5 MW electricity. There two main objectives of developing power plants from oil palm midrib and POME. The objectives are: (i) to produce electricity (either to be privately consumed or to be sold for household lighting) and (ii) to reduce/substitute diesel fuel consumption.

2 Development of electric power plant biogas from palm industry waste

Various studies have been conducted to address issue on energy subsidy. For instance, Moiseyev et al. [3] projected impact of subsidies and carbon pricing on the use of wood biomass for energy in the UK. Another study by Sun et al. [4] investigates subsidies on household biogas use in China, while a study by Gharibnavaz and Waschik [5] investigate the food and energy subsidy reform in Iran. Nauleau et al. [6] argue that subsidy should be differentiated to achieve the social optimum. Chen et al. [7] propose a sewage charge to encourage producers' emphasis on dung disposal. Their implication will lead to an increase on the effect of subsidy policy. Another paper by Zhao et al. [8] finds that renewable energy subsidy generates environmental benefits. Their paper also notes that energy security triggers technology innovation and economic growth. Thus, they conclude that the subsidy policy generates positive impacts. However, Shen and Luo [9] document negative effect of providing subsidy on renewable energy at a certain threshold in China. Therefore, subsidy policy has both positive and negative impacts. In order to generate positive impacts, a subsidy policy should differentiate the tariff level, applicable to renewable energy and on households level, and able to support the environmental benefit.

Instead of merely discussing the impacts and aspects of the subsidy, scholars also address the prerequisite and structural reform of subsidy on energy to meet the optimum level of the policy. A study by Johnston et al. [10] propose a stable, secure and fully functional energy system in the EU due to the important role of energy sector towards economic growth and job creation. Du and Mickiewicz [11] argue that the energy subsidy will be enjoyed more by private and big companies, while the public, small and young firms will enjoy less. Castiblanco et al. [12] recommend that the comprehensive approaches are vital in order to optimize the subsidy on renewable energy. They suggest that the government should ensure that the renewable energy investment is profitable enough. They find that producers of palm oil will gain from the renewable energy investment most in the short term. However, the biodiesel firm will gain more from the renewable energy investment in the long run.

There are two initial conditions before estimating the financial feasibility of the investment. The conditions are: (i) Gaining revenue from selling the electric as the result of the development of the biogas reactor, (ii) Reducing cost by substituting or saving diesel (non-subsidized diesel). The results show that development of biogas electricity generator from POME will be feasible if it serves to substitute diesel (see Table 1 to Table 4 in appendix). On the other hand, the development of POME reactor to produce electricity and sell it to households is not feasible. It is not feasible because electricity production is relatively small and the electricity price is relatively low (compared to the cost). The cost and benefit analysis indicates that the scores are greater than 1. This means that all investments are economically feasible (see Table 5 in appendix).

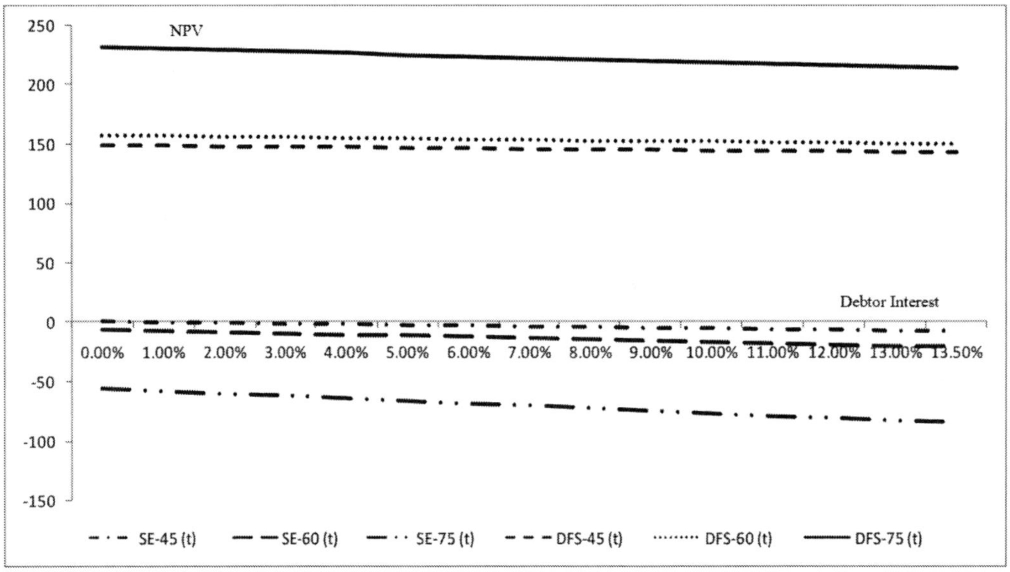

Fig. 1. Debtor interest sensitivity on the net present value (NPV).

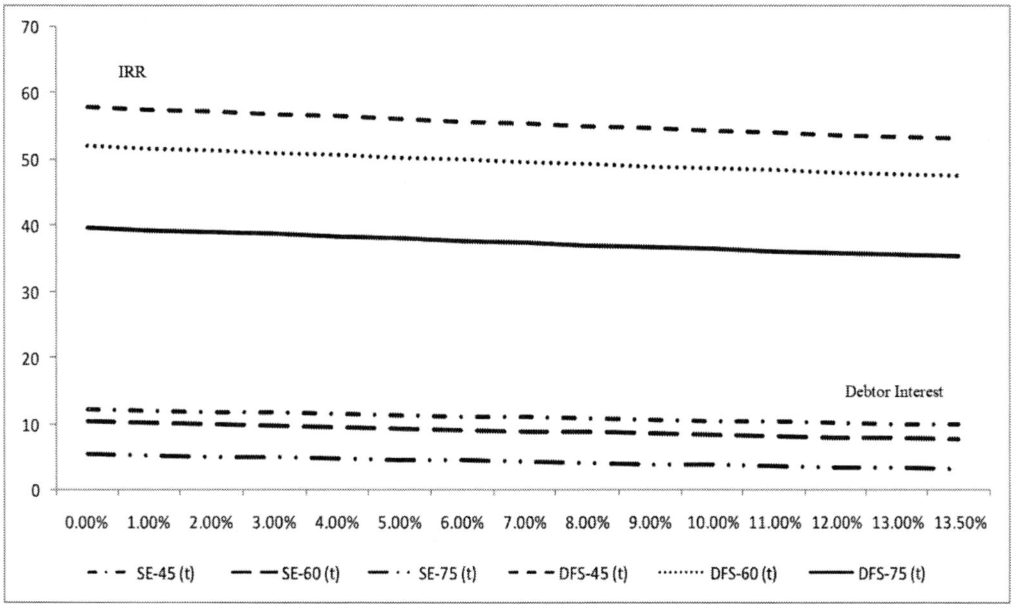

Fig. 2. Debtor interest sensitivity on the internal rate of return (IRR).

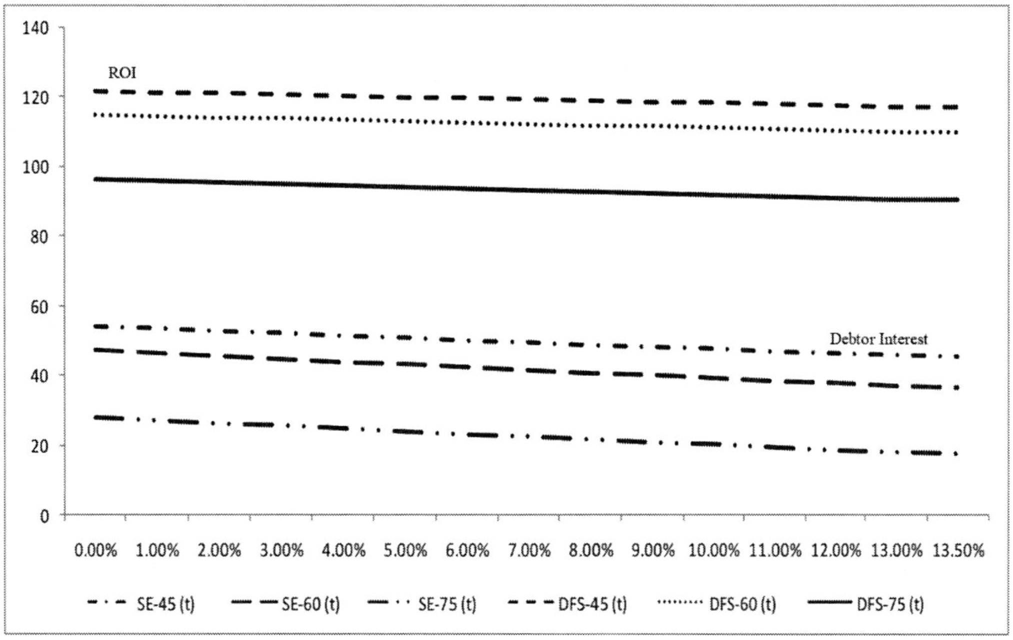

Fig. 3. Debtor interest sensitivity on the return on investment (ROI).

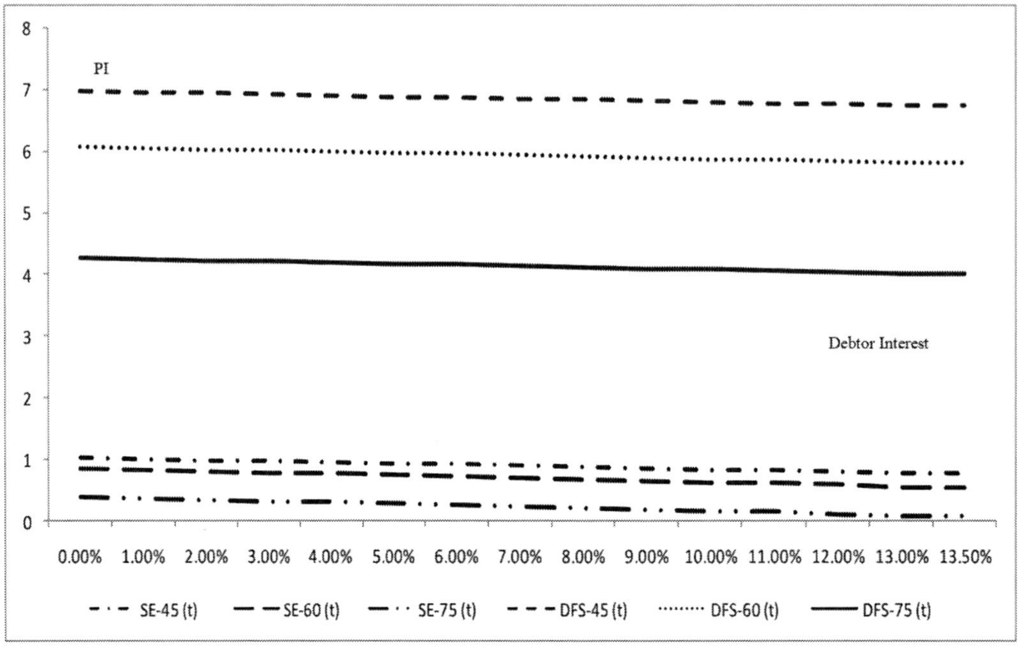

Fig. 4. Debtor interest sensitivity on the profitability index (PI).

Figure 1 to Figure 4 show the sensitivity of the various of debtor interest rate with respect to the value of NPV, IRR, ROI and PI for various capacities of biomass power plant from POME. It is revealed that the higher the debtor interest rate, the lower the value of NPV, IRR, ROI and PI. The analysis presents that NPV, IRR, ROI and RI is much higher for diesel fuel substitution (DFS) compared to the selling electricity (SE), because the price of diesel oil is high and the pollution resulted is also high.

3 Proposed mechanism for financing WTE investment through a credit program

According to the Law No. 23/1999 about Central Bank of Indonesia [13]—as later amended to Law No. 3/2004 [14]—the Central Bank is not allowed to provide credit to support the government priority sectors. Therefore, the responsibility is on the government policy. The policy is Credit Programs that involves financing to support the development of priority sectors. The fund comes from the bank that lends to the borrower with a low interest rate. The difference between the actual interest rate and market interest rates will be paid by the government via interest subsidy.

Many loan programs have been launched by government such as Credit for Food and Energy Security (*Kredit Ketahanan Pangan dan Energi*/KKP-E), Cattle Breeding Credit (*Kredit Usaha Pembibitan Sapi*/KUPS); and Credit for Bio Energy Program and Plantation Revitalization (*Kredit Pengembangan Energi Nabati dan Revitalisasi Perkebunan*/KPEN-RP). There are also loan programs based on a guarantee scheme. One of the programs is People's Business Credit (*Kredit Usaha Rakyat*/KUR). The KUR provides loan for Small and Medium Enterprises (SMEs) and Cooperatives, particularly for feasible but not bankable entities.

The objectives of the WtE investment financing program are: (i) Supporting the government commitment in reducing greenhouse gas emission, (ii) Supporting investment projects in WTE and giving economic benefits to the investors, (iii) Increasing the total funds available for WTE investments, and (iv) Giving financial access to the SMEs and Cooperatives to WTE.

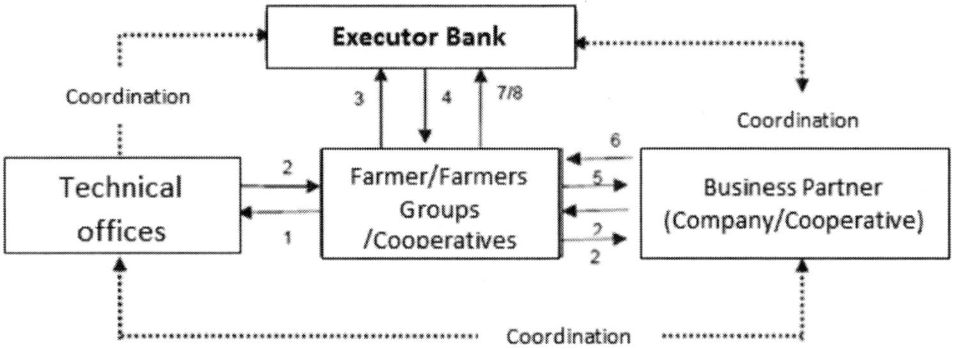

Fig. 5. Procedures of credit program for farmer/farmers group/cooperatives with business partner/s.

Figure 5 describes the channelling scheme of interest subsidy from the banks to debtor/s. The scheme can be elaborated as follows: (i) Individual and group of farmers as the debtor/s prepare loan and business plan assisted by technical assistant from agriculture agency; (ii) The technical assistant endorse the loan and business plan; (iii) The debtor/s submit the plan to the executor bank; (iv) Debtor/s who have partnership with State Owned Enterprise (SOE), Cooperative and private farming companies, can appoint the partner as a loan guarantor; (v) If the contract requests, parts of loan can be overlanded to the guarantor. For instance, cooperatives can act as guarantor of their members; (vi) The partner can guarantee the marketing of products of farmers/farmer groups/cooperatives and assist the debtor/s to repay their loans as well as coordinate with executor bank; and (vii) Debtor/s pay back the credit to the bank.

4 Conclusion

The development of energy generation from POME can benefit society and the government. The role of the government is essential because of the enormous potential electricity and the huge funding. One of the government roles is providing loan interest subsidy. This study finds that the provision of interest subsidies is financially viable if it serves to substitute the use of diesel fuel. The costs and benefits analysis reveals that the interest subsidy generates positive value to the economy. Finally, a mechanism to assist the debtor in accessing the funding is required to implement the interest subsidy to farmers program successfully. The more discussions about the mechanism with the relevant stakeholders are expected to be more beneficial and may produce optimum results.

References

1. Irvan, B. Trisakti, M. Vincent, Y. Tandean. Jurnal Teknik Kimia USU, **1**,2:27–30(2012). [in Bahasa Indonesia]. https://jurnal.usu.ac.id/index.php/jtk/article/view/121
2. Sarono, E.G. Sa'id, O. Suparno, Suprihatin, U. Hasanudin. Jurnal Teknologi Industri Pertanian, **24**,1:11–19(2014). [in Bahasa Indonesia]. http://journal.ipb.ac.id/index.php/jurnaltin/article/view/8083
3. A. Moiseyev, B. Solberg, A.M.I. Kallio. Energy. **76**:161–167(2014). https://www.sciencedirect.com/science/article/pii/S0360544214006173

4. D. Sun, J. Bai, H. Qiu, Y. Cai. Energy Policy, **73**:748–756(2014). https://www.sciencedirect.com/science/article/pii/S0301421514003814
5. M.H. Gharibnavaz, R. Waschik. Journal of Policy Modeling, **37**,5:726–741(2015). https://www.sciencedirect.com/science/article/pii/S0161893815000794
6. M.L. Nauleau, L.G. Giraudet, P. Quirion. Energy Economics, **52**,1:S53–S62(2015). https://www.sciencedirect.com/science/article/pii/S0140988315002479
7. Y. Chen, S.J. Wang, C.C. Tsai, C.J. Zhang. Journal of Cleaner Production, **112**,4:2529–2535(2015). https://www.sciencedirect.com/science/article/pii/S0959652615013189
8. H. Zhao, S. Guo, L.W. Fu. Renewable and Sustainable Energy Reviews, **37**:538–549(2014). https://www.sciencedirect.com/science/article/pii/S1364032114003864
9. J. Shen, C. Luo. Renewable and Sustainable Energy Reviews, **41**:1478–1488(2015). https://www.sciencedirect.com/science/article/pii/S1364032114007801
10. A. Johnston, R.J. Heffron, D. McCauley. Energy Research and Social Science, **3**:1–4(2014). https://www.sciencedirect.com/science/article/pii/S2214629614000632
11. J. Du, T. Mickiewicz. Journal of Business Venturing, **31**,1:22–38(2015). https://www.sciencedirect.com/science/article/abs/pii/S0883902615000622
12. C. Castiblanco, A. Moreno, A. Etter. Energy Economics, **49**:676–686(2015). https://www.sciencedirect.com/science/article/pii/S0140988315000997
13. RI (Republic of Indonesia). *Undang-undang no. 23 tahun 1999 tentang Bank Indonesia*. [Law no. 23/1999 on Central Bank]. Jakarta (1999). [in Bahasa Indonesia]. https://www.bi.go.id/id/tentang-bi/uu-bi/Documents/uu%20bi%2023%20th%2099.pdf
14. RI (Republic of Indonesia). *Undang-undang no. 3 tahun 2004 tentang Perubahan Undang-undang no. 23 tahun 1999 tentang Bank Indonesia* [Law no. 3/2004 on Amendment Law no. 23/1999 on Central Bank]. Jakarta (2004). [in Bahasa Indonesia]. https://www.bi.go.id/id/tentang-bi/uu-bi/Documents/uu_bi_no0304.pdf

APPENDIX

Table 1. NPV estimation.

Debtor Interest	Selling Electricity NPV (10^9 IDR)			Diesel Fuel Substitution NPV (10^9 IDR)		
	45 (t)	**60 (t)**	**75 (t)**	**45 (t)**	**60 (t)**	**75 (t)**
0.0 %	(0.94)	(6.60)	(55.91)	148.84	157.44	231.42
1.0 %	(0.26)	(7.61)	(58.05)	148.39	156.88	230.13
2.0 %	(0.41)	(8.62)	(60.20)	147.94	156.31	228.84
3.0 %	(1.08)	(9.63)	(62.34)	147.48	155.74	227.55
4.0 %	(1.76)	(10.64)	(64.49)	147.03	155.18	226.25
5.0 %	(2.43)	(11.65)	(66.63)	146.58	154.61	224.96
6.0 %	(3.11)	(12.66)	(68.78)	146.12	154.05	223.67
7.0 %	(3.78)	(13.67)	(70.92)	145.67	153.48	222.38
8.0 %	(4.46)	(14.68)	(73.06)	145.22	152.92	221.09
9.0 %	(5.13)	(15.69)	(75.21)	144.76	152.35	219.80
10.0 %	(5.80)	(16.70)	(77.35)	144.31	151.78	218.50
11.0 %	(6.48)	(17.71)	(79.50)	143.85	151.22	217.21
12.0 %	(7.15)	(18.72)	(81.64)	143.40	150.65	215.92
13.0 %	(7.83)	(19.73)	(83.79)	142.95	150.09	214.63
13.5 %	(8.16)	(20.23)	(84.86)	142.72	149.80	213.98

Table 2. IRR estimation.

Debtor Interest	Selling Electricity IRR			Diesel Fuel Substitution IRR		
	45 (t)	**60 (t)**	**75 (t)**	**45 (t)**	**60 (t)**	**75 (t)**
0.0 %	12.26	10.44	5.55	58.02	52.15	39.60
1.0 %	12.07	10.22	5.37	57.64	51.79	39.27
2.0 %	11.89	10.00	5.19	57.27	51.43	38.95
3.0 %	11.70	9.79	5.01	56.90	51.07	38.64
4.0 %	11.52	9.57	4.84	56.53	50.72	38.32
5.0 %	11.34	9.37	4.67	56.16	50.36	38.01
6.0 %	11.17	9.16	4.50	55.80	50.02	37.71
7.0 %	11.00	8.97	4.33	55.44	49.67	37.40
8.0 %	10.83	8.77	4.16	55.08	49.33	37.10
9.0 %	10.66	8.58	3.99	54.72	48.99	36.80
10.0 %	10.49	8.39	3.84	54.37	48.65	36.51
11.0 %	10.33	8.20	3.68	54.02	48.32	36.21
12.0 %	10.17	8.02	3.52	53.67	47.99	35.93
13.0 %	10.01	7.88	3.37	53.33	47.66	35.64
13.5 %	9.93	7.75	3.21	53.16	47.49	35.50

Table 3. ROI estimation

Debtor Interest	Selling Electricity ROI			Diesel Fuel Substitution ROI		
	45 (t)	**60 (t)**	**75 (t)**	**45 (t)**	**60 (t)**	**75 (t)**
0.0 %	54.32	47.45	28.12	121.62	115.01	96.47
1.0 %	53.64	46.58	27.27	121.27	114.63	96.02
2.0 %	52.97	45.73	26.43	120.92	114.25	95.58
3.0 %	52.31	44.89	25.60	120.57	113.87	95.14
4.0 %	51.65	44.06	24.78	120.22	113.50	94.70
5.0 %	51.00	43.24	23.97	119.87	113.12	94.26
6.0 %	50.35	42.43	23.17	119.52	112.75	93.83
7.0 %	49.71	41.62	22.38	119.18	112.38	93.40
8.0 %	49.07	40.83	21.61	118.83	112.01	92.96
9.0 %	48.44	40.04	20.84	118.49	111.64	92.53
10.0 %	47.82	39.26	20.08	118.14	111.27	92.11
11.0 %	47.20	38.50	19.33	117.80	110.90	91.68
12.0 %	46.58	37.74	18.59	117.46	110.54	91.26
13.0 %	45.97	36.98	17.86	117.12	110.17	90.84
13.5 %	45.67	36.61	17.50	116.95	109.99	90.63

Table 4. PI estimation.

Debtor Interest	Electricity Selling PI			Diesel Fuel Substitution PI		
	45 (t)	**60 (t)**	**75 (t)**	**45 (t)**	**60 (t)**	**75 (t)**
0.0 %	1.03	0.85	0.39	6.99	6.08	4.27
1.0 %	1.01	0.83	0.37	6.97	6.06	4.25
2.0 %	0.99	0.81	0.35	6.95	6.04	4.23
3.0 %	0.97	0.78	0.32	6.93	6.02	4.21
4.0 %	0.95	0.76	0.30	6.91	6.00	4.20
5.0 %	0.93	0.74	0.28	6.89	5.98	4.18
6.0 %	0.92	0.71	0.25	6.88	5.97	4.16
7.0 %	0.90	0.69	0.23	6.86	5.95	4.14
8.0 %	0.88	0.67	0.21	6.84	5.93	4.12
9.0 %	0.86	0.65	0.18	6.82	5.91	4.10
10.0 %	0.84	0.62	0.16	6.80	5.89	4.09
11.0 %	0.84	0.62	0.16	6.78	5.88	4.07
12.0 %	0.81	0.58	0.11	6.77	5.86	4.05
13.0 %	0.79	0.55	0.09	6.75	5.84	4.03
13.5 %	0.78	0.54	0.08	6.74	5.83	4.02

Table 5. Cost and benefit analysis of development of biogas reactor from POME (the benefit assumptions are for 20 yr with loan maturities of 5 yr).

No.	Indicators	45 t Palm Oil Fresh Fruit Bunches	60 t Palm Oil Fresh Fruit Bunches	75 t Palm Oil Fresh Fruit Bunches
1.	Initial cost-selling price of electricty (IDR)	42 396 678 573	44 196 687 578	92 220 853 048
2.	Initial cost- saving from diesel fuel (IDR)	29 581 284 210	31 018 593 375	70 806 449 968
3.	Loan period (Year)	5	5	5
4.	Interest Rate by Bank	13.5 %	13.5 %	13.5 %
5.	Simulation			
	Assumption for electricity selling price			
	Cost (C)(IDR)	137 122 560 225	146 746 347 401	293 578 389 012
	Benefit (B) (IDR)	236 398 939 765	254 359 349 049	434 552 531 685
	Net benefit (IDR)	99 276 379 540	107 613 001 648	140 974 142 673
	B per C Ratio (BCR)	1.72	1.73	1.48
	Feasibility (if BCR > 1)	Feasible	Feasible	Feasible
	CO2 Emission Reduction (Ton)	826 818.86	890 604.30	1 447 231.98
	Assumption from saving diesel fuel			
	Cost (C)(IDR)	186 035 035 800	192 966 778 018	370 321 553 481
	Benefit (B) (IDR)	507 344 753 694	526 585 561 403	849 405 525 155
	Net benefit (IDR)	321 309 717 894	333 618 783 385	479 083 971 674
	B per C Ratio (BCR)	2.73	2.73	2.29
	Feasibility (if BCR > 1)	Feasible	Feasible	Feasible
	CO2 Emission Reduction (Ton)	826 818.86	890 604.30	1 447 231.98

Web-Based Robotics Laboratory

Petrus Santoso[1,*], *Handry* Khoswanto[1], and *Iwan* Njoto Sandjaja[2]

[1]Department of Electrical Engineering. Petra Christian University, Siwalankerto, Wonocolo, Surabaya, East Java, 60236, Indonesia
[2]Department of Informatics Engineering, Petra Christian University, Siwalankerto, Wonocolo, Surabaya, East Java, 60236, Indonesia

Abstract. In the education world, the number of web-based system is growing substantially in the past few years. Many web-based teaching tools has been developed to help students expand his knowledge. This paper presents a web-based laboratory to augment learning experiences in the field of robotics. The designed laboratory consists of a robotic arm with laser pointer, projection platform and web-based interface. The laboratory is used to learn about inverse kinematics and forward kinematics problems. Students enter the input parameters through web interface, server calculate output parameters and sent it to the robot. The web interface displays the movement result and turn on the laser pointer to the projection field. Preliminary testing concerning interface usability, access control mechanism and command queueing shows that the system working as expected.

Key words: Laboratory, robotics, web-based.

1 Introduction

Quoting Sir Tim Berners—Lee, "The web is a tremendous platform for innovation, but we face a number of challenges to making it more useful, in particular to people in underserved communities." This statement is given when Sir Tim Berners—Lee announce that he is backing a new project called The World Wide Web Foundation in 2008. The Foundation aims to accelerate the progress of the internet and make it more easily available and accessible in developing nations [1]. In the same spirit, many institutions develop web-based system to be used in our everyday life aspects. In the field of education, a lot of web-based systems have been developed for various purposes. For example: information system, online course, user collaboration, assessment mechanism, and also web-based laboratory (remote experimentation).

Concerning web-based laboratory, the facilities can be offered in three forms [2], namely: Virtual laboratory, remote "hands-on" laboratory, and Hybrid laboratory. Virtual laboratory is simulated version of physical laboratory. The simulation software is executed in the server. There is no actual equipment involved in this kind of laboratory. In remote "hands-on" laboratory, the web gives an interface to the user to manipulate equipment in the physical laboratory. Hybrid laboratory combines both forms of laboratory. User can choose between accessing the simulated version of laboratory or having hands-on experience with physical equipment via web interface.

In the field of robotics, many prototype of internet/web-based robotics laboratories have been implemented. There are internet-based online robot demonstration such as University of Southern California (USC) Mercury and Tele-Garden projects [3–6]. It can be classified as remote "hands-on" laboratory. In the project, an arm robot is operated remotely. The Mercury project consist of an arm robot fitted with charge-coupled device (CCD) camera operated in a sandbox. Tele-Garden allows users to view and interact with a remoted garden filled with living plants. There is also TORUS (Toys Operated Remotely for Understanding Science) project [7]. Beside controlling robot, the project aim is to add remote programming feature of robot.

There is also a study about the feasibility of remote experimentation as part of distance learning mechanism. It is called project ReLAX (Remote Laboratory Experimentation Trial) [8]. It supports the argumentation that the presence of Internet makes remote experimentation feasible. Experiments on real physical equipment can be more affordable and usage of existing laboratory facilities can be more efficient.

*Corresponding author: petrus@petra.ac.id

Most of the mentioned examples involve the operation of robot remotely (teleoperation of robot). It also includes visualization of remote site. Basically, it characterized some form of telepresence mechanism. Telepresence refer to the ability to be present or participate in a distance location without actually being there physically [9]. From several examples about web-based laboratory projects we realize a need to incorporate the laboratory into our robotic course. We conduct a research about web-based robotics laboratory with remote "hands-on" experience. Our objective is to implement a full-scale web-based robotics laboratory with multi-user and multi-robot schema. The aim is to foster ubiquity in engineering education in order to increase student's participation and collaboration in learning. The first prototype result of our web-based robotics laboratory is presented in this paper. Description about the design elaborated after this introduction. It followed by description of experiment to test our prototype, result presentation and discussion.

2 Design

The architectural design of web-based robotics laboratory adopts client-server mechanism. Communication between client and server is done with Hypertext Transfer Protocol (HTTP). Figure 1 depicts the architecture of the system.

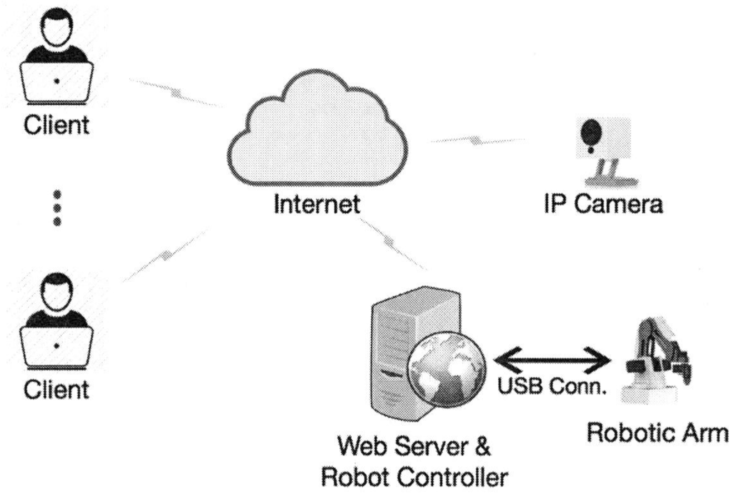

Fig. 1. System architecture.

The main system parts are web server and the controlled robot, for example a robotic arm. Web server also functions as robot controller. Communication between robot controller and robotic arm is done via USB connection. To present robot movements to the user, one or more IP camera are installed in the system. Users access the web-based laboratory via browser client. Multi user can access the server to monitor the robot, but only single user can control the movement of robot at a certain time. Each user has to logon to the system in order to control the robot. Monitoring can be done in guest mode. Figure 2 depicts the design of interface example accessed by browser client. The shown example is concerning about inverse kinematic experiment.

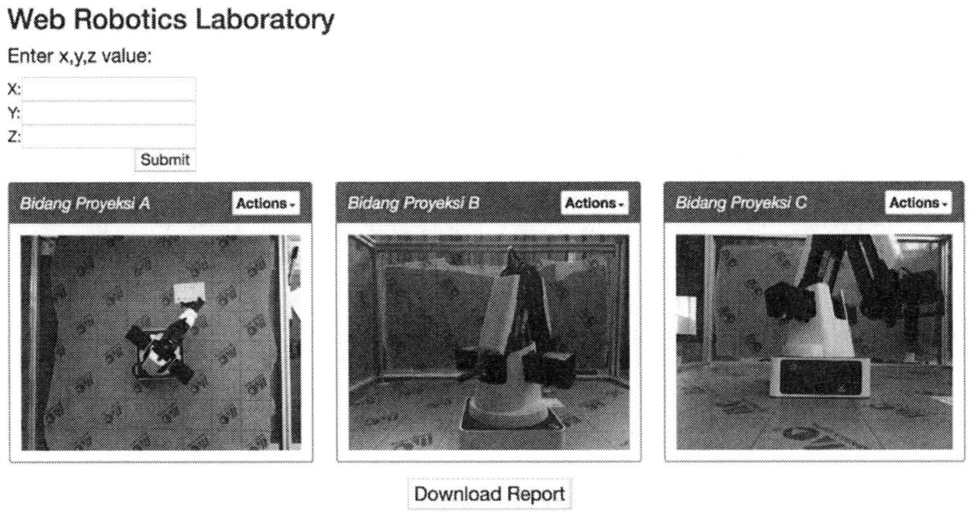

Fig. 2. Interface design.

The interface consists of a form to submits input parameter and robot monitoring area with video streaming feature. After user submits the input parameters, server does a calculation and sends movement commands to the robot. At the end of movement process, server also send command to turn on laser pointer in the robot to visualize robot position in the projection field. Calculation result can be downloaded by user. Internet Protocol (IP) cameras send video streams to the browser client. In this example, there are three IP cameras that represents three projection fields.

Concerning software design, there are two main things need to be addressed properly. The first one is about communication protocol between robot controller and the controlled robot. The protocol should be designed to accommodate various kind of robot. The second one is about access control mechanism. It should accommodate multiple users accessing a single/multiple robot.

To accommodate communication flexibility with various kind of robot. A protocol framework is built based on [9]. The service primitives are grouped into three service elements, namely *movement*, *monitoring* and *auxiliary*. Movement service element deals with the movement of the robot. Monitoring service element handle video monitoring of the robot. Auxiliary service element is used to present command request status and any additional service defined later.

To accommodate multiple users accessing a single/multiple robot, a queue mechanism is built. Commands sent to the robot will be executed one by one with first come first served based mechanism. The queue mechanism makes use of a database system. Each command request from the user entered in the database to form a queue. Each entry has a status flag to represent execution state of command request. System executes each command request in the database in first come first served manner. Figure 3 depicts the prototype of the system. There are still works to be done, but it can represent the proposed system. A single projection field and single laser pointer implemented in this prototype.

Fig. 3. System prototype.

3 Experiment

Some experiments have been done to consider the feasibility of deploying our web-based robotics laboratory prototype in the real application. The first experiment is about the usability of the interface. There are two things considered important in this experiment, namely task completion rate and user satisfaction. The conduct of the experiment is as follow, several users are asked to complete an activity. The activity consists of working on kinematics problem and verify the work using web-based robotics laboratory. At this experiment, access to the server is limited only for a single user each time. All the steps taken by the user is logged in the system. After completing the activity, the completion rate is measured based on the log file. The user also asked to give score to the following questions:

i). Satisfaction with the ease of completing task
ii). Satisfaction with the time of completing task
iii). Satisfaction with the support information during completing task

The score value comes between 1 to 7, with 1 valued as strongly agree and valued as strongly disagree. This scoring method is based on the After-Scenario Questionnaire [10, 11] to rate user satisfaction working with the interface of web-based robotics laboratory. The second experiment is concerning server performance and queue performance. Server performance measured based on the presence of congestion. Queue performance is measured based on the availability of queue slot. To perform the experiment, several users are asked to do an activity with web-based robotics laboratory. There is no limitation on how many users accessing the server each time. The users perform their activity simultaneously in a certain timeframe. In their activity, each user sends several command requests to the server. In this experiment, the expected data results are:

i). Measurement of time needed to execute each command request to the robot.
ii). Number of requests entering the database queue in a certain time.

4 Result and discussion

There are ten users involved in the first experiment. Each user is asked to solve some mathematical problems on kinematics. In the experiment, there are five problems each on forward kinematics and inverse kinematics. The user solved the problem manually, after that, they work with the web-based robotics laboratory to verify the result. There are two kinds of results on the first experiment; task completion rate for each problem and user satisfaction. Task completion rate result is depicted on Table 1. User satisfaction result is depicted on Table 2.

Table 1. Task completion rate

Problem No	Task Completion Rate (%)	Note
1	100	-
2	100	-
3	90	One user failed to finish the problem
4	100	-
5	100	-
6	100	-
7	90	One user failed to finish the problem
8	90	One user failed to finish the problem
9	100	-
10	100	-
Average	**97**	

Table 1 shows that from ten given problem, one user failed to finish problem no 3, 7 and 8. In the log file of the system there are no finish flag in the recorded activities of the corresponding user for the specified problem. When the issue tracked, the user mentioned that there is an intermittent internet connection that affect the video streaming at that time. To address the problem, there should be another mechanism to present visualization of the robot to the user. It is considered to present robot position in the form of time-lapsed image of the robot.

Table 2. User satisfaction

Question	Mean Score
Satisfaction with the ease of completing task	1.32 ± 0.64
Satisfaction with the time of completing task	1.61 ± 0.64
Satisfaction with the support information during completing task	2.54 ± 1.30
Overall score	$\mathbf{1.82 \pm 0.86}$

Table 2 shows a quite good overall score dealing with user satisfaction with web-based robotics laboratory. The score is in the range of 1 to 7, with lower number is the better result. The highest score is concerning the easiness of task completion. Most of the user gives score 1 or 2 about easiness of task completion parameter. The lowest score is about support information during task completion. It is considered as a good score, because there is still little support information available at the time of the experiment.

The second experiment is done in a duration of one hour. There are ten users simultaneously accessing the server. Table 3 depicts the result of average execution time for each command send to the server. Figure 4 depicts the number of command in the queue along the time duration of the experiment.

Table 3. Average execution time

	No of Commands	Average Execution Time (s)
First Quarter	12	6.8
Second Quarter	12	7.2
Third Quarter	11	6.3
Fourth Quarter	7	5.8

From Table 3, it can be seen that the time average for each command execution is less than 8 s. The result is observed every 15 min. It shows that there is no significant deviation from the average value. It means that there is no congestion in the server.

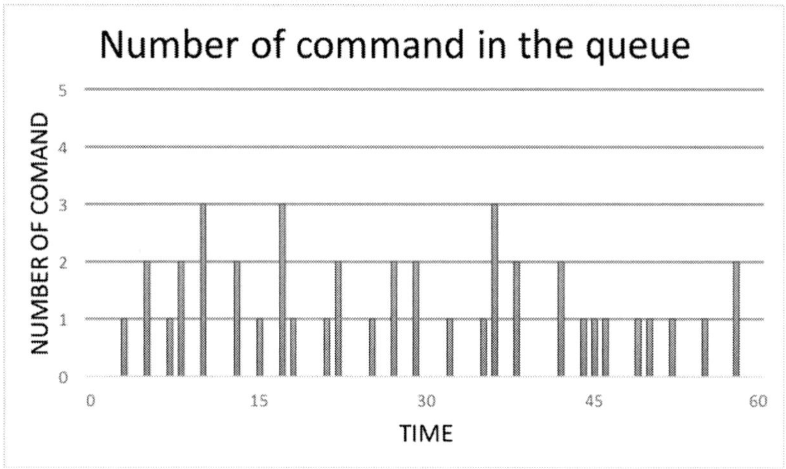

Fig. 4. Command queue.

Figure 4 also confirm that there is no congestion in the server. The largest number in the queue is only 3 at a certain time. The queue mechanism is work quite well. To be more certain, larger experiment must be performed with more user active simultaneously.

5 Conclusion

The web-based robotics laboratory depicted in this paper still has a lot of work to be done. Based on the experiment result, the web interface can be accessed with relative ease. Most command can be executed and the result shown in the interface under 8 s. The queue for robot command has been tested. Testing result showed that maximum value of occupied slots at the given time is only 3. Further testing of web-based laboratory with multiple robots and bigger user capacity still can be done in the future. There are still room for feature improvement in the web-based robotics laboratory. For visualization purpose, there is a need of better mechanism to visualize the robot position in 3D space beside video streaming.

This research is funded by Applied Product Research fund of Indonesian Higher Education Directorate under contract no. 19/SP2H/PDSTRL_PEN/LPPM-UKP/V/2017.

References

1. J. Swaine. *Internet is fostering disinformation, says web's creator.* [Online] from http://www.telegraph.co.uk/technology/3358458/Internet-is-fostering-disinformation-says-webs-creator.html (2008). [Accessed on 1 October 2017].
2. L. Gomes, S. Bogosyan. IEEE Transactions on industrial electronics, **56**(12):4744–4756 (2009). http://ieeexplore.ieee.org/stamp/stamp.jsp?arnumber=5280206
3. K. Goldberg. Algorithmic Foundations of Robotics **VI**:11–16 (2005). https://link.springer.com/chapter/10.1007/10991541_2
4. K. Goldberg, D. Song. *Networked Robotic Cameras for Collaborative Observation of Natural Environments.* International Symposium of Robotics Research (ISRR), 12–15 October (San Francisco, 2005). *Robitcs Research*, pp. 510–519 (2007). https://link.springer.com/chapter/10.1007/978-3-540-48113-3_43
5. S. J. Lu, B.M. Chen, C.C. Ko, S.T. Kee. *Web-based Robot for Remote Experiments*. Proceedings of International Conference on Control and Automation, ICCA, 10–12 June (Montreal, 2003). pp. 158-162 (2003). http://ieeexplore.ieee.org/stamp/stamp.jsp?arnumber=1595004
6. R.C. Luo, K.L. Su, S.H. Shen, K.H. Tsai. *Networked Intelligent Robots Through the Internet: Issues and Opportunities*. Proceedings of the IEEE **91**(3):371–382 (2003). http://ieeexplore.ieee.org/stamp/stamp.jsp?arnumber=1192265
7. G.T. McKee. International Journal of Engineering Education, **19**(3):356-362 (2003). https://www.researchgate.net/publication/228561418_An_Online_robot_system_for_projects_in_robot_intelligence
8. C.S. Tzafestas, N. Palaiologou, and M. Alifragis, IEEE Transactions on education, **49**(3):360-369 (2006). http://ieeexplore.ieee.org/stamp/stamp.jsp?tp=&arnumber=1668280
9. P. Santoso, H. Khoswanto. ARPN J. Eng. Appl. Sci., **9**(12):2437–2440 (2014). http://www.arpnjournals.com/jeas/research_papers/rp_2014/jeas_1214_1352.pdf
10. J.R. Lewis. International Journal of Human-Computer Interaction. **7(1)**, 57–78 (1995). http://www.tandfonline.com/doi/abs/10.1080/10447319509526110
11. J. Sauro, J.S. Dumas. *Comparison of three one-question, post-task usability questionnaires*. Proceedings of the SIGCHI Conference on Human Factors in Computing Systems, CHI, 4–9 April (Boston, 2009). pp. 1599–1608 (2009). https://dl.acm.org/citation.cfm?id=1518946

Biomass and Sugar Content of Some Varieties of Sorghum (*Sorghum Bicolor* L. Moench) on Dry Land Forest as Feedstock Bioethanol

Praptiningsih Gamawati Adinurani[1*], *Sri* Rahayu[1], *Luluk* Sulistiyo Budi[1], *Anggi* Nindita[2], *Peeyush* Soni[3], and *Maizirwan* Mel[4]

[1]Faculty of Agriculture, Merdeka University of Madiun, Jl. Serayu No.79, Pandean, Madiun, Jawa Timur 63133, Indonesia
[2]Department of Agronomy and Horticulture, Faculty of Agriculture, Bogor Agriculture University, Jl. Meranti, Bogor, 16680, Indonesia
[3]Departement of Food, Agriculture and Bioresources, School of Environment, Resources and Development, Asian Institute of Technology, PO Box 4, Klong Luang Pathumthani 12120, Thailand.
[4]Department of Biotechnology Engineering, International Islamic University Malaysia, Jalan Gombak, Kuala Lumpur 53100, Selangor, Malaysia

Abstract. The possibility of sustainable use of sorghum as raw material for bioethanol needs to be supported by evaluation and selection of sorghum varieties for high biomass production and sugar content. An experiment was conducted on forest dry land , altitude 63 m asl. This research aimed to determine the interaction of sorghum varieties and mycorrhiza on biomass production and the high sugar content. The experiment was a two factor (varieties and dosage of mycorrhiza plus) in a randomized complete block design with three replications. The varieties were Suri 3, Kawali, Super 2, Suri 4. Dosage of mycorrhiza plus (5, 10, 15) g per plant. The interaction only significant on a number of internodes and bagasse. There are no effects of dosages mycorrhiza plus, however, varieties of sorghum have significant effects on many variables measured. The highest amount of biomass include the stem height (301.28 cm), stem Dry Weight (DW) is 23.48 t ha^{-1}, leaf DW (4.65 t ha^{-1}), panicle DW (11.35 t ha^{-1}) and biomass DW (39.98 t ha^{-1}) were obtained in varieties Super 2. Sugar content (16.93 %) was obtained in varieties Suri 3 and juice production (2 742.86 L ha^{-1}) in varieties Suri 4.

Keywords: Biomass, sorghum, sugar content, varieties.

1 Introduction

Since the Government of Indonesia has made it mandatory to blend bioethanol and fossil fuels increases the need for bioethanol. Sweet sorghum (*Sorghum bicolor* L. Moench) is a possible candidate for a renewable source of bioethanol. Sweet sorghum is a multiple-purpose crop which has been consumed as either food [1] or feed [2], and industrially cultivated for liquid sugar and ethanol production [3, 4]. Sweet sorghum has been identified as an energy commodity for high sugar content in stem [5, 6]. Sugar content in the juice of sweet sorghum stalks ranging from (8 to 20) % [7] and is capable of producing ethanol (6 000 to 7 000) L ha^{-1} [8, 9]. In Indonesia, the ability of sorghum to produce ethanol ranges between (3 000 to 6 600) L ha^{-1} [10]. The production costs of biofuel from sweet sorghum are cheaper than that from sugarcane in the USA [11]. Ethanol production is determined by the production of biomass and sugar content in stem [12, 10]. Among the parts of the sorghum, stems give contributed most to produce juice as bioethanol feedstock. The average productivity of sorghum stalks ranges (30 to 50) t ha^{-1} and leaf (20 to 40) t ha^{-1} [13].

Sorghum has great potential to be cultivated and developed commercially because it has wide adaptability, high productivity, relatively little input, resistant to pests and plant diseases, drought tolerant, salinity and sour landly [14, 15]. Therefore, efforts to explore the potential of sweet sorghum as a feedstock for ethanol that cultivated on the forest land and popularization of sweet sorghum varieties.

*Corresponding author: praptiningsih.ga@gmail.com

The Vesicular-Arbuscular Mycorrhizal (VAM) is a mutualistic symbiosis between fungi and the roots of plants. Also improved P nutrition by VAM fungi during the periods of water deficit has been postulated as a primary mechanism for enhancing host plant drought tolerance and assists host plants to use N-forms [16] and potential to increase the growth and productivity of plants, especially on marginal lands. The purpose of this research is to know the productivity of biomass and sugar content of several varieties of sorghum cultivated in the forest land.

2 Methods

2.1 Field location

The experiment was conducted at the forest land area village Kampung Baru District of Saradan Madiun, with a height of 63 m asl (above sea level). Soil characteristics consist of C-Organic = 1.59 %; N-total = 1.15 %; C/N ratio = 1.5; P_20_5 available = 86.75 mg kg^{-1}; P_20_5 total = 269.64 mg kg^{-1} and pH 5.37.

2.2 Experimental design

This experiment was arranged in the randomized complete block design (RCBD) with two factors in three replications. The first factor was varieties of sorghum, the varieties consist of Suri 3 (V1), Kawali (V2), Super 2 (V3) and Suri 4 (V4). The second factor was dosage of mycorrhiza plus in three levels, 5g per plant (D1), 10g per plant (D2), and 15 g per plant (D3). The mycorrhiza plus contains mycorrhiza endogen i.e.*Trichoderma* sp., *Pseudomonas fluorescent* and *Bacillus subtilis*.

2.3 Statistical analysis

Analysis of variance (ANOVA) and means comparisons were computed by Statistical Packages for The Social Sciences (SPSS). Duncan range test was used to analyze significant differences between treatments and its combinations.

3 Results and discussion

Analysis of variance showed that combination treatments between sorghum varieties and Mychorrhizal dosage are tended to differ among treatments combination. This resulted in a number of internodes and bagasse fresh weight (Table 1).

Table 1. Sorghum varieties and Mychorrizal means interactions of internode number and bagasse fresh weight.

Treatment Combination	Number of internodes	Bagasse Fresh Weight (t ha^{-1})
V1D1	8.67 abc	90.9 abc
V1D2	8.00 ab	146.4 cde
V1D3	7.11 ab	150.63 cde
V2D1	10.78 bc	122.60 bc
V2D2	8.66 abc	81.27 ab
V2D3	8.0 ab	127.70 bcd
V3D1	11.44.c	62.33 a
V3D2	11.77 c	188.60 ef
V3D3	10.67 bc	96.00 abc
V4D1	9.00 abc	182.00def
V4D2	7.67 ab	104.07 abc
V4D3	9.44 abc	210.00 f

Note: Mean followed by the same letter are not significantly different based on Duncan range test at 0.5 level.

High bagasse fresh weight of sorghum (210 t ha^{-1}) was resulted from treatments combination of V4D3 that is variety of Suri 4 and mychorriza 15 g per plant. This suggests that these varieties are more responsive to mycorrhizal inoculation and respond to mycorrhizal level of treatments. Plant response to mycorrhizal application was affected mainly depends from varieties. Varieties Suri 3 (V1), Super 2 (V3), and Suri 4 (V4) elucidated more responsive result to mychorrizal plus in 15 g per plant of dose. According to [17] it was stated that plant root infections by mychorriza are determined by the compatibility between the plant and mychorriza. The presence of mychorriza has more advantage in the absorption of water and nutrients especially in phosphorus content, therefore resulted to increase the growth and production of plant especially in bagasse weight. The research result of [10] elucidated that 1 kg of bagasse produces (1.29 to 2.13) mL of ethanol depending on sorghum varieties. Variation result of ethanol content indicate a difference in cellulose and lignin content. It was stated [18] that stem baggage of sweet sorghum contains 45 % cellulose, 27 % hemicellulose, and 21 % lignin which can be converted to 5 804 kg of ethanol per ha. The differences in cellulose, lignin and other ingredients content in sorghum, provide a probability to affect the effectiveness of fermentation that affects ethanol production. Another attempt to use sweet sorghum stem bagasse as bioethanol feedstock can be done by enzymatic or acid hydrolysis method [19]. Therefore it can be said that bagasse is one of the criteria for selection of selection of sorghum varieties that potentially produce ethanol. The yield of ethanol was higher than that of the stem sap between (8.6 to 14.2) % and the ethanol estimate of the fermented bagasse between (4.056 to 9.166) L ha^{-1} [10].

Application of mycorrhizal dose plus only has no significant different to all variables. This means that the dose of mycorrhizal plus given has the same effect on the observed plant variables. This is because the dose interval between treatments is only a slight difference so that the effect is no different. The sorghum varieties independently had significant effect on stem height (Table 2), stem Dry Weight (DW), leaf DW, panicle DW and total biomass (Table 3) but not significantly on stem diameter and volume of sap (Table 4).

Table 2. Sorghum variety mean of stem height and stem diameter.

Varieties	Stem height (cm)	Stem diameter (cm)
V1	268.03 b	1.27
V2	192.38 a	1.44
V3	301.28 b	1.39
V4	181.29 a	1.40
		ns

Note: ns = not significantly different; mean followed by the same letter are not significantly different based on the Duncan test at 0.5 level.

Table 3. Variety means of stem DW, leaf DW, panicle DW and total of biomass DW.

Varieties	Stem DW (t ha^{-1})	Leaf DW (t ha^{-1})	Panicle DW (t ha^{-1})	Total of biomass DW (t ha^{-1})
V1	18.07 bc	3.29 a	9.54 bc	30.90 b
V2	15.26 b	4.35 b	8.04 ab	28.11 b
V3	23.48 c	4.65 b	11.35 c	39.98 c
V4	9.27 a	2.89 a	7.12 a	19.57 a

Note: mean followed by the same letter are not significantly different based on the Duncan test at 0.5 level.

Table 4. Variety means of sugar content and juice production.

Varieties	Sugar content (brix, %)	Juice production (L ha^{-1})
Suri 3	16.93 b	2165.08
Kawali	14.38 b	1917.47
Super 2	14.44 b	1415.88
Suri 4	10.39 a	2742.86
		ns

Note: mean followed by the same letter are not significantly different based on the Duncan test at 0.5 level.

Variety of Super 2 (V3) has the highest stem that is 301.28 cm (Table 2) and followed by a high number of total biomass (Table 3), as stated at [20] that plant height is directly proportional to biomass. From 4 different varieties, variety of Super 2 (V3) has the highest result of the dry weight of stem, dry weight of leaf, dry weight of panicle and total of biomass. Biomass potential as an ethanol feedstock varies according to the content of cellulose and hemicellulose that can be converted to simple sugars. But not so with the juice production, the lowest Super 2 varieties are 1415.88 L ha^{-1} (Table 4). The results showed that the sugar content was not directly proportional to the amount of juice produced. This is because there are several factors that affect the production of sap, among others, stem height, stem diameter, harvest time, varieties and sugar content in the sorghum stem.

According to [21] that the sugar content in the stems of the sorghum plant varies for each variety, depending on the environmental conditions, the position of the stem segment, and the stages of the harvest time. The sugar content of the four varieties varied between (10.39 to 16.93) %, the highest on the Suri 3 (V1) varieties (Table 4). The difference between sugar content and its composition in some sweet sorghum varieties will affect the variation of ethanol yield [22, 23].

4 Conclusion

In this experiment, the variety of sorghum tends to differ at 0.5 level from statistical analysis of variance and means comparison. Variety Super 2 (V3) has high total of biomass, this resulted variety Super 2 is potential as a raw material for bioethanol production. Variety of Suri 3 (V1) has the highest sugar content, meanwhile, variety of Suri 4 has the highest juice production.

References

[1] A. Almodares, R. Taheri, S. Adeli. J. Malesian Appl. Bio, **37**:31–36(2008). http://www.mabjournal.com/index.php?option=com_content&view=article&id=335&catid=59:current-view&Itemid=56

[2] H. Fazaeli, H.A. Golmohhammadi, A. Almodares, S. Mosharraf, A. Shaei. Pakistan J. Biol. Sci., **9**:2450–2455(2006). http://docsdrive.com/pdfs/ansinet/pjbs/2006/2450-2455.pdf

[3] A. Almodares, R. Taheri, Chung, M. Fathi. J. Environ. Biol, **29**:849–852(2008). https://pdfs.semanticscholar.org/4cf9/2f2fff743f33372f6e894d3b856cae4830b3.pdf

[4] B.V.S. Reddy, S. Ramesh, P.S. Reddy, B. Ramaiah, P.M. Salimath, R. Kachapur. Int. Sorghum Millets Newslett, **46**:79–86(2005). http://oar.icrisat.org/1234/1/ISMN-46_79-86_2005.pdf

[5] J. Yu, X. Zhang, T. Tan. Biomass and Bioenergy **33**,3:521–526(2009). https://www.researchgate.net/publication/248353675_Optimization_of_media_conditions_for_the_production_of_ethanol_from_sweet_sorghum_juice_by_immobilized_Saccharomyces_cerevisiae

[6] C.S. Wortmann, T. Regassa. *Sweet sorghum as a bioenergy crop for the US great plains*. Lincoln, USA: Department of Agronomy and Horticulture, University of Nebraska-Lincoln (2011). pp. 16. https://www.intechopen.com/books/economic-effects-of-biofuel-production/sweet-sorghum-as-a-bioenergy-crop-for-the-us-great-plains/

[7] G.C. Rains, J.S. Cundiff, D.H. Vaughan. Trans. ASAE **33**,1:56–62(1990). https://www.researchgate.net/profile/Glen_Rains/publication/259971357_Development_of_a_Whole-Stalk_Sweet_Sorghum_Harvester/links/5655cbeb08aeafc2aabdda63/Development-of-a-Whole-Stalk-Sweet-Sorghum-Harvester.pdf

[8] FAO. *Sweet sorghum in China*. Department Agriculture and consumer protection, Food agricultural organization of United Nations (2002). http://www.fao.org/ag/portal/index_en.html

[9] H.B. Dinesh, M.R.G. Rao, A.M. Rao, S.J.S. Naik, H.N. Chetan, C.S. Shantharaja. Research Journal of Agricultural Sciences, **4**,2:184–187(2013). https://www.researchgate.net/profile/Shantharaja_Shivanna/publication/281446275_Evaluation_of_Sweet_Sorghum_Sorghum_bicolor_L_Moench_Cultivars_for_Ethanol_Yield_as_an_Alternate_Source_for_Bio-energy/links/55e7e4bb08ae3e1218421628/Evaluation-of-Sweet-Sorghum-Sorghum-bicolor-L-Moench-Cultivars-for-Ethanol-Yield-as-an-Alternate-Source-for-Bio-energy.pdf

[10] M.B. Pabendon, S. Mas'ud, R.S. Sarungallo, A. Nur. Jurnal Penelitian Pertanian Tanaman Pangan, **31**,1:60–69(2012). [In Bahasa Indonesia]. http://www.ejurnal.litbang.pertanian.go.id/index.php/jpptp/article/view/2880

[11] P. Tamang. *Nitrogen fertilizer requirements for ethanol production from sweet and photoperiod sensitive sorghums in the Texas southern high plains*. [Thesis]. Master of Science Texas Tech University (2010). https://www.researchgate.net/profile/Parikshya_Lama_Tamang2/publication/284690437_Nitrogen_fertilizer_requirements_for_ethanol_production_from_sweet_and_fodder_quality_of_forage_sorghum_Sorghum_bicolor_L_Moench/links/5691ef4408ae0f920dcb92cb/Nitrogen-fertilizer-requirements-for-ethanol-production-from-sweet-and-fodder-quality-of-forage-sorghum-Sorghum-bicolor-L-Moench.pdf

[12] K.J. Han, W.D. Pitman, M. Kim, D.F. Day, M.W. Alison, M.M. Cormick, et al. GCB Bioenergy, 1–9(2012). http://www.lsuagcenter.com/MCMS/RelatedFiles/%7BBE72439E-FBE9-4011-B6F1-C3D1A5BD03DA%7D/Ethanol-production.pdf

[13] A. Almodares, M.R. Hadi. African J. Agri. **4**,9:772–780(2009). http://www.academicjournals.org/journal/AJAR/article-full-text-pdf/6DDEDD738826
[14] M.B. Pabendon, M. Aqil, S. Mas'ud. Iptek Tanaman Pangan, **7**,2:123–129(2012). [In Bahasa Indonesia]. http://pangan.litbang.pertanian.go.id/files/07-Marcia.pdf
[15] J.S. McLaren, N, Lakey, J. Osborne. *Sorghum as a bioresources platform for future renewable resources*. Proceeding 57th Corn and Sorghum Research Conference, CD ROM, 11–13 December 2002 (Illinois, Chicago, 2002). Alexandria, VA, USA: American Seed Trade Association (2003). http://www.worldcat.org/title/proceedings-of-fifty-seventh-annual-corn-sorghum-seed-research-conference-and-proceedings-of-thirty-second-annual-soybean-seed-research-conference/oclc/54070386&referer=brief_results
[16] K.S. Subramanian, P. Santhanakrishnan, P. Balasubramanian. Scientia Horticulturae **107**:245–253(2006). https://www.sciencedirect.com/journal/scientia-horticulturae/vol/107/issue/3
[17] A. Tapwal, R. Kumar, D. Borah. Current Life Sciences, **2**,1:1–8(2016). http://www.journals.tmkarpinski.com/index.php/cls/article/view/366/197
[18] M. Kim, D.F. Day. Journal of Industrial Microbiology and Biotechnology, **38**,7:803–807(2011). https://www.ncbi.nlm.nih.gov/pubmed/20803247
[19] A.M. Kartini, E.S. Pandebesie. Jurnal Purifikasi, **16**,2:118–129(2016). [In Bahasa Indonesia]. http://www.purifikasi.net/index.php/purifikasi/article/download/43/41/
[20] S. Mathur, A.V. Umakhant, V.A. Tonapi, R. Sharma, M.K. Sharma. Biotechnol Biofuels, **10**,146:1–19(2017). https://biotechnologyforbiofuels.biomedcentral.com/articles/10.1186/s13068-017-0834-9
[21] H.A. Qazi, S. Paranjpe, S. Bhargava. J Plant Physiol, **169**,6:605–13(2012). https://www.ncbi.nlm.nih.gov/pubmed/22325624
[22] Y.L. Zhao, A. Dolat, Y. Steinberger, X. Wang, A. Osman, G. H. Xie. Crop Science, **111**,1–2:55–64(2009). https://www.cabdirect.org/cabdirect/abstract/20093080407
[23] T.W. Pfeiffer, M.J. Bitzer, J.J. Toy, J.F. Pedersen. Crop Science, **50**,5:1788–1794(2010). https://pdfs.semanticscholar.org/a235/b0bad3a4e08221bbf310769701f89658d169.pdf

A Mathematical Proof Concerning the Geometrical Aspect of Very Low Index of Difficulty in Multidirectional Tapping Task of the ISO 9241 - Part 411

Reyna Marsya Quita*, and *Romy* Budhi Widodo

Ma Chung University, Informatics Department, Villa Puncak Tidar N-01 Malang, 65151, Indonesia

Abstract. Through mathematics, this paper works to analyse the Index of Difficulty in ISO9241-Part 411: Evaluation methods for the design of physical input devices. It was proven that all the target circles always intersect for very low Index of Difficulty; which conjectured to disturb the experiment or affect the focus of the subject. Some examples are provided, in addition, to support the proof. We hope this proof will contribute to the improvement of ISO9241, where the result might become a special attention to the designer of the experiment in human-computer interaction field; especially in checking the influence of overlap area in the human factor.

Key words: Fitts' law, Human-computer interaction evaluation, Index of difficulty, ISO 9241

1 Introduction

The existence of ISO standard helps the researchers in evaluating pointing devices. In 2012, ISO published ISO/TS 9241-Part 411 that named Ergonomics of human-system interaction: Evaluation methods for the design of physical input devices. This standard helps the researchers to adopt a uniform measurement and avoid the bias of the results; also establish procedures of testing for evaluating pointing devices created by different companies.

The value of ISO9241 standard already widely known by academic researchers. Various studies already apply this standard as a guideline for evaluating non-keyboard input devices. Norman and Norman [1] compared the characteristics of remote pointing devices, i.e. relative versus absolute pointing devices; as an evaluating criterion instrument, they used ISO 9241-9. In [2], Natapov, et al. also use this standard as a basis for comparison between Wii remote and Wii classic controller. MacKenzie, et al. [3] explained theoretical basis, computational techniques and the evaluation of four devices (mouse, trackball, joystick, and touch pad) to validate the measurement; where the tool to evaluate the performance was using ISO 9241-9. Oh, et al. [4] wanted to make an interface with multiuser using modified laser pointer and compare it with the mouse as the baseline; the

* Corresponding author: reynaquita2905@gmail.com

performance evaluation and comparison according to ISO9241-9 standard also presented. In [5], Widodo, et al. was investigating the performance of two laser spot clicking techniques. They also used ISO/TS 9241-411 procedure as a quantitate performance test based on Fitts' one-direction tapping test. Generally speaking, all of these previous papers used ISO 9241 as a basis for evaluating the performance of pointing devices. Evidently, based on these works, ISO has become the attention of the researchers; which make the importance of ISO as the measuring standard is undeniable.

ISO suggested a variety of range of difficulties to test the input devices, which called Index of Difficulty (ID). The ranges of difficulties are high, medium, low, and very low. A problem emerges when a very low range is applied in circular order for multi-directional tapping task; the issue is the appearance of intersection area between targets circles. By cause of this overlapping, it seems ambiguous which next target to be reached; it is surmised that the intersection affects the focus of the subject in tapping test. It implies the effectiveness and efficiency of this paradigm are vague. This intersection develops after some cases had been attempted for very low ID; however, some cases cannot assert as general. To make it general, mathematics is required to prove and analyse the case.

Therefore, the purpose of this paper is to prove and analyse mathematically that all the target circles always intersect for very low ID; which presumed to disturb the experiment or affect the subject's focus. To support the proof, some examples also given. We hope this proof will give a contribution to the enhancement of ISO9241, and the reassessment to find the new solution will be done for a very low index of difficulty classification.

For readers' benefit, a summary of ISO/TS 9241-411 is presented in the following section. Followed by mathematical proof and examples to assist the proof. And lastly, there is a conclusion that can be embraced by researchers.

2 Evaluation of very low index of difficulty

2.1 ISO/TS 9241-411

The relationship between controls and displays in human-factor performance is evaluated in the interface [6]. The evaluation procedures to measure interface's performance using experimental protocol are depicted in ISO 9241. The ISO is composed of nine series, 100 to 900 series. The only series that discusses physical input data is series 400. The method to evaluate the design of physical input data is contained in series 400 part 411. A procedure of evaluation is described in this standard to measure user performance for assessing the efficiency and effectiveness of all input devices.

Performance is measured by task performances on any of these tasks: selecting, pointing, dragging, free-hand input, and tracing. The performances of ISO standard are presented as one-direction tapping task, multi-directional tapping task, dragging task, and tracing task. It is not compulsory to test all of these performances to the input devices; it is decided by the expected use of the device [7].

The main ISO dependent measure is Throughput (TP). TP is the rate of information transfer when an input device is operated by a user to control a pointer on a display. The unit of TP is bits per second (bps), and it merges speed and accuracy of a device in responses.

$$TP = \frac{ID_e}{TM} \tag{1}$$

$$ID_e = \log_2\left(\frac{D + w_e}{w_e}\right) \tag{2}$$

$$w_e = 4.133 \cdot s_x \tag{3}$$

TP is calculated by dividing the effective Index of Difficulty (ID_e , in bits, measures user accuracy required in a test) by the average movement time (TM, in seconds, is calculated from the first movement of input devices to the target). The effective Index of Difficulty (ID_e) was measured from D to w_e , where D is movement distance to the target, and w_e is the effective target width. The standard deviation of tapping task that depends on the directions is denoted as s_x .

ISO recommends that the task has to include many types of difficulty ranges that match the intended use of the input device. There are four precision levels based on the ID (Index of Difficulty), $ID > 6$ as high level, $4 < ID \leq 6$ as medium level, $3 < ID \leq 4$ as low level, and the last, $ID \leq 3$ as very low level. The Index of Difficulty is already defined by the Shannon formulation,

$$ID = \log_2\left(\frac{D}{w} + 1\right) \tag{4}$$

where D , similar as previous, is the movement distance parameter, and w is the target width. The ID units are bits.

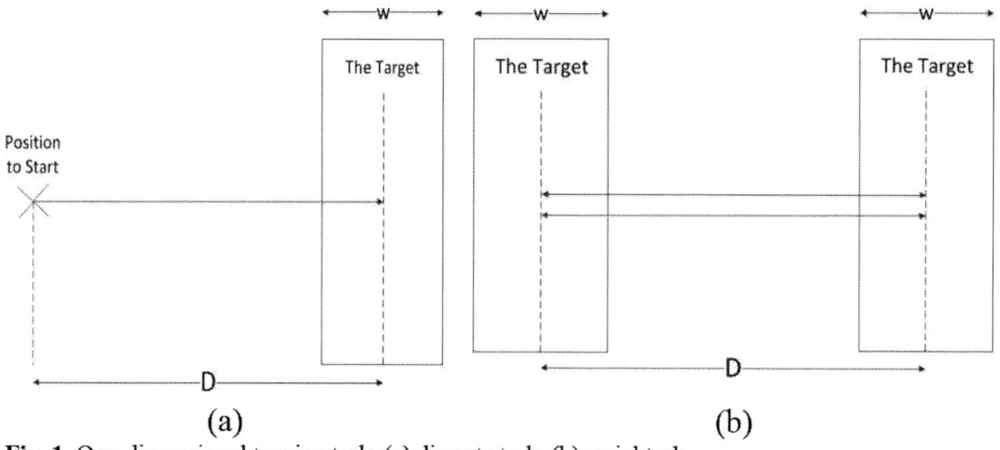

Fig. 1. One-dimensional tapping task, (a) discrete task, (b) serial task.

The first tapping task model was built by Fitts that used the reciprocal tapping apparatus. The schematic drawing of the tool is described in Figure 1. There are two tasks of Fitts' paradigm, Discrete Task and Serial Task. The assignment for the subjects for Discrete Task was to touch the target plate (without touch the either side of the plate) from the starting position. After the subject finally hit the target, the subject needs to go back to starting point and the task is repeated. The Serial Task has the subjects to hit two targets back and forth continuously between the targets. This paradigm is called one-dimensional, considering the movement only limited for a horizontal line. Either way, whether discrete or serial task, this paradigm is rather obsolete because nowadays movement angle of the pointing device is mostly multi-directional.

Another tapping task is multi-directional tapping task, which is described in Figure 2. The task is tapping a small circle that was begun at the top circle and continues clockwise following the ordered number [7, 8]. The benefit of this paradigm is that the movement is not restricted to specific area only, but all of the directions [9].

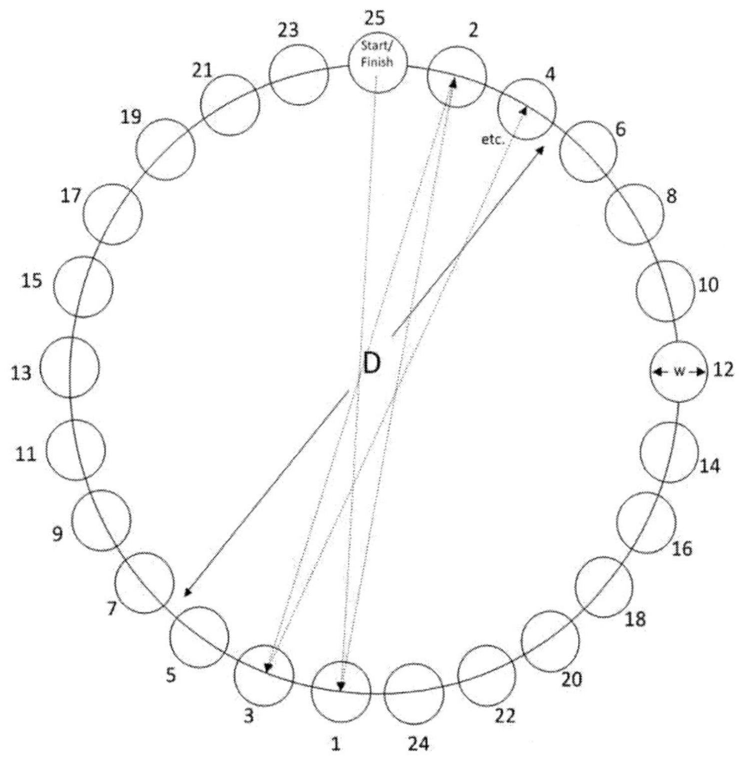

Fig. 2. Multidirectional tapping task.

2.2 Proof of intersection in very low ID

In this section, the aim is to prove when the ID is very low or $ID \leq 3$, then the targets circle in the circular arrangement of ISO standard is always intersecting. First of all, the value of $ID \leq 3$ has to be changed into variable D and w. Based on Equation 4,

$$
\begin{aligned}
& ID = \log_2\left(\frac{D+w}{w}\right) \leq 3 \\
& \Leftrightarrow \frac{D+w}{w} \leq 8 \\
& \Leftrightarrow D + w \leq 8w \\
& \Leftrightarrow D \leq 7w
\end{aligned}
\tag{4}
$$

The second, the area of overlapping is termed as A, see Figure 3; where in the equation to calculate A is already defined by Equation 5 in [10],

$$A = a^2\pi - 2a^2 \tan^{-1}\left(\frac{d}{\sqrt{4a^2 - d^2}}\right) - \frac{1}{2} d\sqrt{4a^2 - d^2} \tag{5}$$

with radii of target circle is a and distance between center points of target circles is d. Based on the value of ISO standard, the value of a is $\frac{w}{2}$, and the value of $d = 0.1253D$ (this number can be obtained by Pythagorean Theorem), thus Equation 5 becomes

$$A = 0.7854w^2 - \frac{w^2}{2}\tan^{-1}\left(\frac{0.1253D}{\sqrt{w^2 - (0.1253D)^2}}\right) - 0.0626D\sqrt{w^2 - (0.1253D)^2} \qquad (6)$$

The idea of the intersection always exists is the same as the value of (6) is constantly positive. Hence, simply prove that A is consistently positive for $ID \leq 3$.

Theorem 1. For every D and w real positive number that satisfy $D \leq 7w$ and $w < D$, then A is always real positive.

Proof: For the lower bound, substitute $D = 7w$ to Equation 6, and the value $A = 0.0394w^2$ is obtained. For the upper bound, simply remove the subtractions from Equation 6. Consequently,

$$0.0394w^2 \leq A < 0.7854w^2$$

which confirms that the value of A is consistently real positive.

The brute force method also validates that the value of A is always positive, nevertheless it is particularly limited for D and w positive integer numbers.

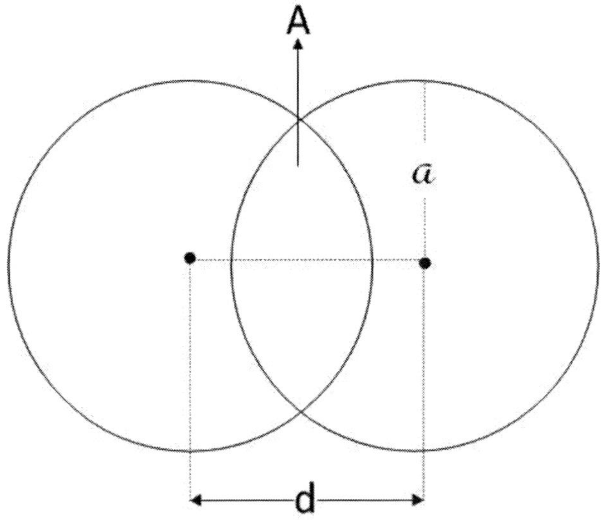

Fig. 3. Description of A as overlapping area, a as radii of target circles, and d as distance of center point between two target circles.

3 Examples

Some examples are provided to assist the understanding of the issue. The C# program has been developed to create the figures. The entire examples were built based on the description in Figure 4. The space for images in the example of 900×900 pixels, where the center of the circle is in (450, 450) coordinate.

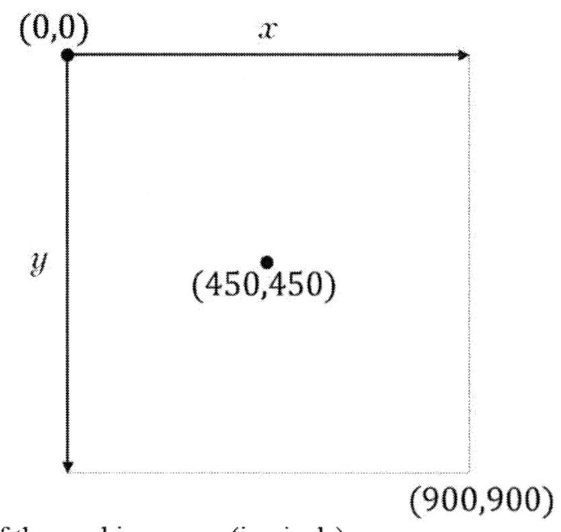

Fig. 4. Description of the working space (in pixels)

All of these cases are very low ID level, or have to comply $D \le 7w$; whereas $w < D$. In the following, it is obvious that the intersection invariably occurs.

1. $D = 350$ and $w = 50$, the result is depicted in Figure 5. Substitute these values to Equation 6 to attain $A = 98.6641394$. Based on Equation 6, the boundary of the area is $98.5 \le A < 1963.5$.
2. $D = 500$ and $w = 80$, the picture is provided in Figure 6. The value of A is 586.647212, where it is bounded by $252.1600 \le A < 5\,026.5600$.

Fig. 5. Multidirectional tapping task for very low *ID*, with $D = 350$ and $w = 50$.

Fig. 6. Multidirectional tapping task for very low *ID*, with $D = 500$ and $w = 80$.

4 Conclusion

This paper is discussing the mathematic proof for overlapping area of multidimensional tapping test in a very low index of difficulty in ISO9241-411. We succeed to prove that when $ID \leq 3$, then the target circles always overlapping with each other. Through this proof, we hope this will be a remarkable condition when design a multi-directional tapping experiment using the ISO standard. The refinement of the effect of overlapping area might be one of the influence conditions in human-computer interaction experiment.

References

1. K.L. Norman, K.D. Norman. *Comparison of relative versus absolute pointing devices* [Online] from http://www.cs.umd.edu/hcil/trs/2010-25/2010-25.pdf (2010). [Accessed on 18 December 2018].
2. D. Natapov, S.J. Castellucci, I.S. MacKenzie. *ISO 9241-9 evaluation of video game controllers*. Graphic Interface 2009 (Kelowna, Canada, 2009). Proceeding of Graphics Interface 2009: 223–230 (2009). pp. 44–45. https://dl.acm.org/citation.cfm?id=1555930
3. I.S. MacKenzie, T. Kauppinenm, M. Silfverberg. *Accuracy measures for evaluating computer pointing devices*. Proc. of the ACM SIGCHI Conference on Human Factors in Computing Systems – CHI 2001 (Seattle, USA, 2001). Proceedings of the SIGCHI Conference on Human Factors in Computing Systems:9–16 (2001). https://dl.acm.org/citation.cfm?id=365028
4. J.Y. Oh, W. Stuerzlinger. *Laser pointers as collaborative pointing devices*. Graphics Interface 2002 (Calgary, Canada, 2002). Proceedings of Graphics Interface 2002:141–150 (2002). http://graphicsinterface.org/proceedings/gi2002/gi2002-17/
5. R.B. Widodo, T. Matsumaru. *Measuring the Performance of Laser Spot Clicking Techniques*. 2013 IEEE International Conference on Robotics and Biomimetics (ROBIO) (Shenzhen, China, 2013). http://ieeexplore.ieee.org/document/6739639/

6. I.S. MacKenzie. *Human-Computer Interaction: An Empirical Research Perspective.* Waltham: Elsevier Inc (2013). pp. 74–86. https://books.google.co.id/books?id=k0kBgyCaokAC&printsec=frontcover&dq=Human-Computer+Interaction:+An+Empirical+Research+Perspective.+Waltham:+Elsevier+Inc&hl=en&sa=X&ved=0ahUKEwjBo_L6qcHZAhVFvo8KHY6sC_QQ6AEIKDAA#v=onepage&q=Human-Computer%20Interaction%3A%20An%20Empirical%20Research%20Perspective.%20Waltham%3A%20Elsevier%20Inc&f=false
7. ISO. *Reference number ISO/TS 9241-411:2012(E)*. International Organization for Standardization (2012). https://www.iso.org/standard/54106.html
8. I.S. MacKenzie. Fitts'law. In: *Handbook of human-computer interaction*. K.L. Norman, J. Kirakowski (Eds.). Wiley: Hoboken, NJ (2018) pp. 349–370. https://www.wiley.com/en-us/The+Wiley+Handbook+of+Human+Computer+Interaction+Set-p-9781118977279
9. R.W. Soukoreff, I.S. MacKenzie. *Int. Journal of Human-Computer Studies,* **61**:751–789 (2004). http://www.yorku.ca/mack/ijhcs2004.pdf
10. E.W. Weisstein. *Lens* [Online] from http://mathworld.wolfram.com/Lens.html (2007). [Accesed on 18 December 2017].

Automatic Essay Scoring in E-learning System Using LSA Method with N-Gram Feature for Bahasa Indonesia

Rico Setiadi Citawan*, *Viny* Christanti Mawardi, and *Bagus* Mulyawan

Faculty of Information Technology, Tarumanagara University, Letjend S. Parman No. 1, West Jakarta 11440, Indonesia

Abstract. In the world of education, e-learning system is a system that can be used to support the educational process. E-learning system is usually used by educators to learners in evaluating learning outcomes. In the process of evaluating learning outcomes in the e-learning system, the form type of exam questions that are often used are multiple choice and short stuffing. For exam questions in the form of essays are rarely used in the evaluation process of educational because of the difference in the subjectivity and time consuming in the assessment process. In this design aims to create an automatic essay scoring feature on e-learning system that can be used to support the learning process. The method used in automatic essay scoring is Latent Semantic Analysis (LSA) with n-gram feature. The evaluation results of the design features automatic essay scoring showed that the accuracy of the average achieved in the amount of 78.65 %, 58.89 %, 14.91 %, 71.37 %, 64.49 % in the LSA unigram, bigram, trigram, unigram + bigram, unigram + bigram + trigram.

Key words: Automatic essay scoring, e-learning, latent semantic analysis, n-gram, singular value decomposition

1 Introduction

Along with advancement of internet technology rapidly allows the application of technology in various fields including one in the education field. One of the technologies that can be utilized to support the learning process is e-learning system. In e-learning system many features are developed to support the learning process such as online exam features who provided by educators to learners in evaluating learning outcomes.

In e-learning system, evaluation of learning outcomes in essay form is important because evaluation results in essay form can be used by educators as an indicator to measure the level of learners understanding of the exams given. Therefore, to solve the problem is designing e-learning system with automatic essay scoring feature that can be used to support the learning process between educators and learners.

There are several methods that can be used to perform assessments in automatic essay scoring such as string matching algorithms like Rabin Karp, Knuth Morris Pratt,

* Corresponding author: rsctvx@gmail.com

Levenshtein distance, etc. However, for this designing is used method Latent Semantic Analysis (LSA) which can be used to find the similarity between answer student essays with answer key model lecturer in automatic essay scoring.

LSA is a method in information retrieval that represents words along with sentences in a matrix with mathematical calculations. Mathematical calculations are performed by mapping the presence or absence of words from word groups in the matrix. LSA method uses a linear algebra technique called Singular Value Decomposition (SVD) to find patterns of relationships between words and contexts that contain the words in semantic matrix.

Generally existing Automatic Essay Scoring (AES) techniques which are using LSA method do not consider word order in a sentence. To solve the problem, the LSA method used in automatic essay scoring for this designing will be added with n-gram feature so that word order in sentence can be considered.

2 Literature Review

In this case, the Latent Semantic Analysis (LSA) method with n-gram feature are used to create an automatic essay scoring in e-learning system.

2.1 Pre-processing

Pre-processing is an early stage in processing input data before entering the main stage process. Pre-processing consists of several stages. The pre-processing stages are performed in the system are case folding, lexical analysis, tokenization. Here is an explanation of the pre-processing steps performed as follows:

i) Case Folding

Case folding is the stage that changes all the letters in the corpus into lowercase. The purpose of case folding is to uniform input data because the input can be lowercase and uppercase.

ii) Lexical Analysis

Lexical analysis is the process of eliminating numbers, punctuation and characters which cannot be read by the system.

iii) Tokenization

Tokenization is the process of cutting or separating words from a collection of text or corpus.

2.2 Latent semantic analysis (LSA)

LSA stands for Latent Semantic Analysis is an information retrieval method that works on a set of texts in which words can be represented along with their context in a matrix with mathematical calculations. The formed matrix is a mapping of the presence or absence of a word or term from a particular group of words or terms. In addition, the context used can be a list of keywords, sentences, even paragraphs.

Latent Semantic Analysis (LSA) was proposed and patented in 1988 by Scott Deerwester, Thomas Launder, and Susan Dumais [1]. This method is widely used in the field of Information Retrieval and Natural Language Processing. One example of the use of the LSA method is the assessment of essay answers. The LSA method uses the mathematical technique of linear algebra called Singular Value Decomposition (SVD) in forming semantic matrix.

The semantic matrix that has been formed is a matrix that contains the pattern of relationship between words with the context in matching between the answer and answer key [2]. LSA methods generally work based on the unigram word occurring simultaneously in certain contexts so that LSA method is more concerned with the keywords contained in a sentence regardless of the word orders and grammar in a sentence, Therefore, to solve the problem, in this LSA method will be added n-gram feature so that LSA method can work on the appearance of word and phrase in certain context so that word order in sentence can be considered [3].

The designing of automatic essay scoring using LSA method, the first step is to represent the student answer and lecturer answer key in a matrix by forming term frequency matrix of student answer and term frequency matrix of lecturer answer key. The term frequency matrix is formed by counting the number of times the word appears on the lecturer answer key. The frequency of occurrence of a word or term that counts can be a set of unigram, bigram, trigram, or all of them.

The formed term frequency matrix consists of two are the term frequency matrix of the lecturer answer key and the frequency term matrix of the student answer. The frequency term matrix for the lecturer answer key consists of rows and columns where each row in the matrix represents a unique word in the lecturer answer key while each column in the matrix represents each sentence of lecturer answer key. In addition, each cell in the matrix represents the number of times the occurrence of a unique word that exists in each sentence of lecturer answer key.

In the term frequency matrix for student answers also consists of rows and columns where each row in the matrix represents a unique word on the lecturer answer key while each column in the matrix represents every student answers sentence then each cell on the matrix represents the number of occurrences of a unique word lecturer answer key is in every student answer sentence. The weighting used in each matrix cell is the frequency of the student's answer and the lecturer's answer key are the weighting of the term frequency (tf).

The next stage is to calculate Singular Value Decomposition (SVD) on the term frequency matrix that has been formed in the previous stage is the term frequency matrix for lecturer answer key and term frequency matrix for student answers. The purpose of SVD is discover a new pattern or relationship "latent" between words and sentences containing these words. The result of the SVD calculation process produces three matrices components are two orthogonal matrices and one diagonal matrix. The factoring of SVD from a matrix A dimension txd is as follows:

$$A_{txd} = U_{txn} \times S_{nxn} \times V_{dxn}^{T} \quad (1)$$

Where:
A: term matrix sized txd.
U: orthogonal matrix sized txn.
S: diagonal matrix sized nxn.
V: orthogonal matrix transpose sized dxn.
t: number of rows of the matrix A.
d: number of columns of the matrix A.
n: the rank value of the matrix A ($\leq$ min(t, d)).

The decomposed of matrix A produces three matrices of the matrix U, S, and VT. The size or dimensions of three matrices generated in the SVD process are different. In the matrix U has the same row as the matrix A, but has fewer columns than the matrix A is n column. In the matrix S has the size of n row and n columns. In the matrix VT has the same column as the matrix A, but has fewer row sizes than matrix A or equal to column matrix A is d row.

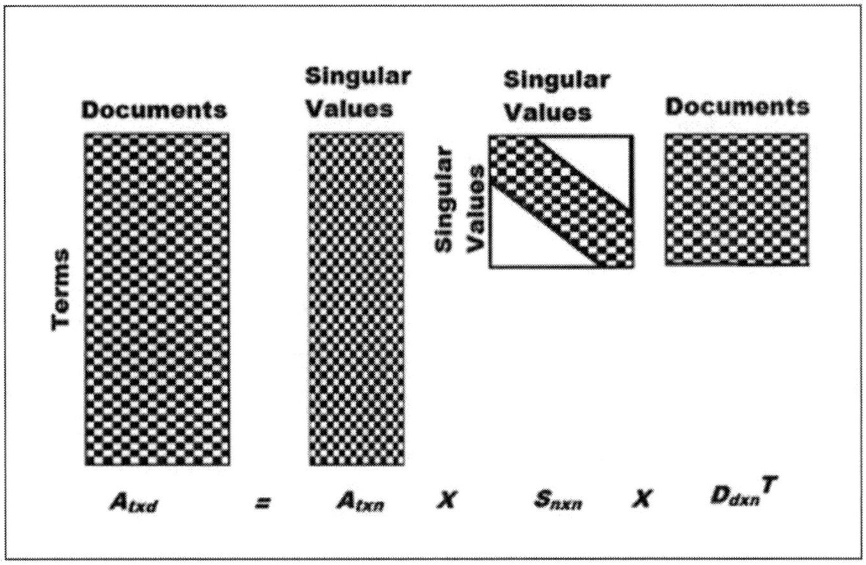

Fig. 1. Singular value decomposition of matrix [2].

Based on Figure 1, the column of the matrix U is an orthogonal eigenvector of A × AT. In column matrix V is an eigenvector of orthogonal $A^T \times A$. In the matrix S is a diagonal matrix whose value is the root of the eigenvalues of the matrix U or V. After doing the SVD process, the next step is to reduce the matrix of SVD calculation result or smoothing process. The purpose of reducing the size or dimension of the matrix is to remove noise or words that are considered unimportant without eliminating the correlation or the relationship between words and sentences [4]. The reduction of the matrix dimension is done by reducing the dimension of the diagonal matrix containing the singular value of the second matrix result of the SVD process.

When reducing the size of the diagonal matrix S containing the singular value, the first step is, choose a value of k. The value of k which can be selected in reducing the matrix size is $k \leq n$. After that the value of k will be used on the matrix of the SVD calculation results by taking the firsts row data and the first column k data on the diagonal matrix containing the singular value [5]. Unselected dimension the singular value on the diagonal matrix S will be set to zero. The reduction in the diagonal matrix (S) also affects both orthogonal matrices U and V.

The result of the reduced SVD matrices can be used for reconstructing the matrix by using a lower dimension (A_k). Reconstructed matrix (A_k) has the same size as the previous matrix (A). However, the reconstructed matrix (A_k) is a matrix with approximation of matrix A using a lower dimension which can show the hidden relationship between words in the sentence so that it can cover all important words and can ignore unimportant words that are not considered.

In addition, the reconstructed matrix can estimate the hidden new relationship of a group of words or terms in a particular sentence so that the word or term group contained in the sentence may be close to or relate to each other in space k although the word or term is not ever present or appear on the sentence. Reconstruction matrix of SVD results can be seen in the Equation 2 and Figure 2.

$$A_{txd} = A_k = U_k \times S_k \times V_k^{\,T} \tag{2}$$

Where:
A_k: reconstruction of term frequency matrix sized k.
U_k: orthogonal matrix sized k.
S_k: diagonal matrix sized k.
V_k: orthogonal matrix transpose sized k.
k: parameter of reduction dimension matrix.

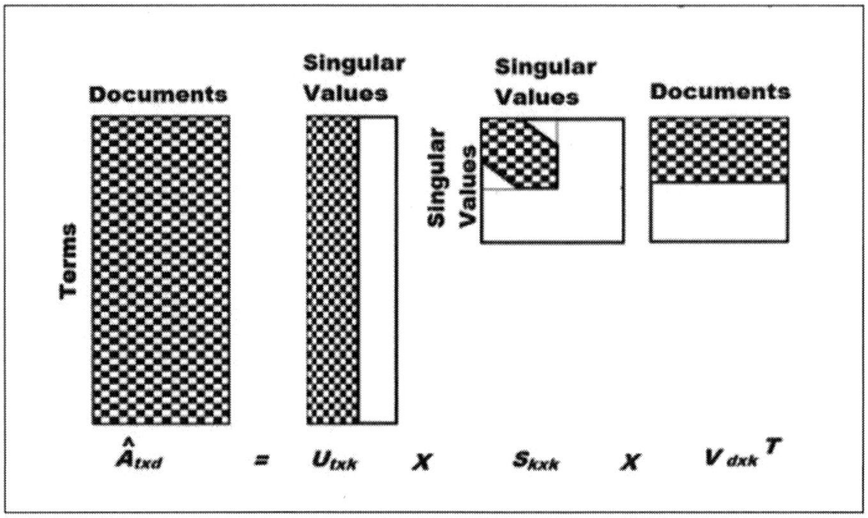

Fig. 2. Reconstruction matrix of singular value decomposition.

After the reconstruction of the student answer matrix and the lecturer answer key matrix has been formed, the next step is to form the answer vector and answer key vector of the matrix result from the student answer and the lecturer answer key who have been reconstructed again using the lower dimension. Reconstruction using the lower dimension will produce a new representation or relationship on the student answer and the lecturer answer [6]. In this case the answer vector is the student answer sentence and the answer key vector is the lecturer answer key sentence. The final stage of the automatic essay scoring using LSA is to measure the similarity between the vector of students answers and the vector of lecturer answer key.

2.3 Cosine similarity

Cosine Similarity is a technique for measuring the similarity of the angle cosine value between document vectors and query vectors. In this case the document vector represents the sentence in the student answer while the query vector represents the sentence in the lecturer answer key. After the document vector (d) and query vector (q) has been formed, the similarity between the document vector and the query vector can be calculated using the Equation (3).

$$\text{CosineSim}(q,d) = \frac{\sum_{j=1}^{t} w_{qj} x w_{dij}}{\sqrt{\sum_{j=1}^{t} (w_{dij})^2} \sqrt{\sum_{j=1}^{t} (w_{qj})^2}} \qquad (3)$$

Where:
q; the student answer vector.
d: the lecturer answer key vector.

2.4. N-gram

Basically, the n-gram model is a probabilistic model designed by mathematicians in the early 20th century and later developed to predict the next item in the order of items. The item can be a sequence letter/character or a word sequence [7]. In the word generation process, n-gram consists of words sequence along n words in a sentence. Where in word, n-gram is can be used to extract pieces of n words from a sentence or paragraph. A n-gram of size 1 is called unigram, for n-gram of size 2 called bigram, for n-gram of size 3 called trigram, whereas for n-gram is a term when it has a size greater than 3. For example, the word sequence "*perangkat keras komputer*" (computer hardware), the word sequence in n-gram as follow.
Unigram : *perangkat, keras, komputer*. (device, hard, computer)
Bigram : *perangkat keras, keras komputer*. (hard device, computer hard)
Trigram : *perangkat keras komputer*. (computer hardware)

2.5. Evaluation

Evaluation of an automated essay scoring system is needed to assess how the Latent Semantic Analysis method works good in assessing or scoring the essay answers. This evaluation is done by comparing the judgments which generated by the system with human judgment, in this case the lecturer. After all data was already obtained, the next step will be analyzing mean absolute error and mean absolute percentage error result. The result of mean absolute error is the average difference between value from lecturer and systems.

$$MAE = \frac{\sum_{i=1}^{n} |x_i - y_i|}{n} \tag{4}$$

Where:
MAE : average value from lecturer and system.
X_i : value from lecturer.
Y_i : value from system.
n : numbers of data.

While the result of mean absolute percentage error is the average difference between value from lecturer and systems. Then the result of mean absolute percentage error calculation can also be measured the success rate of the automatic essay scoring system in assessing or scoring student essay answers.

$$MAE = \frac{\sum_{i=1}^{n} \left| \frac{|x_i - y_i|}{x_i} \right|}{n} \times 100 \tag{5}$$

Where:
MAPE : average percentage error value.
X_i : value from lecturer.
Y_i : value from system.
n : numbers of data.

3 Planning and implementation

3.1. System plan

At this stage will explain the planning that needs to be done in system plan. This stage is done by first determining the purpose and use of the system to be designed. The designed system is an e-learning system with automatic essay scoring feature. The system is built and is intended for students and lecturers in the learning process where in this system planning students can do the exam given by the lecturer in the form of essays while the lecturer can give the test to the student in the form of essay which then will be automatically assessed by the system with the answer key who has been included by lecturer.

The initial stage of the automatic essay scoring system is the preparation stage of the required data such as student answers, questions and models of lecturer answers key. Data consisting of questions and answers key are taken from the book "Discovering Computers 2010: Living in Digital World", websites, ppt and pdf about course material "introductory information technology".

Meanwhile the student answer data is collected by distributing questionnaires containing questions about course material introductory information technology to the students of the information technology faculty Tarumanagara University. In designing automatic essay scoring system that is built, to facilitate the design of the system in assessing essay answers, then the collected data used in the system such as student answers, questions and models of lecturer answer key will be stored in the database.

Automatic essay scoring system designed to receive input in the form of questions, answer keys, and answers essay. Questions and answers were obtained from the lecturer while the essay answers were obtained from the student. Then the answers key and answers will be done pre-processing, after that the system will perform the similarity calculation between the student's essay answers with each model of lecturer's answer key using Latent Semantic Analysis (LSA) where the highest similarity values obtained using cosine similarity will be used to produce the student scores output.

In the automated essay scoring system using LSA designed as shown in Figure 3, this system runs by first managing the data entered by the user consisting of lecturers and students. Data that become system input is lecturer answer key data and student answer data. Once the system gets input from the user, the system goes into the pre-processing stage, the process of calculating the Latent Semantic Analysis algorithm, the result of the student's answer score.

Based on the flow in Figure 3, there is a pre-processing stage. Pre-processing is a series of steps performed to manage input data before entering the next stage. In the pre-processing staged there are several stages performed such as case folding, lexical analysis, and tokenization.

Further data that has been pre-processing this will be input or enter in the process of latent semantic analysis algorithm. Initial stages performed in the process of latent semantic analysis algorithm is the formation of term frequency matrix for answer and term frequency matrix for answer key. The process of forming term frequency matrix by counting the number of words or terms that appear in each sentence in the matrix, then the term frequency matrix that has been formed will be calculated SVD or Singular Value Decomposition that will produce the matrices U, S and V. The result of SVD matrices calculation will be reduction process which then be used to reconstruct the matrix by using a lower dimension.

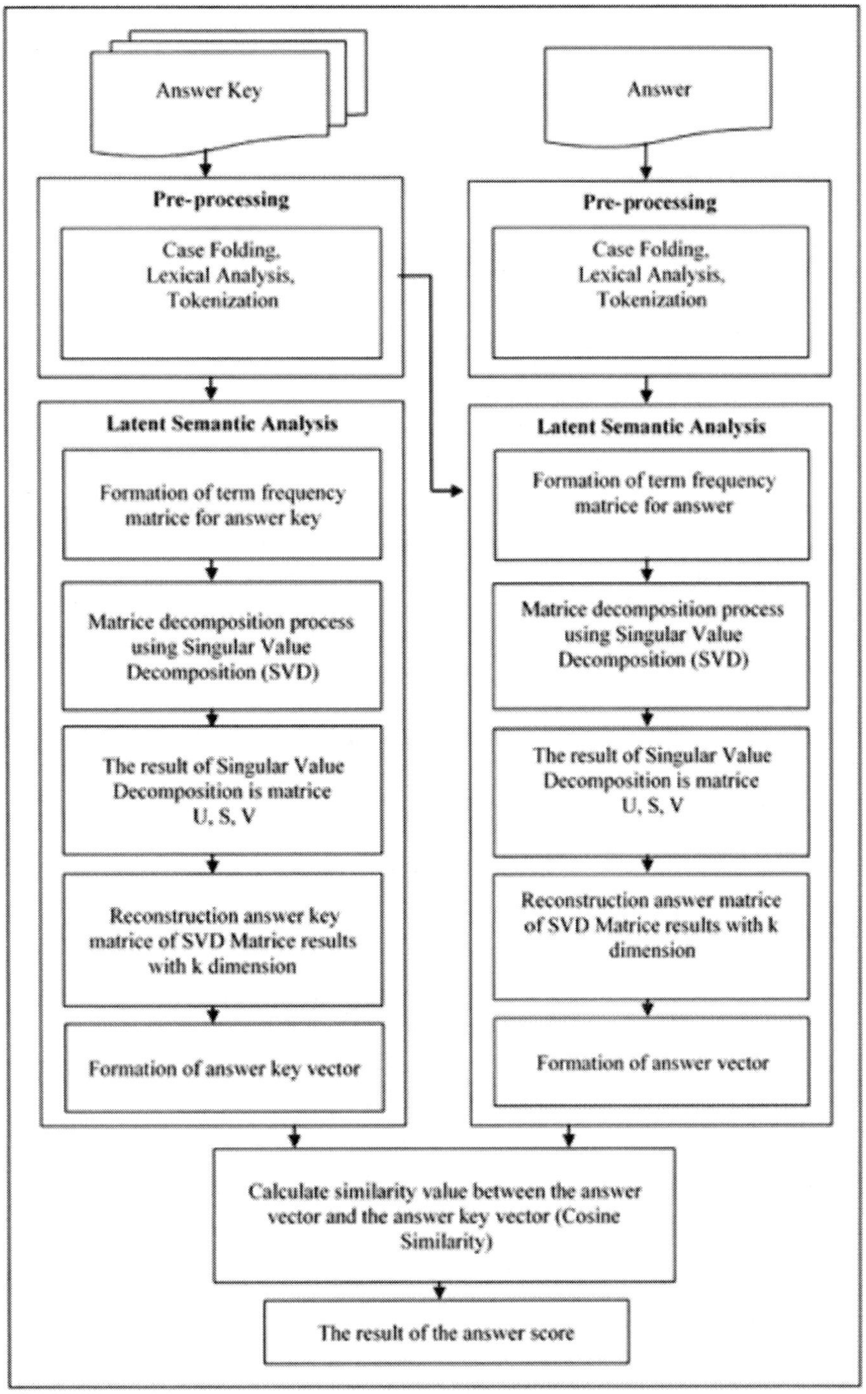

Fig. 3. Similarity answer key and answer using LSA.

In the formation of the term frequency matrix of the answer, the set of terms or words used to calculate the frequency of words occurrence in each sentence answer is a collection of terms or words derived from the pre-processing answers key. Likewise, for the process of forming the term frequency matrix of answer key. If the reconstruction answer matrix and answer key matrix has been formed, then the next process is to form an answer vector and answer key vector.

The answer vector and the answer key vector that has been formed will be calculated by the value of similarity using Cosine Similarity method where a vector formed is a representation of a sentence in the matrix column. Then the value used to evaluate each sentence answer is the value with the highest similarity between answers vector with all the answers key vector.

In the process of assessing student answers, the value to be taken to be the output is the average value obtained from the sum of each value of the highest similarity between the student answer sentences that is compared with all key lecturer answer sentences divided by the number of sentences of student answers. Then the average value of similarity that has range (0 to 1) multiplied by value 100.

3.2. System implementation

After the design phase of the system has been designed then the next stage is to make software adjustments with the system design that has been made before. The first thing to consider in the making of this system is the system needs consisting of hardware and software from the server. Server serves as a mediator during the process of data transfer using internet connection, on the manufacture of the system will use the hosting server.

The hardware used for system development used a computer with IBM Server computer specifications as a server. As for the client side can use a computer that has a web browser like internet explorer, google chrome, mozilla firefox, etc. Software used on the server that is IIS manager and SQL Server Management Studio are used as central data storage server, Matlab used to perform mathematical calculations of linear algebra, and ASP.NET C# and Perl is used as a programming language (back end).

After all the hardware and software that will be used in the manufacture is available, then the creation of the system can be started by first setting up the database needed to store data before and after processing. The existing database will be created using the SQL Server database server.

After the database is created, then the next stage to do is create interface display for each module that has been designed previously. Display interface is made as simple as possible so that users can use the existing program easily. Once the existing interface is created, it will make the program code for the existing interface so that the interface is made to work properly.

If the existing program code has been created, then will be tested against each module that has been made. Testing is made to be known whether the existing program has been running as expected or not. In addition, through the tests made can also be known whether the program is made there is still an error or not.

Once the interface has been completed, program coding will be made available for automatic essay scoring features with the algorithm and the theoretical base described earlier. When the coding program has been completed, it will be tested against the features that have been made. Feature testing is done to find out whether the program has been made output according to the designed.

4 Result and discussion

Testing conducted consist of two stages is black box testing and automatic essay scoring features testing. Black box testing is done to test whether each function in each module has been able to function properly. In testing the automatic essay scoring feature is performed to determine whether the system created can assess the essay answers according with the judgments made by humans.

4.1. Modules testing

This testing is performed on all modules that exist on the system created. Outline, the modules that exist in the system is divided into 2 main modules namely the module for student and modules for lecturer.

4.1.1 Automatic essay scoring modules testing

The results of the testing conducted found that all the functions of the existing automatic essay scoring module had been able to run according with its function. Here is a picture showing the test results from one of the automatic essay scoring modules.

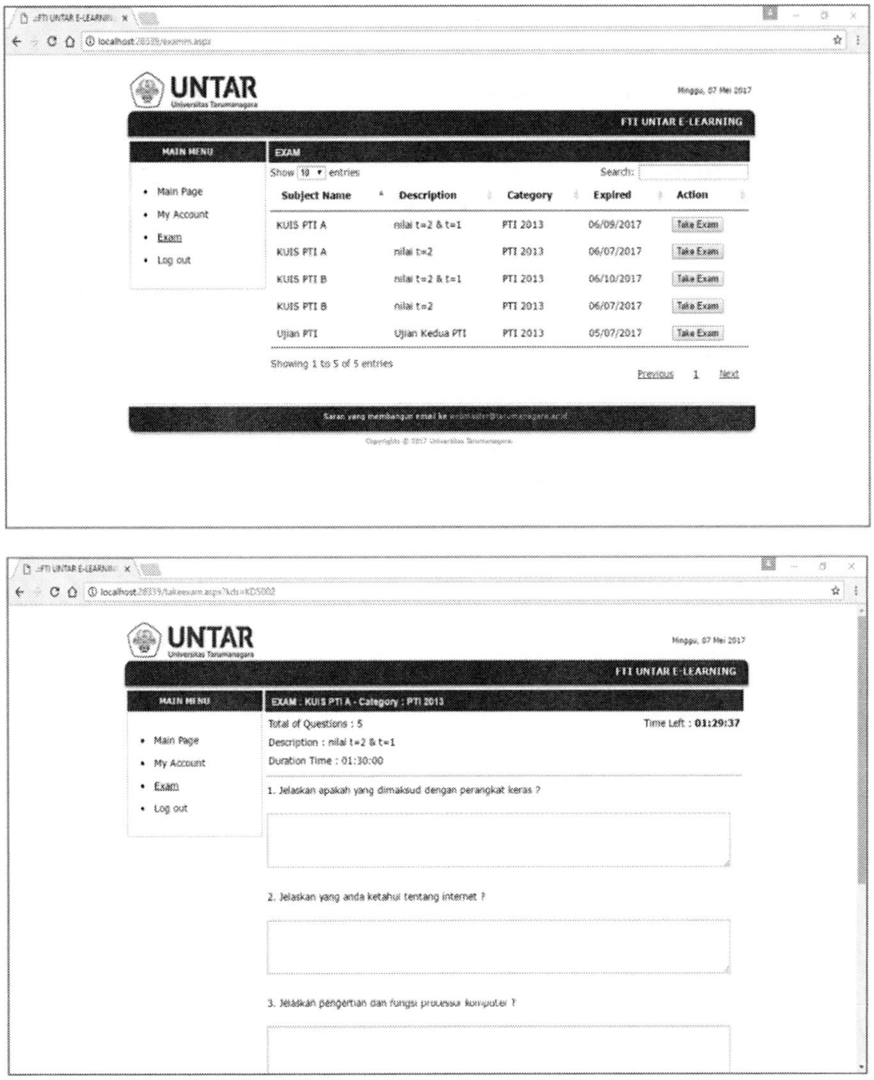

Fig. 4. Testing results of the automatic essay scoring module when the student chooses the exam.

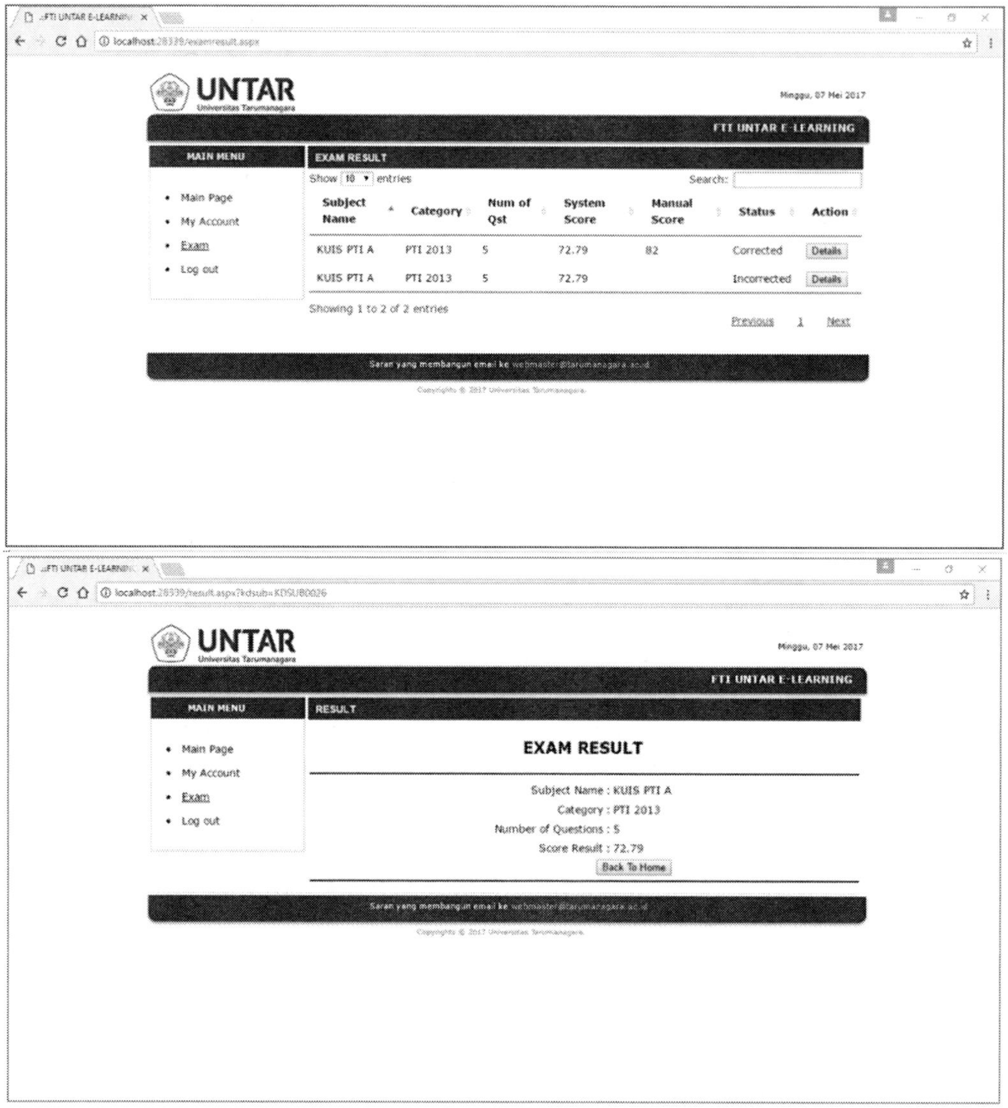

Fig. 5. Testing results of the automatic essay scoring module when the student submits the exam.

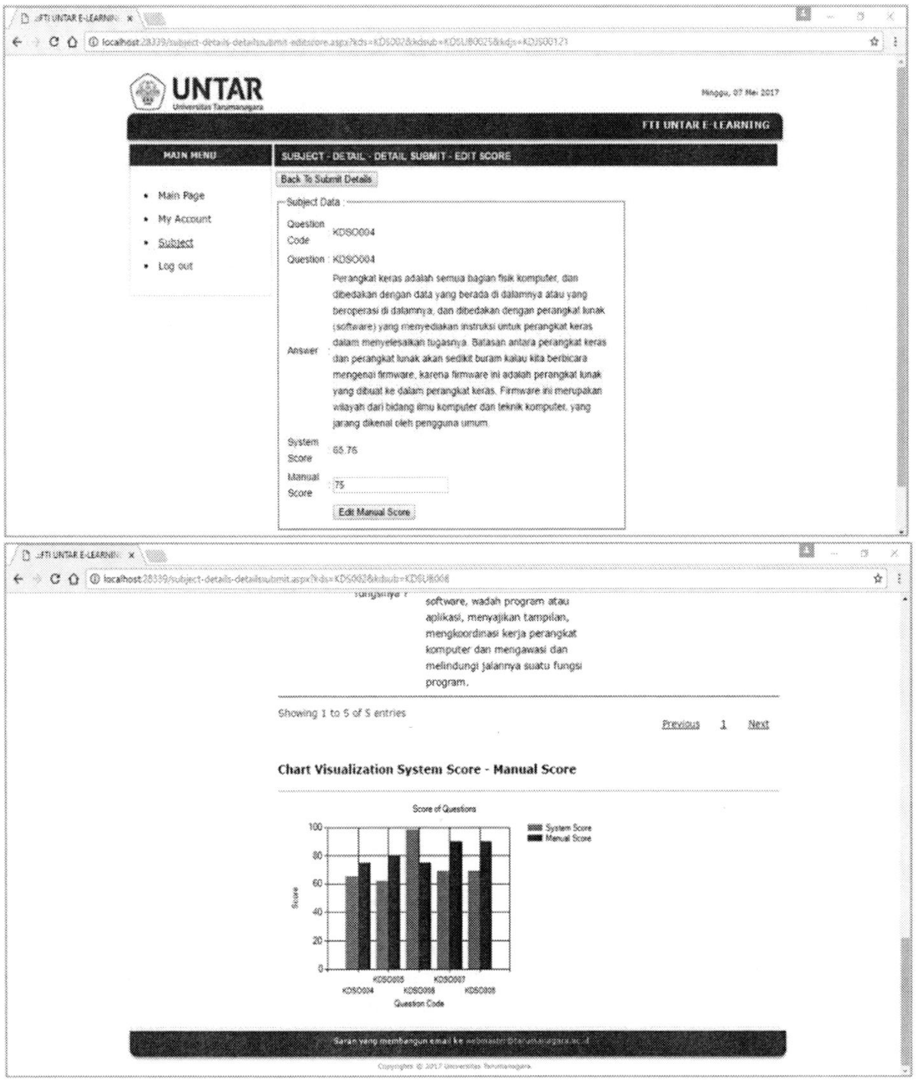

Fig. 6. Testing results of the automatic essay scoring module when the lecturer gives the value manually.

4.2. Automatic essay scoring feature testing

The process of automated essay scoring system is done to find out whether the system created can assess the essay answers according with the assessment conducted by human or lecturers and find out how much the average level of accuracy generated by the automatic essay scoring system. The process of automated essay scoring system test is divided into two parts namely the testing process by the researchers and the testing process by the respondents.

4.2.1 Automatic essay scoring feature testing by researchers

In the process of testing conducted by researcher, the initial process is to collect a set of questions and answers, then the data collected will be tested whether the automatic essay scoring system can assess the essay answers automatically according with the assessment of humans or lecturers. After that the collected data will be validated by Faculty of

Technology Tarumanagara University lecturers. Testing conducted by the researchers there are 2 parts are testing the perfect answer with the same word order and testing the perfect answer with different word order.

4.2.2 Automatic essay scoring feature testing by respondents

In the process of testing by respondents, the testing begins by distributing questionnaires to Faculty of Technology Tarumanagara University students consisting of questions about the course material "Introduction to Information Technology". Total respondents who fill the questionnaire as many as six people while the total answers of students who successfully collected 30 answers. Before the testing started, first the questionnaire will be assessed manually by experts who are lecturers of Faculty of Technology Tarumanagara University. The following are some of the data for questions on the questionnaire:

Table 1. Some of the data for questions on the questionnaire.

No	Questions
1	*Apakah yang dimaksud dengan perangkat keras?* (What is hardware?)
2	*Jelaskan yang anda ketahui tentang internet?* (Explain what you know about the internet?)
3	*Jelaskan yang anda ketahui tentang pengertian dan fungsi processor pada komputer?* (Explain what you know about the meaning and function of the processor on the computer?)
4	*Jelaskan apa yang dimaksud dengan jaringan komputer beserta tujuannya?* (Explain what is meant by computer network and the purpose?)
5	*Apa yang dimaksud dengan sistem operasi pada komputer ? Jelaskan beserta fungsinya?* (What is an operating system on a computer? Describe along with the function?)

Data in the form of questionnaires that have been collected will be tested to find out how much the average mean absolute error between the assessment by the system with the manual assessment by humans and the average mean absolute percentage error of the automatic essay scoring for assessing essay answers. Then with the average level of error percentage can also be measured how much the system accuracy level.

Testing toward the automatic essay scoring feature is conducted through five scenarios, namely:

1. LSA Unigram.
2. LSA Bigram.
3. LSA Trigram.
4. LSA Unigram + Bigram.
5. LSA Unigram + Bigram + Trigram.

Summary results of testing scenarios conducted by respondents can be seen in the Table 2.

Table 2. The results of testing scenarios by respondents.

Number of Answer	Lecturer Score	System Score				
		Scenario 1.	Scenario 2.	Scenario 3.	Scenario 4.	Scenario 5.
1.	70	63.58	43.34	24.15	62.26	55.44
2.	90	41.14	18.78	4.49	36.34	32.68
3.	90	91.76	45.64	45.37	48.46	41.03
4.	90	62.63	20.21	13.61	41.45	36.93
5.	80	68.35	24.88	0	28.86	24.95
..	...	...	...	...	...	...
30.	100	100	52.87	47.82	91.44	86.58

4.2.3 Evaluation of automatic essay scoring feature by researchers

Based on the results of testing conducted by researchers, the system has been able to assess the essay answers with the range (1 to 100). Scores that can be generated system is unigram score, bigram score, trigram score, unigram + bigram score, and unigram + bigram + trigram score. Here is one example of testing conducted by researchers.
Questions:
Apa yang dimaksud dengan perangkat keras?
(What is hardware?)

Answer key:
Perangkat keras merupakan bagian fisik dari komputer yang berfungsi untuk memberi masukan, menampilkan dan mengolah keluaran. Perangkat keras ini digunakan oleh sistem untuk menjalankan suatu perintah yang telah diprogramkan artinya berhubungan dengan perangkat lunak. Perangkat keras ini dibedakan menjadi empat jenis yaitu perangkat input, pemrosesan, output dan penyimpanan.
(Hardware is the physical part of the computer that serves to provide input, display and process the output. This hardware is used by the system to run a command that has been programmed which means it is related to the software. This hardware is divided into four types consisting of input devices, processing, output and storage.)

4.2.3.1 Testing the perfect answer with the same word order

Answer:
Perangkat keras merupakan bagian fisik dari komputer yang berfungsi untuk memberi masukan, menampilkan dan mengolah keluaran. Perangkat keras ini digunakan oleh sistem untuk menjalankan suatu perintah yang telah diprogramkan artinya berhubungan dengan perangkat lunak. Perangkat keras ini dibedakan menjadi empat jenis yaitu perangkat input, pemrosesan, output dan penyimpanan.

(Hardware is the physical part of the computer that serves to provide input, display and process the output. This hardware is used by the system to run a command that has been programmed which means it is related to the software. This hardware is divided into four types consisting of input devices, processing, output and storage.)
Unigram score: 100.
Bigram score: 100.
Trigram score: 100.
Unigram + bigram score: 100.
Unigram + bigram + trigram score: 100.

4.2.3.2 Testing the perfect answer with different word order

Answer:
Keras perangkat merupakan bagian fisik dari komputer yang berfungsi untuk masukan memberi, menampilkan dan mengolah keluaran. Keras perangkat ini digunakan oleh sistem untuk menjalankan suatu perintah yang telah diprogramkan artinya berhubungan dengan lunak perangkat. Keras perangkat ini dibedakan menjadi empat jenis yaitu perangkat input, pemrosesan, output dan penyimpanan.
(Device hard is the physical part of the computer that serves to provide input, display and process the output. This hardware is used by the system to run a command that has been programmed which means it is related to the software. This hardware is divided into four types consisting of input devices, processing, output and storage.)
Unigram score: 100.
Bigram score: 37.04.
Trigram score: 33.90.
Unigram + bigram score: 83.38.
Unigram + bigram + trigram score: 72.91.

4.2.4 Evaluation of automatic essay scoring feature by respondents

Based on the results of testing conducted by respondents, the testing results for the automatic essay scoring system by the respondents can be seen in Table 3 and the level of system accuracy in the test scenario is illustrated in Figure 7.

Table 3. The results of the automatic essay scoring system by respondents.

No	Testing Scenarios LSA	MAE	MAPE
1.	LSA Unigram	16.67267	21.35 %
2.	LSA Bigram	45.06733	58.89 %
3.	LSA Trigram	63.71067	85.09 %
4.	LSA Unigram + Bigram	22.42033	28.63 %
5.	LSA Unigram + Bigram + Trigram	27.38000	35.21 %

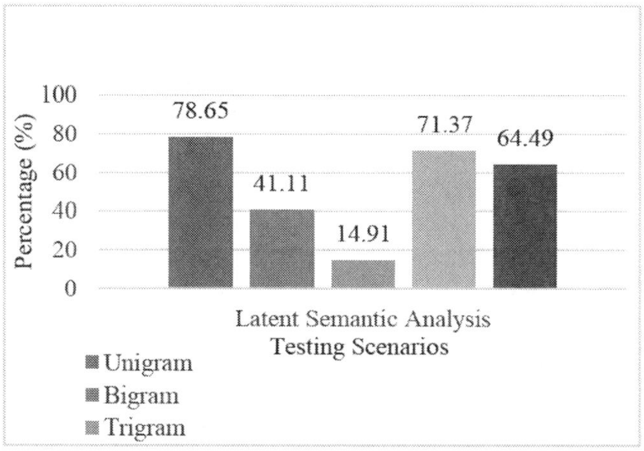

Fig. 7. Graph the average rate of system accuracy percentage by respondents.

Based on the test results the average accuracy rate of the resulting assessment of automatic essay scoring system is quite good or almost similar for value provided by the lecturer. In addition, from five testing scenarios performed, the test with the unigram term gives the best results with an accuracy of 78.65 % or a system error rate of 21.35 % and the mean value difference between the manual value and the system value is 16.672. In the testing process with bigram, trigram, unigram + bigram, unigram + bigram + trigram the resulting accuracy is 58.89 %, 14.91 %, 71.37 %, 64.79 % with average value difference of 45.067, 63.710, 22.420, 27.380. The cause of small accuracy in the testing process of bigram terms and trigram term testing is the rarity of the frequency of occurrence of word or term bigram or trigram found in the lecturer answer key. Another thing that affect the accuracy level of the automatic essay scoring system is:

i) There are still many error words in the answer when the system created can not handle the error correction word.
ii) Besides the other cause is the lack of an alternative answer key that is incorporated into the system.
iii) In addition, from the answers students still use a lot of words abbreviated for example "Internet Protocol" abbreviated to IP.
iv) Another thing that causes the difference of judgment is that the answers key entered by the system can have a similarity of meaning or understanding with other words such as there are similarities of words or words in a foreign language.
v) Another cause is the assessment of the system is very affected on the number of words that exist in each sentence. The results of the system assessment are the average value of similarity between term relationship with the sentence between the student's answer with the lecturer answer key. So that the assessment system will see the completeness of an answer based on each relationship on a term with a sentence whereas in the manual assessment if there is one sentence correct answer then the value given high. This is because the manual assessment sees the completeness of the answer overall than the whole sentence.

5 Conclusion

Based on the results of tests that have been done, can be obtained conclusions on the system that has been made as follows:

i) Each module on the website has been running well.

ii) The automatic essay scoring system has been able to assess student essay answers.
iii) Assessment of the essay answers generated by the automatic essay scoring system is influenced by the presence or absence of key term answers in a sentence, if the more the same term distribution of keywords between answers with answer key then the resulting value will be high, and vice versa.

References

1. S. Deerwester, S.T. Dumais, R. Harshman, *Indexing by latent semantic analysis* [Online] from http://lsa.colorado.edu/papers/JASIS.lsi.90.pdf (1992) [Accessed on 17 September 2017]
2. S. Dikli. *JTLA*, **5**,1 (2006). https://files.eric.ed.gov/fulltext/EJ843855.pdf
3. M.M. Islam, A.S.M. Latiful Hoque. *JCP*, **7**,3:616–626 (2012). http://www.jcomputers.us/index.php?m=content&c=index&a=show&catid=125&id=1969
4. R.H Gusmita, R. Manurung, *Penerapan latent semantic analysis untuk menentukkan kesamaan makna antara kata dalam Bahasa Inggris dan Bahasa Indonesia* [*Applied latent semantic analysis to determine same meaning between words in English and Indonesian*] [Online] from http://digilib.mercubuana.ac.id/manager/t!@file_artikel_abstrak/Isi_Artikel_391792352024.pdf. (2008) [Accessed on 25 January 2018]. [in Bahasa Indonesia]
5. Ch.A. Kumar, S. Srinivas, *CIT*, **17**,3:259–264 (2009). http://cit.fer.hr/index.php/CIT/article/view/1751
6. R.B.A. Pradana, Z.K.A. Baizal, Y. Firdaus. *Automatic essay grading system menggunakan metode latent semantic analysis*, Seminar Nasional Aplikasi Teknologi Informasi (Yogyakarta, Indonesia 2011). Seminar Nasional Aplikasi Teknologi Informasi (SNATI):E78-86 (2011). http://journal.uii.ac.id/index.php/Snati/article/view/2217
7. S.A. Sugianto, Liliana, S. Rostianingsih. *Jurnal Infra*, **1**,2:119–124 (2013). https://www.neliti.com/id/publications/105718/pembuatan-aplikasi-predictive-text-menggunakan-metode-n-gram-based
8. Munir, L.S. Riza, A. Mulyadi. *IJTRD*, **3**,6:403–407 (2016). http://www.ijtrd.com/papers/IJTRD5412.pdf
9. N.T. Thomas, A. Kumar, K. Bijlani. *Procedia Computer Science*, **58**:257–264 (2015). https://ac.els-cdn.com/S1877050915021304/1-s2.0-S1877050915021304-main.pdf?_tid=29855a6a-fed1-11e7-9742-00000aab0f6b&acdnat=1516556184_8c82910250d80802478e13aedd6c965f
10. T. Kakkonen, N. Myller, E. Sutinen. *Applying part-of-speech enhanced LSA to automate essay grading*. Proceedings of the 4th IEEE International Conference on Information Technology: Research and Education (Tel Aviv, Israel, 2006). https://arxiv.org/abs/cs/0610118

Energy Demand Analysis and Design of a Hybrid Power System in Bawean Islands, Indonesia

Ridho Hantoro[1], *Cahyun* Budiono[1], *Ronald* Kipkoech Ketter[2] , and *Nyoman* Ade Satwika[1*]

[1]Department of Physics Engineering, Faculty of Industrial Technology, Sepuluh Nopember Institute of Technology, Surabaya, Indonesia, Indonesia, ITS Street, Sukolilo, Surabaya 60111.
[2]Departement of Physics, Faculty of Mathematics and Science, Carl von Ossietzky Univesity Oldenburg F.R. 26129, Germany

Abstract. Over 70 000 000 people in Indonesia have no access to electricity. This study was carried out in Bawean Islands which are located in the Java Sea about 150 km North of Surabaya, the headquarters of East Java. The study to determine the energy services available in the Bawean Island was done through interviewing a random sample of 72 households in two villages namely Komalasa and Lebak. Based on the average monthly electricity consumption of the sampled households connected to the grid, a hybrid renewable energy based electrical supply system was designed for Gili Timur Island, one of the satellite islands around Bawean Island. The system was designed with the aid of a time step simulation software used to design and analyze hybrid power systems. A sensitivity analysis was also carried out on the optimum system to study the effects of variation in some of the system variables. HOMER suggests that for the expected peak load of 131 kW, an optimum system will consist of 150 kW from PV array, two wind turbines each rated 10 kW, a 75 kW diesel generator and batteries for storage.

Key words: Bawean Island, HOMER, sustainable energy, renewable energy, hybrid power systems

1 Introduction

Over 70 000 000 people in Indonesia do not have access to electricity while over 40 % of households still rely on traditional biomass for cooking. Around 165 000 premature deaths in Indonesia [1] can be attributed to the use of traditional biomass due to the indoor air pollution resulting in respiratory diseases in mainly children and women. Bawean Island is located in the Java Sea approximately 150 km North of Surabaya, the capital of East Java province [1]. Administratively, it is part of Gresik regency and is made up of two sub-districts namely Sangkapura and Tambak. Bawean Island is about 15 km in diameter and has an area of 197 km^2 [2]. It has a population of over 116 000 [3]. A household survey was conducted to obtain current energy consumption data and patterns with the aid of a

* Corresponding author: nyomanadee@gmail.com

questionnaire. This was achieved by choosing a random sample of 72 households in two villages in Sangkapura sub-district [1], Bawean Island and interviewing them through a set of open-ended and closed-ended questions as developed in the pre-designed questionnaire. A simple random sampling method was adopted in choosing the household surveyed. Among the households sampled, 36 were connected to the electricity service provider (PLN Bawean) grid while the other 36 were not connected to the grid.

The data obtained from the study was then analyzed mainly through the use of MS Excel and Hybrid Optimization Model for Electric Renewables (HOMER) software. MS Excel was used for statistical analysis of the data such as frequency distribution, comparison analysis, among others [4]. While HOMER was used to design and analyze an optimal hybrid electrical power system design based on conventional and locally available renewable energy sources [5] that could be exploited for the provision of sustainable electricity supply in Gili Timur Island.

It is a desire to see that the people living in Gili Timur Island enjoy electricity services just like the residents of main Bawean Island. There is also need for the electricity supply to be more reliable, sustainable and cleaner as compared to that of the main island. It is for this reason that this research used the current average electricity consumption demand from the neighbor Bawean Island in the design of the hybrid power system for Gili Timur Island. This research proposed design envisages a hybrid electrical supply system consisting of both renewable and conventional energy sources for environmental and economic sustainability in this paper.

2 Background

2.1 Energy situation in Indonesia

For a long time, the Indonesian economy has relied on oil as the main source of primary energy. However, the decrease in the output of oil as a result of maturing of oil wells and the decreased investment in new exploration as well as the increase in domestic consumption has led to policymakers diversifying to other primary sources available such as coal, biofuels and natural gas [6]. Coal and gas are being fronted as the best primary energy substitutes for generation of electricity while biofuels will play a bigger role in the diversification of transport fuel [7]. Table 1 and show the distribution of primary energy supply by source and the final energy supply by type respectively for the year. Crude oil accounts for about 39 % of the primary energy supply while biomass accounts for 18 % [8].

Currently, the renewable energy sources that are being focused on are geothermal, hydro, solar and wind. Geothermal and large hydro projects are being developed mainly for the central grid while small hydro, solar and wind energy projects are geared towards meeting the needs of the small and mostly remote islands [9]. The potential of the renewable sources in the country as estimated by the Ministry of Energy and Mineral Resources is as shown in Table 2. Hydro, geothermal and biomass have great potential with only a small proportion having been developed.

Table 1. Primary energy supply by sources [8].

Source	**Barrel of Oil Equivalent (BOE)**	**Percentage Share**
Coal	334×10^6	22 %
Crude Oil	592×10^6	39 %
Natural Gas	262×10^6	17 %
Hydropower	31×10^6	2 %
Geothermal	16×10^6	1 %
Biomass	280×10^6	18 %
Total	$1\,516 \times 10^6$	100 %

Table 2. Renewable energy sources [8].

Source	**Potential**	**Installed Capacity**
Hydro Power	75.7 GW	4.2 GW
Geothermal	28.5 GW	1.2 GW
Mini/Micro Hydro	500 MW	86.1 MW
Biomass	49.8 GW	445 MW
Solar	4.8 kWh/m^2/d	14.1 MW
Wind	3 m/s to 6 m/s	1.4 MW

One of the incentives that have been used by the government to encourage the development of renewable energy technologies in Indonesia has been through the use of feed-in-tariffs [10]. The renewable energy sources have different feed-in-tariffs depending on the source of energy, installed capacity and the region where the installation is taking place. A summary of the feed-in-tariffs based on Ministerial Regulations. The tariff also varies depending on whether the plant is connected to a low voltage or medium voltage network [11].

2.2 Energy situation in Bawean Island

Bawean Island has its electricity being supplied by PLN Bawean. PLN Bawean has a centralized power generation consisting of 11 diesel generators with an installed capacity of 5.35 MW. Eight of the diesel engines rated 4.2 MW [6] are owned by private companies subcontracted by PLN and are always in operation. The remaining 1.15 MW, consisting of three diesel engines, are owned by PLN and are on standby and can be brought online in the event of a breakdown in any of those from the private company. According to PLN Bawean statistics, the peak demand in the island currently stands at 3.76 MW. PLN Bawean has a 20 kV transmission grid circumnavigating the island and supplying the load centers located along grid. The electrification ratio based on the number of households connected to the PLN grid is 79 % according to PLN Bawean data for September 2013 [12]. It can be observed from these data that whereas household consumers (social and residential categories) consume 75 % of the generated electricity, they only contribute to 71 % of the revenue [13]. This is attributed to the lower tariffs charged for these customer categories compared to other categories.

Most of the households that are not connected to PLN grid depend on small diesel generators for their electricity needs. The households that own small generators of capacity between 2.4 kVA and 5 kVA of which they tend to supply electricity to their neighbors at a fee based on the number of electrical loads in the household [10].

3 Energy demand analysis in Bawean Island

3.1 Methodology and general sample characteristics

These two villages were chosen because of ease of accessibility. Which, 36 of the randomly sampled households were from grid-connected sub-villages called Komalasa and Tanjung Anyar while the other 36 were from non grid connected sub-villages called Sumur-Sumur and Gunung Mas. The fact that the village elders had been informed of our coming beforehand by the head of the Sangkapura sub-district made our work easy. The total number of people in the surveyed households was 316 giving an average of four people per household. This average is slightly more than that of the official data from the government for the island which puts the average at approximately four people per household.

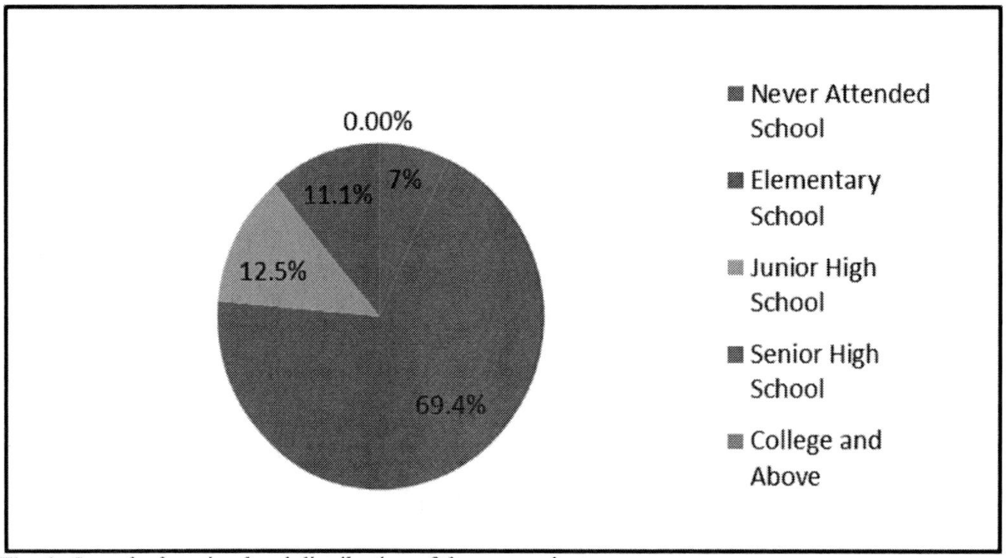

Fig. 1. Overal education level distribution of the respondents.

The overall distribution of the respondents by their level of education is shown in Figure 2. The literacy rate from the surveyed respondents was 93 % which is comparable to those of the national literacy rates according to the government which puts it at 93.25 % [8]

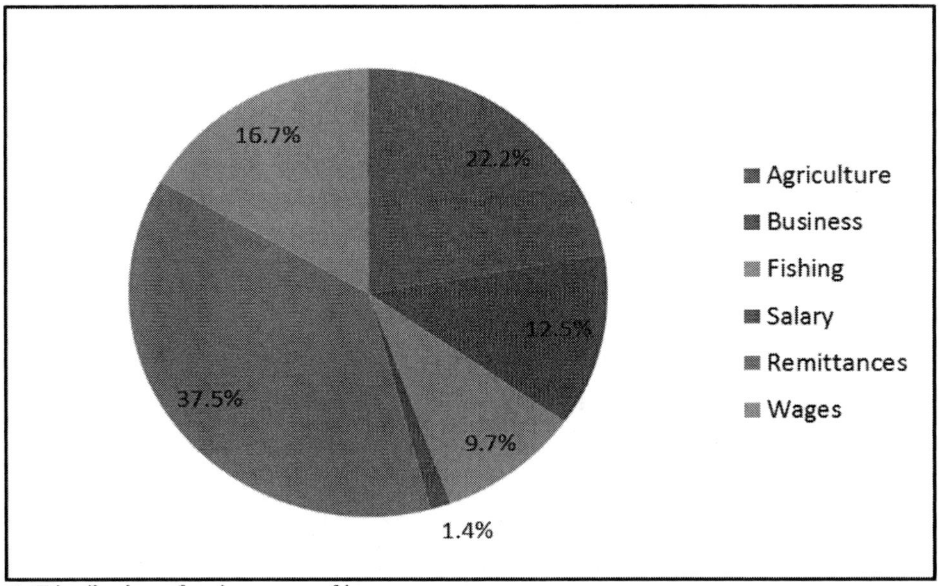

Fig. 2. Distribution of main source of income.

More than one to third of the respondents had their primary source of income is remittances from relatives working abroad. This shows the strong dependence of residents of Bawean Island on remittances. The other main sources of household income were wages, business, fishing, and salary. Figure 3 shows the distribution of main sources of income in the sampled households.

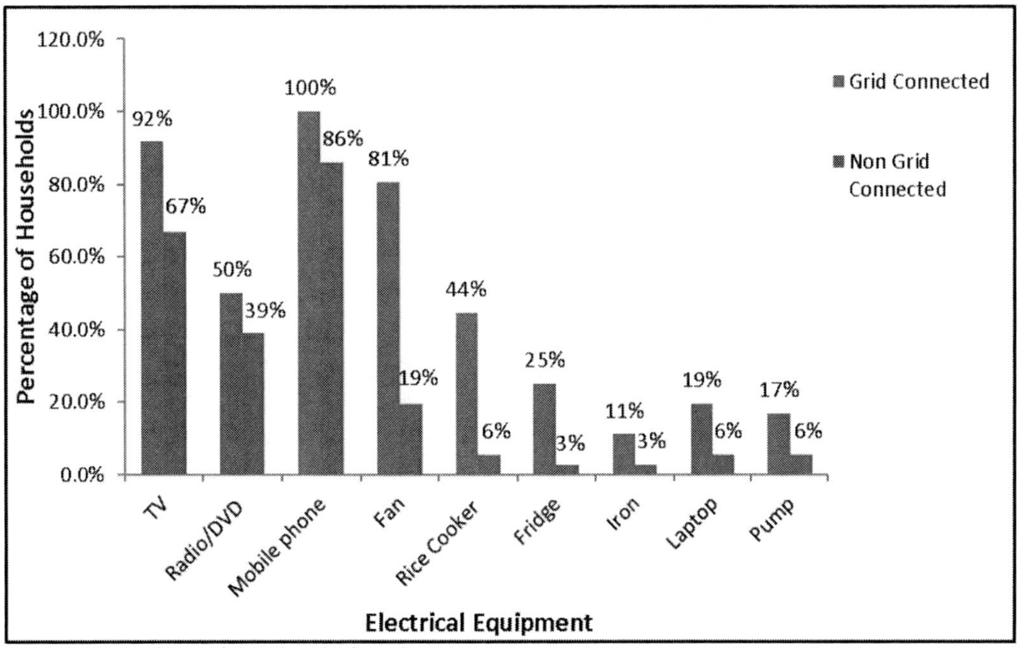

Fig. 3. Comparison of the electrical equipment.

TV, radio/DVD player/speakers, and mobile phones were the most common equipment in both types of households. However, equipment such as fan, rice cooker, refrigerator, laptop, and water pump were more common in the grid-connected households as compared to non grid connected ones. From the survey, it also emerged that for most non grid connected households TV, fan and rice cooker ranks highest as the equipment they would most likely acquire if they were connected to the PLN grid.

3.2 Cooking energy demand

The residents of Bawean Island depend on more than one source of cooking energy, however, the main fuel is firewood. Firewood is easily and freely available to most households since the island has a significant forest cover.

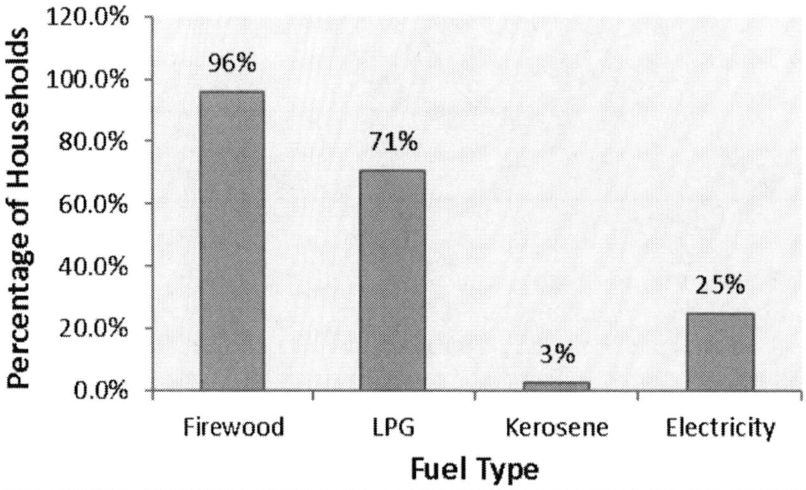

Fig. 4. Sources of cooking energy in the households.

Whereas 96 % of the sampled households used firewood for cooking, 71 % of the total households sampled also had and used LPG. This is remarkable given the remoteness of the Island and shows that the effort that the government of Indonesia has put towards increasing the uptake of LPG for cooking is yielding positive results

4 Results and Discussion

The proposed hybrid power system will be based on a combination of renewable energy sources and diesel generator. The design and optimization of this system were done using HOMER software; time step simulation software used for designing and analyzing the technical and financial viability of a power system based on different technologies and power sources. HOMER is also used to perform sensitivity analysis in order to optimize the system design based on different scenarios or conditions.

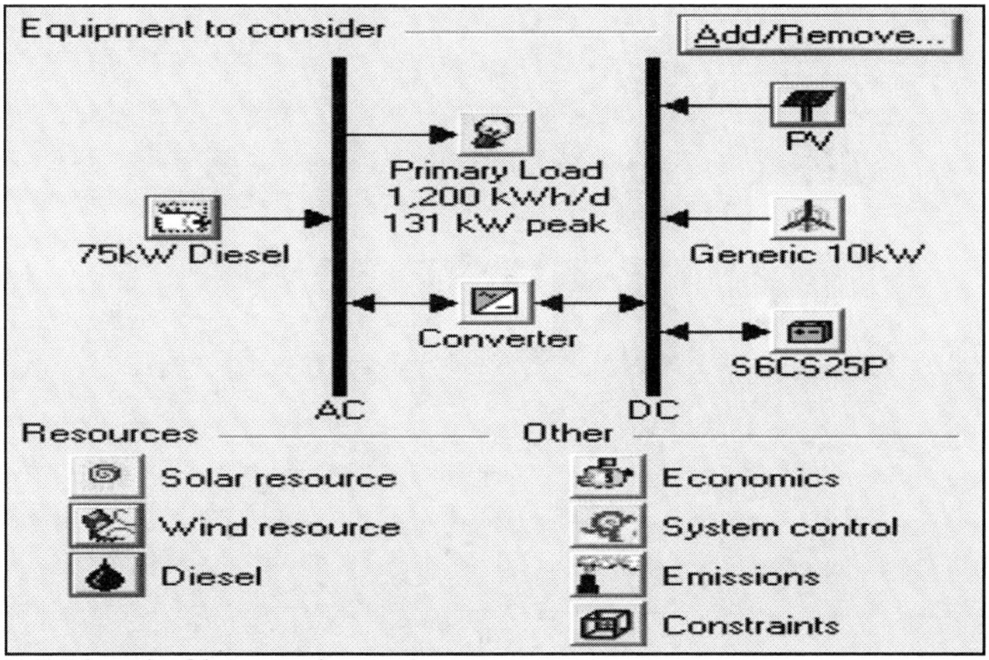

Fig. 5. Schematic of the proposed system.

Production	kWh/yr	%
PV array	269,487	48
Wind turbines	14,422	3
Diesel	280,926	50
Total	564,834	100

Consumption	kWh/yr	%
AC primary load	437,893	100
Total	437,893	100

Quantity	kWh/yr	%
Excess electricity	76,602	13.6
Unmet electric load	107	0.0
Capacity shortage	278	0.1

Quantity	Value
Renewable fraction	0.503

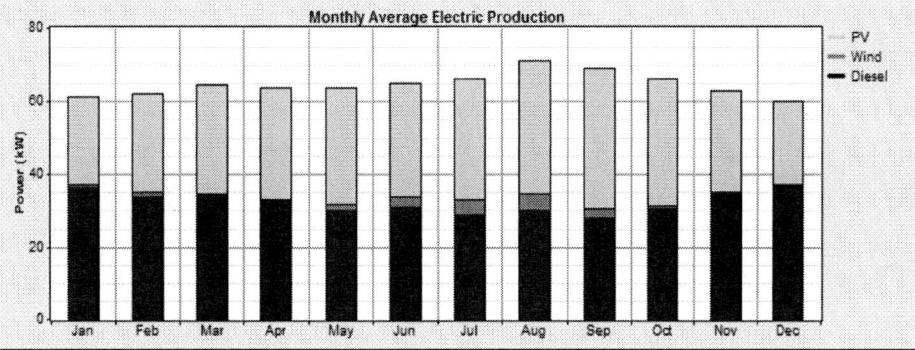

Fig. 6. Electrical power production by source.

It can be observed that it is expected that PV array will contribute the bulk (48 %) of the Renewable energy fraction over the entire year. Wind power output increases marginally in the windy months of June, July, and August. This mini grid electrical power system is expected to generate 565 MWh per year against the expected load demand of 438 MWh per y. For the optimum base system, the diesel generator set will operate for 4 934 h per year; meanwhile the diesel generator set will be replaced six times over the project lifetime given that it has a lifetime of 15 000 operating h. The other significant replacement cost in the project is that of batteries which will be done two times over the project lifetime.

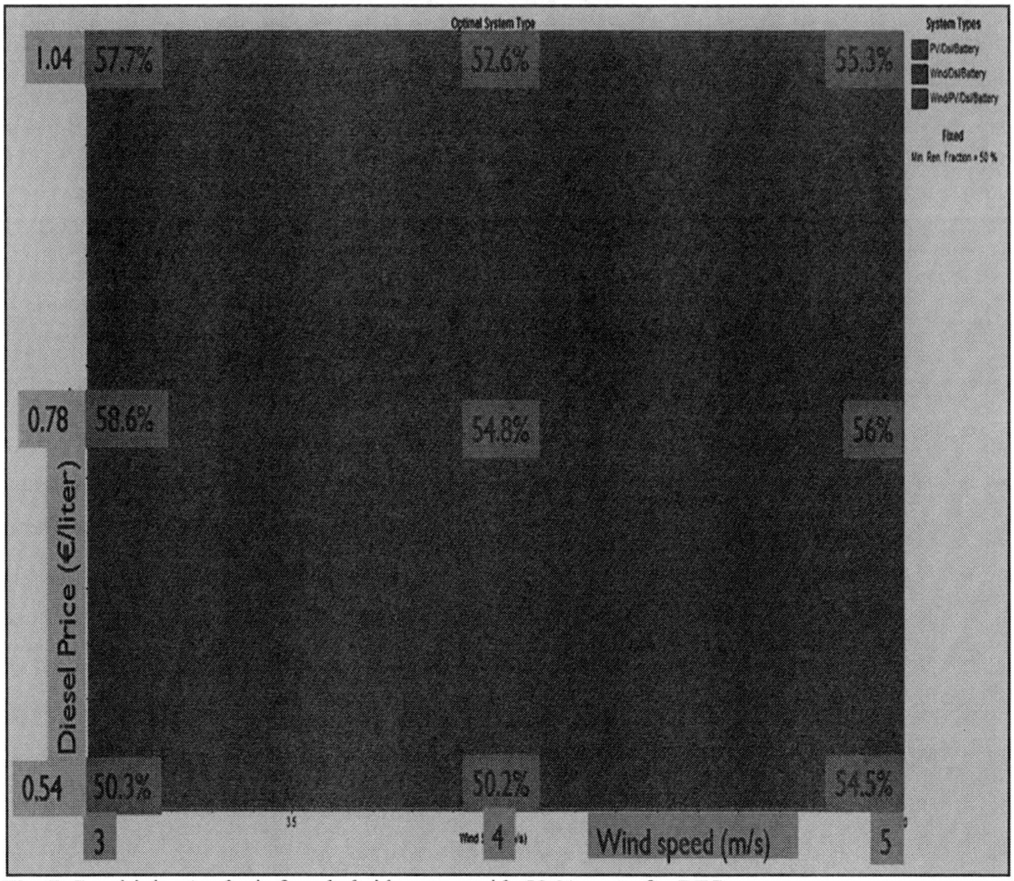

Fig. 7. Sensitivity Analysis for a hybrid system with 50 % quota for RES.

The values in grey boxes of Figure 7 shows the expected fraction of renewable sources electrical production for the various optimum solutions based on the changes in the variables, that is, diesel price and average wind speed. For example, with the average wind speed being 4 m/s and the diesel price being €78, then the optimum system chosen by HOMER will have 54.8 % of the electrical production coming from renewable sources, that is both wind and solar PV for this case. This scenario is based on the simulation giving an optimal hybrid system with at least 50 % electricity production from renewable energy sources (base case scenario).

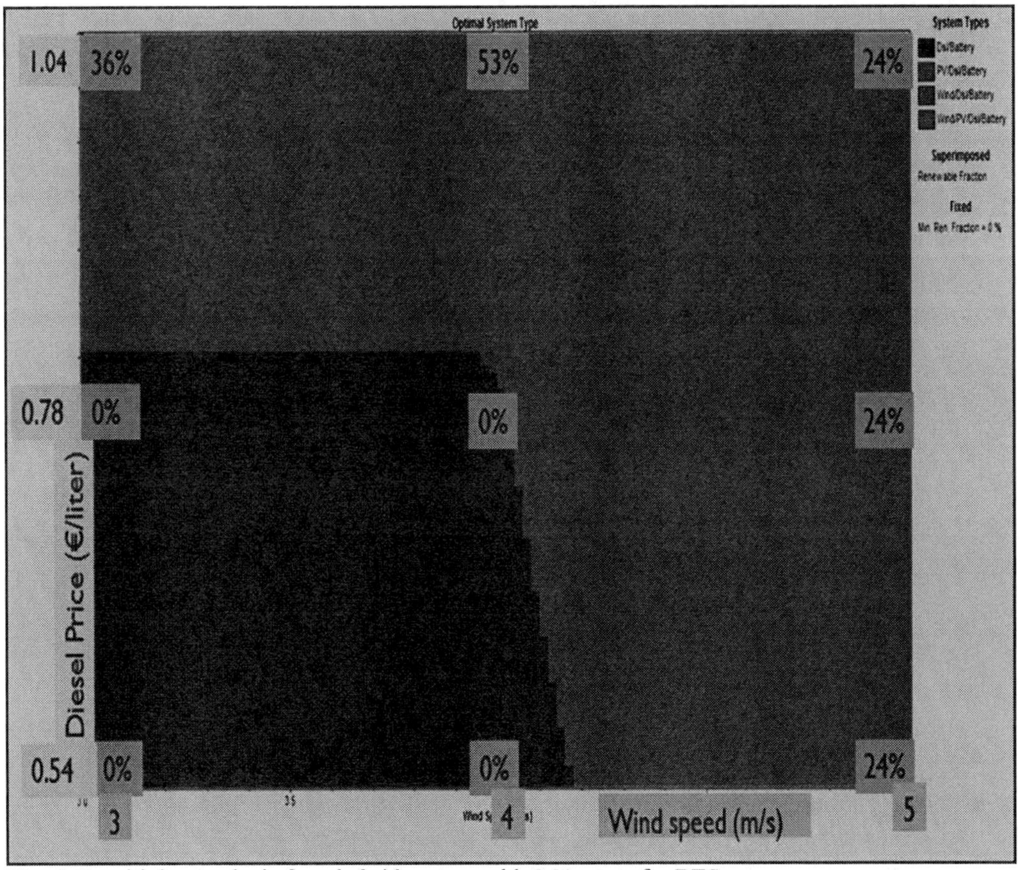

Fig. 8. Sensitivity Analysis for a hybrid system with 0 % quota for RES.

A sensitivity analysis was also carried out on HOMER to determine the effect of a change in battery's lifetime on the levelised cost of energy (LCOE). The battery used in the simulation was assumed to have a conservative lifetime of 7 yr even though the manufacturer's estimate is 12 yr. A sensitivity analysis was done to compare the LCOE for this base case as compared to if the battery had a lifetime of 5 yr or 10 y.r

5 Conclusion

This study was done to determine the current energy demand for the people living in Bawean Islands. Based on the average electricity consumption of 98 kWh per month for the surveyed grid-connected households, a hybrid electrical power system was designed for Gili Timur Island. The proposed system was designed, simulated and optimized using HOMER software. A sensitivity analysis was also carried out on the optimum system to study the effects of variation in some of the system variables. HOMER suggests that for the expected peak load of 131 kW, an optimum system will consist of 150 kW from PV array, two wind turbines each rated 10 kW, a 75 kW diesel generator and batteries for storage. The initial capital needed to set up a hybrid electrical system is relatively high, and the residents of Gili Timur Island may not be in a position to raise the whole amount. It will, therefore, be a great idea if the local or central government could give a subsidized loan or grant towards this noble cause. This way the residents of Gili Timur Island can enjoy the benefits of a 24 h electricity grid just as their neighbors in main Bawean Island.

References

1 Central Intelligence Agency. *The world factbook: Indonesia* [Online] from https://www.cia.gov/library/publications/the-world-factbook/geos/id.html (2013). [Accessed on 23 September 2013].

2 Consulate General of the Republic of Indonesia.*Geography* [Online] from http://indonesiavancouver.org/wp1/index.php/geography/ (2013). [Accessed 24 September 2013].

3 BPS (Central Bureau of Statistics) Gresik. *Gresik dalam angka 2013* [Gresik in figures 2013]. BPS: Gresik (2013). pp 40–65. https://kupdf.com/download/gresik-dalam-angka-2013_59f0a8efe2b6f5ab5ce375f1_pdf . [in Bahasa Indonesia]

4 P.F.A. Ogola, B. Davidsdottir, I.B. Fridleifsson. *Renewable and Sustainable Energy Reviews*, **15**, 8:4067–4079 (2011). https://www.sciencedirect.com/science/article/pii/S1364032111002784

5 A. Brew-Hammond. Energy: the missing millenium development goal. In *Energy for development resources, technologies, environment*. F.L. Toht (Eds). Dordrecht: Springer (2012). pp. 35–43. http://www.springer.com/gp/book/9789400741614

6 R.A. Cabraal, D.F. Barnes, S.G. Agarwal. *Annual Review of Environment and Resources*, **30**:117–144 (2005).

7 K. Kaygusuz. *Renewable and Sustainable Energy Reviews*, **16**, 2:1116–1126 (2012). https://www.sciencedirect.com/science/article/pii/S1364032111005491

8 British Petroleum (BP). *BP Statistical Review of World Energy* [Online] http://www.bp.com/en/global/corporate/about-bp/statistical-review-of-world-energy-2013.html (2013). [Accessed on 25 September 2013]

9 International Institute for Sustainable Development (IISD). *A citizens' guide to energy subsidies in Indonesia*. [Online] from http://www.iisd.org/gsi/sites/default/files/indonesia_czguide_eng_update_2012.pdf (2012). [Accessed on 23 September 2013].

10 International Institute for Sustainable Development (IISD). *A Citizens' Guide to Energy Subsidies in Indonesia* [Online] from http://www.iisd.org/gsi/sites/default/files/indonesia_czguide_eng_update_2012.pdf (2012). [Accessed on 23 September 2013].

11 International Energy Agency. *World energy outlook 2012*. [Online] from http://www.iea.org/publications/freepublications/publication/English.pdf (2012). [Accessed on 2 September 2013]

12 International Energy Agency. "*World Energy Outlook 2012.*" iea.org. November, 2012. http://www.iea.org/publications/freepublications/publication/English.pdf (accessed on 10 September 2013)

13 International Energy Agency (IEA). *Energy for all: Financing access for the poor*. [Online] from http://www.iea.org/papers/2011/weo2011_energy_for_all.pdf (2011). [Accessed on 6 October 2013].

Characterisation of Arabica Coffee Pulp - Hay from Kintamani - Bali as Prospective Biogas Feedstocks

Roy Hendroko Setyobudi[1,*], *Satriyo* Krido Wahono[2,3], *Praptiningsih* Gamawati Adinurani[4], *Ahmad* Wahyudi[5], *Wahyu* Widodo[5], *Maizirwan* Mel[6], *Yogo* Adhi Nugroho[7], *Bayu* Prabowo[8,9], and *Tony* Liwang[7]

[1)]Waste Laboratory of University Muhamadiyah of Malang, Jl. Raya Tlogomas No. 246 Malang, 65114, Indonesia
[2)]Future Industry Institute and School of Engineering, University of South Australia, Mawson Lakes SA 5095, Adelaide, Australia.
[3)]Technical Implementation Unit for Development of Chemical Engineering Processes, Indonesian Institute of Sciences, 55861, Yogyakarta, Indonesia
[4)]Faculty of Agrotechnology, Merdeka University of Madiun, Jl. Serayu No. 79 Madiun 63131, Indonesia
[5)]Faculty of Agricultural and Animal Science, University Muhamadiyah of Malang, Indonesia.
[6]Departement of Biotechnology, Faculty of Engineering, International Islamic University Malaysia (IIUM), Gombak, 50728 Kuala Lumpur, Malaysia
[7)]Plant Production and Biotechnology Division, PT Sinarmas Agroresources and Technology Tbk., Sinar Mas Land Plaza, 2nd Tower 10th Fl. Jl. M.H. Thmrin No. 51, Jakarta 10350, Indonesia
[8)]Department of Renewable Energy Engineering, Universitas Prasetiya Mulya, Tangerang, Banten 15339, Indonesia
[9]Institute of Energy and Power Engineering, Zhejiang University of Technology, Hangzhou, Zhejiang 310014, China

Abstract. The huge amount of coffee pulp waste is an environmental problem. Anaerobic fermentation is one of the alternative solutions. However, availability of coffee pulp does not appear for year-round, whereas biogas needs continuous feedstocks for digester stability. This research uses coffee pulp from Arabica Coffee Factory at Mengani, Kintamani, Bali–Indonesia. The coffee pulp was transformed into coffee pulp-hay product by sun drying for preservations to extend the raw materials through the year. Characterization of coffee pulp-hay was conducted after to keep for 15 mo for review the prospect as biogas feedstocks. Several parameters were analyzed such as C/N ratio, volatile solids, carbohydrate, protein, fat, lignocellulose content, macro-micro nutrients, and density. The review results indicated that coffee pulp-hay is prospective raw material for biogas feedstock. This well-proven preservation technology was able to fulfill the continuous supply. Furthermore, some problems were found in the recent preliminary experiment related to the density and fungi growth in the conventional laboratory digester. Further investigation was needed to implement the coffee pulp – hay as biogas feedstocks.

Key words: Environmental problems, floating feed, hay technology, low density feed, preservation feedstocks, waste to energy

* Corresponding author: roy_hendroko@hotmail.com

1 Introduction

Coffee pulp (CP) is one of the huge wastes which is produced by Coffee Factories (CF). Weight volume of CP is 41 % to 50 % in wet basis [1, 2], or 20 % to 29 % in dry basis [2, 3]. CP is commonly disposed to the river or environment around the CF [4, 5] which produces negative impact since CP contains toxic compound namely caffeine, alkaloids, tannins and polyphenolics [6, 7].

Baier and Hofmann in Bombardiere [8] and reference [9] showed that CP is a prospective organic compound as biogas raw material. Biogas is the renewable energy resource which is needed by CF [10], particularly for reducing fossil energy cost and increasing efficiency. Mulato [11] and Mulato & Suharyanto [12] said that the biogas of CF waste production is able to utilize as energy resources of coffee drying, lighting and circulating pump generator.

However, CP does not available for year-round as biogas feedstock. Coffee harvesting is conducted between June and September every year in Indonesia, so CP is available for 3 mo to 5 mo [13]. Whereas, Steiner [14] stated that the anaerobic digester does not economical when operated less than 8 mo. Some references [12, 13] suggested utilization of cow-dung as replacement feedstocks while there is no availability of CP, but not every CF have stabled cattle ranch. Furthermore, CP replacement by cow-dung and vice versa provide negative impact possibility to anaerobic stability process [15] and disrupt the steady-state/start-up process which conducted for 2 mo to 3 mo [16–18].

Other references [14, 19] suggested to apply silage technology on CP, so biogas feedstock is available for a year. However, it has several drawbacks such as anaerobic storage requirement, component addition (molasses), etc. Therefore, this study was conducted to review effective preservation of CP by sun drying or hay technology.

2 Materials and methods

CP was collected from peeling machine by the wet base system for coffee time processing in July 2016 to August 2016 from Arabica CF at Mengani, Kintamani, Bali, Indonesia. Coffee of Kintamani-Bali is a pioneer plantation product in Indonesia as the first obtained of certifications geographical indications (GI) at 2008 from 10 Indonesian Arabica coffee products [20]. CP was dried under the sunshine for about 5 d on the drying floor until water content about 12 %. Then, the dried pulp or hay pulp (HP) was stored in burlap sacks placed in the warehouse. After 15 mo, HP was characterized in the laboratory of Indonesian Research Institute for Animal Production in Ciawi, Bogor, Indonesia to determine the suitability of HP as biogas feedstock. Analysis methods were shown in Table 1.

Table 1. Laboratory analysis methods of hay pulp as biogas feedstock.

No	Variable	Methods
1	Mg, K, Na, Fe, Ca	Atomic Absorption Spectroscopy (AAS)
2	S, C/N ratio, phenol total	spectrophotometry
3	water, fat, ash, lignin content	gravimetry
4	Protein	destructive auto analysis
5	Neutral Detergent Fiber (NDF)	neutral detergent solvent extraction
6	Acid Detergent Fiber (ADF)	acid detergent solvent extraction
7	Cellulose	acid extraction
8	Carbohydrate, Volatile Solid (VS), N content, hemicellulose	calculation
9	Density	true density

3 Result and Discussions

3.1 C/N ratio

C/N ratio analysis results of arabica coffee HP-GI Kintamani is shown in Table 2. Table 2 shows HP is commonly appropriate as biogas feedstock [21–26], except standard 4 [27, 28]. The previous studies showed that C/N ratio of CP is 40.0 to 71.2 [29, 30]. Furthermore, C/N ratio of cow-dung is 16.67 [31] or 21.00 [32]. It indicates that pulp storage as hay for 15 mo reduce C/N ratio to the ideal value.

Table 2. C/N ratio comparison of coffee pulp-hay

	coffee pulp-hay	**standard**			
		1	**2**	**3**	**4**
C/N ratio	20.06	10 to 30	15 to 25	20 to 30	23 to 32
Reference	This study	[21, 22]	[23, 24]	[25, 26]	[27, 28]

3.2 C/N ratio

Volatile Solid (VS) of arabica coffee HP-GI Kintamani is shown in Table 3. Table 3 shows that VS of HP is appropriate to some references [33–35]. VS is a necessary factor to predict methane amount production [24, 35, 39, 40], wherein the higher ratio of VS produced greater methane [41, 42].

The previous study said that cow-dung is an ideal substrate for anaerobic digestion [43], but other studies stated about vice versa indication that cow-dung produced low yield biogas [44, 45]. The biogas volume of CF waste is 18 times higher than cow-dung [13] which supports also by VS data in Table 3. However, the higher VS was inducted into the digester, also produce the larger amount of volatile acid [39] which influencing digester alkalinity and pH. Therefore, the high VS content had to insert slowly into an anaerobic digester.

Table 3. Volatile solid comparison of coffee pulp-hay

	coffee pulp-hay	**fresh coffee pulp**			**cow-dung**
Volatile Solid	91.02	91.10	92.80	94.00	27.80 to 39.60
Reference	This study	[33]	[34]	[35]	[32, 36–38]

3.3 Carbohydrate, Protein and Fat Contents

Carbohydrate, protein and fat contents of arabica coffee HP-GI Kintamani is shown in Table 4. Table 4 shows that carbohydrate, protein and fat contents of HP after 15 mo storage are appropriate to the references range [5, 48, 49], even particularly for carbohydrate content is higher than references [46, 47]. Moreover, it also shows that HP contents are higher than cow-dung. However, carbohydrate dominant of HP provided negative impact possibility in the anaerobic process. Some references [24, 50, 51] stated that the possibility of buffer capacity is weak, with the impact of problems in the alkalinity of the substrate. It supported by other references [23, 24, 28] which said that carbohydrate dominant produced the low quality of biogas related to the high number of C-atoms in the substrate.

Table 4. Carbohydrate, protein, and fat contents comparison of coffee pulp-hay

	coffee pulp-hay	previous studies	cow-dung
Carbohydrate (%)	65.99	35.00 to 63.20[1)]	41.15
Protein (%)	11.00	0.80 to 15.00[2)]	9.55
Fat (%)	1.54	0.83 to 7.00[3)]	0.40
Reference	This study	[1)][46, 47], [2)][5, 48], [3)][49, 48]	[32]

3.4 Lignocellulose content

Carbohydrate was divided into simple carbohydrate (monosaccharide dan disaccharide) and complex carbohydrate (polysaccharide). Some references [29, 47, 52] stated that CP was categorized rich lignocelluloses as the common characteristic of agricultural wastes [53]. Table 5 shows lignocellulose content consist of cellulose, lignin, and hemicellulose. Table 5 indicates that lignocelluloses of HP are appropriate to some references range [5, 33, 54–57], but lignin content of HP is lower than references [56, 57]. Moreover, cellulose and hemicellulose (a+b) of cow-dung is higher than HP, but it has similar lignin content.

Table 5. Cellulose, lignin, and hemicellulose contents comparison of coffee pulp-hay.

	coffee pulp-hay	previous research	cow-dung
Selulosa (a) (%)	25.84	17.70 to 49.87[1)]	22.28 to 26.59
Hemiselulosa (b) (%)	4.37	2.30 to 21.80[2)]	11.27 to 23.55
Lignin (%)	12.46	17.50 to 31.58 [3)]	11.24 to 12.67
(a) + (b) (%)	30.21	20.00 to 87.00	33.55 to 50.14
Reference		[1][54, 55], [2][5, 33], [3][56, 57]	[31, 32]

3.5 Nutrient

Steiner [14] dan Tadesse & Mebratu [30] stated that CP nutrient is appropriate as biogas feedstocks and met the requirement of C:N:P = 250:10:1, but it did not show nutrient content value. Table 6 shows macronutrient content of HP. Nutrient contents of C, N, P, and S of HP lower than the references requirement [23, 25]. C nutrient was needed by microbes as energy resources [59]. Madigan and Martinko [60] said that 50 % of dry weight cell was carbon. N nutrient was needed to construct cell structure which required 14 % of dry weight of microbes [59, 60].

Table 6 supports references [50, 61] which said that agricultural wastes and or agro-industry were categorized as poor nutrients. However, HP nutrient shows appropriate to previous research range [30, 33, 59], even C nutrient is higher than reference [58]. Based on this data, HP nutrient did not decrease after 15 mo storage and was higher than cow-dung nutrients [32]. It was supported by Higashikawa [62] which found that CP nutrient was higher at N. K, and B variables, but lower at P, Mg, and Mn variables.

Table 6. Macronutrients contents comparison of coffee pulp-hay.

	coffee pulp-hay	**standard 1**	**standard 2**	**previous research**	**cow-dung**
Carbon (%)	35.31	100	500 to 1 000	30.37[1)]	19
Nitrogen (%)	1.76	10	15 to 20	0.80 to 1.90[2)]	0.90
Phosphat (%)	0.20	1	5	0.13 to 0.20[3)]	0.20
Sulphur (%)	0.18	1	3	--	--
Reference	This study	[25]	[23]	[1][58], [2][33, 56], [3][30, 56]	[32]

Table 7 shows that HP contains inhibitors, particularly as micronutrients namely Ca, Mg, and Na. CP was a substance rich in hydroxyl groups, so it had the ability to absorb heavy metal [2, 33, 66–70]. This property caused HP micronutrients were categorized as inhibitors, but microbes had the ability to degrade toxic material [71, 72]. Furthermore, Table 7 also indicates HP contains phenol as an inhibitor. It also supported by some references about CP phenol content [33, 73, 74], but microbes also degraded phenol in anaerobic digestion [75, 76].

Table 7. Micronutrients of P, K, Ca, Mg, Na and total phenol comparison of coffee pulp-hay.

	coffee pulp-hay	**Standard Stimulatory**	**Standard Moderately Inhibitors**
C/P	177	150 to 300[1]	
C/K	11	40 to 100[1]	
K (mg L^{-1})	329	200 to 400[2]	2 500 to 4 500[2]
Ca (mg L^{-1})	4 600	200 to 400[2]	2 500 to 4 500[2]
Mg (mg L^{-1})	1 100	75 to 150[2]	1 000 to 1 500[2]
Na (mg L^{-1})	500	100 to 200[2]	3 500 to 5 500[2]
Phenol (mg L^{-1})	5 500		2 400[3]
Reference		[1][63], [2][64]	[2][64], [3][65]

Fe micronutrient content of HP-GI Kintamani is low which is shown in Table 8. It was lower than stimulatory requirement [77, 78], but it still in previous research range [63, 80], and lower than others previous research [81, 82]. The low Fe content of HP-GI Kintamani was needed further study, it was possibly caused by Kintamani land was categorized Inceptisol [83]. Inceptisol Kintamani was the young land of Batur Volcano eruption. Some references [84, 85] stated about Inceptisol characteristics such as pH was acidic to slightly acidic; soil electrical conductivity (EC) was very low; whereas organic matter, total nitrogen, cation exchange capacity (CEC), saturation bases, potassium potency and Iron Hydrous Oxide were low. Nandini and Narendra [85] found that Fe content of Bangli, Kintamani soil was in the range of 15.0 mg/kg to 18.4 mg/kg which categorized very low

Table 8. Iron nutrient content comparison of coffee pulp-hay.

Fe nutrient of coffee pulp-hay	**Stimulatory**	**Inhibitor**	**Previous Research**
136 mg kg^{-1} or 0.014 %	0.02 % [77] 0.40 % [78]	0.18 % [79]	0.015 % (Bressani in [80]) 0.01 % to 0.50 % [63] 0.025 % [81] 0.287 % [82]

3.6 Density

The true density value of HP-GI Kintamani showed 0.40 g mL^{-1}, which was lower than the bulk density of previous research of 0.53 g mL^{-1} [82]. The low density has a negative impact which was also reported by the previous research of dry husk *Jatropha curcas* Linn. (DH-JcL) with true density of 0.59 g mL^{-1} [32].

Moreover, other problems were obstruction of DH-JcL inclusion since the inlet digester blocked; then DH-JcL floated on the digester substrate, so methanogenic bioconversion process was not optimized. Praptiningsih et al. [86] overcame the floating DH-JcL by utilizing ballast weight. The floating HP problem was confirmed in preliminary studies of biogas using HP-GI Kintamani was conducted in November 2017 to February 2018 at Waste Laboratory of Nutrition and Animal Husbandry Laboratory of Muhamadiyah University of Malang, Indonesia. Another negative impact was the easiness growth of fungi on CP which found when it was drying under the sun as hay on the CF. The fungi were suspected dormant for 15 mo of HP storage process. However, it was grown rapidly when HP was mixed to water diluents in the conventional laboratory digester which is shown in Figure 1.a-d

Figure 1. (a) the floating HP digestate on the substrate; (b) The thickness of HP digestate which blocking biogas goes to gas holder; (c, d) two types of fungi on digestate.

4 Conclusion

Based on the data was concluded that coffee pulp-hay after 15 mo storage was appropriate as biogas feedstock. The further investigation was needed to overcome the dormant fungi problems on the HP storage but grown rapidly when HP was utilized as biogas substrate.

The authors are grateful to Ricky Hendarto Setyobudi and Fitri Ramli, Arabica Coffee Factory at Mengani, Kintamani, Bali – Indonesia for supply the Hay-Pulp as research material.

References

1. B. Janissen, T. Huynh. Resources, Conservation & Recycling **128**, 110–117 (2018). https://www.sciencedirect.com/science/article/pii/S0921344917303154
2. L. Blinova, M. Sirotiak, A. Bartosova, M. Soldan. Slovak University of Technology in Bratislava **25**, 40:91–101 (2017). https://www.degruyter.com/view/j/rput.2017.25.issue-40/rput-2017-0011/rput-2017-0011.xml
3. S. Widyotomo. Review Penelitian Kopi dan Kakao **1**, 1:63–80 (2013). [in Bahasa Indonesia]. https://anzdoc.com/download/potensi-dan-teknologi-diversifikasi-limbah-kopi-menjadi-prod.html?reader=1.
4. J.F. Calzada, O.R. deLeon, M.C. deArriola, F. deMicheo, C. Rolz, C., R. de Leon, et al. Biotechnology Letters **3**, 12:713–716 (1981). https://link.springer.com/article/10.1007/BF00134849
5. T. Widjaja, T. Iswanto, A. Altway, M. Shovitri, S.R. Juliastuti. Methane Production from Coffee Pulp by Microorganism of Rumen Fluid and Cow Dung in Co-digestion. Chemical Engineering Transactions **56**, 1465–1470 (2017). https://www.researchgate.net/profile/Toto_Iswanto/publication/319417335_Methane_Production_from_Coffee_Pulp_by_Microorganism_of_Rumen_Fluid_and_Cow_Dung_in_Co-digestion/links/59a92cd7a6fdcc2398414dd9/Methane-Production-from-Coffee-Pulp-by-Microorganism-of-Rumen-Fluid-and-Cow-Dung-in-Co-digestion.pdf.
6. L. Fan, A.T. Soccol, A. Pandey, C.R. Soccol. Micologia Aplicada International **15**, 15–21 (2003). https://www.researchgate.net/publication/26484135_Cultivation_of_Pleurotus_mushrooms_on_Brazilian_coffee_husk_and_effects_of_caffeine_and_tannic_acid
7. S.R. Juliastuti, T. Widjaja, A. Altway, T. Iswanto. AIP Conference Proceedings 1840, 1 (2017). DOI:10.1063/1.4982341. https://aip.scitation.org/doi/abs/10.1063/1.4982341
8. Y.E. Bombardiere. *The Potensial of Anaerobic Technology to Treat Coffee Waste in Huatusco, Mexico*. [Thesis]. The Center for International Studies of Ohio University, Athens, USA, (2006). pp.85. https://etd.ohiolink.edu/pg_10?0::NO:10:P10_ACCESSION_NUM:ohiou1152557924
9. E. Novita, S. Wahyuningsih. *Teknologi Penanganan Limbah Cair untuk Mewujudkan Lingkungan Perkebunan Kopi Rakyat yang Sehat, Produktif dan Berkelanjutan* [Liquid Waste Technology Process to Develop a Healthy, Productive and Sustainable Peasant Coffee Plantation] [Online] from http://repository.unej.ac.id/bitstream/handle/123456789/73730/Lap_Akhir_Stranas%202015_Elida%20Novita.pdf?sequence=1. (2015). [Accessed on 5 April 2017]. [in Bahasa Indonesia]
10. C. Rolz, J.F. Menchu, F. Calzada, R. de Leon, R. Garcla. Process Biochemistry **17**, 2:8–11 (1982). https://www.cabdirect.org/cabdirect/abstract/19822413679

11. S. Mulato. *Case Study of Biogas Production from Plant-Based Materials and Animal Manure Resources Available In the Cocoa and Coffee Farms*. 2009 International Workshop on Developing Bioenergy and Conserving the Natural Ecosystem in APEC Member Economies (Seoul, Korea, 2009). 2009 APEC Workshop Developing Bioenergy and Conserving the Natural Ecosystem in APEC Member Economies in APEC Member Economies: 79–96 https://apec.org/Publications/2010/02/2009-International-Workshop-on-Developing-Bioenergy-and-Conserving-the-Natural-Ecosystem-in-APEC-Mem
12. S. Mulato, E Suharyanto. Case Study of Biogas Production from Plant-Based Materials and Animal Manure Resources Available in the Coffee Farm. Proceedings of 22th International Conference on Coffee Science, Bali , Indonesia: ASIC 3-8 Oktober 2010 https://www.asic-cafe.org/conference/23rd-international-conference-coffee-science/case-study-biogas-production-plant-based
13. E. Novita. *Desain Proses Pengolahan pada Agroindustri Kopi Robusta Menggunakan Modifikasi Teknologi Olah Basah Berbasis Produksi Bersih* [Process Design of Robusta Coffee Agro Industry Using Wet Processing Technology Modification Based on Cleaner Production. [Dissertation]. Institut Pertanian Bogor, Bogor, Indonesia (2012). p. 325. http://repository.ipb.ac.id/handle/123456789/55728
14. R. Steiner. *Biogas Production of Coffee Pulp & Waste Water* [Online] from www.repic.ch/index.php/download_file/359/358/ (2011). [Accessed on 15 October 2017]
15. R. Bello-Mendoza, M.F. Castillo-Rivera. Anaerobe **4**, 5:219–225 (1998). https://www.sciencedirect.com/science/article/pii/S1075996498901718
16. L.H. Quang. *Making Use of Tannery Chromium Containing Sludge as Feed for Biogas Plant*. [Thesis]. Central Ostrobothnia University of Aplied Sciences (2011) p.92 http://www.theseus.fi/bitstream/handle/10024/29164/Thesis+-+COU+-+Le+Huy+Quang.pdf;jsessionid=508979EDE18F4FE8934D7F9DC4C62613?sequence=1
17. A. Dahiya (Eds). Bioenergy, Biomass to Biofuels. UK: Academic Press (2015). p 619. https://www.amazon.com/Bioenergy-Biomass-Biofuels-Anju-Krivov/dp/0124079091
18. A. Wellinger, J. Patrick Murphy, D. Baxter (Eds). The Biogas Handbook: Science, Production and Applications. UK Woodhead Publishing (2013). p. 512. https://www.amazon.com/Biogas-Handbook-Production-Applications-Publishing/dp/085709498X
19. Hofmann, M. and Baier, U. 2003. Abstract In: Vergärung von Pulpa aus der Kaffee-Produktion. Energieforschung Forschungs- und PhD-Programm Biomass Bundesamts für Energie BFE pp. 33 [in German] http://www.bfe.admin.ch/php/modules/enet/streamfile.php?file=000000007800.pdf&name=230057.pdf
20. Direktorat Jenderal Perkebunan, Kementrian Pertanian. *30 Produk Perkebunan Indikasi Geographis* [30 Plantation Products with Geographical Indication] [Online] from http://ditjenbun.pertanian.go.id/berita-421-30-produk-perkebunan-indikasi-geografis.html (2016). [Accessed on 5 January 2018]. [in Bahasa Indonesia]
21. A.B. Karki, K. Dixit. Biogas fieldbook. Khatmandu: Sahayogi Press (1984). p.171. http://agris.fao.org/agris-search/search.do?recordID=NP8600002
22. M. Schön. *Numerical Modelling of Anaerobic Digestion Processes in Agricultural Biogas Plants*. [Dissertation]. Technische Universität München, Germany, (2009). p. 157.

https://www.uibk.ac.at/umwelttechnik/teaching/phd/diss_schoen_2009_numerical-modelling-of-biogas-plants.pdf

23. D. Deublein, A. Steinhauser. 2008 Biogas from Waste and Renewable Resources; Wiley Online Library: Weinheim, Germany. p. 429. http://onlinelibrary.wiley.com/book/10.1002/9783527621705
24. A. Schnürer, Å. Jarvis. *Microbiological Handbook for Biogas Plants Swedish Waste Management U2009:03 Swedish Gas Centre Report 207* [Online] from http://www.eac-quality.net/fileadmin/eac_quality/user_documents/3_pdf/Microbiological_handbook_for_biogas_plants.pdf (2010. [Accessed on 20 May 2017]
25. G.D. Zupancic, V. Grilc. Anaerobic Treatment and Biogas Production from Organic Waste, In: *Management of Organic Waste*. Sunil K. (Eds). Rijeka, Croatia, Shanghai, China: InTech. (2012). p 28. https://www.intechopen.com/books/howtoreference/management-of-organic-waste/anaerobic-treatment-and-biogas-production-from-organic-wastes
26. K. Fricke , H. Santen , R. Wallmann , A. Hüttner, N. Dichtl . Waste Manag. 2007;**27**(1):30-43 (2007) https://www.ncbi.nlm.nih.gov/pubmed/16860554
27. U. Marchaim. *Biogas Processes for Sustainable Development*. Rome: FAO (1992). p. 254. http://www.fao.org/docrep/t0541e/T0541E00.htm
28. I. Angelidaki, L. Ellegaard. Applied Biochemistry and Biotechnology, **109**, (1-3):95–106 (2003). https://link.springer.com/article/10.1385/ABAB:109:1-3:95
29. N.A. Dzung, T.T. Dzung, V.T. Phuong Khanh. 2013. Resources and Environment **3**, 4:77–82. http://article.sapub.org/10.5923.j.re.20130304.03.html
30. M. Tadesse, A. Mebratu. International Journal of Recent Development in Engineering and Technology, **6**, 1:18–30 (2017). http://www.ijrdet.com/files/Volume6Issue1/IJRDET_0117_04.pdf.
31. G.N. Demirer, S. Chen. Process Biochemistry, **40**, 11:3542–3549 (2005). https://www.sciencedirect.com/science/article/pii/S1359511305001923
32. P.G. Adinurani, R.H. Setyobudi, A. /nindita, S.K. Wahono, M. Maizirwan, A. Sasmito, Y.A. Nugroho, T. Liwang. Energy Procedia **65**:264–273 (2015). https://ac.els-cdn.com/S1876610215000478/1-s2.0-S1876610215000478-main.pdf?_tid=e7f7e647-f845-4103-a871-b25bed4c9de5&acdnat=1521028434_52192956794b4b62ea2502dedc9c71d4
33. G. Corro, L. Paniagua, U. Pal, F. Banuelos, M. Rosas. Energy Conversion and Management **74**:471–481 (2013). https://www.sciencedirect.com/science/article/pii/S0196890413003889
34. E. Fischer, T. Schmidt, S. Hora, J. Giersdorf, W. Stinner, F. Scholwin. *Agro-Industrial Biogas in Kenya. Potentials, Estimates for Tariffs, Policy and Business Recommendations* [Online] from http://kerea.org/wp-content/uploads/2012/12/Agro-Industrial-Biogas-in-Kenya.pdf. (2010). [Accessed on 5 April 2017]
35. C. Nzila, D. Njuguna, D. Madara, J. Githaig, R. Muasya, A. Muumbo, H. Kiriamit. Journal of Emerging Trends in Engineering and Applied Sciences **6**, 5:327–334 (2015). https://www.researchgate.net/publication/308795332_Characterization_of_Agro-Residues_For_Biogas_Production_and_Nutrient_Recovery_In_Kenya
36. J.H. Martin. *An Evaluation of a Mesophilic, Modefied Plug Flow Anaerobic Digester for Dairy Cattle Manure* [Online] from http://www.dvoinc.com/documents/gordondale_report_final.pdf. (2005). [Accessed on 20 May 2017]

37. B.S.U.I. Abubakar, N. Ismail. ARPN Journal of Engineering and Applied Sciences, **7,** 2:169–172 (2012). https://pdfs.semanticscholar.org/88a3/6a207992acfffa045a87a0b8eb04aa1d994e.pdf.
38. J.A. Oleszkiewicz, H.M. Poggi-Varaldo. Journal of Environmental Engineering, **123**, 11:1087–1092 (1997). https://www.researchgate.net/publication/245299570_High-Solids_Anaerobic_Digestion_of_Mixed_Municipal_and_Industrial_Waste
39. M.H. Gerardi. The Microbiology of Anaerobic Digesters. New Jersey: A John Wiley & Sons, Inc. (2003). p. 192. http://onlinelibrary.wiley.com/book/10.1002/0471468967
40. I. Angelidaki, W. Sanders. Reviews in Environmental Science and Bio/Technology, **3**, 2:117–129 (2004). https://link.springer.com/article/10.1007/s11157-004-2502-3
41. S. Goswami. *Optimization of Methane Production from Solid Organic Waste* [Online] (2004) from https://mafiadoc.com/optimization-of-methane-production-from-solid-_59a41c471723dd0a40e084a5.html . [Accessed on 20 May 2012].
42. J.A. Ogejo, Z. Wen, J. Ignosh, E. Bendfeldt, E.E.R. Collins. *Biomethane Technology* [Online] from https://pubs.ext.vt.edu/442/442-881/442-881_pdf.pdf. (2009). [Accessed on 6 April 2017]
43. de Graaf Daniel, and Fendler, R. 2010. Biogas production in Germany. SPIN background paper. p. 29 http://www.spin-project.eu/downloads/0_Background_paper_biogas_Germany_en.pdf
44. H.B. Moller, S.G. Sommer, B.K. Ahring. J. Environ Quality, **33**, 1:27–36 (2004). https://www.ncbi.nlm.nih.gov/pubmed/14964355
45. H.B. Moller, S.G. Sommer, B.K. Ahring. Biomass Bioenergy, **26**, 5:485–495 (2004). https://www.sciencedirect.com/science/article/pii/S0961953403001569
46. M.F. Mahesa. *Esterifikasi Senyawa Polifenol dari Ekstrak Kulit Biji Kopi dengan Asam p-Hidroksibenzoat dengan Menggunakan katalis SiO2 – H2SO4* [Polyphenol Esterification of Skin Coffee Bean Extract Using p-Hydroxybenzoate Acid an SiO2 – H2SO4 Catalyst]. [Thesis]. Universitas Indonesia, Jakarta (2012). p. 103. http://lib.ui.ac.id/file?file=digital/20308463-T31079-Esterifikasi%20senyawa.pdf
47. R. Bressani. *The By-Products of Coffee Berries*. In: Coffee Pulp, Composition, Technology and Utilization. J.E. Braham, R. Bressani (Eds.). Ottawa: International Development Research Centre (1979). pp. 5–10. https://idl-bnc-idrc.dspacedirect.org/handle/10625/6006
48. A. Das, N. Venkatachalapathy. International Journal of Applied and Natural Sciences, **5**, 1:75–82 (2016). https://archive.org/details/10.PROFITABLEEXPLOITATIONOFCOFFEEPULPAREVIEW
49. R. Eka, N. Ahmad, S.C. Titi. 2013. Karakterisasi dan Pre-Treatment Kulit Kopi Hasil Samping Pengolahan Kopi Metode Kering untuk Produksi Bioetanol. [Characterization and Pre-Treatment of Coffee Pulp from Coffee Processing Dry Methods for Bioethanol Production.] Abstrak dan Excecutive Summary.Universitas Jember (2013) p.10 [in Bahasa Indonesia].

    http://repository.unej.ac.id/bitstream/handle/123456789/61192/Eka%20Ruriani_pekerti_dipa_45.pdf;sequence=1
50. W. Parawira. *Anaerobic Treatment of Agricultural Residues and Wastewater Application of High-Rate Reactors*. [Doctoral Dissertation]. Lund University, Sweden (2004). p.60. https://lup.lub.lu.se/search/ws/files/5606523/1472236.pdf.

51. B. Demirel, P. Scherer. Biomass and Engineering, **32**, 3:203–209 (2008). https://www.sciencedirect.com/science/article/pii/S0961953407001523
52. A. Pandey, C.R. Soccol, P. Nigam, D. Brand. Biochem. Eng. J., **6**, 2:153–162 (2000). https://www.ncbi.nlm.nih.gov/pubmed/10959086
53. Y. Chen, J.J. Cheng, K.S. Creamer. Bioresource Technology, **99**, 10:4044–4064 (2008). https://www.sciencedirect.com/science/article/pii/S0960852407001563
54. J.E.G. van Dam, P.F.H. Harmsen. Coffee Residues Utilization. Netherlands: Wageningen UR Food & Biobased Research. p. 75. http://library.wur.nl/WebQuery/wurpubs/503808
55. N.D. Siswati, M. Yatim, R. Hidayanto. *Bioetanol dari limbah kulit kopi dengan proses fermentasi* [Bio-ethanol production from coffee peel waste with fermentation process]. [Online] from https://media.neliti.com/media/publications/134134-ID-none.pdf http://ejournal.upnjatim.ac.id/index.php/tekkim/article/download/80/63 (n.d.).p.4.[Accessed on 6 April 2017]. [in Bahasa Indonesia].
56. E. Houbron, A. Larrinaga, E. Rustria. Water Science & Technology, **48**, 6:255–262 (2003). https://www.ncbi.nlm.nih.gov/pubmed/14640226
57. E. Ruriani, A. Nafi, T.C. Sunarti. *Karakterisasi Kulit Kopi Hasil Samping Pengolahan Kopi Metode Kering untuk Produksi Bioetanol* [Skin Coffee Characterization as By-product of Dry Methods Coffee Processing for Bio-ethanol Production]. Seminar Nasional Perhimpunan Ahli Teknologi Pangan Indonesia (Jember, Indonesia, 2013). http://repository.unej.ac.id/handle/123456789/61192
58. W. Irawaty, H. Hindarso, Felycia E.S., Y. Mulyono, H. Kurniawan. *Utilization of Indonesian Coffee Pulp to Make an Activated Carbon*. Asian Pacific Confederation of Chemical Engineers congress program and abstracts. DOI: 10.11491/apcche.2004.0.452.0 (2004). https://www.jstage.jst.go.jp/article/apcche/2004/0/2004_0_452/_article
59. United Nations. *Updated Guidebook on Biogas Development, Energy Resources Development Series No. 27* [Online] from https://www.ircwash.org/sites/default/files/352.1-84UP-3638.pdf (1984). [Accessed on 6 April 2017]
60. M.T. Madigan, J.M. Martinko. *Brock Biology of Microorganisms*. 11th ed. New Jersey: Pearson Prentice Hall (2006). p. 1056. https://www.amazon.com/Brock-Biology-Microorganisms-11th-J-K/dp/B0028IGIJE
61. R. Zhang, Z. Zhang. Bioresource Technology **68**, 3:235–245 (1999). https://www.sciencedirect.com/science/article/pii/S0960852498001540
62. F.S. Higashikawa, C.A. Silva, W. Bettiol. Revista Brasileira de Ciência do Solo **34**, 5:1743–1752 (2010). http://www.scielo.br/scielo.php?script=sci_arttext&pid=S0100-06832010000500026
63. M. Kayhanian, G. Tchobanoglous, R.C. Brown. *Handbook of Energy Efficiency and Renewable Energy*. USA: CRC Press (2007). Pp. 25.4–25.8. https://www.amazon.com/Efficiency-Renewable-Mechanical-Aerospace-Engineering/dp/0849317304
64. C.P.L. Grady, H.C. Lim. *Biological Wastewater Treatment: Theory and Applications*. New York: Marcel Dekker (1980). p. 963. https://books.google.co.id/books/about/Biological_Wastewater_Treatment.html?id=pDtiQgAACAAJ&redir_esc=y
65. G.F. Parkin, R.E. Speece, C.H.L. Yang, W.M. Kocher. Journal WPCF, **55**, 1:44-53 (1983). https://www.jstor.org/stable/25041796

66. I. Hartati, I. Riwayati, L. Momentum, **7**, 2:25–30 (2011). [in Bahasa Indonesia]
67. U. Zuhail. *Gum Xanthan* [Online] https://ummuzuhail.wordpress.com/dunia/gum-xanthan/ (n.d.). [Accessed on 25 December 2017].
68. I. Riwayati, I. Hartati, H. Purwanto, Suwardiyono. *Adsorpsi Logam Berat Timbal dan Kadmium pada Limbah Batik Menggunakan Biosorbent Pulpa Kopi Terxanthasi* [Adsorption of Lead and Cadmium Metals in Batik Waste Using Biosorbent Xanthate Coffee Pulp]. Prosiding Seminar Nasional Aplikasi Sains & Teknologi (SNAST) 2014 (Yogyakarta, Indonesia, 2014). SNAST 2014:C211–C216 (2014). https://www.researchgate.net/publication/290838755_ADSORPSI_LOGAM_BERAT_TIMBAL_DAN_KADMIUM_PADA_LIMBAH_BATIK_MENGGUNAKAN_BIOSORBENT_PULPA_KOPI_TERXANTHASI
69. LW. Hadayani, I. Riwayati, R.D. Ratnani. Momentum, **11**, 1:19–23 (2015). [in Bahasa Indonesia]. https://publikasiilmiah.unwahas.ac.id/index.php/MOMENTUM/article/view/1077
70. L.S. Oliveira, A.S. Franca, T.M. Alves, S.D.F. Rocha. J. Hazardous Mat. **155**, 3:507–512 (2008). https://www.sciencedirect.com/science/article/pii/S0304389407017177
71. I. Gaime-Perraud, S. Roussos, D. Martínez-Carrera. Micol Neotrop Apl, **6**:95–103 (1993). http://horizon.documentation.ird.fr/exl-doc/pleins_textes/pleins_textes_6/b_fdi_35-36/39745.pdf.
72. T. Jayachandra, C. Venugopal, K.A.A. Appaaiah. Energy Sustain Develop, **15**, 1:104–108 (2011). https://www.infona.pl/resource/bwmeta1.element.elsevier-9ea1f3a7-a107-3fbb-b929-22ae8c49d93a
73. A.K. Kivaisi. Tanz. J. Science, **28**, 2:1–10 (2002). https://www.ajol.info/index.php/tjs/article/view/18349
74. A. Ramakrishnan, R.Y. Surampalli. Bioresource Technology, **123**:352–359 (2012). https://www.ncbi.nlm.nih.gov/pubmed/22940341
75. N.V. Pradepp, S. Anupama, K. Navya, H.N. Shalini, M. Idris, U.S. Hampannavar.. Water Science, **5**, 2:105–112 (2015). https://link.springer.com/article/10.1007/s13201-014-0176-8
76. S.B. Ariyani. Jurnal Biopropal Industri 2 (1): 14–20 (2011). [in Bahasa Indonesia]. http://download.portalgaruda.org/article.php?article=416282&val=8391&title=Decreased%20Levels%20of%20Fenol%20in%20the%20Case%20of%20Traditional%20Herb%20Industry%20using%20Anaerobic%20Activated%20Sludge%20Method
77. L. Hinken, I. Urban, E. Haun, D. Weichgrebe, K.H. Rosenwinkel. Water Sci. Technol. **58**, 7:1453–1459 (2008). https://www.ncbi.nlm.nih.gov/pubmed/18957759
78. N.R. Raju, S.S. Devi, K. Nand. Biotechnol. Lett., **13**, 6:461–464 (1991). https://link.springer.com/article/10.1007/BF01031002
79. F.E. Mosey, D.A. Hughes. Journal Institute Water Pollution Control, **1**:3–24 (1975). https://www.researchgate.net/publication/279573236_The_Toxicity_of_Heavy_Metal_Ions_to_Anaerobic_Digestion
80. L.G. Elias. *Chemical Composition of Coffee-Berry*. In: Coffee Pulp: Composation, Technology, and Utilization. J.E. Braham, R. Bressani (Eds.). Ottawa:The International Development Research Centre (1979). pp. 12–16. https://idl-bnc-idrc.dspacedirect.org/handle/10625/6006
81. F.H. Orozco, J. Cegarra, L.M. Trujillo, A. Roig. Biol Fertil Soils, **22**, 1–2:162–166 (1996). https://link.springer.com/article/10.1007/BF00384449

82. S.N. Avinash, C.A. Srinivasamurthy, S. Bhaskar, N.B. Prakash. International Journal of Current Microbiology and Applied Sciences, **6**, 10:2265–2272 (2017). https://www.researchgate.net/publication/320562129_Characterization_Extraction_and_Foliar_Spray_of_Fortified_Humic_Acid_on_Quality_of_Capsicum
83. W.A. Asfimanto, T. Nurlambang, T. Waryono. *Pengaruh Kondisi Fisik dan Budidaya Terhadap Kualitas Kopi di Kintamani dan Gayo* [Effect of Physical Condition and Cultivation on the Quality Coffee in Kintamani and Gayo] [Online] from http://lontar.ui.ac.id/naskahringkas/2016-04/S47782-Asfirmanto%20W%20A (2013). [Accessed on 20 May 2017]
84. S. Hasibuan, B.K. Djatmo, K.H. Nitimulyo, E. Hanudin. Jurnal Dinamika Pertanian **29**, 1:97–106 (2014). http://journal.uir.ac.id/index.php/dinamikapertanian/article/view/864
85. R. Nandini, B.H. Narendra. Jurnal Penelitian Hutan dan Konservasi Alam, **9**, 3:199–211 (2012). https://www.researchgate.net/publication/319230455_KARAKTERISTIK_LAHAN_KRITIS_BEKAS_LETUSAN_GUNUNG_BATUR_DI_KABUPATEN_BANGLI_BALI
86. P.G. Adinurani, R.H. Setyobudi, S.K. Wahono, M. Mel, A. Nindita, E. Purbajanti, et al.. Proceedings of the Pakistan Academy of Sciences B. Life and Environmental Sciences, **54**, 1:47–57 (2017). http://www.paspk.org/wp-content/uploads/2017/03/Ballast-Weight-Review-of-Capsule-Husk-Jatropha-curcas-Linn.pdf

Revisiting Renewable Energy Map in Indonesia: Seasonal Hydro and Solar Energy Potential for Rural Off-Grid Electrification (Provincial Level)

Ruri Agung Wahyuono[1,]*, and *Miga* Magenika Julian[2,3]

[1]Engineering Physics Department, Institut Teknologi Sepuluh Nopember, Keputih, Sukolilo, Surabaya, 60111, Indonesia
[2]Geodesy and Geomatics Engineering Department, Institut Teknologi Bandung, Lebak Siliwangi, Coblong, Bandung, 40132, Indonesia
[3]Institut Für Geographie, Friedrich-Schiller-University, Löbdergraben 32, 07743 Jena, Germany

Abstract. Regarding the acceleration of renewable energy diffusion in Indonesia as well as achieving the national energy mix target, renewable energy map is essential to provide useful information to build renewable energy system. This work aims at updating the renewable energy potential map, *i.e.* hydro and solar energy potential, with a revised model based on the global climate data. The renewable energy map is intended to assist the design off-grid system by hydropower plant or photovoltaic system, particularly for rural electrification. Specifically, the hydro energy map enables the stakeholders to determine the suitable on-site hydro energy technology (from pico-hydro, micro-hydro, mini-hydro to large hydropower plant). Meanwhile, the solar energy map depicts not only seasonal solar energy potential but also estimated energy output from photovoltaic system.

Key words: Hydro energy, solar energy, off-grid, rural electrification.

1 Introduction

Renewable energy is becoming a global issue as the crisis of fossil energy emerged nowadays. Indonesia as a part of the international community shares the concern on the environment and development issues [1–3]. Indonesia is a country with vast natural resources and significant reserves in oil, gas and coal. It is also abundant in reserves of renewable energy sources. There is also an enormous potential to develop and use clean energy sources such as hydropower (75 000 MW), geothermal (29 164 MW), biomass (49 810 MW), ocean (46 GW), solar (4.80 kW h m^{-2} d^{-1}), and wind energy (3 m s^{-1} to 6 m s^{-1}) [1–5].

*Corresponding author: ruri.tf014@gmail.com, miga.m.julian@gmail.com

Despite these facts, Indonesia is currently facing an energy crisis. The average rate of energy consumption is approximately 7 % in the last decade, while the rate of energy supply is limited. Indonesia is heavily dependent on fossil fuel, particularly on oil. Oil dominates of 50 % of the primary energy mix, followed by coal at 32 %, gas at 19 %, geothermal at 1.3 %, hydro at 2.9 % and the rest is supplied by other renewable energy resources [2, 3]. Moreover, the high growth of fossil energy consumption will lead to environmental problems, particularly in high CO_2 emissions that cause global warming.

Recently, the government of Indonesia committed to reducing greenhouse gasses (GHG) emissions up to 29 % in 2030 through domestic efforts and 41 % with international assistance [1, 2, 6]. Clean energy utilization, termed as renewable energy utilization and energy efficiency according to Presidential Regulation No. 4 and No. 5 year 2010 [1–4] is one of the priority activities in reducing GHG emission in the energy sector: National energy policy involves energy conservation and energy diversification to increase the share of new and renewable energy use in the national primary energy mix. Furthermore, energy mix target focuses to establish 17 % new and renewable energy in energy mix (with an assumption of energy elasticity less than one in 2025 to optimize new renewable energy sources) [2, 3]. To date, the total installed capacity of national electricity is 30 941 MW, with 83 % electricity supplied by the national electricity company (PT. PLN), and the rest by the independent power producers (IPP) at 14 % and private power utility at 3 % [1]. Also, it is estimated that around 93% of Indonesia's inhabitants have access to electricity.

Despite the fact of high electrification ratio achieved in 2017, several areas, *i.e.* coastal and rural area, are facing electricity crisis with electricity demand higher than the supply or no electricity supply into these areas [6]. Since rural areas often face difficulties to get access to national electricity grid due to economic and geographical barriers, utilization of renewable energy resources is likely the only option for generating electricity [6, 7]. Moreover, in order for national energy mix target to achieve acceleration of renewable energy utilization whose technologies are technically and economically proven should be prioritized [6–9]. However, it is known that the renewable energy potential is site-specific and intermittent and hence, temporal (or seasonal) and spatial data of renewable energy potential is required to map the feasible energy generation and the selection of renewable energy technology at different sites. Herein the revised maps of renewable energy potentials, particularly hydro and solar energy, based on the global climate data to support the stakeholders of renewable energy development in Indonesia are presented.

2 Method

2.1 Geographical and climatological data

Data used for this study originated from secondary sources. Climate was represented by precipitation, air temperature, and sunshine duration. Climate data has been obtained from University of East Anglia Climate Research Unit (CRU) (CRU Climatology version 2.0—CRU CL 2.0) [10]. These data provide the mean monthly precipitation, air temperature, and sunshine duration at a (10 × 10) min spatial resolution. The precipitation and air temperature were used for hydrological simulation and later to estimate the hydropower, whilst the sunshine duration was used to estimate the solar power.

Land cover was collected from The Global Land Cover by National Mapping Organizations (GLCNMO) developed by Geospatial Information Authority of Japan (GSI) and Chiba University, Japan. The data were prepared by using MODIS data in a grid of 500 m [11]. The heterogeneous land cover was converted into crop factor which was later used to calculate soil water holding capacity and potential evapotranspiration for hydrological modelling simulation.

The digital elevation model (DEM) was used 30 m—Shuttle Radar Topography Mission (SRTM). The DEM was used to generate slope, river network model, and the natural falling head. For hydrological modelling, DEM should be pre-processed. As the presence of sinks (a pixel value lower than the surroundings) and peaks (a pixel where no adjacent pixels are higher) in DEM might result in an erroneous river flow direction raster, they were filled to ensure proper delineation of river basins and river networks. This step removed small imperfections in the data. After DEM corrected from sinks and peaks, the next step is deriving flow direction. The method of deriving flow direction from a DEM is based on literature [12]. Flow direction was determined by the direction of steepest slope from each cell. Flow direction determined the direction in which water would flow out of the pixel. The accumulated flow was based on the number of pixels that flowing into each pixel. Output pixels with a high flow accumulation were areas of concentrated flow and were used to identify the river network model. In summary, the schematic representation of geographical and climatological data collection and processing is depicted in Figure 1.

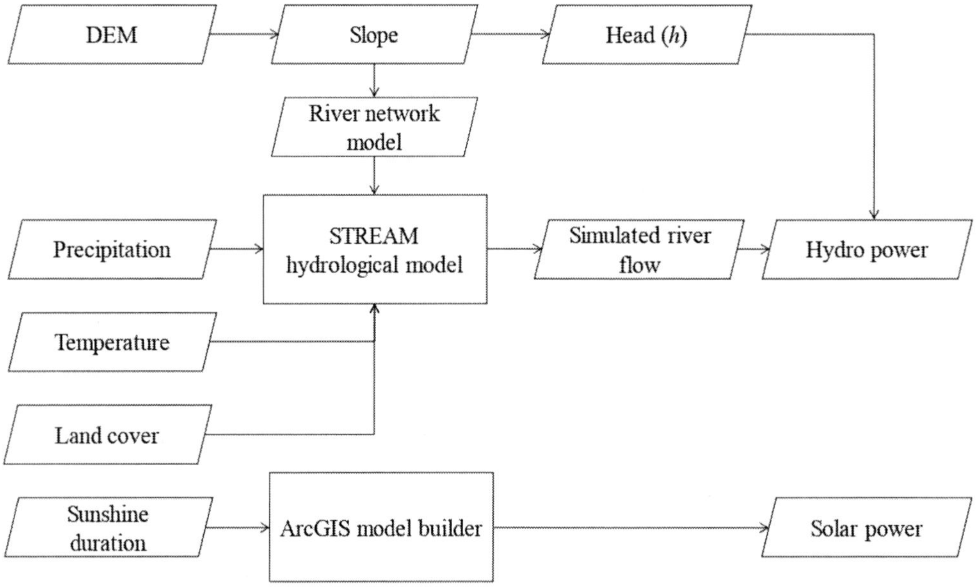

Fig. 1. Flow diagram of global climate data collection and processing for hydro and solar energy estimation.

2.2 Estimation of hydro energy output

Hydro power is classified by the net power output from the system. Typically, hydropower can be classified into picohydro, microhydro, minihydro, small, medium and large hydropower. In order to assess the net power output of the employment hydro energy potential was calculated using the following formula:

$$E_{hydro} = \eta_G \times \eta_T \times \rho \times \dot{\forall} \times g \times h \quad (1)$$

Where η_G is the efficiency of generator, η_T is the efficiency of hydro-turbine, ρ is the density of water (kg m^{-3}), $\dot{\forall}$ is the volumetric flow rate (m^3 s^{-1}), g is the gravitational acceleration (9.8 m s^{-2}), and h is the falling height, head (m). It should be noted that the hydro energy potential estimation in this study doesn't consider the energy sources from hydro kinetic energy. The η_G spans from 0.85 to 0.93, while the η_T spans from 0.75 to 0.95 depending on the type of the turbine used in the system.

The $\dot{\forall}$ was assumed as river discharge flow in drainage network. $\dot{\forall}$ was simulated based on hydrological modelling. STREAM hydrological model is used. STREAM [13] describes the hydrological cycle of a drainage basin as a series of storage compartments and flows. It applies Thornthwaite-Mather's water balance approach to calculate flow discharges along drainage networks derived from a DEM. The main inputs to the model are climate data (maps of precipitation and temperature), a DEM, land cover maps and water holding capacity maps. Potential and actual evapotranspiration are calculated in STREAM at the so-called soil compartment represented by a grid cell. Following this, storage of water in a grid cell is estimated according to the difference between evapotranspiration and precipitation. Finally, discharge per time step is calculated according to excess of water in each grid cell and baseflow from groundwater storage. Calibration of STREAM model has been successfully done and documented in literature [14, 15]. The *h* is estimated based on the different elevation between two pixels on digital elevation model. Firstly, the slope map is generated from the DEM, later the tangent of slope in degree is used to estimate the rise (different height) over the run (spatial resolution of the DEM).

2.3 Estimation of solar energy output

Estimation of solar energy is employed in ESRI ArcGIS version 10 model builder. This allows us for calculating solar power in spatial-temporal scale. The daily energy output (E_{PV}) of photovoltaic (PV) system in this study was revised. In general, the daily energy output from a PV array is calculated using peak hours formula as below:

$$E_{PV} = \frac{P_{rated} \times S}{\Phi_{AM1.5G}} \tag{2}$$

Where P_{rated} is rated peak power of PV panel (Wp), S is insolation (kW h m^{-2} per day), and $\Phi_{AM1.5G}$ is radiative power flux at peak sun (W m^{-2}). This formulation means that a PV panel receives constant $S/\Phi_{AM1.5G}$ peak hours of sun per day (a square-wave function). However, this leads an overestimation of the energy output from PV array since power conversion efficiency of PV declines at lower irradiation. Therefore, the radiative power flux in this work was modelled as a Gaussian wave instead of a square wave.

3 Results and discussion

As a tropical country, the seasonal variation in this work is discussed in the wet and the dry season which occurs approximately from October to March and from April to September, respectively. Therefore, the results of renewable energy potential map are simplified into two maps, *i.e.* the wet and the dry season.

The hydro energy potential is distributed in a manner as shown in Figure 2. It is again worth to note that hydro energy potential estimation neglects the kinetic energy potential by the water flow, instead it is determined from a classical approximation of potential energy due to the natural falling height *h*. Furthermore, the estimated hydro energy potential is used to classify the hydropower plant suitable at certain sites: picohydro (< 5 kW h), microhydro (5 kW h to 100 kW h), minihydro (100 kW h to 1MW h), small hydropower (1 MW h to 25 MW h), medium hydropower (25 MW h to 100 MW h) and large hydropower (>100 MW h) plant [16]. The topographical map of the falling head *h* based on the digital elevation data is depicted in Figure 2a and the hydro energy distribution maps are shown in Figure 2b and Figure 2c.

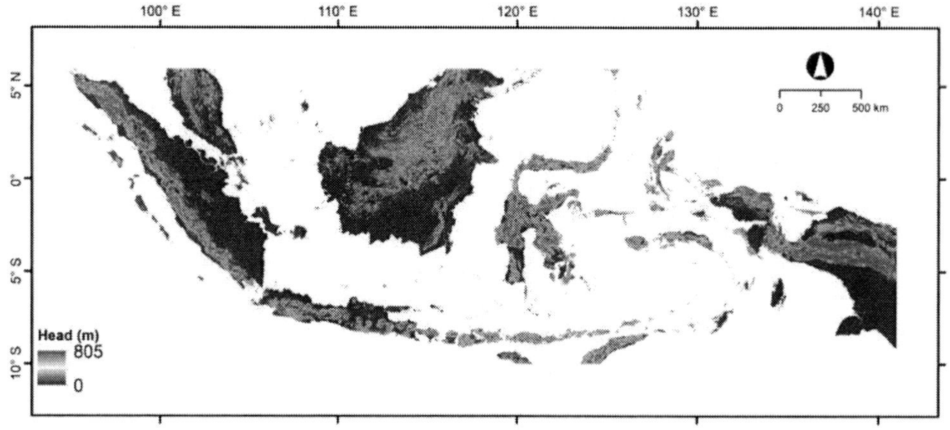

(a)

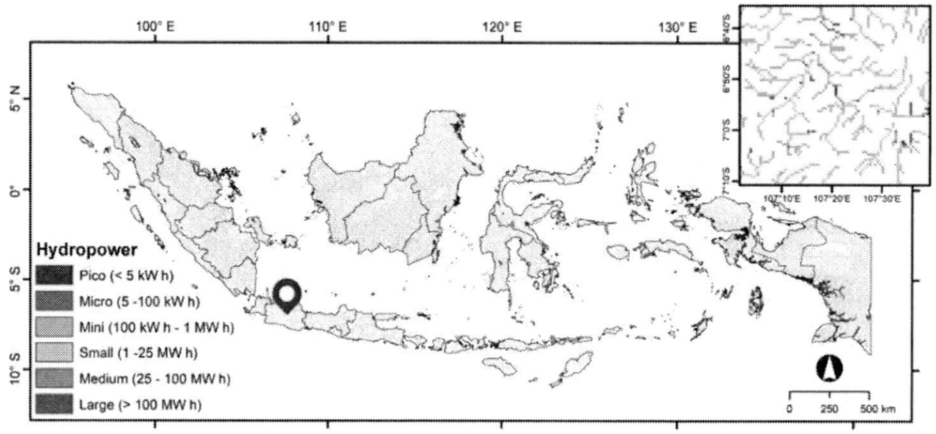

(b)

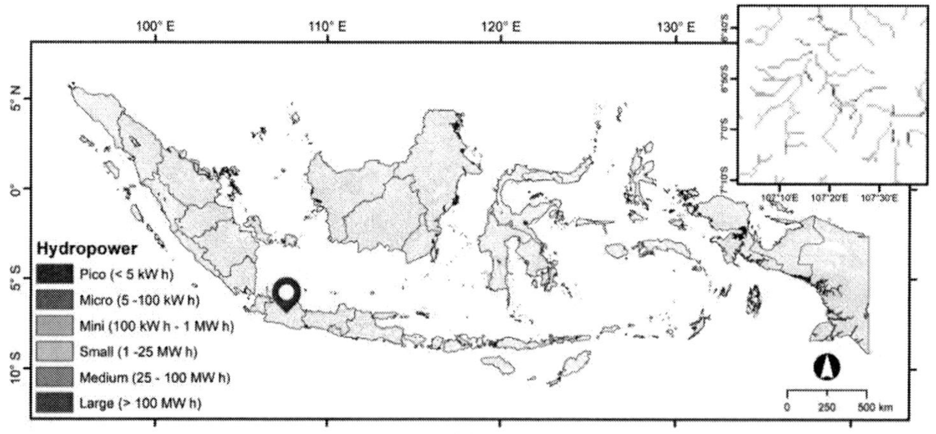

(c)

Fig. 2. (a) Head profile based on digital elevation data. Seasonal hydro energy potential during (b) wet and (c) dry season. Inset of figures depicts an enlarged map of hydropower distribution in west Java as indicated by location symbol (red) in the map.

As shown in the above maps, the hydro energy potential in Indonesia is dominated by the pico to minihydro power plant. A more clear view on how the hydro energy potential changes due to seasonal change in west Java is indicated in the inset of Figure 2b and Figure 2c. The estimated hydro energy potential in this study is verified by other reported works which shows the potential of developing micro and mini hydropower plant [17, 18]. For example, Anugrah et al. [19] evaluating the microhydro power plant in West Sumatera with a capacity of 30 kW to 40 kW in which their system can be improved to yield an annual hydropower spanning from 170 MW h to 275 MW h. Meanwhile, other study by Kumara et al. [20] reports that 43.2 kW h hydropower can be generated in Bali where the hydro energy potential is lower than that in West Sumatera.

Large hydropower plants are only identified in five big islands in Indonesia. The order of the most potential locations is the following: Kalimantan (eastern, middle, and western part), Papua (eastern and middle part), Sulawesi (southeast and middle part), Sumatera (northern and western part), Java (western and middle part). This finding is in good agreement with the study reported by Purwanto and co-workers [21]. The study has concluded that 60 % of total hydropower potentials are located in Kalimantan and Papua. The combination of the high river flows from the large watersheds, especially in the large island, and the variation of topographic slope generates abundant hydropower potential.

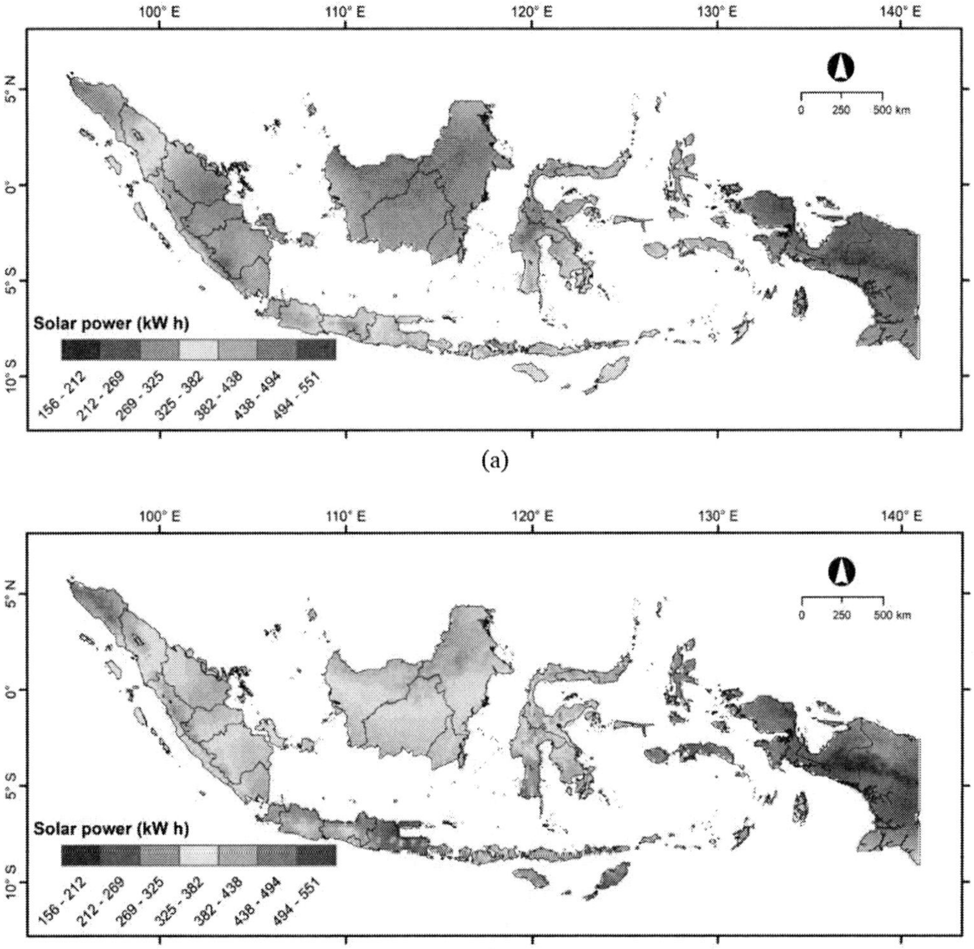

Fig. 3. Profile of estimated solar energy potential in Indonesia during (a) wet and (b) dry season.

The central attention is now turned to the distribution of solar energy potential in Indonesia. In general, solar energy potential in Indonesia is distinguished into two different areas: The Western part of Indonesia features with an average irradiation of (4.50 ± 0.45) kW h m^{-2} per day and the Eastern part of Indonesia is characterized by an average irradiation of (5.10 ± 0.45) kW h m^{-2} d^{-1} [8, 9]. In this work, the solar irradiation is spatially-varying from (1.3 to 3.6) kW h m^{-2} per day (data not shown) and slightly lower than that reported by Rumbayan et al. [22] and Veldhuis and Reinders [23]. The monthly solar irradiation also does not vary significantly within the same season and fluctuates in a moderate extent thought the year.

Figure 3 presents the profile of solar energy available in terms of practical solar energy potential: The solar irradiation potential is already converted into solar energy potential generated in full PV-battery system occupying 350 Wp PV module in 100 m^2 area (DC/AC inverter's efficiency is set to 0.85). As seen in Figure 3, the availability of the solar energy can be used to prioritize the sites for renewable energy development. Some literatures claim that the eastern parts of Indonesia are exposed more solar irradiation than the western part, but the results here indicate that the reported solar energy potential distribution is only partially true. Some of the western were found, *i.e.* south Sumatera, south Kalimantan (Borneo) and Java island, and mid-eastern parts of Indonesia, *i.e.* Bali, East and West Nusa Tenggara, South Sulawesi, have the most stable annual solar-energy potential.

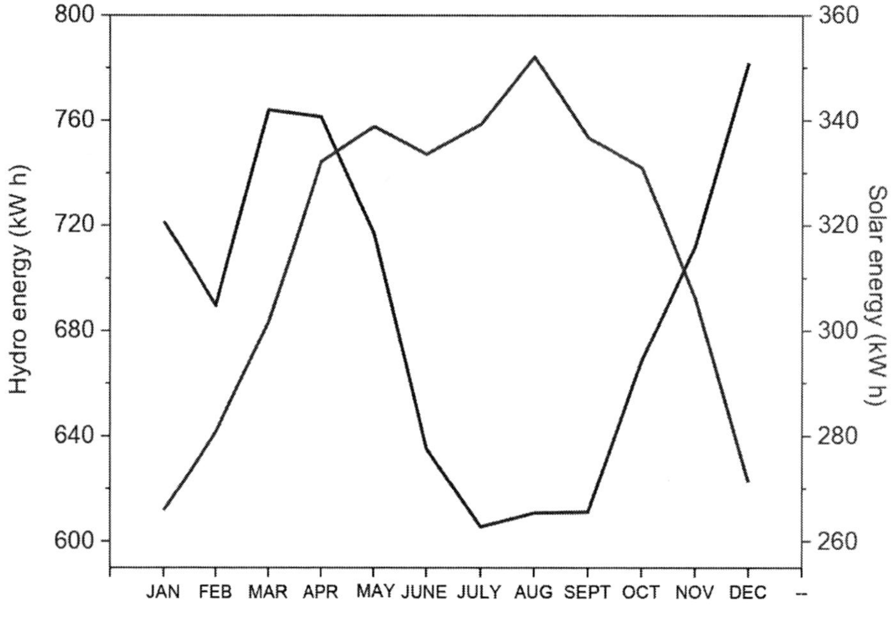

Fig. 4. Monthly potential energy output for hydropower and solar power generation at national level.

The monthly hydro and solar energy potential at national level is shown in Figure 3. It can be clearly seen that the hydro energy potential is lower ((620 ± 10) kW h) during the dry season (approximately starting from May to October), and in contrary the solar energy potential is at the highest level ((335 ± 5) kW h)) during the dry season. Overall, the results show that seasonal variation is not the case for solar energy potential in Indonesia, whilst the hydro energy potential is slightly affected by the seasonal change. Taking the integral of each renewable energy potential in a year, the dry to wet season ratio of total energy for hydro and solar energy is 42 : 58 and 54 : 46, respectively.

Table 1. Hydro and solar energy potential at provincial level during the wet and the dry season.

Province	Hydropower (kW h)		Solar power (kW h)	
	Wet	Dry	Wet	Dry
Aceh Darussalam	7 780	5 168	300	293
Bali	1 133	875	399	491
Bangka Belitung	108	92	295	373
Banten	1 595	1 219	313	436
Bengkulu	2 390	2 129	299	351
Central Java	1 663	1 377	333	436
Central Kalimantan	5 664	4 008	281	361
Central Sulawesi	7 219	5 714	302	345
East Java	1 310	1 013	374	492
East Kalimantan	12 791	9 021	280	337
East Nusa Tenggara	2 510	1 518	355	466
Gorontalo	3 698	2 707	307	317
Jakarta	515	368	317	451
Jambi	3 487	2 976	295	338
Lampung	1 614	1 313	305	387
Maluku	2 895	1 654	301	291
North Maluku	1 862	1 279	317	288
North Sulawesi	2 859	2 289	321	307
North Sumatra	4 980	3 526	336	335
Papua	18 348	10 901	245	251
Riau	2 452	1 965	305	331
South East Sulawesi	4 788	3 186	330	398
South Kalimantan	1 813	1 519	288	381
South Sulawesi	7 760	6 288	306	380
South Sumatra	1 725	1 468	301	365
West Java	2 531	2 303	329	427
West Kalimantan	5 412	3 713	283	356
West Nusa Tenggara	1 413	818	331	423
West Papua	6 491	3 825	260	256
West Sumatra	3 877	3 398	313	334
Yogyakarta Special Region	1 571	1 302	310	397

The hydro and solar energy potential distribution in provincial level is listed in Table 1. The results above support the current government action plan, for example the establishment of solar energy power plant in Nusa Tenggara. In fact, East Java shows promising solar energy to harvest but the availability of area for PV power plant limits the development of large PV system. The levelized cost of (renewable) energy utilizing hydro and solar energy is comparable with the electricity price from PLN. Kumara et al [20] reported that the micro-hydropower plant built in Bali allows the consumer to afford electricity with reasonable price of USD 0.5 per kW h. Furthermore, the use of off-grid PV systems is considered cheaper and profitable than generating electricity by using diesel generator or hybrid diesel/PV system.

4 Conclusion

In this paper, the potential of hydro and solar energy in Indonesia is mapped for predicting off-grid system utilizing renewable energy resources. The present results highlight the seasonal variation of hydro and solar energy potential in Indonesia and show that solar energy potential in Indonesia is stable throughout the year. The hydro energy potential enables mostly the development of hydropower plant in the scale of pico to minihydro. Meanwhile, the solar energy distribution reported here presents a higher and more stable energy potential in Java island, particularly in East Java, than in eastern part of Indonesia which is partially different to the literature. This implies that a thorough calculation and estimation is required for future revised solar energy map.

Financial support by Deutscher Akademischer Austauschdienst (DAAD), funding program No.: 57048249 is gratefully acknowledged.

References

1. E. Wibowo. *Policies and strategies for the development of waste to energy in Indonesia*. Ministry of Energy and Mineral Resources of the Republic of Indonesia, Directorate General of New Renewable Energy and Energy Conservation. 13 November (Jakarta, 2014). http://www.unescap.org/sites/default/files/Session%202_3_MEMR.pdf
2. R. Mulyana. *Government's policy on energy efficiency and renewable energy in buildings*. Director General of New Energy, Renewable Energy and Energy Conservation. Presented at Conference on Energy Efficiency and Renewable Energy Solutions for Building, 31 May 2016 (Jakarta, Indonesia, 2016). http://indonesien.ahk.de/fileadmin/ahk_indonesien/Business_Delegations/Energy_Efficiency/Government_s_Policy_on_Energy_Efficiency_and_Renewable_Energy_in_Buildings.pdf
3. Ministry of Energy and Mineral Resources Republic of Indonesia. *Handbook of energy and economic statistics of Indonesia*. Jakarta: Ministry of Energy and Mineral Resources Republic of Indonesia (2015). pp? https://www.esdm.go.id/assets/media/content/content-handbook-of-energy-economic-statistics-of-indonesia-2015-uwe2cqn.pdf
4. R.A. Wahyuono, M.N. Hakim, S.A. Santoso. Energy Procedia **65**:324–330 (2015). https://www.sciencedirect.com/science/article/pii/S1876610215000612
5. A. Reinders, H. Veldhuis, A. Susandi. *Development of grid-connected PV systems for remote electrification in Indonesia*. The 37th IEEE Photovoltaic Specialists Conference (PVSC), 19–24 June, 2011 (Seattle, WA, USA, 2011). http://ieeexplore.ieee.org/document/6186437/

6. M.H. Hasan, W.K. Muzammil, T.M.I. Mahlia, A. Jannifar, I. Hasanuddin, Renew. Sust. Energ. Rev., **16**(5):3206–3219 (2012). https://www.sciencedirect.com/science/article/pii/S1364032112000871
7. J. Hanafi, A. Riman. Procedia CIRP **29**:444–449 (2015). https://www.sciencedirect.com/science/article/pii/S2212827115004734
8. R.A.Wahyuono. *Dye-Sensitized Solar Cells (DSSC) fabrication with TiO2 and ZnO nanoparticle for high conversion efficiency*. [Master Thesis]. Institut Teknologi Sepuluh Nopember, Indonesia (2013). p. 1. https://www.researchgate.net/publication/273955833_Dye-Sensitized_Solar_Cells_DSSC_Fabrication_with_TiO2_and_ZnO_Nanoparticle_for_High_Conversion_Efficiency
9. A.J. Veldhuis, A.H.M.E. Reinders. Renew. Sust. Energ. Rev., **27**:315–324 (2013). https://www.sciencedirect.com/science/article/pii/S1364032113003870
10. M. New, D. Lister, M. Hulme, I. Makin, Clim. Res. **21**:1–25 (2002). https://crudata.uea.ac.uk/cru/data/hrg/tmc/new_et_al_10minute_climate_CR.pdf
11. R. Tateishi, N.T. Hoan, T. Kobayashi, B. Alsaaideh, G. Tana, D. Xuan Phong, Journal of Geography and Geology **6**(3):99–122 (2014). http://www.cr.chiba-u.jp/~tateishi-lab/pdf/2014/GLCNMO2008JGG.pdf
12. S.K. Jenson, J.O. Domingue. Photogrammetric Engineering Remote Sensing **54**(11):1593–1600 (1998). http://citeseerx.ist.psu.edu/viewdoc/download?doi=10.1.1.138.6487&rep=rep1&type=pdf
13. J.C.J.H. Aerts, M. Kriek, M. Schepel, Physics and Chemistry of the Earth Part B: Hydrology, Oceans and Atmosphere **24**(6): 591–595 (1999). https://www.sciencedirect.com/science/article/pii/S1464190999000490
14. R. Poerbandono, P.J. Ward, M.M. Julian. ITB Journal on Engineering Science **41**, 1:50–64 (2009). http://journal.itb.ac.id/index.php?li=article_detail&id=331
15. M.M. Julian, F. Nishio, Poerbandono, P.J. Ward, International Journal of Technology **2**(1):37–46 (2011). http://www.ijtech.eng.ui.ac.id/old/index.php/journal/article/view/44
16. W.W. Purwanto, N. Afifah. Renew. Energy **93**(C):312–322 (2016) https://econpapers.repec.org/article/eeerenene/v_3a93_3ay_3a2016_3ai_3ac_3ap_3a312-322.htm
17. Darmawi, R. Sipahutar, S.M. Bernas, M.S. Imanuddin, Renew. Sust. Energ. Rev., **17**:213–215 (2013). https://www.sciencedirect.com/science/article/pii/S1364032112005072
18. S. Murni, T Urmee, J. Whale, D. Harries. *The implementation of micro hydro projects in remote villages on the border of Indonesia and Malaysia: Lessons learnt*. International Conference and Utility Exhibition 2014 on Green Energy for Sustainable Development, 19–21 March 2014 (Pattaya, Thailand, 2014). http://ieeexplore.ieee.org/document/6828956/
19. P. Anugrah, A.A. Setiawan, R. Budiarto, Sihana. Energy Proc. **65**:257–263 (2015). https://www.sciencedirect.com/science/article/pii/S1876610215000442
20. Kumara, D.P.D. Suparyawan, W. G. Ariastina, W. Sukerayasa, I.A.D. Giriantari. *Microhydro powerplant for rural area in Bali to generate green and sustainable electricity*. International Conference on Smart Green Technology in Electrical and Information Systems (ICSGTEIS) 5–7 November 2014 (Bali, 2014). IEEE, pp. 113–117. http://ieeexplore.ieee.org/document/7038741/

21. W.W. Purwanto, Y.S. Nugroho, R. Dalimi, A.H. Soepardjo, A. Wahid, D. Supramono, et al. *Indonesia energy outlook and statistics*. Jakarta: PEUI (2006). pp. 93–95. https://kunaifien.files.wordpress.com/2008/12/2006-indonesia-energy-outlook-statistic1.pdf
22. M. Rumbayan, A. Abudureyimu, K. Nagasaka, Renew. Sust. Energ. Rev. **16**:1437–1449 (2012). http://wgbis.ces.iisc.ernet.in/biodiversity/sahyadri_enews/newsletter/issue45/bibliography/Mapping%20of%20solar%20energy%20potential%20in%20indonesia%20using%20artifical.pdf
23. A.J. Veldhuis, A.H.M.E. Reinders. Renew. Sust. Energ. Rev., **52**:757–769 (2015). https://research.utwente.nl/en/publications/reviewing-the-potential-and-cost-effectiveness-of-off-grid-pv-sys

Determination of Generator Steady State Stability Limit for Multimachine System based on Network Losses Concept

Rusilawati[1, 2,*], *Irrine* Budi Sulistiawati [3], *Adi* Soeprijanto [1], and *Rony* Seto Wibowo[1]

[1]Department of Electrical Engineering, Institut Teknologi Sepuluh Nopember, Gedung B, C & AJ Kampus ITS Sukolilo, Surabaya 60111, Indonesia
[2]Department of Electrical Engineering, Akademi Teknik Pembangunan Nasional, Grand Palace Park Jl. A.Yani km 32, Loktabat Banjarbaru 70714, Indonesia
[3]Department of Electrical Engineering, Institut Teknologi Nasional, Jl. Raya Karanglo km 2, Malang 65145, Indonesia

Abstract. In the multimachine circumstances, it is difficult to analyze the steady state stability of each generator. In previous research, analysis of the steady state stability limit has been carried out but only look at the stability of the overall system. Therefore, to analyze the stability of each generator, the multimachine system must be changed into a Single Machine to Infinite Bus (SMIB) system by collecting all the loads into one central load in the infinite bus. The method to change from the multimachine system to SMIB system is presented in this paper. The multimachine system is converted into an equivalent impedance (req and xeq) and an equivalent load based on losses concept. After req and xeq is calculated, then by using steady state stability limit concept, the value of the maximum generation of each generator units can be determined. By means of maximum generation is the maximum output power limit that can be generated without causing unstability. ETAP simulation is used to validate the calculation results of the proposed method. The method was applied to units generator in Java Bali system 500 kV.

Key words: Equivalent reactance, equivalent resistance, generator steady state stability limit, maximum generation, the losses concept

1 Introduction

The power balance between the load and the generator output power is one measure of the power system operation stability. In power system operation, load always changes in the capacity and location at any time, and this mean that the system requires each plant to adjust the output power through the control of the governor and excitation to follow the changes in the system load. If this is not done, it will decrease the power balance and the efficiency of the system causing the system performance deteriorated.

* Corresponding author: habsyi.sila@yahoo.com

Electric power system generally consists of generating units connected to the network to serve the load. Electric power systems that have a lot of machines are usually distribute power to the load through the interconnected system. The main purpose of the interconnected system is to maintain the continuity and the availability for the increasing of the needs of electric power. The growing of the power system can result the poor performance when the system is disturbed. One effect of the interference on the system is the electromechanical oscillations, if not be attenuated can cause disruption of the system and turn out from the area of stability, resulting a worse effect as the total blackout [1, 2].

In recent years, power systems are operated almost at the stability limit due to the use of out of date of the power system infrastructure construction compared to the increase in demand of electric power and the long-distance transmission system. If the load demand beyond the limits of the maximum power (active power and reactive power) that can be generated and transmitted from the source to the load area, and no improvement action is taken, the voltage load area will become unstable and collapse may occur.

Steady-state stability limit of the power system is steady state operating condition in which the power system is still in a stable condition but for a small change of the parameters of the operation will bring the system loses its stability [3]. Initial definition refers to the concept that "the stability of the system to the condition of load changes gradually and slowly change" [4]. Voltage collapse, causing the system to lose synchronism and instability caused by the strengthening of small oscillations of all forms of the steady state instability [5].

Load flow method can be used to determine steady-state stability limit of a power system by increasing the load until the load flow process becomes not convergent. Continuation Power Flow Method (CPF) has also been frequently used to determine the relationship between the loading parameters to voltage at each bus. Both conventional methods have a weakness because they do not incorporate internal reactance generator value in the modelling and analysis. In addition, another weakness is in the computational because the looping iteration process of Load Flow and CPF method require a longer computing time so this method is not suitable to be implemented in the real-time monitoring system. Practical studies to determine the steady state limits have also been developed in Russia to decrease the mathematical equations of the Jacobian Dynamic but this method also requires computation time is much longer [5].

In previous research analysis of the steady-state stability limit has been carried out [5–7], but still these researches only look at the stability of the overall system, making it difficult to analyze the stability of each bus or generator.

In this paper, the losses concept is used to determine the maximum generation of units generator on each generator bus. Maximum generation of generator is influenced by several factors: source voltage, phase angle and networks impedance value [8]. Equivalent network impedance can be determined by knowing the losses in the network, then the multimachine system can be changed into SMIB system with an equivalent impedance and an equivalent load. Note that the determination of equivalent impedance value using losses concept has used in [8] and [9], but the change from the multimachine system to Single Machine to Infinite Bus (SMIB) system is not provided. Maximum generation of generator is a generator steady state stability limit that can be calculated after the network impedance is obtained.

2 Concept of single machine steady state stability

Electric power system is defined as a collection of some of the power stations and substations, which are interconnected by transmitting nets each other. Transmission nets form a unified system known as interconnection system. With the interconnection system, the system will be more reliable because of interconnected systems can assist other systems in sending power requirement if one of the systems in plants have a short fall or trip.

Interconnection system in operating system aims to obtain a combination of electric power generation as economical as possible, so achieving a balance between the power available and the power needed. System interconnection between the generators of the power system shown in Figure 1 [10].

To analyze the steady state stability of each generator, the multimachine system must be changed to SMIB system first. The method to change the multimachine system to SMIB system will discuss in section III.

If the system is considered to have no power loss, the power generated equal to the power delivered to the infinite bus. The equation for P_G written as:

$$P_G = \frac{|E||V|}{X_e} \sin\delta \tag{1}$$

Figure 2 shows a synchronous generator connected to an infinite bus. Bus voltage $|V|$ is the constant magnitude when the net is very large (infinite). Assuming the generator operating at fixed excitation, maintaining fixed E and fixed X_e, then P_G is a function of the power angle δ. Characteristics power- angle shown in Figure 3. The maximum power is delivered to an infinite bus occurred at δ = 90°. Equation (1) can be written as:

$$P_G = P = P_{max} \tag{2}$$

Stable system occurs in less than P_{max} value, which occurs at $\delta < 90$. This can be explained as follows: suppose that the generator works in steady state conditions and transmit power P_G^0 on initial power angle δ_0 as shown in the picture angle-power characteristics in point a in Figure 3. At a point turbine output P_T^0 equal to the power generated (losses ignored). If there were no changes, the steam valve (throttle valve) which controls the turbine generator is opened slowly. Mechanical power input will be higher than the electrical output power. This power is equal to the difference $\Delta P_T = P_T - P_G$.

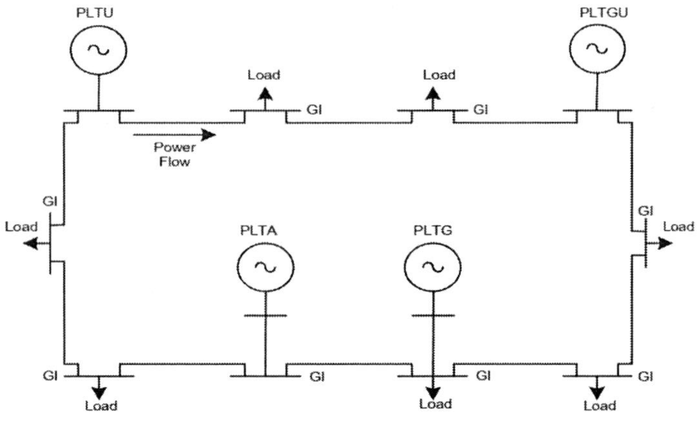

Fig. 1. System interconnection of electric power systems.

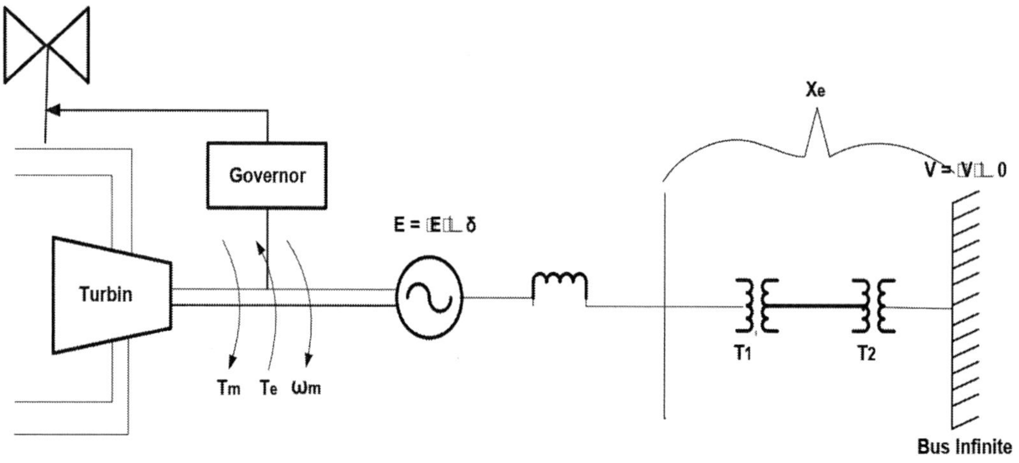

Fig. 2. A machine connected to an infinite bus.

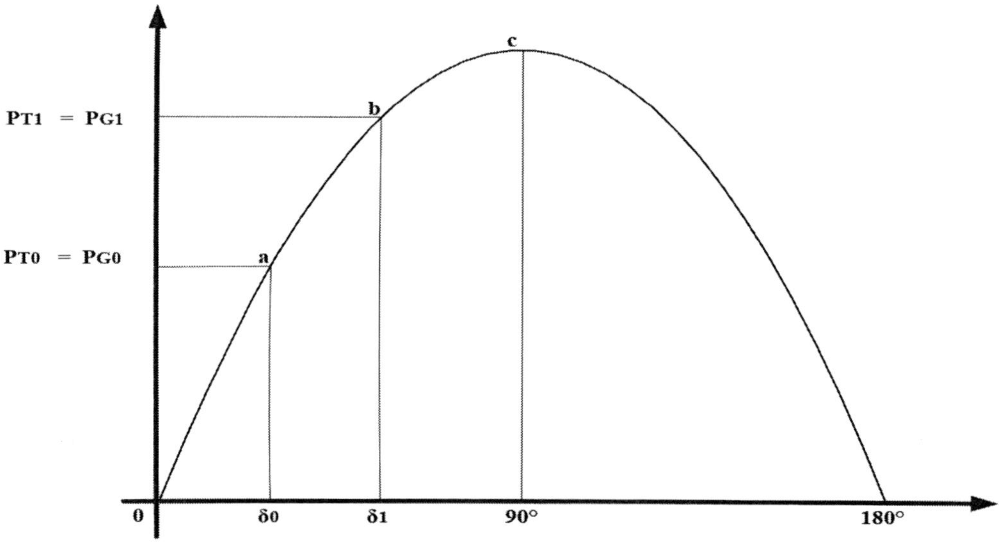

Fig. 3. Characteristics of the real power and the power angle.

Because there is an imbalance of power, then the speed will be slightly up and power angle will also rise. When the power angle δ rise from δ_0, the electric power generator will rise. The increase in power will match with the increase in power output of the turbine. The operating system will be stable with the new power angle δ. Whenever valve steam (water) is opened and steam (water) increases, the output of electric power generators will rise.

Suppose turbine output is increased gradually until the point c (the characteristic power-angle), then the maximum power will be achieved. If the increase of power turbine continues, then the power angle will rise, while the power received by the infinite bus will drop. So that the difference between the input and output increase and will accelerate the rotation generators greater.

When the power angle is increased beyond the angle of 90°, the received power will drop rapidly and becomes zero at the angle of 180°. The acceleration of the generator rotor will increase. In other words, if the power angle is increased beyond 90°, the synchronism is lost.

P_{max} is the steady-state stability limit of the system which is the maximum power that can be delivered under slow disturbance. If an attempt is made to transmit power over this power limit, the synchronism is lost. The maximum power is also referred to as the pull-out power [6].

$$P_{max} = \frac{|E||V|}{X} \tag{3}$$

where X is the reactance transfer between E and V,

$$X = X_d' + X_{eq} \tag{4}$$

$$E = V + j\,I\,X \tag{5}$$

where X_d' is generator reactance, x_{eq} is equivalent reactace, E is generator terminal voltage, I is inducted current and V is generator bus voltage.

It can be concluded that the maximum power that can be transferred by the generator is very dependent on the reactance network. If the generator transfers beyond this maximum power limit, that can be instability as loss of synchronization on the generator. If the load still increases, the stator and rotor magnetic coupling will be loose.

3 Reduction of the multimachine system to SMIB system using losses concept

Electric power system is a large system with multi generators (multimachine). If the generator stability analysis should be carry out in multimachine system, it will be very difficult. Therefore, the multimachine system as shown in Figure 4 must be changed to a Single Machine to Infinite Bus (SMIB) system first.

The procedure to change the multimachine system to SMIB system and the maximum generation calculation procedure (P_{max}) of each generator unit can be explained as follows:

i. Prepare the power system data. Run the load flow with all generators are off except the observed generator (the one that stability will be analyzed and which the equivalent impedance will be calculated).
ii. Calculate the current value I of the observed generator using the following equation:

$$I* = \left(\frac{S_{in}}{\sqrt{3x V_i}} \right) \tag{6}$$

where: S_{in} = generated complex power of generator
Vi = voltage of bus I
S_L = P_L + jQ_L with S_L, P_L and Q_L are complex power losses, active power losses and reactive power losses between two bus, respectively.

iii. Equivalent current is equal with the observed generator current.
iv. Calculate the equivalent value of r_{eq} and x_{eq} using the following equations:

$$Z_{eq} = \frac{S_L}{I^2} = \frac{P_L + jQ_L}{I^2} \tag{7}$$

$$r_{eq} = Z_{eq} \cos \theta \tag{8}$$

and

$$x_{eq} = Z_{eq} \sin\theta \tag{9}$$

v. Calculate E using Equation 5.
vi. Determine the maximum generation of observed generator which is the generator steady-state stability limit using Equation 3.
vii. Repeat this procedure for all generators.

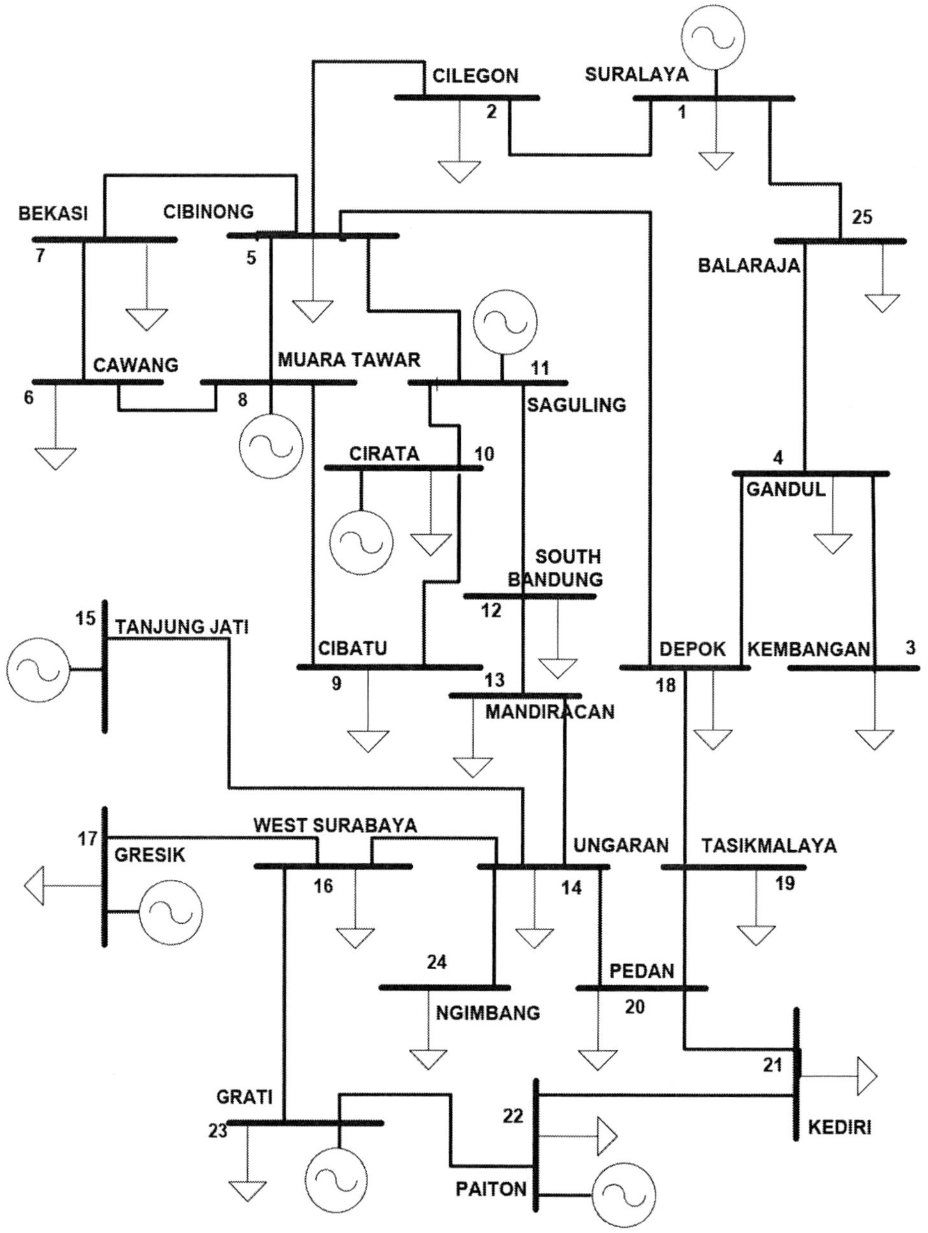

Fig. 4. Java-Bali multimachine system 500 kV.

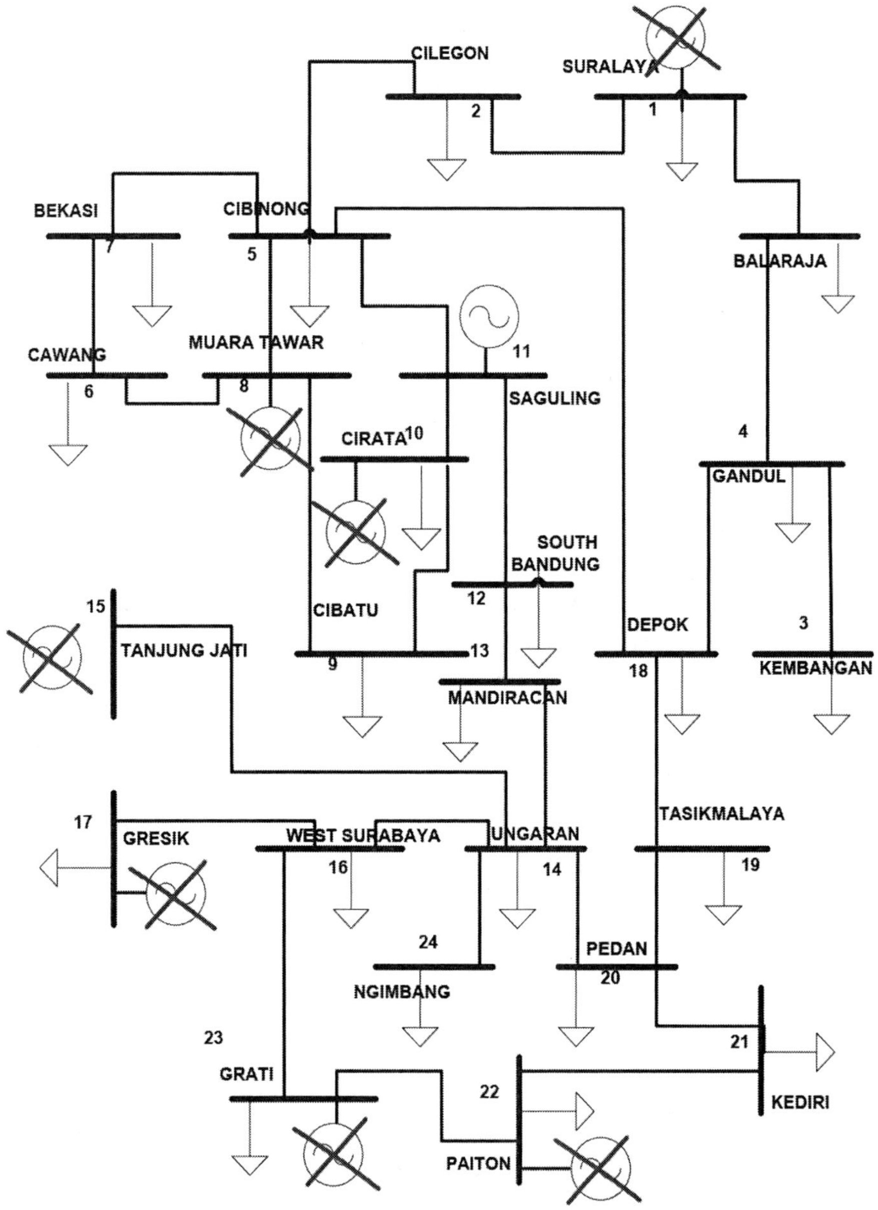

Fig. 5. The procedure to change the multimachine system to SMIB system.

Figure 5 shows the procedure to change the multimachine system to SMIB system. The multimachine system is converted into an equivalent impedance and an equivalent load as shown in Figure 6.

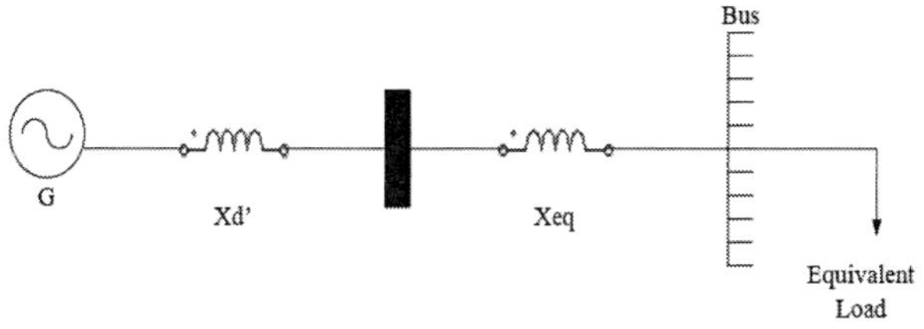

Fig. 6. Single machine to infinite bus (SMIB) system.

4 Simulation and results

The simulation using the 500 kV transmission system of Java-Bali that consisting of one swing bus, seven generator bus and 17 load bus. Figure 4 shows a picture of SLD (Single Line Diagram) of Java-Bali system 500 kV.

There are eight generators in the Java-Bali system 500 kV. The generator is connected to the load bus through the lines with the different conductor type. The Java-Bali system 500 kV data is contained in Table 1, Table 2, and Table 3.

Table 1. Transmission system data of Java-Bali 500 kV.

i -	R (p.u)	X (p.u)	1/2 B (p.u)	*Tap Setting*
1 2	0.000626496	0.007008768	0	1
1 24	0.003677677	0.035333317	0	1
2 5	0.013133324	0.146925792	0.003530571	1
3 4	0.001513179	0.016928308	0	1
4 18	0.000694176	0.006669298	0	1
5 7	0.004441880	0.042675400	0	1
5 8	0.006211600	0.059678000	0	1
5 11	0.004111380	0.045995040	0.004420973	1
6 7	0.001973648	0.018961840	0	1
6 8	0.005625600	0.054048000	0	1
8 9	0.002822059	0.027112954	0	1
9 10	0.002739960	0.026324191	0	1
10 11	0.001474728	0.014168458	0	1
11 12	0.001957800	0.021902400	0	1
12 13	0.006990980	0.067165900	0.006429135	1
13 14	0.013478000	0.129490000	0.012394812	1
14 15	0.013533920	0.151407360	0.003638261	1
14 16	0.015798560	0.15178480	0.003632219	1
14 20	0.009036120	0.086814600	0	1
16 17	0.001394680	0.013399400	0	1
16 23	0.003986382	0.044596656	0	1
18 5	0.000818994	0.007868488	0	1
18 19	0.014056000	0.15724800	0.015114437	1
19 20	0.015311000	0.171288000	0.016463941	1
20 21	0.010291000	0.115128000	0.011065927	1
21 22	0.010291000	0.115128000	0.011065927	1
22 23	0.004435823	0.049624661	0.004769846	1
24 4	0.002979224	0.028622920	0	1
25 14	0.023479613	0.225580588	0.100970352	1
25 16	0.005966652	0.057324466	0	1

Table 2. Generation system data of Java-Bali 500 kV.

Bus No	Generator	Active Power (MW)		ReactivePower (MVAR)	
		Minimum	*Maximum*	*Minimum*	*Maximum*
1	Suralaya	1 500	3 803	–600	2 040
8	Muaratawar	1 040	2 096	–700	1 540
10	Cirata	400	948	–488	488
11	Saguling	400	700	–140	440
15	Tanjung Jati	600	2 808	–240	720
17	Gresik	238	828	–610	660
22	Paiton	1 425	4 710	–840	1 920
23	Grati	150	850	–302	566

Table 3. Generator reactance data of Java-Bali 500 kV.

Bus No	Generator	Ra	Xd'
1	Suralaya	0	0.1418445
8	Muara Tawar	0	0.0498565
10	Cirata	0	0.0982143
11	Saguling	0	0.2820233
15	Tanjung Jati	0	0.4842950
17	Gresik	0	0.1869112
22	Paiton	0	0.1567810
23	Grati	0	0.2630799

The simulations is performed with the load is 11 278 MW. Data loading is presented in Table 4.

The simulation steps in finding the steady state stability limit (P_{max}) for each generator are as follows:

i. The generator on bus 11 is used as observed generator. The load flow result with all generators are off except the observed generator on bus 11 is presented in Table 5.

ii. From Table 5, we can see that the generated power of generator is 536.027 MW and 211.426 MVar. Voltage of bus 11 is 1.00 pu. The active power losses is 1.027 MW and the reactive power losses is –220.448 MVar.

iii. Calculation result for the current value I of the observed generator using Equation 6 is 665.358 A.

iv. The r_{eq} value and the x_{eq} value can calculate using Equation 7, Equation 8 and Equation 9, and we get 0.0000092792– j 0.00199184.

v. We can determine the maximum generation of observed generator which is the generator steady-state stability limit using (3), and be obtained 668.929 MW

vi. Repeat this procedure for all generators. The calculation results of r_{eq} and x_{eq} value using the losses concept as described in section III can be seen in Table 6.

Table 4. Transmission system bus data of Java-Bali 500kV.

Bus No	Bus Name	Bus Type	Voltage		Load	
			Magnitude	Angle	MW	MVAR
1	Suralaya	Slack	1.02	0	153	45
2	Cilegon	Load	1	0	703	227
3	Kembangan	Load	1	0	760	261
4	Gandul	Load	1	0	544	181
5	Cibinong	Load	1	0	697	215
6	Cawang	Load	1	0	760	181
7	Bekasi	Load	1	0	646	170
8	Muaratawar	Generator	1	0	0	0
9	Cibatu	Load	1	0	823	317
10	Cirata	Generator	1	0	680	245
11	Saguling	Generator	1	0	0	0
12	South Bandung	Load	1	0	590	351
13	Mandiracan	Load	1	0	397	136
14	Ungaran	Load	1	0	392	363
15	Tanjung Jati	Generator	1	0	0	0
16	WestSurabaya	Load	1	0	862	317
17	Gresik	Generator	1	0	210	91
18	Depok	Load	1	0	0	0
19	Tasikmalaya	Load	1	0	277	17
20	Pedan	Load	1	0	524	244
21	Kediri	Load	1	0	358	206
22	Paiton	Generator	1	0	839	272
23	Grati	Generator	1	0	130	193
24	Ngimbang	Load	1	0	732	287
25	Balaraja	Load	1	0	264	58
					11 278	4 377

Load flow analysis in ETAP simulation is used to validate the calculation results. The observed generator is turned on and others are turned off. Rated load is increased gradually until reached a state where if the loading value is raised again the load flow process becomes divergent. The generating value that is obtained before the load flow process divergent is the maximum limit of the generation which is a steady state stability limit of the generator.

The calculation results of P_{max} which is a steady state stability limit of each generator unit compared with result of ETAP simulation can be seen in Table 7.

Table 5. The load flow result for observed generator is on bus 11.

Power Flow Solution by Newton-Raphson Method Maximum Power Mismatch = 1.15256e–006 No. of Iterations = 3							
Bus No.	Voltage Mag.	Angle Degree	-------Load------		------Generation------		Injected
			MW	Mvar	MW	Mvar	Mvar
1	0.994	–0.726	7.258	4.440	0.000	0.000	0.000
2	0.994	–0.730	33.349	22.398	0.000	0.000	0.000
3	0.994	–0.697	36.052	25.753	0.000	0.000	0.000
4	0.994	–0.664	25.806	17.859	0.000	0.000	0.000
5	0.995	–0.546	33.064	21.214	0.000	0.000	0.000
6	0.995	–0.572	36.052	17.859	0.000	0.000	0.000
7	0.995	–0.586	30.645	16.774	0.000	0.000	0.000
8	0.966	–0.425	0.000	0.000	0.000	0.000	0.000
9	0.997	–0.298	39.041	31.278	0.000	0.000	0.000
10	0.999	–0.120	32.257	24.174	0.000	0.000	0.000
11	1.000	0.000	0.000	0.000	536.027	211.426	0.000
12	0.999	–0.204	27.988	34.633	0.000	0.000	0.000
13	0.996	–0.732	18.833	13.419	0.000	0.000	0.000
14	0.991	–1.612	15.607	35.817	0.000	0.000	0.000
15	0.992	–1.734	0.000	0.000	0.000	0.000	0.000
16	0.988	–2.001	40.891	31.278	0.000	0.000	0.000
17	0.988	–2.009	9.962	8.979	0.000	0.000	0.000
18	0.995	–0.688	0.000	0.000	0.000	0.000	0.000
19	0.996	–1.248	13.140	1.677	0.000	0.000	0.000
20	0.992	–1.703	24.857	24.075	0.000	0.000	0.000
21	0.990	–1.963	16.983	20.326	0.000	0.000	0.000
22	0.988	–2.109	39.800	26.838	0.000	0.000	0.000
23	0.987	–2.059	6.167	19.043	0.000	0.000	0.000
24	0.994	–0.716	34.724	28.318	0.000	0.000	0.000
25	0.989	–1.957	12.523	5.723	0.000	0.000	0.000
Total			535.000	431.874	536.027	211.426	0.000

Table 6. Calculation result of Z_{eq} using losses concept.

Bus No.	Generator	Z_{eq}	P_{max}
1	Suralaya	0.000157+ j 0.001752	3 574.141
8	Muara Tawar	0.007125 + j 0.068446	2 259.334
10	Cirata	0.0001 + j 0.0023	930
11	Saguling	0.0000092792- j 0.00199184	668.929
15	Tanjungjati	0.012925599 – j 0.21368	2 437.331
17	Gresik	0.0014 + j 0.0083	810
22	Paiton	0.0008 + j 0.0044	4 786.653
23	Grati	0.01004 + j 0.101927	819.2782

Table 7. Calculation result of Z_{eq} using losses concept.

Bus No.	Generator	Calculation result using the proposed method	ETAP simulation result
1	Suralaya	3 574.41	3 650.827
8	Muara Tawar	2 259.334	2 231.407
10	Cirata	930	917.936
11	Saguling	668.929	660.898
15	Tanjungjati	2 437.331	2 586.633
17	Gresik	810	823.246
22	Paiton	4 786.653	4 746.864
23	Grati	819.2782	851.094

5 Conclusion

P_{max} calculation result obtained by the proposed method is not much different compared with the results obtained by the ETAP simulation. It can be concluded that, the method to change multimachine system into SMIB presented in this paper can be applied and determination of r_{eq} and x_{eq} value based on the network losses concept can be done. By using the proposed method, steady state stability limit of each generator in a multimachine system can be determined easily. It will be very useful for guiding the operator in operating their generator safely.

The authors are very grateful to the Power System Simulation Laboratory, Department of Electrical Engineering, Institut Teknologi Sepuluh Nopember (ITS), Surabaya, Indonesia to all facilities provided during this research and the authors are very grateful to Direktur Riset dan Pengabdian Masyarakat, Direktorat Jenderal Penguatan Riset dan Pengembangan through the PDD 2017 Grant Fund.

References

1. C.Thakur, S. Sahu. *Current Trends in Technology and Science*, **II**,VI:330–339 (2013). https://www.ctts.in/assets/upload/8000ctts-415%20vol-2%20iss-6.pdf.
2. Ž. Eleschová, A. Beláň. *AT&P journal PLUS2*:54–57 (2008). https://www.atpjournal.sk/buxus/docs//casopisy/atp_plus/plus_2008_2/plus54_57.pdf.
3. J. Veleba. *Possible steady-state voltage stability analyses of electric power systems* [Online] from http://home.zcu.cz/~tesarova/IP/Proceedings/Proc_2011/Files/Veleba.pdf. (2011). [Accessed on 9 July 2017]
4. K. Himaja, T.S. Surendra, S.T. Kalyani. *IJERT*, **1**,7 (2012). https://www.ijert.org/download/1059/steady-state-stability-analysis-of-a-single-machine-power-system-using-matlab.
5. I.C. Gunadin, M. Abdillah, A.Soeprijanto, O. Penangsang. *WSEAS Transactions On Power Systems*, **7**,3:91–103 (2012). http://repository.unhas.ac.id/handle/123456789/7195
6. J. Lianda. *Analisis batas stabilitas steady state dan transient menggunakan metode Radial Equivalent Independent (Rei) Dimo* [Stability limit analysis of steady state and transient method using Radial Equivalent Independent (REI) Dimo]. [Thesis].

Institut Teknologi Sepuluh Nopember, Surabaya, Indonesia (2011). [in Bahasa Indonesia]. p. 45. http://digilib.its.ac.id/ITS-Undergraduate-3100011042766/15957
7. J. Custer, I. C. Gunadin, O. Penangsang, A. Soeprijanto. *Optimisasi operasi sistem tenaga listrik dengan konstrain kapabilitas operasi generator dan kestabilan steady state* [Optimization of power system operation using capability constraint of generator operation and steady state stability] [Online] from http://digilib.its.ac.id/public/ITS-paper-20168-Paper.pdf. (2011). [Accesed on 29 March 2014]. [in Bahasa Indonesia]
8. P. Kayal, S. Chanda, C.K. Chanda. *International Journal on Electrical Engineering and Informatics*, **4**,2 (2012). http://www.ijeei.org/docs-43441230750358b3a03515.pdf.
9. G.A. Mahmoud. *IET Generation, Transmission & Distribution*, **6**,7 :612–618. http://ieeexplore.ieee.org/document/6235272/
10. I.C. Gunadin, O. Penangsang, A.Soeprijanto. *Influence of load characteristics against voltage collapse phenomena*. Proceeding International Conference on Engineering and Meta-Engineering, (Orlando, USA, 2010). http://www.iiis.org/CDs2010/CD2010IMC/ICEME_2010/index.asp?id=0&area=1

Design and Bandwidth Optimization on Triangle Patch Microstrip Antenna for WLAN 2.4 GHz

Sotyohadi[*], *Riken* Afandi, and *Dony* Rachmad Hadi

Department of Electrical Engineering, National Institute of Technology (ITN) Malang, Jalan Raya Karanglo km 2, Malang 65145, East Java, Indonesia

Abstract. In this paper, single and dual element triangle patch microstrip antenna for WLAN 2.4 GHz is designed, analyzed and fabricated. Both proposed design utilized proximity feeding techniques. Afterwards the design is simulated on HFFS and optimized, which finally the dimension of both design for frequency 2.4 GHz is obtained. The best simulation result for both single and dual element triangle patch microstrip antenna is used as reference for fabrication on FR4 substrate with dielectric constant (□r) = 4.4 and thickness (h) = 1.6 mm. The measurement result showed that the single element can achieve return loss (S11) -51.913 dB and VSWR 1.005 9 at 2.417 GHz, and then for dual element the result for return loss (S1) is -48.213 8 for VSWR 1.007 8 at 2.463 GHz. Compared to coaxial feeding technique, the proximity feeding has better parameter performance.

Key words: Coaxial feeding, HFFS, microstrip antenna, proximity feeding, return loss

1 Introduction

Microstrip antenna becomes more popular recently because of its advantages compared to the conventional antennas, such as Yagi-Uda, horn, helical, and parabolic. Even though they have higher gain and wider bandwidth, but the typical dimensional structure and large size are not applicable for compact wireless devices [1]. In the other hand, the microstrip antenna has several major superiorities such as light weight, low profile, small in size, ease to integrate with Microwave Integrated Circuit (MIC) and Monolithic Microwave Integrated Circuit (MMIC) [2]. Instead of its superiority, the poor bandwidth, low efficiency and gain become the weaknesses of microstrip antenna [3]. There are numerous methods that can be used to overcome this problem. One method that can be used to improve the microstrip antenna parameters is the feeding technique. Previous research has been conducted to analyze the effect of using different feeding technique on microstrip antenna, in which the result showed that the cut feed has better parameter performance compared to coaxial and microstrip line feeding technique [4]. From the previous research for cut feed or microstrip line feed with notch, the bandwidth only up to 60 MHz [5]. Furthermore, since bandwidth is one of the essential parameters for WLAN 2.4 GHz which should cover in the range of 100 MHz [6], better feeding technique should be utilized. In

[*] Corresponding author: sotyohadi@lecturer.itn.ac.id

order to accommodate wider bandwidth, the proximity coupled feeding is one of feeding techniques which has better characteristics in suppressing the spurious feed radiation and enhance bandwidth [7]. Therefore, the use of proximity coupled feeding in present research design on microstrip antenna is considerable.

The aim of this research is to design and analyze a single and dual element triangle patch microstrip antenna utilized proximity coupled feeding. The decision on using triangle patch microstrip antenna is based on the reason that the area of triangle patch has fewer dimensions for the specified operation frequency [8]. Afterwards, the fabricated design is measured and compared to the bandwidth result of triangle patch microstrip antenna which utilized the coaxial feeding technique.

2 Antenna design

The triangle patch microstrip antenna is design to operate for 2.4 GHz. The design is fabricated on the dielectric substrate FR4, which has the dielectric permittivity constant of the substrate (εr) = 4.4 and thickness of the substrate (h) = 1.6 mm.

2.1 Resonant frequency

Resonant frequency determines the dimension of the microstrip antenna. Therefore the corresponding resonance frequency is determine by reference [9]

$$f_r = \frac{ck_{mn}}{2\pi\sqrt{\varepsilon_r}} = \frac{2c}{3a\sqrt{\varepsilon_r}}(m^2 + mn + n^2) \tag{1}$$

Where c is velocity of light in free space and K_{mn} is wave number. The wave number can be determined by reference [9]

$$K_{mn} = \frac{4\pi}{3a}\sqrt{m^2 + mn + n^2}$$

Therefore, from the above equation for lowest order resonance frequency, is given [9]

$$f_r = \frac{2c}{3a\sqrt{\varepsilon_r}} \tag{2}$$

Where:
f_r= resonance frequency
a = length of the side triangular patch
ε_r= relative dielectric constant of substrate

2.2 Triangular patch dimension

The triangular patch has three sides with a length, as shown in Figure 1 [10].

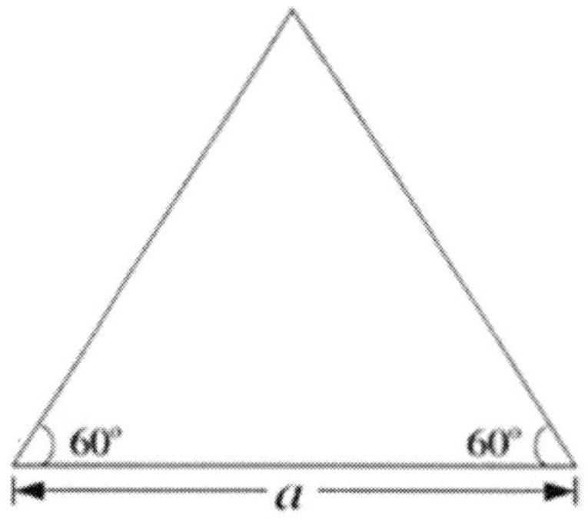

Fig. 1. Triangular patch microstrip antenna.

After substituting the above equation with the given value for f_r = 2.44 GHz as the centre frequency for WLAN, velocity of light $c = 3 \times 10^8\ m\ s^{-1}$, and ε_r = 4.4, the length of a can be calculated. In order to determine length of triangle patch a, the Eq. 2 is utilized which give the result [11].

$$a = \frac{2c}{3f_r\sqrt{\varepsilon_r}} \tag{3}$$

Finally, the value for length of triangle is obtained a = 39.076 3 mm. Thus the height (L_P) is determined by mathematical equation as follow,

$$H = L_p = \sqrt{a^2 - \left(\frac{1}{2} \times a\right)^2} \tag{4}$$

From above Eq.4 for a = 39.076 3 mm, it can be calculated that the height of triangle patch L_P = 33.774 9 mm.

2.3 Ground plane dimension

The ground plane is an area which located in the bottom side. The position of ground plane is shown in Figure 2.

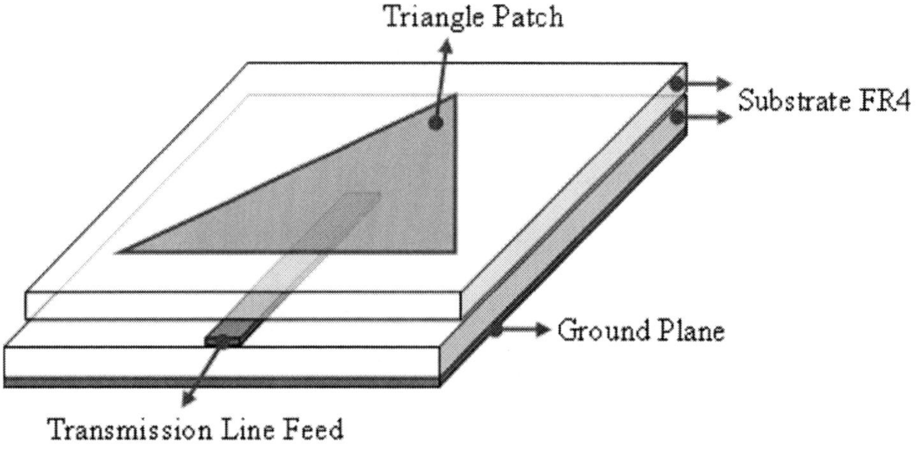

Fig. 2. Ground plane triangular patch microstrip antenna.

According to Punit S. Nakar the size of ground plane is larger than the patch dimensions by approximately six times the height or thickness of the substrate all around the periphery. Hence for the dimension design of the ground plane is determined by reference [12],

$$L_g = 6h + L_p \tag{5}$$

$$L_g = 6\times1.6 + 33.7749 = 43.374\ 9 \text{ mm}$$

$$W_g = 6h + W_p \tag{6}$$

$$W_g = 6\times1.6 + 39.0763 = 48.676\ 3 \text{ mm}$$

2.4 Proximity coupled feeding

In proximity coupled feeding eventually is arrange in stack of substrate layer, which mainly the feeding technique is similar to that microstrip line feeding. The dimension of the microstrip line feeding has important value in order to have matching condition between impedance of the triangle patch microstrip antenna and the transmission line. Therefore the width and length of Z_0 = 50 Ω microstrip feed line for single element can be determined from the following Equation [3],

$$W_f = \frac{2h}{\pi}\left(B - 1 - \ln(2B-1) + \frac{\varepsilon_r - 1}{2\varepsilon_r}\left[\ln(B-1) + 0.39 - \frac{0.61}{\varepsilon_r}\right]\right) \tag{7}$$

Where h = 1.6, B = 5.64 and ε_r = 4.4 then the result for feed line width can be obtained W_f = 3 mm. The following step is calculating of the 50 Ω microstrip feed line which can be obtain from the following Equation [3],

$$L_{f1} = \frac{\lambda_g}{4} = \frac{56.23}{4} = 14.0575\,\text{mm} \tag{8}$$

From Equation 8, where the value for λ_g = 56.23 mm, then the result for L_{f1} = 14.057 5 mm.

For dual element triangle patch, the T-Junction 70.7 Ω is needed to divide the power for both patches [13]. Figure 3 shows for the power divider to connect the both triangle patch microstrip antenna.

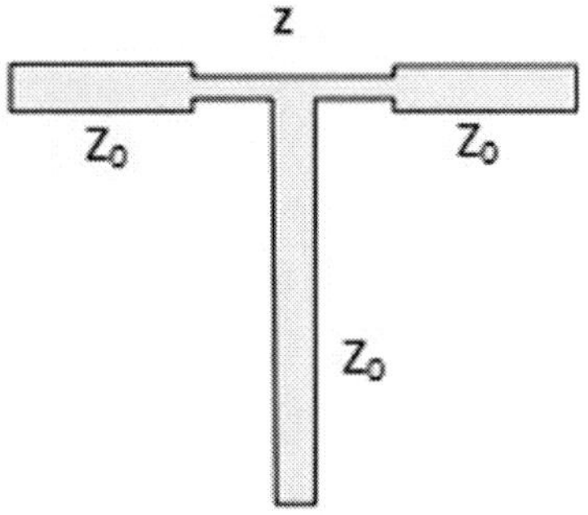

Fig. 3. T-Junction as power divider

In order to maintain the input impedance 50 Ω, ¼ λ transformer is needed. The ¼ λ transformer is an impedance matching technique by providing transmission line impedance Z_t between two non-match transmission channels. To acquire the width of the Z_0 = 70.7 Ω can be determined using Equation 7.

For $B = 3.96$, $\varepsilon_r = 4.4$, and the thickness for substrate $h = 1.6$ mm, the width of the feed line is obtained $W_f = 1.58$ mm. Thus, the length can be obtained by using Equation 8, for $\lambda_g = 43.29$ mm.

$$L_{f2} = \frac{\lambda_g}{4} = \frac{43.29}{4} = 10.8225 \text{ mm}$$

2.5 Distance between two elements

For dual element the distance between both patches should be calculated, this is due to the electromagnetically coupled effect. Therefore, the distance between two elements can be calculated using Equation 9.

$$d = \frac{c}{2f} \tag{9}$$

$$d = \frac{3\times10^8}{2\times2.44\times10^9} = 61.4754 \text{ mm}$$

Finally the distance between two triangle patch microstrip antenna is defined $d = 61.475\,4$ mm.

3 Proposed antenna

3.1 Single element triangle patch

The single element triangle patch microstrip antenna with proximity feeding technique are shown in Figure 4.

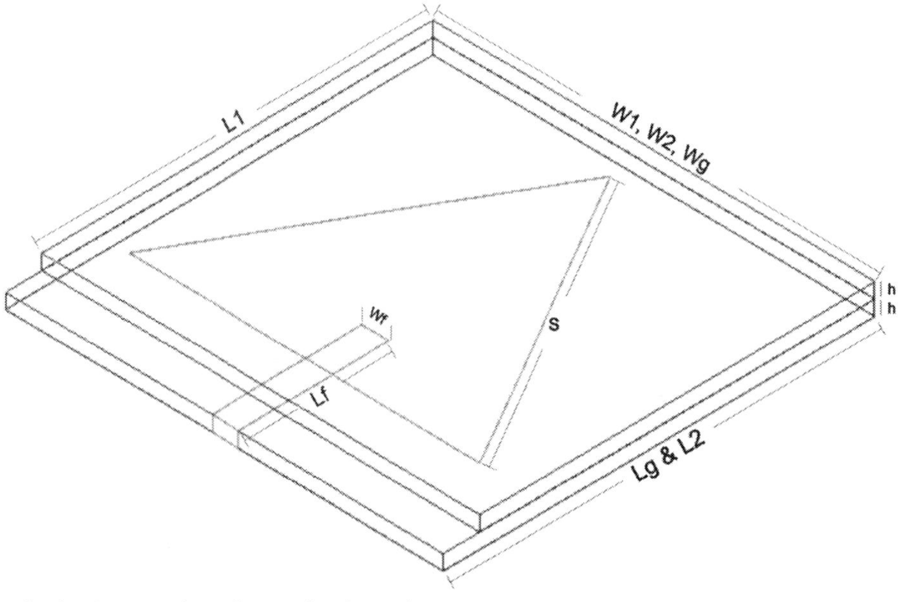

Fig. 4. Single element triangular patch microstrip antenna

From the Figure 4 above, the dimension of proposed antenna for single element is given in the Table 1.

Table 1. Proposed single element triangle patch.

No.	Antenna Dimension	Value (mm)
1	a (length of triangle patch)	39.076 3
2	L_1 (length of upper substrate)	43.374 9
3	L_2 (length of lower substrate)	47.441 0
4	L_g (length of ground plane)	47.441 0
5	W_1 (width of upper substrate)	48.676 3
6	W_2 (width of lower substrate)	48.676 3
7	W_g (width of ground plane)	48.676 3
8	h (thickness of substrate)	1.6
9	L_f (length of microstrip feedline)	16.760 8
10	W_f (width of microstrip feedline)	3.021 6

3.2 Dual element triangle patch

The following Figure 4 is shown for dual element triangle patch microstrip antenna.

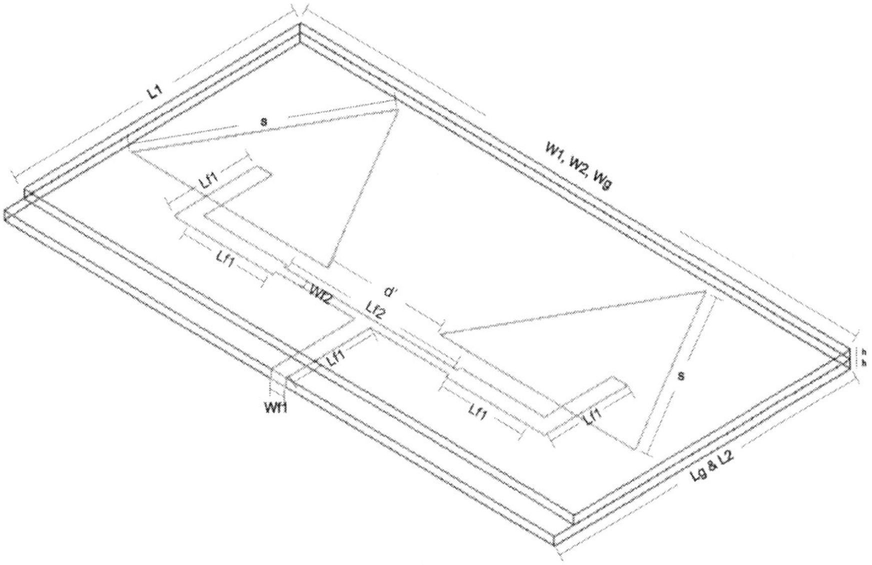

Fig. 5. Dual element triangular patch microstrip antenna.

The dimension of Figure 5 above and include the impedance matching is given in the following Table 2.

Table 2. Proposed dual element triangle patch.

No.	Antenna Dimension	Value (mm)
1	a (length of triangle patch)	39.076 3
2	L_1 (length of upper substrate)	55.601 4
3	L_2 (length of lower substrate)	59.601 4
4	L_g (length of ground plane)	59.601 4
5	W_1 (width of upper substrate)	110.151 7
6	W_2 (width of lower substrate)	110.151 7

Continue on next page

Table 2. Proposed dual element triangle patch (Continue).

No.	Antenna Dimension	Value (mm)
7	W_g (width of ground plane)	110.151 7
8	h (thickness of substrate)	1.6
9	L_{f1} (length of microstrip feedline 50 Ω)	16.760 8
10	W_{f1} (width of microstrip feedline 50 Ω)	3.021 6
11	L_{f2} (length of microstrip feedline 70,7 Ω)	34.507
12	W_{f2} (width of microstrip feedline 70,7 Ω)	1.5734 2
13	d (distance of both patches)	22.399 1

4 Simulation result

4.1 Return loss

For good result, the return loss (S11) should be less than -10 dB. In which the -10 dB is equivalent to VSWR > 2. From Figure 6 it is clear that the simulation result after optimization for single element for S11 is -31.955 6 dB at resonance frequency 2.42 GHz.

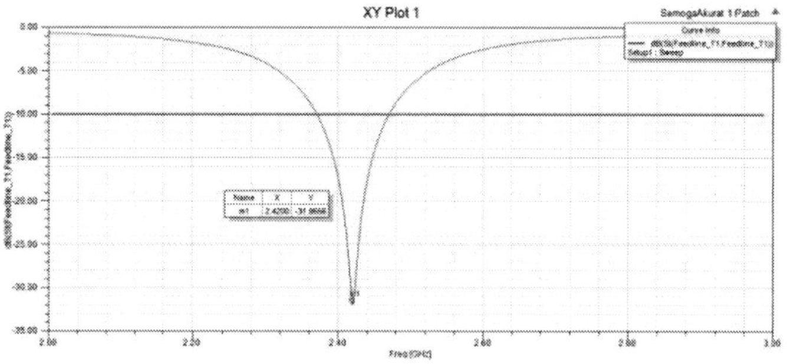

Fig. 6. Return loss (S11) for single element

The following Figure 7 it is depicted the return loss for dual element. After optimization the value of S11 is -24.367 2 dB at resonance frequency 2.43 4 GHz.

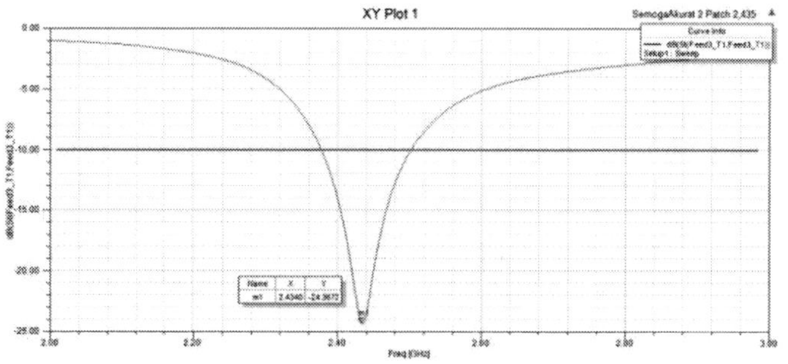

Fig. 7. Return loss (S11) for dual element.

4.2 VSWR

Voltage Standing Wave Ratio (VSWR) is the reflection coefficient. The VSWR for single element is presented in Figure 8, which shows the optimized simulated result for VSWR = 1.051 8, which is less than 2.

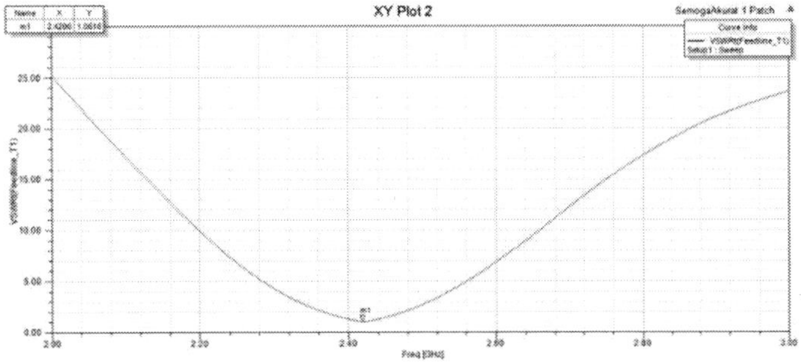

Fig. 8. Simulated VSWR for single element.

In Figure 9, shows the optimized simulation result for dual element VSWR = 1.128 8.

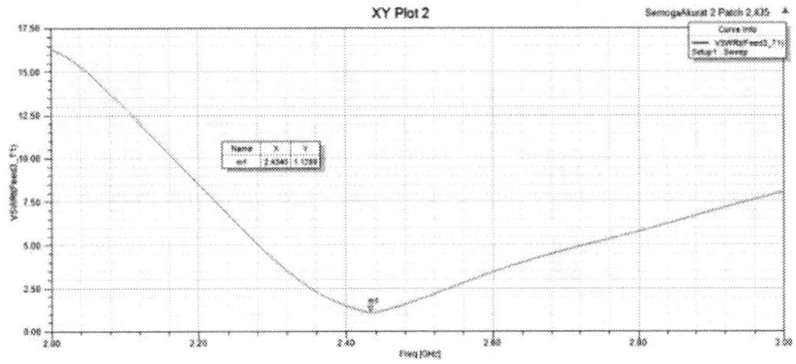

Fig. 9. Simulated VSWR for dual element.

5 Measurement result

5.1 Return loss

The measurement result for return loss (S11) is shown in Figure 10 for single element and Figure 11 for dual element. Both measurements were performed using vector network analyzer (VNA).

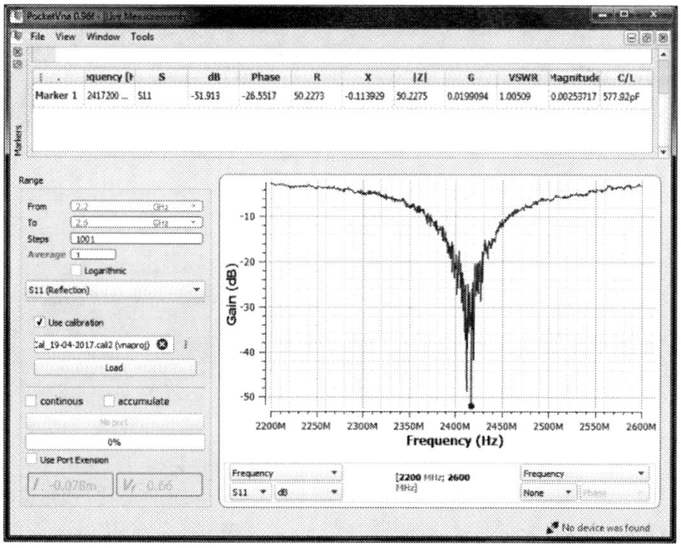

Fig. 10. Return loss for single patch element.

The obtained return loss for measurement in single patch is -51.913 dB at resonant frequency of 2.41 7 GHz.

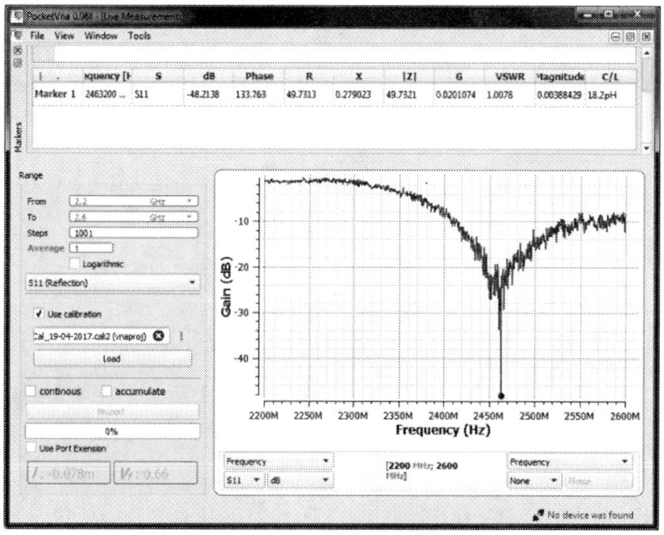

Fig. 11. Return loss for dual patch element.

The measurement result for dual element is -48.213 8 dB at the resonant frequency of 2.46 3 GHz.

5.2 VSWR

For VSWR measurement result is shown in Figure 12 for single element and in Figure 13 for the dual element. The obtained measurement result for single and dual element is 1.005 9 and 1.007 8 respectively.

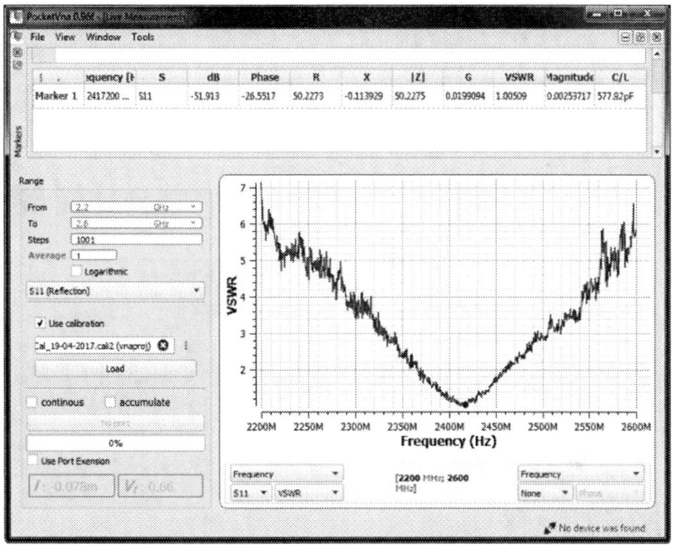

Fig. 12. VSWR for single patch element.

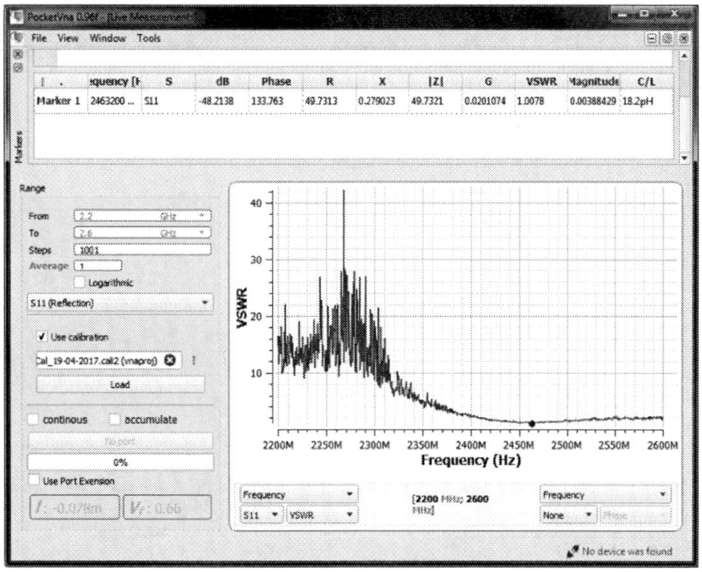

Fig. 13. VSWR for dual patch element.

5.3 Bandwidth

Bandwidth of antenna is capability of an antenna to cope range of frequency within the antenna operation frequency, which is less than -10 dB return loss value. The following Figure 14 and Figure 15 show the bandwidth result for single and dual triangle patch antenna.

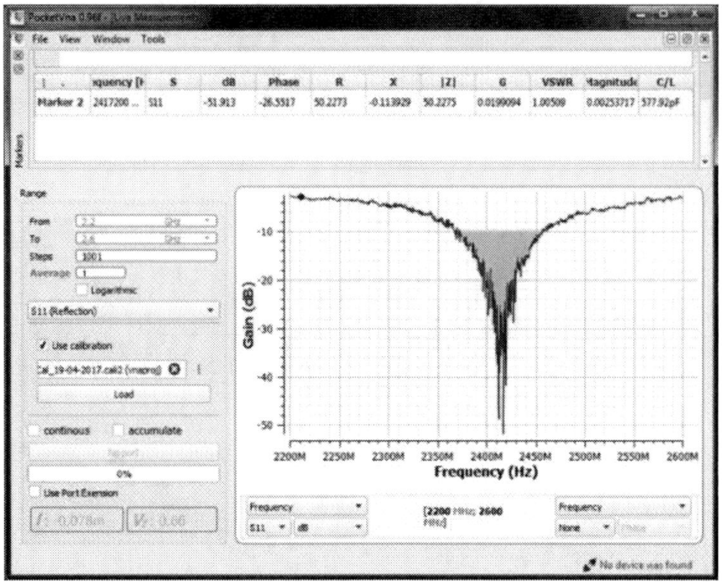

Fig. 14. Bandwidth for single patch element.

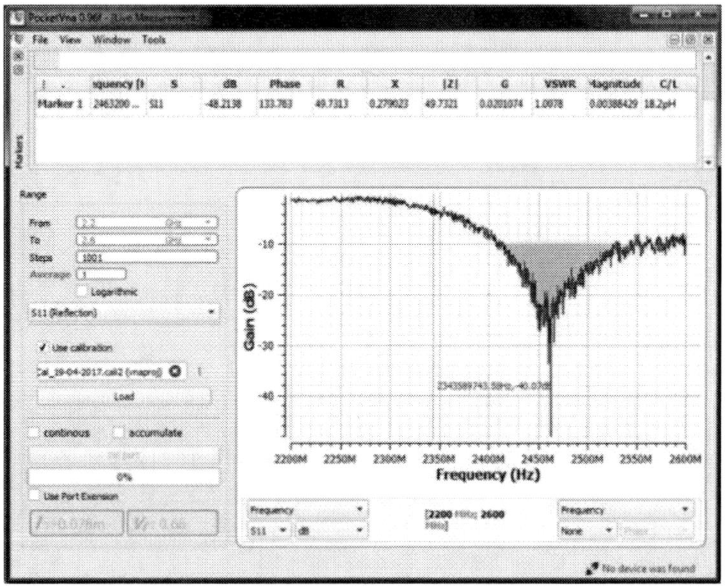

Fig. 15. Bandwidth for dual patch element.

From both figure above, it can be explained that the bandwidth for single element span from 2.372 GHz to 2.456 GHz. In which the bandwidth reaches 84 MHz. In other hand for dual element has range from 2.414 GHz until 2.525 GHz, so that the result is 111 MHz.

5.4 Comparison

The design of single and dual triangle patch microstrip antenna utilizing proximity coupled feeding technique is compared to the single and dual triangle antenna which is used the coaxial probe feeding technique. The result of the comparison is shown in Table 3.

Table 3. Comparison between proximity and coaxial probe feeding.

Parameters	Single Element		Dual Element	
	Coaxial Probe	Proximity	Coaxial Probe	Proximity
Return Loss (dB)	-15.93	-51.913	-19.31	-48.2138
VSWR	1.294	1.005 9	1.24	1.007 8
Bandwidth (MHz)	42	84	28	111
Resonance Frequency (GHz)	2.537	2.417	2.537	2.463

5.5 Fabrication design

The single and dual triangle patch microstrip antenna using proximity coupled feeding technique has been fabricated on a substrate material FR-4, which is shown in Figure 16 and Figure 17 respectively.

Fig. 16. Single triangle patch.

Fig. 17. Dual triangle patch.

6 Conclusion

Finally single and dual element triangle patch microstrip antenna is fabricated and presented. The both proposed antenna is suitable for WLAN 2.4 GHz application. The both fabricated antenna has good performance and almost perfectly impedance matching. It can be concluded that the parameter result of proximity coupled feeding techniques has better performance compare to the coaxial feeding techniques.

Author gratefully thank to National Institute of Technology (ITN) Malang, for their support in funding this research. We also would like to express our gratitude to the head of Telecommunication Laboratory, for their contribution during measurement.

References

1. D. Singh, K.A. Gupta, R.K. Prasad, Design and Analysis of C-Shaped Microstrip Patch Antenna for Wideband Application. In: *Proceedings of the Conference on Advances in Communication and Control Systems-2013 (CAC2S)*. USA : Atlantis Press (2013). pp. 425–428. https://www.atlantis-press.com/proceedings/cac2s-13/6349
2. G. Kumar, K.P. Ray. *Broadband microstrip antennas*, USA: Artech House, Inc. (2005). pp. 3–4. https://books.google.co.id/books/about/Broadband_Microstrip_Antennas.html?id=wfl84429CsEC&redir_esc=y
3. C.A. Balanis. *Antenna theory analysis and design*. 3rd edition. USA: John Willey and Sons (2005). p. 811. https://books.google.co.id/books?id=iFEBCgAAQBAJ&printsec=frontcover&dq=Antenna+Theory+Analysis+and+Design&hl=en&sa=X&ved=0ahUKEwj674m10_7YAhVCuY8KHRFsBqwQ6AEIKDAA#v=onepage&q=Antenna%20Theory%20Analysis%20and%20Design&f=false.
4. K.P. Kumar, K.S. Rao, T. Sumanth, N.M. Rao, R.A. Kumar, Y. Harish. *IJARCCE*, **2**, 2:1276–1281 (2013). https://www.ijarcce.com/upload/february/29-Effect%20of%20feeding%20-tallurisumanth.pdf.
5. S. Sotyohadi, S.H. Pramono, M. Sarosa. Design and fabrication of "Ha" shape-slot microstrip antenna for WLAN 2.4 GHz. In: *Proceedings of Second International Conference on Electrical Systems, Technology and Information 2015 (ICESTI 2015)*. F. Pasila, Y. Tanoto, R. Lim, M. Santoso, N. Pah (Eds). Singapore: Springer (2015). pp. 383–391. https://link.springer.com/chapter/10.1007/978-981-287-988-2_41#citeas
6. H.K. Varshney, M. Kumar, A.K. Jaiswal, R. Saxena, K. Jaiswal. *IJCET*, **4**,3(2014). http://inpressco.com/wp-content/uploads/2014/05/Paper391418-14231.pdf.
7. A. Gupta. *Design and fabrication of dual and triple band microstrip patch antenna using proximity coupling for wireless application*. [Thesis]. Thapar Universiti, Patiala, India (2012). p. 19. http://dspace.thapar.edu:8080/jspui/bitstream/10266/1858/3/1858.pdf
8. V.V.Khairnar, B.V.Kadam, K.R.Khandagle. *Design of equilateral triangular microstrip patch antenna with co-axial feeding technique*. International Conference on Recent Trends in engineering & Technology - 2013(ICRTET'2013) (Kodaikanal, India, 2013). Special Issue of International Journal of Electronics, Communication & Soft Computing Science & Engineering:37–39 (2013). http://www.ijecscse.org/papers/Special%20Issue%202013/Design%20of%20Equilateral%20Triangular%20Microstrip%20Patch%20Antenna%20with%20Co-axial%20Feeding%20Technique.pdf
9. R.K. Vishwakarma, J.A. Ansari, M.K. Meshram. *Indian Journal of Radio Space Physics*, **35**:293–296 (2006). http://www.scirp.org/(S(351jmbntvnsjt1aadkposzje))/reference/ReferencesPapers.aspx?ReferenceID=1846481
10. Y.S.H. Khraisat, M.M. Olaimat, S.N. Abdel-Razeq. *Applied Physics Research*, **4**, 2: 75–81(2012). http://www.ccsenet.org/journal/index.php/apr/article/viewFile/13750/11280.
11. P. Arunagiri, C.N. Kumar, K. Adhavan. *IJRASET*, **4**, IV:88–92 (2016). https://www.ijraset.com/fileserve.php?FID=4397.

12. P.S. Nakar. Design of a compact microstrip patch antenna for use in wireless cellular devices. [Thesis]. Florida State University, Florida, USA (2004). p. 51 http://diginole.lib.fsu.edu/islandora/object/fsu:181039/datastream/PDF/view. page 51.
13. W.D. Pradipta, E. Setijdi, G. Hendrantoro. *Jurnal Teknik ITS*, **1**, 1 (2012). http://ejurnal.its.ac.id/index.php/teknik/article/view/64

The Benefit of Decision Support System as Sustainable Environment Technology to Utilize Coastal Abundant Resources in Indonesia

Surya Hermawan*

Civil Engineering Department, Petra Christian University, Jl. Siwalankerto 121-131, Surabaya, 60234, Indonesia

Abstract. Being the largest archipelagic state in the world (± 81 000 km of coastline), Indonesia has a great potential for developing the aquaculture industry. But, the accomplishment of sustainable practices and management systems are still in its infancy. Therefore, it is vital to improve aquaculture technology and develop management tools that address the need for an eco-friendly production process. In this manuscript, the Decision Support System software is applied for the management of sustainable floating net cage finfish cultures. This software integrates physical, chemical, biological properties and information on coastal uses to determine site selection, production carrying capacity, ecological carrying capacity and socio-economic assessment of 18 cases, focusing on the economic viability of Tiger grouper [*Epinephelus fuscoguttatus* (Forsskål, 1775)], Humpback grouper [*Cromoliptes altivelis* (Valenciennes, 1828)] and Leopard Coral grouper [*Plectropomeus leopardus* (Lacepède, 1802)] at three remote areas in Indonesia, including: Ekas Bay, Talise and Galang Island. The outcomes demonstrate that only Galang Island provides a suitable area of 12 940 ha with the estimated production carrying capacity of (0.5 to 366) t/annual per fish farm along with ecological carrying capacity are limited of (18 393 to 21 727) t/annual and economic evaluation highlighted that all cultures development are economically viable.

Key words: Decision Support System, Indonesia, sustainable.

1 Introduction

Indonesia is the largest aquaculture producer of marine finfish in Southeast Asia [1]. Being the largest archipelagic state in the world with about 81 000 km of coastline, corresponding to approximately 14 % of the world's coastlines, Indonesia has a great potential for developing the aquaculture industry [2]. The expansion of the aquaculture and fishery sector is expected to improve the country's welfare, especially for fishermen and fish farmers that are currently living under the poverty level. On other hand, the accomplishment of sustainable practices and management systems to preserve coastal environments is still in its infancy and more emphasis should be given to it. In particular, the degradation of coastal environments, overlapping and conflicting utilization of the coastal areas and enforcement of laws regarding the management of the marine and coastal environments are not being addressed properly. Therefore, it is essential to improve aquaculture technology and to expand management tools that address the need for an eco-friendly production [3].

During the development, the extensive measurements and monitoring programs along with system application have been successfully implemented to several coastal areas in Indonesia, including Pegametan Bay Bali, Seribu Islands in the Java Sea, Celukan Bawang in Bali and Saleh Bay in Lombok [4, 5]. In this manuscript, the application of the system for the management of sustainable floating net cage finfish cultures of the Decision Support System SYSMAR DSS

*Corresponding author: shermawan@petra.ac.id

software for the sustainable environmental and socio-economic management of floating net cage finfish culture is assessed.

Along with recent developments in SYSMAR DSS, we have turned our attention to the need for substantial and user-friendly software. The lack of measurement data in remote areas has been identified as a major problem for many years and is addressed in this study. This will be complemented with an evaluation of the economic viabilities. The outcomes achieved are going to support decision makers and the public with respect to the selection of best sites, assessment of the impacts and estimation of economic viabilities for the sites under investigation.

2 Material and methods

The investigations will be carried out at three priority sites in Indonesia namely: Talise Island located in the northern most tip of Sulawesi; Galang Island which is part of the Riau Archipelago located opposite of Singapore and Ekas Bay located south of the Lombok Island. The development focuses on the most common high-value finfish species nurtured in floating net cage (FNC) in Indonesia [6–9]. In this study Tiger grouper (*Epinephelus fuscoguttatus* (Forsskål, 1775)), Humpback grouper [*Cromoliptes altivelis* (Valenciennes, 1828)], and Leopard Coral grouper [*Plectropomeus leopardus* (Lacepède, 1802)] are considered.

This software is integrated into a graphical user interface (GUI), which has been constructed in Matrix Laboratory (MATLAB) by van der Wulp et al. [5]. These interfaces have several databases for quick access, and they are linked to a geographic information system (GIS) to process and visualize spatial information. In this paper, the MATLAB version 7.11.0.584 (R2010b), 32 bit (win32) was used.

2.1 Data

When using this system, data input or analysis types are selected by the user through the interface that controls the type of analysis to be made of the model components of the DSS. The compulsory data for the purpose of the DSS is gained from several sources. The hydrodynamic and wave models require bathymetric data along near shore areas in Indonesia which is usually obtained from nautical charts issued by the *Badan Koordinasi Survey dan Pemetaan Nasional* (National Coordinating Agency for Survey and Mapping). General Bathymetric Chart of the Oceans (GEBCO) data is issued by the British Oceanographic Data Centre, U.K. It is usually adopted to provide information in deeper areas. For tidal variations and wind characteristics for diving, the numerical models are extracted from *Total Modal Driver*. The wind data is obtained from the National Centers for Environmental Prediction and the National Center for Atmospheric Research (NCEP/NCAR) reanalysis database. Water quality information is usually obtained from agencies and measurements taken in the vicinity of the selected areas. In many cases, it is supported by analysis of satellite data. Problems resulting from conflicts of integrated coastal zone management or coastal uses and adverse natural environmental conditions are also accounted for in the selection of suitable sites, and for this purpose geographic data of National Development Planning are collected to identify the most relevant problems in the coastal zone.

2.2 Opening screen

Practical information through the SYSMAR DSS is accessible by choosing buttons from the opening screen of the interface, as shown Figure 1. Under the database menu, new database entries can be added, modified or removed. The following windows are shown to illustrate the presentation of SYSMAR DSS. The next selection window is displayed for preparing a DSS input (See Figure 1).

2.3 Farm properties

Figure 2 shows how the window interface of farm properties allows the user to select the FNC grouper culture farm type for decision purposes. The tab allows a specification of farm type, dimensions, investment description, maintenance cost and staff along with wages of a representative FNC grouper culture unit. It contains farm size; estimated investment cost, maintenance cost, as well as staff and technician wages and anticipated farm lifespan. Prices given are valid for the local market.

2.4 Stock properties

In this study, SYSMAR DSS allowed the selection of a combination of one out of three types of grouper species with three feed types. For example, tiger grouper can be selected for species and then combined with feeding by trash fish, pellet, as well as a mix of 30 % pellet and 70 % trash fish. The selected combination of fish species and feed types allows the DSS to establish the production characteristics per ton of production. Site selection criteria are defined in the table shown in Figure 3.

2.5 Site selection criteria interface

Table 1 presents the windows of site selection criteria, which allow the user to input data based on 32 parameters (e.g. physical, chemical and Integrated Coastal Zone Management (ICZM)) related to suitability and sustainability analysis. In this module, the user can define allowable ranges or optimal ranges with respect to the information data.

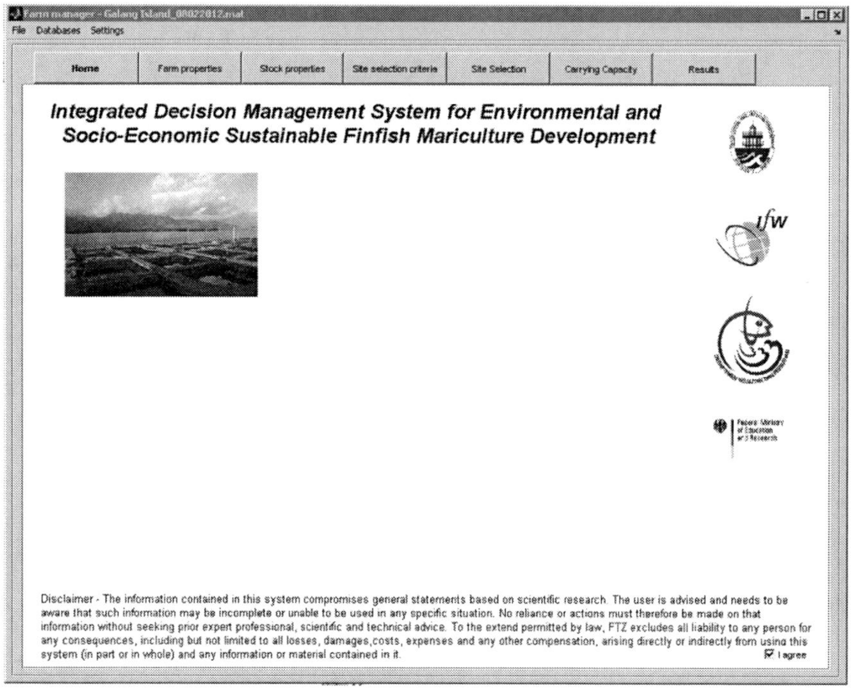

Fig. 1. The opening screen of the SYSMARDSS interface [9].

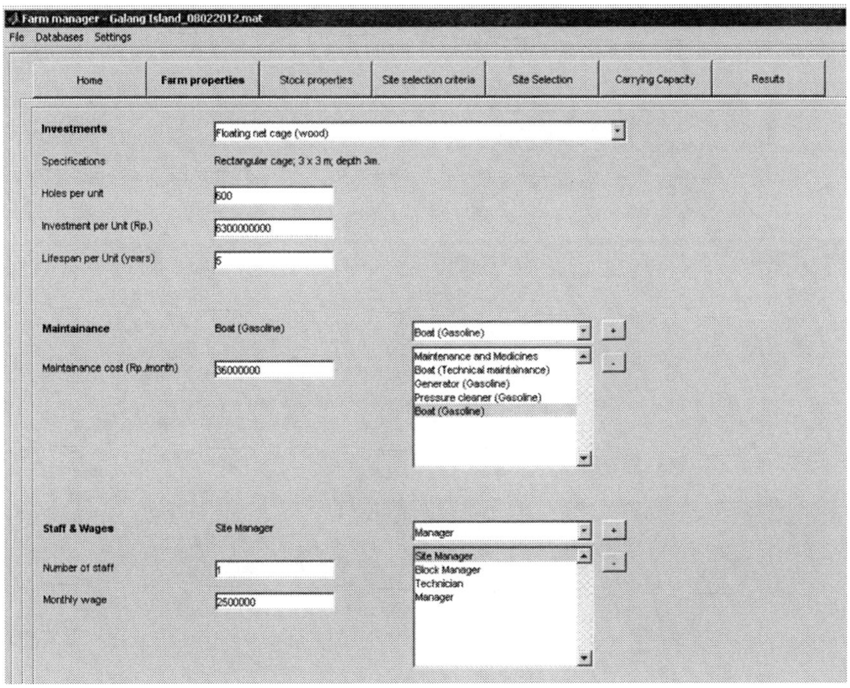

Fig. 2. Farm properties interface.

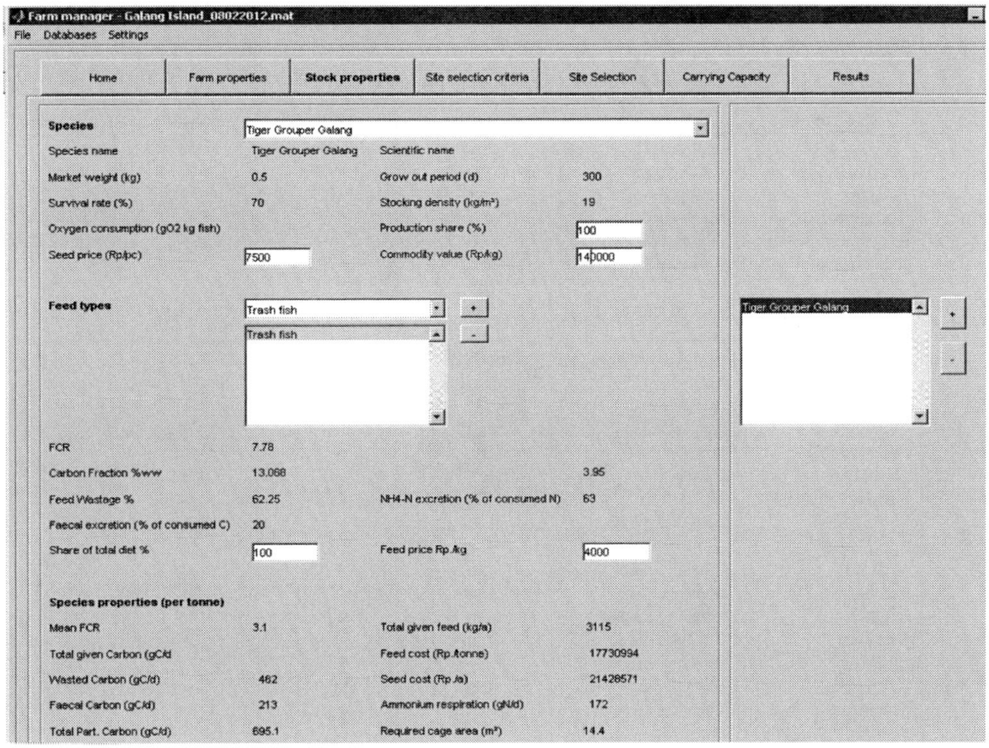

Fig. 3. Stock properties interface

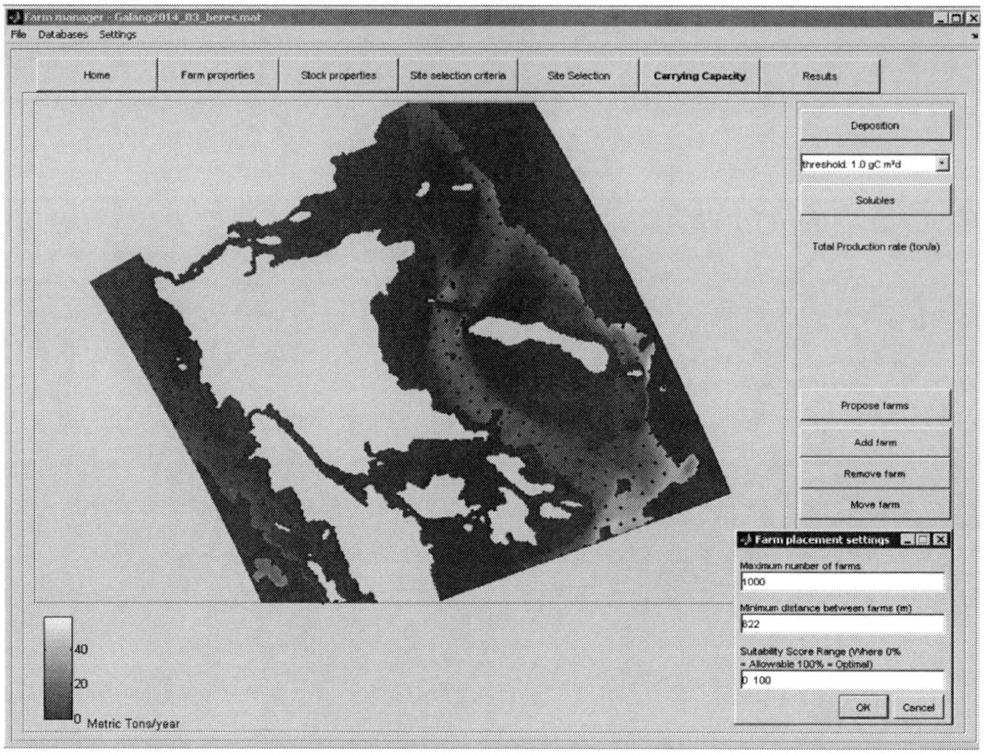

Fig. 4. GIS for carrying capacity.

Table 1. Site selection interface [4, 5, 10–12].

Description	Parameters	Indicators	Units	Unsuitable	Allowable	Optimal
Physical Process	Min. water depth	water depth	m	< 6	> 6	> 8
	Max. mooring	water depth	m	> 25	< 25	< 20
	Flushing	mean current	m s^{-1}	< 0.01	> 0.01	0.2 to 0.5
	Currents	mean current	m s^{-1}	> 1	< 1	0.2 to 0.5
	Exposure to waves	significant wave	m	> 1	< 1	< 0.6
	Exposure to wind	max wind speed	m s^{-1}	> 15	< 15	< 10
Water Quality	Water temperature	water temperature	°C	< 20 or > 35	20 to 35	27 to 31
	Salinity	salinity	nL L^{-1}	< 15 or > 35	15 to 35	26 to 1
	Dissolved oxygen	dissolved oxygen	mgO_2 L^{-1}	< 4	> 4	> 5
	Acid-base balance	pH	-log H^+	< 6 or > 8.5	6 to 7.8	7.8 to 8.5
	Water transparency	Secchi depth	m	< 2	> 2	> 4
	Turbidity	suspended matter	mg L^{-1}	> 10	< 10	< 5
	Ammonium	ammonium	mg NH_4-N L^{-1}	> 1	< 1	< 0.5
	Nitrate	nitrate	mg NO_3-N L^{-1}	> 200	< 200	< 200
	Nitrite	nitrite	mg NO_2-N L^{-1}	> 4	< 4	< 4
	Phosphate	total phosphate	mg P L^{-1}	> 70	< 70	< 70
ICZM						
	Villages	thematic map	m	< 200	> 200	> 500
	Towns	thematic map	m	< 200	> 200	> 500
	Cities	thematic map	m	< 200	> 200	> 500
	Harbours	thematic map	m	< 200	> 200	> 500
	Industry	thematic map	m	< 200	> 200	> 500
	Tourism	thematic map	m	< 200	> 200	> 500
	Streams	thematic map	m	< 200	> 200	> 500
	Rivers	thematic map	m	< 200	> 200	> 500
	Erosive shoreline	thematic map	m	< 200	> 200	> 500
	Semi intensive hatcheries	thematic map	m	< 200	> 200	> 500
	Intensive hatcheries	thematic map	m	< 200	> 200	> 500
	Ponds	thematic map	m	< 200	> 200	> 500
	Sewage discharges	thematic map	m	< 200	> 200	> 500

	Traffic lanes	thematic map	m	< 200	> 200	> 500
	Coastal usage	thematic map	m	< 200	> 200	> 500
	Environmentally protected area	thematic map	m	< 200	> 200	> 500

2.6 GIS for processing and spatial planning data for carrying capacity

Figure 5 shows how the carrying capacity tabs are used to determine carrying capacities with respect to particulate carbon. Locations can be selected by adding farms (manual or auto). For each farm, the suitability analysis and carrying capacity are summarized including needed farm area and economic analysis. This figure has been generated with a particulate carbon deposition threshold of (1 to 2) g cm^{-2} d^{-1}, as well as the settings of the tab for farm placement with the maximum number of farms being adjusted for farms located at a minimum of farm distances of 500 m.

2.7 Economic analysis

It can be seen in Figure 6 below how an overview of the economic flow of development for a FNC tiger grouper culture fed with the pellet is executed under the SYSMAR DSS interface. The capital cost of 600 cages for a 5 yr project is shown by the annual depreciation cost. The variable cost including maintenance, seed and feed are also presented. As can be seen from this figure, the wage costs are defined by one manager, one site manager, two block managers as well as 25 technicians.

The manuscript presents and applies economic models which have been developed as an amendment using SYSMAR DSS in conjunction with a Microsoft Excel spreadsheet program with respect to the cost-benefit analysis technique. All biological data, production cost, and profit are obtained from personal communication and literature data from the development of FNC cultures in Indonesia. Data were obtained from many institutions, including Coral Reef Information And Training Centers (CRITC) COREMAP-LIPI [13] and Indonesian Bank, about progressive tax for domestic agency Indonesian [14]. This method has not been comprehensively reviewed and discussed in previous research with the application of DSS.

Table 2. Economic analysis interface of the SYSMAR DSS.

A	Depreciation		Euro/Year
	Floating net cage (wood) (600 holes,m 16200 m^2)		100 800
B	Variable cost		
	Maintenance	Freshwater	5 760
		Boat (Gasoline)	5 280
		Boat (Technical Maintenance)	2 880
		Generator (Gasoline)	3 840
		Maintenance and Medicines	14 400
	Seed		
		Tiger Grouper (438 000 pcs)	262 800
	Feed		
		Pellet (520 t)	541 158
			836 118
c	Wages		
		Site Manager	2 400
		Manager	4 800
		Technician	33 648
		Block Manager	3 840
D	Revenue		
		Tiger Grouper (197.1 t)	2 207 520
		Total Revenue	2 207 520
		Profit (D-(A+B+C)	1 225 914

3 Results

The performance of this system will be presented through the use of a geographic information system (GIS) as a spatial planning tool. Applying site selection of the SYSMAR DSS shows that Galang Island provides a bright potential for FNC finfish culture development which is indicated by a suitable area of about 12 940 ha (see Figure 5). The results of hydrodynamic and wave numerical models show that Ekas Bay and Talise Island are not suited for FNC finfish culture projects.

Regarding production carrying capacities, the marine environment in the vicinity of Galang Island obviously has a large potential for the development of FNC grouper culture. The findings of this study indicate that the estimation of maximum and minimum production carrying capacity of all potential farms with distances of at least 500 m between farm sites are in the range of (51 to 366) t per farm and (0.5 to 2) t per farm, respectively and estimated production regarding ecological carrying capacity could produce in the range of (18 393 to 21 727) t/yr per community area, respectively (see Figure 5).

The results from the present study have provided vital information on about 18 cases regarding the economic viability of tiger, humpback and leopard coral groupers FNC farming utilizing various feed types and production scales. Every prototype farm consists of 600 cages and 10 cages, respectively in Galang Island with a standard cage size of (3 × 3 × 3) m for width, length, and depth. Different types of feed are also considered, such as trash fish, pellet, as well as mixing 70 % trash fish and 30 % pellet. The study shows that FNC finfish culture developments are economically viable as a whole, because after a 5 yr projection period, positive cumulative cash flow and net present value (NPV), internal rate of return (IRR) at rates above the bank rates, and a payback period (PP) far below the 5 yr projected lifetime of the project are evident.

4 Conclusion

In aquaculture management, the attention to DSS to utilize coastal resources abundant is relatively new along with the development of such a technology will play an increasingly important role in analyzing and planning potential aquaculture site selection, production, environmental impacts and sustainability. SYSMAR DSS intends to help decision makers in Indonesia to collect useful information from a variety of information systems (GIS, remote sensing, online data, etc) for future of sustainable aquaculture development. A possible explanation for some of our results may be the lack of adequate raw data. These results, therefore, need to be interpreted with caution. However, with model simulations, caution must be applied, as the findings might be utilized to identify tasks and make decisions. It is also a priority to develop a management system to ensure that the environmental impact from Indonesian mariculture does not exceed acceptable levels. These results advertise a strategy for the incorporation of aquaculture within the broader ecosystem in a way that supports sustainable development, equity, and the resilience of interlinked social and ecological systems.

The Author gratefully acknowledges the support and generosity of The Centre for International Migration and Development (CIM), and the Deutsche Gesells-chaft für Internationale Zusammenarbeit (GIZ). This study was supported by the Directorate General of Higher Education, Ministry of Education and Culture of Indonesia (DGHE), the German Academic Exchange Service or Deutsche Akademische Austauschdienst (DAAD), the Research and Technology Center Büsum/Forschungs-und Technologie Zentrum Westküste (FTZ)–Büsum and the International Center, Career Center of Christian Albrecht-University in Kiel.

References

1. S.S. De Silva, M.J. Phillips.A review of cage aquaculture: Asia (excluding China). In: *Cage aquaculture–regional reviews and global overview*. M. Halwart, D. Soto, J.R. Arthur (Ed.). FAO Fisheries Technical Paper, 498. Rome: FAO (2007). pp. 18–48. http://www.fao.org/docrep/010/a1290e/a1290e00.htm
2. Ministry Marine Affairs and Fisheries (MMAF) Indonesia. *Indonesian fisheries book 2009*. Jakarta: Japan International Cooperation Agency (2009). pp. 84. http://www.sidik.litbang.kkp.go.id/index.php/searchkatalog/byId/1704
3. S. Hermawan, Syafrani. Adv. Environ. Biol. **9**(7):21–27 (2015). https://www.thefreelibrary.com/An+integrated+decision+support+system+(DSS)+for+the+management+of...-a0440716300
4. S.A. Van der Wulp. *Nutrient mass balance modelling of cage fish farms case study Pulau Serai, Indonesia*. [Thesis] Coastal Research Laboratory Research and Technology Centre Christian Albrechts University Kiel, Germany. pp. 117. [Online] from https://www.slideshare.net/SimonvanderWulp/mscthesissavanderwulp (2007). [Accessed on January 7th, 2017].
5. S.A. Van der Wulp, K.R. Niederndorfer, K-J.Hesse, K-H. Runte, R. Mayerle, A. Hanafi. *Sustainable environmental management for tropical floating net cage mariculture, a modeling approach*. Proceeding XVIIth World Congress of the International Commission of Agricultural Engineering (CIGR) (Quebec, Canada, 2010). http://www.csbe-scgab.ca/docs/meetings/2010/CSBE101056.pdf
6. P.C. Heemstra, J.E. Randal. *FAO species catalogue, Vol.16. Groupers of the world (Family Serranidae, Subfamily Epinephelinae), An annotated and illustrated catalog of the grouper, rockcod, hid, coral grouper and lyretail*

species. Rome: Food and Agriculture of the United Nations (1993). pp. 5. http://www.fao.org/documents/card/en/c/9d54666b-08d2-522c-b593-229651cddc7f/
7. S.Y. Sim, M.A. Rimmer, J.A. Toledo, K. Sugama, I. Rumengan, K.C. Williams, M.J. Philips. *A practical guide to feeds and feed management for cultured grouper*. Bangkok, Thailand: NACA (2005). pp. 18. https://enaca.org/?id=301
8. Y.J. Sadovy, T.J. Donaldson, T.R. Graham, F. McGilvray, G.J. Muldoon, M.J. Phillips, et al. *While stocks last: The live reef food fish trade*. Pacific Studies Series. Manila: Asian Development Bank (2003). pp. 147. https://www.adb.org/sites/default/files/publication/28455/live-reef-complete.pdf
9. Y. Sadovy, C. Thierry, J.H. Choat, A.S. Cabanban. *Cromoliptes altivelis, The IUCN red list of threatened species*. [Online] from http://www.iucnredlist.org/details/39774/0 (2008). [Accessed on December 15th 2015]
10. Batam City Government. *RTRW Kota Batam Tahun 2004–2014 (Perda No. 2 Tahun 2004)*. [Regional Planning of Batam City 2004–2014 (Local Regulations no. 2 of Batam City)] (2004). pp. 116. [in Bahasa Indonesia]. http://perpustakaan.bappenas.go.id/lontar/opac/themes/bappenas4/templateDetail.jsp?id=95378&lokasi=lokal
11. W. Windupranata, R. Mayerle. ITB Journal of Engineering and Technological Sciences, **41**(1):77–96 (2009). http://journals.itb.ac.id/index.php/jets/article/view/118
12. S. Hermawan. Civil Engineering Dimension, Journal of Civil Engineering Science and Application, **18**(2):117–126 (2016). http://ced.petra.ac.id/index.php/civ/article/view/19715
13. Bank Indonesia. *BI 7-day (Reverse) Repo Rate*. [Online] from www.bi.go.id/id/moneter/bi-7day-rr/data/Contents/Default.aspx (2017). [Accessed on October 1st 2017]. [in Bahasa Indonesia].
14. CRITC (Coral Reef Information And Training Centers) COREMAP-LIPI. *Studi potensi pengembangan budidaya perikanan di lokasi COREMAP II Kota Batam*. [Study of the potential aquaculture development in COREMAP II area: Batam City]. pp. 168 (2009). Riau: CRITC LIPI, BPP-PSPL Universitas Riau. [in Bahasa Indonesia]. http://docplayer.info/45213393-Studi-potensi-pengembangan-budidaya-perikanan-di-lokasi-coremap-ii-kota-batam.html

A Study of Mobile Robot Control using EEG Emotiv Epoch Sensor

Timothius Victorio Yasin*, *Felix* Pasila, and *Resmana* Lim

Electrical Engineering Department, Petra Christian University, Jl. Siwalankerto 121-131, Surabaya, 60234, Indonesia

Abstract. The study was using an EEG Emotiv Epoc+ sensor to recognize brain activity for controlling a mobile robot's movement. The study used Emotiv Control Panel software for EEG command identification. The commands will be interfaced inside Mind Your OSCs software and processing software which processed inside an Arduino Controller. The output of the Arduino is a movement command (ie. forward, backward, turn left, and turn right). The training methods of the system composed of three sets of thinking mode. First, thinking with doing facial expressions. Second, thinking with visual help. Third, thinking mentally without any help. In the first set, there are two configurations thinking with facial expression help as command of the mobile robot. Final results of the system are the second facial expressions configuration as the best facial expressions method with success rate 88.33 %. The second facial expression configuration has overall response time 1.60175 s faster than the first facial expressions configuration. In these two methods have dominant signals on the *frontal lobe*. The second facial expressions method have overall respond time 6.12 and 9.53 s faster than thinking with visual, and thinking without help respectively.

Key words: EEG, emotiv epoch sensor, mobile robot control.

1 Introduction

The duration from the beginning of human life, the human always has an actuator, which hands, eyes, feet, mouth and some of the other senses. Without realizing it at the root of this actuator controller itself is the brain, where the development of technology directly to the brain is less developed than others. Then, with increasing awareness of the multiple sides of this, then developed a method of the analysis of brain signals.

Electroencephalography or commonly referred to EEG, is a method of recording electrical activity in the brain to detect or analyze an electrical signal flowing to the brain. EEG using a unit where the voltage will enable the electrodes to record signals (pulse) of the brain [1]. EEG has begun to be used to find and analyze an illness, ranging from Alzheimer's disease, epilepsy, brain tumors, and several other diseases associated with the brain wave signals that are drawn from parts of the head [2]. In another way, EEG testing is also conducted to test the brain stem death (death brain stem), which indicates the presence or absence of the brain's response to stimuli both physically, as well as non-physical. The utilization of EEG sensors has been applied to virtual simulation [3], and also robots in the assistive technologies [4–8], and also applied to face recognition on smartphones [5]. In this project, the Emotiv Epoc+ EEG sensor[9] is used as input to capture facial expressions will give orders to the Arduino[10] as a controller of the mobile robot used.

2 System description

This section will explain about the design of the robot movement control system using Emotiv EEG sensors. Explanation will include the system in general, workflow systems, EEG training process, and design software on the Arduino.

*Corresponding author: timovictorio@gmail.com

2.1 System setup

This system has a sensor input EEG Emotiv Epoc+ to record the activity of brain signals related to a computer via a USB dongle, computer or laptop as the brain of the system for processing input from Emotiv Epoc+, USB serial or Bluetooth from a computer that is connected to the output of the Arduino connected with motor driver to drive the two motors on the mobile robot. Explanation diagrammed through the design of Figure 1.

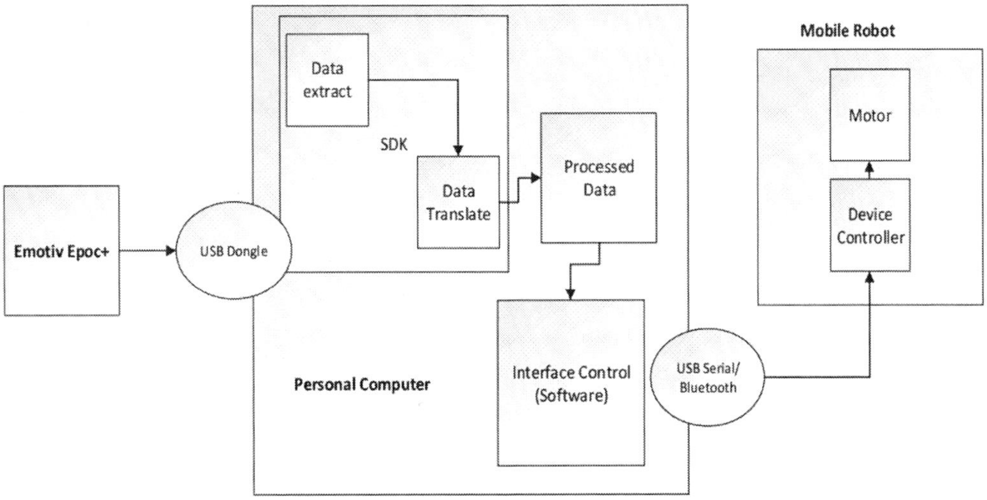

Fig. 1. System diagram.

The system comes up with connection between input, processor, and output, will be shown as Figure 2 below.

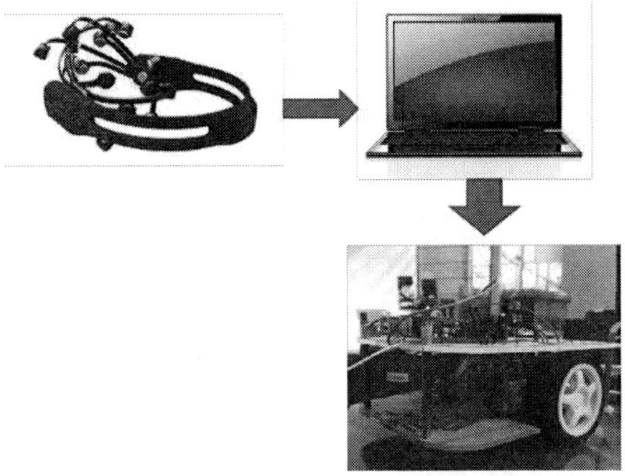

Fig. 2. System hardware diagram.

2.2 EEG training process

In this part there are early initialization commands to do the recording for 8 s through three methods. The record will be stored on each profile in the Emotiv Control Panel, then it will be interfaced to Mind Your OSCs software to send OSC character commands towards Processing software. The Arduino will execute four movement commands through the Processing Software. The third method used is a method of thinking with the help of facial expressions, thinking with the help of visual methods, methods of thinking without assistance. In the method of expression, there are two configurations selected facial expression, and will be tested against two other methods, namely with the aid of visual thinking, thinking without assistance. Movement commands to the method, can be seen in Table 1.

Table 1. Movements command for expression and visual method.

Facial expressions 1	Facial expressions 2	Visual	Movement commands	Description
Eyebrows rose	Smile	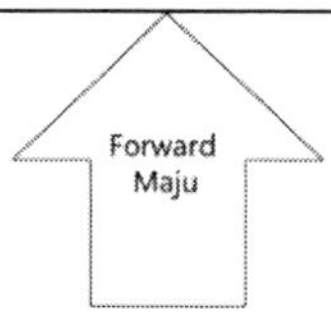	Forward	
See–right towards glanced at	Right eye blinking	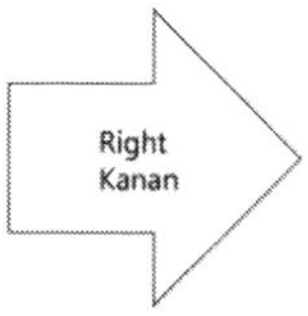	Right	Aided by the right hand as a point of reference (facial expression)
Look–glance towards the left	Left eye blinking	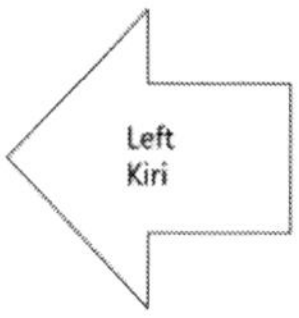	Left	Aided by the left hand as a point of reference (facial expression)
Smile	Eyebrows Rose	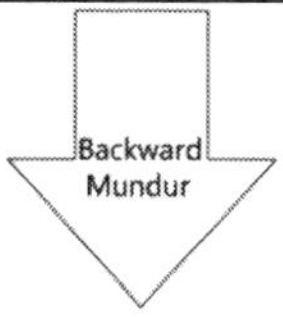	Backward	

On the third method, think without assistance, will be used to think of a direction or movement in a "forward", "backward", "left" or "right".

2.3 Design software on Arduino

On the design of the software or the software on the Arduino, conducted a reading of the injunction through software processing, a message is received in a message of the OSC command which will be known as movement on the robot. The character of the OSC messages described in Table 2 below.

Table 2 . Character table OSC on movement commands.

Movement commands	The character of the OSC transmitted into the Arduino
Forward	/COG/PUSH
Right	/COG/RIGHT
Left	/COG/LEFT
Backward	/COG/PULL

The process of programming in Processing outline is as follows:

(i). Processing software read commands of the OSC messages.

(ii). The commands of the OSC messages has received value in floating point as a representation of power level.

(iii). Power level of a certain command is stored in the variable named "*NilaiBaca*".

(iv). The value in the "*NilaiBaca*" is compared against the threshold as triggers to execute commands the movements of a robot.

(v). After the robot movement command is executed, the system will do a reset (a particular command value = 0).

3 System testing and analysis

3.1 Emotiv Epoc+ methods testing

This test have purpose to find out the best method of time respond using Emotiv Epoc+. In this testing will be done against the three kinds of comparative method. First, the method of facial expression (1st and 2nd configurations), second visual thinking method, and then method of thinking without assistance. This test has the measurements in time (seconds) to see the response time of each method on the given command. Testing through 20 times on any orders from a variety of different methods, the results obtained as in Table 3 below.

Table 3 . The results of the response time average in the four methods.

Command	**Average response time (s)**			
	Expression 1	**Expression 2**	**Visual**	**Mind**
Forward	3.52	3.50	7.90	14.47
Backward	6.21	2.79	9.25	14.56
Left	6.70	4.16	9.44	11.15
Right	4.66	4.23	12.56	12.62
The average overall time (s)	**5.27**	**3.67**	**9.79**	**13.20**

Based on the results of testing on Table 3, it can be seen that the method of facial expression 2 has the response time is much faster than other methods, with an overall average time through 20 times testing on advanced are 3.5 s for forward, 2.79 s for backward, 4.16 s for left and 4.23 s for right.

3.2 Result graphs and mapped figures

The results of testing on every command by a better method, the method of facial expression two generates the image of the brain's signals on the head. An overview of brain signals on this head has a goal to see the signals of the dominant head area when the user performs the method expression on every command. The dominant signals is shown by using EEGLAB software data, which is described as in Figure 3, Figure 4, Figure 5, and Figure 6.

Based on the results of the recording data entered into EEGLAB, the result of dominant channels are 1, 5, 6, 11, 12 (AF3, T7, P7, FC6, F4 respectively), with an analysis on the working frequency *Beta* (12.5 Hz to 30 Hz). Forward command is initialized with a smile and thrilling molars down as well as up, causing the presence of a dominant signal generated on the *Parietal* or parts of the brain that respond to stimuli, one of them is the pressure. This command result is shown in Figure 3 below.

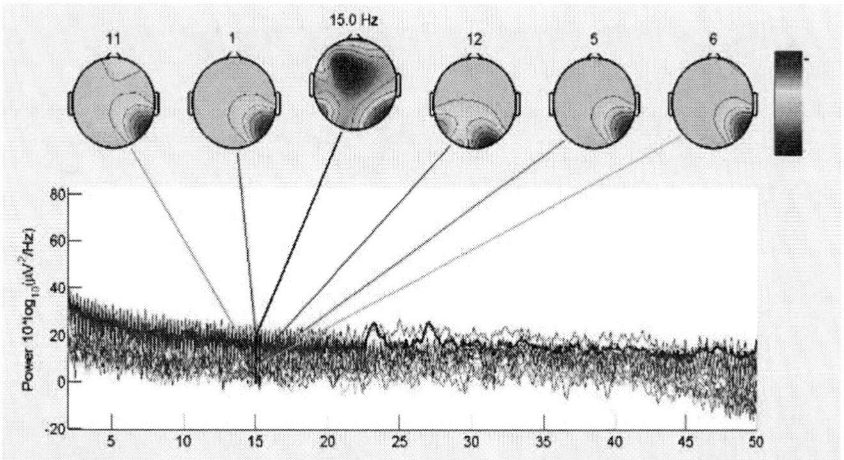

Fig. 3. The results of the *mapping* of the forward command.

The next command is backward, which has the result of dominant channels are 1, 2, 3, 7, 12 (AF3, F3, F7, O1, and F4 respectively). Backward command is initialized with raised eyebrows, so dominant signals generated in result is shown in Figure 4 below.

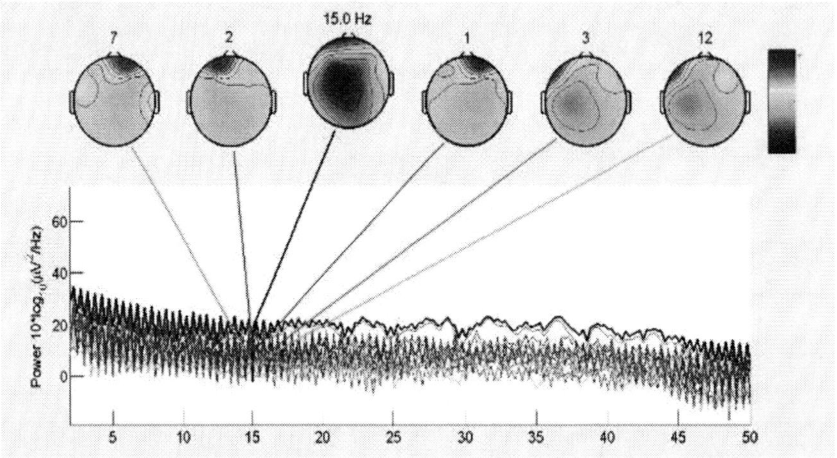

Fig. 4. The results of the *mapping* of the backward command.

In the third command, which is the left command movement, has a result of dominant channels are 1, 3, 4, 7, 12 (AF3, F3, FC5, O1, and AF4 respectively). The left command is initialized with left eye blink, so that the signal generated by the dominant part of the frontal lobe, particularly on the left side of the head. This command result is shown in Figure 5 below.

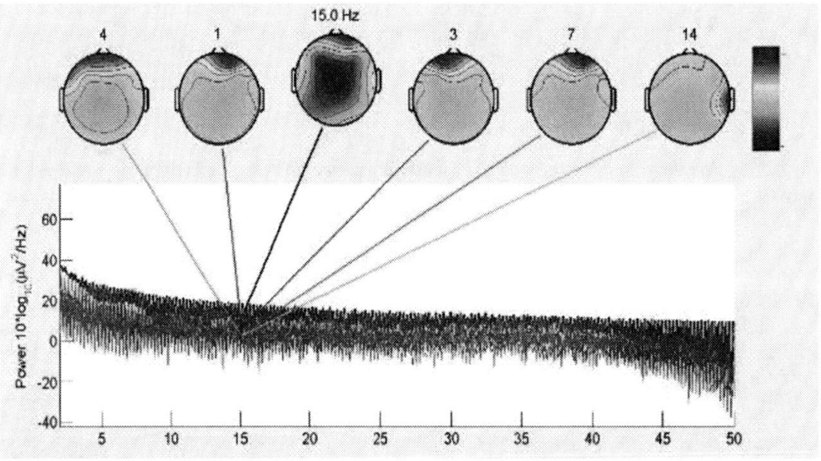

Fig. 5. The results of the mapping of the left command.

In the last command, which is the right command movement, has the result of dominant channels are 1, 3, 4, 7, 9 (AF3, F3, FC5, O1, and P8 respectively). The right command is initialized by right eye blink, so that the dominant signal generated by the part of the frontal lobe, just like the left command, the right command also predominant in the right area. This command result is shown in Figure 6 below.

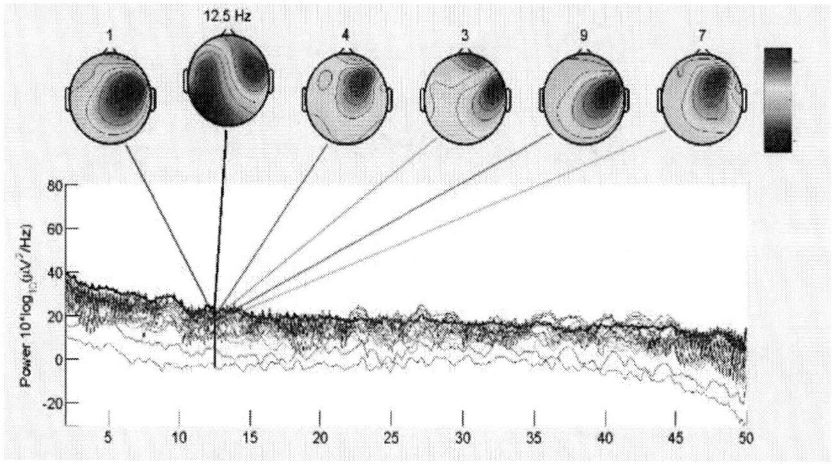

Fig. 6. The results of the mapping of the right command.

3.3 Robot control movement testing

This test is the final process of the system, this test have purpose to find out the mobile robot's movement based on data that has been initialized by the user, and know the standard value (threshold value) against users who have done the training.

3.3.1 The determination of threshold values

At the beginning of this testing, after doing the reading against one user for 8 s (refer to data that is recorded using the TestBench, and length of the *training* data in Emotiv Control Panel), obtained the following results for the fourth reading of the initialized command to move the mobile robot, which is described in the Figure 7, Figure 8, Figure 9 and Figure 10.

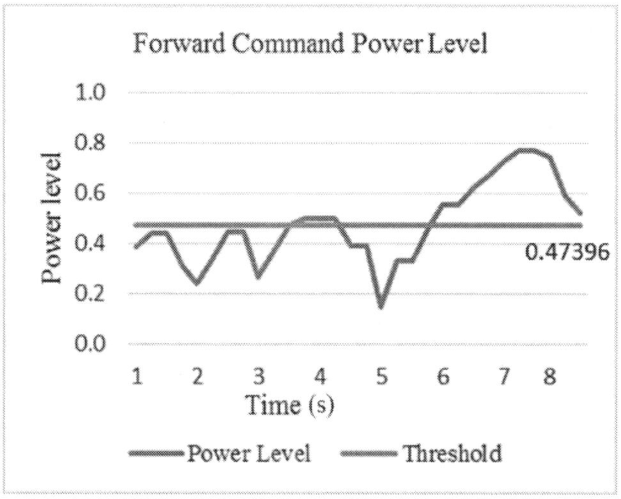

Fig. 7. Forward threshold value determination graph.

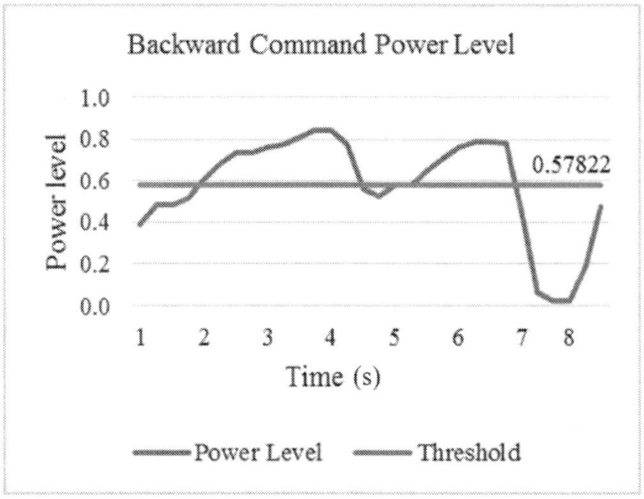

Fig. 8. Backward threshold value determination graph.

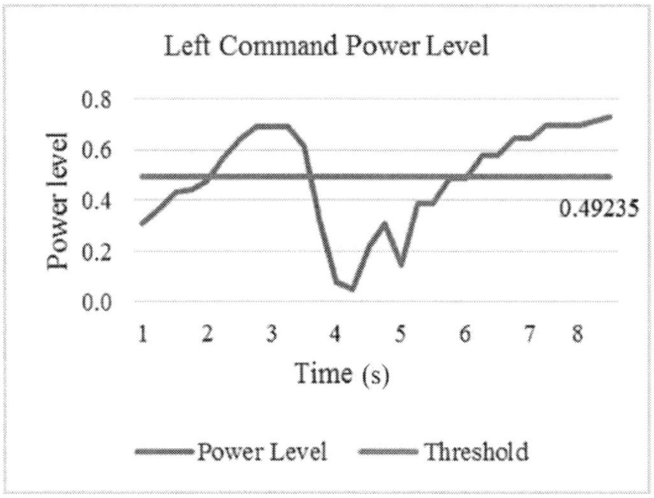

Fig. 9. Left threshold value determination graph.

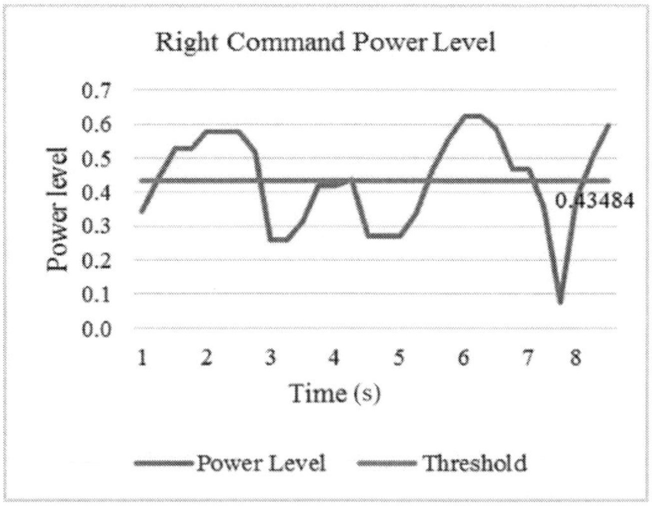

Fig. 10. Right threshold value determination graph.

Based on the results of recording data for 8 s (determined training data for initialization), the data will be averaged to find the threshold value on each command movement. The results of each command are 0.47 396 for forward command, 0.57 822 for backward command, 0.49 235 for left command, 0.43 484 for right command. The value scales are 0 to 1, which represent the power of representing the same command which has been trained before. The closer of the value to 1, it means that the command has the similar pattern or power to the master data. Finally, these values will be used as a trigger to execute a command on a mobile robot's movement.

3.3.2 Testing mobile robots to achieve goals

In this section, the movements of the mobile robot to achieve the goal to be tested in field trials in the form of floor 90 cm × 90 cm with a two-point goal, described through the Figure 11.

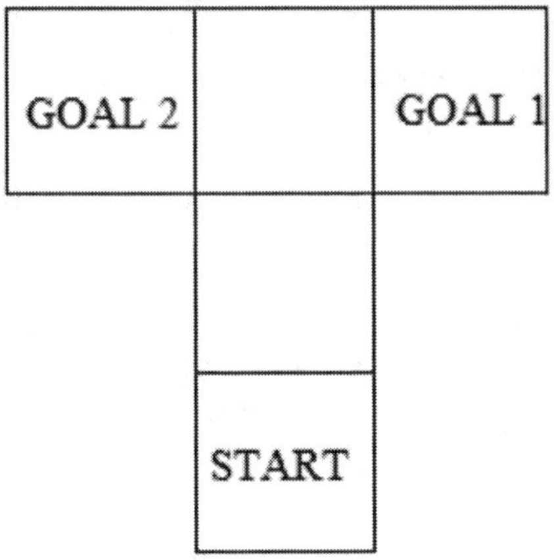

Fig. 11. Field test of the mobile robot movement.

The real field for testing will be shown as Figure 12 below.

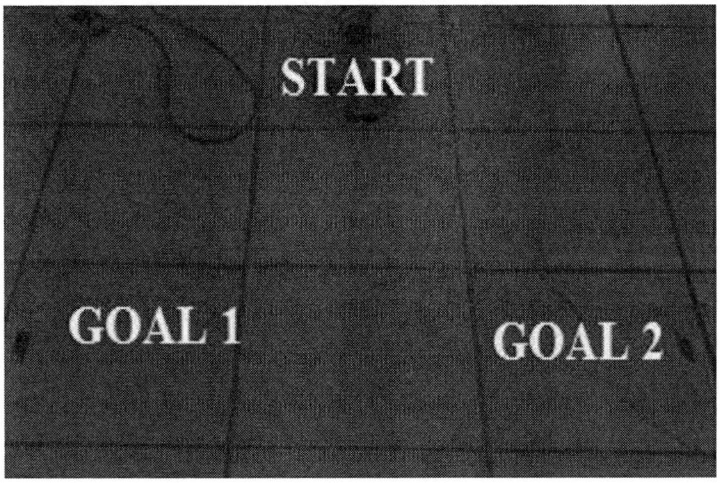

Fig. 12. Images of field test.

Through the configuration of threshold values, some set up have been configured to find the optimum threshold configuration. The configuration can be seen through the Table 4.

Table 4 . Table configuration and the value of the threshold

Configuration	Command	Value Threshold	Description
1	Forward	0.47 396	Initial threshold
	Left	0.49 235	
	Right	0.43 484	
	Backward	0.57 822	
2	Forward	0.45 026	Threshold-5 %
	Left	0.46 773	
	Right	0.4 131	
	Backward	0.54 931	
3	Forward	0.42 656	Threshold-10 %
	Left	0.44 312	
	Right	0.39 136	
	Backward	0.5 204	
4	Forward	0.47 396	Threshold-10 % to the left and right
	Left	0.44 312	
	Right	0.39 136	
	Backward	0.57 822	
5	Forward	0.42 656	Threshold-10 % for Forward and Backward
	Left	0.49 235	
	Right	0.43 484	
	Backward	0.5 204	
6	Forward	0.42 656	Threshold-10 % configuration 3
	Left	0.39 881	
	Right	0.35 222	
	Backward	0.5 204	
7	Forward	0.38 391	Threshold-10 % configuration 6
	Left	0.35 892	
	Right	0.317	
	Backward	0.46 836	
8	Forward	0.34 552	Threshold-10 % 7 configuration
	Left	0.32 303	
	Right	0.2 853	
	Backward	0.42 153	

On Table 4 which is a variation of the value of the threshold, threshold configuration in the early decline of as much as 5 %, 10 %, 10 % for left and right commands, 10 % for forward and backward commands, 10 % against configuration 3, 10 % against configuration 6, 10 % against configuration 7. It decreases gradually committed to see the response given by the car robot in achieving its purpose (reach goals). The results of the mobile robot in achieving the goal is shown as in Table 5 below.

Table 5 . Configuration testing time threshold

Configuration	Test time (s)				
	1st test	2nd test	3rd test	4th test	5th test
1	251.12	237.01	260.83	275.72	263.36
2	230.55	240.1	234.08	286.4	254.08
3	198.47	200.65	191.87	215.83	170.49
4	180.73	190.26	192.24	186.36	190.21
5	194.64	184.34	217.54	199.82	210.36
6	132.30	166.41	140.53	137.28	108.06
7	93.7	64.93	57.5	57.79	77.02
8	113.2	123.38	125.25	146.97	116.53

Based on the test results in Table 5, the test is performed five times, and the average time was obtained from tests on every configuration of threshold as shown in Table 6 below.

Table 6 . Average time of testing the configuration of threshold

Configuration	The average time (s)
1	257.608
2	249.042
3	195.462
4	187.96
5	201.34
6	136.122
7	73.582
8	125,066

Representations of the test results through a graph can be seen in Figure 13 below.

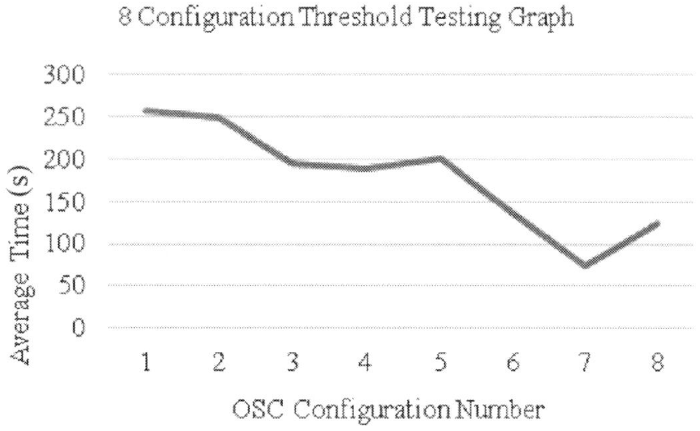

Fig. 13. Threshold variation testing graph.

The results of the test that looks at the Table 6 and Figure 13, indicating the results of optimum threshold is configuration 7. On some previous configuration which have been done, decrement against the initial configuration stopped to the configuration 8, where time for mobile robot can reach a goal go back slower (125.066 s) than the configuration 7 (73.582 s).

4 Conclusion

The conclusion that can be drawn from the results of a study of control of movement of the mobile robot using EEG sensors Emotiv Epoc+ is that feature in command control can use facial expressions, rather than using the methods of thinking with the aid of visual or think without any assistance. With the use of various methods, it was obtained by facial expression 2 as a better method than the methods of facial expression 1, visual, or mind without assistance. The use of the first threshold values of a mobile robot can't make a robot move responsive, it took long enough time for the robot can move towards the goal (about 4 min). These factors caused configuration variations in the value of the threshold. The modification of the first threshold values generates 8 threshold configuration. From eight configurations, generate a configuration which is considered optimum because the average time the resulting car robot in achieve objectives on the test field. It is the configuration 7, which have the values of 0.38391 for forward command, 0.46836 for backward command, 0.35892 for left command, and also 0.31700 for right command.

References

1. E. Niedermeyer, F.H.L. da Silva. *Electroencephalography: Basic principles, clinical applications, and related fields*. Philadelphia: Lippincot Williams & Wilkins (2005). Pp. 17–18. https://books.google.co.id/books/about/Electroencephalography.html?id=tndqYGPHQdEC&redir_esc=y
2. M.E. Drake, H. Padamadan. S.A. Newell. Seizure, **7**(1):39–42 (1998). https://www.ncbi.nlm.nih.gov/pubmed/9548224
3. D. Huang, K. Qian, D.-Y. Fei, W. Jia, X. Chen, O. Bai. IEEE Trans. Neural Syst. Rehabil. Eng., **20**(3):379–388 (2012). https://www.ncbi.nlm.nih.gov/pubmed/22498703
4. J. Svejda, R. Zak, R. Senkerik, R. Jasek. *Using Brain - Computer Interface for Control Robot Movement*. Cd. Proceedings 29th European Conference on Modelling and Simulation '15 (Albena Varna, Bulgaria, 2015). https://www.scs-europe.net/dlib/2015/.../0475-is_ECMS2015_0119.pdf

5. A. Vourvopoulos, F. Liarokapis. Comput. Electr. Eng. **40**(2):714–729 (2014). https://www.sciencedirect.com/science/article/pii/S0045790613002577
6. A.T. Campbell, T. Choudhury, S. Hu, H. Lu, M.K. Mukerjee, M. Rabbi, et al. *NeuroPhone: Brain-mobile phone interface using a wireless EEG headset.* Proceedings of the second ACM SIGCOMM workshop on Networking, systems, and applications on mobile handhelds-MobiHeld '10, pp 3–8 (New Delhi, India, 2010). http://pac.cs.cornell.edu/pubs/neurophone.pdf
7. I.H. Parmonangan, J. Santoso, W. Budiharto, A.A.S. Gunawan. *Fast brain control systems for electric wheelchair using support vector machine.* Proceedings of SPIE, **10011**:100111N (2016). http://spie.org/Publications/Proceedings/Paper/10.1117/12.2243126
8. J. Lin, W. Yang. International Journal of Innovative Computing, Informaion and Control, **8**(9):6011–6024 (2012). http://www.ijicic.org/vol-8(9).htm
9. Emotiv. *Emotiv.* [Online] from http://www.emotiv.com (2015). [Accessed on 28 February 2018].
10. Arduino. *Arduino.* [Online] from https://www.arduino.cc/ (2015). [Accessed on 28 February 2018].

Fuel Saving on Diesel Genset using PV/Battery Spike Cutting in Remote Area Microgrid

Tinton Dwi Atmaja[1,*], *Ant* Ardath Kristi[1], *Agus* Risdiyanto[1], *Bambang* Susanto[1], *Dian* Andriani[1], *Makoto* Fujita[2], and *Atsushi* Hirono[2]

[1]Research Centre for Electrical Power and Mechatronics, Indonesian Institute of Sciences, Komp. LIPI Bandung, Jl. Sangkuriang, Gd. 20, Lt. 2, Bandung 40135, Indonesia
[2]Murata Manufacturing, Co. Ltd. 10-1, Higashikotari 1-chome, Nagaokakyo-shi, Kyoto 617-8555, Japan

Abstract. Diesel Generator set was found to be a favorite power generator in a remote area. In this area, diesel genset usually consumes a significant amount of diesel fuel with higher fuel price than an urban area. Diesel Generator capacity conventionally prepared twice bigger or more than the existing load to prevent any load spike from designated equipment. This work implements an Energy Management System to cut the spike with the support from battery storage unit and photovoltaic module. Once the Energy Management System cut the load spike using battery/photovoltaics, Diesel Generator loads no longer need to be irrelevantly bigger than the existing load. The current experiment in the remote island at Raja Ampat archipelago indicates that the using of 80 kVA Diesel Generator can be reduced to 42 kVA Diesel Generator. This Diesel Generator replacement induces fuel consumption up to 50 %. With this designed work, a smart microgrid with PV-Battery-Diesel can be installed in a designated remote area with lower fuel consumption.

Keywords: Battery storage, diesel generator set, photovoltaic, smart inverter, smart microgrid.

1 Introduction

Microgrid installment in a remote area such as a small island or an isolated village in the middle of the jungle is a very significant aspect for the local people to get electricity. As the lower layer of smart grid [1], the microgrid is self-supplied electricity distributed system consisting a power generation system, having its own storage system, isolated load and limited coverage area. Diesel genset (DG), especially small capacity from 10 kVA to 80 kVA, is the most favorite power generation system in the remote area. DG considered portable to be mobile in harsh condition and easily installed or relocated within remote area far from the main utility grid. Figure 1 shows the 50 kVA DG installed in Lereh, Yadauw, a village 100 km inside Papua jungle, Indonesia.

Fig. 1. Diesel generator set as power sources in remote area.

*Corresponding author: tinton_dwi@yahoo.com

DG has a reasonable price to buy but relatively expensive to maintain. However, its capability to operate at low levels [2] made it a reasonable choice as an off grid power source. Once installed, DG can run continuously [3] with minimum maintenance effort rather than other power generation system. There are some previous researches on increasing DG performance by connecting the additional equipment or integrating the renewable energy (RE) source to assist DG unit. Previous research by Wresta et al.[4] mention that it is highly potential to implement spark ignition DG to increase the DG efficiency. As the potential of RE combination, wind power, and solar energy is the most available renewable sources in the remote area rather than rarely find hydro power or expensive tidal/wave power generation system.

This work was focused in a remote area near the equator line with sufficient solar radiance but low potential of wind power. Therefore, solar power is the main RE that supporting this work. Concentrated solar power (CSP) was once considered as possible energy backup. Previous research has been conducted on CSP installation with designated thermal storage and additional layer [5]. However, the size and the portability of CSP power plant cannot overcome photovoltaic solar farm.

Photovoltaic (PV) systems are considered reliable, cost-effective and environmentally friendly energy power systems especially in remote areas [6]. Figure 2 showed a PV installment in Abar Village, the remote area of Sentani Lake, Papua, Indonesia. Previous research for PV in an equatorial climate has been conducted by K.Y. Lau *et al.*[7]. It comes to attention that PV performance has been effected by the temperature, especially in tropical climate. Furthermore, the electrical efficiency and the power output of a PV module depend linearly on the operating temperature around PV cell [8].

Fig. 2. PV module as renewable energy sources in remote area.

PV was also possible to be installed as building integrated photovoltaic (BIPV) [9]. Therefore, it can be attached in every part of the building aside of the rooftop, such as curtain wall, window sunshade, or balcony side. PV could also increase the energy harnessing by installing in the high vertical position [10]. However, this method only works if there is a highly elevated landscape contour (such as a cliff in sun direction) or high-rise building in the island (such as communication tower).

The main aim of this work is to integrate DG-Battery-PV into one responsive hybrid generation system successfully. The success of this work will bring significant impact on how to utilize solar power in a remote area microgrid. With this integration, there will be a reduction in electricity demand to the DG unit which means a decrease in DG capacity and resulted in fuel consumption reduction. Fuel saving has been considered as one important step to achieve sustainable smart microgrid with green energy sources.

2 System configuration

2.1 Grid configuration

Previous research had described the integration of PV and DG provides greater system reliability and reduces the cost of the generated energy by the system [11]. Another research by Kusakana [12] expressed that significant operation cost could be saved by combining batteries and photovoltaics into diesel genset. The previous design of PV/DG/Battery was provided with simple battery model [13], and optimization was also proposed by Noguera et al. [14]. Our work was designed with similar concept and goal where the primary load was primarily powered by the DG and supported by PV and batteries (Figure 3). The aerial view of the site can be found in Figure 4.

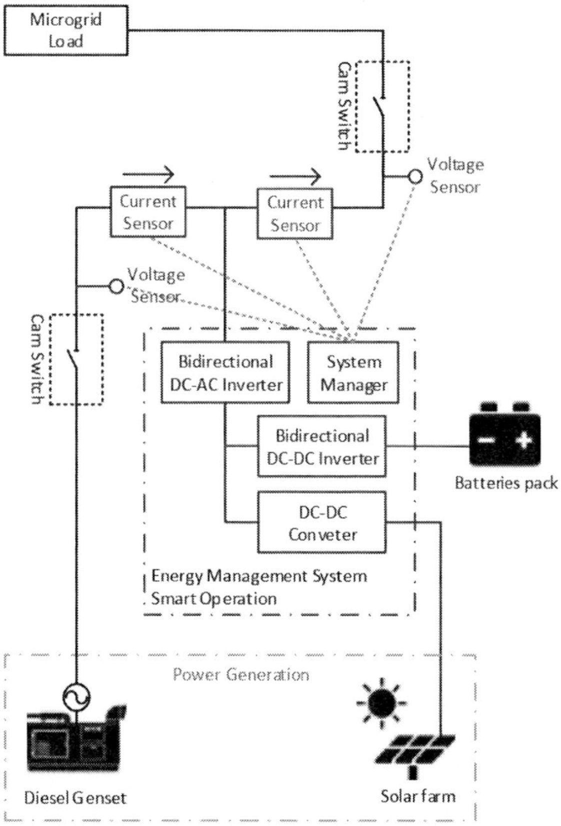

Fig. 3. Grid schematic.

Fig. 4. Aerial view of experimental demo site.

In this site, the load was a research complex of Raja Ampat conservation area located in a remote island approximately 76 km offshore of West Papua mainland. The complex contains several offices, resort, and staff building equipped with air conditioning, refrigerators, and compressors. The main power came from diesel genset unit in the genset house. In this work, a laboratory was built to facilitate integration between the DGs and the renewable source (PV). Inside the laboratory, the smart inverter was installed to harness power from the PV and supplied to the site's microgrid. Battery rack was also placed inside the laboratory as the main energy storage from the solar farm and sometimes from the DG itself.

2.2 Diesel genset and load profile

Installed DG in the demo site was initially set to cover the whole settlement in the island (Figure 5). Furthermore, fuel cost estimation was calculated for a day by the non-linear quadratic function in Equation (1) [15].

$$\sum_{j-1}^{N}\left(aP_{DG(j)}^{2}+bP_{DG(j)}^{2}+2\right) \quad (1)$$

Where N is the number of sampling intervals within the operation range or period of the system; a, b, c is the fuel cost coefficients; j is the jth sampling interval; $P_{DG(j)}$ is the output power from the DG at jth sampling interval; and C_f is the price of 1 L of fuel.

Fig. 5. Diesel generator.

DG usually set to operate within 60 % to 80 % of its maximum capacity so the fuel consumption will be at its optimum rate and increase DG life span. This rate will determine how big is the capacity of the DG should be provided. Figure 6 shows the sample of the load profile of island. In steady condition, the load current will be between 60 A to 100 A, however, because of the distinctive equipment such as compressor and oxygen mixer, there was a spike occurred that highlight the current up to 156 A.

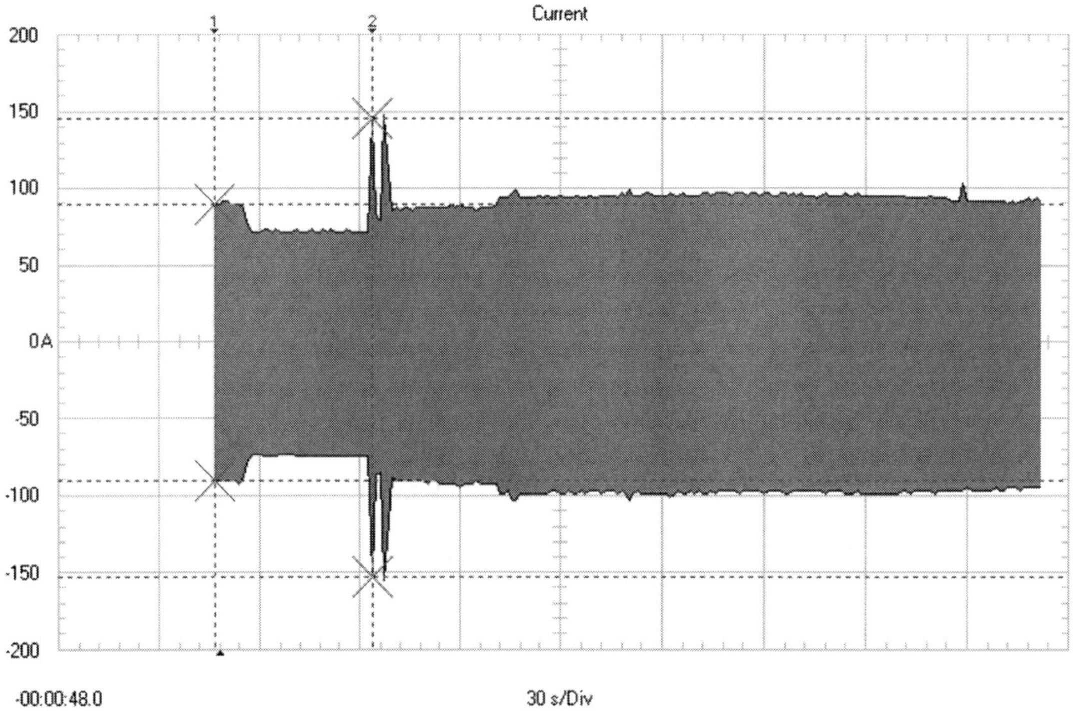

Fig. 6. Load spike.

The spike occurred every time the compressor started. It was happened for at least two to three second per spike. This spike had forced the owner to increase the capacity of the DG. Without the spike, a 42 kVA DG will be sufficient, however, with the spike occurred, the owner should increase DG capacity up to 60 kVA to avoid a possible blackout in the whole island. Even with the increased capacity of the DG, increasing power demand will make the DG operation become unstable and resulted in increased fuel consumption. As the power demand increased, the DG power load also increased and the fuel consumption has increased similarly.

2.3 Energy management system

An energy management system (EMS) was installed in the laboratory to assist the grid to cut the spike. The EMS consists of smart inverter unit and battery pack. The 3 kW Murata Smart Inverter was used in this work in order to facilitate the spike cutting and also later integrate the PV into the microgrid. Murata Smart Inverter was equipped with Murata battery unit. Every three batteries are packed along with one Battery Management System.

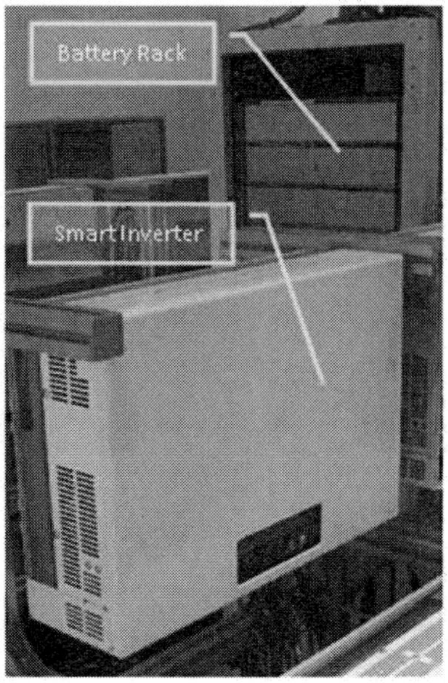

Fig. 7. EMS with smart inverter unit and battery pack.

At the time load spike is occurred, the EMS unit will draw the energy from the batteries –if available– to consume the spike instead of using the energy from the DG. The dynamics of the battery SOC (state of charge) can be expressed in equation (2) [16].

$$SOC_{(J+1)} = SOC_{(J)} - t_s \frac{\eta_{Bat}}{E_{nom}} \times P_{Bat_{(J)}} \tag{2}$$

Where SOC is the state of charge of the battery; h_{Bat} is the battery charging or discharging efficiency; E_{nom} is the battery system nominal energy; and P_{Bat} is the power flowing from the battery system.

2.4 Solar farm to support the EMS

As the island located near the equator, solar power was the most possible available renewable energy on the site. The monocrystalline solar module was installed near the laboratory and integrated to the grid via the EMS unit. The installed capacity reaches up to 9 kWh, and the average power has reached out to 7.4 kWh. The output power of the PV system can be calculated using Equation (3) [17].

$$P_{PV} = A_{PV} \times \eta_{PV} \times \int_{t_0}^{t} I(t) \times f(t) \times dt \tag{3}$$

Where APV is the total area of the photovoltaic generator (m^2); h_{PV} is the module efficiency; I is the hourly irradiance (kWh/m^2); and f(t) is the radiance density.

Fig. 8. Solar farm.

3 Result and discussion

The primary objective of this work was conducting fuel saving from DG unit. The first method was to cut the spike when specific equipment was started. The second method was facilitating renewable energy to support the DG, especially in the peak time so the DG would still work in its optimum workload.

3.1 Cutting the load spike by the EMS

The primary function of EMS unit was to eliminate the load spike occurred when specific equipment was started. The EMS was responsible for cutting the load spike using the energy available in the battery storage unit. The EMS had placed a current sensor on the load side of the microgrid and another current sensor at the power source side of the microgrid. Once the sensor has detected an increasing power demand, the smart inverter would consider that a spike was occurred and would instruct the battery pack to discharge energy in similar amount with the spike. In this condition, the energy amount of the spike would be no longer requested to the DG. Figure 9 illustrates that the spike above a critical point has been cut.

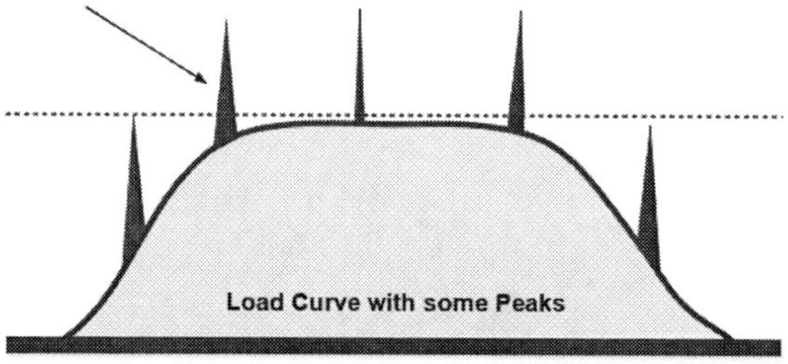

Fig. 9. The illustration of spike cutting by the battery.

As the spike was no longer drawn energy from DG unit, the DG would be operating steadily at its optimum rate. The steady operation means that DG's fuel consumption would also be steady with minimum possibility of sudden increase of fuel consumption.

3.2 RE integration via EMS

The EMS unit can be operated without connected to RE sources. However, with PV connected to the EMS outlet, the electricity supply has increased rather than merely depending on the battery pack. Facilitating the PV as the backup energy for the microgrid was the secondary function of the EMS unit and become significant support to the DG power grid.

There were two scenarios for utilizing the electricity from the solar farm. The first scenario was directly supplied that the electricity harnessed in the daylight—approximately from 8.30 am to 4:30 pm—to the grid. It will help the DG to operate without surpassing DG maximum capacity. In this scenario, battery pack assistance was not necessarily needed.

Figure 10 showed how the electricity from the PV absorbed the demand at the peak time on behalf of the DG. The second scenario was the use of battery pack to store electricity that harnessed in the daylight. This electricity would be used only at the peak time in daytime or nighttime. In this scenario, battery pack was an absolute requirement, and the bigger the capacity of the battery packs the better the coverage of the peak time. Nevertheless, both scenarios would prevent the DG unit to unnecessarily operate at its maximum rate where the fuel consumption was higher.

3.3 Fuel consumption reduction

Cutting spike had reduced the requested peak limit and integrated solar farm had shaved off the peak demand. These two methods change the minimum requirement of DG capacity. Along the reduction of the peak load profile, the operating DG was no longer necessary to be a big one (60 kVA). Altogether, DG unit with 42 kVA capacities was sufficient to cover all the electricity demand of the demo site. Figure 11 showed how DG capacity could be reduced from 60 kVA to 42 kVA. After this capacity reduction, the fuel consumption of smaller DG (42 kVA) had been lower than the higher DG (60 kVA). In this experiment, the fuel saving reduction of smaller DG could reach 30 % to 40 % from the initial bigger DG, respectively.

3.4 Further optimization

Hybrid power generation had a high potential to be implemented in a remote area either in a fixed or mobile platform. The mobile platform of PV-DG-Battery would be suitable for important remote sites such as sea vessel, zero energy building/complex, mobile military compound, or mobile rescue unit. However, previous research by Montreal et al. [18] had mentioned that PV integration would not always give advantages on the mobile microgrid, it depended on how long was the travel period. For 90 d or more travel period, PV panel integration with battery would have sufficient weight to affect a reasonable cost of the travel. However, in shorter traveling time—30 d to 60 d, the optimum system which reaches minimum weigh for reasonable travel cost should not include PV panel.

When it came to fixed/mobile vital facility such as mobile military compound, security should be as much consideration as the hybrid installation. Therefore, part of the research should be covering microgrid security system whether it was online or offline [19]. DG-battery was undeniably favorite combination for off-grid isolated microgrid. However, this combination could not be launched immediately as it needed a slight several second to reach stable condition [20]. Therefore, aside of the hybrid system cost, the use of more sophisticated energy storage system would bring significant advantages. Superconductor (SC) was one of energy storage technology alternative that could resist against the shortage of PV array power and batteries. SC also provided a quick response and extraordinary instantaneous output power. However, SC energy capacity, unfortunately, was shallow and eventually had a high self-discharge current [21].

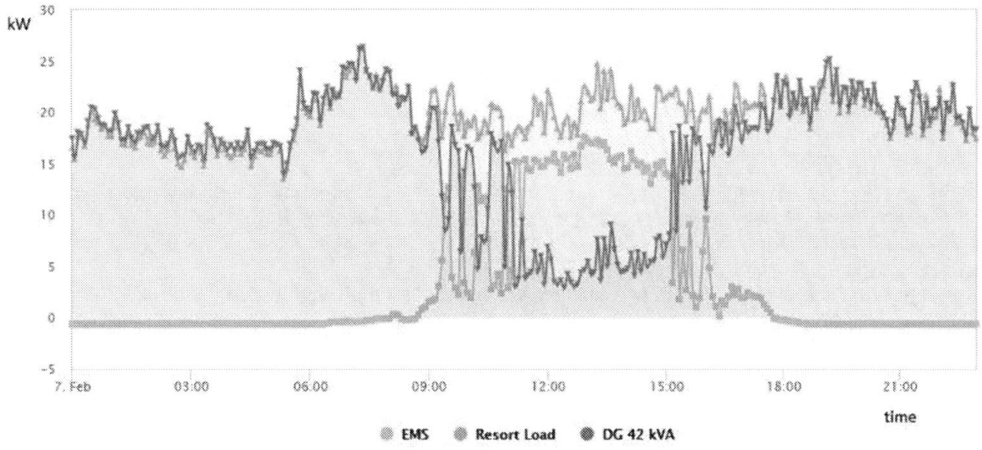

Fig. 10. EMS is facilitating the energy from PV to reduce DG power demand.

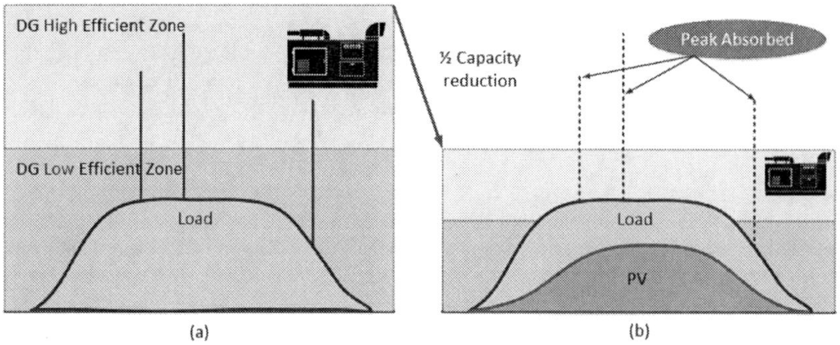

Fig. 11. Diesel genset capacity reduction before (a) and after (b) cutting spike and PV integration.

4 CONCLUSION

This work had integrated PV and battery into DG's power grid to become a hybrid power generation. The integration was using an EMS unit consisted of a smart inverted unit which could cut off any occurring load spike and also facilitated energy supply from solar farm to the DG's microgrid. The spike cut off was conducted by the EMS unit using the available power in the battery to absorb energy spike so it would not burden the DG power output. The EMS unit could help DG unit by absorbing peak energy demand using PV energy directly at the same time or store the energy in the battery and discharge it to be used at any necessary time. The spike cut off and RE integration would reduce the required capacity of the DG. The replacement of 62 kVA DG with the 42 kVA DG means a reduction of fuel consumption regarding DG's capacity difference. The fuel saving was approximately reached 30 % of the previous DG, respectively. This fuel saving would be a significant cost saving which could be relocated into another segment such as investment in more RE sources or extending the battery capacity.

This project was funded by Murata Manufacturing Co.Ltd. and highly supported by Murata engineering team, i.e. Hirofumi Nakata, Toshiya Kawate, Tsuyoshi Matsumoto, Yuta Yamamoto, Hiroyuki Yasui, and Takayuki Miwa. The location to perform the research was provided by Raja Ampat Reseach and Conservation Center (RARCC) at Papua Diving Demo Site owned by Max Ammer. This project was also continuously supported by researchers from Research Centre for Electrical Power and Mechatronics, Indonesian Institute of Sciences (RCEPM-LIPI), i.e. Budi Prawara, Arifin Nur, Rudi Darussalam, Ahmad Rajani, and Dadan Ridwan Saleh.

REFERENCES

[1] H. Farhangi. IEEE Power Energy Mag., **8**(1):18–28 (2010). http://ieeexplore.ieee.org/document/5357331/

[2] P. Bajpai, V. Dash. Renew. Sustain. Energy Rev., **16**(5):2926–2939 (2012). https://www.sciencedirect.com/science/article/pii/S1364032112001025

[3] M. M. Mahmoud, I. H. Ibrik. Renew. Sustain. Energy Rev., **10**(2):128–138 (2006). https://www.sciencedirect.com/science/article/pii/S1364032104001224

[4] A. Wresta, A. Saepudin, A. Santosa, H. Sudibyo, D. Andriani, Kusnadi. J. telecomunication Electron. Comput. Eng., **9**(1–5):6–70 (2017). http://journal.utem.edu.my/index.php/jtec/article/view/1837

[5] T. D. Atmaja, G. Pikra. Energy Procedia, **32**:74–83 (2013). https://www.sciencedirect.com/science/article/pii/S187661021300012X

[6] A. Mohammed, J. Pasupuleti, T. Khatib, W. Elmenreich. Renew. Sustain. Energy Rev., **44**:436–446 (2015). https://www.sciencedirect.com/science/article/pii/S1364032114010879

[7] K. Y. Lau, C. W. Tan, A. H. M. Yatim. Renew. Sustain. Energy Rev., **81**(2):2625–2636 (2018). https://www.sciencedirect.com/science/article/pii/S1364032117310110

[8] E. Skoplaki, J. A. Palyvos. Sol. Energy, **83**(5):614–624 (2009). https://www.sciencedirect.com/science/article/pii/S0038092X08002788

[9] T. D. Atmaja, R. Darussalam, D. Andriani. *Vertical facade PV installation to optimize microgrid system on high rise EV parking lot with AC and DC charging station*. International Conference on Sustainable Energy Engineering and Application (ICSEEA), 23–24 October, 2017 (Jakarta, Indonesia, 2017). IEEE, pp. 164–171 (2018). http://ieeexplore.ieee.org/document/8267703/

[10] T. D. Atmaja. Energy Procedia, **32**:105–114 (2013). https://core.ac.uk/download/pdf/82215540.pdf

[11] H. Tazvinga, X. Xia, J. Zhang. Sol. Energy, **96**:292–299 (2013). https://www.sciencedirect.com/science/article/pii/S0038092X13003046

[12] K. Kusakana, "Operation cost minimization of photovoltaic–diesel–battery hybrid systems," Energy, **85**:645–653 (2015). https://www.sciencedirect.com/science/article/pii/S0360544215004181
[13] E. M. Nfah, J. M. Ngundam, R. Tchinda. Renew. Energy, **32**(5):832–844 (2007). https://www.sciencedirect.com/science/article/pii/S0960148106000760
[14] A.L. Galindo Noguera, L. S. Mendoza Castellanos, E. E. Silva Lora, V. R. Melian Cobas. Energy, **142**:33–45 (2018). https://www.sciencedirect.com/science/article/pii/S036054421731681X
[15] Y. Hu, P. Solana. Renew. Energy, **51**:364–372 (2013). https://www.sciencedirect.com/science/article/pii/S0960148112006313
[16] M. Sechilariu, B.C. Wang, F. Locment. Int. J. Electr. Power Energy Syst., **58**:140–149 (2014). https://www.sciencedirect.com/science/article/pii/S0142061514000313
[17] H. Tazvinga, B. Zhu, X. Xia. Sol. Energy, **108**:412–420 (2014). https://www.sciencedirect.com/science/article/pii/S0038092X14003740
[18] I.R. Cristóbal-Monreal, R. Dufo-López. Energy Convers. Manag., **119**:279–288 (2016). https://www.sciencedirect.com/science/article/pii/S0196890416303004
[19] T.D. Atmaja, Fitriana. *Cyber security strategy for future distributed energy delivery system*. Proceedings of the 2011 International Conference on Electrical Engineering and Informatics (ICEEI) 17–19 July, 2017 (Bandung, Indonesia, 2011). http://ieeexplore.ieee.org/document/6021635/
[20] C. Yin, H. Wu, F. Locment, M. Sechilariu. Energy Convers. Manag., **132**:14–27 (2017). https://www.sciencedirect.com/science/article/pii/S0196890416310135
[21] A. Etxeberria, I. Vechiu, H. Camblong, J.-M. Vinassa. Energy Convers. Manag., **54**(1):113–121 (2012). https://www.sciencedirect.com/science/article/pii/S0196890411002779

V2G Development on Public Vertical Parking Lot to Support Community Energy Management System

Tinton Dwi Atmaja[1,*], *Vita* Susanti[1], *Midriem* Mirdanies[1], and *Aam* Muharam[1, 2]

[1]Research Centre for Electrical Power and Mechatronics, Indonesian Institute of Sciences, Komp. LIPI Bandung, Jl. Sangkuriang, Gd. 20, Lt. 2, Bandung 40135, Indonesia
[2]Dept. of ASEM, Interdisciplinary Graduate School of Engineering and Sciences, Kyushu University, Global Innovation Center Building, 6 Fl. 6-1, Kasuga-Shi, Fukuoka, 816-8580, Japan

Abstract. Vehicle to grid concept emerged as one solution for harnessing the idle power of parked plug-in hybrid electric vehicle. As the public parking lot had been evolving into the vertical parking lot which has more capacity within the same grounding area, a vehicle to building technology provided more available energy to be shared into the designated area around the parking lot. This paper discussed the development of vehicle to grid into a better concept and architecture by integrating the vertical parking lots one another and also with renewable energy sources (photovoltaic) and sophisticated energy storage system. Several standards were suggested in this paper to ensure a steady performance of vehicle to grid parking. At last, the collaboration scenario was proposed between the parking lot management and plug-in hybrid electric vehicle owner to ensure the technical viability of vehicle to grid implementation for both host and participant. This sharing concept optimized community energy management system as the root segment of the smart city and smart grid delivery system.

Keywords: Community energy management system, energy storage system, PHEV, renewable energy, vehicle-to-grid, vertical parking lot.

1 Introduction

Climate change and the depletion of fossil fuel lead to emerging research about sustainable energy in the past two decades. Global policies also point to support green technologies including significant portion of attention on green transportation. Therefore, electric vehicles (EV) becomes a high value exploration commodity amongst engineers and researcher. EVs are projected to contribute up to 60 % of total new car sales in the UK by 2030 [1].

Plug-in hybrid electric vehicle (PHEV) in one unique subject for studying EV connection with the power grid as its ability to connect to the grid and conduct vehicle-to-grid (V2G) operation. Equipped with the power cord to connect to the utility grid, PHEV not only capable of charging electricity from the grid but also discharging electricity to the power grid. Upon this capability, V2G can help provide a sufficient energy to powers buildings from their portable battery store, which can be recharged at a different location [2, 3].

V2G implementation assists the power grid as backup energy storage when its battery pack is used as demand response and reducing system overload. V2G will also improve power quality, simplifying voltage regulation and reducing power outage, injecting reactive and active power to the grid, and escaping the necessity of building new power plants [4]. Previous research conducted on V2G control such as an autonomous distributed V2G control of grid-connected PHEV and EV by coordinating battery condition, use for vehicle, and power system state [5]. Vehicle to grid concept can be seen in Figure 1 [6]. The PHEV is charging or discharging electricity to the charging infrastructure and later send the power output to the house grid or even to the main utility grid. Renewable energy (RE) sources was also an option to be introduced to the V2G system as RE can increase the stability of the microgrid.

*Corresponding author: tinton_dwi@yahoo.com

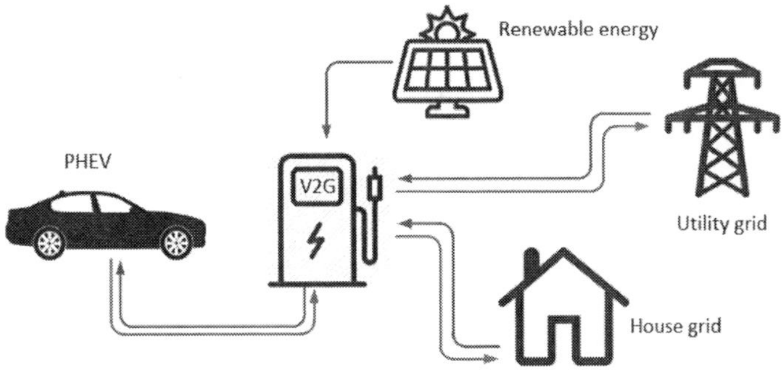

Fig. 1. V2G concept.

Parking garage or parking lot is the most potential facility that can implement V2G concept and deliver the outage power to the nearby building or directly to the utility grid. Evolution of parking lot signs a promising phase to the implementation of V2G. Vertical parking lot have a higher PHEV capacity than on-the-ground parking lot within the same ground area. Higher PHEV capacity means higher electricity capacity to go to the building or to the grid. Figure 2 shows the example of vertical car park [7].

Fig. 2. Vertical parking lot.

Furthermore, V2G parking considerably one of the bases of the emerging concept of community energy management system (CEMS) [8]. Many world class corporation had implemented CEMS to strengthen energy independence and extend the scope of green energy community [9]. Successful CEMS is believed to be one base line which can ensure the steady microgrid among the community which leads to the successfulness of smart grid implementation. The main objective of this work is to study the development of V2G concept within the sophisticated technology lining up in the worldwide research community. Furthermore, this work should improve the implementation of V2G by adding the key components such as RE integration or energy storage system introduction. The following outcome is that the community can have improvement in their CEMS platform by first improving their parking system.

2 V2G vertical parking concept

2.1 V2G parking concept

Previous research by Gough et al. [6] develops a data flow and electricity flow in the V2G parking lot. Preceding research [10] also analyze the proper grid structure which can facilitate AC and DC grid for both AC and DC charging mechanism. Figure 3 shows the conceptual model of this work locating the key components, i.e. the location of the parking lot within the building, parked PHEV, charging/discharging infrastructure, building distribution box, utility meter and the utility grid.

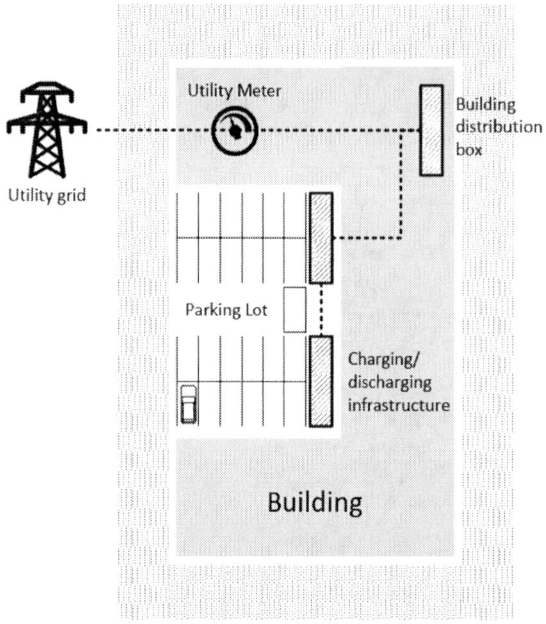

Fig. 3. V2G parking conceptual model illustrating parking location and other key infrastructures.

PHEV in the vertical parking lot connected to the charging infrastructure and further connected into building distribution box. This charging infrastructure is designed to be able to facilitate discharging process from the PHEV into the building/grid. This vehicle-to-building (V2B) process will later be analyzed to bring benefit for both parking lot grid and building grid. The electricity flow also connected into the main utility grid as the main electricity source. The connection is through a bidirectional utility meter to make sure that all incoming and outgoing electricity flow is fairly compensated.

2.2 Charging infrastructure

Charging infrastructure specification on this work was based on standard J1772 by the Society of Automotive Engineering (SAE) which classifies AC charging stations into three categories [11]:

i) Level I: charger is on-board and provides AC voltage 120 V or 240 V with a maximum current of 15 A (standard home outlet), and a maximum power of 3.3 kW.
ii) Level II: charger is on-board and provides AC voltage 240 V with a maximum current of 60 A, and a maximum power of 14.4 kW.
iii) Level III: charger is off-board. The charging station provides DC voltage directly to the battery via a DC connector, with a maximum power of 240 kW.

Level III charging station is a fast charger. At the maximum power, level III charging station should be capable of replenishing more than half of the capacity of an EV battery in less than half an hour. Figure 4 shows the schematic of level III charging infrastructure integrated with the building [12].

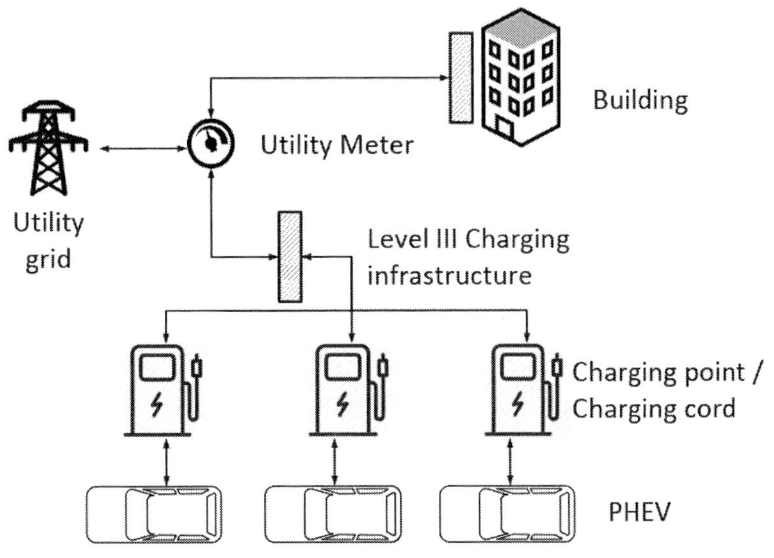

Fig. 4. Schematic of Level III charging infrastructure integrated with a building.

2.3 Charging scenario

The Level III charging station operation models can be developed using adopted model from the work of [12, 13] and assimilated with the unique scenarios from [14]. The scenario will be operated at these following points.

i) When the EV come into the parking spot, the EV driver can choose the available charging cord to park their EV. Once the EV plugged, the EV should not move into another charging cord.
ii) If the EV move to another charging cord, and there is a queue in the line, the moved EV will be placed at the end of the queue as if the EV has just arrived.
iii) An EV can only be charged if arriving with at least 80 % battery state of charge but can be immediately charged if there is no queue in the line.
iv) EV above 80 % can automatically discharge the energy from EV battery into the grid under a specific agreement.
v) Charging will be terminated after the EV battery reach 100 % if there is no queue, and 80 % state of charge if there is a queue
vi) The charging also automatically terminated if the EV disconnected from the charging cord. It is assumed that the driver leaves the parking lot.

2.3 Related standard

Standards related to V2G development on public vertical parking can be seen in Table 1 [15]. Those standards can be used as a reference to the specifications, usage, or characteristics of V2G concept, i.e. connectors, socket outlets, safety standards for EV and HEV, etc. For example, the standardization regarding "Connectors, socket outlets, plugs and vehicle inlets" can refer to IEC 621961: 2014, IEC 621962: 2016, IEC 621963: 2014, BS EN 621961: 2014, and JIS D 621963: 2014. The relevant standard about "Road Vehicles Vehicle to Grid Communication" can refer to ISO 151181: 2013, ISO 151182: 2014, and ISO 151183: 2015. This standardization will facilitate companies in developing V2G. Some companies that are doing research related to V2G are Nissan and Mitsubishi, followed by Ford, Tesla, BMW and Honda [16].

Table 1. Various EVs standard related to V2G parking implementation.

No	Standard	Type and Specification
1	IEC 6185123: 2014	Electric vehicle (EV) conductive charging system Part 23: DC EV charging station
2	IEC 621961: 2014	Vehicle connectors, socket outlets, plugs, and vehicle inlets conductive charging of EVs part 1: general requirements
3	IEC 621962: 2016	Vehicle connectors, socket outlets, plugs, and vehicle inlets conductive charging of EVs part 2: contact tube accessories
4	IEC 621963: 2014	Vehicle connectors, socket outlets, plugs, and vehicle inlets conductive charging of EVs part 3: contact tube vehicle couplers and dimensional compatibility & interchangeability requirements for

Table 1. continue on next page

Table 1. Various EVs standard related to V2G parking implementation (Continued).

No	Standard	Type and Specification
		DC pin
5	IEC 619801: 2015	EV WPT systems - part 1: Basic requirements
6	IEC 6185124: 2014	Part 24 (conductive charging system for EV): To control the DC charging, digitalize communication between a DC supply based EV charging station and an EV.
7	SAE J 1772: 2016	Conductive charge coupler for EV and PHEV
8	SAE J 1773: 2014	SAE inductively coupled charging for EVs
9	SAE J J 537: 2016	Battery storage system
10	SAE J 1797: 2008	Packaging of EV battery modules and recommended practice for.
11	SAE J 1798: 2008	Performance rating of EV battery modules and recommended practice for
12	SAE J 2288: 2008	EV battery modules' life cycle testing
13	SAE J 2464: 2009	Safety and abuse testing of EV and HEV rechargeable ESS
14	SAE J 2758: 2007	Detail description to determine the maximum available power from a RESS on an HEV
15	SAE J 2929: 2013	Safety standard for EV and HEV propulsion battery systems utilizing lithium based rechargeable cells
16	SAE J 2936: 2012	Labelling recommended practice for SAE electrical energy storage device
17	SAE J 2344: 2010	EV safety guidelines
18	SAE J 2894/1: 2011	Plug-in EV chargers required power quality
19	SAE J 2894/2: 2015	Plug-in EV chargers based power quality testing
20	SAE J 2293/1: 2014	Functional requirements and system architectures for EVs energy transfer system (part 1)
21	SAE J 2293/2: 2014	Communication requirements and network architecture for EVs energy transfer system (part 2)
22	SAE J 2841: 2010	Utility factor definitions for PHEV using travel survey data
23	UL 2202: 2009	Edition: 2, Detail of EV charging system equipment
24	UL 22311: 2012	Edition: 2, general requirement of personnel protection systems for EV supply circuits
25	UL 22312: 2012	Edition: 2, particular requirements for protection devices for use in charging systems
26	UL 2251: 2013	Edition: 3, couplers, receptacles and plugs for EVs
27	UL 2734: 2015	Edition: 3, service plugs and outline for connectors for use with on-board EV charging systems
28	UL 2871: 2014	Edition 1: Outline of investigation for and production chargers and EV service
29	UL 9741: 2014	Edition 1: Outline of investigation for bidirectional EV charging system equipment
30	UL 2747: 2012	Outline of investigation for EV power supplies
31	BS EN 618511: 2011	part 1: General requirements for conductive charging system of EVs
32	BS EN 6185121: 2002	Requirements of EV to connect an AC/DC supply in conducting modes
33	BS EN 6185122: 2002	EV charging station based on AC supply
34	BS EN 621961: 2014	General Requirements for vehicle inlets, vehicle connectors, socket outlets, and plugs, for conductive charging of EVs.
35	BS DD CLC/TS 504571: 2008	EVs conductive charging through DC charging station
36	BS DD CLC/TS 504572: 2008	Detail of communication protocol between EV and off board charger for conductive charging of EVs.
37	COC GB/T 18487.1: 2015	Part 1: Details of general requirements for EV conductive charging system
38	COC GB/T 18487.2: 2001	EVs requirements for conductive connection to an AC/DC supply
39	COC GB/T 18487.3: 2001	EV conductive charging system AC/DC EV charging station
40	COC GB/T 20234.1: 2015	Part 1: General requirements for connection set for conductive charging of EVs
41	COC GB/T 20234.2: 2015	Part 2: AC charging coupler for connection set for conductive charging of EVs
42	COC GB/T 20234.3: 2015	Part 2: DC charging coupler for connection set for charging conductive charging of EVs
43	COC GB/T QC/T 895: 2011	Detail of EVs on-board conductive charger
44	COC GB/T QC/T 841: 2010	Conductive charge coupler for EV
45	JIS D 1304: 2004	Efficiency test method of an EV charging system
46	JIS D 6185123: 2014	Part 23: DC EV charging station based EV conductive charging system
47	JIS D 6185124: 2014	EV conductive charging system part 24: To control the DC charging, digital communication between EV and a DC EV charging station
48	JIS D 621963: 2014	General requirements for vehicle inlets, vehicle connectors, socket outlets, and plugs, for conductive charging of EVs.
49	ISO 11955: 2008	ISO/TR 11955 hybrid electric road vehicles guidelines for charge balance measurement
50	ISO 17409: 2015	Electrically propelled road vehicles connection to an external electric power supply safety requirements
51	ISO 151181: 2013	Road vehicles vehicle to grid communication interface part 1: General information and use case definition
52	ISO 151182: 2014	Road vehicles vehicle to grid communication interface part 2: Network and application protocol requirements
53	ISO 151183: 2015	Road vehicles vehicle to grid communication interface part 3: Physical and data link layer requirements

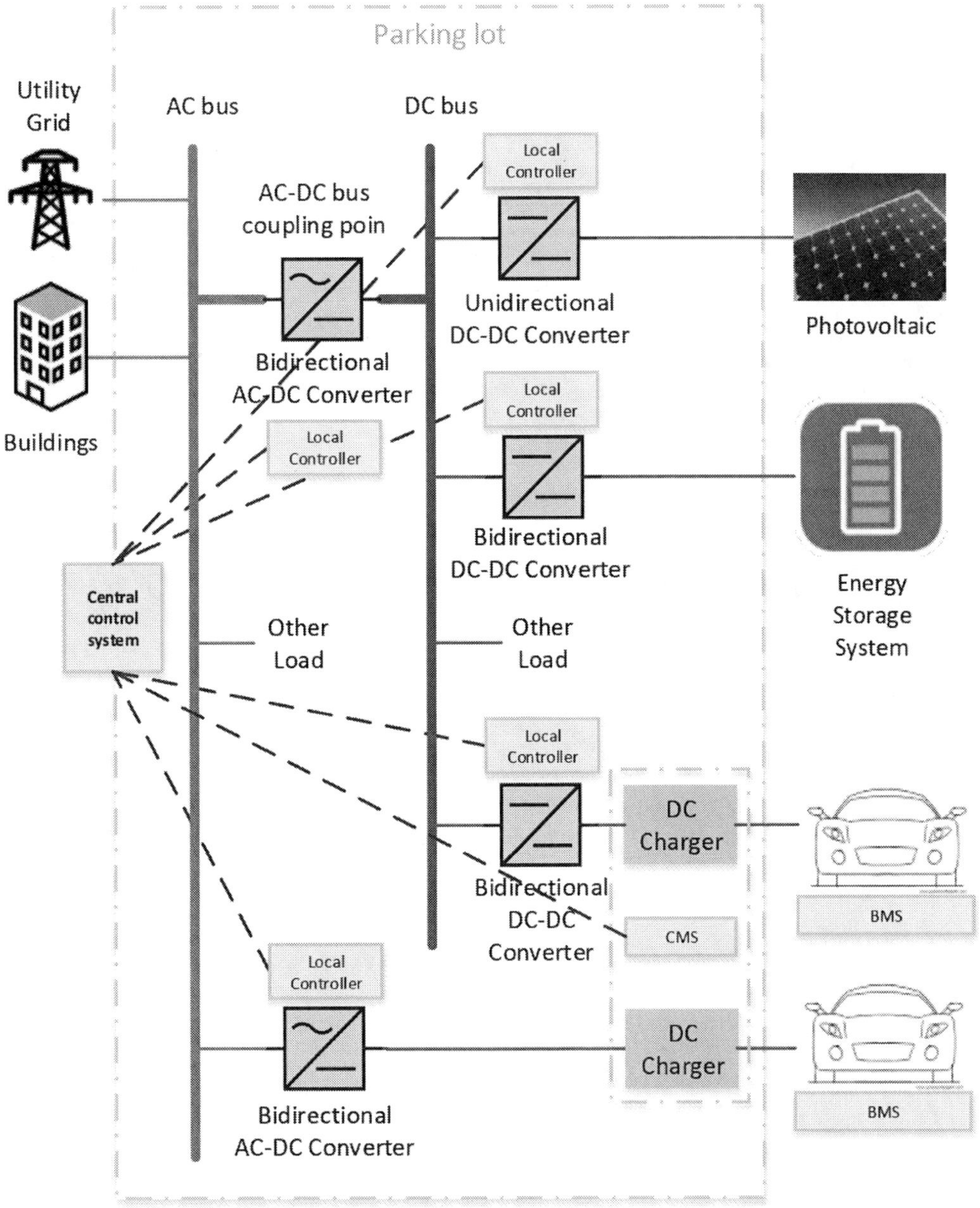

Fig. 5. Control system architecture with PV and ESS for charging mechanism.

3 V2G parking optimization

3.1 Integration with RE and ESS

The parking lot microgrid could not merely depend on the main utility grid as its primary electricity source. Another backup power source should be installed to reduce electricity cost and diminish the dependency of the utility grid. Solar and wind were the most favorite RE sources that available in the urban area. Solar power could be in the form of concentrated solar power (CSP) or photovoltaic (PV). Previous research [17] was implemented a CSP installation with thermal storage media. However, in several cases, CSP size and efficiency has been overcome by PV panel.

Figure 5 showed fast charging mechanism with integrated PV and ESS incorporation [14]. There are many energy storage systems (ESS) that could significantly increase the parking lot microgrid stability. Other previous research had also pointed PV as the potential RE integration because of its flexibility such as in vertical façade installment which is suitable for vertical parking lot [18]. Several types of ESSs integration was also discussed in previous research [19].

3.1 Collaboration possibility

Collaboration between the owner of the EV and the management of the parking lot was the significant social interaction aspect that would support the success and the continuity of V2G implementation. Previous research conducted in Université Laval [20] undertake a mutual collaboration between the EV owner and the parking management. The work was highpoints the benefit of vehicle-to-building (V2B) when the EV was connected to the building microgrid via V2G charging infrastructure.

The work investigated a charging scenario that consist of an agreement that allowed the EV to charge for free in exchange for the right of V2G parking management to control the EV energy [20]. The scenario had utilized Battery management system (BMS) onboard of the EV and the charger management system (CMS) inside the V2G parking infrastructure. When the EV connected, the charging infrastructure not only facilitating power exchange but also the data information exchange. The initiation of V2B process would be determined by the CMS unit. CMS other function was including continuous monitoring of BMS data from the connected EV.

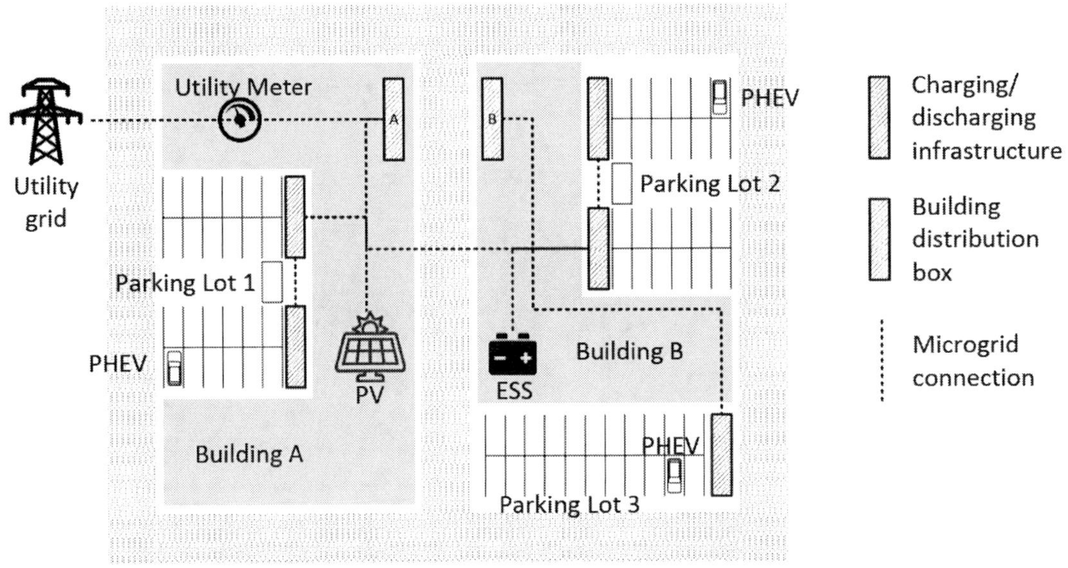

Fig. 6. V2G parking lot integration with buildings, PV, and ESS in detailed location and key infrastructure.

4 Results and discussion

4.1 V2G parking integration with RE and ESS

The integration of RE sources into the V2G Parking microgrid can be seen in Figure 6. Control configuration of PV to the fast charging system has been detailed in Figure 5. ESS was also introduced to the microgrid with an association of battery management system (BMS) and the charger management system (CMS). In this configuration, the addition of ESS was purposed to assist balancing the microgrid. Bidirectional non-isolated DC-DC converter topologies that can be adopted as the DC chargers were also proposed [14]. Vertical facade installation was considered potential because the vertical parking lot has vertical wall that was rarely used for energy source [10]. Further action would be more focused on developing more efficient scheme to accommodate the integration of the EV into the existing microgrid. The smart energy management should consider numerous proposed sophisticated research like deterministic and fuzzy logic algorithms, genetic and particle swarm optimization algorithms, or online operation algorithm that support the improvement of overall efficiency, control, flexibility and security of the system.

4.2 Charging stations integration and building size

Combining several charging stations and buildings was one of the optimization methods since it could reduce PEV demand charge cost by up to 50 % [12]. Figure 6 contains an illustration where several V2G parking was integrated one another and also linked with several buildings. Using higher power charging station such as 240 kW charging infrastructure could shrink the refueling time of the EV. However, it is certain that an increase of connected EV to the grid would increase the demand charges of the building.

When the research was focused on building integration, the high demand charges would reduce the sharing demand charges within the building. It could be seen that when the reserved energy was drawn to the high demand charges, the building would receive a minimum energy sharing. However, this integration would be relative to the actual size of the building. If the building was relatively large enough compared to the parking demand charges, then the building would sufficiently share the demand charges. The integration of fast charging infrastructure would also lead to an increase in the switching rates in the larger buildings.

Overall demand charges cost reductions should be affected significantly by the dynamics and size of the building electricity consumption. High load factor buildings had provided little to no cost benefit, and low load factor buildings might provide savings [12]. Integration with larger building could reduce the chance that the EV charged at the time of building reach its maximum demand, but potential saving might shrink as the building size increased. This was, generally, relative to the building utility and operational cost.

4.3 Collaboration in CEMS

Collaboration between parking management and EV owner on V2B scenario has been investigated in Université Lavalin [20] to aim the beneficial interaction between both parties. The research was examined the possibility of reducing the electricity bill by comparing the implementation of V2B parking with no-V2B parking scenario. Figure 7 shows that there was energy exchange between the parked EV and the microgrid which was happened in between 400 Prius and 16 MW power grid in Université Lavalin [20]. The energy exchange did not happen constantly every day and was not in the similar amount of energy. Nevertheless, it was concluded that the collaboration was reducing the campus electricity bill by 0.9 % and 1.6 % compared to the no-V2B original scenario [20]. If the collaboration can be implemented in every V2G parking in the community area, it is believed that the electricity bill of the community could be reduced.

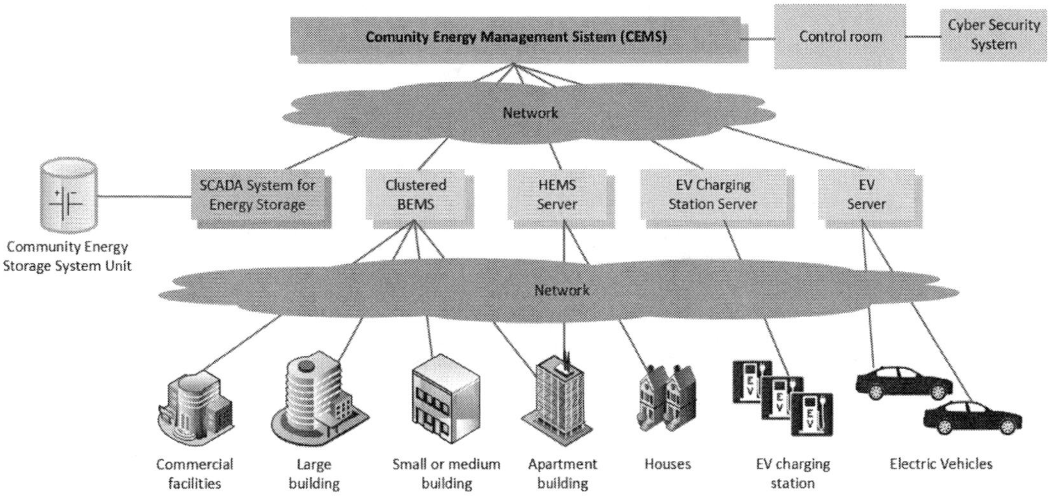

Fig. 8. Brief configuration of CEMS.

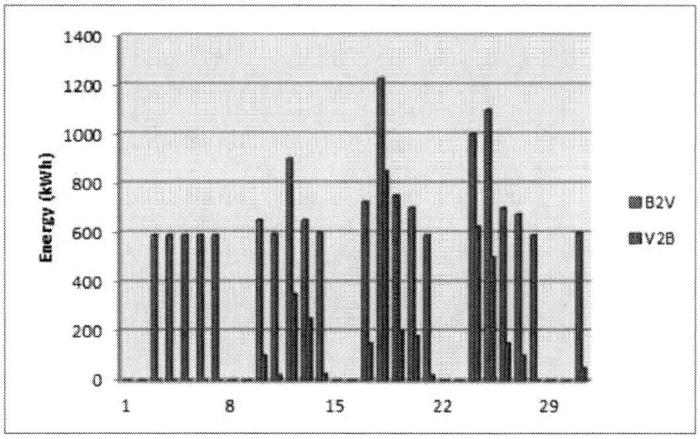

Fig. 7. Energy exchanges between the car and the building for the month of January 2011 at Université Lavalin [20].

Successful collaboration will furthermore support the implementation of CEMS. As mentioned before, there are many corporations that started implementing CEMS in their line of work. Figure 8 is describing the V2G introduction into the CEMS. The concept was adopted from one of CEMS implementation in Yokohama Smart City Project (YSCP) [9]. CEMS project was including the EVs server, EV charging station energy management system, house energy management system (HEMS), building energy management system (BEMS), and energy storage SCADA system.

EV server covered undertakings of dispatched EV within the coverage area of the community or even within the city area. EV server should monitor EVs location, EV power condition, and specific activities such as accidents or depleted EVs. Charging station has its own network and maintained by a server configuring it's charging activity and monitoring the idling potential. Moreover, charging station server should anticipate the possibility of excesses grid demand charges. V2G and V2B implementations were also controlled by this server.

In higher scale, HEMS and BEMS were also integrated to the CEMS server to ensure the grid power demand. These will include small residence, medium house, apartment building, small to medium office, large building, and event commercial facilities within the community. Community energy storage system was installed under specific SCADA system to help the community grid maintain its stability. The whole system was delivered using internet network within the community area. CEMS control room equipped with a designated cyber security system would be a significant addition to the system.

4.3 Further challenges

PV integration and ESS introduction have significantly stabilized the microgrid. However, several challenges would emerge as the large deployment of PHEV connected to the power grid. If EV owners were allowed to charge their PHEV whenever they want, power consumption in the parking lot would increase and created a need for higher peak generation capacity [21]. Moreover, increased generation demand due to the high peaks demand would imply to a more expensive system operation cost [22]. As a final consequence, large fleet of PHEV would require a dumb charging approach which require a massive investment in the distribution grid [23, 24]. Another challenge came from mobility patterns that did not allow EVs to be charged during valley hours. It might increase marginal system cost when intermittent RES generation was low. This would also increase the use of more expensive power generation output and CO2 emissions [25].

5 CONCLUSION

This work introduced the implementation of V2G into parking management system. V2G concept facilitated discharging activity from the plugged EV into the building and power grid. This activity would put EV connected to the grid as energy back up which could share its stored energy when the power grid needs it. This sharing activity had ensured the grid stability and reduced charging demand peak. Vertical parking lot provided higher car capacity within same ground area comparing to the conventional on-ground parking lot. This vertical evolution had also provided higher energy back up capacity. Integrating a renewable energy source and introducing dedicated energy storage system had also provided significant peak demand energy absorption. The stable energy capacity from the plugged EV and the integrated RE could ensure a continuous energy share with the building. V2B would emerge a mutual collaboration between EV owner and the building management. Under the specific agreement, the collaboration could reduce electricity cost of the building. The final affection of implementing V2G within the building in the selected area was supporting the success of CEMS which furthermore cement the solid baseline of smart grid implementation.

The authors would like to express high gratitude to Dian Andriani, Hendri Maja Saputra, and other researchers on Research Centre for Electrical Power and Mechatronics, Indonesian Institute of Sciences, especially in the Industrial Automation Division.

REFERENCES

1. The Committee on Climate Change. *Pathways to high penetration of electric vehicles*. [Final Report]. Cambrigde: University of Aberdeen, Ecolane (2013). pp? https://www.theccc.org.uk/wp-content/uploads/2013/12/CCC-EV-pathways_FINAL-REPORT_17-12-13-Final.pdf
2. C. Guille, G. Gross. Energy Policy, **37**(11):4379–4390 (2009). https://www.sciencedirect.com/science/article/pii/S0301421509003978
3. W. Kempton, J. Tomić. J. Power Sources, **144**(1):268–279 (2005). https://www.sciencedirect.com/science/article/pii/S0378775305000352
4. F. Khosrojerdi, S. Taheri, H. Taheri, and E. Pouresmaeil. *Integration of electric vehicles into a smart power grid: A technical review*. Electrical Power and Energy Conference (EPEC) 12–14 October, 2016 (Ottawa, Canada, 2016). IEEE, pp. 1–6 (2016). http://ieeexplore.ieee.org/document/7771784/
5. Y. Ota, H. Taniguchi, T. Nakajima, K. M. Liyanage, A. Yokoyama. *An autonomous distributed vehicle-to-grid control of grid-connected electric vehicle*. International Conference on Industrial and Information Systems (ICIIS) 28–31 December 2009 (Sri Langka, 2009). IEEE, pp. 414–418 (2010). http://ieeexplore.ieee.org/document/5429826/
6. R. Gough, C. Dickerson, P. Rowley, C. Walsh. Appl. Energy., **192**:12–23 (2017). https://www.sciencedirect.com/science/article/pii/S0306261917301149
7. STMY. *3 or 4 level car parking machine manufacturers vertical car storage*. [Online] from http://www.my-autoparking.com/sale-8227227-3-or-4-level-car-parking-machine-manufacturers-vertical-car-storage.html. [Accessed on 7 July 2017].
8. X. Xu, X. Jin, H. Jia, X. Yu, K. Li. Appl. Energy., **160**:231–243 (2015). https://www.sciencedirect.com/science/article/pii/S0306261915010764
9. Toshiba. *Development of community energy management system*. [Online] from https://www.toshiba.co.jp/rdc/rd/fields/12_e04_e.htm (2010). [Accessed on 31 July 2017].
10. T.D. Atmaja, R. Darussalam, D. Andriani. *Vertical facade PV installation to optimize microgrid system on high rise EV parking lot with AC and DC charging station*. International Conference on Sustainable Energy Engineering and Application (ICSEEA), 23–24 October 2017 (Jakarta, Indonesia, 2017). IEEE, pp. 164–171 (2018). http://ieeexplore.ieee.org/document/8267703/
11. G. Joos, M. de Freige, M. Dubois. *Design and simulation of a fast charging station for PHEV/EV batteries*. Electrical Power & Energy Conference, 25–27 August 2010 (Halifax, Canada, 2010). IEEE, pp. 1–5 (2011). http://ieeexplore.ieee.org/document/5697250/
12. R.J. Flores, B. P. Shaffer, J. Brouwer. Appl. Energy, **191**:367–384 (2017). https://www.sciencedirect.com/science/article/pii/S030626191730017X
13. R.J. Flores, B. P. Shaffer, J. Brouwer. Appl. Energy, **169**:813–830 (2016). https://www.sciencedirect.com/science/article/pii/S0306261916302082
14. R.H. Ashique, Z. Salam, M.J.B.A. Aziz, A. R. Bhatti, Renew. Sustain. Energy Rev., **69**:1243–1257 (2017). https://www.sciencedirect.com/science/article/pii/S136403211631019X
15. F. Ahmad, M.S. Alam, M. Asaad. Sustain. Cities Soc., **35**:552–564 (2017). https://www.sciencedirect.com/science/article/pii/S2210670717310557
16. Fleetcarma. *The latest in vehicle to grid (V2G) charging*. [Online] from https://www.fleetcarma.com/latest-vehicle-grid-v2g-charging/ (2017). [Accessed on 07 November 2017].
17. T. D. Atmaja, G. Pikra. Energy Procedia, **32**:74–83 (2013). https://www.sciencedirect.com/science/article/pii/S187661021300012X
18. T. D. Atmaja. Energy Procedia, **32**:105–114 (2013). https://core.ac.uk/download/pdf/82215540.pdf
19. T. D. Atmaja, Amin. Energy Procedia, **68**:429–437 (2015). https://www.sciencedirect.com/science/article/pii/S1876610215005809
20. K. Tanguy, M.R. Dubois, K.L. Lopez, C. Gagné. Sustain. Cities Soc., **26**:496–506 (2016). https://www.sciencedirect.com/science/article/pii/S2210670716300439
21. J. Kiviluoma, P. Meibom. Energy, **36**(3):1758–1767 (2011). https://www.sciencedirect.com/science/article/pii/S0360544210007590
22. C. Fernandes, P. Frías, L. Olmos, A. Ramos, T. Gómez. *Economic impact of plug-in hybrid electric vehicles on power systems operation*. The 33rd IAEE International Conference, 6–9 June, 2010 (Rio de Janeiro, Brazil, 2010). https://www.iit.comillas.edu/publicacion/mostrar_publicacion_conferencia.php.en?id=10823
23. J.A.P. Lopes, F.J. Soares, P.M.R. Almeida, *Identifying management procedures to deal with connection of Electric Vehicles in the grid*. Bucharest PowerTech, 28 June to 2 July, 2009 (Bucharest, Romania, 2009). IEEE, pp. 1–8 (2009). http://ieeexplore.ieee.org/document/5282155/

24. L.P.Fernandez, T.G.S. Roman, R. Cossent, C. Mateo Domingo, P. Frias. *Assessment of the Impact of Plug-in Electric Vehicles on Distribution Networks*. Trans. Power Syst., **26**(1):206–213 (2011). http://ieeexplore.ieee.org/document/5471115/
25. C. Fernandes, P. Frías, J. M. Latorre. Appl. Energy, **96**:194–202 (2012). https://www.sciencedirect.com/science/article/pii/S0306261911007641

Spelling Correction for Text Documents in Bahasa Indonesia Using Finite State Automata and Levinshtein Distance Method

Viny Christanti Mawardi*, *Niko* Susanto, and *Dali* Santun Naga

Faculty of Information Technology, Tarumanagara University, Letjend S. Parman No.1, West Jakarta 11440, Indonesia

Abstract. Any mistake in writing of a document will cause the information to be told falsely. These days, most of the document is written with a computer. For that reason, spelling correction is needed to solve any writing mistakes. This design process discuss about the making of spelling correction for document text in Indonesian language with document's text as its input and a .txt file as its output. For the realization, 5 000 news articles have been used as training data. Methods used includes Finite State Automata (FSA), Levenshtein distance, and N-gram. The results of this designing process are shown by perplexity evaluation, correction hit rate and false positive rate. Perplexity with the smallest value is a unigram with value 1.14. On the other hand, the highest percentage of correction hit rate is bigram and trigram with value 71.20 %, but bigram is superior in processing time average which is 01:21.23 min. The false positive rate of unigram, bigram, and trigram has the same percentage which is 4.15 %. Due to the disadvantages at using FSA method, modification is done and produce bigram's correction hit rate as high as 85.44 %.

Key words: Finite state automata, Levenshtein distance, N-gram, spelling correction

1 Introduction

Language is one of the most important component in human life, which could be expressed by either spoken word or written text. As a text, language became an important element in document writing. Any mistake in document writing will cause the information told falsely. Nowadays, most of the document is written with a computer. In its writing process, there could be some mistakes happened because of human error. The mistake or error can be caused by either the letters from the adjacent keyboard keys, errors due to mechanical failure or slip of the hand or finger. Error when writing a document is often occurred. Especially nowadays, people's awareness to pour his idea into the article, scientific journals, college assignment or other documents have increased. For that reason, spelling correction is needed to solve any writing mistakes. This research aim to objectify spelling correction on Indonesian text documents, to overcome non-word error. This system helps

* Corresponding author: viny@untar.ac.id

the user to overcome document text writing errors, input on this system is a text document and its output is new document text which error of writing have been corrected.

FSA method is used to determine which letter caused error in a word. Levenshtein distance method is used to calculate the difference between the word error and the word suggestion. The word suggestion sequence is determined by the probability of N-gram.

2 Literature review

In this case, the Finite State Automata, Levenshtein distance and N-gram methods are used to create application spelling correction for document text.

2.1 Pre-processing

Pre-processing is the initial stage in processing input data before entering the main stage process of spelling correction for Indonesian text documents. Pre-processing consists of several stages. The pre-processing stage is done case folding, eliminating numbers, punctuation and characters other than the alphabet letter, tokenization.

The pre-processing step are explained below:

(i) Case folding

Case folding is the stage that changes all the letters in the document into lowercase. Only the letters 'a' to 'z' are accepted. Case folding is done for inputs, because the input can be capitalized letter or non capitalized letter. For example from the input "i just Want to Eat ", we'll get output "i just want to eat ".

(ii) Eliminating numbers, punctuation and characters other than the alphabet

Eliminating numbers, punctuation and characters other than the alphabet is done because the characters are considered as delimiters and have no effect on text processing. There are exceptions to the eliminating punctuation because it will affect the process of building N-grams, the examples is ". (dots) "and", (comma) ".

(iii) Tokenization

Tokenization is commonly understood as "splitting text into words." using white space characters as delimiters and isolate punctuation symbols when necessary [1]. For example from input text "i just want to eat ", we can get tokens "i", "just", "want", "to", "eat ".

2.2 Finite state automata (FSA)

Finite State Automata (FSA) is a mathematical model that can accept inputs and outputs with two values that are accepted and rejected. The FSA has a limited number of states and can move from one state to another by input and transition functions. The FSA has no storage or memory, so it can only remember the current state [2].

There are two types of FSA, the first is Deterministic Finite State Automata (DFA) expressed by five tuples:

$M = (Q, \Sigma, \delta, S, F)$

Q = Finite set of states

Σ = Finite set of input symbols called the alphabet

δ = Transition function $\delta : Q \times \Sigma$

S = Initial or start state, $S \in Q$

F = Final state, $F \subseteq Q$

The second is the Nondeterministic Finite State Automata (NFA) which differs from the Deterministic Finite State Automata (DFA) only in the transition function $Q \times (\Sigma \cup \{\varepsilon\})$.

That means, for each state there may be more than one transition, and each may lead to a different state. Finite State Automata is a good data structure for representing natural language dictionaries. FSA is used to represent dictionaries and word errors to facilitate Levenshtein distance calculations [3].

2.3 Levenshtein distance

Levenshtein distance, could also be referred to as edit distance, is a measurement (metric) by calculating number of difference in the two strings. The Levenshtein distance from two strings is the minimum number of point mutation required to replace a string with another string. Point mutations consist of:

(i) Substitutions: substitutions is an operation to exchange a character with another character. For example the author writes the string "eat" become "eay", in this case the character "t" is replaced with the character "y".
(ii) Insertions: insertions is the addition of characters into a string. For example the string "therfor" becomes "therefore" with an addition of the character "e" at the end of the string. The addition of characters is not restricted at the end of a word, but can be added in the beginning or middle of the string.
(iii) Deletions: deletions is deleting the character of a string. For example the string "womanm" become "woman", in this operation the character "m" is deleted [4].

Distance is the number of changes needed to convert a string into another string. The following equation or algorithm used to calculate the Levenshtein distance between two words $a = a_1....a_n$ and $b = b_1....b_m$ are:

$$d_{i0} = \Sigma_{k=1}^{i} w_{del}(b_k), \quad \text{for } 1 \leq i \leq m \tag{1}$$

$$d_{0j} = \Sigma_{k=1}^{j} w_{ins}(a_k), \quad \text{for } 1 \leq j \leq m \tag{2}$$

$$d_{ij} = \begin{cases} d_{i-1,j-1} & \text{for } 1\, a_j = b_j \\ \min \begin{cases} d_{i-1,j} + w_{del}(b_k) \\ d_{i-1,j} + w_{ins}(a_j) \\ d_{i-1,j-1} + w_{sub}(a_j, b_j) \end{cases} & \text{for } 1 \leq i \leq m, 1 \leq j \leq n \quad \text{for } a_j \neq b_j \end{cases} \tag{3}$$

Where : a = Words represented as rows
b = Words represented as columns
i = Letter index of word a
j = Letter index of word b
n = Letter length of the word a
m = Letter length of the word a
w = The value of deletions, insertions, or substitutions (w = 1)

This algorithm start from the top left corner of a two-dimensional array that has filled in a number of initial sring characters and target strings with cost. The cost at the lower right end becomes the levenshtein distance value, that describes the number of differences between the two strings.

2.4 N-gram

N-gram is a probabilistic language model to predict the next item in sequence. The N-gram model is widely used in probability, communication theory, linguistic computing (e.g., statistical natural language processing), biological computing (e.g., biological sequence analysis), and data compression. There are two benefits of the N-gram model that is simple and scalability [5].

The number of N-grams in a sentence can be calculated using the following equations:

$$\text{N-gram}_k = X - (N - 1) \tag{4}$$

Where: X = Number of words in a sentence k
N = Number of N-grams

The easiest way to calculate the probability is with Maximum Likelihood Estimation (MLE), by taking the number of corpus and dividing to produce interval [0,1]. For example, to calculate the probability of bigram the word y against x is by calculating amount number of bigrams c (xy) of the corpus and dividing by the number of corpus x. Here is the equation used to calculate the probability bigram:

$$P\langle W_n \mid W_{n-1}\rangle = \frac{c(W_1 W_n)}{c(W_{n-1})} \tag{5}$$

Where: P = N-gram probabilities
w = Word
n = Index
c = Word frequency

For the general case of MLE N-gram parameter estimation :

$$P\langle W_n \middle| W_{n-N+1}^{n-1}\rangle = \frac{c\left(W_{n-N+1}^{n-1} \big/ W_n\right)}{\left(W_{n-N+1}^{n-1}\right)} \tag{6}$$

The probability of N-gram can be zero, due to the limitations of the corpus. Therefore modification of Maximum Likelihood Estimation (MLE) is required, the modification is called smoothing.

2.5 Add-one smoothing

There are many smoothing techniques for Maximum Likelihood Estimation (MLE) that can be done from the simplest (add-one smoothing) to the sophisticated smoothing techniques, such as Good-Turing discounting or back-off models. Some of these smoothing methods work by determining a distribution value of N-grams and using Bayesian inference to calculate the probability of N-grams produced. However, more sophisticated smoothing methods usually does not use the method but through independent considerations instead [6].

Spelling correction for document text using add-one smoothing, because add-one smoothing is the simplest method to implement. Add-one smoothing is a very simple smoothing algorithm, which adds a value of one at all frequencies and normalizes the denominator because of this addition. The unigram probability equation is as follows :

$$p(W_i) = \frac{c_i}{N} \tag{7}$$

Where c_i is the number of words i and N is the total number of words. The unigram probability equation after smoothing using the add one method is as follows :

$$P_{addone}(W_i) = \frac{c_i + 1}{N + V} \tag{8}$$

Where V is the number of words (unique). Bigram probability equation after smoothing :

$$P_{addone}\langle W_n \mid W_{n-1} \rangle = \frac{c(W_1 W_n) + 1}{c(W_{n-1}) + V} \tag{9}$$

2.6 Perplexity

The correct way to evaluate the performance of a language model N-gram is to embed it in an application. There are some methods to evaluate this performance. One of these methods is in vivo evaluation. But this method is very wasteful in time which may take hours or even days. Perplexity (PP) is the most common evaluation metric for N-gram language models.

The intuition of the perplexity depends on two probabilistic models. The better model is the one that has tighter fit to the test data also predict better details on the test data. A better prediction depends on the probability. If the probability of test data is high the model is good. If the probability of the word sequence is high, then the perplexity is then low. Minimizing the perplexity is equal to maximizing the probability [7].

The mathematical concept of the perplexity of language model on a test set is function of probability normalized by the number of words. The perplexity of a test set W=w1w2…wN is in Equation 12:

$$pp(\mathrm{W}) = p(w_1 w_2 \ldots\ldots w_N)^{-\frac{1}{N}} \tag{10}$$

$$pp(\mathrm{W}) = \sqrt[N]{\frac{1}{p(w_1 w_2 \ldots\ldots w_N)}} \tag{11}$$

$$pp(\mathrm{W}) = \sqrt[N]{\Pi_{i=1}^{N} \frac{1}{p(w_1 w_2 \ldots\ldots w_N)}} \tag{12}$$

Where: W = Test set (sentence)
N = Number of words in W
P = w probabilities
i = Indeks

2.7 Correction hit rate and false positive rate

Correction hit rate, it is the ratio between the number of typos corrected and the total number of typos [8].

$$\text{Correction hit rate} = \frac{\Sigma \text{typos corrected}}{\Sigma \text{typos}} \times 100\% \quad (13)$$

The higher the percentage of correction hit rate, the higher the accuracy of spelling correction is done. In addition to looking for a correction hit rate that indicates the accuracy of the designed spelling correctio system, it also determines the false positive rate. False positive rate, it is the ratio between the number of false positives (i.e., correct words that are wrongly detected as typos) the total number of correct words in the tested sentences. The lower, the better [9].

$$\text{False positive rate} = \frac{\Sigma \text{false positive}}{\Sigma \text{correct words}} \times 100\% \quad (14)$$

3 Planning and implementation

3.1 System plan

The designed system is a web-based spelling correction for text documents. The system is designed to allow users to manually and automatically perform the correction. Users can input text documents in the spelling correction system, then the system will display the contents of the document and mark the location of the error word with red color.

Manual correction can be done by clicking on a word that has a mark and the system will give word suggestions for the error word, where the user can choose the word suggestion that he/she consider as the correct word. Automatic correction can be done only by clicking a button, then manual or automatic correction will result in the output of a text document whose error has been corrected.

Spelling correction system is designed using System Development Life Cycle (SDLC). Systems development methods are methods, procedures, job concepts, rules that will be used as guidelines for how and what to do during this development. Method is a systematic way to do things. A step-by-step list of instructions for solving any instance of the problem is known as algorithm [10].

3.1.1 Initiation

Initiation is the initial planning stage for the designed system. At the stage of the initiation described the data needed in the design of spelling correction for text documents system .

There are two data that must be prepared first before step into the design of spelling correction system text documents, the first is the dictionary and the second is news articles. The data dictionary (Kamus Besar Bahasa Indonesia or KBBI) obtained manually with pdf form. Specification of data dictionary used can be seen in Table 1.

Table 1. Dictionary data specification.

Description	Specification
Source	http://jurnal-oldi.or.id/public/kbbi.pdf
Edition	Fourth (2008)
Document size	8.71 MB
Number of pages	1 490
Word count	426 774

We used news articles as training data that is consist of 5 000 Indonesian. News articles obtained from online news www.kompas.com. The news articles consist of various categories, the categories are regional, megapolitan, national, entertainment, soccer, economics, international, automotive, travel, property, technology, health, female, science and education.

3.1.2 Analyzing system

This section discusses the specifications or devices that will be used in the design of this system, the device is hardware and software. Hardware specifications (laptop) used in this design are :

1. Model : Acer Aspire E5-473G
2. Processor : Intel i5 7200U 2.5 GHz
3. Memory : RAM 8GB
4. Hard Disk : 1 TB
5. Graphics Card : NVIDIA GeFOrce 940MX 2GB

The software specifications used in this design are:

1. Operating System : Windows 10
2. Web Browser : Google Chrome
3. Text Editor : Padre and dreamweaver
4. Programming Languages: Perl and PHP

3.1.3 System design

The next step after analyzing system is system design. Design stage is a system workflow designed. This stage is divided into several sections. They consist of process and data flow design and application program interface design.

3.1.3.1 Design process

The design process describe the process of application program communicating with the System and how the system runs. The design of the process and the flow of data in the design is explained with flowchart and state transition diagram. Flowchart spelling correction system designed can be seen in Figure 1.

The state transition diagram illustrates how the system works through state. The state transition diagram illustrates the actions performed due to a particular event. Figure 2 shows the state transition diagram of the designed spelling correction system.

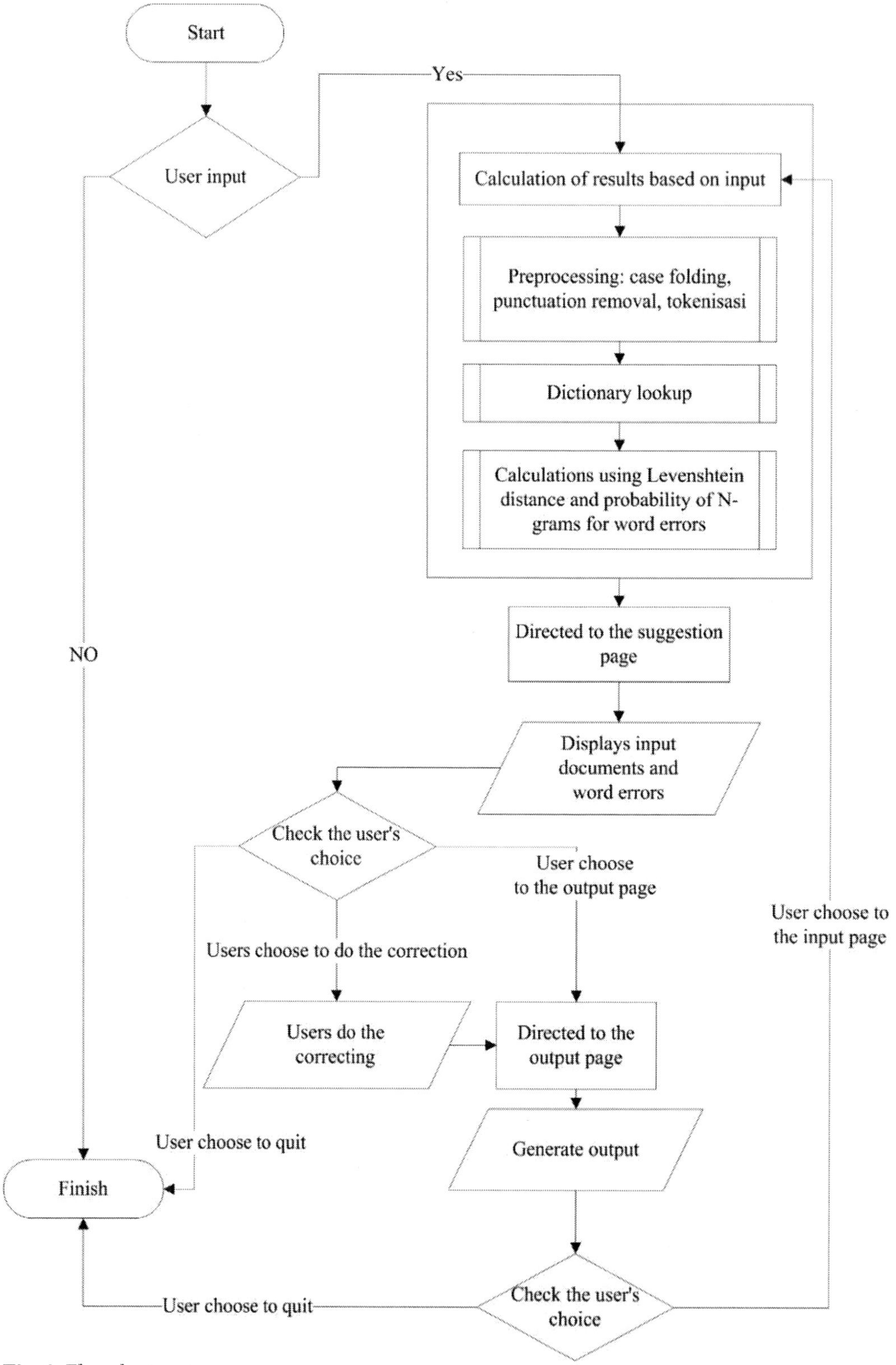

Fig. 1. Flowchart system.

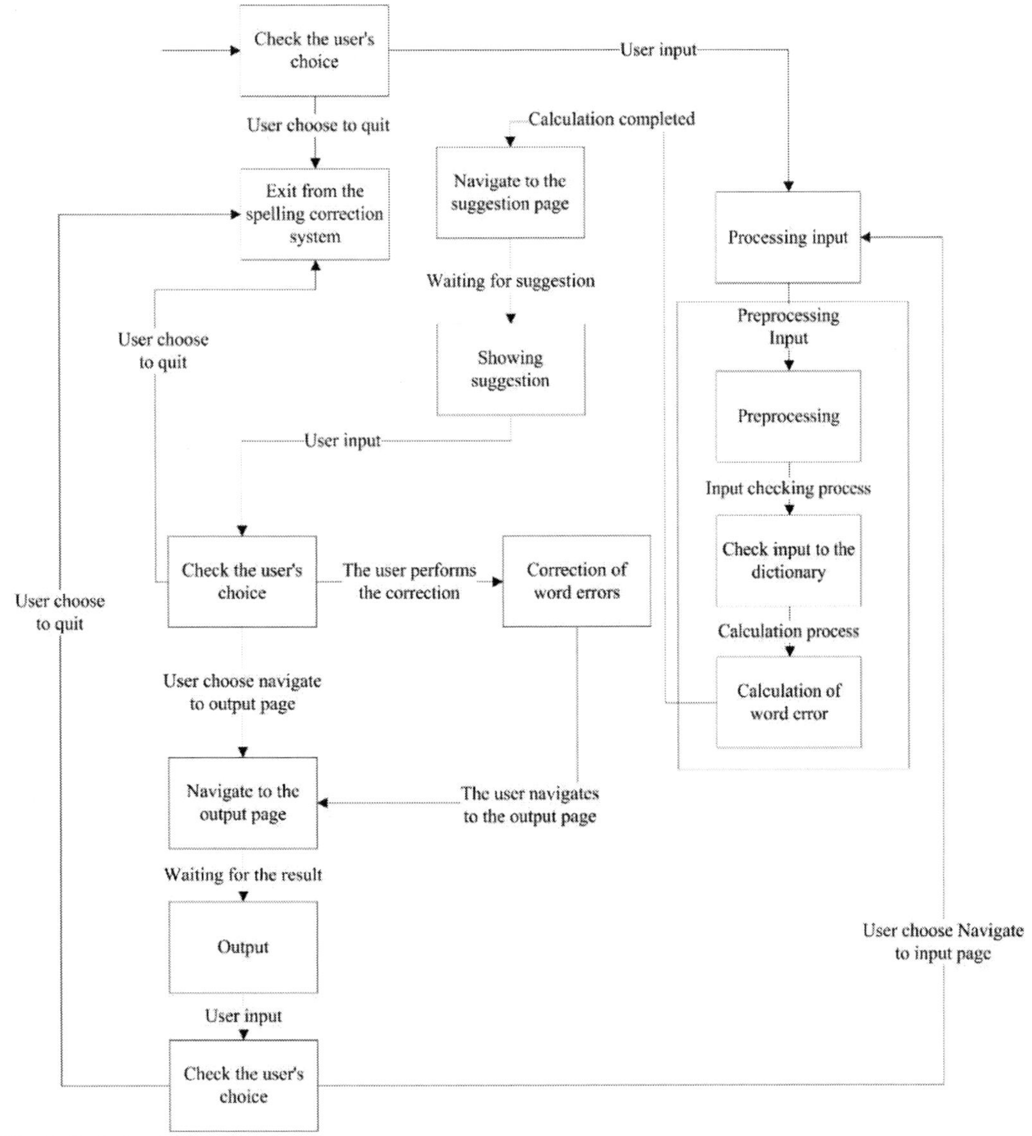

Fig. 2. State transition diagram.

3.1.3.2 Dialog design

In this section described what dialogues exist in the designed system. There are three dialogues on the designed system, the first is the front page dialogue, the second is the suggestion page dialogue, and the last is the output dialogue. More details can be seen in Figure 3 which shows the hierarchy of the designed spelling correction system.

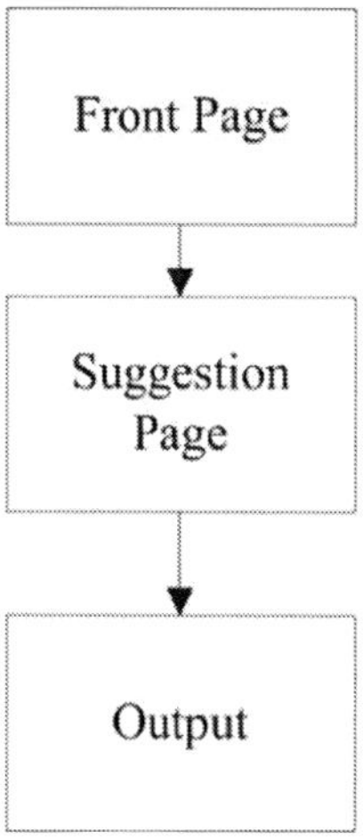

Fig. 3. Hierarchy diagram program.

3.1.3.3 Interface design

Interface Design is a media that connects users and systems which designed to communicate. In this spelling correction system there are four modules:

(i). Front Page Module
This module is the main module of the web-service. User can input the text document which he/she want to check in this module.

(ii). Suggestion Page Module
This module displays the contents of the input document which already marked for word errors. User can perform both automatic or manual correction.

(iii). Manual Output Module
This module displays the correction results manually which could be downloaded by the user.

(iv). Manual Automatic Module
This module displays the correction results automatically which could be downloaded by the user.

3.1.3.4 Implementation system

The next stage is the system implementation. System implementation is a software adjustment with the system design that has been made before. The hardware and software of the server is required in the system implementation. Server acts as a mediator during the process of data transfer using internet connection. Implementation of the system will use a hosting server.

(iv) Result and discussion

4.1 Testing method

Testing process are performed on the website, the method used, and the results of the correction. The tests are performed by the developer to determine how well the method is used in the system, and the output results.

4.1.1 Website testing

Website testing are done on every module on the website. Testing performed for each component contained in the module to test whether it is running properly or not. The tests include the following modules:

4.1.1.1 Front page module

In the middle of the front page there is a "Pilih File" button to select a text document and next to the "Pilih File" button there is a textbox that displays the name of the text document. At the bottom of "Pilih File" there is "UPLOAD" button to upload the file.

Fig. 4. Front page module.

4.1.1.2 Suggestion page module

There is a text area that displays the contents of a text document that has been uploaded by the user where the error word will be highlighted in red. If a highlighted word is clicked, it will create a suggestion word pop-up. The user then choose the word that is considered correct from the pop-up. When the word suggestion is selected, the highlighted word will be replaced with the suggested word that has been selected. Below the text area is a "KOREKSI MANUAL" button to navigate user to the manual output page module. Below the "KOREKSI MANUAL" button is the "KOREKSI OTOMATIS" button to navigate user to the automatic output page module.

Fig. 5. Suggestion page module.

4.1.1.3 Manual output page module

The manual output page module contains the results of the manually performed correction. The result are displayed inside the text area, where the word error with a red highlight in the previous module will turn green as a mark that the word has been corrected. In this module, there is a "DOWNLOAD" button to download the result of manual correction into .txt file. After the "DOWNLOAD" button is clicked, it will create a thank you pop-up with an "OK" button to return to the front page module.

Fig. 6. Manual output page module.

4.1.1.4 Automatic output page module

The automatic output page module contains the results of the automatic correction. The results are displayed inside the text area. The highlight will turn into green if the error word has been successfully corrected, otherwise it will remains red. Below the text area there are "<" and ">" buttons. The ">" button is used to navigate to next corrected document's page and the "<" button is used to navigate to previous corrected document's page Below the "<" and ">" buttons is a "DOWNLOAD" button to download the results of automatic correction into .txt file. After the "DOWNLOAD" button is clicked, it will create a thank you pop-up with an "OK" button to return to the front page module.

Fig. 7. Automatic output page module.

All functions in the modules have been working properly.

4.2 Perplexity testing

The testing result of N-grams method generated from training documents can be seen on Table 2. From the table, we can conclude that the smallest perplexity value is unigram (1.14 823 655), bigram (1.165 909), and trigram (1.167 692).

Table 2. Perplexity evaluation results.

N-Gram	Perplexity
Unigram	1.14 823 655
Bigram	1.165 909
Trigram	1.167 692

4.3 Correction hit rate and false position rate testing

At this stage the system will be tested against the results of the spelling correction by unigram, bigram and trigrams. The document used for testing is one of Indonesian text document from training document, which has been manipulated in such a way as to have a non-real word error.

The test was conducted on 15 documents, with different size. The highest correction hit rate on bigram is 75.36 %, trigram is 74.46 % and unigram is 64.59 %. While the highest total hit correction hit by bigram and trigram is 71.20 %. The false positive rate on unigram, bigram, and trigram has the same percentage of 4.43 %. The fastest processing time for spelling correction is unigram with 01:20.73 min, after that is bigram with 01:21.23 min, then trigram with 01:32.80 min.

There is also a test on correction hit rate and false positive rate for adjoined or sequenced word consist of two or three error words. The spelling correction results then compared between unigram, bigram and trigram. The highest corrected hit rate is bigram with 75 %, followed by unigram with 73.68 % and trigram with 69.73 %. From here, we can conclude that bigram is better than unigram and trigram for either adjoined or non-adjoined error words.

After that, there was a test on the modificated results in order to improve the correction hit rate on the designed spelling correction system. From the previous tests showed that bigram is the better N-gram method than unigram or trigram, therefore the tests and modifications are made to bigram. The comparison of results between correction hit rate and false positive rate correction spelling Bigram with FSA, without FSA, and modificated results can be seen in Table 3.

Table 3. Comparison of bigram test results with FSA, without FSA, and modifications.

Testing Category	With FSA	Without FSA	Modifications
Total documents	15	15	15
Total size document	255 kb	255 kb	255 kb
Total words	34 919	34 919	34 919
Total word error	316	316	316
Total words corrected correctly	225	276	270
Total words corrected wrongly	91	40	46
Total false Positive	1 436	1 436	1 436
Total correction Hit rate	71.20 %	87.34 %	85.44 %
Average correction hit rate	75.63 %	83.75 %	85.80 %
Total false positive rate	4.15 %	4.15 %	4.15 %
Average false positive rate	4.43 %	4.43 %	4.43 %
Total time spelling correction process	20:18.48 min	07:31:46.87 h	27:42.00 min
Average time of spelling correction process	01:21.23 min	30:07.12 min	01:50.80 min

5 Conclusions

Based on the test results, it can be concluded as follows :

- Text document spelling correction can resolve non-word error, using FSA and Levenstein distance methods.

- Bigram has greater correction hit rate than unigram and trigram, with the adjoining word error that is 75 %. While the non adjoining word error, bigram and trigram have the same correction hit rate that is 71.20 %.
- FSA method can be used to shorten the spelling correction processing time.
- The modification results show an increase in correction hit rate from 71.20 % to 85.80 %, but the average processing time becomes longer by 29.57 s.

References

1. L. Michelbacher. *Multi-word tokenization for natural language processing*. [PhD dissertation]. University of Stugartt, Stugartt, Germany (2013). pp. 27–28. https://d-nb.info/1046313010/34
2. Global Komputer. *Finite automata* [Online] from http://www.globalkomputer.com/Bahasan/Teori-Bahasa-dan-Otomata/Topik/Finite-Automata.html (2006). [Accessed on 10 January 2017]. [in Bahasa Indonesia]
3. J. Daciuk, D. Weiss. *Theoretical Computer Science,* **450**,7:10–21 (2012). https://www.sciencedirect.com/science/article/pii/S0304397512003787
4. N.M.M. Adriyani. *JELIKU,* **1**,1 (2012). https://ojs.unud.ac.id/index.php/JLK/article/view/2800
5. W. Zhang. *Comparing the effect of smoothing and n-gram order: Finding the best way to combine the smoothing and order of n-gram*. [PhD dissertation]. Florida Institute of Technology, Melbourne, Florida, pp. 1–6 (2015). https://pdfs.semanticscholar.org/ac6b/aabe681737c3baecf7315b629c7ab4c23577.pdf
6. D., Jurafsky, J.H. Martin. *Speech and language processing volume 3* [Online] from http://www.cs.colorado.edu/~martin/SLP/Updates/1.pdf (2014) [Accessed on 18 December 2016]
7. T.M. Allam, H. Abdelkader, E. Sallam. *IAJeT,* **4**, 2:94–102 (2015). http://www.iajet.org/iajet_files/vol.4/no.2/5-58594_formatted.pdf
8. D. Fossati, B. Di Eugenio. A mixed trigrams approach for context sensitive spell checking. In: *Computational linguistics and intelligent text processing*. A. Gelbukh. (Eds). CICLing 2007. Lecture Notes in Computer Science. Volume 4394. Heidelberg: Springer. pp. 623–633. https://link.springer.com/chapter/10.1007/978-3-540-70939-8_55
9. F. Kurniawan. *Implementasi algoritme fonetik untuk koreksi ejaan bahasa indonesia* [Implementation of phonetic algorithms for Indonesian spelling corrections] [Online] from http://studylibid.com/doc/94649/implementasi-algoritme-fonetik-untuk-koreksi-ejaan (2010). [Accessed on 14 January 2017]. [in Bahasa Indonesia]
10. B. Miller, D. Ranum. *Problem Solving with Algorithms and Data Structures*. [Online] from https://www.cs.auckland.ac.nz/courses/compsci105s1c/resources/ProblemSolvingwithAlgorithmsandDataStructures.pdf (2013). [Accessed on 25 January 2017].

MATEC Web of Conferences **164**, 01048 (2018) https://doi.org/10.1051/matecconf/201816401048
ICESTI 2017

Implementation of Winnowing Algorithm Based K-Gram to Identify Plagiarism on File Text-Based Document

Yanuar Nurdiansyah[1*], *Fiqih* Nur Muharrom[1] ,and *Firdaus*[2]
[1]Sistem Informasi, Program Studi Sistem Informasi, Universitas Jember (UNEJ), Jl. Kalimantan 37, Jember 68121, Indonesia
[2]Advances Informatics School, Universiti Teknologi Malaysia, Level 5, Menara Razak, Jalan Sultan Yahya Petra, 54100 Kuala Lumpur, Malaysia

Abstract. Plagiarism occurs when the students have tasks and pursued by the deadline. Plagiarism is considered as the fastest way to accomplish the tasks. This reason makes the author tried to build a plagiarism detection system with Winnowing algorithm as document similarity search algorithm. The documents that being tested are Indonesian journals with extension .doc, .docx, and/or .txt. Similarity calculation process through two stages, the first is the process of making a document fingerprint using Winnowing algorithm and the second is using Jaccard coefficient similarity. In order to develop this system, the author used iterative waterfall model approach. The main objective of this project is to determine the level of plagiarism. It is expected to prevent plagiarism either intentionally or unintentionally before our journal published by displaying the percentage of similarity in the journals that we make.

Key words: Jaccard's coefficient, plagiarism, Winnowing algorithm

1 Introduction

The rapid technology improvement does give not only positive effect on daily life but also gives negative influences that cannot be avoided. In this era, information is easy to get and influence people. One of the negative impacts is the great number of plagiarism [1]. Plagiarism often occurs when the students have tasks and pursued by the deadline. The students consider that conducting plagiarism is the fastest way to accomplish the assignment [2].

Students regard that doing plagiarism is the instant way to accomplish their assignments [3]. Those factors influence the result of the evaluation. This issue also makes an obstacle for teachers in detecting plagiarism regarding the numerous task file and the scientific work. One of the functions of technology is that it can be used as an alternative to identifying plagiarism regarding that has been so many scientific works published in electronic. Thus the identifying process becomes much easier.

[*] Corresponding author: yanuar_pssi@unej.ac.id

The technology is used, which means the author uses the computer application to do the calculation of text- document similarity [4]. The algorithm selection on text-document similarity search is very affecting [5]. A mistake in algorithm selection may decrease the accuracy of document similarity calculation [6]. Winnowing algorithm is a method of word similarity search in a document by comparing the fingerprint on the document [7], the algorithm input is the text document which is processed and result in output in the form of hash value. That hash value is then called as the fingerprint. This is the fingerprint which is used to compare the similarity of each document.

There are some basic needs that are used by winnowing algorithm in detecting the document similarity. The basic needs which have to be accomplished by detection algorithm are [8, 9]:

i) Whitespace insensitivity, it is a word search which is not influenced by space, punctuation, type of letter (capital or normal), etc.
ii) Noise suppression, the function is to avoid the finding of short word and not the common word such as 'the'
iii) Position independence, it is a similarity finding that does not have to depend on the word position, so words with different order still can be recognized if there is a similarity. Generally, the work principles of the algorithm in the document-similarity detection are (in a few steps):
    i) Both the target text and the original text are assumed as string s with the length t
    ii) Conducting the cleaning of punctuation, space, etc. which refer to the basic needs of detection algorithm
    iii) Dividing the document to be k- gram, that is as parameter selected by the user. K-Gram is the sub-string that is alongside with the length of character k.
    iv) Finding Hash Value from each k-gram
    v) Selecting some hash result to be the fingerprint document.

The difference of Winnowing Algorithm and another algorithm of similarity detector is in the selection process of its fingerprint. The result of hash value calculation is divided into window w in which the smallest value will be taken from each window to be the document fingerprint.

2 Research method

This research used the designing method and system development method. To do that method, we use software for life cycle development by adopting the iterative waterfall model.

2.1 System requirements analysis

The analysis system is needed at the early stage in designing and developing the system to determine the needs of plagiarism detection system that will build. On this stage, the researcher conducted literature study that learnt the retrieval information system and fingerprint document method using winnowing algorithm to identify the similarity of text document through all sorts of media, those are the internet, journals and books refer to plagiarism and text processing to get the view of winnowing algorithm that is going to be used on the system as the algorithm to detect the document similarity and what data needed to build that system.

a) Winnowing Algorithm as Algorithm of document similarity search

The selected result of winnowing algorithm as the algorithm of document similarity search was based on the accuracy stage and the time speed of the process by referring to the previous research that is written in the bibliography. The stage of winnowing algorithm process that is implemented in the system is described in Figure 1 below.

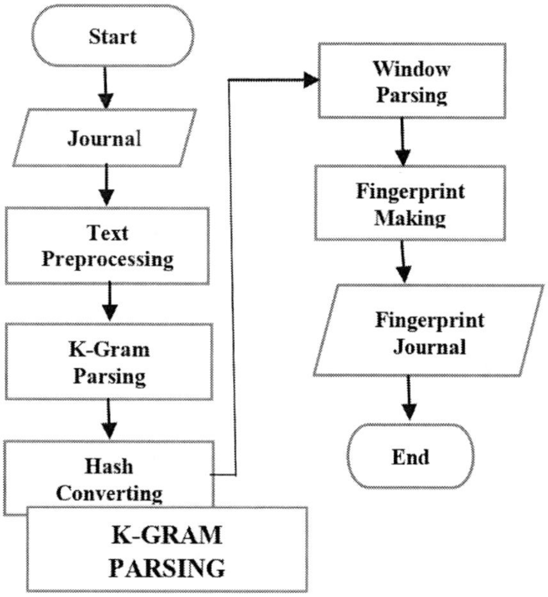

Fig. 1. Stage of the fingerprint makes using winnowing algorithm.

b) Data needed by system

The data used to build the system of plagiarism detection is Journal Data. The journal data of the system will be renewed by both administration and student as a user non-administrator. However, the student can only upload a journal which has been approved by the administrator. If the journal is already approved, it can be saved in the database and used as the reference by other students for next verification in order to avoid the damage of the journal data in the database. Database for the journal is divided into two table:

i) Table of field study

It is a table that saves the data of field study category which functions to divide the journal based on each category of its field study.

ii) Table of Journal

Table of journal is a table that saves journal data both specifically about the journal or the fingerprints as the result of processing using winnowing algorithm.

2.2 System design

Stage of the system designing which is going to build uses UNIFIED Modeling Language (UML) that supports the model concept of programming based on Object-Oriented Programming (OOP) as will be applied to program code writing – stage. This stage will result in modeling documentation; those are Business Process, Use Case Diagram, Use Case Scenario, Sequence Diagram, Activity Diagram, Class Diagram, and Entity Relationship Diagram (ERD).

2.3 Implementation

Implementation stage is the conversion process of the system design into the program code. A system that is going to be built is written by language program of Page Hypertext Pre-Processor (PHP) using CodeIgniter framework that has applied Object Oriented Programming concept (OOP). This system also uses local server and database to save the data that is needed anytime and can be re-accessed. The local server uses XAMPP application which supports apache to build an application based on web and database that was used MySql (PhpMyadmin).

2.3 Testing

After the implementation process, the next stage is system testing. This research conducted two methods of system testing; those are white box testing and black box testing. White Box Testing is testing on the module of program coding to guarantee that the program code is clear from syntax or logical error. Black Box Testing is a testing that emphasizes on system functionality testing in order to get the expectation result.

3 The design and the planning

The design and the planning of the plagiarism detection systems using winnowing algorithm as the algorithm on similarity document search explained the functional need and also non-functional need, use case diagram, and Entity Relationship Diagram (ERD).

1. The functional need-system is a need that has to be owned by the system. The functional need- system of the plagiarism detection used winnowing algorithm as below:
i) The system which used login feature to authenticate the access right of its user.
ii) The system can save the user's data on user register feature.
iii) The system can update the user's data.
iv) The system can show the user's data in the database.
v) The system can manage the journal data (insert, update, delete).
vi) The system can show the journal data of the database.
vii)The system can show the log activity of the user.
viii) The system is available in calculating the similarity of the journal document that is uploaded to the system.
ix) The system is available to show the calculation result of the journal document similarity which is uploaded.

2. The Non- Functional need is the addition need to complete the system. The non – functional needs are:
i) System based on web.
ii) System that uses CodeIgniter framework.

3. Entity Relationship Diagram is a data structure data and the relation of the data. The object in ERD is usually described in an entity which has attributes that relate to other entities. The process of system making in this research used nine entities. Those entities have been normalized to collect the data in the database that is related using one to many relations. Entity relationship diagram of plagiarism detector can be seen in Figure 2 and Figure 3 below.

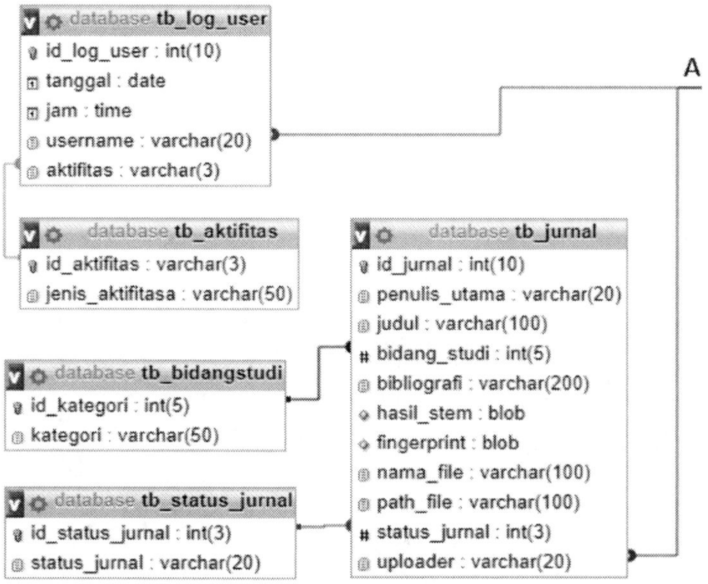

Fig. 2. Entity relationship diagram.

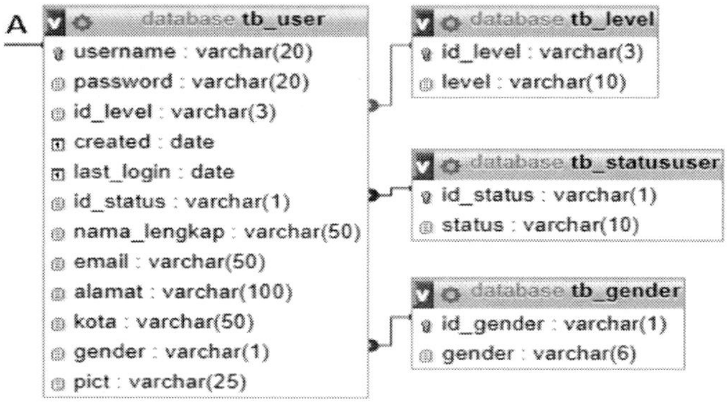

Fig. 3. Entity relationship diagram.

4 Discussion

Winnowing algorithm implementation in this system is also feature of new journal data that can be accessed by the user administration and on the feature that checks the journal plagued in which can be accessed by user students. Those two features have the fingerprint making process that uses winnowing algorithm. Every word of the journal file is uploaded first to through the filtering process, that is the cleaning process of punctuation, space, etc. by referring to the basic need of algorithm detector. In this research, the writer added the stemming process that functions to change every word in the journal to be a basic word.

4.1 Stemming and filtering

Stemming is the part of retrieval (IR) information process; it changes the word into its basic word before doing the indexing process [10]. The stemming of Indonesian is different from the stemming of English. The stemming process of Indonesian is more complicated because Indonesian has prefixes, infixes, suffixes, and combination between confix.

The stemming and filtering process of the system are included in stemmer and filtering function method. Before processing the file using those methods, the file has to be processed into document extraction process. This stage is conducted in order to get the content of the document file. The process of content extraction is included into get_content() method that can be seen in Figure 4.

Fig. 4. Get_content() method.

Get_content() method needs a parameter in the form of file extension and saved file location. Furthermore, the file extension will be checked. If the file extension accomplishes the system certainty, it will be processed into extraction of the document file content. The output of this process is string in document file content which is placed in variable '$isi_file'.

The next process is stemming process and filtering process which is implemented into stemmer and filtering function method. Those methods can be seen on Figure 5 and Figure 6 below

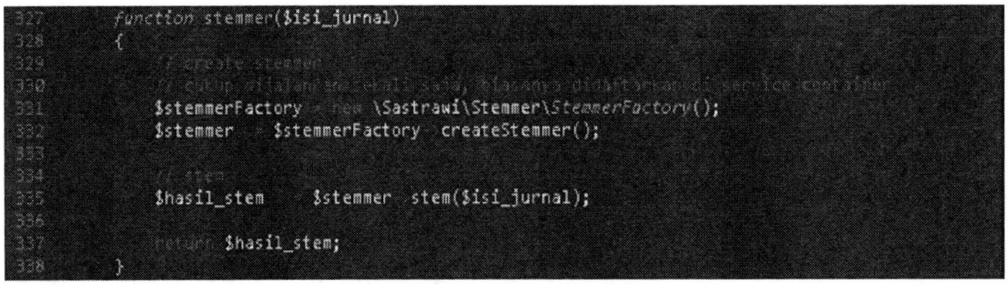

Fig. 5. Stemmer method.

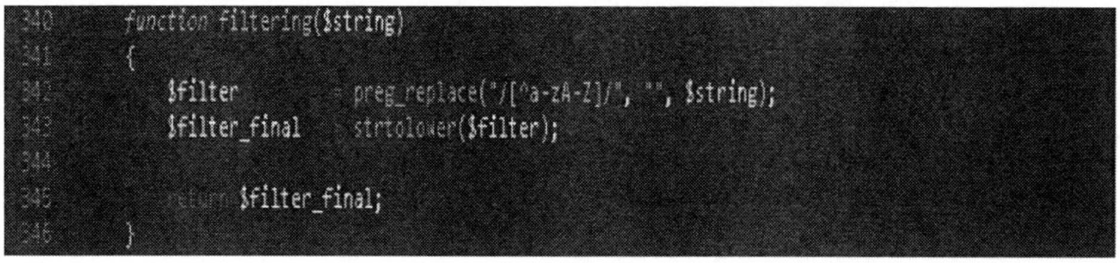

Fig. 6. Filtering method.

The stemming process on the system needs parameter input as string that is collected from the extraction process of document file content. The result of stemming process is placed in variable $hasil_stem. While the filtering process cleans the sentences from punctuation, space, the conversion of capital letters, and the number elimination.

4.2 Process of K-Gram forming

K-Gram forming is a process that converts string into sub–string gram. K-Gram is a substring series that is along with length k.

The process of gram forming on the system is included in the function method of parsing_gram. Gram forming process needs two parameters. Those parameters are string of the stemming process and the filtering process and also value k. Value k functions to check whether the result of every gram is suitable with value k that has been determined. The parsing_gram method can be seen on Figure 7.

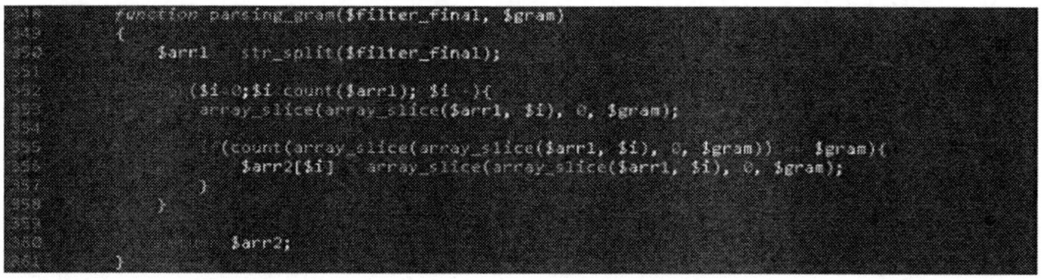

Fig. 7. Parsing_gram method.

Those are the result gram forming process showed by the system to ensure that the gram forming is suitable with the concept of winnowing algorithm. The appearance of gram forming on the comparison sentence file that has been processed on stemming can be seen on Figure 8 below.

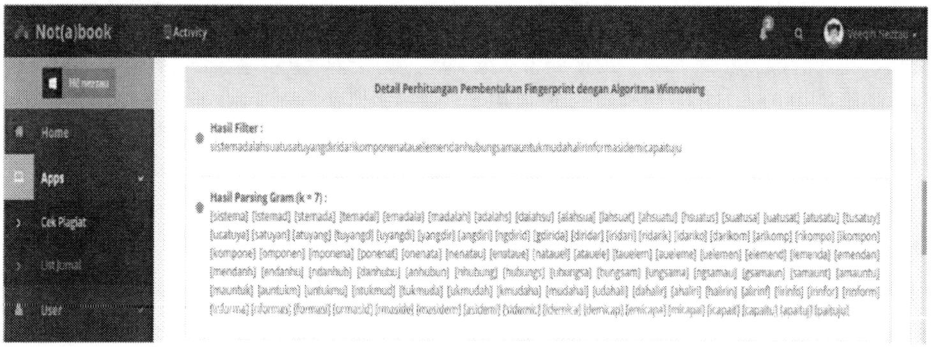

Fig. 8. The result appearance of gram forming on the system.

4.2 The conversion process of Hash value

Firstly, every character in gram is converted into value ASCII. It is done before doing the calculation of rolling hash value. Hash formulation is defined as Equation 1.

$$H_{cl..ck} = c1 \times b^{(k-1)} + c2 \times b^{(k-2)} + \ldots + c(k-1) \times b + c^{k} \quad (1)$$

Explanation:
c: value ASCII character
b: basis of primes
k: value k-gram/many characters on

Rolling Hash Gram has an advantage to search the hash $H_{(c2...ck+1)}$ by using the earned value on hash $H_{c1...ck}$ function hash $H_{(c2...ck+1}$ can be done by Equation 2.

$$H_{(c2..ck+1)} = \left(H_{(c1..ck)} - c1 \times b^{(k-1)}\right) \times b + c_{(k+1)} \quad (2)$$

The forming process of the window on the system is included into the parsing_window function. Window process needs two parameters. Those are each conversion of hash value and value w. The value w functions to check whether the window forming result is suitable with value w that has been determined.

The conversion process uses the looping process for each conversion in each gram into hash value. Every character in each gran is converted into ASCII value with the help of function that has been given by language program php 'ord function'. Next, hash value is put into the array and next it is showed by the system.

4.4. The forming process of *Window w*

Forming window is a conversion process of hash value into windows. The window forming process of the system is included into parsing_window function method. Window forming method needs two parameters. First, it is the result of hash value and value w conversion. Value w functions to check whether the result of window forming is already suitable with value w that has been determined.

The result of window forming process is showed by the system to ensure the window forming is suitable with the winnowing concept.

4.5. The process of fingerprint selection

Fingerprint selection is the forming fingerprint process. It is conducted by selecting the minimum hash value of each different window that has been made before. If there are similar values in a different window, just choose one of those value to be the fingerprint.

The fingerprint selection process of the system is included into function fingerprint method. The fingerprint selection process needs the parameter of window w forming result. This process uses the looping function to select the minimum value on each window and array_unique function to ensure that there is no similar value on the array as the result of fingerprint selection. The fingerprint method can be seen on Figure 9

```
function fingerprint($parsing_window)
{
    $t = 0;
    while($t < count($parsing_window)){
        $arr5[] = min($parsing_window[$t]);
        $t++;

    }

    $fingerprint = array_unique($arr5);

        return $fingerprint;
    }
}
```

Fig. 9. Fingerprint method.

The result of fingerprint selection process is showed by the system to ensure that the fingerprint selection is suitable with winnowing algorithm system.

4.6. The calculation process of document similarity

The similarity calculation using Jaccard coefficient similarity. Jaccard Coefficient Similarity is similarity measurement standard that compares two sets, P and Q [11]. The general pattern of Jaccard's Coefficient Similarity formulation can be seen in equation 3.

$$Jacc(P,Q) = \frac{P \cap Q}{P \cup Q} \tag{3}$$

Explanation:
Jacc (P, Q) : similarity value
$|P \cap Q|$: the similar fingerprints number of P and Q
$|P \cup Q|$: fingerprint p that does n ot have Q is added by number of fingerprint Q, that does not belong to P is added by the number of similar fingerprint between P and Q.

The similarity calculation process on the system is included into proses_hitung method (process_calculation). System searches the difference of the value in both array using function array_diff and then count the number of array using count function. The result of similarity calculation process can be seen in Figure 10 below.

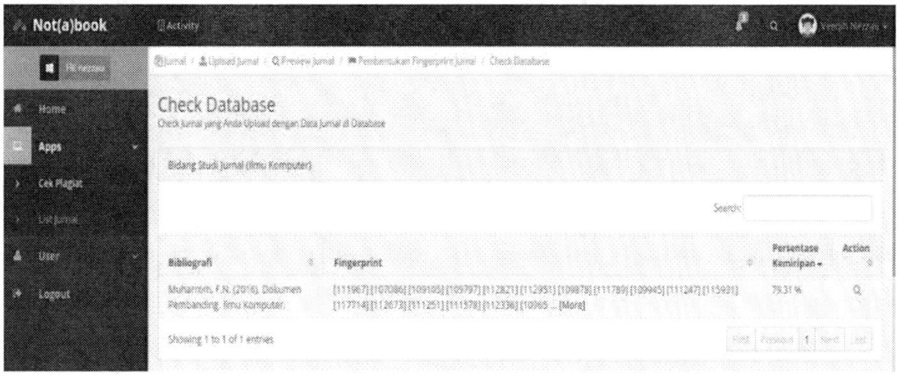

Fig. 10. The program code of similarity calculation.

5 Summary

i) This application is free and can be used for every journal, daily tasks and final task that is written in Bahasa Indonesia as the priority. Users can make their own database that can check plagiarism from every journals, daily tasks and final task that is written before.

ii) Winnowing algorithm as the algorithm fingerprint document and Jaccard coefficient similarity as the similarity measurement standard can be applied in finding the similarity percentage of text document. The journal document as the input process using winnowing algorithm for the document's fingerprint-forming. The fingerprint of each document is calculated using Jaccard coefficient similarity formulation in order to get the similarity percentage. The researcher also added the stemming process to winnowing algorithm in order to get higher accuracy.

iii) Winnowing algorithm error value with stemming process has less error value 1.63 %, whereas Winnowing algorithm without stemming process has error value 0.69 %

Hopefully, the advice below can be used for further research to reach a better result:

a. The addition process of undescriptive word elimination, such as "yang", "dan", "di", "dari", etc. may give a higher accuracy.

b. The journal document can be processed by a more diverse system by adding the document in .pdf extension which has been suitable for the journal writing format (two column).

Determination of gram value an window value uses a more relevant method in order to get higher accuracy.

References

1 Z. Ercegovac, J.V. Richardson Jr.. Academic dishonesty, plagiarism included, in the digital age; a literature review. *College & Research Libraries*, **65**, 4:301–318. https://crl.acrl.org/index.php/crl/article/view/15673/17119

2 C. Liu, C. Chen, J. Han, P.S. Yu. *GPLAG: detection of software plagiarism by program dependence graph analysis*. Proceedings of the 12th ACM SIGKDD International Conference on Knowledge Discovery and Data Mining (Philadelphia, USA, 2006). Proceedings of the 12th ACM SIGKDD International Conference on Knowledge Discovery and Data Mining:872–881. https://dl.acm.org/citation.cfm?id=1150522

3 Republik Indonesia. Peraturan menteri pendidikan nasional No. 17 tahun 2010 ([Online] [National minister of education regulation 2010 no. 17] from http://mahasiswa.ut.ac.id/images/stories/artikel/osmb/Permendiknas_Pencegahan_Plagiat_2010.pdf (2010). [Accessed on 3 April 2017]. [in Bahasa Indonesia]

4 G.V. Dhivyabharathi, S. Kumaresan. *A survey on duplicate record detection in real world data*. 2016 3rd International Conference on Advanced Computing and Communication Systems (ICACCS) (Coimbatore, India, 2016). ICACCS:1–5. http://ieeexplore.ieee.org/document/7586397/

5 P. Shukla, A.K. Somani. *Context-aware duplicate detection in semi-structured data streams*. 2014 IEEE World Congress on Services (Anchorage, USA, 2014). 2014 IEEE World Congress on Services:216–223. http://ieeexplore.ieee.org/document/6903268/

6 C. Rong, Y.N. Silva, C. Li. *Frontiers of Computer Science*, **11**,2:307–319 (2017). https://link.springer.com/article/10.1007/s11704-016-5231-1

7 P. Cornic. *Software plagiarism detection using model-driven software development in Eclipse platform.* [Thesis]. University of Manchester, Manchester (2008), pp. 1-101. http://studentnet.cs.manchester.ac.uk/resources/library/thesis_abstracts/MSc08/Abstracts/CornicPierre-fulltext.pdf

8 S. Scheleimer, D.S. Wilkerson, A. Aiken. (2003). *Winnowing: Local Algorithm for Document Fingerprinting*. Proceedings of the 2003 ACM SIGMOD International Conference (San Diego, California, 2003). Proceedings of the 2003 ACM SIGMOD International Conference on Management of Data:76–85. https://dl.acm.org/citation.cfm?id=872770

9 J. Oetsch, J. Pührer, M. Schwengerer, H. Tompits. *Theory and Practice of Logic Programming*, **10**, 4–6:759-775 (2010). https://arxiv.org/abs/1007.4971
10 A.Z. Arifin, I.A. Mahendra, H.T. Ciptaningtyas. *Enhanced confix stripping stemmer and ants algorithm for classifying news document in indonesian language*. The 5th International Conference on Information & Communication Technology and System (Melaka, Malaysia, 2017). The 5th International Conference on Information & Communication Technology and System:149–158. *https://www.researchgate.net/publication/228416000_ENHANCED_CONFIX_STRIPPING_STEMMER_AND_ANTS_ALGORITHM_FOR_CLASSIFYING_NEWS_DOCUMENT_IN_INDONESIAN_LANGUAGE*
11 F. Naumann, H. Melanie. (2010). *An Introduction to Duplicate Detection.* Morgan & Claypool Publisher: Canada. pp. 57–61. http://www.morganclaypool.com/doi/abs/10.2200/S00262ED1V01Y201003DTM003

The Design of E-Commerce System in the Shrimp Paste Industry using the Method of Structured Analysis and Design Technique (SADT) to Increase Marketing

Yanuar Nurdiansyah[1,*], *Feri* Wijayanto[2], and *Firdaus*[3]

[1]Sistem Informasi, Program Studi Sistem Informasi, Universitas Jember (UNEJ), Jl. Kalimantan 37, Jember 68121, Indonesia
[2]Institute for Computing and Information Science, Radbound University Comenisulaan 4, 6525 HP Nijmegen The Netherlands
[3]Advances Informatics School, Universiti Teknologi Malaysia, Level 5, Menara Razak, Jl. Sultan Yahya Petra, 54100 Kuala Lumpur Malaysia

Abstract. The E-Commerce system in the shrimp paste industry is designed to increase the marketing and branding of Payangan shrimp paste. The shrimp paste produced by KUB (*Kelompok Usaha Bersama*—Business Group) and Poklahsar (*Kelompok Pengolah Pemasaran*—Marketing Processing Group) consisting of a number of joint household industries is yet to meet the sales number set. Shrimp paste has several variants, such as the processed one, the raw one and one in the form of powder which constitute the result of the development of maritime research group of Universitas Jember. The target market of the product is both national and international, especially for the powder shrimp paste which is the recent innovation of the maritime research group. It is considered to be a possibility to increase the sales figures and to decrease the marketing costs by optimizing the use of the internet. In order to do so, a system should be design using Structured Analysis and Design Technique (SADT) to build an e-commerce application. It is expected that the E-Commerce application can increase the sales of the shrimp paste and reach a wider number of consumers.

Key words: E-commerce, integration definition language 0 (IDEF-0), Payangan Shrimp Paste, structured analysis and design technique (SADT),

1 Introduction

Coastal area is an area which serves a number of functions (multiple use zones). Payangan, located in Sumberrejo Village, Sub-district of Ambulu, is one of the coastal areas in the District of Jember - Indonesia which constitutes the second largest area for seafood processing business in Jember. The local people are mostly fishermen and seafood processors. The business of seafood processing is mostly household of which mostly produce: black shrimp paste, shrimp paste, smoked fish, and salted fish [1].

*Corresponding author: yanuar_pssi@unej.ac.id

The products of household industry in Payangan, Watu Ulo Village, Sumberejo Village, Sub-district of Ambulu, District of Jember, East Java, have not been professionally maintained in order to produce quality and hygienic products. As a matter of fact, a lot of people have become familiar to the taste of the shrimp paste [2, 3]. It means that the marketing opportunity for the shrimp paste remains open. At present, Payangan Shrimp Paste Industry has not managed to meet the sales figures as set. The targeted market of Payangan Shrimp Paste Industry is the internet. With the development of online marketing system, a wider number of consumers can eventually be familiar with the product. By selling the product through the internet, it allows the increase of sales figures and the decrease of marketing costs. To achieve the goal, it is required a marketing system using Structured Analysis and Design Technique (SADT) to build an online-based E-Commerce application. The cost of E-Commerce business is affordable it means that by building a business on the internet, the company will get feedback from the customers.

2 Research method

This research used the designing SADT method and system development method [4]. To do that method, the software of life cycle development was used by adopting the iterative waterfall model.

2.1. Structured analysis and design technique (SADT)

Structured Analysis and Design Technique (SADT) was further supported and developed by Softech Corporation since 1974. SADT views a system as an object (objects, documents, data) and event (activities performed by people, machines or software). Moreover, SADT also uses two types of diagrams: activity diagrams or actigrams (also used in process-oriented approach) and data diagrams or datagrams (also used in data/object-oriented approach).

SADT simply uses two diagrams in both process- and object-oriented approaches; that are actigram and datagrams. Compared to the other two approaches, SADT is commonly used due to the presence of a separate control activity or control II-21 activity and the fact that it is able to confirm actigrams with datagrams that the database structure is more valid. Process actigram can be seen in Figure 1.

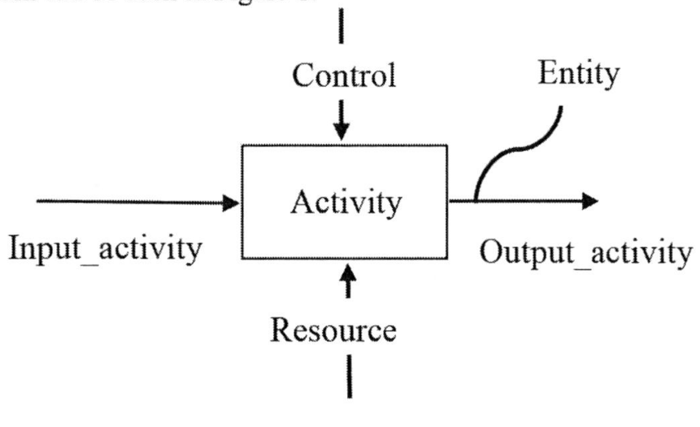

Fig. 1. Actigrams.

In Actigrams (activity diagram in SADT), there are two symbols: box indicates the activities and arrow indicates the data used by the activity (input data), data generated by the activity (output data), control data (constraints), support mechanisms shows the department or individual which is in charge of the activity.

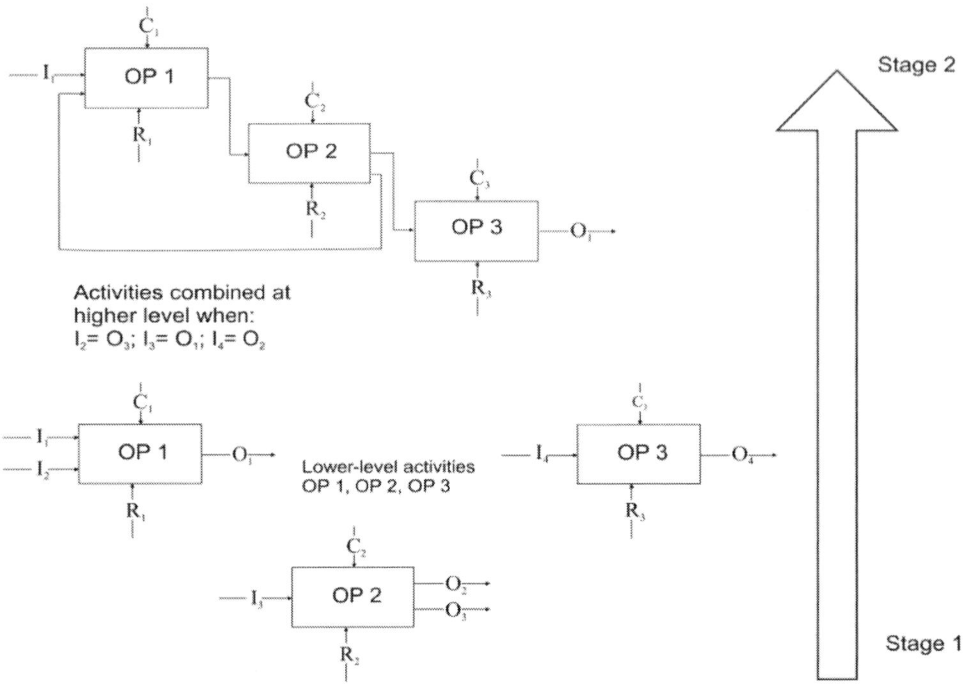

Fig. 2. Datagrams.

In Datagrams (data diagram in SADT), there are two symbols: box indicates the data and arrow indicates the activity. Control Activity limits the data generating activity and the activity that uses II-22 data. The storage mechanism is the outer storage file used to obtain the data. Such control activity limits the data-generating activity and data-oriented activity as well as corrects the existing structured data used in the process involved (process-oriented activity). Thus, the generated database is in accordance with the system. Datagram can be seen in Figure 2.

SADT has the following advantages:

i). Easy to learn;
ii). A suitable communication means between system analysis and system users in the process of system development;
iii). Providing system design documentation; and
iv). Producing similar solutions with precise design specifications for system designers.

However, SADT has the following disadvantages:

i). Time consuming and more personnel needed;
ii). In general, the method is suitable for analysis and design, but in terms of detailed design, the system analysis must employ another methodology;
iii). The application requires expertise and experience of the analyst.

2.2. E-Commerce

Electronic Commerce or generally known as E-Commerce is a new concept or process of buying and selling goods or services on the internet [5]. The implementation of Electronic Commerce began in the early 1970s with the innovation of electronic transfers (EFT) [6]. At that time, the application was limited to large companies, financial institutions, and few small companies. Electronic Data Interchange (EDI) was established which evolves from financial transaction to other transaction and enlarges the number of the participating companies, at the same time [7]. Therefore, the term E-Commerce is a narrow term for few people. Many prefer to use the term e-business, which refers to the broad definition of E-Commerce, which means that it does not merely revolves around selling and buying, but also serving customers and collaborating with business partners, as well as electronic transaction within an organization.

In the history, only few numbers of innovations were noted to gain many potential advantages as E-Commerce. The global technology nature, low cost, the chance of reaching to millions of people, the interactive nature, and the rapid development have gained many benefits for organizations, individuals and communities.

3. Discussion

3.1. System design

This stage of study provides a general overview about the identification regarding the needs of the data information. It is used to design the outline of the system. The model was formulated as a function which describes the relationship among the objects in the process of the e-commerce system [8]. The system was designed and developed using website-based PHP programming language of which users consist of two entities: the seller/admin and the customer/user. In the application, the login form is available for two user accesses in which the application can run in different PC, be it computer, laptop, or mobile. The processes for each user are:

i). Seller/admin: to facilitate the data entry regarding the shrimp paste which is available to purchase; to display the report data to be printed.

ii). Customer/user: to facilitate the data entry regarding the shrimp paste purchased using a digital cart which accommodates a number of items ordered along with the shipping cost.

3.2. Data diagram

In SADT, the data diagram also uses box and arrow symbols. The box symbol indicates the data and the arrow symbol indicates the activity associated with the data. Datagram of Shrimp Paste E-Commerce can be seen on Figure 3.

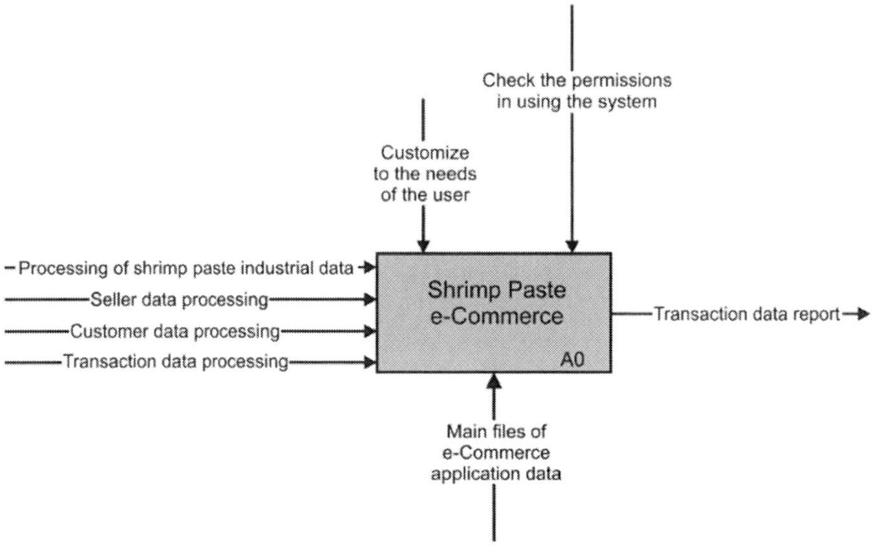

Fig. 3. Datagram of shrimp paste E-Commerce

In the Payangan Shrimp Paste E-commerce datagram, there are a number of data processing inputs performed by the system, including the data processing of shrimp paste by the industry, the seller data, the customer data and the transaction which is controlled by the system access based on the needs of the user [9, 10]. The output is in the form of transaction data which constitutes the report of the transaction data. All input and output data are stored in the database of the E-Commerce application. Actigram SADT of shrimp paste data management can be seen on Figure 4 and Actigram SADT of transaction data can be seen on Figure 5.

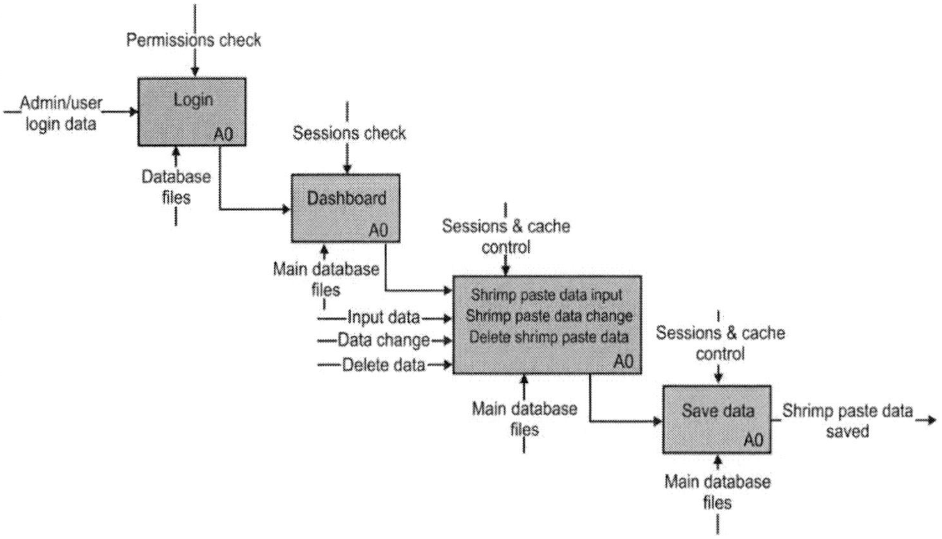

Fig. 4. Actigram SADT of shrimp paste data management.

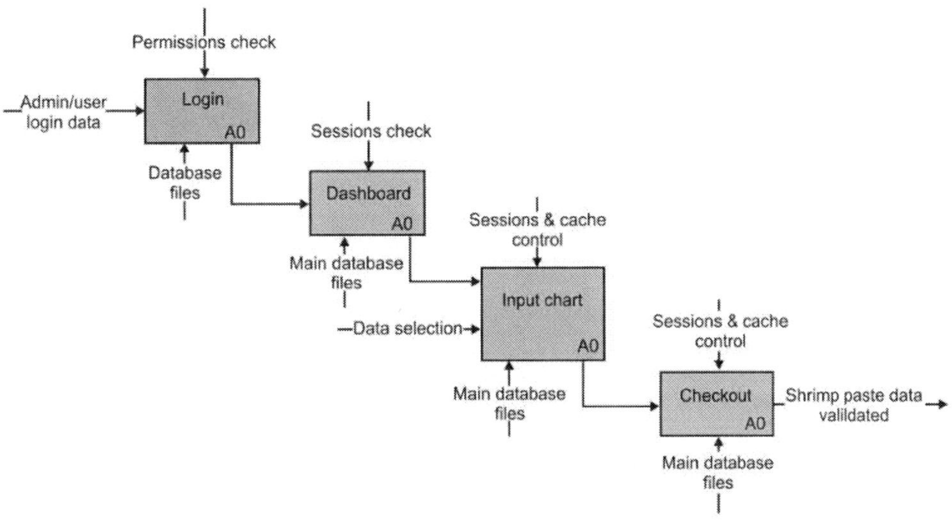

Fig. 5. Actigram SADT of transaction data.

Furthermore, the E-Commerce datagram is divided using the integration definition language 0 (IDEF-0) technique to generate the actigram from each business process performed within [11, 12]. There are two main business activities in the E-Commerce system of Payangan Shrimp Paste: the shrimp paste data management and the transaction data management.

The process of shrimp paste data management, which is conducted completely by the seller of the shrimp paste products, includes the management of the shrimp paste along with the price. Meanwhile, the transaction data management includes the role of the customer (user) and the seller (admin) in which the customer orders the shrimp paste product by selecting the item, then proceed to the checkout to see the cost to pay including the shipping cost; afterwards, order verification is conducted by the seller and the shrimp paste is ready for delivery to the customer.

4. Conclusion

A number of conclusions are drawn from the design and the implementation of the Payangan shrimp paste E-commerce.

i. Payangan shrimp paste E-Commerce which was developed can help increase the sales performance by providing digital information which is accessible for everyone.

ii. Structured Analysis and Design Technique (SADT) model using Integration Definition Language 0 (IDEF0) approach, a language of definition and graphic model (syntax and semantics) which describes a comprehensive methodology to develop the model, is applicable to this application because it structurally models the whole business processes from the lowest to the highest level.

References

1 B. Sobhi, M.N. Adzahan, M.S.A. Karim, R. Karim. Journal of Food, Agriculture and Environment **8**,1:38–40 (2010).

https://www.researchgate.net/publication/292566565_Physicochemical_and_sensory_properties_of_a_traditional_chilli_shrimp_paste
2 J. Pongsetkul, S. Benjakul, P. Sumpavapol, O. Kazufumi, N. Faithong. International Aquatic Research, **6**,3:155-166 (2014). https://link.springer.com/article/10.1007%2Fs40071-014-0076-4
3 J. Pongsetkul, S. Benjakul, P. Sumpavapol, K. Osako., N. Faithong. Journal of Food Processing and Preservation, **40**,4:636–646 (2015a). https://onlinelibrary.wiley.com/doi/abs/10.1111/jfpp.12643
4 M.E. Dickover, C.L. Mcgowan, D.T. Ross. *Software design using: SADT*. ACM '77 Proceedings of the 1977 annual conference. 16–19 October 1977. (Seattle, Washington, 1977). ACM, pp. 125–133 (1977). https://dl.acm.org/citation.cfm?id=810192
5 Y.A. Nanehkaran. International Journal Of Scientific & Technology Research, **2**,4:190–193 (2013). http://www.ijstr.org/final-print/apr2013/An-Introduction-To-Electronic-Commerce.pdf
6 M. Niranjanamurthy, D. Chahar. International Journal of Advanced Research in Computer and Communication Engineering, **2**,7:1–12 (2013). https://www.ijarcce.com/upload/2013/july/69-o-Niranjanamurthy%20-The%20study%20of%20E-Commerce%20Security%20Issues%20and%20Solutions.pdf
7 D. Pandey, V. Agarwal. International Journal of Advanced Research in Computer Science and Software Engineering, **4**,3:669–671 (2014). https://www.researchgate.net/publication/291903546_E-commerce_Transactions_An_Empirical_Study
8 M.O. El-fitouri. International Journal of Engineering Research and Applications, **5**,1(Part 1):102–115 (2015). https://pdfs.semanticscholar.org/f86b/37506f7972d0c46694d5f94c035a5d2a0279.pdf
9 J. Singh. International Journal of Innovative Research in Computer and Communication Engineering, **2**,2:2850–2858 (2014). http://www.ijircce.com/upload/2014/february/1_Review.pdf
10 Y.Y. Zhu. International Journal of Security and Its Applications, **7**,6:259–268 (2013). https://pdfs.semanticscholar.org/485a/96ef603d0ddaa906469fb7fd8080840eeb73.pdf
11 C.-H. Kim, R.H. Weston, A. Hodgson, K.-H. Lee. Computers in Industry, **50**,1:35–56 (2003). https://www.sciencedirect.com/science/article/pii/S0166361502001458
12 J.A.B. Montevechi, F. Leal, A.F. De Pinho, R.F. Da Silva Costa, M.L.M. De Oliveira, A.L.F. Da Silva. *Conceptual modeling in simulation projects by mean adapted IDEF: An application in a Brazilian Tech Company*. Proceedings of the 2010 Winter Simulation Conference. 5–8 December 2010 (Baltimore, Maryland, 2010). pp. 1624–1635. https://dl.acm.org/citation.cfm?id=2433708&dl=ACM&coll=DL

AUTHOR INDEX

Aam, Muharam 446
Adi, Purnama 253
Adi, Soeprijanto 391
Adri, Gabriel Sooai 275
Aep, Saepul Uyun 106, 217
Agung, Alfiansyah 1
Agung, Setyawan 186
Agus, Risdiyanto 437
Agus, Zainudin 253
Ahmad, Wahyudi 367
Akh, Farid 204
Ali, Ikhwan 253
Ali, Mahmudi 19
Alie, Bamahry 217
Amin, Hariyadi Mokhamad 30
Anas, Azhar 1
Anggi, Nindita 327
Annas, Vijaya 30
Ant, Ardath Kristi 437
Anthony, Anci 36
Arief, Budiman 265
Aris, Winaya 275
Aryo, Nugroho 275
Aryuato, Soetedjo 132
Atsushi, Hirono 437
Bagus, Mulyawan 340
Bambang, Prio Hartono 132
Bambang, Susanto 437
Bayu, Prabowo 367
Bobby, Putra Emas Wijaya 167
Boonchoo, Jitnupong 52
Cahyun, Budiono 357
Dali, Santun Naga 457
Daniel, Rohi 212
Dany, Perwita Sari 64
David, Boy Tonara 194
Dian, Andriani 437
Dony, Rachmad Hadi 404
Doris, Caliz 123
Ega, Dwiputra Albertus 8
Ellysa, Nursanti 93
Emmalia, Adriantantri 204
Erlanda, Augupta Pane 159
Erma, Suryani 72
Fathul, Nugroho 84
Fazia, Adyani Ahmad Fuad 259
Felix, Pasila 140, 426
Feri, Wijayanto 484
Fiqih, Nur Muharrom 473
Firdaus 473, 484
Fouad, Riyad Hussein Abdeen 259
Fourry, Handoko 93
Gatot 93
Hamzah, Mohd Salleh 259
Handry, Khoswanto 8, 321
Harisno 186
Heri, Saptono Warpindyasmoro 100
Herry, Susanto 106
Hestiasari, Rante 123
Ichwana 235
Indar, Sugiarto 140
Irrine, Budi Sulistiawati 391
Iskandar, Dzulqornain Muhammad 286
Ismail 159
Iwan, Njoto Sandjaja 321
Jalinas 167
Jarot, Sembodo Suroso 186
Jason, Reynaldo 194
Joseph, Dedy Irawan 204
Julianus, Hutabarat 93
Julius, Sentosa Setiadji 212
Kamaruddin, Abdullah 106, 217
Kanyanut, Homsapaya 225
Kartika, Gunadi 100
Kiman, Siregar 235
Komang, Somawirata I 132
Kustamar 93
Lalu, Mulyadi 93
Lande, Sudianto 245
Lily, Puspa Dewi 72
Lim, Kok Kuan 253
Luluk, Sulistiyo Budi 327
Maftuchah 253, 275
Maizirwan, Mel 259, 327, 367
Makoto, Fujita 437
Maria, Magdalena Widiantari 265
Martinus, Edwin Tjahjadi 93
Michael 19
Michael, Lund 123
Midriem, Mirdanies 446
Miga, Magenika Julian 380
Mizanul, Achlaq Mochamad 275
Murtiyanto, Santoso 297
Niko, Susanto 457
Nobel, Cristian Siregar 235
Noor, Al-Azam Moh 275
Noor, Syaifudin 84, 302, 312
Nurkholis 302, 312
Nyoman, Ade Satwika 357
Ohm, Sornil 225
Peeyush, Soni 327
Petrus, Santoso 321
Petrus, Simon 245
Phillip, Fasrter Eka Adipraja 72
Praptiningsih, Gamawati Adinurani 327, 367
Rahayu Sri 327
Rangga, Handika 302, 312
Raymond, Sutjiadi 8, 297
Resmana, Lim 8, 297, 426
Reyna, Marsya Quita 332

AUTHOR INDEX

Rico, Setiadi Citawan 340
Ridho, Hantoro 357
Riken, Afandi 404
Rino, Imanda 217
Rizal, Alamsyah 235
Romy, Budhi Widodo 332
Ronald, Kipkoech Ketter 357
Rony, Seto Wibowo 391
Roy, Hendroko Setyobudi 259, 302, 312, 367
Rully, Agus Hendrawan 72
Ruri, Agung Wahyuono 380
Rusilawati 391
Salma, Angreani Linda 30
Saminuddin, Tou 235
Sany, Izan Ihsan 259
Satriyo, Krido Wahono 367
Sentot, Achmadi 19
Sholihati 235
Soleh 159
Sotyohadi 404
Sukaridhoto Sritrusta 286
Surya, Hermawan 418
Syukri, Muhammad Nur 106, 217
Teguh, Herbasuki 132
Teuku, Meurah Indra Mahlia 106, 217
Timothius, Victorio Yasin 426
Tinton, Dwi Atmaja 437, 446
Tony, Liwang 367
Trianggoro, Wiradinata 36
Tuga, Mauritsius 186
Udin, Harun Al Rasyid M. 286
Viny, Christanti Mawardi 340, 457
Vita, Susanti 446
Wahyu, Kusuma Raharja 167
Wahyu, Widodo 367
Waraporn, Jirachiefpattana 52
Yanuar, Nurdiansyah 473, 484
Yoanne, Flantine Mozes 212
Yogo, Adhi Nugroho 367
Yun-Shang, Chiou 64